D1796740

LIBRARY
COPY

DO NOT
REMOVE

Thomas Hobbes

International Library of Essays in the History of Social and Political Thought
Series Editor: Tom Campbell

Thomas Hobbes

Edited by

Gabriella Slomp
University of St Andrews, UK

ASHGATE

© Gabriella Slomp 2008. For copyright of individual articles please refer to the Acknowledgements.

All rights reserved. No part of this publication may be reproduced, stored in a retrieval system or transmitted in any form or by any means, electronic, mechanical, photocopying, recording or otherwise without the prior permission of the publisher.

Wherever possible, these reprints are made from a copy of the original printing, but these can themselves be of very variable quality. Whilst the publisher has made every effort to ensure the quality of the reprint, some variability may inevitably remain.

Published by
Ashgate Publishing Limited
Gower House
Croft Road
Aldershot
Hampshire GU11 3HR
England

Ashgate Publishing Company
Suite 420
101 Cherry Street
Burlington, VT 05401-4405
USA

Ashgate website: http://www.ashgate.com

British Library Cataloguing in Publication Data
Thomas Hobbes. - (International library of essays in the
   history of social and political thought)
   1. Hobbes, Thomas, 1588-1679
   I. Slomp, Gabriella
   192

Library of Congress Cataloging-in-Publication Data
Thomas Hobbes / edited by Gabriella Slomp.
          p. cm – (International library of essays in the history of social and
political thought)
   Includes index.
   ISBN 978-0-7546-2702-9 (alk. paper)
   1. Hobbes, Thomas, 1588-1679. I. Slomp, Gabriella.

   B1247.T36 2008
   192–dc22

                                                                                                           200704567

ISBN: 978 0 7546 2702 9

Mixed Sources
Product group from well-managed
forests and other controlled sources
www.fsc.org Cert no. SGS-COC-2482
© 1996 Forest Stewardship Council

Printed and bound in Great Britain by
TJ International Ltd, Padstow, Cornwall

Contents

Acknowledgements

The editor and publishers wish to thank the following for permission to use copyright material.

Blackwell Publishing for the essays: Michael Oakeshott (1975), 'Introduction to *Leviathan*', in *Hobbes on Civil Association*, Oxford: Basil Blackwell, pp. 1–74. Copyright © 1975 Michael Oakeshott; J.W.N. Watkins (1955), 'Philosophy and Politics in Hobbes', *The Philosophical Quarterly*, **5**, pp. 125–46; Tom Sorell (1990), 'Hobbes's Persuasive Civil Science', *The Philosophical Quarterly*, **40**, pp. 342–51.

Terence Ball for the essay: Terence Ball (1985), 'Hobbes' Linguistic Turn', *Polity*, **17**, pp. 739–60.

Brill for the essay: Arrigo Pacchi (1989), 'Some Guidelines into Hobbes's Theology', *Hobbes Studies*, **2**, pp. 87–103.

Cambridge University Press for the essay: Quentin Skinner (1964), 'Review: Hobbes's "Leviathan"', *The Historical Journal*, **7**, pp. 321–33. Copyright © 1964 Cambridge University Press; Quentin Skinner (1966), 'Thomas Hobbes and his Disciples in France and England', *Comparative Studies in Society and History*, **8**, pp. 153–67. Copyright © Society for the Comparative Study in Society and History, published by Cambridge University Press.

Carole Pateman for the essay: Carole Pateman (1989), '"God Hath Ordained to Man a Helper": Hobbes, Patriarchy and Conjugal Right', *British Journal of Political Science*, **19**, pp. 445–63. Copyright © 1989 Carole Pateman.

Copyright Clearance Center for the essays: Patrick Neal (1988), 'Hobbes and Rational Choice Theory', *The Western Political Quarterly*, **4**, pp. 635–52; Russell Hardin (1991), 'Hobbesian Political Order', *Political Theory*, **19**, pp. 156–80. Copyright © 1991 Sage Publications, Inc; Kinch Hoekstra (1997), 'Hobbes and the Foole', *Political Theory*, **25**, pp. 620–54. Copyright © 1997 Sage Publications, Inc.; Keith Brown (1978), 'The Artist of the *Leviathan* Title-Page', *British Library Journal*, **4**, pp. 24–36. Copyright © 1978 The British Library Board; Patricia Springborg (1995), 'Hobbes's Biblical Beasts: *Leviathan* and *Behemoth*', *Political Theory*, **23**, pp. 353–75. Copyright © 1995 Sage Publications, Inc.

Imprint Academic for the essay: George Klosko and Daryl Rice (1985), 'Thucydides and Hobbes's State of Nature', *History of Political Thought*, **6**, pp. 405–9. Copyright © 1985 Imprint Academic, Exeter, UK.

The Johns Hopkins University Press for the essay: Edwin Curley (1996), 'Calvin and Hobbes, or, Hobbes as an Orthodox Christian', *Journal of the History of Philosophy*, **34**, pp. 257–71. Copyright © 1996 Journal of the History of Philosophy, Inc.

Oxford University Press for the essay: Noel Malcolm (2002), 'Hobbes's Theory of International Relations', in *Aspects of Hobbes*, Oxford: Oxford University Press, pp. 432–56.

Simon and Schuster for the essay: J.G.A. Pocock (1971), 'Time, History and Eschatology in the Thought of Thomas Hobbes', in Politics, Language and Time: Essays on Political Thought and History, New York: Atheneum Publishers, pp. 148–201.

University of Chicago Press for the essays: Leo Strauss (1953), 'On the Spirit of Hobbes's Political Philosophy', in *Natural Right and History* reprinted in K.C. Brown (ed.) (1965), *Hobbes Studies*, Oxford: Basil Blackwell, pp. 1–29. Copyright © 1953 Chicago University Press; Norberto Bobbio (1993), 'Hobbes and Natural Law Theory' in Daniela Gobetti (trans.), *Thomas Hobbes and the Natural Law Tradition*, Chicago and London: The University of Chicago Press, pp. 149–71. Copyright © 1993 by the University of Chicago Press.

University of Pennsylvania Press for the essay: Richard Schlatter (1945), 'Thomas Hobbes and Thucydides', *Journal of the History of Ideas*, **6**, pp. 350–62. Reprinted with permission of the University of Pennsylvania Press.

Every effort has been made to trace all the copyright holders, but if any have been inadvertently overlooked the publishers will be pleased to make the necessary arrangement at the first opportunity.

Series Preface

The International Library of Essays in the History of Social and Political Thought brings together collections of important essays dealing with the work of major figures in the history of social and political thought. The aim is to make accessible the complete text with the original pagination of those essays that should be read by all scholars working in that field. In each case, the selection is made from the extensive available literature by an established expert who has a keen sense of the continuing relevance of the history of social and political thought for contemporary theory and practice. The selection is made on the basis of the quality and enduring significance of the essays in question. Every volume has an introduction that places the selection made in the context of the wider literature, the historical period, the contemporary state of scholarship and the editor's particular interests.

TOM CAMPBELL
Series Editor
Centre for Applied Philosophy and Public Ethics (CAPPE)
Charles Sturt University
Canberra

Introduction

Hobbesian scholarship is immense and selecting just a handful of excellent essays is a daunting task. Every inclusion requires hundreds of exclusions that are difficult to justify. Previous collections of essays on Hobbes published by Ashgate (Shaver, 1999; Finkelstein, 2005) consider the relevance of different works to the formation and development of, and challenge to, an understanding of Hobbes's moral and political theory, defined by Robert Shaver as the 'received view' (explained below). This was used as the criterion for selection, and as a criterion it was inspired in so far as it enabled Shaver to single out milestones of twentieth century Hobbesian scholarship, namely essays by Taylor, Warrender, Macpherson, Goldsmith, Skinner, Curley, Gauthier, Kavka and Hampton among others.

Having been entrusted with the task of selecting another small set of seminal essays on Hobbes, I had the choice of either following Shaver's approach, namely to supplement his collection with other writers' arguments for or against the 'received view' of Hobbes's theory, or of adopting a different criterion of inclusion and exclusion. The appeal of the first option is that we know that such an approach worked wonders for Shaver; the disadvantage is that Shaver did his job very well and the most famous and influential essays for and against the 'received view' have already been selected. Hence I decided to use a different approach that could catch a number of seminal essays of the twentieth century that had escaped Shaver's net.

We may recall Hobbes's exhortation to the reader in the *Elements of Philosophy*:

> Or imitate the creation: if you will be a philosopher in good earnest, let your reason move upon the deep of your own cogitations and experience; those things that lie in confusion must be set asunder, distinguished, and every one stamped with its own name set in order; that is to say, your method must resemble that of the creation. The order of the creation was, *light, distinction of day and night, the firmament, the luminaries, sensible creatures, man*; and, after the creation, *the commandment*. Therefore the order of contemplation will be, *reason, definition, space, the stars, sensible quality, man*; and after man is grown up, *subjection to command*.[1]

Unsympathetic readers have criticized the above passage because Hobbes invites the philosopher to follow God's 'order of creation', but refers to the creation of light as the first divine act. Genesis tells us that '[i]n the beginning God created the heavens and the earth' and not light. Only after having noticed that 'the earth was formless and empty' and that 'darkness was over the surface of the deep', did God say 'let there be light'. Why would Hobbes get the order of creation wrong? Why would he invite the philosopher-reader to mess up things right from the start?

But a more sympathetic reading of Hobbes suggests that the philosopher-reader is invited to follow God not in the 'order of creation' but in the 'creation of order'.

---

1 Hobbes, *Elements of Philosophy*, The First Section, Concerning Body, in *The English Works of Thomas Hobbes*, ed. William Molesworth,1839, vol. 1, p. xiii; emphasis in the original.

Indeed, the creation of order in every field of endeavour seems to have been Hobbes's ultimate aim; his ambition as expressed in the *Elements of Philosophy*, in *De Cive* and elsewhere was to create a philosophical system that explained everything that could be explained, from cosmology to morals, from natural science to politics.

His contemporaries tended to think that in this respect Hobbes had been successful: both his few admirers and his many detractors seemed to agree that his materialism, morality, theology (or lack thereof) and politics were all components of a single whole.[2]

As from the end of the nineteenth century, however, the bearing of Hobbes's cosmology and theory of motion on his political thought became a matter of great controversy; in particular, a materialistic interpretation of his moral and political theory was seriously questioned. Could and should Hobbes's moral and political philosophy be seen as a mere derivation of his natural science? This question grabbed the attention of interpreters of the first half of the twentieth century and gave rise to the epic interpretations of Leo Strauss, Howard Warrender and Michael Oakeshott, among others.

Over time, however, the interest in the unity of Hobbes's system diminished. The belief that one cannot understand Hobbes's political theory without a proper understanding of his natural science and of his theory of motion became less and less widespread and more and more qualified. Indeed, although there is room for debate, one can argue that after the 1960s the prevailing tendency in the twentieth century was to devote attention to aspects, perspectives, dimensions and features of Hobbes's philosophy, rather than its bold central claims.

In the late 1980s a number of interpreters began to denounce and lament what can be termed as the 'fragmentation' of Hobbes studies. Some looked for 'internal' reasons for such a fragmentation, blaming analytical philosophy or game theory, or pointing the finger at contextualism. Others looked for 'external' explanations. It was remarked that Hobbes was increasingly being studied in Politics departments and that this explained the lack of interest in his general philosophy; it was observed that the twenty-page format of journal essays prevented the study of anything bigger or wider than 'fragments of Hobbes'; it was said that time constraints on the writing of monographs accounted for the limited ambitions and modest aims of Hobbesian studies in the second half of the twentieth century.

Although there is ample scope for debate as to the ultimate reasons for the fragmentation of Hobbes studies in the twentieth century, any claim that such a fragmentation did not take place will have the weight of evidence and opinion against it: it seems that the 1960s heralded an end to the age of grand interpretations of Hobbes.

The collection that we are proposing aims at capturing this trend of fragmentation, offering a taste of early epic studies that engaged with the whole of Hobbes's theory, and a taste of later studies interested in capturing more limited narratives and at recounting parallel stories that seem to be running through Hobbes's works. The rest of this introduction hopes to offer a compass to orient the reader's journey through the collection.

---

2   An interesting survey of the reactions of Hobbes's contemporaries to his theories can be found in Mintz (1962).

Hobbes's System of Natural and Political Science

As I mentioned above, the belief in the unity of Hobbes's philosophy and the related view that Hobbes derives morality entirely from his materialistic psychology have been dominant over the centuries and have been endorsed by the finest minds, last but not least because there is a wealth of passages throughout Hobbes's writings which support such a reading. Robert Shaver summarized this majority understanding or 'received view' of Hobbes's moral, political and natural philosophy thus:

> We are self-interested, valuing our self-preservation above everything else. This leads us, in the state of nature, to a war of all against all, in which there is no right or wrong. Moral philosophy is no different than prudence; it tells us how to avoid this war. The laws of nature are justified because following them lets us preserve ourselves. They could have no other justification, for all value is subjective, stemming from our interests, and reason is purely instrumental. Neither value from some other source nor the pronouncements of other beings, such as God, are relevant All obligations are self-imposed. The most important law of nature tells us to establish a sovereign, to keep peace between us. For the sovereign to succeed in this task, and because the sovereign represents each of us, the sovereign must be absolute. It does not follow, however, that we have no right to defend ourselves against the sovereign; this right is inalienable (Shaver, 1999, p. xi).

The question whether Hobbes did indeed support the above view of morality and justice acquired special significance between the 1920s and the 1950s. If one could argue that Hobbes derived politics exclusively from his mechanistic notion of nature, if one could show that Hobbes explained moral behaviour entirely in terms of prudence and survival, if one could prove that Hobbes identified all morality with state morality, then one could claim that as much as Machiavelli[3] was a precursor of Fascism and the total state, so was Hobbes. Indeed Hobbes's notion of absolute unlimited indivisible state power and his condemnation of political factions seemed to appeal to the European Far Right, so much so that in the 1920s and 1930s Carl Schmitt often suggested he was a modern re-incarnation of Thomas Hobbes. On the other hand, if it could be proven that in Hobbes's writings there is a notion of justice and morality that is independent of his natural science, that for Hobbes there are limits to a state's power and authority, that the Leviathan and its citizens are accountable to God, then any association between Hobbes and fascism or totalitarianism could be seriously questioned.

This ideological context provided the background for the interpretations of Leo Strauss, A.E. Taylor and Howard Warrender. In different ways, all three interpreters put forward a reading of Hobbes that opposed any association of his thought with fascist ideology. All three rejected the view that there is any relevant link between Hobbes's natural science and his political theory. They argued that despite Hobbes's claims to the contrary, his political theory is unrelated to and richer than his natural science. In 1936, Leo Strauss said that the 'particular object' of his book on Hobbes's political philosophy was to show 'that the real basis of Hobbes's political philosophy is not modern science' (Strauss, [1936] 1963, p. ix).

---

3   In the 1920s and 1930s, a number of writers claimed that a link existed between Italian Fascism and Machiavelli's patriotism and love for ancient Rome. Among these writers, Carl Schmitt singles out Machiavelli as a precursor of the nationalist myth famously described by Mussolini in October 1922 before the March on Rome (Schmitt, 1988, p. 43).

Using a very different perspective, in 1938 A.E. Taylor also strongly rejected Hobbes's claim that there is unity between his natural science and his political theory. He contended that Hobbes's ethical theory is a very strict deontology 'disengaged' from the rest of his philosophy 'with which it has no logically necessary connection' (Taylor, 1938, p. 408). In the same vein, in 1957 Howard Warrender argued that Hobbes's theory of obligation must be separated analytically from his natural philosophy and his psychology and that if in fact Hobbes wanted to derive his moral theory from an empirical theory 'he must be held to have failed in his main enterprise' (Warrender, [1957] 1976, p. xx). According to the so-called 'Warrender-Taylor thesis', there is more to Hobbes's morality than prudence and self-interest and more to his political theory than materialism. Important contributions to the debate that took place can be found in Keith Brown's *Hobbes Studies* published in 1965. Of course, the debate never died but persisted with a long string of fine writers continuing to champion the claim that there is more to Hobbes than materialism and prudential morality.[4]

Shaver's collection includes Taylor's seminal essay of 1938 as well as an essay on the Hobbesian notion of morality by Warrender (1962). In the present collection we are including the chapter on Hobbes from Leo Strauss's *Natural Right and History* (1953).

In 1946, however, Michael Oakeshott took a distinctive and different position to that of Strauss, Taylor and Warrender. Unlike interpreters who denied or asserted the derivation of Hobbes's political philosophy from his natural science, Oakeshott argued that it was not the content but the particular *form* of reasoning which unifies the entire Hobbesian construction. Oakeshott rejects the view that Hobbes was one of the founders of a new philosophy of materialism or scientific mechanism; for Oakeshott, Hobbes is in the tradition of St Augustine, Montaigne and Pascal, a tradition of moralists aware of the limits of philosophical enquiry. Oakeshott maintains that in order to understand Hobbes's texts we need to re-unite them with their intellectual context and that the intellectual context of Leviathan is the philosophical reasoning of his day, namely a late scholastic view of philosophy. Oakeshott's 'Introduction to *Leviathan*' (Chapter 1 in this volume) is regarded as a classic of Hobbesian scholarship, and possibly one of the most inspired and stimulating reading of that work.[5]

Writing in the 1950s and 1960s, scholars such as Richard Peters, John Watkins, and Thomas Spragens went further than Oakeshott in claiming that Hobbes's philosophy was not only influenced by the form, but also by the content of his natural philosophy. Arguing against Strauss, Taylor and Warrender, these interpreters were prominent members of the school of thought which maintains that although Hobbes's political theory was not, and could not be, logically deduced from his cosmology, it should nevertheless not be considered as a self-contained whole totally independent from the rest of Hobbes's natural philosophy. In 1965, Watkins confidently stated that 'some of Hobbes's political ideas are implied by some of his philosophical ideas,' (Watkins, 1965, p. 8). In a similar vein, in 1973 Spragens summarized his position as follows: 'My view, like that of Watkins, is that there is considerable interaction

---

4 Although the Warrender-Taylor thesis has few supporters nowadays, the claim that one can find a notion of justice which is independent of civil law in Hobbes is still being made regularly and competently in journals and books by a small but persistent number of interpreters who can point to (selected) textual evidence to support their views. See, for example, State (1991), Boonin-Vail (1994), Shelton (1992) and Ewin (1991).

5 For an example of interesting work on Oakeshott's interpretation of Hobbes, see Tregenza (2003).

between [Hobbes's natural philosophy and his political philosophy] and that the results of this intersection are significant for the final content of Hobbes's political theory' (Spragens, 1973, p. 36). Watkins' essay on philosophy and politics in Hobbes, published in 1955, is reproduced here (Chapter 3).

Hobbes's scientific concerns and ambitions were of course taken seriously by other writers in the 1960s. Worthy of particular attention are Maurice Goldsmith, F.S. McNeilly, C.B. Macpherson and David Gauthier.[6]

Even though the interest in the link between Hobbes's natural philosophy and his political theory persisted throughout the twentieth century and is still present today (Sorrell, 1986, pp. 24–26; Malcolm, 2002, pp. 146–55), after the Sixties the issue lost the special ideological significance that it had in the century's opening decades. Indeed it has been argued (see below) that such an interest has become superficial since the 1980s.

Hobbes's Political Theory

In 1886, G.C. Robertson argued that Hobbes's political views were, in fact, derived from 'his personal circumstances and the events of his time' (Robertson, 1886, p. vi). On the one hand, this claim had profound effects on Hobbesian scholarship in that it put in question the bearing of Hobbes's cosmology and theory of motion on his political thought. On the other hand, this claim urged interpreters to look at a type of historical context that Hobbesian scholarship would largely ignore for the next sixty years or so.

Indeed in his book on Hobbes, Richard Tuck points out that whereas between 1885 and 1930, writers such as George Croom Robertson, Ferdinand Toennies and Frithiof Brandt revealed historical sensitivity in their work on Hobbes, 'the period from about 1930 to about 1965 was remarkable for the widespread lack of interest' in the 'close investigation of Hobbes's relationship with his contemporaries and of the historical circumstances in which he composed his works' (Tuck, 1989, p. 214). Tuck explains that 'this is not to say, however, that the writers of the period 1930–65 had no interest in historical issues: the project of understanding Hobbes, and his relationship with broadly defined traditions of thought, continued' (ibid).

Of course, one can find exceptions to Tuck's verdict; in this collection we are including an important essay written by Richard Schlatter in 1946 (an essay that eventually was used as an introduction to Hobbes's translation of Thucydides). Schlatter (Chapter 4) does not simply engage with the history of ideas or with what Tuck regards as 'historical issues' but also examines the perception of Thucydides in Hobbes's times.

According to Tuck, works displaying 'interest in historical issues' but no real interest in Hobbes's relationship with his contemporaries are those by Leo Strauss and C.B. Macpherson. In Shaver's collection one can find the seminal essay by Macpherson that Tuck regards as an example in point. Here we are including an essay by Norberto Bobbio (Chapter 5) who locates Hobbes in the history of ideas as the founder of the modern doctrine of natural law: whereas the medieval theory of natural law implied a notion of reason which is associated with an immutable world order, the modern concept of natural law interprets reason as the order of factual conditions.

---

6   Shaver's collection contains famous contributions from Goldsmith, Macpherson and Gauthier.

From the mid-1960s onwards, a new way of contextualising Hobbes's work became dominant; the work of Quentin Skinner became prominent, so much so that we witness a proper revolution in the way in which texts are approached. The history-of-ideas approach was increasingly criticized for its abstractness.

In Shaver's collection one can find Skinner's seminal article of 1966 on the ideological context of Hobbes's political thought. Here we are including two essays by Skinner (Chapters 6 and 7) published in 1964 and 1965 where his distinctive brand of contextualism is in action. We are also including an essay by Tuck (Chapter 8).

Fragmented Hobbesian Scholarship

Of Man and Commonwealth

I have mentioned above that in the second half of the twentieth century the objects of analysis of many works on Hobbes are more limited than in the first half. The engagement with the whole of Hobbes's system is usually confined to an introductory chapter or even merely to a few remarks. Gregory Kavka's book on Hobbes (Kavka, 1986) exemplifies works that on the one hand still address the issue of whether Hobbes's moral and political philosophy can be separated from his materialistic-deterministic metaphysics and on the other hand show that the interest in such a question is superficial; as the engagement with Hobbes's system of philosophy is slight, so is the engagement with the whole of Hobbes's political theory.

Interpreters of this period concentrate more and more on Hobbes's *Leviathan*, and within it they consider almost exclusively the first two parts, and of the first two parts they examine mainly the chapters on the state of nature and on the social contract. The rest of Hobbes's political and natural philosophy seems to represent an interesting and yet largely irrelevant background. This phenomenon was noticed and lamented by a number of Hobbesian scholars in the 1980s.

In 1988, in the *International Hobbes Association Newsletter*, Robert Kraynak denounced the 'striking change' of Hobbesian studies in the second half of the century (Kraynak, 1988). He pointed out that the study of Hobbes 'has evolved from a kind of "heroic age" of bold and original interpretations to a more prosaic age of modest and highly professionalized studies' (p. 3). He lamented the end of the great debates of the past: 'The great debates engendered by Strauss's thesis about Hobbes's moral basis and transformation of the natural law tradition or by Macpherson's thesis about the origins of possessive individualism or by the Taylor-Warrender thesis about moral obligation in Hobbes seem to have subsided'. He denounced 'a fragmented field of books that reflect the interests of contemporary philosophers, usually guided by the problems of analytical philosophy or the Rawlsian revival of contract theory'. He commented that 'Such scholars do not seek to advance grand interpretive theses about Hobbes but more modestly seek to illuminate 'useful' problems in his works or more simply wish to hone their analytical teeth, as it were, on the bones of the dead master' (Kraynak, 1988, p. 8).

Kraynak does not openly criticize the game-theoretical approach to Hobbes's texts that commenced in the 1960s, but of course this approach is particularly responsible for the fragmentation of Hobbes's works. From Gauthier to Kavka, and from Jean Hampton to Iain

McLean and Russell Hardin, game-theorists are mainly interested in two moments of Hobbes's theory, namely in the dynamics of the state of nature and in the nature of contracts.

Game-theoretical readings of Hobbes caused strong feelings among interpreters in the Eighties and divided them in two opposing camps. In an ironic and harsh review of Hampton (1986), William Sacksteder (1987) voiced the serious concerns that many Hobbesian readers had with game-theoretic interpretations. He denounced the game-theorists' tendency to slight Hobbes's methodology, metaphysics and natural philosophy; he criticized their propensity to ignore the coexistence of many narratives within his discourse; he argued that it was clearly flawed to try and single out 'almost aggressively one argument, one account, one reading, and to argue that if that reading does not work not even with the assistance of game-theoretic techniques, Hobbes's failure is exposed' (Sacksteder, 1987, p. 6).

In Shaver's collection we have the most famous game-theoretical interpretations of Hobbes, namely those by Gauthier, Kavka and Hampton; here we are including a well-known essay by Russell Hardin (Chapter 12), where he joins 'the enterprise of re-reading Hobbes as a proto-game theorist' and has no hesitation to claim that '[f]rom Gauthier to Kavka, our understanding of Hobbes has been remade and clarified' (p. 267). We include also an important plea by Patrick Neal (Chapter 10) for a return to reading Hobbes's text in its full flavour. Neal contends that a game-theoretical reading cannot reap that which Hobbes tried to sow.

In addition to analytical and game-theoretical studies, in the 1980s, feminist interpretations also tended to isolate and emphasize only aspects or sections of Hobbes's argument. Carole Pateman, Susan Okin, Diane Coole and many others are examples in point. While earlier writers had pointed out that in the history of ideas Hobbes could be regarded as the philosopher who had dismantled patriarchalism as a basis of political power, feminists tended to devote attention to Hobbes's specific comments on women and wives in his account of the state of nature and in the political state. Here we include an essay by Carole Pateman (Chapter 11) exemplifying the feminist approach to Hobbes's writings in the 1980s.

We are also including essays (by George Klosko and Daryl Rice (Chapter 9), and by Kinch Hoekstra (Chapter 13)) that show a great interest in 'fragments of Hobbes' and in particular in the state of nature and yet do not share the approach or perspective that Kraynak blames for the fragmentation of Hobbes studies. These essays illustrate how the process of fragmentation has fostered excellent scholarship.

Of a Christian Commonwealth

Hobbes's contemporaries tended to regard Hobbes as an atheist – an accusation that he often resisted. For most of the twentieth century, in spite of a few exceptions (see, for example, Eisenhach, 1982; Haliday, 1983; Pacchi, 1989; Brown, 1962; and Pocock, 1971), interpreters have shown little interest in Hobbes's theology. Writing in 1989, Tuck remarked that '[s]o far, there is remarkably little of quality written on Hobbes's religious ideas' (Tuck, 1989, p. 238).

The prevailing view among interpreters until the 1980s is captured by McNeilly's remark made in the 1960s that Hobbes 'preserved theology only by pickling it in political vinegar' (McNeilly, 1968, p. 24).

Even interpreters such as A.E. Taylor and Warrender, who had argued that there was more to Hobbes's notion of morality than prudential calculation, had not insisted on Hobbes being a traditional Christian. One notable exception was the work of F.C. Hood (1964), who tried to argue that Hobbes believed in Christianity and tried to combine Christianity with materialism.

Since the 1990s, a growing number of writers have devoted their attention to Hobbes's views on religion. It has been pointed out that both text and context point to the relevance of theology in Hobbes's work. After all, Part 2 and Part 3 of *Leviathan* are devoted to a detailed discussion of the Scriptures. Moreover, the religious debates of the time must surely have had an impact on Hobbes.

Among the works in the 1990s that attach great importance to the religious element of Hobbes's political theory (Baumgold, 1988; Lloyd, 1992; Pangle, 1992; Curley, 1996; Fuller, 1992; Letwin, 1976; and Pocock, 1990), it is worth mentioning A.P. Martinich's *The Two Gods of Leviathan* (1992). Opposing the tradition of writers that understood Hobbes as a secular figure, Martinich argues that Hobbes's thinking can only be understood within the religious context of his time and that Hobbes's goal was to 'show the distinctively religious content of the bible could be reconciled with the new science of Copernicus and Galileo' (Martinich, 1992, p. 5). In this collection we are including an essay on Hobbes's theology by J.G A. Pocock (Chapter 14) that has been defined as 'pathbreaking' as well as seminal essays by Arrigo Pacchi (Chapter 15) and Edwin Curley (Chapter 16).

The Rhetoric of Leviathan

Kraynak was not the only one to lament the change and fragmentation of Hobbesian scholarship. In 1989, in a review of *Perspectives on Thomas Hobbes* (Rogers and Ryan, 1988), Robert Orr made similar claims to Kraynak's, but pointed to a different culprit:

> Whereas the Hobbes exegetes of twenty to thirty years ago – Oakeshott, Warrender, Macpherson, Goldsmith, Watkins – searched for system, coherence and overall logic, the current inclination is to get busy elaborating sub-systems, to accept tacitly, if not explicitly Skinner's belief that logic in Hobbes is largely instrumental to the exigencies of rhetorical purpose (Orr, 1989, p. 2).

For Orr, a volume such as *Perspectives* was likely to accelerate further 'the fragmentation of Hobbes studies, to discourage renewed attempts to find a system in Hobbes' (Orr, 1989, p. 5). Orr makes us reflect on the appropriateness of the title (perspectives) to capture the mood not just of the volume but also of the times. He points out that in spite of acknowledgements by the editors that

> Hobbes is one of the few English philosophers, and perhaps the only one of note who has constructed what can be seen as a grand philosophic system' ... all the contributors betray and sometime state a readiness to recognize rather than a determination to resolve the long-known tensions in Hobbes. Even Alan Ryan, who stands by the older thesis that there is a conceptual linkage between Hobbes's mechanistic materialism and his epistemological individualism sees the connection only as an indirect affinity (Orr, 1989, p. 2).

For Orr, works by Richard Tuck, Noel Malcolm and Tom Sorell, among others, reflect the drift that took place in Hobbesian scholarship, moving from systems towards subsystems and details.

Whereas Krynak had blamed analytical philosophy for the fragmentation of Hobbes's studies, Robert Orr lays responsibility at the door of Skinner.

Unfortunately, Orr does not elaborate on this claim and so one wonders why he thought that 'Skinner's belief that logic in Hobbes is largely instrumental to the exigencies of rhetorical purpose' could foster fragmentation. Prima facie, a concern with rhetoric might encourage a comprehensive approach to a text, rather than its fragmentation.

What Orr is perhaps suggesting is that, because of Skinner's influence, we now regard Hobbes's claim to have built a philosophical system as merely rhetorical; hence we consider any search for a systematic version of Hobbes's philosophy as pointless; we tend to think that any attempt such as Watkins's or even Goldsmith's or McNeilly's to elucidate Hobbes's system of ideas is misguided and misleading; instead, we concentrate on those aspects of Hobbes's arguments where advocacy rather than explanation comes to the fore; we pay special attention to specific works by Hobbes (for example, the *Leviathan*, rather than *De Cive* or *Elements of Law*) and to specific parts of these works (the *Leviathan*'s Review or Conclusion, the Letter to the reader) where rhetoric is more obvious.

It is worth noticing that, before Skinner, many writers in the twentieth century had made the point that Hobbes cared a great deal about his audience and was well aware that communication is as relevant as explanation. From Strauss to Oakeshott, from Charles Tarlton (1977) to Keith Brown (1978, Chapter 17 in this volume), from Terence Ball (1985, Chapter 18 in this volume) to George Shulman (1989), from David Johnston (1986)[7] to Charles Cantalupo (1991) and Raia Prokhovnik (1991), a long list of interpreters discussed the role of rhetoric in Hobbes's writings. Skinner's work on Hobbes's rhetoric, however, had an impact (see Schuhmann, 1998) that previous studies did not, in that it questioned the belief that Hobbes was serious when he wrote that he had provided us with a scientific demonstration of the need for government that could be 'understood by all thinking men of sound judgement, in prose that was simple and direct, *not in rhetoric*'.[8]

We are including essays by Keith Brown (Chapter 17), Terence Ball (Chapter 18), Tom Sorell (Chapter 19) and Patricia Springborg (Chapter 20) as examples of Hobbesian scholarship's strong interest in Hobbes's 'rhetoric'.[9]

International Relations

During the twentieth century, the greatest interest in 'fragments of Hobbes', rather than his whole natural and political philosophy, has been shown by specialists of international relations. From Hans Morgenthau (1946, 1948) to Kenneth Waltz (1959), from Edward Carr (1946) to Hedley Bull (1977), from Michael Doyle (1997) to Jack Donnelly (2000), scholars associate Hobbes with the so-called realist tradition in IR. His qualifying credentials for

---

7   Johnston argues that Hobbes studied the rhetorical method of his times and used them to reach an audience. For Johnston, *Leviathan* is Hobbes's attempt 'to synthesise the new science methods of reason as applied to politics with the older lessons of the rhetorical tradition' (Johnston, 1986, p. 25).

8   Hobbes, 'The Prose Life', in *Human Nature and De Corpore Politico*, ed. J.C.A. Gaskin, 1994, p. 250; emphasis added.

9   I am using the term in a broad sense. For an interpretation of the mysteries of plates and pictures in Hobbes's works, see Goldsmith (1981, 1990). See also Condren (1990), Malcolm (2002, pp. 200–229), Musolff (2006), Tralau (2007), Sacksteder (1984), and Whelan (1981).

belonging to this tradition are his negative notion of human nature, his concept of anarchy and state sovereignty and his claim that a law without sanctions is no law at all. In particular, IR specialists are fond of the following quotation from Hobbes's *Leviathan*:

> But though there had never been any time, wherein particular men were in a condition of warre one against another; yet in all times, Kings, and Persons of Soveraigne authority, because of their Independency, are in continuall jealousies, and in the state and posture of Gladiators; having their weapons pointing, and their eyes fixed on one another; that is, their Forts, Garrisons, and Guns upon the Frontiers of their Kingdomes; and continuall Spyes upon their neighbours; which is a posture of War (Hobbes, [1651] 1991, p. 90).

Specialists of Hobbes have shown mixed feelings about the association of Hobbes with IR in general and with Realism in particular.[10]

On the one hand, a growing number of Hobbesian interpreters, including David Gauthier, Timo Airaksinen, Martin Bertman, Murray Forsyth and Peter Caws, have shown interest in the implications of Hobbes's theory for international affairs.

On the other hand, Noel Malcolm (Chapter 22) leads the camp that is worried and irritated by misuses and abuses of Hobbes by IR specialists. Malcolm claims that the portrayal of Hobbes by IR theorists 'appears to be based, for the most part, on a handful of passages in one or two of his works (ignoring many comments on international affairs elsewhere in his writings); and even those few passages have been misunderstood' (p. 502).

Murray Forsyth (Chapter 21) and R. John Vincent (Chapter 23) complete the discussion on the international dimension of Hobbes's theory in this volume.

Conclusion

In this brief Introduction I have argued that we have witnessed a progressive fragmentation of Hobbes's studies in the twentieth century. A number of external and internal causes may have contributed to the gradual disappearance of epic interpretations of Hobbes's system of ideas. Among internal causes, some interpreters have singled out contextualism, analytical philosophy and game theory as the driving forces that led readers to disregard the whole of Hobbes's philosophy.

Reflecting on his own work, in 1963 Carl Schmitt wrote that 'the age of the great systems is now over' and that at present only two modes of thought are available, namely either 'a retrospective historical glance' or the 'aphoristic style' (Schmitt, 2002, p. 13). For Schmitt, a grand theory such as Hobbes's could not be emulated in the twentieth century.

Following Schmitt, we could say that the certainties of Strauss, Warrender and Macpherson escape present interpreters. Those writers agreed only on one thing, namely that each of them alone understood the whole of Hobbes's theory. Nowadays, the dominant tendency among interpreters is to agree that there are many ways of understanding Hobbes, many readings of *Leviathan*, many aspects, many perspectives, many discourses, many narratives; in the case of Hobbes, as with so many other things, there are as many interpretations as interpreters.

---

10 See for example C. Navari (1982), D.W. Hanson (1984), Bull (1981) and Williams (1996).

It is difficult to predict whether grand interpretations of Hobbes will return in the twenty-first century. It is perhaps tempting to hope that there are still other, sweeping interpretations of Hobbes's whole system to be found. For the man himself, surely, there was only one interpretation of his work, and the modern trends leading towards fragmentation perhaps lose sight of the aim to find this most important of interpretations.

Acknowledgements

I should like to thank Chris Brown, Iain Hampsher-Monk and John Horton for discussing the ideas of this Introduction with me. I am particularly grateful to Camillo La Manna and to the Series Editor Tom Campbell for detailed and constructive comments on earlier drafts.

Hobbes's Main Works

Hobbes, Thomas, *Behemoth, or The Long Parliament* [1679], ed. Ferdinand Tönnies (London, 1889, ed. Stephen Holmes, Chicago 1990).

Hobbes, Thomas, *The Correspondence*, 2 vols, ed. Noel Malcolm, Clarendon Edition of the Works of Hobbes, vols. 6 and 7 (Oxford, Clarendon Press, 1994).

Hobbes, Thomas, *De cive, On the Citizen*, ed. and trans. Richard Tuck and Michael Hobbes, Thomas, *The Elements of Law Natural and Politic*, ed. Ferdinand Tönnies (1889), reissued with a new Introduction by M. M. Goldsmith (London, Cass, 1969).

Hobbes, Thomas, *The English Works of Thomas Hobbes*, 11 vols, ed. Sir William Molesworth (London, Bohn, 1839–45).

Hobbes, Thomas, *Leviathan* [1651], ed. Richard Tuck, (Cambridge University Press, 1991).

Hobbes, Thomas, *Opera Philosophica quae Latine scripsit omnia*, 5 vols, ed. Sir William Molesworth (London, Bohn, 1839–45).

Hobbes, Thomas, 'The Prose Life', in Thomas Hobbes, *Human Nature and De Corpore Politico*, edited by J.C.A. Gaskin (Oxford, Oxford University Press, 1994), pp. 245–53.

Hobbes, Thomas [1642], *Thomas White's 'De Mundo' Examined*, trans. Harold Whitmore Jones (Bradford, Bradford University Press, 1976).

Selected Bibliography and References

Aubrey, John (1898), *'Brief Lives', chiefly of Contemporaries, set down by John Aubrey between the Years 1669 & 1696*, 2 vols. Edited from the Authors mss. by Andrew Clark, Oxford.

Airaksinen, Timo and Bertman, Martin (eds) (1989), *Hobbes: War Among Nations*, Aldershot: Avebury.

Ashcraft, Richard (1988), 'Political Theory and Practical Action: A reconsideration of Hobbes's State of Nature', *Hobbes studies*, 1, pp. 63–88.

Baumgold, Deborah (1988), *Hobbes's Political Theory*, Cambridge: Cambridge University Press.

Beitz, Charles (1979), *Political Theory and International relations*, Princeton, NJ: Princeton University Press.

Bertman, Martin A. (1976), 'Equality in Hobbes, with reference to Aristotle', *Review of Politics*, **28**, pp. 534–44.

Bertman, Martin A. (1981), *Hobbes: The Natural and the Artifacted Good*, Bern: Peter Lang.

Bertman, Martin A. (1991), *Body and Cause in Hobbes: Natural and Political*, Wakefield, NH: Longwood Academic.

Blits, Ian H. (1989), 'Hobbesian Fear', *Political Theory*, **17**, pp. 417–31.

Bobbio, Norberto (1993), *Thomas Hobbes and the Natural Law Tradition*, Chicago: University of Chicago Press.

Boonin-Vail, David (1994), *Thomas Hobbes and the Science of Moral Virtue*, Cambridge: Cambridge University Press.

Boucher, David (1998), *Political Theories of International relations, from Thucydides to the Present*, Oxford: Oxford University Press.

Brandt, Frithiof (1927), *Thomas Hobbes' Mechanical Conception of Nature*. Copenhagen: Levin and Munksgaard.

Bredekamp, Horst (1999), 'From Walter Benjamin to Carl Schmitt, via Thomas Hobbes', *Critical Inquiry*, **25**, pp. 247–66.

Brown C.W. (1987), 'Thucydides, Hobbes, and the Derivation of Anarchy', *History of Political Thought*, **8**, pp. 33–62.

Brown, C.W. (1989), 'Thucydides, Hobbes and the Linear Causal Perspective', *History of Political Thought*, **10**, pp. 215–56.

Brown, Keith (1962), 'Hobbes's Grounds for Belief in a Deity', *Philosophy*, **37**, pp. 344–66.

Brown, Keith (ed.) (1965), *Hobbes Studies*, Oxford: Blackwell.

Bull, Hedley (1977), *The Anarchical Society: a Study of Order in World Politics*, London: Macmillan.

Bull, Hedley (1981), 'Hobbes and the International Anarchy', *Social research: an International Quarterly of the Social Sciences*, **48**, pp. 717–38.

Burgess, G. (1990), 'Contexts for the Writing and Publication of Hobbes's *Leviathan*', *History of Political Thought*, **11**(4), pp. 675–702.

Cantalupo, Charles (1991), 'A Literary Leviathan: Thomas Hobbes's Masterpiece of Language', London and Toronto: Associated University Presses.

Carr, E.H. (1946), *The Twenty Years Crisis 1919–1939*, London.

Catlin, G. (1922), *Thomas Hobbes, as Philosopher, Publicist and Man of Letters*, Oxford: Blackwell.

Caws Peter (ed.) (1989), *The Causes of Quarrel: Essays on Peace, War, and Thomas Hobbes*, Boston, MA: Beacon Press.

Coady, C.A.J. (1990), 'Hobbes and "the Beautiful Axiom"', *Philosophy*, **65**, pp. 5–17.

Collins, Jeffrey R. (2005), *The Allegiance of Thomas Hobbes*, Oxford: Clarendon Press.

Condren, C. (1990), 'On the Rhetorical Foundations of *Leviathan*', *History of Political Thought*, **11**(4), pp. 703–20.

Cranston, Maurice and Richard Peters (eds) (1965), *Hobbes and Rousseau*, New York: Doubleday.

Dietz Mary(ed.) (1990), *Thomas Hobbes and Political Theory*, Lawrence, KS: University Press of Kansas.

Donnelly, Jack (2000), *Realism and International Relations*, Cambridge: Cambridge University Press.

Doyle, Michael (1997), *Ways of War and Peace*, New York: Norton & Co.

Eisenach, E.J. (1982), 'Hobbes on Church, State and Religion', *History of Political Thought*, **3**, pp. 675–703.

Ewin R.E. (1991), *Virtues and Rights. The Moral Philosophy of Thomas Hobbes*, Boulder, CO: Westview Press.

Finkelstein, Claire (ed.) (2005), *Hobbes on Law*, Philosophers and Law Series, Aldershot: Ashgate.

Foisneau, L. and Sorell, T. (eds) (2004), *Leviathan After 350 Years*, Oxford : Clarendon Press.

Foisneau Luc and George Wright (eds) (2005), *New Critical Perspectives on Hobbes's Leviathan Upon the 350th Anniversary of Its Publication*, Milan: Franco Agnelli.

Frohnen, Bruce P. (1990), 'Oakeshott's Hobbesian Myth: Pride, Character and the Limits of Reason', *Western Political Quarterly*, **43**, pp. 789–809.

Fuller, Timothy (1992), 'The Idea of Christianity in Hobbes's *Leviathan*', *Jewish Political Studies Review*, **4**(2), pp. 141–61.

Gauthier, David P. (1969), *The Logic of Leviathan. The Moral and Political Theory of Thomas Hobbes*, Oxford: Clarendon Press.

Gauthier, David P. (1977), 'The Social Contract as Ideology', *Philosophy and Public Affairs*, **6**, pp. 130–64.

Gert, Bernard (1965), 'Hobbes, Mechanism and Egoism', *Philosophical Quarterly*, **15**, pp. 341–49.

Gert, Bernard (1967), 'Hobbes and Psychological Egoism', *Journal of the History of Ideas*, **28**, pp. 503–20.

Gert, Bernard (1972), 'Introduction', *Thomas Hobbes. Man and Citizen*, New York: Doubleday.

Goldie, Mark (1991), 'The Reception of Hobbes', in J.H. Burns and Mark Goldie (eds), *The Cambridge History of Political Thought, 1450–1700*, Cambridge: Cambridge University Press, pp. 589–615.

Goldsmith, Maurice (1966), *Hobbes's Science of Politics*, New York: Columbia University Press.

Goldsmith, Maurice (1969), 'Introduction', in Thomas Hobbes, *Behemoth or the Long Parliament*, 2nd edn, ed. Ferdinand Tönnies, London: Frank Cass, pp. v–xiv.

Goldsmith, Maurice (1980), 'Hobbes's Mortall God: Is There a Fallacy in Hobbes's Theory of Sovereignty?', *History of Political Thought*, **1**, pp. 33–50.

Goldsmith, Maurice (1981), 'Picturing Hobbes's Politics: the Illustrations to the *Philosophicall Rudiments*', *Journal of the Warburg and Courtauld Institutes*, **44**, pp. 231–37.

Goldsmith, Maurice (1990), 'Hobbes's Ambiguous Politics', *History of Political Thought*, **11**, pp. 639–73.

Halliday, R.J., Kenyon, T. and Reeve, A. (1983), 'Hobbes's Belief in God', *Political Studies*, **31**, pp. 418–33.

Hampton, Jean (1986), *Hobbes and the Social Contract Tradition*, Cambridge: Cambridge University Press.

Hanson, D.W. (1984), 'Thomas Hobbes's Highway to Peace', *International Organization*, **38**(2), pp. 329–54.

Herbert, Gary B. (1976), 'Thomas Hobbes's counterfeit equality', *Southern Journal of Philosophy*, **14**, pp. 269–82.

Herbert, Gary B. (1989), *Thomas Hobbes. The Unity of Scientific and Moral Wisdom*, Vancouver: University of British Columbia Press.

Heyed, David (1982), 'The Place of Laughter in Hobbes's Theory of Emotions', *Journal of History of Ideas*, **43**, pp. 285–95.

Hoekstra, Kinch (2003), 'Hobbes on Law, Nature, and Reason', *Journal of the History of Philosophy*, **41**(1), pp. 111–20.

Hoffman, Stanley (1965), *The State of War: Essays on the Theory and Practice of International Politics*, New York: Praeger.

Hood, F. (1964), *The Divine Politics of Thomas Hobbes*, Oxford: Clarendon Press.

Hungerland, Isabel C. and George R. Vick (1973), 'Hobbes's Theory of Signification', *Journal of the History of Philosophy*, **11**, pp. 459–82.

James, D.G. (1949), *The Life of Reason: Hobbes, Locke, Bolingbroke*, London: Longmans.

Johnston, David (1986), *The Rhetoric of Leviathan*, Princeton, NJ: Princeton University Press.

Kavka, Gregory (1983), 'Hobbes's War of All Against All', *Ethics*, **93**, pp. 291–310.

Kavka, Gregory (1986), *Hobbesian Moral and Political Theory*, Princeton, NJ: Princeton University Press.

Kavka, Gregory (1990), 'Nuclear Weapons and World Government', *Monist*, **70**, pp. 298–315.

Kidder, Joel (1983), 'Acknowledgements of Equals: Hobbes's Ninth Law of Nature', *Philosophical Quarterly*, **33**, pp. 133–46.

King, Preston (1974), *The Ideology of Order*, London: Allen & Unwin.

Kraynak, Robert (1988), *International Hobbes Association Newsletter*, Colorado Springs, Co., No. 7 (June), pp. 8–10.

Kraynak, Robert P. (1990), *History and Modernity in the Thought of Thomas Hobbes*, Ithaca, NY: Cornell University Press.

Laird J. (1934), *Hobbes*, London: Benn.

Letwin, S.R. (1976), 'Hobbes and Christianity', *Daedalus: Journal of the American Academy of Arts and Sciences*, **105**, pp. 1–21.

Leyden, Wolfgang von (1981), *Hobbes and Locke: The Politics of Freedom and Obligation*, London: Macmillan.

Lloyd, S.A. (1992), *Ideas as Interests in Hobbes Leviathan: the Power of Mind over Matter*, Cambridge: Cambridge University Press.

Lund William R. (1992), 'Hobbes on Opinion, Private Judgment and Civil War', *History of Political Thought*, **13**, pp. 51–72.

Macpherson, C.B. (1962), *The Political Theory of Possessive Individualism. Hobbes to Locke*, London: Oxford University Press.

Malcolm, Noel (2002), *Aspects of Hobbes*, Oxford: Clarendon Press.

Martinich, A.P. (1992), *The Two Gods of Leviathan: Thomas Hobbes on Religion and Politics*, Cambridge: Cambridge University Press.

Martinich, A.P. (1995), *A Hobbes Dictionary*, Oxford: Blackwell.

Martinich, A.P. (1996), 'On the Proper Interpretation of Hobbes's Philosophy', *Journal of the History of Philosophy*, **34**, pp. 273–83.

Mastnak, Thomaz (ed) (2003), 'Hobbes's *Behemoth*', *Filozofski Vestnik (Acta Philosophica)*, **24**(2), special issue.

McLean, Iain (1981), 'The Social Contract in *Leviathan* and the Prisoner's Dilemma Supergame', *Political Studies*, **29**, pp. 339–51.

McNeilly, F.S. (1968), *The Anatomy of Leviathan*, London: Macmillan.

Mill, David van (2001), *Liberty, Rationality and Agency in Hobbes's Leviathan*, State University of New York Press.

Milton, P. (1993), 'Hobbes, Heresy and Lord Arlington', *History of Political Thought*, **14**(4), pp. 501–46.

Minogue, Kenneth (1973), 'Introduction', Thomas Hobbes, Leviathan, London: Dent.

Mintz, Samuel I. (1962), *The Hunting of Leviathan*, Cambridge: Cambridge University Press.

Morgenthau, Hans (1946), *Scientific Man versus Power Politics*, Chicago, IL: University of Chicago Press.

Morgenthau, Hans (1948), *Politics among Nations: Tthe Struggle for Power and Peace*, New York.

Musolff, Andreas (2006), 'Ignes fatui or Apt Similitudes? – the Apparent Denunciation of Metaphor by Thomas Hobbes', in *Hobbes Studies*, **17**, pp. 96–113.

Nagel, Thomas (1959), 'Hobbes's Concept of Obligation', *Philosophical Review*, **68**(1), pp. 68–83.

Navari, C. (1982), 'Hobbes and "the Hobbesian Tradition" in International Thought', *Millenium: Journal of International Studies*, **2**, pp. 203–22.

Oakeshott, Michael (1937), *Hobbes on Civil Association*, Oxford: Blackwell.

Orr, Robert (1989), *International Hobbes Newsletter*, No. 10, pp. 2–5.

Orr, Robert (1987), 'Hobbes on the Regulation of Voluntary Motion', in G. Feaver and F. Rosen (eds), *Lives, Liberty and the Public Good*, London: Macmillan, pp. 45–60.

Pacchi, Arrigo (1987), 'Hobbes and the Passions', *Topoi*, **6**, pp. 111–19.

Pangle, Thomas (1992), 'A Critique of Hobbes's Critique of Biblical and Natural Religion in Leviathan, *Jewish Political Studies Review*, **4**(2), pp. 25–57.

Peters, Richard (1956), *Hobbes*, Harmondsworth: Penguin.

Plamenatz, John (1963), *Man and Society*, Vol. I: *Political and Social Theory: Machiavelli through Rousseau*, New York: McGraw-Hill.

Pocock, J.G. (1990), 'Thomas Hobbes: Atheist or Enthusiast? His Place in a Restoration Debate', *History of Political Thought*, **11**(4), pp. 737–49.

Prokhovnik, Raia (1991), *Rhetoric and Philosophy in Hobbes' Leviathan*, London: Garland.

Raphael, D.D. (1977), *Hobbes: Morals and Politics*, London: Allen & Unwin.

Reik, Miriam (1977), *The Golden Lands of Thomas Hobbes*, Detroit, MI: Wayne State University Press.

Robertson, G.C. (1886), *Hobbes*, Edinburgh: Blackwood.

Rogers, G.A.J. and Ryan, Alan (eds) (1988), *Perspectives on Thomas Hobbes*, Oxford: Clarendon Press.

Rogers, G A J., and Sorell, Tom (2000), *Hobbes and History*, London: Routledge.

Rogow, Arnold A. (1986), *Thomas Hobbes. Radical in the Service of Reaction*, New York: Norton.

Ryan, Alan (1983), 'Hobbes, Toleration and the Inner Life', in David Miller and Larry Seidentop (eds), *The Nature of Political Theory*, Oxford: Clarendon Press.

Ryan, Alan (1988), 'A more tolerant Hobbes', in Susan Mendus (ed.), *Justifying Tolerction*, Cambridge: Cambridge University Press.

Sacksteder, William (1981), 'Hobbes' Geometrical Objects', *Philosophy of Science*, **48**, pp. 573–90.

Sacksteder, William (1982), *Hobbes Studies (1879–1979): a Bibliography*, Bowling Green, OH: Ohio State University Press.

Sacksteder, William (1984), 'Hobbes: Philosophical and Rhetorical Artifice', *Philosophy and Rhetoric*, **17**, pp. 30–46.

Sacksteder, William (1987), *International Hobbes Association Newsletter*, No. 6, Colorado Springs, CO, pp. 6–10.

Sarasohn, L.T. (1985), 'Motion and Morality: Pierre Gassendi, Thomas Hobbes and the Mechanical World-view', *Journal of the History of Ideas*, **46**, pp. 363–79.

Schlatter, Richard (1975), 'Introduction', in R. Schlatter (ed.), *Hobbes's Thucydides*, New Brunswick, NJ: Rutgers University Press, pp. xi–xxviii.

Schmitt, Carl (1988), *The Crisis of Parliamentary Democracy*, Cambridge, MA: MIT Press.

Schmitt, Carl (1996), *The Leviathan in the State Theory of Thomas Hobbes*, Westport, CT: Greenwood Press.

Schmitt, Carl (2002), Foreword to the 1963 German edition of Carl Schmitt, *Der Begriff des Politischen*, 7th edn, Berlin.

Schuhmann, Karl (1988), 'Hobbes and Telesio', *Hobbes Studies*, **1**, pp. 109–33.

Schuhmann, Karl (1998), 'Skinner's Hobbes', *British Journal of the History of* Philosophy, **6**(1), pp. 115–25.

Shaver, Robert (ed.) (1999), *Hobbes*, Ashgate: Aldershot.

Shelton, George (1992), *Morality and Sovereignty in the Philosophy of Hobbes*, New York: St Martin Press.

Shulman, George (1989), 'Metaphor and Modernization in the Political Thought of Thomas Hobbes', *Political Theory*, **17**(3), pp. 392–416.

Skinner, Quentin (1966), 'The Ideological Context of Hobbes's Political Thought', *The Historical Journal*, **9**, pp. 286–317.

Skinner, Quentin (1978), *The Foundations of Modern Political Thought*, vol. 2: *The Age of* Reformation, Cambridge: Cambridge University Press.

Skinner, Quentin (1990), 'Thomas Hobbes on the Proper Signification of Liberty', *Transactions of the Royal Historical Society*, **40**, pp. 121–51.

Skinner, Quentin (1990), 'Thomas Hobbes: Rhetoric and the Construction of Morality', *Proceedings of the British Academy*, **76**, pp. 1–61.

Skinner, Quentin (1996), *Reason and Rhetoric in the Philosophy of Hobbes*, Cambridge: Cambridge University Press.

Skinner, Quentin (2002), *Visions of Politics*, 3 vols, Cambridge: Cambridge University Press.

Slomp, Gabriella (1994), 'Hobbes and the Equality of Women', *Political Studies*, **42**(3), pp. 441–52.

Slomp, Gabriella (1998), 'From Genus to Species: The Unravelling of Hobbesian Glory', *History of Political Thought*, **19**(4), pp. 552–69.

Slomp, Gabriella (1990), 'Hobbes, Thucydides and the Three Greatest Things', *History of Political Thought*, **11**, pp. 565–86.

Slomp, Gabriella (2000), *Thomas Hobbes and the Political Philosophy of Glory*, Basingstoke: Macmillan.

Slomp, Gabriella (2003), 'Hobbes's *Behemoth* on Ambition, Greed, and Fear', *Filozofski Vestnik (Acta Philosophica)*, special issue on Hobbes's *Behemoth*, ed. Tomaz Mastnak, **24**(2), pp. 189–204.

Slomp Gabriella (2007), 'Hobbes on Glory and Civil Strife', in *The Cambridge Companion to Hobbes's Leviathan*, ed. P. Springborg, Cambridge: Cambridge University Press, pp. 181–98.

Slomp, Gabriella (2007), 'Kant Against Hobbes: Reasoning and Rhetoric', *Journal of Moral Philosophy*, **4**(2), pp. 208–23.

Slomp, Gabriella and La Manna, M. (1994), 'Leviathan: Revenue-Maximizer or Glory-Seeker', *Constitutional Political Economy*, **92**, pp. 159–72.

Slomp, Gabriella and La Manna, M. (1996), 'Hobbes, Harsanyi and the Edge of the Abyss', *Canadian Journal of Political Science*, **29**(1), pp. 159–72.

Sommerville, Johan P. (1992), *Thomas Hobbes: Political Ideas in Historical Context*, London: Palgrave Macmillan.

Sorell, Tom (1986), *Hobbes*, London: Routledge.

Sorell, Tom (ed.) (1996), *The Cambridge Companion to Hobbes*, Cambridge: Cambridge University Press.

Sorell, Tom and Foisneau, Luc (eds) (2004), *Leviathan after 350 Years*, Oxford: Clarendon Press.

Spragens, Thomas (1973), *The Politics of Motion. The World of Thomas Hobbes*, London: Croom Helm.

Springborg, Patricia (1994), 'Hobbes, Heresy and the *Historia Ecclesiastica*', *Journal of the History of Ideas*, **55**(4), pp. 553–71. (Reprinted in *Great Political Thinkers*, Vol. 3, ed. John Dunn and Ian Harris, Cheltenham: Elgar, 1997, pp. 599–61.)

Springborg, Patricia (2003), '*Behemoth* and Hobbes's "Science of *Just* and *Unjust*"', *Filozofski vestnik (Acta Philosophica)*, special issue on Hobbes's *Behemoth*, ed. Tomaz Mastnak, **24**(2), pp. 267–89.

Springborg, Patricia (ed.) (2007), *Cambridge Companion to Hobbes's Leviathan*, New York: Cambridge University Press.

State, Steven (1991), *Thomas Hobbes and the Debate over Natural Law and Religion*, London: Garland.

Stephen, Leslie (1904), *Hobbes*, London: Macmillan.

Strauss, Leo (1952), *The Political Philosophy of Hobbes*, Chicago.

Strauss, Leo (1953), *Natural Right and* History, Chicago: University of Chicago Press.

Strauss, Leo (1963 [1936]), *The Political Philosophy of Hobbes. Its Basis and its Genesis*, Chicago and London: University of Chicago Press.

Strauss, Leo (1964), *The City and Man*, Chicago: Chicago University Press.

Strong, Tracy (1993), 'How to Write Scripture: Words, Authority, and Politics in Thomas Hobbes', *Critical Inquiry*, **20**, pp. 128–59.

Tarlton, Charles (1977), 'Levitating Leviathan: Glosses on a theme in Hobbes', *Ethics*, **88**(1), pp. 1–19.

Tarlton, Charles (1978), 'The Creation and Maintenance of Government: A Neglected Dimension of Hobbes's *Leviathan*', *Political Studies*, **26**, pp. 307–27.

Taylor, A.E. (1938), 'The Ethical Doctrine of Hobbes', *Philosophy*, **13**, pp. 406–24.

Tralau, Johan (2007), 'Leviathan, the Beast of Myth. Medusa, Dionysos, and the Riddle of Hobbes's Sovereign Monster', in Patricia Springborg (ed.), *Cambridge Companion to Hobbes's Leviathan*, Cambridge: Cambridge University Press, pp. 61–81.

Tregenza, Ian (2003), *Michael Oakeshott on Hobbes. A Study in the Renewal of Philosophical Ideas*, Exeter: Imprint Academic.

Tuck, Richard (1979), *Natural Rights Theories: Their Origin and Development*, Cambridge: Cambridge University Press.

Tuck, Richard (1989), *Hobbes*, Oxford: Oxford University Press.

Tuck, Richard (1990), 'Hobbes and Locke on Toleration', in Mary G. Dietz (ed.), *Thomas Hobbes and Political Theory*, Lawrence, KS: University Press of Kansas, pp. 153–71.

Verdon, Michel (1982), 'On the Laws of Physical and Human Nature: Hobbes's Physical and Social Cosmologies', *Journal of the History of Ideas*, **43**, pp. 653–63.

Waltz, Kenneth (1959), *Man, the State and War*, New York: Columbia University Press.

Warrender, Howard (1970 [1957]), *The Political Philosophy of Hobbes. His theory of Obligation*, Oxford: Clarendon Press.

Warrender, Howard (1962), 'Hobbes's Conception of Morality', *Rivista critica di storia della filosofia*, **17**, pp. 434–49.

Watkins, John (1970), 'Imperfect Rationality', in R. Borger and F. Cioffi (eds), *Explanation in the Behavioural Sciences*, Cambridge: Cambridge University Press.

Watkins, John (1973), *Hobbes's System of Ideas: A Study in the Political Significance of Philosophical Theories*, 2nd edn, London: Hutchinson.

Whelan, F.G. (1981), 'Language and its Abuses in Hobbes's Political Philosophy', *American Political Science Review*, **75**, pp. 59–75.

Williams, M.C. (1996), 'Hobbes and International Relations: a Reconsideration', *International Organization*, **50**, pp. 213–36.

Part I
Hobbes's System of Natural and Political Science

[1]

Introduction to Leviathan

Michael Oakeshott

'We are discussing no trivial subject, but how a man should live.'
—Plato, *Republic*, 352D.

I. BIOGRAPHICAL

Thomas Hobbes, the second son of an otherwise undistinguished vicar of Westport, near Malmesbury, was born in the spring of 1588. He was educated at Malmesbury where he became an exceptional scholar in Latin and Greek, and at Oxford where in the course of five years he maintained his interest in classical literature and became acquainted with the theological controversies of the day, but was taught only some elementary logic and Aristotelian physics.

In 1608 he was appointed tutor (and later became secretary) to the son of William Cavendish, first Earl of Devonshire. For the whole of his adult life Hobbes maintained a close relationship with the Cavendish family, passing many of his years as a member of the household either at Chatsworth or in London. In these circumstances he came to meet some of the leading politicians and literary men of his day, Bacon and Jonson among them. The year 1610 he spent in France and Italy with his charge, getting a first glimpse of the intellectual life of the continent and returning with a determination to make himself a scholar. The next eighteen years, passed mostly at Chatsworth, were the germinating period of his future intellectual interests and activities. There is little record of how precisely they were spent, and the only literary product of this period of his life was the translation of Thucydides, published in 1629: but there can be no doubt that philosophy occupied his mind increasingly.

On the death of the second Earl of Devonshire in 1628, Hobbes accepted the position of tutor to the son of Sir Gervase Clinton, with whom he stayed three years, two of which were spent on the continent. It was at this time that Hobbes discovered for himself the intellectual world of mathematics and geometry, a world so important to the continental philosophers of his time, but of which hitherto he had been entirely ignorant. The discovery gave renewed impetus and fresh direction to his philosophical reflections, and from then philosophy dominated his mind.

In 1631 Hobbes returned to the Cavendish household as tutor to the new earl, with whom he made his third visit to the continent (1634–7). It was on this visit that he met Galileo in Florence and became acquainted with the circle of philosophers centred round Mersenne in Paris, and particularly with Gassendi. And on his return to England he completed in 1640 (but did not publish until 1650) his first important piece of philosophical writing, the *Elements of Law*. He was fifty-two years old, and he had in his head the plan of a philosophy which he desired to expound systematically.

The next eleven years were spent in Paris, free for a while from extraneous duties. But instead of embarking at once on the composition of the most general part of his philosophy—his philosophy of nature—he wrote *De Cive*, an exposition of his political philosophy, which was published in 1642. Paris for Hobbes was a society for philosophers; but in 1645 it became the home of the exiled court of Charles, Prince of Wales, and Hobbes was appointed tutor to the prince. His mind still ran on the philosophy of politics, and in 1651 his masterpiece, *Leviathan*, was published.

In 1652 he returned to England, took up his place (which he was never again to leave) in the household of the Earl of Devonshire, and set about the composition of the rest of his philosophical system. In 1655 was published *De Corpore*, and in 1658 *De Homine*. He had still twenty years to live. They were years of incessant literary activity and of philosophical,

Introduction to Leviathan 3

mathematical, theological and political controversy. After the
Restoration he was received at Court, and he spent much of
his time in London. In 1675, however, perceiving that he must
soon retire from the world, he retired to Chatsworth. He died
in the winter of 1679 at the age of ninety-one.

II. THE CONTEXT OF *LEVIATHAN*

Leviathan is the greatest, perhaps the sole, masterpiece of
political philosophy written in the English language. And the
history of our civilization can provide only a few works of
similar scope and achievement to set beside it. Consequently,
it must be judged by none but the highest standards and must
be considered only in the widest context. The masterpiece
supplies a standard and a context for the second-rate, which
indeed is but a gloss; but the context of the masterpiece itself,
the setting in which its meaning is revealed, can in the nature
of things be nothing narrower than the history of political
philosophy.

Reflection about political life may take place at a variety
of levels. It may remain on the level of the determination of
means, or it may strike out for the consideration of ends. Its
inspiration may be directly practical, the modification of the
arrangements of a political order in accordance with the perception of an immediate benefit; or it may be practical, but
less directly so, guided by general ideas. Or again, springing
from an experience of political life, it may seek a generalization of that experience in a doctrine. And reflection is apt to
flow from one level to another in an unbroken movement,
following the mood of the thinker. Political philosophy may
be understood to be what occurs when this movement of
reflection takes a certain direction and achieves a certain level,
its characteristic being the relation of political life, and the
values and purposes pertaining to it, to the entire conception
of the world that belongs to a civilization. That is to say, at all
other levels of reflection on political life we have before us the
single world of political activity, and what we are interested in

is the internal coherence of that world; but in political philosophy we have in our minds that world and another world,
and our endeavour is to explore the coherence of the two
worlds together. The reflective intelligence is apt to find itself
at this level without the consciousness of any great conversion
and without any sense of entering upon a new project, but
merely by submitting itself to the impetus of reflection, by
spreading its sails to the argument. For, any man who holds
in his mind the conceptions of the natural world, of God, of
human activity and human destiny which belong to his civilization, will scarcely be able to prevent an endeavour to assimilate these to the ideas that distinguish the political order in
which he lives, and failing to do so he will become a philosopher (of a simple sort) unawares.

But, though we may stumble over the frontier of philosophy
unwittingly and by doing nothing more demonstrative than
refusing to draw rein, to achieve significant reflection, of
course, requires more than inadvertence and more than the
mere acceptance of the two worlds of ideas. The whole impetus
of the enterprise is the perception that what really exists is a
single world of ideas, which comes to us divided by the abstracting force of circumstances; is the perception that our
political ideas and what may be called the rest of our ideas
are not in fact two independent worlds, and that though they
may come to us as separate text and context, the *meaning*
lies, as it always must lie, in a unity in which the separate
existence of text and context is resolved. We may begin, probably we must begin, with an independent valuation of the text
and the context; but the impetus of reflection is not spent
until we have restored in detail the unity of which we had
a prevision. And, so far, philosophical reflection about politics
will be nothing other than the intellectual restoration of a
unity damaged and impaired by the normal negligence of
human partiality. But to have gone so far is already to have
raised questions the answers to which are not to be found in
any fresh study of what is behind us. Even if we accept the
standards and valuations of our civilization, it will be only by
putting an arbitrary closure on reflection that we can prevent

Introduction to Leviathan 5

the consideration of the meaning of the general terms in which those standards are expressed; good and evil, right and wrong, justice and injustice. And, turning, we shall catch sight of all that we have learned reflected in the *speculum universitatis*.

Now, whether or not this can be defended as a hypothetical conception of the nature of political philosophy, it certainly describes a form of reflection about politics that has a continuous history in our civilization. To establish the connections, in principle and in detail, directly or mediately, between politics and eternity is a project that has never been without its followers. Indeed, the pursuit of this project is only a special arrangement of the whole intellectual life of our civilization; it is the whole intellectual history organized and exhibited from a particular angle of vision. Probably there has been no theory of the nature of the world, of the activity of man, of the destiny of mankind, no theology or cosmology, perhaps even no metaphysics, that has not sought a reflection of itself in the mirror of political philosophy; certainly there has been no fully considered politics that has not looked for its reflection in eternity. This history of political philosophy is, then, the context of the masterpiece. And to interpret it in the context of this history secures it against the deadening requirement of conformity to a merely abstract idea of political philosophy.

This kind of reflection about politics is not, then, to be denied a place in our intellectual history. And it is characteristic of political philosophers that they take a sombre view of the human situation: they deal in darkness. Human life in their writings appears, generally, not as a feast or even as a journey, but as a predicament; and the link between politics and eternity is the contribution the political order is conceived as making to the deliverance of mankind. Even those whose thought is most remote from violent contrasts of dark and light (Aristotle, for example) do not altogether avoid this disposition of mind. And some political philosophers may even be suspected of spreading darkness in order to make their light more acceptable. Man, so the varied formula runs, is the dupe

6   *Introduction to* Leviathan

of error, the slave of sin, of passion, of fear, of care, the enemy
of himself or of others or of both—

> *O miseras hominum mentes, O pectora caeca*

—and the civil order appears as the whole or a part of the
scheme of his salvation. The precise manner in which the
predicament is conceived, the qualities of mind and imagination and the kinds of activity man can bring to the achievement of his own salvation, the exact nature and power of
civil arrangements and institutions, the urgency, the
method and the comprehensiveness of the deliverance—these
are the singularities of each political philosophy. In them
are reflected the intellectual achievements of the epoch or
society, and the great and slowly mediated changes in intellectual habit and horizon that have overtaken our civilization.
Every masterpiece of political philosophy springs from a new
vision of the predicament; each is the glimpse of a deliverance
or the suggestion of a remedy.

It will not, then, surprise us to find an apparently contingent element in the ground and inspiration of a political
philosophy, a feeling for the exigencies, the cares, the passions
of a particular time, a sensitiveness to the dominant folly of
an epoch: for the human predicament is a universal appearing
everywhere as a particular. Plato's thought is animated by the
errors of Athenian democracy, Augustine's by the sack of
Rome, and what stirs the mind of Hobbes is 'grief for the present calamities of my country', a country torn between those
who claimed too much for Liberty and those who claimed too
much for Authority, a country given over into the hands of
ambitious men who enlisted the envy and resentment of a
'giddy people' for the advancement of their ambitions.[1, 2] And
not being surprised at this element of particularity, we shall
not allow it to mislead us into supposing that nothing more is
required to make a political philosopher than an impression-
able political consciousness; for the masterpiece, at least, is

---

[1] *E.W.*, II, i–xxiv.

[2] *L.*, pp. 3, 274, 549. Hobbes had also in mind the situation in late
sixteenth-century France.

Introduction to Leviathan 7

always the revelation of the universal predicament in the local and transitory mischief.[3]

If the unity of the history of political philosophy lies in a pervading sense of human life as a predicament and in the continuous reflection of the changing climate of the European intellectual scene, its significant variety will be found in three great traditions of thought. The singularities of political philosophies (like most singularities) are not unique, but follow one of three main patterns which philosophical reflection about politics has impressed upon the intellectual history of Europe. These I call traditions because it belongs to the nature of a tradition to tolerate and unite an internal variety, not insisting upon conformity to a single character, and because, further, it has the ability to change without losing its identity. The first of these traditions is distinguished by the master-conceptions of Reason and Nature. It is coeval with our civilization; it has an unbroken history into the modern world; and it has survived by a matchless power of adaptability all the changes of the European consciousness. The master-conceptions of the second are Will and Artifice. It too springs from the soil of Greece, and has drawn inspiration from many sources, not least from Israel and Islam. The third tradition is of later birth, not appearing until the eighteenth century. The cosmology it reflects in its still unsettled surface is the world seen on the analogy of human history. Its master-conception is the Rational Will, and its followers may be excused the belief that in it the truths of the first two traditions are fulfilled and their errors find a happy release. The masterpiece of political philosophy has for its context, not only the history of political philosophy as the elucidation of the predicament and deliverance of mankind, but also, normally, a particular tradition in that history; generally speaking it is the supreme expression of its own tradition. And, as Plato's *Republic* might be chosen as the representative of the first tradition, and Hegel's *Philosophie des Rechts* of the third, so *Leviathan* is the head and crown of the second.

Leviathan is a masterpiece, and we must understand it

[3] *L.*, p. 271.

8 *Introduction to* Leviathan

according to our means. If our poverty is great, but not ruinous, we may read it not looking beyond its two covers, but intent to draw from it nothing that is not there. This will be a notable achievement, if somewhat narrow. The reward will be the appreciation of a dialetical triumph with all the internal movement and liveliness of such a triumph. But *Leviathan* is more than a *tour de force*. And something of its larger character will be perceived if we read it with the other works of Hobbes open beside it. Or again, at greater expense of learning, we may consider it in its tradition, and doing so will find fresh meaning in the world of ideas it opens to us. But finally, we may discover in it the true character of a masterpiece—the still centre of a whirlpool of ideas which has drawn into itself numberless currents of thought, contemporary and historic, and by its centripetal force has shaped and compressed them into a momentary significance before they are flung off again into the future.

III. THE MIND AND MANNER

In the mind of a man, the σύνολον of form and content alone is actual; style and matter, method and doctrine, are inseparable. And when the mind is that of a philosopher, it is a sound rule to come to consider the technical expression of this unity only after it has been observed in the less formal version of it that appears in temperament, cast of mind and style of writing. Circumstantial evidence of this sort can, of course, contribute nothing relevant to the substantiation of the technical distinctions of a philosophy; but often it has something to contribute to the understanding of them. At least, I think this is so with Hobbes.

Philosophy springs from a certain bent of mind which, though different in character, is as much a natural gift as an aptitude for mathematics or a genius for music. Philosophical speculation requires so little in the way of a knowledge of the world and is, in comparison with some other intellectual pursuits, so independent of book-learning, that the gift is apt to

Introduction to Leviathan   9

manifest itself early in life. And often a philosopher will be found to have made his significant contribution at an age when others are still preparing themselves to speak or to act. Hobbes had a full share of the *anima naturaliter philosophica*, yet it is remarkable that the beginning of his philosophical writing cannot be dated before his forty-second year and that his masterpiece was written when he was past sixty. Certainly there is nothing precocious in his genius; but are we to suppose that the love of reasoning, the passion for dialectic, which belong to the gift for philosophy, were absent from his character in youth? Writers on Hobbes have been apt to take a short way with this suggestion of a riddle. The life of Hobbes has been divided into neat periods, and his appearance as a philosopher in middle life has been applauded rather than explained. Brilliant at school, idle at the university, unambitious in early life, later touched by a feeling for scholarship and finally taking the path of philosophy when, at the age of forty, the power of geometric proof was revealed to him in the pages of *Euclid*: such is the life attributed to him. It leaves something to be desired. And evidence has been collected which goes to show that philosophy and geometry were not coeval in Hobbes's mind, evidence that the speculative gift was not unexercised in his earlier years.[4] Yet it remains true that when he appears as a philosophical writer, he is already adult, mature in mind; the period of eager search of tentative exploration, goes unreflected in his pages.

The power and confidence of Hobbes's mind as he comes before us in his writings cannot escape observation. He is arrogant (but it is not the arrogance of youth), dogmatic, and when he speaks it is in a tone of confident finality: he knows everything except how his doctrines will be received. There is nothing half-formed or undeveloped in him, nothing in progress; there is no promise, only fulfilment. There is self-confidence, also, a Montaigne-like self-confidence; he has accepted himself and he expects others to accept him on the same terms. And all this is understandable when we appreciate that Hobbes is not one of those philosophers who allow us to

[4] L. Strauss, *The Political Philosophy of Hobbes.*

see the workings of their minds, and that he published nothing
until he was fifty-four years old. There are other, more technical, reasons for his confidence. His conception of philosophy
as the establishment by reasoning of hypothetical causes saved
him from the necessity of observing the caution appropriate
to those who deal with facts and events.[5] But, at bottom, it
springs from his maturity, the knowledge that before he spoke
he was a match for anyone who had the temerity to answer
back. It belonged to Hobbes's temperament and his art, not
less than to his circumstances, to hold his fire. His long life
after middle age gave him the room for change and development that others find in earlier years; but he did not greatly
avail himself of it. He was often wrong, especially in his light-
hearted excursions into mathematics, and he often changed
his views, but he rarely retracted an opinion. His confidence
never deserted him.

But if the first impression of Hobbes's philosophical writing
is one of maturity and deliberateness, the second is an impression of remarkable energy. It is as if all the lost youth of
Hobbes's mind had been recovered and perpetuated in this
pre-eminently youthful quality. One of the more revealing
observations of Aubrey about him is that 'he was never idle;
his thoughts were always working.' And from this energy flow
the other striking characteristics of his mind and manner—
his scepticism, his addiction to system and his passion for controversy.

An impulse for philosophy may originate in faith (as with
Erigena), or in curiosity (as with Locke), but with Hobbes
the prime mover was doubt. Scepticism was, of course, in the
air he breathed; but in an age of sceptics he was the most
radical of them all. His was not the elegiac scepticism of Montaigne, nor the brittle net in which Pascal struggled, nor was
it the methodological doubt of Descartes; for him it was both
a method and a conclusion, purging and creative. It is not the
technicalities of his scepticism (which we must consider later)
that are so remarkable, but its ferocity. A medieval passion
overcomes him as he sweeps aside into a common abyss of

[5] *L.*, p. 554.

absurdity both the believer in eternal truth and the industrious seeker after truths; both faith and science. Indeed, so
extravagant, so heedless of consequences, is his scepticism,
that the reader is inclined to exclaim, what Hobbes himself
is said to have exclaimed on seeing the proof of the forty-
seventh theorem in *Euclid*, 'By God, this is impossible.' And
what alone makes his scepticism plausible is the intrepidity
of Hobbes himself; he has the nerve to accept his conclusions
and the confidence to build on them. Both the energy to
destroy and the energy to construct are powerful in Hobbes.

A man, it is generally agreed, may make himself ridiculous
as easily by a philosophical system as by any other means. And
yet, the impulse to think systematically is, at bottom, nothing
more than the conscientious pursuit of what is for every philosopher the end to be achieved. The passion for clearness and
simplicity, the determination not to be satisfied with anything
inconsequent, the refusal to relieve one element of experience
at the cost of another, are the motives of all philosophical
thinking; and they conduce to system. 'The desire of wisdom
leadeth to a kingdom.' And the pursuit of system is a call, not
only upon fine intelligence and imagination, but also, and
perhaps pre-eminently, upon energy of mind. For the principle in system is not the simple exclusion of all that does not
fit, but the perpetual re-establishment of coherence. Hobbes
stands out, not only among his contemporaries, but also in the
history of English philosophy, as the creator of a system. And
he conceived this system with such imaginative power that,
in spite of its relatively simple character, it bears comparison
with even the grand and subtle creation of Hegel. But if it
requires great energy of mind to create a system, it requires
even greater not to become the slave of the creation. To become the slave of a system in life is not to know when to 'hang
up philosophy', not to recognize the final triumph of incon-
sequence; in philosophy, it is not to know when the claims of
comprehension outweigh those of coherence. And here also the
energy of Hobbes's mind did not desert him. When we come
to consider the technicalities of his philosophy we shall observe
a moderation that, for example, allowed him to escape an

atomic philosophy, and an absence of rigidity that allowed him to modify his philosophical method when dealing with politics; here, when we are considering informally the quality of his mind, this ability appears as resilience, the energy to be perpetually freeing himself from the formalism of his system.

Thinking, for Hobbes, was not only conceived as movement, it was felt as movement. Mind is something agile, thoughts are darting, and the language of passion is appropriate to describe their workings. And the energy of his nature made it impossible for him not to take pleasure in controversy. The blood of contention ran in his veins. He acquired the lucid genius of a great expositor of ideas; but by disposition he was a fighter, and he knew no tactics save attack. He was a brilliant controversialist, deft, pertinacious and imaginative, and he disposed of the errors of scholastics, Puritans and Papists with a subtle mixture of argument and ridicule. But he made the mistake of supposing that this style was universally effective, in mathematics no less than in politics. For brilliance in con-troversy is a corrupting accomplishment. Always to play to win is to take one's standards from one's opponent, and local victory comes to displace every other consideration. Most readers will find Hobbes's disputatiousness excessive; but it is the defect of an exceptionally active mind. And it never quite destroyed in him the distinction between beating an opponent and establishing a proposition, and never quite silenced the conversation with himself which is the heart of philosophical thinking. But, like many controversialists, he hated error more than he loved truth, and came to depend overmuch on the stimulus of opposition. There is sagacity in Hobbes, and often a profound deliberateness; but there is no repose.

We have found Hobbes to possess remarkable confidence and energy of mind; we must consider now whether his mind was also original. Like Epicurus, he had an affectation for originality. He rarely mentions a writer to acknowledge a debt, and often seems over-sensitive about his independence of the past in philosophy. Aristotle's philosophy is 'vain', and scholas-ticism is no more than a 'collection of absurdities'. But, though

Introduction to Leviathan 13

he had certainly read more than he sometimes cared to admit —it was a favourite saying of his that if he had read as much as other men he should have known no more than other men —he seems to have been content with the reading that happened to come his way, and complained rather of the inconvenience of a want of conversation at some periods in his life than of a lack of books. He was conscious of being a self-taught philosopher, an amateur, without the training of a Descartes or the background of a Spinoza. And this feeling was perhaps strengthened by the absence of an academic environment. One age of academic philosophy had gone, the next was yet to come. The seventeenth century was the age of the independent scholar, and Hobbes was one of these, taking his own way and making his own contacts with the learned world. And his profound suspicion of anything like authority in philosophy reinforced his circumstantial independence. The guidance he wanted he got from his touch with his contemporaries, particularly in Paris; his inspiration was a native sensitiveness to the direction required of philosophy if it were to provide an answer to the questions suggested by contemporary science. In conception and design, his philosophy in his own. And when he claimed that civil philosophy was 'no older than my own book *De Cive*',[6] he was expressing at once the personal achievement of having gone afresh to the facts of human consciousness for his interpretation of the meaning of civil association, and also that universal sense of newness with which his age appreciated its own intellectual accomplishments. But, for all that, his philosophy belongs to a tradition. Perhaps the truth is that Hobbes was as original as he thought he was, and to acknowledge his real indebtedness he would have required to see (what he could not be expected to see) the link between scholasticism and modern philosophy which is only now becoming clear to us. His philosophy is in the nature of a palimpsest. For its author what was important was what he wrote, and it is only to be expected that he should be indifferent to what is already there; but for us both sets of writing are significant.

[6] *E.W.*, I, ix.

14   *Introduction to* Leviathan

Finally, Hobbes is a *writer*, a self-conscious stylist and the
master of an individual style that expresses his whole personality; for there is no hiatus between his personality and his
philosophy. His manner of writing is not, of course, foreign
to his age; it belongs to him neither to write with the infor-
mality that is the achievement of Locke, nor with the simplicity that makes Hume's style a model not to be rejected
by the philosophical writer of today. Hobbes is elaborate in
an age that delighted in elaboration. But, within the range of
his opportunities, he found a way of writing that exactly
reflected his temperament. His controversial purpose is large
on every page; he wrote to convince and to refute. And that
in itself is a discipline. He has eloquence, the charm of wit,
the decisiveness of confidence and the sententiousness of a
mind made up: he is capable of urbanity and of savage irony.
But the most significant qualities of his style are its didactic
and its imaginative character. Philosophy in general knows
two styles, the contemplative and the didactic, although there
are many writers to whom neither belongs to the complete
exclusion of the other. Those who practice the first let us into
the secret workings of their minds and are less careful to send
us away with a precisely formulated doctrine. Philosophy for
them is a conversation, and, whether or not they write it as
a dialogue, their style reflects their conception. Hobbes's way
of writing is an example of the second style. What he says is
already entirely freed from the doubts and hesitancies of the
process of thought. It is only a residue, a distillate that is
offered to the reader. The defect of such a style is that the
reader must either accept or reject; if it inspires to fresh
thought, it does so only by opposition. And Hobbes's style is
imaginative, not merely on account of the subtle imagery
that fills his pages, nor only because it requires imagination to
make a system. His imagination appears also as the power to
create a myth. *Leviathan* is a myth, the transposition of an
abstract argument into the world of the imagination. In it
we are made aware at a glance of the fixed and simple centre
of a universe of complex and changing relationships. The
argument may not be the better for this transposition, and

what it gains in vividness it may pay for in illusion. But it is an accomplishment of art that Hobbes, in the history of political philosophy, shares only with Plato.

IV. THE SYSTEM

In Hobbes's mind, his 'civil philosophy' belonged to a system of philosophy. Consequently, an enquiry into the character of this system is not to be avoided by the interpreter of his politics. For, if the details of the civil theory may not improperly be considered as elements in a coherence of their own, the significance of the theory as a whole must depend upon the system to which it belongs, and upon the place it occupies in the system.

Two views, it appears, between them hold the field at the present time. The first is the view that the foundation of Hobbes's philosophy is a doctrine of materialism, that the intention of his system was the progressive revelation of this doctrine in nature, in man and in society, and that this revelation was achieved in his three most important philosophical works, *De Corpore, De Homine* and *De Cive*. These works, it is suggested, constitute a continuous argument, part of which is reproduced in *Leviathan*; and the novel project of the 'civil philosophy' was the exposition of a politics based upon a 'natural philosophy', the assimilation of politics to a materialistic doctrine of the world, or (it is even suggested) to the view of the world as it appeared in the conclusions of the physical sciences. A mechanistic-materialist politics is made to spring from a mechanistic-materialist universe. And, not improperly, it is argued that the significance of what appears at the end is determined at least in part by what was proved or assumed at the beginning. The second view is that this, no doubt, was the intention of Hobbes, but that 'the attempt and not the deed confounds him'. The joints of the system are ill-matched, and what should have been a continuous argument, based upon a philosophy of materialism, collapses under its own weight.

Both these views are, I think, misconceived. But they are the product not merely of inattention to the words of Hobbes; it is to be feared that they derive also from a graver fault of interpretation, a false expectation with regard to the nature of a philosophical system. For what is expected here is that a philosophical system should conform to an architectural analogue, and consequently what is sought in Hobbes's system is a foundation and a superstructure planned as a single whole, with civil philosophy as the top storey. Now, it may be doubted whether any philosophical system can properly be represented in the terms of architecture, but what is certain is that the analogy does violence to the system of Hobbes. The coherence of his philosophy, the system of it, lies not in an architectonic structure, but in a single 'passionate thought' that pervades its parts.[7] The system is not the plan or key of the labyrinth of the philosophy; it is, rather, a guiding clue, like the thread of Ariadne.[8] It is like the music that gives meaning to the movement of dancers, or the law of evidence that gives coherence to the practice of a court. And the thread, the hidden thought, is the continuous application of a doctrine about the nature of philosophy. Hobbes's philosophy is the world reflected in the mirror of the philosophic eye, each image the representation of a fresh object, but each determined by the character of the mirror itself. In short, the civil philosophy belongs to a philosophical system, not because it is materialistic but because it is philosophical; and an enquiry into the character of the system and the place of politics in it resolves itself into an enquiry into what Hobbes considered to be the nature of philosophy.

For Hobbes, to think philosophically is to reason; philosophy is reasoning. To this all else is subordinate; from this all else derives. It is the character of reasoning that determines the range and the limits of philosophical enquiry; it is this

---

[7] Confucius said, 'T'zu, you probably think that I have learned many things and hold them in my mind.' 'Yes,' he replied, 'is that not true?' 'No,' said Confucius; 'I have one thing that permeates everything.' —Confucius, *Analects*, XV, 2. *L.*, p. 19.

[8] *E.W.*, II, vi.

Introduction to Leviathan 17

character that gives coherence, system, to Hobbes's philosophy. Philosophy, for him, is the world as it appears in the mirror of reason; civil philosophy is the image of the civil order reflected in that mirror. In general, the world seen in this mirror is a world of causes and effects: cause and effect are its categories. And for Hobbes reason has two alternative ends: to determine the conditional causes of given effects, or to determine the conditional effects of given causes.[9] But to understand more exactly what he means by this identification of philosophy with reasoning, we must consider three contrasts that run through all his writing: the contrast between philosophy and theology (reason and faith), between philosophy and 'science' (reason and empiricism) and between philosophy and experience (reason and sense).

Reasoning is concerned solely with causes and effects. It follows, therefore, that its activity must lie within a world composed of things that are causes or the effects of causes. If there is another way of conceiving this world, it is not within the power of reasoning to follow it; if there are things by definition causeless or ingenerable, they belong to a world other than that of philosophy. This at once, for Hobbes, excludes from philosophy the consideration of the universe as a whole, things infinite, things eternal, final causes and things known only by divine grace or revelation: it excludes what Hobbes comprehensively calls theology and faith. He denies, not the existence of these things, but their rationality.[10] This method of circumscribing the concerns of philosophy is not, of course, original in Hobbes. It has roots that go back to Augustine, if not further, and it was inherited by the seventeenth century (where one side of it was distinguished as the heresy of Fideism: both Montaigne and Pascal were Fideists) directly from its formulation in the Averroism of Scotus and Occam. Indeed, this doctrine is one of the seeds in scholasticism from which modern philosophy sprang. Philosophical explanation, then, is concerned with things caused. A world of such things is, necessarily, a world from which teleology is excluded; its internal movement comprises the impact of its parts upon one

[9] *E.W.*, I, 65–6, 387. [10] *L.*, p. 80; *E.W.*, I, 10, 410.

another, of attraction and repulsion, not of growth or development. It is a world conceived on the analogy of a machine,
where to explain an effect we go to its immediate cause, and
to seek the result of a cause we go only to its immediate
effect.[11] In other words, the mechanistic element in Hobbes's
philosophy is derived from his rationalism; its source and
authority lie, not in observation, but in reasoning. He does
not say that the natural world is a machine; he says only that
the rational world is analogous to a machine. He is a scholastic, not a 'scientific' mechanist. This does not mean that the
mechanistic element is unimportant in Hobbes; it means only
that it is derivative. It is, indeed, of the greatest importance,
for Hobbes's philosophy is, in all its parts, pre-eminently a
philosophy of *power* precisely because philosophy is reasoning, reasoning the elucidation of mechanism and mechanism
essentially the combination, transfer and resolution of forces.
The end of philosophy itself is power—*scientia propter
potentiam.*[12] Man is a complex of powers; desire is the desire
for power, pride is illusion about power, honour opinion
about power, life the unremitting exercise of power and death
the absolute loss of power. And the civil order is conceived as
a coherence of powers, not because politics is vulgarly observed to be a competition of powers, or because civil philosophy must take its conceptions from natural philosophy, but
because to subject the civil order to rational enquiry unavoidably turns it into a mechanism.

In the writings of Hobbes, philosophy and science are not
contrasted *eo nomine*. Such a contrast would have been impossible in the seventeenth century, with its absence of differentiation between the sciences and its still unshaken hold
on the conception of the unity of human knowledge. Indeed,
Hobbes normally uses the word science as a synonym for
philosophy; rational knowledge is scientific knowledge. Nevertheless, Hobbes is near the beginning of a new view of the
structure and parts of knowledge, a change of view which became clearer in the generation of Locke and was completed
by Kant. Like Bacon and others before him, Hobbes has his

[11] *E.W.,* II, xiv.   [12] *E.W.,* I, xiv; *O.L.,* I, 6.

Introduction to Leviathan 19

own classification of the *genres* of knowledge,[13] and that it is a classification which involves a distinction between philosophy and what we have come to call 'science' is suggested by his ambiguous attitude to the work of contemporary scientists. He wrote with an unusually generous enthusiasm of the great advances made by Kepler, Galileo and Harvey; 'the beginning of astronomy', he says, 'is not to be derived from farther time than from Copernicus';[14] but he had neither sympathy nor even patience for the 'new or experimental philosophy', and he did not conceal his contempt for the work of the Royal Society, founded in his lifetime. But this ambiguity ceases to be paradoxical when we see what Hobbes was about, when we understand that one of the few internal tensions of his thought arose from an attempted but imperfectly achieved distinction between science and philosophy. The distinction, well known to us now, is that between knowledge of things as they appear and enquiry into the fact of their appearing, between a knowledge (with all the necessary assumptions) of the phenomenal world and a theory of knowledge itself. Hobbes appreciated this distinction, and his appreciation of it allies him with Locke and with Kant and separates him from Bacon and even Descartes. He perceived that his concern as a philosopher was with the second and not the first of these enquiries; yet the distinction remained imperfectly defined in his mind. But that philosophy meant for Hobbes something different from the enquiries of natural science is at once apparent when we consider the starting-place of his thought and the character of the questions he thinks it necessary to ask. He begins with sensation; and he begins there, not because there is no deceit or crookedness in the utterances of the senses, but because the fact of our having sensations seems to him the only thing of which we can be indubitably certain.[15] And the question he asks himself is, what *must* the

---

[13] *L.*, p. 64.   [14] *E.W.*, I, viii.

[15] It will be remembered that the brilliant and informal genius of Montaigne had perceived that our most certain knowledge is what we know about ourselves, and had made of this a philosophy of introspection.

world be like for us to have the sensations we undoubtedly
experience? His enquiry is into the cause of sensation, an enquiry to be conducted, not by means of observation, but by
means of reasoning. And if the answer he proposes owes something to the inspiration of the scientists, that does nothing to
modify the distinction between science and philosophy inherent in the question itself. For the scientist of his day the
world of nature was almost a machine, Kepler had proposed
the substitution of the word *vis* for the word *anima* in physics;
and Hobbes, whose concern was with the rational world (by
definition also conceived as the analogy of a machine), discovered that some of the general ideas of the scientists could
be turned to his own purposes. But these pardonable appro-
priations do nothing to approximate his enquiry to that of
Galileo or Newton. Philosophy is reasoning, this time contrasted, not with theology, but with what we have come to
know as natural science. And the question, What, in an age
of science, is the task of philosophy? which was to concern
the nineteenth century so deeply, was already familiar to
Hobbes. And it is a false reading of his intention and his
achievement which finds in his civil philosophy the beginning
of sociology or a science of politics, the beginning of that
movement of thought that came to regard 'the methods of
physical science as the proper models for political'.[16]

But the contrast that finally distinguishes philosophy and
reveals its full character is that between philosophy and what
Hobbes calls experience. For in elucidating this distinction
Hobbes shows us philosophy coming into being, shows it as
a thing generated and relates it to its cause thereby establishing it as itself a proper subject of rational consideration. The
mental history of a man begins with sensation, 'for there is
no conception in a man's mind, which hath not at first, totally,
or by parts, been begotten upon the organs of sense'.[17] Some
sensations, perhaps, occupying but an instant, involve no
reference to others and no sense of time. But commonly, sensations, requiring a minimum time of more than a single

16 J. S. Mill, *Autobiography*, p. 165.
17 *L.*, p. 11.

instant, and reaching a mind already stored with the relics
of previous sensations, are impossible without that which gives
a sense of time—memory.[18] Sensation involves recollection,
and a man's experience is nothing but the recollected after-
images of sensations. But from his power to remember man
derives another power, imagination, which is the ability to
recall and turn over in the mind the decayed relics of past
sensation, the ability to experience even when the senses
themselves have ceased to speak. Moreover imagination,
though it depends on past sensations, is not an entirely servile
faculty; it is capable of compounding together relics of sensations felt at different times. Indeed, in imagination we may
have in our minds images not only of what we have never
actually seen (as when we imagine a golden mountain though
we have seen only gold and a mountain), but even of what we
could never see, such as a chimera. But imagination remains
servile in that 'we have no transition from one imagination
to another whereof we never had the like before in our
senses'.[19] Two things more belong to experience; the fruits of
experience. The first is History, which is the ordered register
of past experiences. The second is prudence, which is the
power to anticipate experience by means of the recollection of
what has gone before. 'Of our conceptions of the past, we
make a future.'[20] A full, well-recollected experience gives the
'foresight' and 'wisdom' that belong to the prudent man, a
wisdom that springs from the appreciation of those causes and
effects that time and not reason teaches us. This is the end
and crown of experience. In the mind of the prudent or sagacious man, experience appears as a kind of knowledge. Governed by sense, it is necessarily individual, a particular
knowledge of particulars. But, within its limits, it is 'absolute
knowledge';[21] there is no ground upon which it can be
doubted, and the categories of truth and falsehood do not
apply to it. It is mere, uncritical 'knowledge of fact': 'experience concludeth nothing universal'.[22] And in all its characteristics it is distinguished from philosophical knowledge,

[18] *E.W.*, I, 393.   [19] *L.*, p. 18.
[20] *E.W.*, IV, 16.   [21] *L.*, p. 64.   [22] *E.W.*, IV, 18.

which (because it is reasoned) is general and not particular, a knowledge of consequences and not of facts, and conditional and not absolute.

Our task now is to follow Hobbes in his account of the generation of rational knowledge from experience. In principle, experience (except perhaps when it issues in history) is something man shares with animals and has only in a greater degree: memory and imagination are the unsought mechanical products of sensation, like the movements that continue on the surface of water after what disturbed it has sunk to rest. In order to surmount the limits of this sense-experience and achieve reasoned knowledge of our sensations, we require not only to have sensations, but to be conscious of having them; we require the power of introspection. But the cause of this power must lie in sense itself, if the power is to avoid the imputation of being an easy *deus ex machina*. Language satisfies both these conditions: it makes introspection possible, and springs from a power we share with animals, the physical power of making sounds. For, though language 'when disposed of in speech and pronounced to others'[23] is the means whereby men declare their thoughts to one another, it is primarily the only means by which a man may communicate his own thoughts to himself, may become conscious of the contents of his mind. The beginning of language is giving names to after-images of sensations and thereby becoming conscious of them; the act of naming the image is the act of becoming conscious of it. For, 'a name is a word taken at pleasure to serve as a mark that may raise in our minds a thought like some thought we had before'.[24]

Language, the giving of names to images, is not itself reasonable, it is the arbitrary precondition of all reasoning:[25] the generation of rational knowledge is by words out of experience. The achievement of language is to 'register our thoughts', to fix what is essentially fleeting. And from this achievement follows the possibility of definition, the conjunc-

[23] *E.W.*, I, 16.   [24] *E.W.*, I, 16.
[25] This is why introspection that falls short of reasoning is possible. *E.W.*, I, 73.

Introduction to Leviathan 23

tion of general names, proposition and rational argument, all of which consist in the 'proper use of names in language'. But, though reasoning brings with it knowledge of the general and the possibility of truth and its opposite, absurdity,[26] it can never pass beyond the world of names. Reasoning is nothing else but the addition and subtraction of names, and 'gives us conclusions, not about the nature of things, but about the names of things. That is to say, by means of reason we discover only whether the connections we have established between names are in accordance with the arbitrary convention we have established concerning their meanings.'[27] This is at once a nominalist and a profoundly sceptical doctrine. Truth is of universals, but they are names, the names of images left over from sensations; and a true proposition is not an assertion about the real world. We can, then, surmount the limits of sense-experience and achieve rational knowledge; and it is this knowledge, with its own severe limitations, that is the concern of philosophy.

But philosophy is not only knowledge of the universal, it is a knowledge of causes. Informally, Hobbes describes it as 'the natural reason of man flying up and down among the creatures, and bringing back a true report of their order, causes and effects.'[28] We have seen already how, by limiting philosophy to a knowledge of things caused (because reasoning itself must observe this limit) he separates it from theology. We have now to consider why he believed that the essential work of reasoning (and therefore of philosophy) was the demonstration of the cause of things caused. Cause for Hobbes is the means by which anything comes into being. Unlike any of the Aristotelian causes, it is essentially that which, previous in time, brings about the effect. A knowledge of cause is, then, a knowledge of how a thing is generated.[29] But why must philosophy be a knowledge of this sort? Hobbes's answer would appear to be, first, that this sort of

---

[26] Since truth is of propositions, its opposite is a statement that is absurd or nonsensical. Error belongs to the world of experience and is a failure in foresight. *L.*, p. 34.

[27] *O.L.*, V, 257.   [28] *E.W.*. I. xiii.   [29] *E.W.*, VII, 78.

knowledge can spring from reasoning while it is impossible
to mere experience, and, secondly, that since, *ex hypothesi*,
the data of philosophy are effects, the only possible enlarge-
ment of our knowledge of them must consist in a knowledge
of their causes. If we add to the experience of an effect a
knowledge of its generation, a knowledge of its 'constitutive
cause',[30] we know everything that may be known. In short, a
knowledge of causes is the pursuit in philosophy because
philosophy is reasoning.[31]

The third characteristic of philosophical knowledge, as distinguished from experience, is that it is conditional, not
absolute. Hobbes's doctrine is that when, in reasoning, we conclude that the cause of something is such and such, we can
mean no more than that such and such is a possible efficient
cause, and not that it is the actual cause. There are three
criteria by which a suggested cause may be judged, and proof
that the cause actually operated is not among them. For
reasoning, a cause must be 'imaginable', the necessity of the
effect must be shown to follow from the cause, and it must
be shown that nothing false (that is, not present in the effect)
can be derived.[32] And what satisfies these conditions may be
described as an hypothetical efficient cause. That philosophy
is limited to the demonstration of such causes is stated by
Hobbes on many occasions; it applies not only to the detail
of his philosophy, but also to the most general of all causes, to
body and motion. For example, when he says that the cause
or generation of a circle is 'the circumduction of a body whereof one end remains unmoved', he adds that this gives 'some
generation [of the figure], though perhaps not that by which
it was made, yet that by which it might have been made'.[33]
And when he considers the general problem of the cause of
sensations, he concludes, not with the categorical statement
that body and motion are the only causal existents, but that

[30] *E.W.*, II, xiv.
[31] Hobbes gives the additional reason that a knowledge of causes is
useful to mankind. *E.W.*, I, 7–10.
[32] *Elements of Law*, Appendix II, § 1, 168.
[33] *E.W.*, I, 6, 386–7.

Introduction to Leviathan 25

body (that is, that which is independent of thought and which fills a portion of space) and motion are the hypothetical efficient causes of our having sensations. If there were no body there could be no motion, and if there were no motion of bodies there could be no sensation; *sentire semper idem et non sentire ad idem recidunt.*[34] From beginning to end there is no suggestion in Hobbes that philosophy is anything other than conditional knowledge, knowledge of hypothetical generations and conclusions about the names of things, not about the nature of things.[35] With these philosophy must be satisfied, though they are but fictions. Indeed, philosophy may be defined as the establishment by reasoning of true fictions. And the ground of this limitation is, that the world being what it is, reasoning can go no further. 'There is no effect which the power of God cannot produce in many several ways,'[36] verification *ad oculos* is impossible because these causes are rational not perceptible, and consequently the farthest reach of reason is the demonstration of causes which satisfy the three rational criteria.

My contention is, then, that the system of Hobbes's philosophy lies in his conception of the nature of philosophical knowledge, and not in any doctrine about the world. And the inspiration of his philosophy is the intention to be guided by reason and to reject all other guides: this is the thread, the hidden thought, that gives it coherence, distinguishing it from Faith, 'Science' and Experience. It remains to guard against a possible error. The lineage of Hobbes's rationalism lies, not (like that of Spinoza or even Descartes) in the great Platonic-Christian tradition, but in the sceptical, late scholastic tradition. He does not normally speak of Reason, the

[34] *O.L.*, I, 321.

[35] *L.*, pp. 49–50.

[36] *E.W.*, VII, 3. It may be observed that what is recognized here is the normally unstated presupposition of all seventeenth-century science: the Scotist belief that the natural world is the creation *ex nihilo* of an omnipotent God, and that therefore categorical knowledge of its detail is not deducible but (if it exists) must be the product of observation. Characteristically adhering to the tradition, Hobbes says that the only thing we can know of God is his omnipotence.

divine illumination of the mind that unites man with God;
he speaks of reasoning. And he is not less persuaded of its
fallibility and limitations than Montaigne himself.[37] By means
of reasoning we certainly pass beyond mere sense-experience,
but when imagination and prudence have generated rational
knowledge, they do not, like drones, perish; they continue
to perform in human life functions that reasoning itself
cannot discharge. Nor, indeed, is man, in Hobbes's view,
primarily a reasoning creature. This capacity for general
hypothetical reasoning distinguishes him from the animal,
but he remains fundamentally a creature of passion, and it
is by passion not less than by reasoning that he achieves his
salvation.[38]

We have considered Hobbes's view of philosophy because
civil philosophy, whatever else it is, is philosophy. Civil philosophy, the subject of *Leviathan*, is precisely the application of
this conception of philosophy to civil association. It is not the
last chapter in a philosophy of materialism, but the reflection
of civil association in the mirror of a rationalistic philosophy.
But if the *genus* of civil philosophy is its character as
philosophy, its *differentia* is derived from the matter to be
considered. Civil philosophy is settling the generation or constitutive cause of civil association. And the kind of hypothetical
efficient cause that civil philosophy may be expected to demonstrate is determined by the fact that civil association is an
artifact: it is artificial, not natural. Now, to assert that civil
association is an artifact is already to have settled the question
of its generation, and Hobbes himself does not begin with
any such assertion. His method is to establish the artificial
character of civil association by considering its generation.
But in order to avoid false expectations it will be wise for us
to anticipate the argument and consider what he means by
this distinction between art and nature.

Hobbes has given us no collected account of his philosophy
of artifice; it is to be gathered only from scattered observations. But when these are put together, they compose a co-

[37] *L.*, p. 34.   [38] *L.*, p. 98.

Introduction to Leviathan 27

herent view. A work of art is the product or effect of mental activity. But this in itself does not distinguish it securely from nature, because the universe itself must be regarded as the product of God's mental activity, and what we call 'nature' is to God an artifact;[39] and there are products of human mental activity which, having established themselves, become for the observer part of his natural world. More firmly defined, then, a work of art is the product of mental activity considered from the point of view of its cause. And, since what we have to consider are works of human art, our enquiry must be into the kind of natural human mental activity that may result in a work of art; for the cause of a work of art must lie in nature; that is, in experience. It would appear that the activities involved are willing and reasoning. But reasoning itself is artificial, not natural; it is an 'acquired' not a 'native' mental activity,[40] and therefore cannot be considered as part of the generation of a work of art.[41] We are left, then, with willing, which, belonging to experience and not reasoning, is undoubtedly a natural mental activity. The cause (hypothetical and efficient, of course) of a human work of art is the will of a man. And willing is 'the last desire in deliberating', deliberating being mental discourse in which the subject is desires and aversions.[42] It is a creative activity (not merely imitative), in the same way as imagination, working on sensations, creates a new world of hitherto separated parts. Both will and imagination are servile only in that their products must be like nature in respect of being mechanisms; that is, complexes of cause and effect.[43] Moreover, will creates not only when it is single and alone, but also in concert with other wills. The product of an agreement between wills is no less a work of art than the product of one will. And the peculiarity of civil association, as a work of art, is its generation from a number of wills. The word 'civil', in Hobbes, means artifice spring-

[39] *L.,* p. 5.   [40] *L.,* p. 29.

[41] The expression 'natural reason' is not absent from Hobbes's writings, but it means the reasoning of individual men contrasted with the doubly artificial reasoning of the artificial man, the Leviathan. e g. *L.,* pp. 5, 42, 233, 242; *E.W.,* I, xiii.

[42] *L.,* p. 38.   [43] *L.,* p. 8.

ing from more than one will. Civil history (as distinguished
from natural history) is the register of events that have sprung
from the voluntary actions of man in commonwealths.[44] Civil
authority is authority arising out of an agreement of wills,
while natural authority (that of the father in the family) has
no such generation and is consequently of a different character.[45] And civil association is itself contrasted on this account
with the appearance of it in mere natural gregariousness.[46]

Now, with this understanding of the meaning of both 'civil'
and 'philosophical', we may determine what is to be expected
for a civil philosophy. Two things may be expected from it.
First, it will exhibit the internal mechanism of civil association as a system of cause and effect and settle the generation
of the parts of civil association. And secondly, we may expect
it to settle the generation, in terms of an hypothetical efficient
cause, of the artifact as a whole; that is, to show this work of
art springing from the specific nature of man. But it may be
observed that two courses lie open to anyone, holding the
views of Hobbes, who undertakes this project. Philosophy, we
have seen, may argue from a given effect to its hypothetical
efficient cause, or from a given cause to its possible effect.
Often the second form of argument is excluded; this is so with
sensations, when the given is an effect and the cause is to seek.
But in civil philosophy, and in all reasoning concerned with
artifacta, both courses are open; for the cause and the effect
(human nature and civil association) are both given, and the
task of philosophy is to unite the details of each to each in
terms of cause and effect. Hobbes tells us[47] that his early thinking on the subject took the form of an argument from effect
(civil association) to cause (human nature), from art to nature;
but it is to be remarked that, not only in *Leviathan*, but also
in all other accounts he gives of his civil philosophy, the form
of the argument is from cause to effect, from nature to art.
But, since the generation is rational and not physical, the
direction from which it is considered is clearly a matter of
indifference.

[44] *L.*, p. 64.   [45] *L.*, p. 153.
[46] *L.*, p. 130.   [47] *E.W.*, II, vi, xiv.

Introduction to Leviathan   29

V. THE ARGUMENT OF *LEVIATHAN*

Any account worth giving of the argument of *Leviathan*
must be an interpretation; and this account, because it is an
interpretation, is not a substitute for the text. Specific comment is avoided; but the implicit comment involved in
selection, emphasis, the alteration of the language and the
departure from the order of ideas in the text, cannot be
avoided.

The nature of man is the predicament of mankind. A knowledge of this nature is to be had from introspection, each man
reading himself in order to discern in himself, mankind. Civil
philosophy begins with this sort of knowledge of the nature
of man.[48]
 Man is a creature of sense. He can have nothing in his mind
that was not once a sensation. Sensations are movements in
the organs of sense which set up consequent movements in the
brain; after the stimulus of sense has spent itself, there remain in the mind slowly fading relics of sensations, called
images or ideas. Imagination is the consciousness of these
images, we imagine what was once in the senses but is there
no longer. Memory is the recollection of these images. A man's
experience is the whole contents of his memory, the relics of
sensations available to him in recollection. And Mental Discourse is images succeeding one another in the mind. This
succession may be haphazard or it may be regulated, but it
always follows some previous succession of sensations. A typical regulated succession of images is where the image of an
effect calls up from memory the image of its cause. Mental

[48] Man is a mechanism; but a mechanism may be considered at different levels of abstraction. For example, the working of a watch may
be described mathematically in terms of quantities, or in the mechanical terms of force and inertia, or in terms of its visible parts, springs
and cogs. And to choose one level does not deny the possibility of the
others. In selecting introspection as the sort of knowledge of man required in civil philosophy, Hobbes is doing no more than to choose
what he considers to be the relevant level of abstraction.

discourse becomes Prudence or foresight when, by combining
the recollection of the images of associated sensations in the
past with the present experience of one of the sensations, we
anticipate the appearance of the others. Prudence is natural
wisdom. All these together may be called the *receptive* powers
of a man. Their cause is sensation (into the cause of which we
need not enquire here), and they are nothing other than
movements in the brain.[49]

But, springing from these there is another set of movements
in the brain, which may be called comprehensively the *active*
powers of a man; his emotions or passions. These movements
are called voluntary to distinguish them from involuntary
movements such as the circulation of the blood. Voluntary
activity is activity in response to an idea, and therefore it has
its beginning in imagination. Its undifferentiated form is
called Endeavour, which, when it is towards the image from
which it sprang is called Desire or Appetite, and when it is
away from its originating image is called Aversion. Love corresponds to Desire; Hate to Aversion. And whatever is the
object of a man's desire he calls Good, and whatever he hates
he calls Evil. There is, therefore, nothing good or evil as such;
for different men desire different things, each calling the
object of his desire good, and the same man will, at different
times, love and hate the same thing. Pleasure is a movement
in the mind that accompanies the image of what is held to be
good, pain one that accompanies an image held to be evil.
Now, just as the succession of images in the mind is called
Mental Discourse (the end of which is Prudence), so the succession of emotions in the mind is called Deliberation, the
end of which is Will. While desire and aversion succeed one
another without any decision being reached, we are said to be
deliberating; when a decision is reached, and desire is concentrated upon some object, we are said to will it. Will is the
last desire in deliberating. There can, then, be no final end,
no *summum bonum*,[50] for a man's active powers; human con-

---

[49] *L.*, chs. i–iii.

[50] There is, however, a *summum malum*, and it is death; its opposite,
being alive, is only a 'primary good'. *L.*, p. 75; *O.L.*, II, 98.

Introduction to Leviathan   31

duct is not teleological, it is concerned with continual success
in obtaining those things which a man from time to time
desires, and success lies not only in procuring what is desired,
but also in the assurance that what will in the future be desired will also be procured. This success is called Felicity,
which is a condition of movement, not of rest or tranquillity.
The means by which a man may obtain this success are called,
comprehensively, his Power; and therefore there is in man a
perpetual and restless desire for power, because power is the
conditio sine qua non of Felicity.[51]

The receptive and the active powers of man derive directly
from the possession of the five senses; the senses are their efficient cause. And since we share our senses with the animals,
we share also these powers. Men and beasts do not have the
same images and desires; but both alike have imagination and
desire. What then, since this does not, differentiates man from
beast? Two things: religion and the power of reasoning. Both
these are at once natural and artificial: they belong to the
nature of man because their generation is in sense and emotion, but they are artificial because they are the products of
human mental activity. Religion and reasoning are mankind's
natural inheritance of artifice.

The character of reasoning and its generation from the invention of speech has already been described. Here it need only
be added that, just as Prudence is the end-product of imagination and Felicity of emotion, so Sapience is the end-product of
reasoning; and Sapience is a wealth of general hypothetical
conclusions or theorems, found out by reasoning, about the
causes and consequences of the names of sensations.[52]

The seed of religion, like that of reasoning, is in the nature
of man, though what springs from that seed, a specific set of
religious beliefs and practices, is an artifact. The generation of
religion is the necessary defect of Prudence, the inexperience
of man. Prudence is foresight of a probable future based upon
recollection, and insight into a probable cause also based upon
recollection. Its immediate emotional effect is to allay anxiety

[51] *L.*, chs. vi, xi.
[52] *L.*, chs. iv, v.

and fear, fear of an unknown cause or consequence.[53] But
since its range is necessarily limited, it has the additional effect
of increasing man's fear of what lies beyond that limit. Prudence, in restricting the area in the control of fear, increases
the fear of what is still to be feared; having some foresight,
men are all the more anxious because that foresight is not
complete. (Animals, having little or no foresight, suffer only
the lesser evil of its absence, not the greater of its limitation.)
Religion is the product of mental activity to meet this situation. It springs from prudent fear of what is beyond the power
of prudence to find out,[54] and is the worship of what is feared
because it is not understood. Its contradictory is Knowledge;
its contrary is Superstition, worship springing from fear of
what is properly an object of knowledge. The perpetual fear
that is the spring of religion seeks an object on which to concentrate itself, and calls that object God. It is true that per-
severance in reasoning may reveal the necessity of a First
Cause, but so little can be known about it that the attitude
of human beings towards it must always be one of worship
rather than knowledge. And each man, according to the restriction of his experience and the greatness of his fear, renders
to God worship and honour.[55]

The human nature we are considering is the internal structure
and powers of the individual man, a structure and powers
which would be his even if he were the only example of his
species: we are considering the character of the solitary. He
lives in the world of his own sensations and imaginations,
desires and aversions, prudence, reason and religion. For his
thoughts and actions he is answerable to none but himself. He
is conscious of possessing certain powers, and the authority for
their exercise lies in nothing but their existence, and that
authority is absolute. Consequently, an observer from another

---

[53] For Hobbes, fear is aversion from something believed to be hurtful. *L.*, p. 43.
[54] *L.*, p. 82. The limitations of reasoning also produce fear, a rational
fear of what is beyond the power of reason to discern.
[55] *L.*, ch. xii.

Introduction to Leviathan 33

world, considering the character of our solitary, would not improperly attribute to him a natural freedom or right of judgement in the exercise of his powers of mind and body for the achievement of the ends given in his nature.[56] In the pursuit of felicity he may make mistakes, in his mental discourse he may commit errors, in his reasoning he may be guilty of absurdity, but a denial of the propriety of the pursuit would be a meaningless denial of the propriety of his character and existence. Further, when our solitary applies his powers of reasoning to find out fit means to attain the ends dictated by his emotional nature, he may, if his reasoning is steady, light upon some general truths or theorems with regard to the probable consequences of his actions. It appears, then, that morally unfettered action (which may be called a man's natural right to exercise his natural powers), and the possibility of formulating general truths about the pursuit of felicity, are corollaries of human nature.

Two further observations may be made. First, in the pursuit of felicity certain habits of mind and action will be found to be specially serviceable, and these are called Virtues. Other habits will hinder the pursuit, and these are called Defects. Defects are misdirected virtues. For example, prudence in general is a virtue, but to be over-prudent, to look too far ahead and allow too much care for the future, reduces a man to the condition of Prometheus on the rock (whose achievements by night were devoured by the anxieties of the day), and inhibits the pursuit.[57] And the pre-eminently inhibiting defect from which human beings may be observed to suffer is Pride. This is the defect of Glory, and its other names are Vanity and Vain-glory. Glory, which is exultation in the mind based upon a true estimate of a man's powers to procure felicity, is a useful emotion; it is both the cause and effect of well-grounded confidence. But pride is a man's false estimate

[56] Freedom, for Hobbes, can be properly attributed only to a body whose motion is not hindered. *L.*, p. 161. And the 'right' derives, of course, not from the authority of a natural law, but from the character of the individual as an *ens completum*.

[57] *L.*, p. 82.

of his own powers, and is the forerunner of certain failure. Indeed, so fundamental a defect is pride, that it may be taken as the type of all hindrances to the achievement of felicity.[58] Secondly, it may be observed that death, the involuntary cessation of desire and the pursuit which is the end of desire, is the thing of all others the most hateful; it is the *summum malum.* And that which men hate they also fear if it is beyond their control. Prudence tells a man that he will die, and by taking thought the prudent man can sometimes avoid death by avoiding its probable occasions, and, so far, the fear of it will be diminished. But death will outdistance the fastest runner; in all its forms it is something to be feared as well as hated. Yet it is to be feared most when it is most beyond the control of prudence: the death to be most greatly feared is that which no foresight can guard against—sudden death.[59] It would appear, then, that Pride is the type of all hindrances to the achievement of felicity, and death the type of all Aversion.

Now, the element of unreality in the argument so far is not that the solitary, whose character we have been considering, is an abstraction and does not exist (he does exist and he is the real individual man), but that he does not exist alone. This fact, that there is more than one of his kind, must now be recognized; we must turn from the nature of man to consider the natural condition of man. And it is at this point that the predicament of mankind becomes apparent; for, apart from mortality, the character of the solitary man presents nothing that could properly be called a predicament.

The existence of others of his kind, and the impossibility of escaping their company, is the first real impediment in the pursuit of felicity; for another man is necessarily a competitor.

[58] *L.,* pp. 44, 88.

[59] In *Leviathan* death itself is taken to be the greatest evil; the refinement about sudden death is an interpretation of the view that appears in the *De Cive* and elsewhere that the greatest evil is *violent* death at the hands of another. This not only terminates the pursuit of felicity, but does so in a manner shameful to the victim; it convicts him of inferiority.

Introduction to Leviathan   35

This is no mere observation, though its effects may be seen by any candid observer; it is a deduction from the nature of felicity. For, whatever appears to a man to belong to his felicity he must strive for with all his powers, and men who strive for the possession of the same object are enemies of one another. Moreover, he who is most successful will have the most enemies and be in the greatest danger. To have built a house and cultivated a garden is to have issued an invitation to all others to take it by force, for it is against the common view of felicity to weary oneself with making what can be acquired by less arduous means. And further, competition does not arise merely when two or more happen to want the same thing, for when a man is among others of his kind his felicity is not absolute but comparative; and since a large part of it comes from a feeling of superiority, of having more than his fellow, the competition is essential, not accidental. There is, at best, a permanent potential enmity between men, 'a perpetual contention for Honour, Riches and Authority'.[60] And to make matters worse, each man is so nearly the equal of each other man in power, that superiority of strength (which might set some men above the disadvantage of competition: the possibility of losing) is nothing better than an illusion. The natural condition of man is one of the competition of equals for the things (necessarily scarce because of the desire for *superiority*)[61] that belong to felicity. But equality of power, bringing with it, not only equality of fear, but also equality of hope, will urge every man to try to outwit his neighbour. And the end is open conflict, a war of all against all, in which the defects of man's character and circumstances make him additionally vulnerable. For, if pride, the excessive estimate of his own powers, hinders a man in choosing the best course when he is alone, it will be the most crippling of all handicaps when played upon by a competitor in the race. And in a company of enemies, death, the *summum malum*, will be closer than felicity. When a man is among men, pride is more dangerous and death more likely.[62]

But further, the relationship between these self-moved

---

[60] *L.*, p. 547.   [61] *L.*, p. 130.   [62] *L.*, ch. xiii.

seekers after felicity is complicated by an ambiguity. They are
enemies but they also need one another. And this for two
reasons: without others there is no recognition of superiority
and therefore no notable felicity; and many, perhaps most of
the satisfactions which constitute a man's felicity are in the
responses he may wring from others. The pursuit of felicity,
in respect of a large part of it, is a procedure of bargaining
with others in which one seeks what another has got and for
which he must offer a satisfaction in return.

The predicament may now be stated precisely. There is a
radical conflict between the nature of man and the natural
condition of mankind: what the one urges with hope of
achievement, the other makes impossible. Man is solitary;
would that he were alone. For the sweetness of all he may
come by through the efforts of others, is made bitter by the
price he must pay for it, and it is neither sin nor depravity
that creates the predicament; nature itself is the author of his
ruin.

But, like the seeds of fire (which were not themselves warm)
that Prometheus brought mankind, like the first incipent
movements (hardly to be called such) that Lucretius, and after
him Hobbes, supposes to precede visible movement, the deliverance lies in the womb of nature. The saviour is not a
visitor from another world, nor is it some god-like power of
Reason come to create order out of chaos; there is no break
either in the situation or in the argument. The remedy of the
disease is homeopathic.[63]

The precondition of the deliverance is the recognition of
the predicament. Just as, in Christian theory, the repentance
of the sinner is the first indispensable step towards forgive-
ness and salvation, so here, mankind must first purge itself
of the illusion called pride. So long as a man is in the grip of
this illusion he will hope to succeed tomorrow where he
failed today; and the hope is vain. The purging emotion (for
it is to emotion that we go to find the beginning of deliverance) is fear of death. This fear illuminates prudence; man
is a creature civilized by fear of death. And what is begun in

[63] *L.*, p. 98.

Introduction to Leviathan 37

prudence is continued in reasoning; art supplements the gifts of nature.

For, as reasoning may find out truths for the guidance of a man in his pursuit of felicity when he is alone, so it is capable of uncovering similar truths in respect of his competitive endeavour to satisfy his wants. And since what threatens to defeat every attempt to procure felicity in these circumstances is the unconditionally competitive character of the pursuit (or, in a word, war), these truths found out by reason for avoiding this defeat of all by all may properly be called the articles of Peace. Such truths, indeed, have been uncovered, and they are all conditions qualifying the competitive pursuit of felicity which, if they are observed by all, will enhance the certainty, if not the magnitude of the satisfaction of each. They are sometimes called the 'laws of nature', but this is a misnomer except in special circumstances (to be considered later) when they are recognized to be the commands of a God or of a civil sovereign. Properly speaking, they are only theorems, the product of reasoning about what conduces to the optimum satisfaction of human wants.[64] And they are fruitless until they are transformed from mere theorems into maxims of human conduct and from maxims into laws; that is, until they are recognized as valid rules of conduct of known jurisdiction, to be subscribed to by all who fall within that jurisdiction and to which penalties for non-subscription have been annexed and power to enforce them provided. But this transformation also lies within the scope of human art. Such rules of conduct are neither more nor less than the product of an agreement to recognize them as rules, and human beings endowed with the faculty of speech may not only communicate their thoughts to one another but also make agreements; indeed, their association is solely in terms of agreements. In short, moved by fear of ill-success in procuring the satisfaction of their wants, instructed by the conclusions of reasoning about how this ill-success may be mitigated and endowed with the ability to set these conclusions to work, human beings enjoy the means of escaping from the predicament of mankind.

[64] *L.*, 122, 205.

The substantial conclusions of human reasoning in this matter Hobbes sums up in a maxim: *do not that to another, which thou wouldest not have done to thyself.*[65] But, more important than this, is its formal message, namely, that where there is a multitude of men each engaged in unconditional competition with the others to procure the satisfaction of his own wants, and of roughly equal power to obtain each what he seeks, they may succeed in their respective endeavours only when its unconditionality is abated. The abrogation of the competition is, of course, impossible; there can be no common or communal felicity to which they might be persuaded to turn their attention. But this race in which each seeks to come first and is also unavoidably and continuously fearful of not doing so, must have some rules imposed upon it if it is not to run everyone into the ground. And this can be done only in an agreement of those concerned.

Now, in the day-to-day transactions in which human beings seek the satisfaction of their wants this message of reason may often be listened to and acted upon. They make *ad hoc* agreements about procedures of bargaining, they enter into formal relationships, they even make and accept promises about future actions and often keep them. And although such arrangements cannot increase the magnitude of their felicity they may make its pursuit less chancy. But this abatement of uncertainty is at best marginal and at worst delusive. These *ad hoc* formal relationships of mutual agreement between assignable persons are evanescent; remotely they may reflect generally accepted theorems about rational conduct, but as rules they are the products of specific and temporary agreements between the persons concerned. And further, they are always liable to be undermined by the substantial relationship of competitive hostility. And even if such agreements contain penalty clauses for the non-observance of the conditions they impose upon the conduct of a transaction, these (in the absence of an independent means of enforcing them) add nothing to the certainty of the sought-for outcome. And this is particularly the case where a promise to respond in the

---

[65] *L.,* p. 121.

future is made by one who has already received a conditional benefit: the abatement of uncertainty it purports to offer depends upon the expectation of its being fulfilled, that is, upon whether or not it is in the interest of the respondent to keep his promise when the time comes to do so. And this, in Hobbes's view, must always be insufficiently certain for a reasonable man to bank upon it. In short, these *ad hoc* devices to increase the certainty of the satisfaction of wants, when taken alone, are themselves infected with uncertainty; where there is a present and substantial agreement about mutual interests they may be a convenience, where this is absent they provide merely an illusion of security.

What, then, is lacking here, and what is required for a 'constant and lasting' release from the impediments which frustrate the common pursuit of individual felicity, is settled and known rules of conduct and a power sufficient to coerce those who fall within their jurisdiction to observe them. How may this condition of things be imagined to be 'caused' or 'generated'? First, it can be the effect only of an agreement among the human beings concerned. It is human beings associated in a particular manner, and all human association is by agreement. Secondly, it can be the effect of only a particular kind of agreement; namely, one in which a number of men, neither small nor unmanageably large, associate themselves in terms of a covenant to authorize an Actor to make standing rules to be subscribed to indifferently in all their endeavours to satisfy their wants and to protect the association from the hostile attentions of outsiders, and to endow this Actor with power sufficient to enforce these conditions of conduct and to provide this protection. Or, if this is not the only imaginable cause of the desiderated condition of peace and security, then at least it is a possible cause.[66]

Such a covenant requires careful specification if it is to be shewn not itself to inhibit the pursuit of felicity and not to conflict with the alleged characters of those who enter into it. And it is susceptible of various descriptions. It may, in general, be recognized as an agreement of many to submit their

[66] *L.,* ch. xvii.

Introduction to Leviathan

wills every one to the will of an Actor in respect of 'all those things which concern the common peace and safety'.[67] More precisely it may be identified as an agreement in which each participator surrenders his natural right to 'govern himself' (or, 'to be governed by his own reason')[68] which derives from his natural right to the unconditional pursuit of his own felicity. But if so, the character of this surrender must be specified: it must be not a mere laying down of this right, but a giving up of it to another. The right of each to 'govern himself' (that is, to determine the conditions upon which he may pursue his felicity) is transferred to an Actor; that is, to one authorized in the agreement to exercise it. But who must this Actor be? Not a natural person, one among those who covenant to surrender their right to govern themselves, for that would be merely to place the government of their conduct in the hands of one moved only by his appetite to satisfy his own wants. The Actor is an artificial man who represents or 'bears the person' of each of those who, by agreeing among themselves to do so, creates him and authorizes all his actions. What is created and authorized in this covenant is an Office which, although it may be occupied by one or by more than one office-holder, remains single and sovereign in all its official actions and utterances. Thus, the condition of peace and security is said to be the effect of 'a covenant of every man with every man, in such manner, as if every man should say to every man, *I authorize and give up my right of governing myself, to this man, or to this assembly of men, on this condition, that thou give up thy right to him, and authorize all his actions in like manner'.*[69] Or again, it may be recognized as a covenant in which the covenanters agree among themselves 'to confer all their strength and power upon one [artificial] man', thus providing the power to enforce recalcitrants to submit to the will and the judgement of an office-holder authorized to deliberate and to decide upon the conditions to be observed by all in their several adventures in pursuit of felicity. And here it is a covenant not merely to transfer a right (which could notionally be effected in a single once-

[67] *L.*, p. 131.   [68] *L.*, p. 99.   [69] *L.*, p. 131.

Introduction to Leviathan 41

for-all pronouncement), but to be continuously active in sup-
plying the power required to exercise it—for the Office can
have no such resources of its own.

This covenant, then, purports to create an artifact composed of a sovereign Ruler authorized and empowered by
covenanters who thereby become 'united in one person',
transform themselves into Subjects and thus release themselves from the condition of war of all against all. This artifact is called a Commonwealth or *civitas*.

This is Hobbes's account of the hypothetical efficient cause
of civil association. There are refinements I have not mentioned and, no doubt, also, difficulties; but the rest of the
civil philosophy consists of an exhibition of this artifact as a
system of internal causes and effects, joining where necessary
parts of its structure to particular features of the predicament
from which it is designed to rescue mankind. This may be
conveniently considered under four heads: (1) the constitution of the sovereign authority, (2) the rights and 'faculties' of
the sovereign authority, (3) the obligations and liberties of
subjects, (4) the civil condition.

(1) The recipient of the transferred rights, whatever its
constitution, is a single and sovereign authority. But this
Office may be occupied by one or by many, and if by more
than one either by some or by all. Thus a civil authority may
have a monarchical, an aristocratic (or oligarchical) or a democratic constitution. Which it is to be, is solely a matter of
which is most likely to generate the peace for which civil
association is instituted. The advantages of monarchy are
obvious. But if the Office is occupied by an assembly of men,
this cannot be because such an assembly is more likely to
'represent' the variety of opinion among subjects, for a ruler
is not the interpreter of the various wants of his subjects but
the custodian of their will for peace. However, no kind of
constitution is without its defects. Reason gives no conclusive
answer, but tells us only that the main consideration is not
wise but authoritative rule.[70]

(2) The rights of the occupant of the sovereign office are

[70] *L.*, ch. xix.

those which the covenanters confer upon him.[71] They are the right to rule and the right to enjoy the support of those who, in the agreement, have created themselves Subjects. These rights are both limited and unconditional. The covenanters have not surrendered their right to pursue felicity; they have surrendered only their right each to do this unconditionally, or (which is the same thing) on conditions which each decides for himself. But the rights with which they have endowed the sovereign are not retractable, and since he is not himself a party to any agreement he does not 'bear their persons' on condition that he observes the terms of an agreement. Nor may any man exclude himself from the condition of Subject, on the grounds that he did not himself assent to the covenant, without declaring himself an 'outlaw' and forfeiting the protection of the sovereign. The right to rule is the right to be the sole judge of what is necessary for the peace and security of subjects.

The business of ruling is the exercise of this right. And the most important part of it is to make rules for the conduct of Subjects.[72] In a *civitas* the sovereign is the sole legislative authority; nothing is law save what he declares to be law, and it is law solely in virtue of that declaration. A law, in Hobbes's understanding of it, is a command, the expression of the Will of the Sovereign. Not every command of the sovereign is law, but only those commands which prescribe a rule of conduct to be subscribed to indifferently by all Subjects.

In general, the contents of civil law corresponds to the theorems which natural reason has uncovered about what conduces to peaceful relationships between human beings. In certain circumstances (with which we are not now concerned) these theorems may properly be called 'natural laws' and the legal virtue or validity of the declarations of a civil sovereign may be thought to derive, at least in part, from their correspondence with these 'natural laws'; but here the civil sovereign has nothing but theorems of natural reason to guide him and the legal validity of the rules he makes lies solely in their being his commands. In short, in civil association the validity

[71] *L.*, ch. xviii.　　　　[72] *L.*, p. 137, ch. xxvi.

Introduction to Leviathan 43

of a law lies neither in the wisdom of the conditions it imposes upon conduct, nor even in its propensity to promote peace, but in its being the command of the sovereign and (although this is obscure) in its being effectively enforced. There may be unnecessary laws and even laws which increase rather than diminish contention, and these are to be deplored, but no valid law can, strictly speaking, be 'unjust'. 'Just' conduct is identifiable only in terms of law and in civil association there is none but civil law. And if, as Hobbes suggests, the law which identifies the conditions upon which a man may rightfully call anything his own and upon which he may recognize the rights of others in this respect is the most important branch of civil law, this is because in each man coming to know what he may call his own and in being protected in his enjoyment of it the most fruitful cause of human contention is abated.[73]

Together with the right to make laws goes the right to interpret them, to administer them and to punish those who do not observe them. All law requires interpretation; that is, decision about what it means in contingent circumstances. This decision must be authoritative. And, in Hobbes's view, laws lose all their virtue if their observance is not enforced by inescapable penalties. This 'faculty' of the civil sovereign is exercised in courts of law presided over by himself or his agents. The sovereign's relationship to civil law is that as its maker he is *legibus solutus* (having unconditional authority to make or to repeal), but in respect of his judicial office he is bound by the law as it is. He may pardon some offences.[74]

Besides the sole right to make, repeal, interpret, administer and enforce rules, the sovereign is the judge of what is necessary for the peace and security of his subjects in respect of threats to the association coming from without: the right to negotiate, make war, conclude peace, levy taxes to defray the expenses of war and raise an army of volunteers of such dimensions as he shall think fit. He has the right to choose his

[73] *L.*, pp. 111, 137.
[74] *L.*, p. 137.

own counsellors and agents, and he is himself the commander-in-chief of such military force as the association disposes.[75]

Lastly, the civil sovereign, although he cannot dictate the beliefs of his subjects, has the right to inspect and to govern all expressions of opinion or doctrine among his subjects (especially those addressed to large audiences) in relation to their propensity to promote or to disrupt the peace of the association. This censorship is not directly concerned with the truth or falsity of the opinions uttered, but 'a doctrine repugnant to peace, can no more be true, than peace and concord can be against the law of nature'.[76]

It should be noted that the office of Sovereign has no rights of 'lordship'; its *dominium* is solely *regale*.

(3) Civil Subjects are persons who, in a mutual agreement, have transferred the right of each to govern himself to a sovereign Actor; they have covenanted with one another to authorize all his actions, each to avouch every such action as his own, to submit their judgements and wills to his judgement and will in all that concerns their peace and security, to obey his commands and to pledge all their strength and power to support the exercise of his authority. Thus, in a mutual agreement, they have each and all undertaken an obligation. Each in agreement with all others has bound himself in advance to a specified course of conduct in relation to one another and in relation to a ruler and his acts of ruling. In what respect may a civil Subject be said to be free?[77]

Freedom means the absence of external impediment to movement; and a man, whose movement is the performance of actions he has willed to perform, is properly said to be free when 'in those things, which by his strength and wit he is able to do, [he] is not hindered to do what he has willed to do.'[78] Human freedom is a quality of conduct itself, not of will. To find no external stop in doing what he has a will to do is to be a free man.

Cives, however, are subject to artificial impediments which stand in the way of their doing what they wish to do; namely,

[75] *L.*, pp. 137–8.
[77] *L.*, ch. xxi.
[76] *L.*, p. 136, ch. xlii.
[78] *L.*, p. 161.

Introduction to Leviathan 45

civil laws and the penalties which attach to not observing them, even the penalty of death, which is a stop to all conduct. They are in a situation of being compelled to do what they may not wish to do. And in this respect their freedom is curtailed.

But, it may be observed, first, that this situation is one of their own choosing; they may have chosen it out of fear of the alternative (the perpetual and unregulated obstruction of their actions by others), but this does not make the covenant any the less a free action. Whatever impediments they suffer on this account have been authorized by themselves. And further, their covenant was an act designed to emancipate them from certain external impediments to the pursuit of felicity, and if it were to be conscientiously observed by all there would be a net gain of freedom; fewer and less disastrous impediments to their willed actions.

More to the point, however, are the following considerations. Civil authority, the regulation of human conduct by law, does not and cannot prescribe the whole of any man's conduct. Apart from the fact that rules can be observed only in choosing to perform actions which they do not themselves prescribe, there is always an area of the conduct of civil Subjects which, on account of the silence of the law, they are free to occupy on their own terms; to do and to forebear each at his own discretion. And the 'greatest liberty' of civil subjects derives from the silences of the law.[79] Furthermore, civil subjects enjoy a freedom which Hobbes calls their 'true freedom', which derives from the precise form of the covenant; in specifying their obligations the covenant specifies also a freedom. Each covenanter has surrendered his right to govern himself and has undertaken to *authorize* the actions of the sovereign ruler as if they were his own. The terms of the covenant exclude, and are designed to exclude, any undertaking to surrender rights which cannot be given up without a man risking the loss of all that he designed to protect in making the covenant; that is, his pursuit of felicity and even his life.[80] Thus, the covenanter authorizes the sovereign to arraign him

[79] *L.*, pp. 162, 168.　　　　[80] *L.*, p. 167.

before a court for an alleged breach of the law, but he has no obligation to accuse himself without the assurance of pardon. And although, if convicted, he authorizes the infliction upon himself of the lawful penalty, even the penalty of death, he is not obliged to kill himself or any other man. And it is in the enjoyment of all those rights which he has not surrendered that the 'true freedom' of the Subject lies. Finally, although he cannot himself retract the authorization he has given, he retains the right to protect himself and his interests by such strength as he may have if the authorized ruler is no longer able to protect him.[81]

(4) The civil condition is an artifact. And since it is human beings associated in terms of the authorization of the decisions and the actions of a single Sovereign, Hobbes calls it an Artificial Man. It is association articulated in terms of settled and known laws which define the conditions of a 'just' relationship between its members. And since 'justice', strictly speaking, is a function of having rules which cannot be breached with impunity, and since in default of a *civitas* there are no rules with penalties annexed to them but only unconditional competition for the satisfaction of wants together with some theorems about how this competition might become more fruitful from which nothing more than general maxims of prudent conduct may be rationally derived, 'justice' and the civil condition may be said to be coeval.

But if human beings may find in civil association a condition of 'peace' in which the frustrations and anxieties of an unconditional competition between men for the satisfaction of wants are relieved, these are not the only anxieties they suffer and this is not the only 'peace' they seek. They are dimly aware of inhabiting a world in which nothing happens without a cause and they think and speak of this world, metaphorically, as the 'natural kingdom of God', the first or master cause of all that happens being identified as the will of this God. But they are acutely aware of their ignorance of the efficient causes of occurrences and of their consequent inability to move about this world with confidence, assured of

[81] *L.*, p. 170.

Introduction to Leviathan 47

achieving the satisfaction of their wants. They are gnawed by an anxiety, distinguishable from that which arises from their lack of power to compete unconditionally with their fellows, and they seek relief not only in a *pax civilis* but in a *pax dei.* They attribute to this God nothing but what is 'warranted by natural reason', they acknowledge his power (indeed his omnipotence), they do not (or should not) dishonour him by disputing about his attributes, and they address him in utterances of worship—and all this in a design to ingratiate themselves with what they cannot control and thus abate their anxieties. In the civil condition this worship may be in secret and thus of no concern to the civil sovereign, or by private men in the hearing of others and thus subject to the conditions of civility. But since a civil association is a many joined in the will and authorized actions of a Sovereign authority it must display this unity in the worship of this God. He is to be recognized and honoured in a public *cultus* and in utterances and gestures determined by the civil Sovereign. In a *civitas* the *pax dei* is an integral part of the *pax civilis.*[82]

Now, even an attentive reader might be excused if he supposed that the argument of *Leviathan* would end here. Whatever our opinion of the cogency of the argument, it would appear that what was projected as a civil philosophy had now been fulfilled. But such is not the view of Hobbes. For him it remains to purge the argument of an element of unreality which still disfigures it. And it is not an element of unreality that appears merely at this point; it carries us back to the beginning, to the predicament itself, and to get rid of it requires a readjustment of the entire argument. It will be remembered that one element of unreality in the conception of the condition of nature (that is, in the cause of civil association) was corrected as soon as it appeared; the natural man was recognized to be, though solitary, not alone. But what has remained so far unacknowledged is that the natural man is, not only solitary and not alone, but is also the devotee of a positive religion; the religion attributed to him was something

[82] *L.,* ch. xxi.

less than he believed. How fundamental an oversight this was we shall see in a moment; but first we may consider the defect in the argument from another standpoint. In the earlier statement, the predicament was fully exhibited in its universal character, but (as Hobbes sees it) the particular form in which it appeared to his time, the peculiar folly of his age, somehow escaped from that generality; and to go back over the argument with this in the forefront of his mind seemed to him a duty that the civil philosopher owed to his readers. The project, then, of the second half of the argument of *Leviathan* is, by correcting an error in principle, to show more clearly the local and transitory mischief in which the universal predicament of mankind appeared in the seventeenth century. And both in the conception and in the execution of this project, Hobbes reveals, not only his sensitiveness to the exigencies of his time, but also the medieval ancestry of his way of thinking.

The Europe of his day was aware of three positive religions: Christianity, the Jewish religion and the Moslem. These, in the language of the Middle Ages, were *leges*,[83] because what distinguished them was the fact that the believer was subject to a *law*, the law of Christ, of Moses or of Mahomet. And no traditionalist would quarrel with Hobbes's statement that 'religion is not philosophy, but law'.[84] The consequence in civil life of the existence of these 'laws' was that every believer was subject to two laws—that of his *civitas* and that of his religion: his allegiance was divided. This is the problem that Hobbes now considers with his accustomed vigour and insight. It was a problem common to all positive religions, but not unnaturally Hobbes's attention is concentrated upon it in relation to Christianity.[85]

The man, then, whose predicament we have to consider is, in addition to everything else, a Christian. And to be a Christian means to acknowledge obligation under the *law* of God. This is a real obligation, and not merely the shadow of one,

[83] Cf. the *De Legibus* of William of Auvergne, Bishop of Paris, d. 1249.

[84] *E.W.,* VII, 5.

[85] *L.,* ch. xxxii.

Introduction to Leviathan 49

because it is a real law—a command expressing the will of God. This law is to be found in the Scriptures. There are men who speak of the results of human reasoning as Natural Laws, but if we are to accept this manner of speaking we must beware of falling into the error of supposing that they are laws because they are rational. The results of natural reasoning are no more than uncertain theorems,[86] general conditional conclusions, unless and until they are transformed into laws by being shown to be the will of some authority. If, in addition to being the deliverance of reasoning, they can be shown to be the will and command of God, then and then only can they properly be called laws, natural or divine; and then and then only can they be said to create obligation.[87] But, as a matter of fact, all the theorems of reasoning with regard to the conduct of men in pursuit of felicity are to be found in the scriptures, laid down as the commands of God. Now, the conclusion of this is, that no proper distinction can be maintained between a Natural or Rational and a Revealed law. All law is revealed in the sense that nothing is law until it is shown to be the command of God by being found in the scriptures. It is true that the scriptures may contain commands not to be discovered by human reasoning and these, in a special sense, may be called revealed; but the theorems of reasoning are laws solely on account of being the commands of God, and therefore their authority is no different from that of the commands not penetrable by the light of reasoning. There is, then, only one law, Natural and Divine; and it is revealed in scripture.

But Scripture is an artifact. It is, in the first place, an arbitrary selection of writings called canonical by the authority that recognized them. And secondly, it is nothing apart from interpretation. Not only does the history of Christianity show that interpretation is necessary and has been various, but any consideration of the nature of knowledge that is not entirely perfunctory must conclude that 'no line is possible between what has come to men and their interpretation of what has come to them.'[88] Nothing can be more certain than that, if the

---

[86] *E.W.*, IV, 285.   [87] *L.*, p. 122; *E.W.*, IV, 285.
[88] Hort, *The Way, the Truth and the Life*, p. 175.

50   *Introduction to* Leviathan

law of God is revealed in scripture, it is revealed only in an interpretation of scripture.[89] And interpretation is a matter of authority; for, whatever part reasoning may play in the process of interpretation, what determines everything is the decision, *whose* reasoning shall interpret? And the far-reaching consequences of this decision are at once clear when we consider the importance of the obligations imposed by this law. Whoever has the authority to determine this law has supreme power over the conduct of men, 'for every man, if he be in his wits, will in all things yield to that man an absolute obedience, by virtue of whose sentence he believes himself to be either saved or damned'.[90]

Now, in the condition of nature there are two possible claimants to this authority to settle and interpret scripture and thus determine the obligations of the Christian man. First, each individual man may claim to exercise this authority on his own behalf. And this claim must at once be admitted. For, if it belongs to a man's natural right to do whatever he deems necessary to procure felicity, it will belong no less to this right to decide what he shall believe to be his obligations under the law natural and divine. In nature every man is 'governed by his own reason.'[91] But the consequences of this will be only to make more desperate the contentiousness of the condition of nature. There will be as many 'laws' called Christian as there are men who call themselves Christian; and what men did formerly by natural right, they will do now on a pretended obligation to God. A man's actions may thus become conscientious, but conscience will be only his own good opinion of his actions.[92] And to the secular war of nature will be added the fierceness of religious dispute. But secondly, the claim to be the authority to settle and interpret the scriptures may be made on behalf of a special spiritual authority, calling itself, for the purpose, a church. And a claim of this sort may be made either by a so-called universal church (when the claim will be to have authority to give an interpretation to be accepted by all Christians everywhere), or by a church whose

[89] *L.*, ch. xxxiii.   [90] *E.W.*, II, 283–97.
[91] *L.*, p. 99.   [92] *L.*, p. 224.

authority is limited to less than the whole number of Christians. But, whatever the form of the claim, what we have to enquire into is the generation of the authority. Whence could such an authority be derived? We may dispose at once of the suggestion that any spiritual authority holds a divine commission to exercise such a faculty. There is no foundation in history to support such a suggestion; and even if there were, it could not give the necessary ground for the authority. For, such an authority could only come about by a transfer of natural right as a consequence of a covenant; this is the only possible cause of any authority whatever to order men. But we have seen already that a transfer of rights as a consequence of a covenant does not, and could not, generate a special spiritual authority to interpret scripture; it generates infallibly a civil society. A special spiritual authority for settling the law of God and Nature, cannot, then, exist; and where it appears to exist, what really exists is only the natural authority of one man (the proper sphere of which is that man's own life) illegitimately extended to cover the lives of others and masquerading as something more authoritative than it is; in short, a spiritual tyranny.

There is in the condition of nature, where Christians are concerned, a law of nature; and it reposes in the scriptures. But what the commands of this law are no man can say except in regard to himself alone; the public knowledge of this law is confined to the knowledge of its bare existence.[93] So far, then, from the law of nature mitigating the chaos of nature, it accentuates it. To be a 'natural' Christian adds a new shadow to the darkness of the predicament of the condition of nature, a shadow that will require for its removal a special provision in the deliverance.

The deliverance from the chaos of the condition of nature as hitherto conceived is by the creation of a civil association or Commonwealth; indeed, the condition of nature is the hypothetical efficient cause of a Commonwealth. And when account is taken of this new factor of chaos, the deliverance must be by the creation of a Christian Commonwealth; that

[93] *L.*, p. 275.

is, a civil association composed of Christian subjects under a Christian sovereign authority. The creation of this requires no new covenant; the natural right of each man to interpret scripture and determine the law of God on his own behalf will be transferred with the rest of his natural right, for it is not a separable part of his general natural right. And the recipient of the transferred right is the artificial, sovereign authority, an authority which is not temporal *and* spiritual (for, '*Temporal* and *Spiritual* government are but two names brought into the world to make men see double, and mistake their lawful sovereign'),[94] but single and supreme. And the association represented in his person is not a state *and* a church, for a true church (unlike the so-called churches which pretended their claims to be independent spiritual authorities in the condition of nature) is 'a company of men professing Christian Religion, united in the person of one Sovereign'. It cannot be a rival spiritual authority, setting up canons against laws, a spiritual power against a civil, and determining man's conduct by eternal sanctions,[95] because there is no generation that can be imagined for such an authority and its existence would contradict the end for which society was instituted. And if the Papacy lays claim to such an authority, it can at once be pronounced a claim that any other foreign sovereign might make (for civil associations stand in a condition of nature towards one another), only worse, for the Pope is a sovereign without subjects, a prince without a kingdom: 'if a man consider the original of this great Ecclesiastical Dominion, he will easily perceive, that the Papacy, is no other, than the *ghost* of the deceased *Roman Empire*, sitting crowned on the grave thereof: For so did the Papacy, start up on a sudden out of the ruins of that great Heathen Power.'[96]

It remains to consider what it means to be a Christian sovereign and a Christian subject. The chief right of the sovereign as Christian is the right to settle and interpret scripture and thus determine authoritatively the rules that belong to the Law of God and Nature. Without this right it is impossible for him to perform the functions of his office. For, if he does

[94] *L.*, p. 306.   [95] *L.*, p. 214.   [96] *L.*, p. 457.

not possess it, it will be possessed either by no one (and the chaos and war of nature will remain) or by someone else who will then, on account of the pre-eminent power this right gives, wield a supremacy both illegitimate and destructive of peace. But it is a right giving immense authority, for the laws it determines may be *called* God's laws, but are in fact the laws of the sovereign. With this right, the sovereign will have the authority to control public worship,[97] a control to be exercised in such a way as to oblige no subject to do or believe anything that might endanger his eternal salvation.[98] He may suppress organized superstition and heresy,[99] because they are destructive of peace; but an inquisition into the private beliefs of his subjects is no part of his right. And, as with other rights of sovereignty, he may delegate his right of religious instruction to agents whom he will choose, or even (if it be for the good of the society) to the Pope;[1] but the authority thus delegated is solely an authority to instruct, to give counsel and advice, and not to coerce.[2] But if the sovereign as Christian has specific rights, he has also obligations. For in the Christian Commonwealth there exists a law to which the sovereign is, in a sense, obliged. What had previously been merely the rational articles of peace, have become (on being determined in scripture) obligatory rules of conduct. The sovereign, of course, has no obligations to his subjects, only functions; but the law of God is to him (though he has made it himself), no less than to his subjects, a command creating an obligation. And iniquity, which in a heathen sovereign could never be more than a failure to observe the conclusions of sound reasoning, in the Christian sovereign becomes a breach of law and therefore a sin, punishable by God.

The subject as Christian has a corresponding extension of his obligation and right. The rule of his religion, as determined by the authoritative interpretation of scripture, creates no new and independent obligations, but provides a new sanction for the observation of all his obligations. The articles of peace are for him no longer merely the conclusions of reason-

[97] *L.*, p. 136, ch. xlii.   [98] *L.*, ch. xliii.

[99] *L.*, p. 453.   [1] *L.*, pp. 421, 427   [2] *L.*, p. 384.

ing legitimately enforced by the sovereign power; they are the laws of God. To observe the covenant he has made with his fellows becomes a religious obligation as well as a piece of prudential wisdom. The freedom of the Christian subject is the silence of the law with regard to his thoughts and beliefs; for if it be the function of the sovereign to suppress controversy, he has no right to interfere with what he cannot in fact control and what if left uncontrolled will not endanger peace. 'As for the inward *thought* and *belief* of men, which human governors take no notice of (for God only knoweth the heart), they are not voluntary, nor the effect of the laws, but of the unrevealed will and of the power of God; and consequently fall not under obligation.'[3] It is a darkly sceptical doctrine upon which Hobbes grounds toleration.

The argument is finished: but let no one mistake it for the book. The skeleton of a masterpiece of philosophical writing has a power and a subtlety, but they are not to be compared with the power and subtlety of the doctrine itself, clothed in the irony and eloquence of a writer such as Hobbes.

VI. SOME TOPICS CONSIDERED

(1) *The Criticism of Hobbes.* Most great philosophers have found some defenders who are prepared to swallow everything, even the absurdities; but Hobbes is an exception. He has aroused admiration in some of his readers, horror in others, but seldom affection and never undiscriminating affection. Nor is it surprising that this should be so. He offended against taste and interest, and his arrogance invited such a consequence. He could not deny himself the pleasure of exaggeration, and what were remembered were his incautious moments, and the rest forgotten. His doctrines, or some of them, have received serious attention and criticism from the time when they first appeared; but his critics have for the most part been opponents, and his few defenders not conspicuous

[3] *L.,* p. 364.

Introduction to Leviathan 55

for their insight into his meaning. On the whole it remains true that no great writer has suffered more at the hands of little men than Hobbes.

His opponents divide themselves into two classes; the emotional and the intellectual. Those who belong to the first are concerned with the supposed immoral tendencies of his doctrines; theirs is a practical criticism. The second are concerned with the theoretical cogency of his doctrines; they wish to shed light and sometimes succeed in doing so.

With the critics of the first class we need not greatly concern ourselves, though they still exist. They find in Hobbes nothing but an apostle of atheism, licentiousness and despotism, and express a fitting horror at what they find. The answers to *Leviathan* constitute a library, its censors a school in themselves. Pious opinion has always been against him, and ever since he wrote he has been denounced from the pulpit. Against Hobbes, Filmer defended servitude, Harrington liberty, Clarendon the church, Locke the Englishman, Rousseau mankind and Butler the Deity. And a writer of yesterday sums up Hobbes's reflections on civil philosophy as 'the meanest of all ethical theories united with unhistorical contempt for religion to justify the most universal of absolutisms.' No doubt some responsibility for all this attaches to Hobbes himself; he did not lack caution, but like all timid men he often chose the wrong occasion to be audacious. It is true that his age excused in Spinoza what it condemned in Hobbes; but then Spinoza was modest and a Jew, while Hobbes was arrogant and enough of a Christian to have known better. And that the vilification of Hobbes was not greater is due only to the fact that Machiavelli had already been cast for the part of scapegoat for the European consciousness.

The critics of the second class are more important, because it is in and through them that Hobbes has had his influence in the history of ideas. They, also, are for the most part his opponents. But, in the end, if Hobbes were alive today he would have some reason to complain (as Bradley complained) that even now he must 'do most of his scepticism for himself.' For his critics have shown a regrettable tendency to fix their

attention on the obvious errors and difficulties and to lose
sight of the philosophy as a whole. There has been a deplor-
able over-confidence about the exposure of faults in Hobbes's
philosophy. Few accounts of it do not end with the detection
of a score of simple errors, each of which is taken to be destructive of the philosophy, so that one wonders what claim Hobbes
has to be a philosopher at all, let alone a great one. Of course
there are inconsistencies in his doctrines, there is vagueness
at critical points, there is misconception and even absurdity,
and the detection of these faults is legitimate and useful criticism; but niggling of this sort will never dispose of the philosophy. A writer like Bentham may fall by his errors, but not
one such as Hobbes. Nor is this the only defect of his critics.
There has been failure to consider his civil philosophy in the
context of the history of political philosophy, which has
obscured the fact that Hobbes is not an outcast but, in purpose
though not in doctrine, is an ally of Plato, Augustine and
Aquinas. There has been failure to detect the tradition to
which his civil philosophy belongs, which has led to the misconception that it belongs to none and is without lineage or
progeny. And a large body of criticism has been led astray by
attention to superficial similarities which appear to unite
Hobbes to writers with whom, in fact, he has little or nothing
in common.

The task of criticism now is to make good some of these
defects. It is not to be expected that it can be accomplished
quickly or all at once. But a beginning may be made by recon-
sidering some of the vexed questions of the civil philosophy.

(2) *The Tradition of Hobbes.* Hobbes's civil philosophy is
a composition based upon two themes, Will and Artifice. The
individual who creates and becomes the subject of civil authority is an *ens completum*, an absolute will. He is not so much a
'law unto himself' as free from all law and obligation which is
the creature of law. This will is absolute because it is not
conditioned or limited by any standard, rule or rationality
and has neither plan nor end to determine it. This absence of
obligation is called by Hobbes, natural right. It is an original
and an absolute right because it derives directly from the

Introduction to Leviathan 57

character of will and not from some higher law or from Reason. The proximity of several such individuals to one another is chaos. Civil association is artificial, the free creation of these absolute wills, just as nature is the free creation of the absolute will of God. It is an artifice that springs from the voluntary surrender of the unconditional freedom or right of the individual, and consequently it involves a replacement of freedom by law and right by obligation.[4] In the creation of civil association a sovereignty corresponding to the sovereignty of the individual is generated. The Sovereign is the product of will, and is himself representing the wills of its creators. Sovereignty is the right to make laws by willing. The Sovereign, therefore, is not himself subject to law, because law creates obligation, not right. Nor is he subject to Reason, because Reason creates nothing, neither right nor obligation. Law, the life of civil association, is the command of the Sovereign, who is the Soul (the capacity to will), not the head, of civil association.[5]

Now, two things are clear about such a doctrine. First, that its ruling ideas are those that have dominated the political philosophy of the last three hundred years. If this is Hobbes's doctrine, then Hobbes said something that allied him to the future. And secondly, it is clear that this doctrine is a breakaway from the great Rational-Natural tradition of political philosophy which springs from Plato and Aristotle and found embodiment later in the Natural Law theory. That tradition in its long history embraced and accommodated many doctrines, but this doctrine of Hobbes is something it cannot tolerate. Instead of beginning with right, it begins with law and obligation, it recognizes law as the product of Reason, it finds the only explanation of dominion in the superiority of Reason, and all the various conceptions of nature that it has entertained exclude artifice as it is conceived by Hobbes. For these reasons it is concluded that Hobbes is the originator of a new tradition in political philosophy.[6]

But this theory of Hobbes has a lineage that stretches back

[4] *L.*, ch. xxi.   [5] *L.*, pp. 8, 137.
[6] Strauss, *op. cit.*, ch. viii.

into the ancient world. It is true that Greek thought, lacking the conception of creative will and the idea of sovereignty, contributed a criticism of the Rational-Natural theory which fell short of the construction of an alternative tradition: Epicurus was an inspiration rather than a guide. But there are in the political ideas of Roman civilization and in the politico-theological ideas of Judaism strains of thought that carry us far outside the Rational-Natural tradition, and which may be said to constitute beginnings of a tradition of Will and Artifice. Hobbes's immediate predecessors built upon the Roman conception of *lex* and the Judaic-Christian conception of will and creation, both of which contained the seeds of opposition to the Rational-Natural tradition, seeds which had already come to an early flowering in Augustine. And by the end of the middle ages this opposition had crystallized into a living tradition of its own. Hobbes was born into the world, not only of modern science, but also of medieval thought. The scepticism and the individualism, which are the foundations of his civil philosophy, were the gifts of late scholastic nominalism; the displacement of Reason in favour of will and imagination and the emancipation of passion were slowly mediated changes in European thought that had gone far before Hobbes wrote. Political philosophy is the assimilation of political experience to an experience of the world in general, and the greatness of Hobbes is not that he began a new tradition in this respect but that he constructed a political philosophy that reflected the changes in the European intellectual consciousness which had been pioneered chiefly by the theologians of the fifteenth and sixteenth centuries. *Leviathan*, like any masterpiece, is an end and a beginning; it is the flowering of the past and the seed-box of the future. Its importance is that it is the first great achievement in the long-projected attempt of European thought to re-embody in a new myth the Augustinian epic of the Fall and Salvation of mankind.

(3) *The Predicament of Mankind.* In the history of political philosophy there have been two opposed conceptions of the source of the predicament of man from which civil society

Introduction to Leviathan 59

springs as a deliverance: one conceived the predicament to arise out of the nature of man, the other conceived it to arise out of a defect in the nature of man. Plato, who went to what he believed to be the nature of man for the ground and structure of the *polis*, is an example of the first. And Spinoza, with his insistence on the principle that nothing in nature must be attributed to a defect of it,[7] adheres, in his different convention, to the same project of deducing civil society from 'the very condition of human nature'.[8] For Augustine, on the other hand, the predicament arises from a defect in human nature, from sin. Where does Hobbes stand in this respect? The widely-accepted interpretation of Hobbes's view is that, for him, the predicament springs from the egoistical character of man and that therefore it is vice and depravity that create the chaos. Moreover, it is a genuinely original depravity, for the Fall of man (or anything to take its place) is no part of Hobbes's theory. But when we look closer, what was distinguished as egoism (a moral defect) turns out to be neither moral nor a defect; it is only the individuality of a creature shut up, without hope of immediate release, within the world of his own imagination. Man is, by nature, the victim of solipsism; he is an *individua substantia* distinguished by incommunicability. And when this is understood, we are in a position to accept Hobbes's own denial of a doctrine of the natural depravity of man;[9] and he appears to take his place, on this question, beside Plato and Spinoza, basing his theory on the 'known natural inclinations of mankind'.[10] But not without difficulty. First, the striving after power which is characteristic of the human individual may, in Hobbes's view, be evil; it is so when it is directed by Pride. And Pride is so universal a defect in human nature that it belongs to the constitutive cause of the predicament. And, if by interpreting it as illusion Hobbes deprives Pride of moral significance, it still remains

---

[7] Spinoza, *Ethica*, Pars, III, Praefatio.
[8] Spinoza, *Tractatus Politicus*, § 4.
[9] *E.W.*, II, xvi–xvii; *L.*, pp. 97, 224, 480.
[10] *L.*, p. 554.

a defect. And since Pride (it will be remembered) is the Augustinian interpretation of the original sin, this doctrine of Hobbes seems to approximate his view to the conception of the predicament as springing from, not nature, but defect in nature. But secondly, the predicament for Hobbes is actually caused, not by an internal defect in human nature, but by something that becomes a defect when a man is among men. Pride in one may inhibit felicity, but it cannot produce chaos. On this point, then, I think our conclusion must be that Hobbes's conception of the natural man (apart from his defects) is such that a predicament requiring a deliverance is created whenever man is in proximity to man, and that his doctrine of Pride and the unpermissible form of striving after power only increases the severity of the predicament.

(4) *Individualism and Absolutism.* Individualism as a gospel has drawn its inspiration from many sources, but as a reasoned theory of society it has its roots in the so-called nominalism of late medieval scholasticism, with its doctrines that the nature of a thing is its individuality, that which makes it *this* thing, and that both in God and man will is precedent to reason. Hobbes inherited this tradition of nominalism, and more than any other writer passed it on to the modern world. His civil philosophy is based, not on any vague belief in the value or sanctity of the individual man, but on a philosophy for which the world is composed of *individuae substantiae*. This philosophy, in Hobbes, avoided on the one hand atomism (the doctrine that the individual is an indestructible particle of matter) and on the other hand universalism (the doctrine that there is but one individual, the universe), and involved both Hobbes and his successors in the conception of a scale of individuals in which the individuality of sensations and images was preserved while the individuality of the man was asserted. The human being is first fully an individual, not in respect of self-consciousness, but in the activity of willing.[11]

---

[11] Briefly, it may be said that the doctrine that sprang from the reflections of medieval philosophical thinkers distinguished two elements in personality, a rational element and a substantial element. The standard definition of *persona* was that of Boëthius—'the individual sub-

Introduction to Leviathan 61

Between birth and death, the self as imagination and will is an indestructible unit, whose relations with other individuals are purely external. Individuals may be collected together, may be added, may be substituted for one another or made to represent one another, but can never modify one another or compose a whole in which their individuality is lost. Even reason is individualized, and becomes merely the reasoning of an individual without power or authority to oblige acceptance by others: to convince a man is not to enjoy a common understanding with him, but to displace his reason by yours.[12] The natural man is the stuff of civil association which, whatever else it is, is an association that can comprehend such individuals without destroying them. Neither before nor after the establishment of civil association is there any such thing as the *People*, to whom so much previous theory ascribed sovereignty. Whatever community exists must be generated by individual acts of will directed upon a single object, that is, by agreement: the essence of agreement is, not a common will (for there can be no such thing), but a common object of will. And, since these individual wills are in natural opposition to one another, the agreement out of which *civitas* can spring must be an agreement not to oppose one another, a will not to will. But something more is required; merely to agree not to will is race suicide. The agreement must be for each to transfer his right of willing in some specific respect, to a single artificial Representative, who is thenceforth authorized to will and to act in place of each individual. There is in this association no concord of wills, no common will, no common good;

---

stance of a rational nature.' In later medieval thought this definition suffered disruption. Emphasis upon the rational element in personality resulted, finally, in the Cartesian doctrine of the primacy of cognition and of self-consciousness as the true ground of personality. While emphasis upon the substantial element made the most of the opposition between personality and rationality and resulted in what may be called the romantic doctrine of personality with its assertion of the primacy of will—the person is that which is separate, incommunicable, eccentric or even irrational. This second emphasis was the work of the late medieval nominalists, and it is the emphasis that is dominant in Hobbes.

[12] *L.*, p. 33.

its unity lies solely in the singleness of the Representative, in the *substitution* of his one will for the many conflicting wills.[13] It is a collection of individuals united in one Sovereign Representative, and in generation and structure it is the only sort of association that does not compromise the individuality of its components.

Now, the common view is that though Hobbes may be an individualist at the beginning, his theory of civil association is designed precisely to destroy individualism. So far as the generation of civil association is concerned, this is certainly not true. To authorize a representative to make a choice for me does not destroy or compromise my individuality; there is no confusion of wills, so long as it is understood that my will is in the authorization of the representative and that the choice he makes is not mine, but his on my behalf. Hobbes's individualism is far too strong to allow even the briefest appearance of anything like a general will.[14]

Nor is the effect generated, the Leviathan, a designed destruction of the individual; it is, in fact, the *minimum* condition of any settled association among individuals. The Sovereign is absolute in two respects only, and neither of them is destructive of individuality: first, the surrender of natural right to him is absolute and his authorization is permanent and exclusive; and secondly, there is no appeal from the legitimacy of his command. The natural right surrendered is the unconditional right, on all occasions, to exercise one's individual will in the pursuit of felicity.[15] Now, an absolute right, if it is surrendered at all, is necessarily surrendered absolutely: Hobbes refused the compromise which suggests that a part of the right had to be sacrificed, not because he was an absolutist in government, but because he knew a little elementary logic. But to surrender an absolute right to do something on all occasions, is not to give up the right of doing it on any occasion. For the rest, Hobbes conceives the Sovereign

---

[13] *L.,* pp. 126, 167.

[14] Thus, Hobbes does not say that the criminal *wills* his own punishment, but that he is the *author* of his own punishment. *L.,* p. 167.

[15] *L.,* p. 99.

Introduction to Leviathan 63

as a law-maker and his rule, not arbitrary, but the rule of law. And we have already seen that law as the command of the Sovereign holds within itself a freedom absent from law as Reason or custom: it is Reason, not Authority, that is destructive of individuality. And, of course, the silence of the law is a further freedom; when the law does not speak the individual is sovereign over himself.[16] What, indeed, is excluded from Hobbes's *civitas* is not the freedom of the individual, but the independent rights of spurious 'authorities' and of collections of individuals such as churches, which he saw as the source of the civil strife of his time.

It may be said, then, that Hobbes is not an absolutist precisely because he is an authoritarian. His scepticism about the power of reasoning, which applied no less to the 'artificial reason' of the Sovereign than to the reasoning of the natural man, together with the rest of his individualism, separate him from the rationalist dictators of his or any age. Indeed, Hobbes, without being himself a liberal, had in him more of the philosophy of liberalism than most of its professed defenders.[17] He perceived the folly of his age to lie in the distraction of mankind between those who claimed too much for Authority and those who claimed too much for Liberty. The perverse authoritarians were those who forgot, or never understood, that a moral authority derives solely from an act of will of him who is obliged, and that, since the need for authority springs from the passions of men, the authority itself must be commensurate with what it has to remedy, and who therefore claimed a ground for authority outside the wills and desperate needs of mortal men. The perverse libertarians were those whose illusions led them to cling to a natural right in religion which was destructive of all that was achieved by

[16] *L.*, p. 163; cf. Aristotle, *Nic. Eth.*, V, xi, 1.

[17] Hobbes stood in contrast to both the rationalist and the 'social instinct' ethics of his contemporaries, and was attacked by representatives of both these schools. The rationalists nurtured the doctrines of anti-liberalism. And it was Richard Cumberland with his 'social instinct' and later Adam Smith with his 'social passions' who bewitched liberalism by appearing to solve the problem of individualism when they had really only avoided it.

the surrender of the rest of natural right.[18] *Autres temps,
autres folies*: if Hobbes were living today he would find the
universal predicament appearing in different particulars.

(5) *The Theory of Obligation*. Under the influence of
distinctions we are now accustomed to make in discussing
questions of moral theory, modern critics of Hobbes have
often made the mistake of looking for an order and coherence
in his thoughts on these questions which is foreign to the
ideas of any seventeenth-century writer. Setting out with
false expectations, we have been exasperated by the ambiguity
with which Hobbes uses certain important words (such as,
obligation, power, duty, forbid, command), and have gone
on, in an attempt to understand his theory better than he
understood it himself, to interpret it by *extracting* from his
writings at least some consistent doctrine. This, I think, is
the error that lies in attributing to him a theory of civil obligation in terms of self-interest; which is an error, not because
such a theory cannot be extracted from his writings, but
because it gives them a simple formality which nobody supposes them to possess. Even if we confine ourselves to *Leviathan*, we are often met with obscurity and ambiguity; but
Hobbes is a writer who encourages the expectation of consistency, and the most satisfactory interpretation will be that
which gives as coherent a view as is consistent with all of
what Hobbes actually wrote.

Hobbes begins with the natural right of each man to all
things. Now, this right is always at least as great as a man's
power to enjoy it; for, when power is sufficient a man acts,[19]
and nothing that a man does can exceed what he has a natural
right to do. It follows that power and natural right are equal
to one another only when the power is irresistible.[20] This is so
with God, in whom right and power are equal because his
power is as absolute as his right.[21] But it is not so with men;
for, in the unavoidable competition, a man's power, so far

[18] *L.*, p. 337; *E.W.*, VI, 190.
[19] *E.W.*, I, 128. Power is another name for cause, act for effect.
[20] *Elements of Law*, p. 56.
[21] *L.*, p. 276.

from being irresistible, is merely equal to the power of any other man. Indeed, his natural right, which is absolute, must be vastly greater than his power which, in the circumstances, is small because it is uncertain. It appears, then, that while natural right is absolute, power is a variable quality. Natural right and the power to enjoy it are, therefore, two different considerations; neither is the cause of the other, and even where (as in God) they are equal, they are still not identifiable with one another. Might and Right are never the same thing.

According to Hobbes, for a man to be 'obliged' is for him to be bound, to be constrained by some external impediment imposed, directly or indirectly, by himself. It is to suffer some specific self-inflicted diminution of his freedom which may be in respect of his right to act or of both his right and his power to act. And in this connection to do and not to do are alike to act.

First, then, were a man to be constrained from willing and performing a certain action because he judged its likely consequences to be damaging to himself, he would suffer no external constraint and therefore could not properly be said to be 'obliged' to refrain from this action. Here the so-called constraint is internal, a combination of rational judgement and fear, which is aversion from something believed to be hurtful. Neither his right to do what he wills to do nor his power to do it have suffered any qualification: he remains 'governed by his own reason'. Thus, no man may be said to be 'obliged' to act rationally so long as rationality is understood in terms of theorems about the likely consequences of actions; and fear, even if it is fear of being thwarted by the power of another man, is, as we have seen, a reason for acting or refraining from a particular action, not an external constraint upon conduct. Secondly, were a man to will to perform an action which he is unable to perform from his own lack of power to do so (e.g. to lift a weight beyond his capacity to lift), he could not properly be said to be 'obliged' to refrain from the action. He is deprived of nothing: his right to will remains intact and he never had the power he lacks. And thirdly, a man prevented by the power (and not merely the

66   *Introduction to* Leviathan

fear of the power) of another from performing an action he
has willed and is otherwise able to perform, or one compelled
by another to move in a manner he has not chosen to move, is
certainly constrained, and his freedom is in some specific respect diminished. But here the constraint is solely in respect
of this power; it leaves unimpaired his right to do as he wills.
He is deprived of one of the qualities of a free man, the exercise of his ability to do as he wishes. But, although the constraint here is certainly external and although his freedom
is substantially diminished, this constraint and this diminution are not self-imposed and consequently he cannot properly
be said to be 'obliged' to do what he is compelled to do or to
desist from what he is prevented from doing.

In order to be obliged, then, or (avoiding the confusion of
common speech) in order to have an obligation, a man must
himself perform an action which obligates him: there is,
strictly speaking, 'no obligation on any man, which ariseth
not from some act of his own'.[22] This act must be one which
acknowledges or imposes constraint upon his unconditional
right to do whatever he wills and has power to do, thus diminishing his natural freedom. The constraint imposed or acknowledged must be limited and specific: to surrender his
right completely would be to obliterate himself and there
would be nothing left to be obligated. That is, the act must
be a surrender not of the right but of the unconditionality of
the right. Further, if (as it must be) this constraint is to be
external it cannot arise from merely putting-by the unconditionality of the right; it must be the giving up of whatever
is given up to another who then has the right to enjoy it. And
lastly, an obligation undertaken cannot lapse merely by a
failure to fulfil it; it can be ended only in an agreement that
it shall be terminated or (if it is temporary) in reaching its
natural terminus—a promise fulfilled.

Now, since to undertake an obligation is always to perform
a voluntary act of self-denial, it must always be done in the
hope of acquiring some benefit. No man can voluntarily
'despoil' himself of any part of his unconditional right know-

[22] *L.*, p. 166.

ing that it will be to his disadvantage. And the only 'good' any man can recognize is the satisfaction of his wants and the avoidance of that greatest of all dissatisfactions, death. It is to this end that men bind themselves, undertake duties and become capable of injustice or injury to others which are the outcomes of not observing obligations. Thus, they make promises to one another and enter into agreement of mutual trust, designing thereby to make more secure the satisfaction of their wants. These obligations are genuine; they are voluntary undertakings which, on that account, *ought* not to be made void by those who undertake them. Nevertheless, the situation of one who accepts a promise or one who is the first performer in an agreement of mutual trust, remains hazardous, for the *strength* of the bonds of obligation lies not in themselves but in the fear of the evil consequences of breaking them. And, in the circumstances, these evil consequences are nothing more than what lies within the power of the party bilked to impose and the fear of them is, therefore, not notably compelling.

But there is a way in which human beings may acquire less transitory obligations, although these also are the outcome of voluntary actions. If the theorems of natural reason about prudent conduct (theorems such as 'honesty is, on the whole, the best policy') were to be recognized as the *laws* of a God, and if further this God were to be recognized as their God and they to lie within the jurisdiction of these rules, they would have acknowledged their conduct to be subject to these rules and would have obligated themselves to observe them. In this situation they are alike bound by a known external impediment to the exercise of their unconditional right to do what each wills and has power to do. In a voluntary act of acknowledgement they would have submitted themselves to the rule of divine commands. They have not authorized God to make rules for their guidance and they have not endowed him with power to enforce these rules, but they know that he exists, that he is a law-giver and omnipotent, and they have acknowledged themselves to be his Subjects. Henceforth the reason why, for example, they *ought* to keep the agreements they have undertaken is not merely that they ought not 'to make void voluntary acts of their own' but that God has ruled that agreements made ought to be kept. And the advantage they hope to gain from this acknowledgement is the benefit of the approval of the ruler of the universe and perhaps also 're- ward in heaven' for obeying his commands. What they have handed over in this acknowledgement is the right of each to rule himself according to his own natural reason. But they remain free to disobey these divine laws and, so far as life on earth is concerned, with a fair chance of impunity. This God is omnipotent, but he has no agents on earth equipped with power to enforce penalties for disobedience. This obligation, and transitory obligations such as those which arise from mak- ing promises to private persons, may be said to be examples of pure but imperfect 'moral' obligation. Nothing is given up save the right of a man to govern his own conduct; nothing is provided save a bare rule of conduct.

What, then, is *civil* obligation? Like all other obligations, it arises from a voluntary act. This act is a notional covenant between many in which the right of each to govern himself by his own reason is surrendered and a sovereign Actor (the occupant of an artificially created office) is authorized to exer- cise it on their behalf; that is, to declare, to interpret and to administer rules of conduct which the covenanters pledge themselves in advance to obey. The persons concerned are under no obligation to make any such agreement among them- selves; they are merely instructed to do so by reason and fear. Thus, civil obligation is a 'moral' obligation; it arises from a genuine surrender of *right*. Furthermore, it comprehends all other moral obligation. It is true that the subjects of a civil sovereign may have acknowledged themselves to be obligated to the laws of a God known to them by their natural reason and even to one whose will is also revealed in prophetic utter- ances (scripture). But first, a civil subject cannot know where his duty lies if he understands himself to be obligated by two possibly divergent sets of laws; and secondly, God has not himself provided an authoritative apparatus (a court of law) for deciding the meaning of his laws in contingent circum-

Introduction to Leviathan 69

stances, and while this is so the obligations they entail remain imperfectly specified; what they mean is almost anybody's guess. Consequently, on both these counts, it falls to the civil sovereign to specify his subjects' obligations; he must assimilate divine to civil law and he must provide an official interpretation of the meaning in contingent circumstances of all the rules which govern his subjects' conduct. And there is something more which distinguishes civil obligation. In addition to binding themselves each to surrender his right to govern himself, the covenanters who thus create a *civitas* pledge themselves to use all their strength and power on behalf of the civil sovereign; that is, they obligate themselves not only in respect of their right to govern themselves, but in respect also of the use of their power. This, then, is the unique characteristic and special virtue of civil obligation and civil association: a subject obligated both in respect of his right to act and his power to act, and an association equipped with known and authoritative rules of conduct which cannot be breached with impunity.

(6) *Civil Theology.* Long before the time of Hobbes the severance of religion from civil life, which was one of the effects of early Christianity, had been repealed. But the significant change observable in the seventeenth century was the appearance of states in which religion and civil life were assimilated to one another as closely as the universalist tradition of Christianity would permit. It was a situation reminiscent at least of the ancient world, where religion was a communal *cultus* of communal deities. In England, Hooker had theorized this assimilation in the style of a medieval theologian; it was left to Hobbes to return to a more ancient theological tradition (indeed, a pagan tradition) and to theorize it in a more radical fashion.

In the later middle ages it had become customary to divide Theology, the doctrine concerning divine things, into a part concerned with what is accessible by the light of natural reason (and here the doctrine was largely Aristotelian in inspiration), and a part concerned with what is known only through the revelation of scripture. Theology, that is, was both

70   *Introduction to* Leviathan

Rational and Revealed. This way of thinking had sprung, by
a long process of mediation, from the somewhat different view
of the *genera theologiae* that belonged to the late Roman
world for which the contrast was between Rational Theology
(again largely derived from Aristotle) and Civil Theology.[23]
This last was the consideration of the doctrines and beliefs
of religions actually practised in civil communities. It was not
concerned with philosophic speculation or proof, with first
causes or the existence of God, but solely with the popular
beliefs involved in a religious *cultus*. It is to this tradition
that Hobbes returned. Of course, the immediate background
of his thought was the political theology of the late middle
ages and the Reformation; and, of course, scripture was the
authoritative source to which he went to collect the religious
beliefs of his society. And it is not to be supposed that he made
any conscious return to an earlier tradition, or that his way of
thinking was unique in his generation. What is suggested is
that he has more in common with the secular theologians of
the Italian Renaissance than with a writer such as Erastus,
and that he treats the religion of his society as he finds it in the
scriptures, not in the style of a Protestant theologian, but
rather in the style of Varro.

Hobbes's doctrine runs something like this. Religious belief
is something not to be avoided in this world, and is something
of the greatest practical importance. Its generation is from fear
arising out of the unavoidable limits of human experience and
reasoning. There can be no 'natural knowledge of man's estate
after death',[24] and consequently there can be no natural
religion in the accepted meaning of the term. Natural religion
implies a universal natural Reason; but not only is reasoning
confined to what may be concluded from the utterances of the
senses, but it is never more than the reasoning of some individual man. There is, then, first, the universal and necessary
lack of knowledge of things beyond the reach of sense;
secondly, innumerable particular expressions of this lack of
knowledge in the religious fears of human beings; and thirdly,

[23] Augustine, *De Civitate Dei*, Bk. VI.
[24] *L.*, p. 113.

Introduction to Leviathan 71

the published collection in the Christian scriptures of the fears of certain individuals, which has become the basis of the religious idiom of European civilization. And the result is confusion and strife; confusion because the scriptures are at the mercy of each man's interpretation, strife because each man is concerned to force his own fears on other men or on account of them to claim for himself a unique way of living.

To those of Hobbes's contemporaries for whom the authority of medieval Christianity was dead, there appeared to be two possible ways out of this chaos of religious belief. There was first the way of natural religion. It was conceived possible that, by the light of natural Reason, a religion, based upon 'the unmoveable foundations of truth',[25] and supplanting the inferior religions of history, might be found in the human heart, and receiving universal recognition, become established among mankind. Though their inspiration was older than Descartes, those who took this way found their guide in Cartesian rationalism, which led them to the fairyland of Deism and the other fantasies of the *saeculum rationalisticum*, amid the dim ruins of which we now live. The other way was that of a civil religion, not the construction of reason but of authority, concerned not with belief but with practice, aiming not at undeniable truth but at peace. Such a religion was the counterpart of the sovereign civil association. And civil philosophy, in its project of giving this civil association an intellectual foundation, could not avoid the responsibility of constructing a civil theology, the task of which was to find in the complexities of Christian doctrine a religion that could be an authorized public religion, banishing from civil association the confusion and strife that came from religious division. This was the way of Hobbes. He was not a natural theologian, the preconceptions of natural theology and natural religion were foreign to his whole philosophy; he was a civil theologian of the old style but in new circumstances. For him, religion was actual religious beliefs, was Christianity. He was not concerned to reform those beliefs in the interest of some universal, rational truth about God and the world to come, but to remove from

[25] Herbert of Cherbury, *De Veritate*, p. 117.

them the power to disrupt society. The religion of the seventeenth century was, no less than the religion of any other age,
a religion in which fear was a major constituent. And Hobbes,
no less than others of his time—Montaigne and Pascal, for
example—felt the impact of this fear; he died in mortal fear
of hell-fire. But whereas in an earlier age Lucretius conceived
the project of releasing men from the dark fears of their religion by giving them the true knowledge of the gods, no such
project could enter the mind of Hobbes. That release, for him,
could not come from any knowledge of the natural world; if
it came at all it must be the work of time, not reason. But
meanwhile it was the less imposing task of civil theology to
make of that religion something not inimical to civilized life.

(7) *Beyond Civility.* Political philosophy, I have suggested,
is the consideration of the relation between civil association
and eternity. The *civitas* is conceived as the deliverance of a
man observed to stand in need of deliverance. This, at least,
is the ruling idea of many of the masterpieces of political
philosophy, *Leviathan* among them. In the Preface to the
Latin edition Hobbes says: 'This great Leviathan, which is
called the State, is a work of art; it is an artificial man made
for the protection and salvation of the natural man, to whom
it is superior in grandeur and power.' We may, then, enquire
of any political philosophy conceived on this plan, whether the
gift of civil association to mankind is, in principle, the gift of
salvation itself, or whether it is something less, and if the
latter, what relation it bears to salvation. The answers to these
questions will certainly tell us something we should know
about a political philosophy; indeed, they will do more, they
will help us to determine its value.

When we turn to make this enquiry of the great political
philosophies, we find that, each in its own convention, they
maintain the view that civil association is contributory to the
fulfilment of an end which it cannot itself bring about; that
the achievement in civil association is a tangible good and not,
therefore to be separated from the deliverance that constitutes
the whole good, but something less than the deliverance itself.
For both Plato and Aristotle civil association is not man's high-

Introduction to Leviathan 73

est activity, and what is achieved in it must always fall short of
the best life, which is a contemplative, intellectual life. And
the contribution of the *civitas* to the achievement of this end
is the organization of human affairs so that no one who is able
may be prevented from enjoying it.[26] For Augustine the *justitia*
and *pax* that are the gifts of civil association are no more than
the necessary remedy for the immediate consequences of the
original sin; they have a specific relation to the justice of
God and the *pax coelestis*, but they cannot themselves bring
about that 'perfectly ordered union of hearts in the enjoyment
of God and one another in God'.[27] For Aquinas a *communitas
politica* may give to man a natural happiness, but this, while
it is related to the supernatural happiness, is not itself more
than a secondary deliverance from evil in the eternal life of
the soul. And Spinoza, who perhaps more completely than
any other writer adheres to the conception of human life as a
predicament from which salvation is sought, finds in civil
association no more than a second-best deliverance, giving a
freedom that cannot easily be dispensed with, but one not to
be compared with that which belongs to him who is delivered from the power of necessity by his knowledge of the
necessary workings of the universe.[28]

Now, in this matter Hobbes is perhaps more suspect than
any other great writer. This alleged apostle of absolutism
would, more than others, appear to be in danger of making
civil association a hell by conceiving it as a heaven. And yet
there is little justification for the suspicion. For Hobbes, the
salvation of man, the true resolution of his predicament, is
neither religious nor intellectual, but emotional. Man above
all things else is a creature of passion, and his salvation lies,
not in the denial of his character, but in its fulfilment. And
this is to be found, not in pleasure—those who see in Hobbes
a hedonist are sadly wide of the mark—but in Felicity, a
transitory perfection, having no finality and offering no repose.
Man, as Hobbes sees him, is not engaged in an undignified

[26] Plato, *Republic*, 614 *sq.*; Aristotle, *Nic. Eth.*, X, vii–ix.
[27] Augustine, *De Civitate Dei*, xix, 13.
[28] Spinoza, *Ethica*, Pars, V.

scramble for suburban pleasures; there is the greatness of great passion in his constitution. The restless desire that moves him is not pain,[29] nor may it be calmed by any momentary or final achievement;[30] and what life in another world has to offer, if it is something other than Felicity, is a salvation that has no application to the man we know.[31] For such a man salvation is difficult; indeed what distinguishes Hobbes from all earlier and most later writers is his premise that a man is a moving 'body', that human conduct is inertial, not tele-ological movement and that his 'salvation' lies in 'continual success in obtaining those things which a man from time to time desires'. And certainly civil association has no power to bring this about. Nevertheless, what it offers is something of value relative to his salvation. It offers the removal of some of the circumstances that, if they are not removed, must frus-trate the enjoyment of Felicity. It is a negative gift, merely making not impossible that which is sought. Here, in civil association, is neither fulfilment nor wisdom to discern fulfil-ment, but peace, the only condition of human life that can be permanently established. And to a race condemned to seek its perfection in the flying moment and always in the one to come, whose highest virtue is to cultivate a clear-sighted vision of the consequences of its actions, and whose greatest need (not supplied by nature) is freedom from the distraction of illusion, the Leviathan, that *justitiae mensura atque ambi-tionis elenchus*, will appear an invention neither to be despised nor over-rated. 'When the springs dry up, the fish are all together on dry land. They will moisten each other with their dampness and keep each other wet with their slime. But this is not to be compared with their forgetting each other in a river or a lake.'

1946 and 1974

[29] Locke, *Human Understanding*, II, xxi, 32.
[30] Aquinas, *Summa Theologica*, II, i, 1. Q. 27. 1.
[31] *L.*, p. 48.

[2]

ON THE SPIRIT OF HOBBES'S POLITICAL PHILOSOPHY

Leo Strauss

THOMAS HOBBES regarded himself as the founder of political philosophy or political science. He knew, of course, that the great honour which he claimed for himself was awarded, by almost universal consent, to Socrates. Nor was he allowed to forget the notorious fact that the tradition which Socrates had originated was still powerful in his own age. But he was certain that traditional political philosophy 'was rather a dream than science'.[1]

Present-day scholars are not impressed by Hobbes's claim. They note that he was deeply indebted to the tradition which he scorned. Some of them come close to suggesting that he was one of the last Schoolmen. Lest we overlook the wood for the trees, we shall reduce for a while the significant results of present-day polymathy into the compass of one sentence. Hobbes was indebted to tradition for a single, but momentous, idea: he accepted on trust the view that political philosophy or political science is possible or necessary.

To understand Hobbes's astonishing claim means to pay proportionate attention to his emphatic rejection of the tradition, on the one hand, and to his almost silent agreement with it, on the other. For this purpose one must first identify the tradition. More precisely, one must first see the tradition as Hobbes saw it and forget for a moment how it presents itself to the present-day historian. Hobbes mentions the following representatives of the tradition by name: Socrates, Plato, Aristotle, Cicero, Seneca, Tacitus, and Plutarch.[2] He then tacitly identifies the tradition of political philosophy with a particular tradition. He identifies it with that tradition whose basic premises may be stated as follows: the noble and the just are fundamentally distinguished from the

---

[1] *Elements of Law*, Ep. ded.; I, 1, sec. 1; 13, sec. 3, and 17, sec. 1. *De Corpore*, Ep. ded.; *De Cive*, Ep. ded. and praef.; *L.W.* I, p. xc. *Leviathan*, XXXI (p. 241) and XLVI (p. 438).

[2] *De Cive*, praef., and XII, 3; *L.W.* V, pp. 358–59.

2   LEO STRAUSS

pleasant and are by nature preferable to it; or, there is a natural
right that is wholly independent of any human compact or
convention; or, there is a best political order which is best because
it is according to nature. He identifies traditional political
philosophy with the quest for the best regime or for the simply
just social order, and therefore with a pursuit that is political not
merely because it deals with political matters but, above all,
because it is animated by a political spirit. He identifies traditional
political philosophy with that particular tradition that was public
spirited or—to employ a term which is loose indeed but at present
still easily intelligible—that was 'idealistic'.

When speaking of earlier political philosophers, Hobbes does
not mention that tradition whose most famous representatives
might be thought to be 'the sophists', Epicurus and Carneades.
The anti-idealistic tradition simply did not exist for him—as a
tradition of political philosophy. For it was ignorant of the very
idea of political philosophy as Hobbes understood it. It was
indeed concerned with the nature of political things and especially
of justice. It was also concerned with the question of the right
life of the individual and therefore with the question of whether
or how the individual could use civil society for his private, non-
political purposes: for his ease or for his glory. But it was not
political. It was not public spirited. It did not preserve the
orientation of statesmen while enlarging their views. It was not
dedicated to the concern with the right order of society as with
something that is choiceworthy for its own sake.

By tacitly identifying traditional political philosophy with the
idealistic tradition, Hobbes expresses, then, his tacit agreement
with the idealistic view of the function or the scope of political
philosophy. Like Cicero before him, he sides with Cato against
Carneades. He presents his novel doctrine as the first truly
scientific or philosophic treatment of natural law; he agrees with
the Socratic tradition in holding the view that political philosophy
is concerned with natural right. He intends to show 'what is law,
as Plato, Aristotle, Cicero, and divers others have done'; he does
not refer to Protagoras, Epicurus, or Carneades. He fears that his
Leviathan might remind his readers of Plato's *Republic*; no one could
dream of comparing the *Leviathan* to Lucretius' *De rerum natura*.[3]

---

[3] *Elements*, Ep. ded.; *Leviathan*, XV (pp. 94–95), XXVI (p. 172), XXXI (p. 241),
and XLVI (pp. 437–38).

THE SPIRIT OF HOBBES'S POLITICAL PHILOSOPHY 3

Hobbes rejects the idealistic tradition on the basis of a fundamental agreement with it. He means to do adequately what the Socratic tradition did in a wholly inadequate manner. He means to succeed where the Socratic tradition had failed. He traces the failure of the idealistic tradition to one fundamental mistake: traditional political philosophy assumed that man is by nature a political or social animal. By rejecting this assumption, Hobbes joins the Epicurean tradition. He accepts its view that man is by nature or originally an a-political and even an a-social animal, as well as its premise that the good is fundamentally identical with the pleasant.[4] But he uses that a-political view for a political purpose. He gives that a-political view a political meaning. He tries to instil the spirit of political idealism into the hedonistic tradition. He thus became the creator of political hedonism, a doctrine which has revolutionized human life everywhere on a scale never yet approached by any other teaching.

The epoch-making change which we are forced to trace to Hobbes was well understood by Edmund Burke: 'Boldness formerly was not the character of atheists as such. They were even of a character nearly the reverse; they were formerly like the old Epicureans, rather an unenterprising race. But of late they are grown active, designing, turbulent, and seditious.'[5] Political atheism is a distinctly modern phenomenon. No pre-modern atheist doubted that social life requires belief in, and worship of, God or gods. If we do not permit ourselves to be deceived by ephemeral phenomena, we realize that political atheism and political hedonism belong together. They arose together in the same moment and in the same mind.

For in trying to understand Hobbes's political philosophy we must not lose sight of his natural philosophy. His natural philosophy is of the type classically represented by Democritean-Epicurean physics. Yet he regarded, not Epicurus or Democritus,

---

[4] *De Cive*, I, 2; *Leviathan*, VI (p. 33). Hobbes speaks more emphatically of self-preservation than of pleasure and thus seems to be closer to the Stoics than to the Epicureans. Hobbes's reason for putting the emphasis on self-preservation is that pleasure is an 'appearance' whose underlying reality is 'only motion', whereas self-preservation belongs to the sphere not only of 'appearance' but of 'motion' as well (cf. Spinoza, *Ethics*, III, 9 schol. and 11 schol.). Hobbes's emphasizing self-preservation rather than pleasure is then due to his notion of nature or of natural science and has therefore an entirely different motivation than the seemingly identical Stoic view.

[5] *Thoughts on French Affairs*, in *Works of Edmund Burke* ('Bohn's Standard Library', Vol. III), p. 377.

4   LEO STRAUSS

but Plato, as 'the best of the ancient philosophers'. What he
learned from Plato's natural philosophy was not that the universe
cannot be understood if it is not ruled by divine intelligence.
Whatever may have been Hobbes's private thoughts, his natural
philosophy is as atheistic as Epicurean physics. What he learned
from Plato's natural philosophy was that mathematics is 'the
mother of all natural science'.[6] By being both mathematical and
materialistic-mechanistic, Hobbes's natural philosophy is a
combination of Platonic physics and Epicurean physics. From
his point of view, pre-modern philosophy or science as a whole
was 'rather a dream than science' precisely because it did not think
of that combination. His philosophy as a whole may be said to
be the classic example of the typically modern combination of
political idealism with a materialistic and atheistic view of the
whole.

Positions that are originally incompatible with one another
can be combined in two ways. The first way is the eclectic
compromise which remains on the same plane as the original
positions. The other way is the synthesis which becomes possible
through the transition of thought from the plane of the original
positions to an entirely different plane. The combination effected
by Hobbes is a synthesis. He may or may not have been aware
that he was, in fact, combining two opposed traditions. He was
fully aware that his thought presupposed a radical break with all
traditional thought, or the abandonment of the plane on which
'Platonism' and 'Epicureanism' had carried on their secular
struggle.

Hobbes, as well as his most illustrious contemporaries, was
overwhelmed or elated by a sense of the complete failure of
traditional philosophy. A glance at present and past controversies
sufficed to convince them that philosophy, or the quest for
wisdom, had not succeeded in transforming itself into wisdom.
This overdue transformation was now to be effected. To succeed
where tradition had failed, one has to start with reflections on the
conditions which have to be fulfilled if wisdom is to become
actual: one has to start with reflections on the right method. The
purpose of these reflections was to guarantee the actualization of
wisdom.

---

[6] *Leviathan*, XLVI (p. 438); *E.W.* VII, p. 346.

THE SPIRIT OF HOBBES'S POLITICAL PHILOSOPHY   5

The failure of traditional philosophy showed itself most clearly in the fact that dogmatic philosophy had always been accompanied, as by its shadow, by skeptical philosophy. Dogmatism had never yet succeeded in overcoming skepticism once and for all. To guarantee the actualization of wisdom means to eradicate skepticism by doing justice to the truth embodied in skepticism. For this purpose, one must first give free rein to extreme skepticism: what survives the onslaught of extreme skepticism is the absolutely safe basis of wisdom. The actualization of wisdom is identical with the erection of an absolutely dependable dogmatic edifice on the foundation of extreme skepticism.[7]

The experiment with extreme skepticism was then guided by the anticipation of a new type of dogmatism. Of all known scientific pursuits, mathematics alone had been successful. The new dogmatic philosophy must therefore be constructed on the pattern of mathematics. The mere fact that the only certain knowledge which was available is not concerned with ends but 'consists in comparing figures and motions only' created a prejudice against any teleological view or a prejudice in favour of a mechanistic view.[8] It is perhaps more accurate to say that it strengthened a prejudice already in existence. For it is probable that what was foremost in Hobbes's mind was the vision not of a new type of philosophy or science, but of a universe that is nothing but bodies and their aimless motions. The failure of the predominant philosophic tradition could be traced directly to the difficulty with which every teleological physics is beset, and the suspicion arose quite naturally that, owing to social pressures of various kinds, the mechanistic view had never been given a fair chance to show its virtues. But precisely if Hobbes was primarily interested in a mechanistic view, he was inevitably led, as matters stood, to the notion of a dogmatic philosophy based on extreme skepticism. For he had learned from Plato or Aristotle that if the universe has the character ascribed to it by Democritean-Epicurean physics, it excludes the possibility of any physics, of any science, or, in other words, that consistent materialism necessarily culminates in skepticism. 'Scientific

---

[7] Compare Hobbes's agreement with the thesis of Descartes's first *Meditation*.

[8] *Elements*, Ep. ded., and I, 13, sec. 4; *De Cive*, Ep. ded.; *Leviathan*, XI (p. 68); cf. Spinoza, *Ethics*, I, Appendix.

6   LEO STRAUSS

materialism' could not become possible if one did not first
succeed in guaranteeing the possibility of science against the
skepticism engendered by materialism. Only the anticipatory
revolt against a materialistically understood universe could make
possible a science of such a universe. One had to discover or to
invent an island that would be exempt from the flux of mechanical
causation. Hobbes had to consider the possibility of a natural
island. An incorporeal mind was out of the question. On the
other hand, what he had learned from Plato and Aristotle made
him realize somehow that the corporeal mind, composed of very
smooth and round particles, with which Epicurus remained
satisfied, was an inadequate solution. He was forced to wonder
whether the universe did not leave room for an artificial island,
for an island to be created by science.

The solution was suggested by the fact that mathematics, the
model of the new philosophy, was itself exposed to skeptical
attack and proved capable of resisting it by undergoing a specific
transformation or interpretation. To 'avoid the cavils of the
skeptics' at 'that so much renowned evidence of geometry. . . .
I thought it necessary in my definitions to express those motions
by which lines, superficies, solids, and figures, were drawn and
described'. Generally stated, we have absolutely certain or
scientific knowledge only of those subjects of which we are the
causes, or whose construction is in our own power or depends on
our arbitrary will. The construction would not be fully in our
power if there were a single step of the construction that is not
fully exposed to our supervision. The construction must be
conscious construction; it is impossible to know a scientific truth
without knowing at the same time that we have made it. The
construction would not be fully in our power if it made use of
any matter, i.e., of anything that is not itself our construct. The
world of our constructs is wholly unenigmatic because we are
its sole cause and hence we have perfect knowledge of its cause.
The cause of the world of our constructs does not have a further
cause, a cause that is not, or not fully, within our power; the world
of our constructs has an absolute beginning or is a creation in the
strict sense. The world of our constructs is therefore the desired
island that is exempt from the flux of blind and aimless causation.[9]

---

[9] *E.W.* VII, pp. 179 ff.; *De Homine*, X, 4–5; *De Cive*, XVIII, 4, and XVII, 28; *De
Corpore*, XXV, 1; *Elements*, ed. Tönnies, p. 168; fourth objection to Descartes's

THE SPIRIT OF HOBBES'S POLITICAL PHILOSOPHY 7

The discovery or invention of that island seemed to guarantee the possibility of a materialistic and mechanistic philosophy or science, without forcing one to assume a soul or mind that is irreducible to moved matter. That discovery or invention eventually permitted an attitude of neutrality or indifference toward the secular conflict between materialism and spiritualism. Hobbes had the earnest desire to be a 'metaphysical' materialist. But he was forced to rest satisfied with a 'methodical' materialism.

We understand only what we make. Since we do not make the natural beings, they are, strictly speaking, unintelligible. According to Hobbes, this fact is perfectly compatible with the possibility of natural science. But it leads to the consequence that natural science is and will always remain fundamentally hypothetical. Yet this is all we need in order to make ourselves masters and owners of nature. Still, however much man may succeed in his conquest of nature, he will never be able to understand nature. The universe will always remain wholly enigmatic. It is this fact that ultimately accounts for the persistence of skepticism and justifies skepticism to a certain extent. Skepticism is the inevitable outcome of the unintelligible character of the universe or of the unfounded belief in its intelligibility. In other words, since natural things are, as such, mysterious, the knowledge or certainty engendered by nature necessarily lacks evidence. Knowledge based on the natural working of the human mind is necessarily exposed to doubt. For this reason Hobbes parts company with pre-modern nominalism in particular. Pre-modern nominalism

Meditations. The difficulty to which Hobbes's view of science is exposed is indicated by the fact that, as he says, all philosophy or science 'weaves consequences' (cf. *Leviathan*, IX) while taking its beginning from 'experiences' (*De Cive*, XVII, 12), i.e., that philosophy or science is ultimately dependent on what is given and not constructed. Hobbes tried to solve this difficulty by distinguishing between the sciences proper, which are purely constructive or demonstrative (mathematics, cinematics, and political sciences), and physics, which has a lower status than the former (*De Corpore*, XXV, 1; *De Homine*, X, 5). This solution creates a new difficulty, since political science presupposes the scientific study of the nature of man, which is a part of physics (LEVIATHAN, chap. ix in both versions; *De Homine*, Ep. ded.; *De Corpore*, VI, 6). Hobbes apparently tried to solve this new difficulty in the following manner: it is possible to know the causes of the political phenomena both by descending from the more general phenomena (the nature of motion, the nature of living beings, the nature of man) to those causes and by ascending from the political phenomena themselves, as they are known to everyone from experience, to the same causes (*De Corpore*, VI, 7). At any rate, Hobbes emphatically stated that political science may be based on, or consist of, 'experience' as distinguished from 'demonstrations' (*De Homine*, Ep. ded.; *De Cive*, praef.; *Leviathan*, Introd. and XXXII, beginning).

8   LEO STRAUSS

had faith in the natural working of the human mind. It showed
this faith especially by teaching that *natura occulte operatur in
universalibus*, or that the 'anticipations' by virtue of which we take
our bearings in ordinary life and in science are products of nature.
For Hobbes, the natural origin of the universals or of the anticipations was a compelling reason for abandoning them in favour of
artificial 'intellectual tools'. There is no natural harmony between
the human mind and the universe.

Man can guarantee the actualization of wisdom, since wisdom
is identical with free construction. But wisdom cannot be free
construction if the universe is intelligible. Man can guarantee the
actualization of wisdom, not in spite of, but because of, the fact
that the universe is unintelligible. Man can be sovereign only
because there is no cosmic support for his humanity. He can be
sovereign only because he is absolutely a stranger in the universe.
He can be sovereign only because he is forced to be sovereign.
Since the universe is unintelligible and since control of nature
does not require understanding of nature, there are no knowable
limits to his conquest of nature. He has nothing to lose but his
chains, and, for all he knows, he may have everything to gain.
Still, what is certain is that man's natural state is misery; the
vision of the City of Man to be erected on the ruins of the City of
God is an unsupported hope.

It is hard for us to understand how Hobbes could be so hopeful
where there was so much cause for despair. Somehow the
experience, as well as the legitimate anticipation, of unheard of
progress within the sphere which is subject to human control
must have made him insensitive to 'the eternal silence of those
infinite spaces' or to the crackings of the *moenia mundi*. In fairness
to him, one must add that the long series of disappointments
which subsequent generations experienced have not yet succeeded
in extinguishing the hope which he, together with his most
illustrious contemporaries, kindled. Still less have they succeeded
in breaking down the walls which he erected as if in order to limit
his vision. The conscious constructs have indeed been replaced
by the unplanned workings of 'History.' But 'History' limits
our vision in exactly the same way in which the conscious
constructs limited the vision of Hobbes: 'History,' too, fulfils
the function of enhancing the status of man and of his 'world'

THE SPIRIT OF HOBBES'S POLITICAL PHILOSOPHY 9

by making him oblivious of the whole or of eternity.[10] In its final stage the typically modern limitation expresses itself in the suggestion that the highest principle, which, as such, has no relation to any possible cause or causes of the whole, is the mysterious ground of 'History' and, being wedded to man and to man alone, is so far from being eternal that it is coeval with human history.

To return to Hobbes, his notion of philosophy or science has its root in the conviction that a teleological cosmology is impossible and in the feeling that a mechanistic cosmology fails to satisfy the requirement of intelligibility. His solution is that the end or the ends without which no phenomenon can be understood need not be inherent in the phenomena; the end inherent in the concern with knowledge suffices. Knowledge as the end supplies the indispensable teleological principle. Not the new mechanistic cosmology but what later on came to be called 'epistemology' becomes the substitute for teleological cosmology. But knowledge cannot remain the end if the whole is simply unintelligible: *Scientia propter potentiam.*[11] All intelligibility or all meaning has its ultimate root in human needs. The end, or the most compelling end posited by human desire, is the highest principle, the organizing principle. But if the human good becomes the highest principle, political science or social science becomes the most

---

[10] Two quotations taken from authors who belong to opposed camps but to the same spiritual family may serve as illustrations. We read in Friedrich Engels' *Ludwig Feuerbach und der Ausgang der deutschen klassischen Philosophie*: 'nichts besteht vor [der dialektischen Philosophie] als der ununterbrochene Prozess des Werdens und Vergehens, des Aufsteigens *ohne Ende* vom Niedern zum Höhern. . . . Wir brauchen hier nicht auf die Frage einzugehn, ob diese Anschauungsweise durchaus mit dem jetzigen Stand der Naturwissenschaft stimmt, die der Existenz der Erde selbst ein mögliches, ihrer Bewohnbarkeit aber *ein ziemlich sicheres Ende* vorhersagt, die also auch der Menschengeschichte nicht nur einen aufsteigenden, sondern auch einen absteigenden Ast zuerkennt. Wir befinden uns *jedenfalls noch ziemlich weit von dem Wendepunkt*'. We read in J. J. Bachofen's *Die Sage von Tanaquil*: 'Der Orient huldigt dem Naturstandpunkt, der Occident ersetzt ihn durch den geschichtlichen. . . Man könnte sich versucht fühlen, in dieser *Unterordnung der göttlichen unter die menschliche Idee* die letzte Stufe des Abfalls von einem früheren erhabeneren Standpunkte zu erkennen. . . . Und dennoch enthält dieser Rückgang den Keim zu einem sehr wichtigen Fortschritt. Denn als solchen haben wir jede Befreiung unseres Geistes aus den lähmenden Fesseln einer kosmischphysischen Lebensbetrachtung anzusehen. . . . Wenn der Etrusker bekümmerten Sinnes an die Endlichkeit seines Stammes glaubt, so freut der Römer sich der *Ewigkeit seines Staates, an welcher zu zweifeln er gar nicht fähig ist*'. (The italics are not in the originals.)

[11] *De Corpore*, I, 6. The abandonment of the primacy of contemplation or theory in favour of the primacy of practice is the necessary consequence of the abandonment of the plane on which Platonism and Epicureanism had carried on their struggle. For the synthesis of Platonism and Epicureanism stands or falls with the view that to understand is to make.

important kind of knowledge, as Aristotle had predicted. In the
words of Hobbes, *Dignissima certe scientiarum haec ipsa est, quae ad
Principes pertinet, hominesque in regendo genere humano occupatos.*[12]
One cannot leave it, then, at saying that Hobbes agrees with the
idealistic tradition in regard to the function and scope of political
philosophy. His expectation from political philosophy is incom-
parably greater than the expectation of the classics. No Scipionic
dream illumined by a true vision of the whole reminds his readers
of the ultimate futility of all that men can do. Of political philosophy thus understood, Hobbes is indeed the founder.

It was Machiavelli, that greater Columbus, who had discovered
the continent on which Hobbes could erect his structure. When
trying to understand the thought of Machiavelli, one does well to
remember the saying that Marlowe was inspired to ascribe to
him: 'I . . . hold there is no sin but ignorance.' This is almost a
definition of the philosopher. Besides, no one of consequence
ever doubted that Machiavelli's study of political matters was
public spirited. Being a public spirited philosopher, he continued
the tradition of political idealism. But he combined the idealistic
view of the intrinsic nobility of statesmanship with an anti-
idealistic view, if not of the whole, at any rate of the origins of
mankind or of civil society.

Machiavelli's admiration for the political practice of classical
antiquity and especially of republican Rome is only the reverse
side of his rejection of classical political philosophy. He rejected
classical political philosophy, and therewith the whole tradition of
political philosophy in the full sense of the term, as useless:
Classical political philosophy had taken its bearings by how man
ought to live; the correct way of answering the question of the
right order of society consists in taking one's bearings by how
men actually do live. Machiavelli's 'realistic' revolt against
tradition led to the substitution of patriotism or merely political
virtue for human excellence or, more particularly, for moral
virtue and the contemplative life. It entailed a deliberate lowering
of the ultimate goal. The goal was lowered in order to increase
the probability of its attainment. Just as Hobbes later on abandoned the original meaning of wisdom in order to guarantee the
actualization of wisdom, Machiavelli abandoned the original

---

[12] Aristotle *Nicomachean Ethics* 1141ª20–22; *De cive*, praef.; cf. *L.W.* IV, pp. 487–
88: the only serious part of philosophy is political philosophy.

THE SPIRIT OF HOBBES'S POLITICAL PHILOSOPHY   **11**

meaning of the good society or of the good life. What would happen to those natural inclinations of man or of the human soul whose demands simply transcend the lowered goal was of no concern to Machiavelli. He disregarded those inclinations. He limited his horizon in order to get results. And as for the power of chance, Fortuna appeared to him in the shape of a woman who can be forced by the right kind of men: chance can be conquered.

Machiavelli justified his demand for a 'realistic' political philosophy by reflections on the foundations of civil society, and this means ultimately by reflections on the whole within which man lives. There is no superhuman, no natural, support for justice. All human things fluctuate too much to permit their subjection to stable principles of justice. Necessity rather than moral purpose determines what is in each case the sensible course of action. Therefore, civil society cannot even aspire to be simply just. All legitimacy has its root in illegitimacy; all social or moral orders have been established with the help of morally questionable means; civil society has its root not in justice but in injustice. The founder of the most renowned of all commonwealths was a fratricide. Justice in any sense is possible only after a social order has been established; justice in any sense is possible only within a man-made order. Yet the founding of civil society, the supreme case in politics, is imitated, within civil society, in all extreme cases. Machiavelli takes his bearings not so much by how men live as by the extreme case. He believes that the extreme case is more revealing of the roots of civil society and therefore of its true character than is the normal case.[13] The root or the efficient cause takes the place of the end or of the purpose.

It was the difficulty implied in the substitution of merely political virtue for moral virtue or the difficulty implied in Machiavelli's admiration for the lupine policies of republican Rome[14] that induced Hobbes to attempt the restoration of the moral principles of politics, i.e., of natural law, on the plane of Machiavelli's 'realism'. In making this attempt he was mindful of the fact that man cannot guarantee the actualization of the right social order if he does not have certain or exact or scientific knowledge of both the right social order and the conditions of its actualization. He attempted, therefore, in the first place a rigorous

---

[13] Cf. Bacon, *Advancement of Learning* ('Everyman's Library' ed.), pp. 70–71.
[14] *De Cive*, Ep. ded.

12   LEO STRAUSS

deduction of the natural or moral law. To 'avoid the cavils of the
skeptics', natural law had to be made independent of any natural
'anticipations' and therefore of the *consensus gentium*.[15] The predominant tradition had defined natural law with a view to the
end or the perfection of man as a rational and social animal. What
Hobbes attempted to do on the basis of Machiavelli's fundamental
objection to the utopian teaching of the tradition, although in
opposition to Machiavelli's own solution, was to maintain the
idea of natural law but to divorce it from the idea of man's perfection; only if natural law can be deduced from how men actually
live, from the most powerful force that actually determines all
men, or most men most of the time, can it be effectual or of
practical value. The complete basis of natural law must be sought,
not in the end of man, but in his beginnings,[16] in the *prima
naturae* or, rather, in the *primum naturae*. What is most powerful in
most men most of the time is not reason but passion. Natural law
will not be effectual if its principles are distrusted by passion or
are not agreeable to passion.[17] Natural law must be deduced
from the most powerful of all passions.

But the most powerful of all passions will be a natural fact,
and we are not to assume that there is a natural support for justice
or for what is human in man. Or is there a passion, or an
object of passion, which is in a sense antinatural, which marks
the point of indifference between the natural and the non-
natural, which is, as it were, the *status evanescendi* of nature and
therefore a possible origin for the conquest of nature or for
freedom? The most powerful of all passions is the fear of death
and, more particularly, the fear of violent death at the hands of
others: not nature but 'that terrible enemy of nature, death', yet
death insofar as man can do something about it, i.e., death insofar
as it can be avoided or avenged, supplies the ultimate guidance.[18]

---

[15] Ibid., II, 1.
[16] In the alternative title of the *Leviathan* (*The Matter, Form, and Power of a Commonwealth*) the end is not mentioned. See also what Hobbes says about his method in
the Preface to *De Cive*. He claims that he deduced the end from the beginning. In
fact, however, he takes the end for granted; for he discovers the beginning by
analyzing human nature and human affairs with that end (peace) in view (cf. *De Cive*,
I, 1, and *Leviathan*, XI beginning). Similarly, in his analysis of right or justice,
Hobbes takes for granted the generally accepted view of justice (*De Cive*, Ep. ded.).
[17] *Elements*, Ep. ded.
[18] Ibid., I, 14, sec. 6; *De Cive*, Ep. ded., I, 7, and III, 31; *Leviathan*, XIV
(p. 92) XXVII (p. 197). One would have to start from here in order to understand
the role of the detective story in present-day moral orientation.

THE SPIRIT OF HOBBES'S POLITICAL PHILOSOPHY 13

Death takes the place of the *telos*. Or, to preserve the ambiguity of Hobbes's thought, let us say that the fear of violent death expresses most forcefully the most powerful and the most fundamental of all natural desires, the initial desire, the desire for self-preservation.

If, then, natural law must be deduced from the desire for self-preservation, if, in other words, the desire for self-preservation is the sole root of all justice and morality, the fundamental moral fact is not a duty but a right; all duties are derivative from the fundamental and inalienable right of self-preservation. There are, then, no absolute or unconditional duties; duties are binding only to the extent to which their performance does not endanger our self-preservation. Only the right of self-preservation is unconditional or absolute. By nature, there exists only a perfect right and no perfect duty. The law of nature, which formulates man's natural duties, is not a law, properly speaking. Since the fundamental and absolute moral fact is a right and not a duty, the function as well as the limits of civil society must be defined in terms of man's natural right and not in terms of his natural duty. The state has the function, not of producing or promoting a virtuous life, but of safeguarding the natural right of each. And the power of the state finds its absolute limit in that natural right and in no other moral fact.[19] If we may call liberalism that political doctrine which regards as the fundamental political fact the rights, as distinguished from the duties, of man and which identifies the function of the state with the protection or the safeguarding of those rights, we must say that the founder of liberalism was Hobbes.

By transplanting natural law on the plane of Machiavelli, Hobbes certainly originated an entirely new type of political doctrine. The premodern natural law doctrines taught the duties of man; if they paid any attention at all to his rights, they conceived of them as essentially derivative from his duties. As has frequently been observed, in the course of the seventeenth and eighteenth centuries a much greater emphasis was put on rights than ever had been done before. One may speak of a shift of emphasis from natural duties to natural rights.[20] But quantitative

---

[19] *De Cive*, II, 10 end, 18–19; III, 14, 21, 27 and annot., 33; VI, 13; XIV, 3; *Leviathan*, XIV (p. 84, pp. 86–87), XXI (pp. 142–43), XXVIII (p. 202), and XXXII (p. 243).

[20] Cf. Otto von Gierke, *The Development of Political Theory* (New York, 1939), pp. 108, 322, 352; and J. N. Figgis, *The Divine Right of Kings* (2nd ed.; Cambridge:

14   LEO STRAUSS

changes of this character become intelligible only when they are
seen against the background of a qualitative and fundamental
change, not to say that such quantitative changes always become
possible only by virtue of a qualitative and fundamental change.
The fundamental change from an orientation by natural duties to
an orientation by natural rights finds its clearest and most telling
expression in the teaching of Hobbes, who squarely made an
unconditional natural right the basis of all natural duties, the
duties being therefore only conditional. He is the classic and the
founder of the specifically modern natural law doctrine. The
profound change under consideration can be traced directly to
Hobbes's concern with a human guaranty for the actualization of
the right social order or to his 'realistic' intention. The actualization of a social order that is defined in terms of man's duties is
necessarily uncertain and even improbable; such an order may
well appear to be utopian. Quite different is the case of a social
order that is defined in terms of the rights of man. For the rights
in question express, and are meant to express, something that
everyone actually desires anyway; they hallow everyone's self-
interest as everyone sees it or can easily be brought to see it. Men
can more safely be depended upon to fight for their rights than
to fulfil their duties. In the words of Burke: 'The little catechism
of the rights of men is soon learned; and the inferences are in the
passions.'[21] With regard to Hobbes's classic formulation, we add
that the premises already are in the passions. What is required to
make modern natural right effective is enlightenment or propaganda rather than moral appeal. From this we may understand
the frequently observed fact that during the modern period natural
law became much more of a revolutionary force than it had been
in the past. This fact is a direct consequence of the fundamental
change in the character of the natural law doctrine itself.

The tradition which Hobbes opposed had assumed that man
cannot reach the perfection of his nature except in and through
civil society and, therefore, that civil society is prior to the
individual. It was this assumption which led to the view that the
primary moral fact is duty and not rights. One could not assert

At the University Press, 1934), pp. 221–23. For Kant it is already a question why
moral philosophy is called the doctrine of duties and not the doctrine of rights (see
Metaphysik der Sitten, ed. Vorlaender, p. 45).

---

[21] *Thoughts on French Affairs*, p. 367.

THE SPIRIT OF HOBBES'S POLITICAL PHILOSOPHY 15

the primacy of natural rights without asserting that the individual is in every respect prior to civil society: all rights of civil society or of the sovereign are derivative from rights which originally belonged to the individual.[22] The individual as such, the individual regardless of his qualities—and not merely, as Aristotle had contended, the man who surpasses humanity—had to be conceived of as essentially complete independently of civil society. This conception is implied in the contention that there is a state of nature which antedates civil society. According to Rousseau, 'the philosophers who have examined the foundations of civil society have all of them felt the necessity to go back to the state of nature'. It is true that the quest for the right social order is inseparable from reflection on the origins of civil society or on the prepolitical life of man. But the identification of the prepolitical life of man with 'the state of nature' is a particular view, a view by no means held by 'all' political philosophers. The state of nature became an essential topic of political philosophy only with Hobbes, who still almost apologized for employing that term. It is only since Hobbes that the philosophic doctrine of natural law has been essentially a doctrine of the state of nature. Prior to him, the term 'state of nature' was at home in Christian theology rather than in political philosophy. The state of nature was distinguished especially from the state of grace, and it was subdivided into the state of pure nature and the state of fallen nature. Hobbes dropped the subdivision and replaced the state of grace by the state of civil society. He thus denied, if not the fact, at any rate the importance of the Fall and accordingly asserted that what is needed for remedying the deficiencies or the 'inconveniences' of the state of nature is, not divine grace, but the right kind of human government. This antitheological implication of 'the state of nature' can only with difficulty be separated from its intra-philosophic meaning, which is to make intelligible the primacy of rights as distinguished from duties: the state of nature is originally characterized by the fact that in it there are perfect rights but no perfect duties.[23]

[22] *De Cive*, VI, 5–7; *Leviathan*, XVIII (p. 113) and XXVIII (pp. 202–3).
[23] *De Cive*, praef.: 'conditionem hominum extra societatem civilem (quam conditionem appellare liceat statum naturae).' Cf. Locke, *Treatises of Civil Government*, II, sect. 15. For the original meaning of the term, cf. Aristotle *Physics* 246ª10–17; Cicero *Offices* i. 67; *De finibus* iii. 16, 20; *Laws* iii. 3 (cf. also *De Cive*, III, 25). According to the classics, the state of nature would be the life in a healthy civil society and not

16   LEO STRAUSS

If everyone has by nature the right to preserve himself, he necessarily has the right to the means required for his self-preservation. At this point the question arises as to who is to be the judge of what means are required for a man's self-preservation or as to which means are proper or right. The classics would have answered that the natural judge is the man of practical wisdom, and this answer would finally lead back to the view that the simply best regime is the absolute rule of the wise and the best practicable regime is the rule of gentlemen. According to Hobbes, however, everyone is by nature the judge of what are the right means to his self-preservation. For, even granting that the wise man is, in principle, a better judge, he is much less concerned with the self-preservation of a given fool than is the fool himself. But if everyone, however foolish, is by nature the judge of what is required for his self-preservation, everything may legitimately be regarded as required for self-preservation: everything is by nature

the life antedating civil society. The conventionalists assert, indeed, that civil society is conventional or artificial, but this implies a depreciation of civil society. Most conventionalists do not identify the life antedating civil society with the state of nature: they identify the life according to nature with the life of human fulfilment (be it the life of the philosopher or the life of the tyrant); the life according to nature is therefore impossible in the primeval condition that antedates civil society. On the other hand, those conventionalists who identify the life according to nature, or the state of nature, with the life antedating civil society, regard the state of nature as preferable to civil society (cf. Montaigne, *Essais*, II, 12, *Chronique des lettres françaises*, III, 311). Hobbes's notion of the state of nature presupposes the rejection of both the classic and the conventionalist view, for he denies the existence of a natural end, of a *summum bonum*. He identifies, therefore, the natural life with the 'beginning', the life dominated by the most elementary wants; and at the same time he holds that this beginning is defective and that the deficiency is remedied by civil society. There is, then, according to Hobbes, no tension between civil society and what is natural, whereas, according to conventionalism, there is a tension between civil society and what is natural. Hence, according to conventionalism, the life according to nature is superior to civil society, whereas, according to Hobbes, it is inferior to it. We add that conventionalism is not necessarily egalitarian, whereas Hobbes's orientation necessitates egalitarianism. According to Thomas Aquinas, the *status legis naturae* is the condition in which man lived prior to the revelation of the Mosaic law (*Summa theologica* II. 1. qu. 102, *a.* 3 ad 12). It is the state in which the Gentiles live and therefore a condition of civil society (cf. Suarez, *Tr. de legibus* I, 3, sec. 12; III, 11 ['in pura natura, vel in gentibus']; III, 12 ['in statu purae naturae, si in illo esset respublica verum Deum naturaliter colens']; also Grotius *De jure belli* ii. 5, sec. 15. 2 uses 'status naturae' in contradistinction to the 'status legis Christianae'; when Grotius [iii. 7, sec. 1] says: 'citra factum humanum aut primaevo naturae statu', he shows, by the addition of 'primaevo', that the state of nature as such is not 'citra factum humanum' and hence does not essentially antedate civil society. However, if the human law is regarded as the outcome of human corruption, the *status legis naturae* becomes that condition in which man was subject to the law of nature alone, and not yet to any human laws (Wyclif, *De civili dominio*, II, 13, ed. Poole, p. 154). For the prehistory of Hobbes's notion of the state of nature cf. also Soto's doctrine as reported by Suarez, op. cit., II, 17, sec. 9.

just.[24] We may speak of a natural right of folly. Furthermore, if everyone is by nature the judge of what is conducive to his self-preservation, consent takes precedence over wisdom. But consent is not effective if it does not transform itself into subjection to the sovereign. For the reason indicated, the sovereign is sovereign not because of his wisdom but because he has been made sovereign by the fundamental compact. This leads to the further conclusion that command or will, and not deliberation or reasoning, is the core of sovereignty or that laws are laws by virtue, not of truth or reasonableness, but of authority alone.[25] In Hobbes's teaching, the supremacy of authority as distinguished from reason follows from an extraordinary extension of the natural right of the individual.

The attempt to deduce the natural law or the moral law from the natural right of self-preservation or from the inescapable power of the fear of violent death led to far-reaching modifications of the content of the moral law. The modification amounted, in the first place, to a considerable simplification. Sixteenth- and seventeenth-century thought in general tended toward a simplification of moral doctrine. To say the least, that tendency easily lent itself to absorption in the broader concern with the guaranty for the actualization of the right social order. One tried to replace the 'unsystematic' multiplicity of irreducible virtues by a single virtue, or by a single basic virtue from which all other virtues could be deduced. There existed two well-paved ways in which this reduction could be achieved. In the moral teaching of Aristotle, 'whose opinions are at this day, and in these parts of greater authority than any other human writings' (Hobbes), there occur two virtues which comprise all other virtues or, as we may say, two 'general' virtues: magnanimity, which comprises all other virtues in so far as they contribute to the excellence of the individual, and justice, which comprises all other virtues in so far as they contribute to man's serving others. Accordingly, one could simplify moral philosophy by reducing morality either to magnanimity or else to justice. The first was done by Descartes, the second by Hobbes. The latter's choice had the particular advantage that it was favourable to a further simplification of

[24] *De Cive*, I, 9; III, 13; *Leviathan*, XV (p. 100) and XLVI (p. 448).
[25] *De Cive*, VI, 19; XIV, 1 and 17; *Leviathan*, XXVI (p. 180); cf. also Sir Robert Filmer, *Observations concerning the Original of Government*, Preface.

18   LEO STRAUSS

moral doctrine: the unqualified identification of the doctrine of
virtues with the doctrine of the moral or natural law. The moral
law, in its turn, was to be greatly simplified by being deduced
from the natural right of self-preservation. Self-preservation
requires peace. The moral law became, therefore, the sum of
rules which have to be obeyed if there is to be peace. Just as
Machiavelli reduced virtue to the political virtue of patriotism,
Hobbes reduced virtue to the social virtue of peaceableness.
Those forms of human excellence which have no direct or unambiguous relation to peaceableness—courage, temperance, magnanimity, liberality, to say nothing of wisdom—cease to be virtues
in the strict sense. Justice (in conjunction with equity and charity)
does remain a virtue, but its meaning undergoes a radical change.
If the only unconditional moral fact is the natural right of each
to his self-preservation, and therefore all obligations to others
arise from contract, justice becomes identical with the habit of
fulfilling one's contracts. Justice no longer consists in complying
with standards that are independent of human will. All material
principles of justice—the rules of commutative and distributive
justice or of the Second Table of the Decalogue—cease to
have intrinsic validity. All material obligations arise from the
agreement of the contractors, and therefore in practice from the
will of the sovereign.[26] For the contract that makes possible all
other contracts is the social contract or the contract of subjection
to the sovereign.

If virtue is identified with peaceableness, vice will become
identical with that habit or that passion which is per se incompatible with peace because it essentially and, as it were, of set
purpose issues in offending others; vice becomes identical for all
practical purposes with pride or vanity or *amour-propre* rather than
with dissoluteness or weakness of the soul. In other words, if
virtue is reduced to social virtue or to benevolence or kindness or
'the liberal virtues', 'the severe virtues' of self-restraint will lose
their standing.[27] Here again we must have recourse to Burke's
analysis of the spirit of the French Revolution; for Burke's

---

[26] *Elements*, I, 17, sec. 1; *De Cive*, Ep. ded.; III, 3–6, 29, 32; VI, 16; XII, 1; XIV,
9–10, 17; XVII, 10; XVIII, 3; *De Homine*, XIII, 9; *Leviathan*, XIV (p. 92), XV
(pp. 96, 97, 98, 104), and XXVI (p. 186).
[27] 'Temperantia privatio potius vitiorum quae oriuntur ab ingeniis cupidis
(*quibus non laeditur civitas*, sed ipsi) quam virtus moralis (est)' (*De Homine*, XIII, 9).
The step from this view to 'private vices, public benefits', is short.

THE SPIRIT OF HOBBES'S POLITICAL PHILOSOPHY 19

polemical overstatements were and are indispensable for tearing away the disguises, both intentional and unintentional, in which 'the new morality' introduced itself: 'The Parisian philosophers . . . explode or render odious or contemptible, that class of virtues which restrain the appetite. . . . In the place of all this, they substitute a virtue which they call humanity or benevolence.'[28] This substitution is the core of what we have called 'political hedonism'.

To establish the meaning of political hedonism in somewhat more precise terms, we must contrast Hobbes's teaching with the nonpolitical hedonism of Epicurus. The points in which Hobbes could agree with Epicurus, were these: the good is fundamentally identical with the pleasant; virtue is therefore not choiceworthy for its own sake but only with a view to the attainment of pleasure or the avoidance of pain; the desire for honour and glory is utterly vain, i.e., sensual pleasures are, as such, preferable to honour or glory. Hobbes had to oppose Epicurus in two crucial points in order to make possible political hedonism. In the first place, he had to reject Epicurus' implicit denial of a state of nature in the strict sense, i.e., of a prepolitical condition of life in which man enjoys natural right; for Hobbes agreed with the idealistic tradition in thinking that the claim of civil society stands or falls with the existence of natural right. Besides, he could not accept the implication of Epicurus' distinction between natural desires which are necessary and natural desires which are not necessary; for that distinction implied that happiness requires an 'ascetic' style of life and that happiness consists in a state of repose. Epicurus' high demands on self-restraint were bound to be utopian as far as most men are concerned; they had therefore to be discarded by a 'realistic' political teaching. The 'realistic' approach to politics forced Hobbes to lift all restrictions on the striving for unnecessary sensual pleasures or, more precisely, for the *commoda hujus vitae*, or for power, with the exception of those restrictions that are required for the sake of peace. Since, as Epicurus said, 'Nature has made [only] the necessary things easy to supply', the emancipation of the desire for comfort required that science be put into the service of the satisfaction of that desire. It required, above all, that the function of civil society be radically redefined: 'the good life', for the sake

[28] Letter to Rivarol of June 1, 1791.

of which men enter civil society, is no longer the life of human excellence but 'commodious living' as the reward of hard work. And the sacred duty of the rulers is no longer 'to make the citizens good and doers of noble things' but to 'study, as much as by laws can be effected, to furnish the citizens abundantly with all good things . . . which are conducive to delectation.'[29]

It is not necessary for our purpose to follow Hobbes's thought on its way from the natural right of everyone, or from the state of nature, to the establishment of civil society. This part of his doctrine is not meant to be more than the strict consequence from his premises. It culminates in the doctrine of sovereignty, of which he is generally recognized to be the classic exponent. The doctrine of sovereignty is a legal doctrine. Its gist is not that it is expedient to assign plenitude of power to the ruling authority but that that plenitude belongs to the ruling authority as of right. The rights of sovereignty are assigned to the supreme power on the basis not of positive law or of general custom but of natural law. The doctrine of sovereignty formulates natural public law.[30] Natural public law—*jus publicum universale seu naturale*—is a new discipline that emerged in the seventeenth century. It emerged in consequence of that radical change of orientation which we are trying to understand. Natural public law represents one of the two characteristically modern forms of political philosophy, the other form being 'politics' in the sense of Machiavellian 'reason of state'. Both are fundamentally distinguished from classical political philosophy. In spite of their opposition to each other,

---

[29] *De Cive*, I, 2, 5, 7; XIII, 4–6; *Leviathan*, XI (pp. 63–64) and XIII end; *De Corpore*, I, 6.

[30] LEVIATHAN, chap. xxx, the third and fourth paragraphs of the Latin version; *De Cive*, IX, 3; X, 2 beginning, and 5; XI, 4 end; XII, 8 end; XIV, 4; cf. also Malebranche, *Traité de morale*, ed. Joly, p. 214. There is this difference between natural law in the ordinary sense and natural public law, that natural public law and its subject matter (the commonwealth) are based on a fundamental fiction, on the fiction that the will of the sovereign is the will of all and of each or that the sovereign represents all and each (*De Cive*, V, 6, 9, 11; VII, 14). The will of the sovereign has to be *regarded* as the will of all and of each, whereas, in fact, there is an essential discrepancy between the will of the sovereign and the wills of the individuals, the only wills that are natural: to obey the sovereign means precisely to do what the sovereign wills, not what I will. Even if my reason should habitually tell me to will what the sovereign wills, this rational will is not necessarily identical with my complete will, my actual or explicit will (cf. the reference to the 'implicit wills' in *Elements*, II, 9, sec. 1; cf. also *De Cive*, XII, 2). On the basis of Hobbes's premises, 'representation' is then not a convenience but an essential necessity.

they are motivated by fundamentally the same spirit.[31] Their origin is the concern with a right or sound order of society whose actualization is probable, if not certain, or does not depend on chance. Accordingly, they deliberately lower the goal of politics; they are no longer concerned with having a clear view of the highest political possibility with regard to which all actual political orders can be judged in a responsible manner. The 'reason of state' school replaced 'the best regime' by 'efficient government'. The 'natural public law' school replaced 'the best regime' by 'legitimate government'.

Classical political philosophy had recognized the difference between the best regime and legitimate regimes. It asserted, therefore, a variety of types of legitimate regimes; that is, what type of regime is legitimate in given circumstances depends on the circumstances. Natural public law, on the other hand, is concerned with that right social order whose actualization is possible under all circumstances. It therefore tries to delineate that social order that can claim to be legitimate or just in all cases, regardless of the circumstances. Natural public law, we may say, replaces the idea of the best regime, which does not supply, and is not meant to supply, an answer to the question of what is the just order here and now, by the idea of the just social order which answers the basic practical question once and for all, i.e., regardless of place and time.[32] Natural public law intends to give such a universally valid solution to the political problem as is meant to be universally applicable in practice. In other words, whereas, according to the classics, political theory proper is essentially in need of being supplemented by the practical wisdom of the statesman on the spot, the new type of political theory solves, as such, the crucial practical problem: the problem of what order is just here and now. In the decisive respect, then, there is no

---

[31] Cf. Fr. J. Stahl, *Geschichte der Rechtsphilosophie* (2d. ed.), p. 325: 'Es ist eine Eigentümlichkeit der neuern Zeit, dass ihre Staatslehre (das Naturrecht) und ihre Staatskunst (die vorzugsweise sogenannte Politik) zwei völlig verschiedene Wissenschaften sind. Diese Trennung ist das Werk des Geistes, welcher in dieser Periode die Wissenschaft beherrscht. Das Ethos wird in der Vernunft gesucht, diese hat aber keine Macht über die Begebenheiten und den natürlichen Erfolg; was die äusserlichen Verhältnisse fordern und abnöthigen, stimmt gar nicht mit ihr überein, verhält sich feindlich gegen sie, die Rücksicht auf dasselbe kann daher nicht Sache der Ethik des Staates sein'. Cf. Grotius *De jure belli*, Prolegomena, sec. 57.

[32] Cf. *De Cive*, praef. toward the end, on the entirely different status of the question of the best form of government, on the one hand, and the question of the rights of the sovereign, on the other.

22   LEO STRAUSS

longer any need for statesmanship as distinguished from political theory. We may call this type of thinking 'doctrinairism', and we shall say that doctrinairism made its first appearance within political philosophy—for lawyers are altogether in a class by themselves—in the seventeenth century. At that time the sensible flexibility of classical political philosophy gave way to fanatical rigidity. The political philosopher became more and more indistinguishable from the partisan. The historical thought of the nineteenth century tried to recover for statesmanship that latitude which natural public law had so severely restricted. But since that historical thought was absolutely under the spell of modern 'realism', it succeeded in destroying natural public law only by destroying in the process all moral principles of politics.

As regards Hobbes's teaching on sovereignty in particular, its doctrinaire character is shown most clearly by the denials which it implies. It implies the denial of the possibility of distinguishing between good and bad regimes (kingship and tyranny, aristocracy and oligarchy, democracy and ochlocracy) as well as of the possibility of mixed regimes and of 'rule of law'.[33] Since these denials are at variance with observed facts, the doctrine of sovereignty amounts in practice to a denial not of the existence, but of the legitimacy, of the possibilities mentioned: Hobbes's doctrine of sovereignty ascribes to the sovereign prince or to the sovereign people an unqualified right to disregard all legal and constitutional limitations according to their pleasure,[34] and it imposes even on sensible men a natural law prohibition against censuring the sovereign and his actions. But it would be wrong to overlook the fact that the basic deficiency of the doctrine of sovereignty is shared, if to different degrees, by all other forms of natural public law doctrines as well. We merely have to remind ourselves of the practical meaning of the doctrine that the only legitimate regime is democracy.

[33] *De Cive*, VII, 2–4; XII, 4–5; *Leviathan*, XXIX (p. 216). See, however, the reference to legitimate kings and to illegitimate rulers in *De Cive*, XII, 1 and 3. *De Cive*, VI, 13 end, and VII, 14, show that natural law, as Hobbes understands it, supplies a basis for objectively distinguishing between kingship and tyranny. Cf. also ibid., XII, 7, with XIII, 10.

[34] As for the discrepancy between Hobbes's doctrine and the practice of mankind, see *Leviathan*, XX end, and XXXI end. As for the revolutionary consequences of Hobbes's doctrine of sovereignty, see *De Cive*, VII, 16, and 17 as well as *Leviathan*, XIX (p. 122) and XXIX (p. 210): there is no right of prescription; the sovereign is the present sovereign (see *Leviathan*, XXVI, p. 175).

THE SPIRIT OF HOBBES'S POLITICAL PHILOSOPHY 23

The classics had conceived of regimes (*politeiai*) not so much in terms of institutions as in terms of the aims actually pursued by the community or its authoritative part. Accordingly, they regarded the best regime as that regime whose aim is virtue, and they held that the right kind of institutions are indeed indispensable for establishing and securing the rule of the virtuous, but of only secondary importance in comparison with 'education', i.e., the formation of character. From the point of view of natural public law, on the other hand, what is needed in order to establish the right social order is not so much the formation of character as the devising of the right kind of institutions. As Kant put it in rejecting the view that the establishment of the right social order requires a nation of angels: 'Hard as it may sound, the problem of establishing the state [i.e., the just social order] is soluble even for a nation of devils, provided they have sense', i.e., provided that they are guided by enlightened selfishness; the fundamental political problem is simply one of 'a good organization of the state, of which man is indeed capable'. In the words of Hobbes, 'when [commonwealths] come to be dissolved, not by external violence, but intestine disorder, the fault is not in men, as they are the *matter*, but as they are the *makers*, and orderers of them'.[35] Man as the maker of civil society can solve once and for all the problem inherent in man as the matter of civil society. Man can guarantee the actualization of the right social order because he is able to conquer human nature by understanding and manipulating the mechanism of the passions.

There is a term that expresses in the most condensed form the result of the change which Hobbes has effected. That term is 'power'. It is in Hobbes's political doctrine that power becomes for the first time *eo nomine* a central theme. Considering the fact that, according to Hobbes, science as such exists for the sake of power, one may call Hobbes's whole philosophy the first philosophy of power. 'Power' is an ambiguous term. It stands for *potentia*, on the one hand, and for *potestas* (or *jus* or *dominium*), on the other.[36] It means both 'physical' power and 'legal' power.

---

[35] *Leviathan*, XXIX (p. 210); Kant, *Eternal Peace*, Definitive Articles, First Addition.

[36] Cf., e.g., the headings of chap. x in the English and Latin versions of the *Leviathan*, and the headings of *Elements*, II, 3 and 4, with those of *De Cive*, VIII and IX. For an example of the synonymous use of *potentia* and *potestas* see *De Cive*, IX, 8. A comparison of the title of the *Leviathan* with the Preface of *De Cive* (beginning of the section on method) suggests that 'power' is identical with 'generation'. Cf. *De Corpore*, X, 1: *potentia* is the same as *causa*. In opposition to Bishop Bramhall, Hobbes insists on the identity of 'power' with 'potentiality' (*E.W.*, IV, p. 298).

24   LEO STRAUSS

The ambiguity is essential: only if *potentia* and *potestas* essentially
belong together, can there be a guaranty of the actualization of the
right social order. The state, as such, is both the greatest human
force and the highest human authority. Legal power is irresistible
force.[37] The necessary coincidence of the greatest human force
and the highest human authority corresponds strictly to the
necessary coincidence of the most powerful passion (fear of violent
death) and the most sacred right (the right of self-preservation).
Potentia and *potestas* have this in common, that they are both
intelligible only in contradistinction, and in relation, to the *actus:*
the *potentia* of a man is what a man *can* do, and the *potestas* or,
more generally expressed, the right of a man, is what a man *may*
do. The predominance of the concern with 'power' is therefore
only the reverse of a relative indifference to the *actus*, and this
means to the purposes for which man's 'physical' as well as his
'legal' power is or ought to be used. This indifference can be
traced directly to Hobbes's concern with an exact or scientific
political teaching. The sound use of 'physical' power as well as
the sound exercise of rights depends on *prudentia*, and whatever
falls within the province of *prudentia* is not susceptible of exactness.
There are two kinds of exactness: mathematical and legal. From
the point of view of mathematical exactness, the study of the *actus*
and therewith of the ends is replaced by the study of *potentia*.
'Physical' power as distinguished from the purposes for which it
is used is morally neutral and therefore more amenable to mathematical strictness than is its use: power can be measured. This
explains why Nietzsche, who went much beyond Hobbes and
declared the will to power to be the essence of reality, conceived
of power in terms of 'quanta of power'. From the point of view
of legal exactness, the study of the ends is replaced by the study of
potestas. The rights of the sovereign, as distinguished from the
exercise of these rights, permit of an exact definition without any
regard to any unforeseeable circumstances, and this kind of
exactness is again inseparable from moral neutrality: right
declares what is permitted, as distinguished from what is honourable.[38] Power, as distinguished from the end for which power is

---

[37] *De Cive*, XIV, 1, and XVI, 15; *Leviathan*, X (p. 56).
[38] *De Cive*, X, 16, and VI, 13 annot. end. Cf. *Leviathan*, XXI (p. 143), for the
distinction between the permitted and the honourable (cf. Salmasius, *Defensio regia*
[1649], pp. 40–45). Cf. *Leviathan*, XI (p. 64) with Thomas Aquinas *Summa
contra Gentiles* III. 31.

used or ought to be used, becomes the central theme of political reflections by virtue of that limitation of horizon which is needed if there is to be a guaranty of the actualization of the right social order.

Hobbes's political doctrine is meant to be universally applicable and hence to be applicable also and especially in extreme cases. This indeed may be said to be the boast of the classic doctrine of sovereignty: that it gives its due to the extreme case, to what holds good in emergency situations, whereas those who question that doctrine are accused of not looking beyond the pale of normality. Accordingly, Hobbes built his whole moral and political doctrine on observations regarding the extreme case; for the experience on which his doctrine of the state of nature is based is the experience of civil war. It is in the extreme situation, when the social fabric has completely broken down, that there comes to sight the solid foundation on which every social order must ultimately rest: the fear of violent death, which is the strongest force in human life. Yet Hobbes was forced to concede that the fear of violent death is only 'commonly' or in most cases the most powerful force. The principle which was supposed to make possible a political doctrine of universal applicability, then, is not universally valid and therefore is useless in what, from Hobbes's point of view, is the most important case—the extreme case. For how can one exclude the possibility that precisely in the extreme situation the exception will prevail?[39]

To speak in more specific terms, there are two politically important phenomena which would seem to show with particular clarity the limited validity of Hobbes's contention regarding the overwhelming power of the fear of violent death. In the first place, if the only unconditional moral fact is the individual's right of self-preservation, civil society can hardly demand from the individual that he resign that right both by going to war and by submitting to capital punishment. As regards capital punishment, Hobbes was consistent enough to grant that, by being justly

[39] *Leviathan*, XIII (p. 83) and XV (p. 92). One may state this difficulty also as follows: In the spirit of the dogmatism based on skepticism, Hobbes identified what the skeptic Carneades apparently regarded as the conclusive refutation of the claims raised on behalf of justice, with the only possible justification of these claims: the extreme situation—the situation of the two shipwrecked men on a plank on which only one man can save himself—reveals, not the impossibility of justice, but the basis of justice. Yet Carneades did not contend that in such a situation one is compelled to kill one's competitor (Cicero *Republic* iii. 29–30): the extreme situation does not reveal a real necessity.

and legally condemned to death, a man does not lose the right to
defend his life by resisting 'those that assault him': a justly condemned murderer retains—nay, he acquires—the right to kill his
guards and everyone else who stands in his way to escape, in
order to save dear life.[40] But, by granting this, Hobbes in fact
admitted that there exists an insoluble conflict between the rights
of the government and the natural right of the individual to self-
preservation. This conflict was solved in the spirit, if against the
letter, of Hobbes by Beccaria, who inferred from the absolute
primacy of the right of self-preservation the necessity of abolishing
capital punishment. As regards war, Hobbes, who proudly
declared that he was 'the first of all that fled' at the outbreak of the
Civil War, was consistent enough to grant that 'there is allowance
to be made for natural timorousness'. And as if he desired to
make it perfectly clear to what lengths he was prepared to go in
opposing the lupine spirit of Rome, he continues as follows:
'When armies fight, there is on one side, or both, a running away:
yet when they do it not out of treachery, but fear, they are not
esteemed to do it unjustly, but dishonourably'.[41] But, by granting
this, he destroyed the moral basis of national defence. The only
solution to this difficulty which preserves the spirit of Hobbes's
political philosophy is the outlawry of war or the establishment
of a world state.

There was only one fundamental objection to Hobbes's basic
assumption which he felt very keenly and which he made every
effort to overcome. In many cases the fear of violent death proved
to be a weaker force than the fear of hell fire or the fear of God.
The difficulty is well illustrated by two widely separated passages
of the *Leviathan*. In the first passage Hobbes says that the fear of
the power of men (i.e., the fear of violent death) is 'commonly'
greater than the fear of the power of 'spirits invisible', i.e., than
religion. In the second passage he says that 'the fear of darkness
and ghosts is greater than other fears'.[42] Hobbes saw his way to
solve this contradiction: the fear of invisible powers is stronger
than the fear of violent death as long as people believe in invisible
powers, i.e., as long as they are under the spell of delusions about

---

[40] *Leviathan*, XXI (pp. 142–43); cf. also *De Cive*, VIII, 9.
[41] *Leviathan*, XXI (p. 143); *E.W.* IV, p. 414. Cf. *Leviathan*, XXX (p. 227)
and *De Cive*, XIII, 14, with Locke's chapter on conquest.
[42] *Leviathan*, XIV (p. 92) and XXIX (p. 215); cf. also ibid., XXXVIII beginning;
De Cive, VI, 11; XII, 2, 5; XVII, 25 and 27.

THE SPIRIT OF HOBBES'S POLITICAL PHILOSOPHY 27

the true character of reality; the fear of violent death comes fully into its own as soon as people have become enlightened. This implies that the whole scheme suggested by Hobbes requires for its operation the weakening or, rather, the elimination of the fear of invisible powers. It requires such a radical change of orientation as can be brought about only by the disenchantment of the world, by the diffusion of scientific knowledge, or by popular enlightenment. Hobbes's is the first doctrine that necessarily and unmistakably points to a thoroughly 'enlightened', i.e., a-religious or atheistic society as the solution of the social or political problem. This most important implication of Hobbes's doctrine was made explicit not many years after his death by Pierre Bayle, who attempted to prove that an atheistic society is possible.[43]

It is, then, only through the prospect of popular enlightenment that Hobbes's doctrine acquired such consistency as it possesses. The virtues which he ascribed to enlightenment are indeed extraordinary. The power of ambition and avarice, he says, rests on the false opinions of the vulgar regarding right and wrong; therefore, once the principles of justice are known with mathematical certainty, ambition and avarice will become powerless and the human race will enjoy lasting peace. For, obviously, mathematical knowledge of the principles of justice

---

[43] A good reason for connecting Bayle's famous thesis with Hobbes's doctrine rather than with that of Faustus Socinus, e.g., is supplied by the following statement of Bayle (*Dictionnaire*, art. 'Hobbes', rem. D): 'Hobbes se fit beaucoup d'ennemis par cet ouvrage [*De cive*]; mais il fit avouer aux plus clairvoyants, qu'on n'avait jamais si bien pénétré les fondements de la politique'. I cannot prove here that Hobbes was an atheist, even according to his own view of atheism. I must limit myself to asking the reader to compare *De cive*, XV, 14, with *E.W.* IV, p. 349. Many present-day scholars who write on subjects of this kind do not seem to have a sufficient notion of the degree of circumspection or of accommodation to the accepted views that was required, in former ages, of 'deviationists' who desired to survive or to die in peace. Those scholars tacitly assume that the pages in Hobbes's writings devoted to religious subjects can be understood if they are read in the way in which one ought to read the corresponding utterances, say, of Bertrand Russell. In other words, I am familiar with the fact that there are innumerable passages in Hobbes's writings which were used by Hobbes and which can be used by everyone else for proving that Hobbes was a theist and even a good Anglican. The prevalent procedure would merely lead to historical errors, if to grave historical errors, but for the fact that its results are employed for buttressing the dogma that the mind of the individual is incapable of liberating itself from the opinions which rule his society. Hobbes's last word on the question of public worship is that the commonwealth *may* establish public worship. If the commonwealth fails to establish public worship, i.e., if it allows 'many sorts of worship', as it may, 'it cannot be said . . . that the commonwealth is of any religion at all' (cf. *Leviathan*, XXXI [p. 240] with the Latin version [p.m. 171]).

(i.e., the new doctrine of natural right and the new natural public law that is built on it) cannot destroy the wrong opinions of the vulgar, if the vulgar are not apprised of the results of that mathematical knowledge. Plato had said that evils will not cease from the cities if the philosophers do not become kings or if philosophy and political power do not coincide. He had expected such salvation for mortal nature as can reasonably be expected, from a coincidence over which philosophy has no control but for which one can only wish or pray. Hobbes, on the other hand, was certain that philosophy itself can bring about the coincidence of philosophy and political power by becoming popularized philosophy and thus public opinion. Chance will be conquered by systematic philosophy issuing in systematic enlightenment: *Paulatim eruditur vulgus.*[44] By devising the right kind of institutions and by enlightening the citizen body, philosophy guarantees the solution of the social problem, whose solution cannot be guaranteed by man if it is thought to depend on moral discipline.

Opposing the 'utopianism' of the classics, Hobbes was concerned with a social order whose actualization is probable and even certain. The guaranty of its actualization might seem to be supplied by the fact that the sound social order is based on the most powerful passion and therewith on the most powerful force in man. But if the fear of violent death is truly the strongest force in man, one should expect the desired social order always, or almost always, to be in existence, because it will be produced by natural necessity, by the natural order. Hobbes overcomes this difficulty by assuming that men in their stupidity interfere with the natural order. The right social order does not normally come about by natural necessity on account of man's ignorance of that

---

[44] *De Cive*, Ep. ded.; cf. *De Corpore*, I, 7: the cause of civil war is ignorance of the causes of wars and of peace; hence the remedy is moral philosophy. Accordingly Hobbes, characteristically deviating from Aristotle (*Politics* 1302ª35 ff.), seeks the causes of rebellion chiefly in false doctrines (*De Cive*, XII). The belief in the prospects of popular enlightenment—*De Homine*, XIV, 13; *Leviathan*, XVIII (p. 119), XXX (p. 221, 224–25), and XXXI end—is based on the view that the natural inequality of human beings in regard to intellectual gifts is inconsiderable (*Leviathan*, XIII [p. 80] and XV [p. 100]; *De Cive*, III, 13). Hobbes's expectation from enlightenment seems to be contradicted by his belief in the power of passion, and especially of pride or ambition. The contradiction is solved by the consideration that the ambition which endangers civil society is characteristic of a minority: of 'the rich and potent subjects of a kingdom, or those that are accounted the most learned'; if 'the common people', whom necessity 'keepeth attent on their trades, and labour,' are properly taught, the ambition and avarice of the few will become powerless. Cf. also *E.W.* IV, pp. 443–44.

THE SPIRIT OF HOBBES'S POLITICAL PHILOSOPHY 29

order. The 'invisible hand' remains ineffectual if it is not supported by the *Leviathan* or, if you wish, by the *Wealth of Nations*.

There is a remarkable parallelism and an even more remarkable discrepancy between Hobbes's theoretical philosophy and his practical philosophy. In both parts of his philosophy, he teaches that reason is impotent and that it is omnipotent, or that reason is omnipotent because it is impotent. Reason is impotent because reason or humanity have no cosmic support: the universe is unintelligible, and nature 'dissociates' men. But the very fact that the universe is unintelligible permits reason to rest satisfied with its free constructs, to establish through its constructs an Archimedean basis of operations, and to anticipate an unlimited progress in its conquest of nature. Reason is impotent against passion, but it can became omnipotent if it co-operates with the strongest passion or if it puts itself into the service of the strongest passion. Hobbes's rationalism, then, rests ultimately on the conviction that, thanks to nature's kindness, the strongest passion is the only passion which can be 'the origin of large and lasting societies' or that the strongest passion is the most rational passion. In the case of human things, the foundation is not a free construct but the most powerful natural force in man. In the case of human things, we understand not merely what we make but also what makes our making and our makings. Whereas the philosophy or science of nature remains fundamentally hypothetical, political philosophy rests on a nonhypothetical knowledge of the nature of man.[45] As long as Hobbes's approach prevails, 'the philosophy concerned with the human things' will remain the last refuge of nature. For at some point nature succeeds in getting a hearing. The modern contention that man can 'change the world' or 'push back nature' is not unreasonable. One can even safely go much beyond it and say that man can expel nature with a hayfork. One ceases to be reasonable only if one forgets what the philosophic poet adds, *tamen usque recurret*.

[45] Cf. n. 9 above.

[3]

PHILOSOPHY AND POLITICS IN HOBBES[1]

J.W.N. Watkins

I. INTRODUCTION

> If a thing is divided into parts, there is nothing against its having the property
> of unity.   *Plato.*

For Bacon, the philosopher's job is to discover the principles common
to the special sciences, to develop a *natural* philosophy, or ' universal science '
which stands to the special sciences as a tree-trunk to its branches. For
Locke, on the contrary, the philosopher is not a super-scientist such as the
' incomparable Mr. Newton ' ; the philosopher does not examine the external
world, even in its most universal aspects. His job is ' to examine our own
abilities ', i.e. to conduct a *critical* second-order enquiry into the mental
processes and methods involved in first-order enquiries.

This shift from natural philosophy to critical philosophy is uncompleted
in Hobbes' thought. What he says about philosophy echoes Bacon ; what
he does when he is philosophising largely foreshadows Locke. His definition
of philosophy equates it with science (*De Corp.*, i, 2 ; *E.W.*, ii, p. iv ; *Lev.*
p. 367), and the title of his major philosophic work, *De Corpore*, suggests
a study of nature. Such a study, however, occurs only in Part Four (' The
Phenomena of Nature ') which is in any case largely occupied by an analysis
of sensation. The earlier and more important Parts are concerned with such
typical second-order topics as : the methods of physics, geometry and civil
philosophy ; the *meaning* of ' cause ' and ' effect ' ; the nature of language
and the status of universals. Hobbes is the author of a rudimentary natural
philosophy of the world, and also of a full-fledged and highly distinctive
critical philosophy of our knowledge of the world.

Students of Hobbes who have asked, ' What do his political doctrines
owe to his philosophy ? ' have mostly confined themselves to the question
of a relation between his politics and his *natural* philosophy, i.e. his materialism.[2] This is no doubt largely due to Hobbes himself. As we have seen,

---

[1]References to the *Leviathan* are to the first edition (the pagination of which is given
in the Oxford edition). The spelling of quotations has been modernised.

[2]Professor Leo Strauss's brilliant, influential and, I believe, misguided work is
discussed in the text. G. C. Robertson (*Hobbes*, p. 57), A. E. Taylor (*Thomas Hobbes*,
p. 44), John Laird (*Hobbes*, pp. 244-5), B. E. Jessup (*Ethics*, lviii, 3, 1948), and S. P.
Lamprecht (*De Cive*, N.Y., Introduction, p. xvii) all held that Hobbes' psychology
and politics are autonomous because they were not, and could not have been, derived
from his materialism. On the other hand, G. E. G. Catlin (*Thomas Hobbes, as Philosopher,
Publicist, and Man of Letters*, p. 14 and article on ' Hobbes ' in *The Encyclopaedia of
the Social Sciences*) and Leslie Stephen (*Hobbes*, p. 73) held that Hobbes' psychology
and politics are *not* autonomous because they *were* derived from his materialism. Stephen,
however, quoted a passage from Hobbes which rules out his own interpretation : ' the
principles of natural science . . . cannot teach us our own nature ' (p. 151). In Professor Oakeshott's Introduction to *Leviathan* (pp. xviii-xix) we have, for the first time

126   J. W. N. WATKINS

his definition of philosophy diverts attention to his conception of nature ; and in the ' Preface to the Reader ' in *De Cive* Hobbes suggests that he had once intended to derive from his conception of nature his conception of human nature, and from his conception of human nature his conception of government. And this does suggest that the question, ' What do Hobbes' political doctrines owe to his philosophy ? ' can be re-formulated as, ' What does his psychology owe to his materialism ? ' Now the answer to *this* question is obvious. Psychological conclusions about thoughts, feelings and wants cannot be deduced from materialistic premisses about bodily movements : therefore Hobbes must have made a fresh start when he turned from nature to psychology and politics. And this answer appears to be clinched by Hobbes' further statement in the same Preface that ' approaching war . . . ripened and plucked from me this third part. Therefore it happens that what was last in order, is yet come forth first in time, and the rather, because I saw that grounded on its own principles sufficiently known by experience it would not stand in need of the former sections '.

I wish to answer the wider question , ' What do Hobbes' political doctrines owe to his *whole* philosophy, both natural and critical ? ' My thesis will be that the skeleton of Hobbes' argument in Parts I and II of *Leviathan* can (except for one empirical assumption) be derived from his whole philosophical system. In section II I shall show that Hobbes' main philosophical notions were temporally prior to his political theorising. Then I shall turn from his intellectual development to the finished system of ideas at which he arrived. This I shall reconstruct by showing the connections between his philosophic notions and by drawing out (in sections III to VI) the psychological, moral and juridical consequences of those philosophical notions. These consequences will be marshalled together in section VII. In section VIII I shall consider the significance of the interdependence of Hobbes' ideas.

II. THE DEVELOPMENT OF HOBBES' THOUGHT

Hobbes published his translation of Thucydides in 1628. There runs through Thucydides' own work the rough notion of the constancy of human nature, and this notion Hobbes later sharpened and expanded into a universal doctrine (see section VI). It was on such a notion that Machiavelli had based his belief in the induction of remedial political principles from a study of history (*Discourses*, i, 39) ; and in his ' Preface to the Readers ' Hobbes similarly writes of ' the principal and proper work of history being to instruct, and enable men by the knowledge of actions past, to bear themselves prudently in the present, and providently towards the future '. But in his later work Hobbes entirely subordinates prudence derived from historical experience to power derived from scientific knowledge (see *Lev.*,

I believe, the suggestion that Hobbes' thought is neither a disunity because the politics were not derived from his materialism, nor a unity because the politics were derived from his materialism, but a system because it is controlled by a critical, second-order philosophical theory.

p. 135, and section V below). His later political theory is scarcely fore-shadowed in his first work.

His next work, which Tönnies discovered and entitled *A Short Tract on First Principles*, appears to have been written in 1630. It shows that Hobbes had sketched out a distinctive philosophy several years before he circulated the first version of his political theory in 1640. The ideas of the *Tract*, greatly expanded and somewhat altered (though not in essentials), reappear in *De Corpore*.

Professor Leo Strauss has devoted a well-known book to the thesis that ' Hobbes's political philosophy is really, as its originator claims, based on a knowledge of men which is deepened and corroborated by the self-knowledge and self-examination of the individual, and not on a general scientific or metaphysical theory ' (*The Political Philosophy of Hobbes*, p. 29). Now Strauss mention the *Tract* but not its contents—an omission which, I shall now show, is fatal to his claim that Hobbes worked out his political theory on the basis of his knowledge of men and manners *before* he became interested in philosophy.

The purpose of the *Tract* is to explain perceptions of distant bodies. Hobbes begins by laying down as self-evident the key principle that ' That which is in no way touched by another, hath nothing added to it nor taken from it '—it ' remains in the same state it was '. That change is caused by nothing but push remained Hobbes' central metaphysical belief through-out his life.[3] (We shall find that its psychological and ethical consequences are impressive.) In the light of his key principle Hobbes explains the per-ception of a distant body in two stages : first, a physical theory about the diffusion of species emitted by the body and their passage, with diminishing power, to the eye of the observer ; and secondly, a physiological-cum-psychological theory describing how the pressure on the eye is conducted to the observer's ' animal spirits ' (i.e. his nervous system) which react by projecting an image of the distant body.

In section 3 Hobbes turns from perception to motivation. Since all change is caused by bodily push, so-called ' final ' causes must be efficient causes in disguise. ' Good ' says Hobbes in the *Tract*, ' is to every thing that, which hath power to attract it. . . . Appetite is a motion of the animal spirits towards the object that moveth them. . . . The object is the efficient

---

[3] In *De Corpore* it re-appears as : ' All mutation consists in motion only. . . . There can be no cause of motion, except in a body contiguous and moved ' (ix, 6-7). Hobbes, of course, accepts the obvious implication that the sense of touch is basic and that the other senses are more complicated versions of the sense of touch. Professor Strauss, however, always keen to scent a moral and pre-philosophic motive in Hobbes, claims that ' the preference for the sense of touch . . . is already implied in Hobbes's original view of the fundamental antithesis between vanity and fear ' (*op. cit.*, p. 166). Pre-sumably, Strauss means that, for Hobbes, vanity involves visual imagining whereas we become afraid when we feel the world physically resisting us ; and preferring fear to vanity, he prefers touch to sight. This is ingenious ; but Hobbes does not ' prefer ' touch to sight—he merely says that seeing is an indirect and complicated sort of touch-ing. Nor does he correlate fearful with tactile experiences—e.g. fear of the unknown (a cause of religion) is not due to touch. Nor is there any mention of fear or vanity in the *Tract* where Hobbes first outlined his touch-theory of vision.

cause, or agent, of desire '. If an object excites me towards itself it is good for me ; if it repels you from itself, it is evil for you. This thorough-going subjectivism, which plays a decisive role in Hobbes' political theory, is already laid down in the *Tract*.

Indeed the *Tract* is fairly bursting with consequences which are drawn out in Hobbes' subsequent political writings. The *Tract* asserts, in so many words, that man is a part of ' meer nature ' and that his behaviour must be explained by the same sort of causal principles as explain other natural phenomena. Since nature is normless and non-hierarchical, the state of nature will clearly be likewise. Since the brain is activated only after the sense-organs have been impinged on by the external world, it follows that Hobbes' theory of knowledge must be basically empiricist. And from this, together with Hobbes' need to provide a causal explanation of thinking and language, follows (as I shall show in sections IV and V) Hobbes' nominalism, with all its consequences for his conception of the human situation and for his ethics and jurisprudence.

All this is ignored by Strauss. Moreover, if we follow Strauss's concluding recommendation and go to the least mature version of Hobbes' political theory for the best understanding of it, we find that *The Elements of Law*, far from being the work of a non-philosophical student of men, politics and history, conspicuously displays Hobbes' main philosophical notions in the influential opening chapters. His belief that the motion of bodies is the reality which causes sentients to project secondary qualities on to those bodies, his account of the physical process by which objects generate images in sentients, and his account of the endeavours towards or away from the object which these images arouse in sentients—all this is expanded from the *Tract*, together with a consequent subjectivist analysis of ' good ' and ' evil '. A causal theory of thinking, necessitated by Hobbes' physiological psychology, is also developed in *The Elements of Law*, based on a theory of signs and marks which leads to Hobbes' nominalism. His main theological tenets are also outlined : God is First Cause, and infinite both in the physical sense that he is omnipotent, and in the logical sense that he is unlimited by any characteristics.[4] Hence, all that men can know of him is that he exists and is omnipotent, unimaginable and incomprehensible (*El. of L.*, I, xi, 2).

Two years later, in *De Cive*, Hobbes added to the foregoing a theory of truth whose reliance on stipulative definitions has obvious political over-tones (see section V). To the English translation he prefixed an informal account of his method, which he afterwards described systematically in *De Corpore* (on which Hobbes worked between 1636 and 1654, a period which embraces the shorter period during which he elaborated his political theory). I want now to turn to his method, for I think I have said enough to show that Hobbes was a philosopher before he became a political theorist and that his philosophy is in the forefront of his early political work.

---

[4] Hobbes' ' God ' is almost indistinguishable from Aristotle's ' unformed matter '. See *E.W.*, iv, p. 313.

III. HOBBES' METHOD

> They say that in describing the generation of the world they are doing as a geometer does in constructing a figure, not implying that the universe ever really came into existence, but facilitating understanding by exhibiting the object, like the figure, in process of formation.
>
> *Aristotle.*

Harvey and Galilei were men whose work won Hobbes' rare admiration. Each had, in his view, created a new science—a science of the human body and a science of moving bodies—just as he, Hobbes, had created a new science of the body politic.

When someone is deeply impressed by thinkers in other fields we can expect their work to influence him in two main ways. First, he will be tempted to take up their basic concepts and extend them beyond their original contexts. This Hobbes did. Galilei's great advance was made possible by the fact that he drew his dividing line not, as Aristotle had done, between motion and rest, but between accelerated motion and uniform motion (of which rest is a special case) : thus everything is in some sort of motion.

The idea of motion permeates all Hobbes' thought : geometry studies motion ; thought is motion ; imagination and memory are made possible by the law of inertia ; ' life itself is but motion ' ; social life is like a race ; tranquil happiness is impossible ; a good object is one which arouses motion towards itself. If the *Republic* may be called the political expression of the Pythagorean theory of the tuned lyre, the *Leviathan* may be called the political expression of the Galilean theory of motion.

The main impression given by Harvey's account of the motion of the heart and blood is of a system of pumps, tubes and valves. Hobbes (like that other enthusiastic admirer of Harvey, Descartes) extends this mechanical interpretation to the whole body, and even to the mind. Harvey had said that ' every affection of the mind . . . is the cause of an agitation whose influence extends towards the heart, and there induces change ', a change which in turn modifies the behaviour of the body (*De Motu*, xv). Hobbes' psychology is an elaboration of this remark.[5]

The second main way in which a pupil may be influenced by masters in other fields is by the example of their *method*, for a method of enquiry may be fruitfully employed outside the discipline in which it was developed. In Hobbes' time, nearly all philosophers stressed the need for a sure method of acquiring and formulating knowledge, and attempted to meet that need.[6] But Hobbes chose (not a method worked out *a priori* by his philosopher-acquaintances, Bacon and Descartes, but) the resolutive-compositive method which had actually been practised by his scientific friends. Harvey

[5] ' The original of life being in the heart, that motion in the sentient, which is propagated to the heart, must necessarily make some alteration or diversion of vital motion . .' (*De Corp.*, xxv, 12). He refers to Harvey in his next paragraph. Hobbes' theory of motivation is discussed in section IV below.

[6] See, e.g., Bacon's *Novum Organon*, Descartes' *Discours*, Harvey's ' Manner and Order of Acquiring Knowledge ', Spinoza's *On the Improvement of the Understanding*, Leibnitz' ' Logic of Invention ', Newton's ' Rules of Philosophizing '.

and Galilei, with extraordinary fruitfulness. Their method has a common origin and background in the University of Padua, where Harvey was a student when Galilei was a professor. Thus any influence of Hobbes' method on his political theory (and I shall argue that it was considerable) is a consequence of the fact that Hobbes attached himself to the successful scientific tradition, and thereby had his method determined for him.

To elucidate the nature of this method I shall first briefly consider Harvey's use of it. Harvey's *De Motu Cordis et Sanguinis* is an *argument*, and not a description, because the blood-system itself cannot be observed. His first task, occupying many years, was to establish, by dissection and inspection, the character of the system's constituent elements—the structure, capacity, and movement of the heart, the one-way valves in the veins, etc. On this knowledge of its parts he based a hypothetical reconstruction of the whole system : the existence of the one-way valves refuted the ebb-and-flow theory of the blood's movement, and the fact that, in half an hour, the left ventricle pumped an amount of blood into the aorta at least equal to the amount of blood in the whole body, sufficiently refuted the theory that blood is continuously ingested and digested. The only hypothesis about the nature of the whole system which seemed consistent with the observed nature of its parts was that there is ' a motion, as it were, in a circle '. This hypothetical reconstruction was then tested and confirmed by observing the effects of, for instance, amputations, ligatures and infections.

Having shown the ' resolutive-compositive ' (or, as it might be re-named for Harvey, the ' dissection-reconstruction ') method at work, I will now outline its previous formulation,[7] in order to show what a well-wrought instrument Hobbes inherited.

Like Aristotle, the creators of this method drew a sharp distinction between the order of experience and the order of nature and, consequently, between the order of discovery and the order of demonstration or exposition. Our senses acquaint us with *effects*, with confused and colourful situations, with the surface-manifestations of a system invisibly governed by simple and universal principles. These principles are the constitutive causes into which effects have to be resolved. A touch of genius is necessary to penetrate to the causes underlying an effect, for they are not rationally self-evident, nor, of course, are they implied by the effect ; they have to be conjectured.

Our next step is to reconstruct the whole situation, transforming a confused effect with which we had previously been merely acquainted, into an intelligible system. Having dismantled the effect and having postulated the nature of its elements, we now have to put it together again by combining the constituent principles, or causes, and deducing the effect from them. In short, the scientist has to *axiomatise* his subject-matter.

Before I turn to Hobbes' conception and employment of this method

---

[7]The following two paragraphs are mainly based on the famous article by J. H. Randall, jr., ' Scientific Method in the School of Padua ', *Jour. History of Ideas*, i, 2, 1940.

there is a further feature of it which needs to be elucidated because it exerted an important influence on Hobbes' formulation of his political theory : namely, the fact that once several factors at work in a complex situation have been isolated and defined, intellectual experiments can be performed by idealising the situation, that is, by imagining certain factors which are actually always present in some degree to be diminished to zero. Inferring the consequences of the remaining factors may lead to the discovery of a new principle. It was in this manner that, for example, Stevinius showed that the pull of equal weights along inclined planes of equal heights must vary inversely with the lengths of the inclined planes. But the classic examples are Galilei's discovery of the Law of Inertia and his analysis of the trajectory of a cannon-ball. Having shown that, assuming no friction, ' a body which descends along any inclined plane and continues along a plane inclined upwards will, on account of the momentum acquired, ascend to an equal height above the horizontal ' (*Two New Sciences*, p. 217), Galilei now imagines the slope of the second plane, and consequently the deceleration of the body, to be gradually reduced to zero—and then the body's speed would be uniform. Having thus established the Law of Inertia, Galilei imagines the body to pass over the edge of the horizontal plane. Its velocity can now be resolved into the original uniform horizontal motion and the newly acquired uniform downwards acceleration (assuming no air resistance). When these two motions are mathematically recomposed, the resultant is a semi-parabola. It is further deduced that a projectile fired at an angle will describe a full parabola, and that a cannon has a maximum range when its elevation is 45°. Galilei was already *acquainted* with this fact ' from accounts given by gunners ' ; but now, having resolved the trajectory into its constituent principles, he can, by deduction from them, both explain this maximum range and also predict the decreases in range at other elevations.

Having surveyed the development of what Galilei called the *metodo resolutivo* and the *metodo compositivo* we can now turn to Hobbes' account and employment of it. Hobbes took his method more seriously than most of his commentators have done.

Hobbes follows tradition by distinguishing the method of invention or discovery from the method of teaching or demonstration (*De Corp.*, vi, 10). The process of discovery is not recorded in a didactic work of exposition (thus the *Leviathan* opens with an account of the premises and not with an account of how Hobbes arrived at them). In a scientific enquiry we start with what is ' more known to us ', namely, the whole amalgam of qualities presented to our senses (vi, 2). This is the effect of a singular configuration of causes, or intersection of principles, each of which is simple, universal, and ' more known to nature '. The causes into which we try to resolve the effect are the conditions which are necessary and sufficient to generate the effect. To understand an effect with which our senses have acquainted us, is to know a recipe for producing it. Knowledge is power

' The subject of philosophy is every body of which we can conceive any generation . . . or which is capable of composition and resolution ' (i, 8). The resolutive-compositive method can be applied to words, to physical situations, to geometrical figures, and to human situations. Let us begin with its application to words.

If we wish to explicate a compound term such as ' man ' we must, says Hobbes, go on resolving it until we reach the unanalysable constituents of its meaning such as ' body ', ' animated ', ' sentient ', and ' rational ' ; then we compose these together into a definition (vi, 15).

In physics we are acquainted with effects and we know, according to Hobbes, that they are caused by some sort of motion. But precisely *what* motion generates thunder, say, or the tides, has to be conjectured because it cannot be known *a priori*. We have to resolve the effect into those hypothetical mechanical principles from which the effect can, and anything contrary to experience cannot, be deduced (xxx, 15). Hobbes claims that his own explanations of natural phenomena are demonstrated from ' suppositions not absurd ' (*Ep. Ded.*).

Euclid's definition of a sphere is a genetic definition, a recipe for constructing spheres (*Bk.* xi, *def.* 14).[8] According to Hobbes it is therefore a prototype for all geometrical definitions, since geometry demonstrates how figures are generated by the motions of points and lines. To understand a geometrical figure we have to resolve it into its elements and then deductively recompose it. But whereas in the analysis and definition of compound words the whole process takes place, so to speak, before our eyes, and whereas in physics we are only acquainted with the effect and have to guess the causes, in geometry we know the whole figure and we can find out its simple constituents, but we cannot know the routes they followed when the whole figure was actually constructed. We can only postulate a hypothetical generation of the known whole from its known parts (*De Corp.*, i, 5). I mention this because the methodological situation in civil philosophy is analogous.

In the Preface to *De Cive* Hobbes gives an informal account of the way he used his method in civil philosophy :

> Concerning my method . . . I took my beginning from the very matter of civil government, and thence proceeded to its generation and form, and the first beginnings of justice ; for everything is best understood by its constitutive causes. For as in a watch, or some such small engine, the matter, figure, and motion of the wheels cannot well be known, except it be taken in sunder, and viewed in parts ; so to make a more curious search into the rights of states, and duties of subjects, it is necessary (I say not to take them in sunder, but yet that) they be so considered, as if they were dissolved.

In seventeenth century science the idea of resolution had come to mean division of a system either into its physical parts (Harvey's procedure) or into the simple and universal principles governing it (Galilei's procedure). Hobbes' idea of resolution combines both procedures. He resolves civil

---

[8]I think—though I am not sure—that the fact that these basic definitions are *genetic* means that they may be synthetic and not analytic. On this question see F. Brandt, *Thomas Hobbes' Mechanical Conception of Nature*, pp. 192-7.

society into its physical parts, solitary individuals. This is an intellectual experiment in which Hobbes ' idealises ' the human situation by imagining away the factors of authority and justice. He then lays down the universal principles which govern individual behaviour. These principles are the constitutive causes of the State. And in civil philosophy, as in geometry, it is enough to know the original causes and their final product, and merely postulate a route by which the causes might have led to the effect. Aristotle had resolved the *polis* into its elements ; but his explanation of why these coalesce into a self-sufficient whole turns into a typical history of their evolution. Hobbes, on the other hand, is indifferent to historical development. The state of nature is an ideal limit : it depicts ' what manner of life there *would* be, where there were no common power to fear ' (*Lev.*, p. 63), and where men have ' sprung out of the earth, and suddenly (like mushrooms) come to full maturity ' (*De Cive*, viii, 1). And Hobbes' account of their progress to civil society describes the most direct route they could have taken from one extreme to its opposite, whereas the routes which have been followed in history have been long and circuitous, seldom starting from the former extreme and often failing to reach the latter.

Such failures give the resolutive-compositive method a special function in political science. When one applies it to a physical effect or to a geometrical figure the recomposed whole, which one now understands, is still the whole with which one had previously only been acquainted. But when this method is applied to society the recomposed whole may very well differ from the original. An actual society may be inconsistent, at war with itself. But when a system of political authority is rationally reconstructed by deduction from the nature of the system's elements it will obviously be consistent with them. To apply the resolutive-compositive method to society is to discover what men *are* and what the State *ought to be* to be consistent with their nature. The method has a normative function. Thus in the Preface to *De Cive* already quoted Hobbes says that the object of the method is ' to make a more curious search into the rights of states, and the duties of subjects '. And in *De Corpore* he says that the method is used in civil philosophy to determine questions of justice and injustice (vi, **7**).

We are now in a position to consider how Hobbes' method shaped his political philosophy.

First, society is to be resolved into nothing but individuals, and the principles governing their behaviour provide the sole premises from which the right state is subsequently reconstructed.

Secondly, Hobbes' didactic purpose in his political theory will be ' only to put men in mind of what they know already, or may know by their own experience ' (*El. of L.*, I, i, 2).[9] His theory will demonstrate the type of state which is alone consistent with their natures. The *Leviathan* would be a redundant book if men understood themselves and the logic of their

---

[9] Hence his statement : ' Neither was it rashly nor inadvisedly said by Plato of old, that knowledge was memory ' (*De Cive*, xviii, 4).

situation. Such understanding, however, requires ' deep study ' which most men cannot perform for themselves, especially when the shelter of authority lulls them into forgetting the evils which would follow its disappearance. According to Sextus Empiricus, when a king died the Persians used to be left without law for five hair-raising days to teach them their desperate need of authority. Hobbes draws a graphic picture of the state of nature to remind men of the same lesson.

Thirdly, Hobbes' method requires that his conception of natural law takes the form it does take.[10] Hitherto, two main conceptions had prevailed, one deriving from Plato and the other from Aristotle. The first depicted natural law as a sort of ' brooding omniscience in the sky ' ; the second, as the essential core common to all historic systems of civil law. Hobbes dismisses the first as something ' built in the air ' (*El. of L.*, p. xviii). His method does not allow any appeal to transcendent norms because it requires that psychological axioms alone shall provide the premises for a rational reconstruction of the state.[11] Nor does his method allow any appeal to common practice, since the behaviour of men which is based on received opinions may be inconsistent with how they would behave if they had a true knowledge of themselves and their situation (*De Cive*, ii, 1).

If natural laws are neither transcendental norms nor immanent in legal systems, but are nevertheless some kind of imperative which is both prior to political authority and found out by reason ; and if psychological axioms are the only permissible premises ; then natural laws must be hypothetical imperatives deduced from psychological principles, instructing us what we must do if we are to be consistent with our own nature. Since all men shun unnatural death ' by a certain impulsion of nature, no less than that whereby a stone moves downward ' (for a reason given in section IV below) the laws of nature dictate ' those duties they are necessarily to perform towards others in order to their *own* preservation ' (*De Cive*, ii, 2, my italics).

Fourthly, since Hobbes' method, and consequently the laws of nature, teach man what behaviour is consistent with his nature and situation, a man who rationally promises to behave in a certain way and fails to do so, a man who behaves inconsistently and irrationally, is contravening natural law. ' For as it is . . . called an absurdity, to contradict what one maintained in the beginning : so . . . it is called injustice, and injury, voluntarily to undo that, which from the beginning he had voluntarily done ' (*Lev.*, p. 65). The rational propriety of fulfilling promises is the basis of Hobbes' moral system.

In a word, Hobbes' method required that his political theory should be anthropocentric from start to finish. Unlike episcopalians and presbyterians who claimed authority from God, and unlike common lawyers who claimed authority for a system of maxims which had grown into something largely

---

[10]Here, I am considering Hobbes' natural laws *qua* ' dictates of reason '. I shall consider them *qua* dictates of God in section V.

[11]The requirement is re-inforced by Hobbes' nominalism. See section V below.

independent of human will, Hobbes' sovereign was *man*-made : ' I ground the civil right of sovereigns, and both the duty and liberty of subjects, upon the known natural inclinations of mankind ' (*Lev.*, p. 394). As Dewey pointed out in an excellent study,[12] Hobbes' contemporaries did not object to his principle of absolute authority but to the merely human source of that authority. Before Locke, Hobbes was generally regarded as subversive rather than totalitarian.

IV. THE NATURE OF MAN

> Man, be he learned or ignorant, is a part of nature.   *Spinoza*.

Professor Strauss concedes[13] that the application of Hobbes' method to political societies, whereby ' what was at first an " irrational " whole is " rationalised " ' had a significant effect on Hobbes' political philosophy :

> It would seem that the characteristic contents of Hobbes's political philosophy —the absolute priority of the individual to the state, the conception of the individual as asocial, of the relation between the state of nature and the State as an absolute antithesis, and finally of the State itself as Leviathan—is [*sic*] determined by and, as it were, implied in the method.

But, he continues,

> Precisely on the assumptions of the ' resolutive-compositive ' method . . . the question of the aim and quality of the individual will, of man's will in the state of nature, becomes decisive for the concrete development of the idea of the State.

Strauss goes on to argue that Hobbes derived his conception of human will from his experience of, and insight into, human nature, and not from scientific or philosophic considerations.

But a rational act of will, which is the source of political authority for Hobbes, is, according to him, the outcome of a process of deliberation involving experience, language, reasoning and wanting, and his epistemological and psychological analyses of these clearly affected his conception of human will. Moreover, his psychology and epistemology were in their turn affected by his conception of the causal relationship between the human organism and the external world. Thus Hobbes' conception of nature and causation did *indirectly* affect his conception of human will although the latter was not, and could not have been, deduced from the former. At any rate, this is the thesis which I shall now try to substantiate.

The great dividing line for Hobbes is not between mind and matter but between art and nature.[14] Civil society is a product of art—' we make the commonwealth ourselves ' ; but *we* are a part of nature. Our ideas, memory, and desires have a natural genesis which can be depicted by a mechanical model ; and while language and reasoning are not inborn, they have a technological genesis which can be depicted by an improved version of the same model. God, so to speak, equipped us with Mark I minds which we have expanded into Mark II minds. Hobbes' mechanical model of the mind

---

[12]' The Motivation of Hobbes's Political Philosophy ', *Studies in the History of Ideas*, Dept. of Philosophy, Columbia University, N.Y., 1918, i.

[13]*Op., cit.*, pp. 2-3.

[14]See Professor Oakeshott's lucid account of Hobbes' philosophy of artifice, *op. cit.*, p. xxviii,

does not entail the *contents* of his psychological doctrine, but it does narrowly limit the possible contents of that doctrine.

It is, in fact, a quasi-mechanical model because, while Hobbes pretends to be giving a thoroughly materialist account of the mind's workings, he actually gives, as one would expect, an epiphenomenalist account. He really regards thoughts and feelings as the shadows and overtones *of* movements in the brain, though he claims they *are* those movements. This self-deception, and his transitions from physical to mental language, are rendered easier by the fact that Hobbes (like Freud in our own time) uses terms which are ambiguously susceptibile to a physiological or a psychological interpretation, e.g. : 'compulsion', 'disturbance', 'tranquillity', 'celerity', 'dullness', 'agitation', 'stirrings', 'phantasm'. But the most important example of a term to which he tacitly gives a dual function is 'endeavour', which Hobbes defines as 'motion made through the length of a point, and in an instant or point of time' (*De Corp.*, xv, 2) ; but since it obviously suggests *conatus*, it becomes plausible for Hobbes to say that voluntary action begins as an endeavour.

We must now see what consequences this causal and epiphenomenalist theory of the mind has for Hobbes' theory of knowledge and motivation, and so for his conception of human will.

First, for Hobbes the mind cannot be (as it could be for Plato and Spinoza) self-moved—or, to put it in his own terms, the animal spirits in the nervous system have no inherent power of movement.[15] Ideas cannot spring spontaneously into consciousness. The mind can only be set in motion by pressure from without—by pressure exerted on the sense-organs either directly by a body touching them or by the ether being vibrated by a distant body. The motion set up in the sentient is transmitted first to the brain which reacts by projecting outwards an image of the distant body, and then to the heart where it sets up an endeavour towards or away from the object. This endeavour is (accompanied by) desire or aversion respectively. By the Law of Inertia, the perturbation subsides only gradually, and remains capable of causing after-images (accompanied by hope or fear) in the absence of the object. If nothing intervenes, the endeavour will be amplified into large-scale bodily movement towards or away from the object.

This is the simplest kind of voluntary action and it occurs in men and animals. But in more sophisticated kinds of voluntary action only the premeditation becomes more complex ; the motivation remains the same. The heart always dominates the brain in the sense that its final *pro* or *con* endeavour determines the course of action. Thus all striving, according to Hobbes, is shown to be the effect of efficient and not final causes.

From his analysis two principles follow which re-appear as premises in his account of the state of nature. First, since the vital motions of the heart can only be excited by the prospect of some bodily change in its owner, all

---

[15]This key principle was already established in the *Tract* : 'the animal spirits are moved locally, by another' (iii, *conc.* 2).

motivation is egocentric ; merely moral considerations which do not refer to such a change cannot affect behaviour (*Lev.*, p. 66). Secondly, since aversion is aroused when the vital motions are hindered, the prospect of their stoppage, i.e. of death, will arouse the most violent aversion of all.

V. HOBBES' NOMINALISM

I can see a horse, Plato, but I cannot see its horseness.   *Antisthenes.*

Rational behaviour, like all purposeful behaviour, has, according to Hobbes, a causal genesis, and it involves experience, language and reasoning. We must now follow his attempt to provide a mechanical model to explain these. Then we shall see what consequences this model of the mind has for his epistemology and what consequences this epistemology has for his ethics and jurisprudence.

For Hobbes, the sense-organs are the only conduits between the brain and the external, primordial world which ' depends not upon our thought ' ; and this entails his fundamental empiricism. Sensory images are the only bricks with which he can build his theory of knowledge ; for him, ' cognition ', ' imagination ', ' idea ', ' conception ' all mean imagery (*El. of L.*, I, iv, 6) ; and ' there is no conception in a man's mind, which hath not at first, totally, or by parts, been begotten upon the organs of sense. The rest are derived from that original ' (*Lev.*, p. 3). To remember is to revive an image ; and if the image of one thing (e.g. fire) is frequently succeeded by the image of another thing (e.g. ashes), the two images become associated and the occurrence of one will revive the other. Experience is the sum of such remembrances ' of the succession of one thing to another ', the ability to recognise certain things as signs of other things ; and ' prudence ' means ' taking signs of experience warily '. Animals possess prudence[16] as well as men. But the utility of pre-linguistic experience is limited, because it only operates when a natural sign is actually sensed, and because chains of associations cannot be summarised in a general formula but have to be re-experienced link by link on each occasion. We must now turn to Hobbes' account of what he considers one of men's greatest technological triumphs, the creation of language.

For Hobbes, the universe consists of singular things, the singular images caused by those things touching (directly or indirectly) on sense-organs, and images compounded from the original images.[17] Hence if words are to find a place in this universe, they too must be *things*. What sort of things ? We have already seen that two things may come to be regarded as signs of one another if images of them get associated. Thus heavy cloud is a sign of rain. This, however, is a *natural* sign. We also recognise artificial signs, or marks, such as those placed on submerged rocks or outside pawn-brokers' shops. Now names, according to Hobbes, are just such marks : ' A name is a

---

[16]And so do Professor Grey Walter's electrical tortoises, which suggests that Hobbes was right to suppose that he was giving a *causal* explanation of this sort of behaviour.

[17]For simplicity of exposition I omit the feelings which accompany the images. They will be introduced later.

word taken at pleasure to serve for a mark, which may raise in our mind a thought [i.e. image] like to some thought we had before, and which being disposed in speech and pronounced to others, may be to them a sign of what thought the speaker had . . . before his mind ' (*De Corp.*, ii, 4).

We are following Hobbes' attempt to give a causal explanation, compatible with his mechanical conception of nature, of rational behaviour ; but at this point the role of words in merely prudent behaviour may be mentioned. Here, words greatly increase the number of signs which evoke responses (e.g. grabbing the fire-extinguisher on hearing ' Fire ! ' as well as on seeing smoke). Words also make possible a register of experience, or history, so that we no longer have to rely each on our own small experience. And words enable us to summarise the lessons of experience in inductive generalisations (e.g. ' Punishment follows crime '). But prudent human behaviour is only a more efficient version of prudent animal behaviour, and it suffers from the fundamental defect that induction cannot yield certain and universal principles. ' For though in all places of the world, men should lay ·the foundations of their houses on the sand, it could not thence be inferred that so it ought to be ' (*Lev.*, p. 107). On the contrary, ' where men build on false grounds, the more they build, the greater is the ruin ' (p. 140). Maxims based on custom and precedent are therefore dangerously unreliable.[18] This general condemnation has a particular target : Hobbes is, of course, trying to torpedo the common law.[19]

Having traced Hobbes' causal analysis of prudent behaviour we must now see how he extends this analysis to that much more powerful and efficacious kind of conduct, rational or scientific behaviour. Words, as we have seen, are physical marks or, as Hobbes also calls them, counters. In pre-rational thinking these counters get added together only if the things they denote get associated in experience. But in rational thinking counters are added to and subtracted from one another, not according to experience, but according to *rules*. These rules, or definitions, specify permissible substitutions between counters. In brief, Hobbes interprets deductive science on the model of arithmetic (*De Corp.*, i, 2-3), and the human mind engaged in deduction on that of an adding-machine or abacus. Rational conduct consists in calculating the consequences of alternative actions and in then doing that action the imagined consequences of which arouse the strongest *pro* endeavour.

Hobbes' causal interpretation of names as physical marks which get tied, by association, to the things they denote, applies well enough to proper names like ' Charles I ', but what of universal terms like ' Man ' ? There is no room in Hobbes' world for universal essences or natures for it consists only of singular things and images. Nor is it possible for a man to entertain

---

[18]Cp. Bacon, *Works* (1819), i, p. 13.

[19]See *Lev.*, p. 50 and *E.W.*, vi. Contrast Lord Eldon : ' Dumpor's case always struck me as extraordinary ; but if you depart from Dumpor's case, what is there to prevent a departure in every direction ? ' (Quoted by Bagehot, *Literary Studies* (Everyman), i, p. 10).

a universal *concept*, for images are individual and particular, and when images get amalgamated the resultant is still a singular compound : ' They err, that say the idea of anything is universal ; as if there could be in the mind an image of a man, which were not the image of some man, but a man simply, which is impossible ; for every idea is one, and of one thing ' (*De Corp.*, v, 8).

Thus Hobbes' materialism implies that universal words cannot denote anything universal outside the mind, and his causal theory of image-thinking implies that they cannot denote anything universal inside the mind. Therefore, there is ' nothing in the world universal but names ' (*Lev.*, p. 13). ' Charles I ' is the name of one individual ; ' Stuart ' is the name of several individuals ; and ' Man ' is the name of many individuals. A universal is a sort of sur-surname. It does not *connote* a meaning ; it only *denotes* particular items in the universe. This is Hobbes' nominalism, whose impressive consequences must now be unfurled.

For Aristotle, a person is a configuration of properties which inhere in matter which persists through change. Socrates' essential property, his reason, is also his least distinctive property, for it belongs to *all* members of his species. His more distinctive properties, his snub nose and irony, for instance, are merely accidental ; but even these do not distinguish him from all other men. What individuates this particular configuration of rationality, snub-nosedness, irony, etc., from all possible similar configurations is the sheer characterless, incomprehensible matter in which they inhere. Thus for Aristotle a man is an individual in virtue of something valueless and a member of a community in virtue of his highest properties ; which readily suggests that individual ends must be subordinated to the common good.

But according to Hobbes' nominalism, these common properties do not exist. There are only things and the names which denote them. The universe is an aggregate of distinct things, and society of distinct individuals.[20]

In order to understand a further consequence of Hobbes' nominalism I must introduce the reader to a complication in Hobbes' theory of language whose significance has been generally overlooked. ' Names ', Hobbes writes, ' are signs not of things, but of our cogitations ' (*De Corp.*, ii, 5). The word ' stone ' does not denote stones but the stoney images in the minds of people who pronounce, write, hear, read, or imagine the word (*De Corp.*, vi, 11). This doctrine is inescapable if, with Hobbes, we assume that words denote but do not connote ; that the universe consists only of existent things ; and that we can nevertheless imagine and speak meaningfully of non-existent things, or fictions, such as centaurs and future or impossible events. A platonist would say that ' centaur ', ' to-morrow ', etc., have a connotation or meaning, although they do not denote anything existent ; but Hobbes cannot say this. Meaningful words must denote *something* existent, and the only available candidates are our *images* of centaurs, future events, etc. Moreover,

[20]See Professor Oakeshott's excellent remarks on the connection between nominalism and individualism, *op. cit.*, p. lv.

the function of words, according to Hobbes, is mnemonic : a word is invented so that the thought of it may arouse in the thinker's mind its associated image and so that his pronunciation of it may arouse similar images in the minds of his hearers. For this reason also Hobbes asserts that words ' are signs of our conceptions . . . not signs of the things themselves ' (ii, 5).

To understand one consequence of this imagine a number of adjoining prison-cells, each occupied by a prisoner who has never met the others and who can communicate with them only by tapping signals on the wall. The prisoners can exchange information and they may even be able to work out a concerted plan of action, but they cannot establish any *rapport* or em-pathetic understanding between themselves. They are shut off from each other by the medium through which they send their signals. Each remains fundamentally solitary.

Hobbes' theory of communication places us all in the prisoners' situation. According to it, there are no common thoughts or purposes which we can share. I have a private thought, I transmit a public signal, and then you have a private thought—that is the closest we can get. Thus Hobbes' nominalism implies, not only that society is an aggregate of separate indi-viduals, but also that each individual is inescapably lonely and self-reliant even when he acts in concert.

Now consider the ethical consequences of Hobbes' nominalism. In a world consisting only of particular things, images, and accompanying feelings, there is no place for a transcendent moral order to which moral terms refer. Yet Hobbes accepts that we use the words ' good ' and ' evil ' meaningfully. Now on his view, as we have seen, a meaningful word denotes something—something *inside* the mind. The mind contains only images and the feelings of desire and aversion set up by the images. If I say ' Hitler is evil ', ' Hitler ' denotes my image of the man, not the man himself. What, then, does ' evil ' denote ? It must be something in my mind and not some-thing in Hitler ; and the only thing in my mind remaining to be denoted is the feeling of aversion aroused by my image of Hitler. Thus Hobbes' nominalism leads to his ethical subjectivism. In nature there are no common moral principles ; no moral properties inhere in objective situations ; moral statements describe the state of their authors, not of the objects to which they refer (*Lev.*, p. 24).

This doctrine is—to borrow Professor Wisdom's adjective for the equally iconoclastic verification-principle of the 1930's—' smashing '. It blows up Platonism, Aristotelianism, Stoicism, Thomism and any other classical systems which assert that moral standards which are independent of men and their passions provide the premises from which men can infer what they ought to do. It does this quite simply by saying that moral terms, or names, denote only subjective passionate feelings, feelings which vary between men and within the same man at different times: ' and therefore such names can never be true grounds of any ratiocination ' (*Lev.*, p. 17).

The original motive of the mediaeval nominalists had been to dissolve the alleged web of mental fictions which had been interposed by their opponents between the investigator and the real world of things.[21] But Hobbes carried this attack on verbal fictions into new territory : ethics too must study matter (that is, the passions which moral terms denote) and not words and opinions. But ethics should not merely *describe* human passions— that, according to Hobbes, was the defect of Greek moral philosophy (*Lev.*, p. 369). Hobbes defines ethics as knowledge of the *consequences* of the passions of men.

We have already seen, in section III, that Hobbes' method requires that psychological axioms be the premises from which the nature of the rightly ordered state is deduced[22] ; and we now see that Hobbes' nominalism re-inforces that methodological requirement by entailing that there is nothing else which *could* provide those premises. We also saw that his method requires that natural laws take the form of hypothetical imperatives deduced from a psychological axiom (*Lev.*, p. 80). Yet these hypothetical imperatives are also divine imperatives and so are properly called Laws after all : ' the Law of Nature is a Divine Law '. We must now consider how this is so.

Hobbes' nominalism and subjectivism assert that moral terms only denote private feelings ; consequently, a power sufficient to cause all men constantly to fear the same thing would cause them all to call that thing evil. Thus, while interpersonal moral principles have no autonomous existence, they can be *created* by a super-personal power. A persistent search for antecedent causes leads men to realise that the First Cause, Immortal God, must be such a power ; and we know that he has caused us all to fear unnatural death above all else, and so to call it the supreme evil which ought always to be avoided. That men must try to avoid unnatural death is a product of God's art ; but to us it is a natural law, because ' the Art whereby God hath made and governs the world ' is, to us, ' Nature ' (*Lev.*, p. 1).

The strategy for avoiding unnatural death is, of course, for men mutually to promise to transfer their rights to a sovereign ; and this mortal god will likewise possess the super-personal power with which to fill the moral vacuum by creating interpersonal moral principles. He will cause all his subjects to fear doing actions defined as penal by his laws. The words ' just ' and ' unjust ' have no connotation ; but the sovereign will pump meaning into them by *causing* them to have a uniform denotation.

The affinity between mathematics and jurisprudence was very obvious to seventeenth century natural lawyers : both disciplines are deductive, universal, and independent of fact. But what is the status of their premises ? Are they synthetic *a priori* principles, timeless and shiningly self-evident

[21]Cf. Bacon : ' Here therefore is the first distemper of learning, when men study words, and not matter ' (*Op. cit.*, i, p. 28).

[22]' To reduce this doctrine [of justice and policy] to the rules and infallibility of reason, there is no way, but first to put such principles down for a foundation, as passion not mistrusting, may not seek to displace ; and afterward to build thereon . . . the law of nature ' (*El. of L., Ep. Ded.*).

142   J. W. N. WATKINS

truths ? Or merely stipulative definitions ? Grotius replied as a platonist.
Hobbes replies as a nominalist : truth is made by definitions and uniform
standards of justice between men can only be created by the definitions of
a single authority above men. Hobbes' nominalism and his stipulative
theory of truth leads obviously to a command theory of justice. ' Before
there was any government just and unjust had no being, their nature only
being relative to some command ' (*De Cive*, xii, 1).

Finally, it is clear that Hobbes' nominalism requires that such unambiguous and non-conflicting commands should be issued by a single determinate
body. In a society consisting of nothing but separate individuals authority
can be assigned only to one of them or to one group of them. There is no
immaterial entity (such as Law, or a General Will, or a Constitution) to
whom it could be assigned. The civil authority, says Hobbes, must be
visible, not ghostly (*Lev.*, p. 171).[23]

VI. THE UNIFORMITY OF MEN

No single thing is so like another, so exactly its counterpart, as all of us are to
one another.   *Cicero.*

According to Hobbes, we can only imagine some particular man ; yet
in *Leviathan* he imagines a prototype-Man. Now if an Aristotelian can admit
that men are very diverse, having only certain essential features in common,
surely a nominalist ought to say that ' Man ' denotes many separate beings
with *nothing* in common but the name ?

Of course, for Hobbes to admit that men may be differently motivated
would have been fatal to his project of a political science deduced from
universal psychological principles. Who could infer the outcome of a state
of nature peopled by introverted dreamers and extraverted alcoholics ?
But in fact Hobbes' belief that men are basically similar (*De Corp.*, i, 7)
not only does not conflict with his nominalism but is actually required by
it. True, all that men share is the name. But why were all of them, and
nothing else, given it ? Having no common properties they must have been
given the same name because they *resemble* one another : ' one universal
name is imposed on many things for their *similitude* ' (*Lev.*, p. 13).

Let me pursue this a little further. Universal terms which are least
amenable to a nominalist interpretation are terms (like ' weapon ', ' game ',
' mammal ') whose instances (e.g. atom-bombs and daggers, chess and
football, kangaroos and whales) do not overtly resemble each other at all,
for here we seem to be driven to find the explanation of the common name
in a common property.[24] The kind of term which is most amenable to

[23]In this article I am concerned with the consequences of Hobbes' philosophical
notions for the secular part of his civil philosophy. But I may mention here that he
explicitly derives the need for the Erastian control of religious worship from his nominalism. See *De Cive* xv, 17.

[24]In this paper my object is to show the connections between Hobbes' ideas, not
to criticise them ; but having got so far, I may as well add that Hobbes himself gave the
game away when he said that things are given a common name if they are similar
in virtue of some ' *accident* '. Descartes complained that Hobbes left the distinction

a nominalist interpretation is a trade-name given to a line of almost identical products. It is plausible to imagine the Chairman saying, ' Let that ' (pointing) ' and anything very similar to it be called a " Daimler Conquest " ' ; and this is the way in which Hobbes supposes all universals to come into existence. Thus, while the nominalist begins by, so to speak, fragmenting the universe into discrete and distinct singulars, he goes on to exaggerate the resemblance between those which share a common name because obvious resemblance is the only ground for giving them a common name.

There is a further philosophic reason for Hobbes' belief in the uniformity of human nature. Like Leonardo, Hobbes sees men as engines—as engines of a similar design (*Lev.*, p. 1).[25] Since they all operate according to the same principles, the only significant difference between them will be the *speed* at which they operate ; and the only difference between men which Hobbes allows is precisely ' this difference of quickness ' in the movements of their minds (*Lev.*, pp. 32-3 ; *El. of L.*, I, x, 3).

A man is a mechanical part of nature and his internal movements are hidden from other men's sight, i.e. encased ; but there is, so to speak, an inspection-window to which he alone has access, and through which he can observe the motions of his mind. In principle, Hobbes claims, such motions could always be deduced from a knowledge of the structure of the human mechanism and of the input it receives from its environment ; but it is much easier to introspect them. ' The causes of the motions of the mind are known, not only by ratiocination, but also by the experience of every man that takes the pains to observe these motions in himself ' (*De Corp.*, vi, 7). The popular assertion that Hobbes' psychology and politics are logically independent of his philosophy is, of course, true if it means only that Hobbes did not deduce introspectible data from mechanical premises. But Hobbes' belief that introspection can provide data for political science is itself a consequence (not of introspection but) of a belief which, as we have just seen, is philosophically grounded, namely, his belief in the uniformity of human nature. Only this latter belief entitles Hobbes to assert : ' For the similitude of the thoughts and passions of one man, to the thoughts, and passions of another, whosoever looketh into himself, and considereth what he doth, when he does think, opine, reason, hope, fear, &c, and upon what grounds ; he shall thereby read and know, what are the thoughts and passions of all other men, upon the like occasions ' (*Lev.*, p. 2).

between accident and substance unexamined (Haldane and Ross, ii, p. 65). I do not think this complaint is justified—the distinction was drawn in the *Tract* (i, *princs.* 15-16) and elaborated in *De Corpore* (viii)—but Descartes was directing attention to a crucial weakness in Hobbes' nominalism. For if an accident, as Hobbes says, is not itself a substance although it inheres in a substance, it is nothing but Aristotle's universal *in re* ; i.e. Hobbes' nominalism presupposes Aristotle's realism.

[25]Hobbes does not shirk the suggestion that such engines point to an engineer : ' it is very hard to believe ', he says, ' that to produce male and female, and all that belongs thereto . . . could be the work of anything that had not understanding ' (*E.W.*, vii, p. 175).

144   J. W. N. WATKINS

VII. SUMMARY

Hobbes' political radicalism springs from a logical radicalism.

Ernst Cassirer.

I shall now assemble the various consequences of Hobbes' philosophy for his political theory.

He will begin by resolving existing political society into men in a state of nature (section III) which is normless (section II). These men are very similar to each other (section VI) and the universal principles of human nature alone provide the axioms from which natural laws, and the reconstruction of the State, can be deduced (section III). All men are solitary, self-reliant creatures whose moral utterances merely describe their own desires and aversions (section V) ; their emotions are aroused only by the (direct or indirect) prospect of some bodily good or ill to themselves (see, e.g., *Lev.*, p. 27). Bodily good is movement forward, and the extreme bodily ill is death (section IV). Hence men can be tranquil only in death which they fear above all. But in the state of nature (granted the obvious fact that goods and power are scarce and that men are in contact with one another) men's egocentricity, and the lack of standard rules (sections II and V) to modify relations between them result in strife : ' What this man commends (that is to say, calls good) the other undervalues, as being evil. . . . Whilst thus they do, necessary it is there should be discord and strife ' (*De Cive*, iii, 31). It follows (granted the obvious fact that unrestricted strife may lead to killing) that men in a state of nature are continuously threatened by what they fear most. But they can speak and calculate (section V). Natural laws tell them the only logical way of removing that threat. The compositive part of Hobbes' political theory describes how men would erect a political authority if they obeyed natural law. This reconstructed State is neither what existing political society is nor what it ought to be according to some external criterion. It is the kind of state which is alone consistent with human nature (section III).

All this is implied by Hobbes' philosophy together with a few obvious empirical facts. But now an empirical *assumption* has to be introduced ; for men might try to remove the threat of being killed by trying to dominate the others ; and Hobbes, like Epicurus before him, argues that this will lead to a cumulatively self-aggravating situation in which the risk of death is increased by attempts to reduce it. This argument depends on the assumption that in a natural struggle for power the strongest is equal to the weakest in the sense that neither can insure himself against the risk of being killed.

This crude equality of men is, no doubt, *suggested* by Hobbes' belief in the similarity of men (section VI) and, more remotely, by his anti-Aristotelian conception of a non-hierarchical universe (section II). But I do not wish to spoil my argument by claiming too much, and I think that Hobbes regarded the equal spread of the risk of being killed in the state of nature as a brute fact and not as a consequence of more general features of the universe.

With this empirical assumption introduced, we can continue to reconstruct the skeleton of Hobbes' argument in Parts I and II of *Leviathan* by wiring together the consequences of his philosophy. Since the assumption that one is of superior power is unrealistic and will, if acted on, endanger one's life, it is a natural law ' that every man acknowledge other for his equal by nature ' (*Lev.*, p. 77). This acknowledged, the only remaining way to remove the threat of death is mutually to promise to transfer the causes of that threat to, and to obey, an arbitrator ; and this is dictated by a law of nature. This arbitrator, or sovereign, is the necessary product of merely human needs (section III). He must be a single determinate body who will fill the natural moral vacuum by issuing commands or laws which will create moral distinctions and regulate relations between men (section V). To disobey these laws is to break one's previous rational promise, and such inconsistent behaviour is forbidden by a law of nature (section III).

VIII. CONCLUSION

I have tried to show that Hobbes' thought is systematic : if we trace certain consequences of his natural and critical philosophy, and then assemble these consequences together and add one empirical assumption, we achieve an (admittedly thin) *précis* of the secular part of his political theory. To show the significance of this systematic character of Hobbes' thought I must draw a well-worn distinction between its form and its content. Much of the content is plainly false. I will confine myself to two criticisms.

First, Hobbes saw that explanations of social phenomena must be in terms of the activities of individuals ; and he saw that ill-informed or irrational activities may have social effects which are both unintended and unwanted, such as civil war. He did not see, however, that the unintended effects of skilful and intelligent activities may be, for good or ill, far more significant than the intended effects they also produce. He imported a sociological version of Descartes' axiom that ' an effect cannot be more perfect than its cause ' into his political theory, where the causes are human wills. His consequent emphasis on the wilful creation of a moral and political order, *ex nihilo* so to speak, exerted (through Rousseau) an influence whose direction is suggested by the fact that he was called ' the father of us all ' by Marx and the ' true father of revolutionary philosophy ' by Comte.

Secondly, Hobbes' attempt to provide a causal account of human thinking and language was bound to fail. Professor K. R. Popper has recently shown that even the simplest semantical relation, i.e. the relation between a proper name and the object it names, cannot be causally represented, because it is impossible, without interpretation, to distinguish the beginning of the causal sequence (the appearance of the object) and its completion (the naming of the object) from other phases of the causal sequence. He concludes : ' The name-relation is therefore clearly not to be realized by, say, an association model, or a conditioned reflex model. . . Naming is by far the simplest case of a descriptive use of words. Since no causal realization of the name-relation is possible, no causal physical theory of the des-

146   J. W. N. WATKINS

criptive and argumentative functions of language is possible '.[26] Of course,
Hobbes' nominalism could be freed from the causal theory of the mind which
engendered it ; but I hope to show on another occasion that it is impossible,
not only to interpret ordinary language nominalistically, but even to construct a nominalist language in which empirical assertions can be made.

But the very fact that such abstract criticisms are relevant to the author
of the *Leviathan* shows the importance of the systematic character of his
thought. The more a body of ideas is connected, the more it can be tested.
The more it can be tested, the more reliable it is if the tests are satisfactory,
and the more corrigible it is if they are unsatisfactory. Other seventeenth
century political writers—Prynne, Selden, and Parker, for instance—reached
conclusions about sovereignty and Erastianism broadly similar to Hobbes'.
But whereas his are the upshot of a whole system of thought which can be
tested and corrected at many levels, their's are not and are now mainly of
historical interest. Hobbes possessed two of the qualities which make a
great scientist : a synoptic vision of the whole situation and the ability to
unfold it logically and in detail. (The third quality, humility before facts
and criticisms, he did not possess.) His vision of a world in which men
strive to subordinate to their wills the environment which determines their
wills was, perhaps, paradoxical ; and his detailed elaboration of that vision
laid him open to cogent objections. But the extent of his failure is a measure
of the greatness of his attempt ; and that attempt to integrate political
thought into a more broadly based system is an example we seem to have
lost the courage to follow.

J. W. N. WATKINS

London School of Economics and Political Science.

[26]' Language and the Body-Mind Problem ', *Proceedings of the XIth International Congress of Philosophy*, vii, p. 106.

Part II
Hobbes's Political Theory

[4]

THOMAS HOBBES AND THUCYDIDES

By Richard Schlatter

Thomas Hobbes began his career of scholar, man of letters, and philosopher by translating Thucydides. Why did he choose Thucydides? How successful was his translation? In what way did his careful study of the historian affect his own thought?[1] The answer to the last question is especially interesting: *The History of the Peloponnesian War* apparently crystallized for Hobbes many of the ideas fundamental in his later political philosophy.

In translating and studying Thucydides Hobbes was carrying on the Renaissance tradition of turning to the Greek and Roman historians with the expectation of learning how to solve the problems of modern politics. The first known Latin translation of Thucydides was made by Lorenzo Valla about 1452, and his preface pointed to the usefulness of true history.[2]

Bishop Seyssel of Marseilles, afterwards Archbishop of Turin, was the first to put the *History of the Peloponnesian War* into a modern language. Using Valla's faulty Latin version he made an even more inaccurate French version.[3] Nevertheless, the Bishop's French made good reading.

Seyssel too, in the fashion of his day, valued Thucydides most for his political teachings. In his prologue he records that this is one of the translations he has done for the use of Louis XII who has found in the ancient historians useful lessons for a modern monarch; and Thucydides is the best of them all for this purpose.[4]

[1] Ferdinand Tönnies, *Thomas Hobbes*, 3rd ed. (Stuttgart, 1925), refers to a work by Arturo Bersano, *Per le fonti di Hobbes* (Bologna, 1908), emphasizing Hobbes' debt to Thucydides. I have been unable to find this work in the United States or England.

[2] I have used the edition in the Harvard College Library which was probably printed at Venice about 1485 (Hain-Cop. *15511). Valla's version was reprinted at Cologne in 1543 by Konrad Heresbach. The *Editio Princeps* of Thucydides was printed by Aldus in 1502.

[3] Henri Estienne said of it: "ut Valla plerumque divinum potius quam interpretem Thucydidis egerat, ita hic episcopus vicissim Vallae sensum divinabat potius quam interpretabatur." Estienne printed a revised version of Valla's Latin together with the Greek text and his introduction examines the errors of both Valla and Seyssel; this edition, a folio, was printed at Paris in 1564. The passage occurs in this introduction (*iii^b).

[4] The Bishop's translation was printed in 1527 by command of Francis I. "au prouffit et edification de la noblesse et subiects de son Royaulme." A preface by the poet and Royal Secretary, Jacques Colin, emphasized again the importance of the

In the half-century after Seyssel's edition Thucydides was translated and retranslated into several modern languages[5] and Thomas Hobbes was, consequently, working in a well established tradition when he began his translation in the 1620's.   In fact, as Hobbes knew, an English version already existed.   In 1550, Thomas Nicolls, a former Cambridge scholar, and then a barrister, published *The hystory writtone by Thucydides the Athenyan of the warre, whiche was betwene the Peloponesians and the Athenyans, translated oute of Frenche in to the Englysh language by Thomas Nicolls Citezeine and Goldesmyth of London.   Imprinted the XXV. day of July in the yeare of oure Lorde God a Thousande, fyve hundredde and fyftye.*   So for seventy-five years before Hobbes' edition, Englishmen had been able to read an English Thucydides translated from the French of Seyssel which in turn had been taken from the Latin translation of Valla.   No doubt Hobbes was right in saying that Thucydides had been traduced rather than translated into English.   Nicolls was sometimes careless as when in his description of the plague he mistook "puys" for "pays" and translated it "countrey," or read "cave" for "eaue" (eau) and translated it "cave."   Sometimes he was betrayed by the simple lack of an English equivalent, a lack which later translators supplied by coining new words, thereby enriching our language and our thinking.   For example, when Nicolls read "patrie" he could find no corresponding English word: English patriotism was developing rapidly but in the days of Edward VI it still had no word to connote both the nation and the feeling which a loyal citizen had for it.   Seventy-five years later, Hobbes could use "countrey" where Nicolls could do no better than "patrie."[6]

Nevertheless Nicolls succeeded in making a book which conveyed the meaning of Thucydides after a fashion; and he wrote at a time when the English language, whatever its inadequacies as a vehicle of classical thought, had a freshness and immediacy of its own which the more scholarly English of later ages often lacked.

---

study of history for rulers and noblemen and recommended Thucydides as the best of historians.   *L'Histoire de Thucydide Athenien, de la guerre, qui fut entre les Peloponnesiens et Atheniens (Paris, 1527)*.   A second edition, claiming to be corrected by the Greek text, was published in 1559.   Seyssel said he had been aided in his work by the famous scholar Jean Lascaris.

[5] An Italian translation by Francesco di Soldo Strozzi of Florence, dedicated to Cosimo de' Medici, was published in Venice in 1545, with a second edition in 1550; a Spanish translation by "el Secretario Diego Gracian" was printed at Salamanca in 1564; William Smith, in the *Preface* to his translation published in London in 1753, refers to a German translation of 1533 (not listed in Panzer or the British Museum Catalogue); a second French translation was published at Leyden in 1600 by Louis Jaussaud who used the revised Greek and Latin text of Estienne.

[6] In the Funeral Oration and in the Melian Dialogue.   The N.E.D. gives 1566 as the date when "country" was first used in the sense of "fatherland."

352   RICHARD SCHLATTER

Even on the score of accuracy, Nicolls does not deserve total condemnation except insofar as the French text he used was itself corrupt. For Nicolls belonged to the school of translators presided over by Sir John Cheke who emphasized the virtues of literal accuracy. In a letter to Cheke, printed as an introduction to the *History,* Nicolls says he has attempted to translate plainly and truly and requests Cheke to make corrections from the Greek text. In dedicating his work to Cheke, the tutor of Edward VI, Nicolls may well have had in mind the use which might be made of it in educating the young king. At any rate, he took care to translate and print the prologues of Seyssel and Colin where it was said that Louis XII and Francis I had found practical lessons in the historian.

If Nicolls' work was unsatisfactory, he could have said in its defense that competent scholars scorned translations and that it was his version or none. For even as late as 1550, just as conservative priests feared that the Church would be vulgarized if the Bible were translated, and aristocratic rulers feared that governments would become popular if parliaments inquired into the mysteries of state, so conservative scholars feared that the temple of learning would be profaned if the classics were translated. But in England the tide was slowly beginning to flow in the direction of popular religion, popular government, and popular literature. In the generation after Nicolls', translation became a respectable art, a host of translators turned the classics of Greece and Rome into classics of English literature, and a few years later produced the greatest monument of English prose, the King James Bible.[7]

Consequently, when Thomas Hobbes decided to translate Thucydides, he was deciding to carry on a respected and living tradition of thought and language. His predecessors had not doubted that they were enriching English literature, and improving the morals and minds of their countrymen. To their imaginations the classics were as living and pertinent as contemporary literature and the translator was doing a great and even patriotic job in presenting them to his fellow citizens. Philemon Holland wrote in the preface of his version of Pliny, published in 1600, that the few old-fashioned scholars who still objected to translations "thinke not so honourably of their native countrey and mother tongue as they ought."[8]

By the time Hobbes turned to Greek and Roman history many transla-

[7] See F. O. Matthiessen, *Translation, an Elizabethan Art* (Cambridge, Mass., 1931), and the works cited there for the story of translation in England after 1550. C. H. Conley, *The First English Translators* (Yale, 1927), shows Nicolls as one of the group of young protestants whose translations were frowned on by the Universities and by conservative Catholic scholars, clergymen, and statesmen. During the reaction under Mary almost no translations were published.

[8] Matthiessen, *op. cit.,* 179.

tions had already appeared.[9] He knew of Nicolls' translation and in his preface stated his opinion that a new English version made directly from the revised Greek text of his own day was needed to replace the old English version taken at three removes from the imperfect Greek text of Valla's day. He also said that the reader of Thucydides needs maps and his was the first edition to supply them.

Even if Nicolls had not been inaccurate, Hobbes might still have thought him insufficient: the English language itself had developed so rapidly between 1550 and 1625 that Nicolls' book was entirely out of date, just as a century later Hobbes was considered out of date, though not yet inaccurate. In 1753, the Rev. William Smith wrote in the preface of his translation of Thucydides:

Mr. Hobbes, however sorry and mischievous a philosopher, was undoubtedly a very learned man. He hath shewn it beyond dispute in his translation of Thucydides . . . [but] he cannot now be read with any competent degree of pleasure. He is faithful, but most servilely so, to the letter of his author. . . . Too scrupulous an attachment to the letter of the original hath made the copy quite flat and heavy, the spirit is evaporated, the lofty and majestic air hath intirely disappeared. Too many low and vulgar expressions are used, which Thucydides ever studiously avoided. Such frequently occur in the midst of some grand circumstance, which they throw into a kind of burlesque, and may excite a reader's laughter. The English language hath gone through a great variation, hath been highly polished, since Mr. Hobbes wrote. Hence, tho' his terms be in general very intelligible, yet they have not that neatness, precision, and dignity, to which the polite and refined writers within the last century have habituated our ears.[10]

In any case, a large part of Hobbes' task was to make a modern as well as an accurate translation to replace that of Nicolls. Because he had the fortune to be writing in a period when the tradition of English writing and translating was good, Hobbes was able to modernize without denaturing, without losing the sense of life and pertinence which Nicolls had captured. A few sentences from their descriptions of the Plague are proof that Hobbes

[9] For example, Henry Savile, *Tacitus* (1592); North, *Plutarch* (1579); Holland *Livy* (1600), *Suetonius* (1606), *Ammianus Marcellinus* (1609); Rich, *Herodotus* (1584); Watson, *Polybius* (1568); Heywood, *Sallust* (1608).

[10] An example of Smith's refinement occurs in I, 8: he writes, "the combatants engage with scarfs round their loins" where Hobbes had written, "the combattants, about their privie parts, weare breeches." A fourth edition of Hobbes' work was printed in 1822 and in 1829. Rev. S. T. Bloomfield noted in the preface to his translation that Smith was out of fashion and Hobbes was again the preferred translation. Bloomfield, following the new fashion of his day, objected to the artificial diction of Smith which lacked the "native strength" of plain, idiomatic English.

Hobbes used the Greek and Latin text of Estienne as revised by Aemilius Portus and printed at Frankfort in 1594. For his accuracy see the notes to the edition by Sir William Molesworth, 2 vols. (London, 1843). The translation is said to have been revised by Ben Jonson and Sir Robert Ayton.

could correct and bring up to date and yet still translate in the great tradition which Nicolls had had a hand in creating.

NICOLLS

And to them, that were infected with other sickenes, yt tourned into this selfe same. And those, that were in full helth, founde thē soubdainly taken, without that, there was any cause precedinge, that might be knowin. And furste they felte a great heate in the hedde, whereby their eyes became redde and inflamed. And withinfourthe, their tongue and their throte, became all redde, & their breath became stinkynge and harshe. Whereupon, there ensued a continual neysinge and therof thair voice became hoerse. Anone after that, yt descended into the stomacke, whyche caused a greate coughe, that did righte sharply payne them, and after that the matter came to the partes of the harte, it provokedde them to a vomyte. By meane whereof, wyth a peyne yet more vehemente, they avoyded by the mouthe, stynkinge and bitter humors. And wyth that, some dyd fall into a yeskynge, whereupon they came incontynently into a palsey, whyche passed from some forthwyth, and with othere endured longer. And althoughe, that, to touche and se them wythoute, and throughe the bodyes: they were not exceedinge hotte nor pale, but that their skynne was, as redde colour adusted, full of a lytle thynne blaynes: yet they feeled winfourthe so marvailous a heate, that they might not indure, one onely clothe of lynnen upon their fleshe, but they must of necessytie be all bare. . . . But the woorste that was in this, was that men loste their harte, & hope incontynently, as they feeled themself attaincted. In suche sort, that many, for despaire, holdinge themselves for dead, habandoned and forsoke thēself, & made no provisyon nor resistence againste the sickenes. And an other great evill was, that the malady was so cōtagious, that those, that went for to visitt the sicke, were taken and infected, lyke as the shepe be, one after an other. By occasyon whereof, many dyed for lacke of succours. Whereby it happened that many howses stoode voyde, and they that went to se theym, dyed also. And specially the most honnest & honorable people, whiche toke it for shame, not to go to se nor succour their parentes and their frendes. And loved better to putt and sett fourth themselfe to manyfest danger, than to faile them at thair necessitie.

HOBBES

If any man were sicke before, his disease turned to this; if not, yet suddenly, without any apparent cause preceding, and being in perfect health, they were taken first with an extreame ache in their heads, rednesse and inflammation of the eyes; and then inwardly, their throats and tongues, grew presently bloody, and their breath noysome, and unsavory. Upon this, followed a sneezing and hoarsenesse, and not long after, the paine, together with a mighty cough, came downe into the breast. And when once it was settled in the stomacke, it caused vomit, and with great torment came up all manner of bilious purgation that Physitians ever named. Most of them had also the Hickeyexe, which brought with it a strong convulsion, and in some ceased quickly, but in others was long before it gave over. Their bodies outwardly to the touch, were neither very hote nor pale, but reddish livid, and beflowred with little pimples and whelkes; but so burned inwardly, as not to endure any the lightest cloathes or linnen garment, to be upon them, nor any thing but meere nakednesse. . . . But the greatest misery of all was, the deiection of mind, in such as found themselves beginning to be sicke (for they grew presently desperate, and gave themselves over without making any resistance) as also their dying thus like sheepe, infected by mutuall visitation; for the greatest mortality proceeded that way. For if men forbore to visite them, for feare; then they dyed forlorne, whereby many Families became empty, for want of such as should take care of them. If they forbore not, then they died themselves, and principally the honestest men. For out of shame, they would not spare themselves, but went in unto their friends.[11]

As in these passages, so throughout his translation Hobbes modernized the punctuation and spelling and substituted new words and new forms for Nicoll's obsolete ones. Where Nicolls expanded, Hobbes compressed. He shortened or omitted the elaborate connectives and used one word where Nicolls wrote doublets. "Putt and set fourth themselve," "honnest and honorable," "their parentes and their frendes," "lost harte and hope" became "went in unto," "honestest," "friends," "grew presently desperate." Nicolls elaborated and suggested more than he said; Hobbes pared down and strove for exact statement. Both versions are good reading, but Hobbes' terse directness may well have approached more nearly the simplicity and force of the original. In any case, if Hobbes had had no other purpose than to provide his generation with a readable version of a famous classic, his choice of Thucydides and his translation were both justified.

In choosing Thucydides, however, Hobbes may well have been responding to the changing historical taste of his contemporaries. For the humanists of the sixteenth century, who believed the classics of Greece and Rome should be read for their ethical values, Thucydides was not the ideal ancient historian. His reluctance to point a moral and his scepticism about the influence of ethical principles on human behavior must have disturbed the grave, moral scholars of Tudor England. Roger Ascham and his master, Sir John Cheke, did not recommend Thucydides as one of the necessary books for the good student who wanted to grow to a good man; Ascham preferred reading Livy.[12] The preference for Livy as a teacher of political virtues is implied in the preface to Holland's translation and even as late as 1625, Degory Wheare, Camden Reader of History at Oxford, gave his highest praise to Livy with particular mention of his fearless moral judgments.[13]

But the literature of the Jacobean Age is evidence that among some

[11] All references are to the 1st ed., London, 1629.

[12] See Matthiessen, *op. cit.*, 14, 55; Ascham, *Scholemaster*, Bk. 11 and *Report and Discourse of the Affairs of Germany*, both in vol. III of *The Whole Works* (London, 1864).

[13] *The Method and Order of Reading both Civil and Ecclesiastical Histories*, 2nd ed. (London, 1694), 86–9.

RICHARD SCHLATTER

groups in England scepticism in the realm of faith and morals and a belief in self-interest as the dominant motive in human affairs were growing stronger; that Thucydides' popularity should increase at the same time is readily understood. Bacon could find in Thucydides grounds for making an unprovoked attack upon Spain.[14] He also considered the *History of the Peloponnesian War* the most perfect type of historical writing.[15] In the Second Book of the *Advancement of Learning* he states that the business of the historian is to describe events and allow the reader to draw his own conclusions from them; such a view of the historian's task would lead the critic to prefer Thucydides to Livy or any of the other classic historians.

Again in the Second Book of the *Advancement of Learning* Thucydides is mentioned as one of the historians worthy of being incorporated without alteration or omission into a Universal History. Thus it is entirely possible that Hobbes' translation is a part of Bacon's grand plan for collecting and digesting all knowledge as a preparation for its advancement. The tendency of recent scholarship has been to minimize Hobbes' debt to Bacon.[16] But the biographical evidence (given in Tönnies, *Thomas Hobbes*) and the obvious similarity of many of their political ideas—Hobbes probably made the Latin translation of the essay "Of the True Greatness of Kingdoms and Estates" which is the fullest statement of Bacon's mature political philosophy—indicate that Hobbes saw in Bacon a shrewd political thinker if not a great philosopher. And it was the political lessons they found in Thucydides which led both men to admire him.

In the dedication of his translation, Hobbes refers to the late Earl of Devonshire, his patron, as a reader of that which "best deserveth the pains and hours of great persons, history and civil knowledge." To the new Earl, his former pupil, Hobbes recommends the reading of Thucydides as "profitable instruction for noblemen and such as may come to have the managing of great and weighty actions," especially in the present age when the political virtues are so little understood. In short, Hobbes was continuing the tradition of reading the classic historians for the light which they threw on contemporary politics. What political lessons did he learn from Thucydides?

In the preface "To the Readers" he explains that Thucydides is the best of historians: "for the principal and proper work of history being to instruct and enable men by the knowledge of actions past to bear themselves prudently in the present and providently towards the future, there is not extant any other (merely human) that doth more fully and naturally perform it

[14] *Works,* ed. Spedding, Ellis, and Heath, XIV (London, 1874), 474.

[15] *Works,* IV (1870), 304–5.

[16] Leo Strauss, *The Political Philosophy of Hobbes* (Oxford, 1936), does emphasize Bacon's influence, but does not attach this to the *Essays,* from which Hobbes may well have taken many of his religious and political ideas.

then this of my author.'' In the text itself Hobbes makes a marginal note, "the use of this history,'' where Thucydides claimed that "he that desired to look into the truth of things done and which (according to the condition of humanity) may be done again, or at least their like, he shall find enough herein to make him think it profitable'' (13).

In marking this passage by a marginal note, Hobbes was emphasizing a concept which was fundamental in his own thinking as well as in that of Thucydides. The idea of an unchanging human nature, the constant element in history, the common denominator which enables the historian to compare one event with another and construct a formula or pattern which is intelligible and useful, was a basic assumption of the science of history as Thucydides expounded it.[17] Hobbes devotes the first third of the *Leviathan* to a detailed description of human nature which served as the foundation for his political philosophy. Moreover, Hobbes found in Thucydides concrete examples of how human nature performs: the descriptions in the *Leviathan* of how men act read like generalizations from these examples.

In the beginning of the war, the Athenian ambassadors at Sparta defended their empire by claiming, as Hobbes interprets it, "that at first we were forced to advance our dominion to what it is out of the nature of the thing itself, as chiefly for fear, next for honor, and lastly for profit.'' They went on to argue that if "overcome by three of the greatest things, honor, fear, and profit, we have accepted the dominion delivered to us and refuse again to surrender it we have therein done nothing to be wondered at nor beside the manner of men.'' They have merely followed the "natural inclination of man'' (41). In the *Leviathan* Hobbes observes that the three motives of human nature which led men to quarrel and to subdue one another are desire of profit, fear, and love of honor—the respect of the inferior for his superior: "so that in the nature of man, we find three principal causes of quarrel. First, competition; secondly, diffidence; thirdly, glory'' (Pt. I, ch. 13). Of these three, fear was the cause of the Peloponnesian War (Hobbes marks Thucydides' statement of the fact by two marginal notes, pp. 14 and 46), and its absence—when men no longer feared human or divine punishment—was responsible for the anarchy of the time of the Plague. Both instances support the doctrine of the *Leviathan* that fear breeds war between nations and the lack of it breeds anarchy within nations.

Again, in the speech of the Athenian ambassadors at Sparta at the beginning of the war, Hobbes reads "it hath been ever a thing fixed for the weaker to be kept under by the stronger. . . . You now fall to allegation of equity, a thing which no man that had the occasion to achieve anything by strength ever so far preferred as to divert him from his profit'' (41). Hobbes notes in the margin (175) that the Spartans in the course of the

[17] J. H. Finley, Jr., *Thucydides* (Cambridge, Mass., 1942), 108–10.

whole war never "esteemed of justice at all when it crossed their own interest or passion." Finally, in the Melian Dialogue, Hobbes reads the Athenian argument

that in human disputation, justice is then only agreed on when the necessity is equal. Whereas they that have odds of power exact as much as they can and the weak yield to such conditions as they can get. . . . [We think] of men, that for certain, by necessity of nature, they will everywhere reign over such as they be too strong for. Neither did we make this law, nor are we the first that use it made, but as we found it, and shall leave it to posterity forever, so also we use it. Knowing that you likewise, and others that should have the same power which we have, would do the same" (341, 344).

In the preface "Of the Life and History of Thucydides" Hobbes expresses his approval of the Athenian generals at Melos who refused to discuss the justice of their invasion—as soldiers their proper function was to carry out the will of the Athenian State by fair means or foul. As to whether the action of the state was just in this case, Hobbes puts aside the question with the observation that it "was not unlike to divers other actions that the people of Athens openly took upon them."

Thus the judgment of history and the opinions of Athenian statesmen supported Hobbes' contention that by the law of nature the strong should rule the weak, and that justice is an empty word in international relations or wherever here is no sovereign power (*Leviathan*, Pt. I, ch. 13). The revolution in Corcyra was, of course, an excellent example of a time when particular men lived in a state of war and the same chapter of the *Leviathan* referred to periods of civil war as typical of the state of nature.

The *Leviathan* goes on to explain in a famous chapter that political liberty and freedom are no more than the power of the independent, sovereign state to wage successful war against its enemies. Athens is cited as an illustration: the Athenians were free, although they had not the liberty of refusing to obey their government, because their government could resist or invade other peoples (Pt. II, ch. 21). The translation of Thucydides had already anticipated this view: the Boeotian commander Pagondas says, "For liberty with all men is nothing else but to be a match for the cities that are their neighbors," and Hobbes notes in the margin, "So that so soon as a state hath a neighbor strong enough to subdue it, it is no more to be thought a free state" (262).

Without doubt, Hobbes found in Thucydides' descriptions of the nature of men and the motives which lead them to act a great deal that he himself accepted as true. But for both men the analysis of human nature was only a part of the solution of a problem which they had set themselves; given the nature of man, how can the good society be set up and kept going? Thucydides had seen the good society in Periclean Athens and his history can be taken as a record and analysis of its decline. Hobbes apparently

THOMAS HOBBES AND THUCYDIDES   359

found the good society in Jacobean and Stuart England and he saw with prophetic eye that it needed to learn the lessons of history—particularly from Thucydides—if it too was not to decline.[18] Thucydides offered no solution to his problem, but he did make clear that the cause of Athens' downfall was political disunity at home, faction and rebellion. Perhaps he was sceptical of any ideal solution: he stated that the horrors of the revolution in Corcyra "have been before and shall be ever as long as human nature is the same." But when Hobbes translated that phrase he was already thinking of his ideal solution of the problem. He accepted the opinion that the problem was one of political unity; and he found in Thucydides' magnificent history the outlines of his answer.

In the preface "Of the Life and History of Thucydides" Hobbes writes,

For his opinion touching the government of the state it is manifest that he least of all liked the democracy. And upon divers occasions he noteth the emulation and contention of the demagogues for reputation and glory of wit; with their crossing of each others counsels to the damage of the public; the inconstancy of resolutions caused by the diversity of ends, and power of rhetoric in the orators; and the desperate actions undertaken upon the flattering advice of such as desired to attain, or to hold what they had attained of authority and sway amongst the common people.

Here was another reason for Hobbes to prefer Thucydides among the classics and to translate him as a political textbook for his contemporaries. *The History of the Peloponnesian War* was a necessary antidote to the poison of ancient political theory: the *Leviathan* complains that men have adopted the political opinions of Aristotle, Cicero, and other classical writers whose false notions of democracy and liberty lead directly to sedition and rebellion. "I think I may truly say there was never anything so dearly bought as these western parts have bought the learning of the Greek and Latin tongues" (Pt. II, ch. 21). In *Behemoth* Hobbes cites as the ultimate cause of the Civil Wars the teaching in the Universities of political theory taken from Aristotle, Plato, Cicero, Seneca, and the classical historians.[19]

Hobbes continues his discussion of the historian's politics by remarking, "Nor doth it appear that he magnifieth any where the authority of the few, amongst whom he saith every one desireth to be chief, and they that are undervalued beare it with less patience than in a democracy; whereupon sedition followeth, and the dissolution of the government." A note in the margin of the text reads: "Ambition of the oligarchicals amongst themselves overthroweth their government" (521). Here again Hobbes has found in

[18] For an account of Hobbes' views of contemporary politics, see Julius Lips, *Die Stellung des Thomas Hobbes zu den Politischen Parteien der Grossen Englischen Revolution* (Leipzig, 1927).

[19] *Behemoth* (London, 1680), 31, 57, 74. In the *Leviathan*, Pt. II, ch. 25, Hobbes states that democracy is workable only in special circumstances; the circumstances he cites are obviously derived from Thucydides.

RICHARD SCHLATTER

Thucydides an opinion which he himself maintained in his later works; an aristocracy is perhaps better than a democracy but is still liable to break up into warring factions.[20]

The summary of Thucydides' politics concludes: "He praiseth the government of Athens when it was mixed of the few and the many; but more he commendeth it, both when Pisistratus reigned (saving that it was an usurped power) and when in the beginning of this war it was democratical in name, but in effect monarchical under Pericles. So that it seemeth that as he was of regal descent, so he best approved of the regal government." In the text of the *History* the statement that Athens under Pericles had in fact a government of one man is italicized by Hobbes.

The matured political theory of Hobbes, of course, denied the possibility of "mixed government:" did he then arrive at this opinion sometime after his translation had been published? The text of the translation itself provides some evidence that Hobbes did not regard the government of the Five Thousand as a "mixed government" in the sense that the sovereign power was divided. He translates: "The Athenians . . . called an Assembly . . . in which, having deposed the Four Hundred, they decreed the Sovereignty to the Five Thousand" (528). But if the Five Thousand had the sovereignty (later translators do not use this word here—Crawley writes "government") then according to Hobbes' later thinking the government was not mixed, but a simple aristocracy. In fact, the creation of the aristocracy of the Five Thousand by the Athenian people is a perfect illustration from history of Hobbes' later description of how a true, unmixed, aristocratic government is instituted: the people come together and agree to give the sovereignty by majority vote to a particular group of men. Because he chose to use in this passage the word "sovereignty"—a word so central in all his political thinking—we may surmise that Hobbes read here no more than a praise of a particular aristocratic government which, unlike the aristocracy of the Four Hundred, was properly instituted by the whole people and ruled well; if he calls it "mixed" that is a paraphrase of Thucydides and not his own opinion. If the surmise is correct, Hobbes found nothing here to conflict with his later political thinking.

In any case, his reading into the *History* a preference for monarchy is clear evidence that Hobbes himself, whatever Thucydides may have in fact preferred, had already thought out his solution of the political problem— government by one man. The objection that the power of Pisistratus was usurped does not indicate that Hobbes' opinion of legitimacy was not yet fully developed. In the first place, he was here again paraphrasing what

---

[20] *Elements of the Law* (Cambridge, 1928), Pt. II, ch. 5. Hobbes notes here that the Venetians have improved the Greek and Roman model of aristocracy (*Leviathan*, Pt. II, ch. XIX). *Behemoth*, 219, observes that the Rump might have ruled England successfully if the members had had more honesty and wit.

he took to be the opinion of Thucydides; secondly, the idea of legitimacy implied here is not in any way inconsistent with the doctrine of the *Leviathan* which teaches very clearly how to institute legitimate governments and why rebellion and usurpation are crimes against the law of nature.   That successful usurpers may become legitimate monarchs does not make usurpation good.

In fact, Thucydides' account of the tyrants of Greece seems to have provided Hobbes with one of his principal arguments in favor of absolute monarchy and in opposition to classical political theories.   His translation of the passage in the *History* defines tyranny as an unlimited monarchy as distinguished from the older Greek "kingdoms with honors limited"; the latter were "hereditary," which suggests that the succession was settled by law while in the tyrannies the sovereign had the power to name his successor. Hobbes writes in the margin beside this passage, "The difference between tyranny and regal authority" (9).   Thus the tyrant of Thucydides appears to be identical with the ideal monarch of Hobbes—an unlimited sovereign whose powers include that of naming his own successor.   In the *Leviathan* Hobbes states explicitly that his ideal monarchy is not hereditary and that his ideal monarch choses his own heir;[21] in the same place he points to the kingdom of Sparta—the older type of hereditary Greek kingdom as distinguished from the newer tyrannies—as an example of a government which was not a true monarchy (Pt. II, ch. 19).   But if a tyrant is no other than the ideal monarch, the arguments of Aristotle and his successors against tyranny fall to the ground—tyrannicide is the same as regicide and consequently wrong.   This argument, since it rests on the definition of words, is the kind that appealed to Hobbes and he used it more than once in combatting the opinion that rebellion is justified if the government is tyrannical (*Leviathan*, Pt. II, ch. 19, 29 and Pt. IV, ch. 46; *Behemoth*, 4, 31).   The reading of the political theory of the ancients led to civil war and rebellion, but a proper reading of Thucydides would lead men to obey their sovereign —another reason for providing Englishmen with a good translation of the *History of the Peloponnesian War*.

Finally, Hobbes found in Thucydides an opinion of religion which fitted nicely his own religious beliefs.   His preface relates that the historian belonged to the school of Anaxagoras "whose opinions, being of a strain above the apprehension of the vulgar, procured him the estimation of an atheist, which name they bestowed upon all men that thought not as they did of their ridiculous religion."   Anaxagoras and his pupil Socrates, Hobbes says, were put to death as atheists, and some critics have fastened the name on

[21] Strauss is clearly wrong in saying, (59) "at all stages in his development Hobbes considered hereditary absolute monarchy as the best form of the state." In general, his discussion of Hobbes and Thucydides is less convincing than the other parts of his book.

Thucydides. In fact, Hobbes continues, Thucydides was not an atheist; he objected to superstition and he blamed Nicias for losing the war by being so punctilious in observing religious customs, but he also praised Nicias for his piety at other times. "So that in his writings our author appeareth to be on the one side not superstitious, on the other side not an atheist." Hobbes might have written all this of himself. He too was not an atheist; he despised superstition and regarded popular Christianity as ridiculous; his opinions got him the reputation of being an atheist and in 1666 he thought his life was being threatened on that account.

Thus it appears that Hobbes' reading of Thucydides confirmed for him, or perhaps crystallized for him, the broad outlines and many of the details of his own thought. As an individual, he was said to have read little but to have digested thoroughly what he did read. As a translator, he was working in a great tradition which assumed that classical history was to be read as a preparation for political action. When he turned to Thucydides—perhaps at the suggestion of Francis Bacon—he had been meditating on political affairs for some time. Parliament and King were debating fiercely about royal power, men were taking sides, and Hobbes, in his late thirties, must have already thought out some of the major premises which sustained his political philosophy consistently during the next forty years. Turning to Thucydides he found precisely the view of human nature and the state which he himself had been constructing. No doubt in his eagerness he strained the meaning of Thucydides at times; but the result was an example of the thing which happens when a great mind, on the verge of a great discovery, suddenly happens upon the book which crystallizes its ideas. Hobbes was henceforth saturated with Thucydides and cited examples from the *History* throughout his later works. When he wrote in his Latin verse autobiography that he had found Thucydides the best reading of all the classics and that he had translated him as a political lesson to his countrymen, the old philosopher was no doubt remembering accurately in spite of his eighty-four years.

Harvard College.

[5]

Hobbes and Natural Law Theory

Noberto Bobbio

1. It is commonly held that the history of natural law theory should be divided into two periods. The first includes classical and medieval natural law theory; the second, the modern version. But it seems to me that in recent years there has been a shift in the evaluation of when this change occurred, even if supporters of the two natural law theories have not been fully aware of it. Until a few years ago the prevailing doctrine, already firmly in place at the end of the seventeenth century and the beginning of the eighteenth through the work of Pufendorf, Thomasius, and Barbeyrac, was that Grotius was the initiator of the modern theory of natural law. The perspective has now changed. The conviction is spreading that modern natural law theory begins with Hobbes rather than Grotius. Two things have happened. On the one hand, Grotius's philosophical originality has been called into question, and scholars have studied more carefully and confirmed his links with the premodern tradition, in particular with the philosophy of late scholasticism. On the other hand, Hobbes's legal thought has come out of quarantine and is being studied with curiosity and with the growing conviction that it constitutes an illuminating anticipation of theories which are, rightly or wrongly, considered innovative.

Hobbes and Natural Law Theory

Let us take into consideration the criteria which are most frequently used by both sides to establish and justify a distinction
between medieval and modern natural law theory.[1] All these
criteria pass a rigorous historical test only if their point of reference is the philosophy of Hobbes. If we test them against
Grotius's natural law theory, they almost completely lose their
argumentative strength and become unacceptable. We might
say in jest that, in the dispute between old and new natural law
theorists, an irresistible and inevitable *reductio ad Hobbesium* of
all possible arguments has occurred.

I take into consideration the four criteria that are most frequently used. They can be classified according to whether they
are employed to argue for or against the superiority of medieval over modern natural law theory, and whether they rely on
ideological or methodological arguments. We shall label these
four criteria 1a and 1b, and 2a and 2b. The former two are more
frequently employed by defenders of medieval natural law
theory; the latter two, by defenders of modern natural law theory. In both pairs, the first argument is mostly methodological
(1a and 2a), while the second is mostly ideological (1b and 2b).

1a.   Medieval natural law theory is superior to the modern
version because it has never attempted to build a complete system of prescriptions, which might be deduced *more geometrico*
[in geometric fashion] from an abstract human nature, established once and for all. The natural law of medieval natural law
theory consists of a few general principles, or even of one principle (*bonum faciendum, male vitandum* [that good is to be done
and evil avoided]), which must be historically completed or
specified.[2] Modern natural law theory is the fruit of an abstract
rationalism, which does not make any concession to the histor-

1. It is better to leave classical natural law theory aside, for it can be employed to support both the medieval and the modern versions, depending on
the situation.
2. Through secondary natural law or human positive law. Rommen speaks
of natural law as providing a frame for norms, which does not make human
legislators superfluous. *Lo stato nel pensiero cattolico* (Milan: Giuffrè, 1959),
pp. 78–79.

Hobbes and Natural Law Theory

ical development of humankind; while medieval natural law theory is the fruit of a moderate rationalism which, by conceiving the truth as the on-going adaptation of human reason to universal reason, accepts and justifies historical development. The most war-hardened Catholic natural law theorists do not accept defeat and are, on the contrary, again on the offensive more than ever in these years. We know well how insistent they are in asserting that modern natural law theory is anti-historical and that scholastic natural law theory, which is reconciled to history, is more modern than the doctrines that proclaim themselves modern.

If we consider this argument, we may say that the first thinker who attempted to build a deductive legal system deriving secondary prescriptions (the derived natural laws) from an original ethical postulate (the fundamental law of nature) was not Grotius, but rather Hobbes. In his *Prolegomena* (section eight), Grotius did not aim at formulating an eternal code, but merely at drawing a broad and flexible list of common rules such as abstaining from things that belong to others, returning what belongs to others, keeping promises, repairing damage done, and subjecting one's self to the punishment for transgression of laws. In the second and third chapters of *De Cive*, and the fourteenth and fifteenth of *Leviathan*, on the contrary, Hobbes, with much confidence and some presumption, presents real tables of the laws of nature, among which he even lists, in *De Cive*, the prohibition against drunkenness. No matter what people say of eighteenth-century abstract rationalism and its claims to fix natural rights once and for all, I do not know of any thinker who has been more audacious than Hobbes in taking upon himself the ungrateful role of universal legislator.

1b. Modern natural law theory no longer starts from the assumption that human beings are social by nature, but emphasizes their selfishness, and takes into consideration the individual isolated in the state of nature, rather than the individual in society. Medieval natural law theory is thus superior to its modern counterpart, because the latter has expressed a

Hobbes and Natural Law Theory

conception of man which is narrow, particularistic, atomistic, and so forth. And it has given life to a particular political theory, that is, liberalism, which is everywhere in decline. Supporters of scholastic natural law theory present it as an ethics of the person, in opposition to an ethics of the individual, which is typical of the Enlightenment and utilitarianism. They represent it as a communitarian conception of society, in opposition to the atomistic conception. And they contend that such a conception provides a view of human beings and history more in tune with the tasks of the modern state, which are positive, and no longer merely negative.

From this point of view, and even more clearly than with respect to point 1a, it is Hobbes, and not Grotius, who represents the moment of change. If we consider this criterion of distinction between medieval and modern natural law theory, Grotius is clearly irrelevant, while Hobbes is fully relevant. Grotius's scarcely rigorous starting assumption was that of *appetitus societatis* [desire for society]. This was a vaguer version of the notion of Aristotle and Thomas's *zoon politikon* [political animal], still shared by the scholastics of the sixteenth century. Hobbes starts with the asocial individual of the state of nature, who lives with the constant suspicion of being deceived and offended by others, who does not comply with the laws of nature for fear that others may violate them before he does, and who is perpetually moved by the will to harm others (quite the opposite of *appetitus societatis!*). Hobbes says all this, as usual for him, from the first pages of *De Cive*, while replying in a note to the second edition to the chorus of objections which the traditionalists had made to him: "For they who shall more narrowly look into the causes for which men come together, and delight in each other's company, shall easily find that this happens not because naturally it could happen no otherwise, but by accident."[3]

2a.   Modern natural law theory is superior to the medieval one because the former relies on a new concept of reason,

3. *De Cive,* I, 2, p. 3.

Hobbes and Natural Law Theory

which is more pliable and suitable to the new conception of man in the universe. It also relies on a new conception of nature, which is no longer the universal order created by God, but is simply the set of environmental, social, and historical conditions which individuals must take into account in order to regulate their social life. It has been said that, with the change in the concepts of reason and nature, "natural law ceases to be the path through which human communities can participate in the cosmic order or contribute to it, and it becomes a rational technique of social life."[4]

Such a criterion of distinction between old and new natural law theory might not have been conceived, had Hobbes's philosophy not existed. Once more, Hobbes is the obligatory step. Hobbes is the first to construct a theory of reason as calculation. In particular, reason is, for human beings in society, a calculus of utilities, which induces us to join with others through a compact, and to form civil society. It is a calculation which induces us to create the conditions for transforming natural laws, which are indeed good, but ineffective, into positive laws, which are good, that is advantageous, merely because they are at least effective, and ensure the implementation of the supreme value of peace. Hobbes is the first thinker who does not merely ascribe very general precepts to the law of nature, as his predecessors, including Grotius, had done. But he draws a long list of natural laws, which he derives mostly from the law of war. He thus tests his thesis that the laws of nature are nothing other than the product of the calculus of utilities,[5] and devices made by reason in order to make peaceful social life possible. In Grotius's work there exists no theory of reason, except as a pale reflection of the discussions going on at that time. Even the famous sentence "*etsi daremus non esse Deum*" [even if God did not exist], is a scholastic saw, as Fasso has successfully shown. As for the law of nature, this was still for Grotius the major bulwark against utilitarianism and moral

4. N. Abbagnano, *Dizionario di filosofia* (Turin: Utet, 1961), s.v. "Diritto," p. 254b.

5. And it is in this new sense that they are *dictamina rectae rationis* [dictates of right reason].

Hobbes and Natural Law Theory

skepticism. For he saw it as a reflection of an unchangeable rational order, in which man participates. In Grotius's eyes, the correspondence of the law of nature to a nature understood as divine order,[6] ensured its universal validity in comparison to the historical validity of civil law.

2b.   Modern natural law theory is superior to medieval natural law theory, because the latter considers the law of nature almost exclusively from the point of view of the duties which derive from that law; whereas the former considers the rights which that law grants.[7] All accept that the function of natural law theory has always been that of setting limits to the sovereign's power. But according to the traditional conception, natural law theory fulfilled this function by stating that the sovereign was bound not to violate the laws of nature. Modern natural law theory, however, recognizes to subjects, at first, the right to resist a sovereign who has violated the laws of nature, thus transforming the sovereign's duty from an imperfect to a perfect one, from an internal to an external one. At a later stage, modern natural law theory no longer considers the sovereign's duty to respect the laws of nature as the original foundation of the limits of the power of the state. Instead that foundation is provided by a greater or lesser set of individual rights which precede the rise of the state. These are the so-called natural rights, which are seen as the reason why the sovereign has the duty to respect the laws of nature.

Scholars agree unanimously on this point. The theory of natural rights is born with Hobbes. There is no trace of it in Grotius. When Grotius discusses sovereignty, the presumed founder of natural law theory is mainly concerned to refute the opinions of those who hold that sovereignty always has a foundation in the people. In order to deny this thesis, Grotius resorts to all

---

6. Even if this order was created by divine reason rather than divine will.

7. See L. Strauss, *Natural Right and History* (Chicago: University of Chicago Press, 1953), pp. 182–83, and the authors cited therein. See also Alessandro Passerin d'Entrèves, *La dottrina del diritto naturale* (Milan, Edizioni di Comunità, 1954), pp. 76ff.

Hobbes and Natural Law Theory

sorts of arguments, including the one which Aristotle used to justify slavery. In a famous passage from *De Cive*, repeated in *Leviathan*, Hobbes faced without qualms the question of the distinction between *lex* and *jus*, by observing that "law is a *fetter*, right is *freedom*; and they differ like contraries."[8] The sphere of liberty, which is opposed to the sphere regulated by laws (here to be taken as civil laws), is the state of nature. This condition is therefore characterized by the existence of rights, not duties. Prominent among these rights are the rights to life and to all things which are indispensable to preservation. It is true that with the institution of civil society the individual is forced to give up his natural liberty and most of his natural rights. But this is a problem which for the time being must not concern us. What matters, if we are to show that Hobbes is an innovator,[9] is that he is the first to elaborate a complete theory of the state of nature. This condition would become the main device for those who wished to ground the theory of the limits of sovereignty on the perfect rights of citizens, rather than on the imperfect duty of the prince.

If we wish to draw all the consequences of the theses which we have presented and briefly discussed, we should conclude that Hobbes and only Hobbes is the initiator of modern natural law theory. Nonetheless, there is an interpretation of his thought and position in the history of legal theory which considers him to be the precursor of legal positivism. If I am not mistaken, this is also the prevailing interpretation.[10] Modern natural law theory would thus pass through a thinker in whom there also begins the dissolution of natural law theory. This would indeed be a rather embarrassing predicament, out of which we might follow two paths. We can either maintain that the so-called modern natural law theory no longer has any-

8. *De Cive*, XIV, 3, p. 186.

9. And his innovation will have many consequences, even if contrary to the ones at which he aimed.

10. For a detailed history of the historiography on Hobbes's legal theory, see M. Cattaneo, *Il positivismo giuridico inglese: Hobbes, Bentham, Austin* (Milan: Giuffrè, 1962), pp. 46ff. The author of this essay emphasizes that Hobbes is a natural law theorist, but in the end considers him "the first representative of British legal positivism" (p. 46).

Hobbes and Natural Law Theory

thing to do with medieval natural law theory; the former is
rather the antithesis of the latter. (This is the path recently
taken by Piovani.) Or we can show that Hobbes, despite a few
concessions to legal positivism, which are more substantive
than formal, is a strong defender of natural law theory. He
is substantively a natural law theorist more than people are
usually willing to believe. (And this path is followed authoritatively by Warrender.) I incline toward the less drastic conviction that we can solve the problem when we realize the
following:

1. The concepts "natural law theory" and "legal positivism" are quite ambiguous terms. (As are, by the
   way, all terms that label great currents of constantly
   recurring ideas.) There are various ways of being a
   natural law theorist or a legal positivist, which are not
   all antithetical to one another.
2. Despite his splendid conceptual armor, Hobbes is
   more vulnerable to inconsistency than would seem at
   first sight. And he is more vulnerable than I myself
   believed or have led my readers to believe in previous
   studies.[11]

I call "natural law theories" those conceptual systems in
which at least the two following statements are recurrent:

1. Besides positive law (which no philosopher has ever
   dared to deny) there is natural law.
2. Natural law is superior to positive law. (In the sense
   that I shall specify below.)

I think that, from a historical point of view, we can find these
two essential conditions in three different philosophical and
juridical systems. They can be distinguished from one another
because they conceive the relationship of superiority between

11. Cattaneo is right in saying: "Hobbes's thought contains a few basic
contradictions—in particular the conflict between the natural right to self-
preservation and sovereignty, principles which are both tendentially absolute.
It is also so complex that it becomes impossible to draw from it extreme and
unilateral conclusions" (ibid., pp. 119–20).

Hobbes and Natural Law Theory

natural and positive law in different ways. I therefore think it necessary, in order to avoid confusion and misunderstanding, to distinguish three kinds of natural law theories, by formulating three broad theses:

1. Natural law and positive law are in the relation of the starting point to the conclusion (or of general maxims to applications).
2. Natural law determines the content of legal norms, while positive law makes them effective, by making them binding.
3. Natural law constitutes the foundation of validity of the positive legal order, taken as a whole.

These three possible theories of natural law rest on different understandings of how natural law is *superior to* positive law. A law[12] can be said to be superior to another law either in the sense of a static theory, or in that of a dynamic theory, according to Kelsen's well-known terminology. That is, the inferior law draws from the superior one either its content (as a logical conclusion follows from an evident premise), or its validity. In both cases the inferior norm does not have the power to abrogate the superior one. But in the former case, the inferior norm that is incompatible with the superior one is said to be unjust; in the latter case, it is said to be invalid. We may distinguish the three kinds of natural law theories depending on whether natural law is superior to positive law because it provides both content and validity to the latter (system 1); because it only provides the content (system 2); or because it only provides the ground of validity (system 3).

1. In St. Thomas, human law is conceived as a conclusion reached from the general maxims of natural law, and it draws both content and the ground of its validity from natural law.[13]
2. In a system which attributes to positive law the func-

12. By "law" I here refer both to one norm and to an entire legal order.
13. The case of human laws conceived as *determinationes* of the law of nature is different: for these only does Thomas say that "they derive their validity from the human law alone" (*Summa Theologica*, I, II, q. 95, art. 2).

Hobbes and Natural Law Theory

    tion of ensuring that the norms of natural law are effective,[14] the individual norms of positive law derive their content from natural law, but not their ground of validity.

3. Finally, in a system in which natural law provides the ground of validity of the legal order as a whole, natural law is superior to positive law because, unlike in system 2, positive law does not depend on natural law for its content, but rather for its validity.

    As already remarked, Hobbes's thought is far from being simple, and contains on the contrary much roughness under its smooth surface. Nonetheless, the letter of Hobbes's system nearly always—and its spirit, in my opinion, always—prompts me to interpret it as a natural law theory of the third type. I have illustrated this thesis on another occasion.[15] But I have deemed it opportune to revive this discussion by adding some clarifications and also some nuances,[16] because recent interpreters such as Warrender and, within limits, Cattaneo have reevaluated Hobbes as a natural law theorist.

    2.   Hobbes's main aim in elaborating his political theory is to give solid foundations to civil power. The ideological import of natural law theory was at the time very vigorous. Hobbes therefore thought that the best way to found civil power was to show that the obligation to obey the sovereign was a duty derived from a law of nature. He stated that the main theme of his work was the law of nature, although in it he aimed to justify a maximum of sovereignty together with a minimum of resistance. But his entire discourse on the law of nature could be reduced to the assertion that the obligation to obey the sovereign is established by the laws of nature. Consequently, once the state has been instituted, there is no natural (or moral) duty for subjects, except for cases which are exceptional and cir-

---

14. We can consider Locke's theory as an example of this case, although with a certain approximation.

15. See the previous chapter.

16. For which I am grateful to those who think differently from me.

Hobbes and Natural Law Theory

cumscribed, other than that of obedience. In this respect, at least two passages from *De Cive* are irrefutable: "By the virtue of the natural law which forbids breach of covenant, the law of nature commands us to keep all the civil laws" and "Our Saviour hath not showed subjects any other laws for the government of a city, beside those of nature, that is to say, beside the command of obedience."[17]

Even the most important work on Hobbes's political thought which has appeared in recent years confirms this thesis.[18] Howard Warrender's aim is not to assign Hobbes either to the tradition of natural law theory, or to legal positivism, which would be a futile enterprise. It is rather to show that the law of nature plays an indispensable function in Hobbes's thought. More precisely, Warrender's aim is to refute those interpreters who have repeatedly noted in Hobbes's system the lack or ineffectiveness of a natural (or moral) obligation, as distinct from a civil obligation. Nonetheless, Warrender's favorite argument in support of his thesis is that Hobbes's entire theory of political obligation would have collapsed, if he had not accepted a moral obligation preceding and independent of civil obligation. Moral obligation derives from the law of nature that prescribes keeping one's promises, first and foremost the promise made in the compact from which political obligation derives.

In Hobbes's works, there are also hints and passages which may induce us to interpret Hobbes's natural law theory as a theory of the second type, that is, as a theory in which the law of nature provides the content of the norm, and positive law guarantees that the norm will be effective. Hobbes begins his discussion as follows: The laws of nature exist in the state of nature, but they are usually ineffective because of the condition of insecurity which characterizes relations among individuals. We thus need a firm and unquestioned power which makes it possible for human beings to carry out the laws of nature, thus ensuring their safety. This beginning would justify

17. *De Cive*, XIV, 10, pp. 190–91; XVII, 11, p. 267.
18. H. Warrender, *The Political Philosophy of Hobbes: His Theory of Obligation* (Oxford: Clarendon Press, 1957).

Hobbes and Natural Law Theory

us in believing that Hobbes aimed to construct a legal system
in which the laws of nature would constitute the substantive or
primary norms; whereas positive law constitutes the set of the
secondary or sanctioning norms. We can interpret in the same
fashion Hobbes's version of the theory which maintains that
the gaps in the legal system can be filled by resorting to the
laws of nature.[19] In the case where a positive norm is missing,
the law of nature reemerges. If this is true, it is argued, this is a
sign that the law of nature has never been superseded by a positive law. On the contrary, a norm of the law of nature under-
lies, or must underlie every corresponding norm of positive
law. Indeed, remarks Hobbes, "the *civil law* . . . also pun-
isheth those who knowingly and willingly do actually trans-
gress the *laws of nature*."[20]

Hobbes thus leads us to understand that the laws of nature
are always in force, as substantive norms regulating conduct.
This is so even if the laws of nature cannot oblige *in foro externo*,
and are thus ineffective, unless the legislator acknowledges
them once and for all; or unless the judge acknowledges them,
in case of a gap, that is, if there is a case which the legislator
did not foresee. From the point of view of the letter of Hobbes's
text, there is one passage which is highly complicated and has
created problems even for Warrender (even if for other reasons), and is especially favorable to this interpretation. This is
the passage from chapter XXVI of *Leviathan* in which Hobbes
says that the law of nature and the civil law contain one another and are coextensive. He then goes on to remark that the
laws of nature are not really laws until the state exists, "for it is
the sovereign power that obliges men to obey them." He concludes: "Civil, and natural laws are not different kinds, but different parts of law; whereof one part being written, is called
civil the other unwritten, natural."[21]

In my opinion, there are, however, more decisive reasons
for believing that Hobbes's version of natural law theory is

19. *De Cive*, XIV, 14, p. 194; *Leviathan*, XXVI, p. 183.
20. *De Cive*, XIV, 14, p. 194.
21. *Leviathan*, XXVI, p. 174.

Hobbes and Natural Law Theory

ultimately of the third type. There is, first of all, a general argument, which we can infer from the spirit of Hobbes's system. The conception of natural law theory of the second type is historically the ideology of the limited or liberal state, and of the theories of resistance. But Hobbes aims with all his energies at supporting the reasons for the absolute state. This is a state in which power encounters as few limits as possible in the rights of others; and it is the state where absolute obedience reigns, that is, an obedience than which no greater can be given.[22] As we shall see, the version of natural law theory of the third type serves very well the purpose of rationally founding the ideology of the absolute state. The essential feature of the third type consists of rejecting the law of nature as a source of prescriptive content, and of accepting it exclusively as the source of the content of norms.

We can easily document Hobbes's aversion to the law of nature as a set of substantive norms, which are valid as such even after the institution of civil society. The decisive passage is in *De Cive,* on the basis of which we could legitimately count Hobbes among the purest representatives of ethical positivism. This is the doctrine according to which the law is just merely because it is the law.

> Since therefore it belongs to kings to discern between *good* and *evil,* wicked are those, though usual, sayings, *that he only is a king who does righteously,* and *that kings must not be obeyed unless they command us just things;* and many other such like. Before there was any government, *just* and *unjust* had no being, their nature only being relative to some command: and every action in its own nature is indifferent; that it becomes *just* or *unjust,* proceeds from the right of the magistrate. Legitimate kings therefore make the things they command just, by commanding them, and those which they forbid, unjust, by forbidding them.[23]

22. *De Cive,* VI, 13, p. 80.
23. Ibid., XII, 1, p. 158. In *Leviathan:* "It is manifest, that the measure of good and evil actions, is the civil law; and the judge the legislator, who is always representative of the commonwealth" (XXIX, p. 211).

Hobbes and Natural Law Theory

This statement is so serious that it may induce us to seek moderating hints. Hobbes appears to be referring to all possible actions. Nonetheless, we might contend that the sovereign's power to establish what is good and what is evil only regards indifferent actions, that is, those actions that are neither commanded nor prohibited by the laws of nature. This would be confirmed by another passage:

> That which is prohibited by the divine law cannot be permitted by the *civil*; neither can that which is commanded by the *divine law*, be prohibited *by the civil*. Notwithstanding, that which is permitted by the *divine right*, that is to say, that which may be done by *divine right* doth no wit hinder why the same may not be forbidden by the *civil laws*; for *inferior laws* may restrain the liberty allowed by the *superior*, although they cannot enlarge them.[24]

However, against this thesis we can adduce the curious and provocative thesis of *De Cive*, which Hobbes often repeats, and which concerns precisely necessary actions, that is, those that are commanded or prohibited by the law of nature. This thesis shows that for Hobbes it pertains only to the sovereign to establish the legality or illegality of actions, even if these are already regulated by the law of nature. "Theft, murder, adultery, and all injuries, are forbid by the laws of nature; but what is to be called *theft*, what *murder*, what *adultery*, what *injury* in a citizen, this is not to be determined by the natural, but by the civil law."[25] From this premise Hobbes draws the marvellously

---

24. *De Cive*, XIV, 3, pp. 185–86. Cattaneo offers another interpretation. Wishing to acquit Hobbes of the charge of ethical positivism, he draws arguments from the definition of law given in *Leviathan*, at the beginning of chap. XXVI, and from a few other passages, in order to show that Hobbes employs "just" and "unjust" instead of "legal" or "illegal" (*Il positivismo giuridico inglese*, pp. 106ff.). It seems to me that Cattaneo's thesis is acceptable for the definition offered in *Leviathan*, but cannot be applied to the passage which I have quoted in the text, and which Cattaneo does not take into consideration.

25. *De Cive*, VI, 16, pp. 85–86. Thus in XIV, 10, pp. 190–91; XVII, 10, pp. 265–66.

Hobbes and Natural Law Theory

bold conclusion that "no civil law whatsoever, which tends not to a reproach of the Deity . . . can possibly be against the law of nature."[26] If we take this statement literally,[27] we should interpret it as meaning that the sovereign never errs, and is always right, no matter what he commands or prohibits. The laws of nature are so general, and the sovereign's freedom to interpret them so absolute that every civil law always conforms to the law of nature.

In brief, according to the second version of natural law theory, civil law incorporates the law of nature, and therefore depends on it. But according to this passage from Hobbes, civil law *shapes* the law of nature, thus subjecting it to its own ends. In the former case the sovereign resembles more a mechanic who starts a machine that is already perfect; in the latter case, he resembles more a sculptor, who makes the statue out of raw material.

But it is not the thesis cited above (which disappears from *Leviathan*) that offers the strongest argument in favor of the thesis that the civil law is substantively independent of the law of nature. It is rather the argument that derives from Hobbes's theory of obedience, which is one of the essential elements of his system. In several places Hobbes calls the obedience which the subject owes to the sovereign "simple obedience." Absolute sovereignty is not an unlimited power (only God's power is), but rather the power "than which a greater command cannot be imagined."[28] In the same way, simple obedience, which Hobbes also calls absolute, is not an unlimited obedience, but it is the one than which "a greater cannot be performed."[29] By simple obedience Hobbes means the obedience owed to the command as command, independently of its content. Such obedience is founded on our promise to do, without questioning, all the commands of the person to whom we have transferred the right to command. It is the same obedience that the

26. Ibid., XVII, 10, p. 190.
27. But we shall have to accept a few exceptions.
28. Ibid., VI, 6, p. 75.
29. Ibid., VI, 13, p. 158.

Hobbes and Natural Law Theory

slave owes to the master,[30] and Adam and Eve to God in the Garden of Eden.[31] This type of obedience, by the way, distinguishes the law as command from advice: "Now when obedience is yielded to the laws, not for the thing itself, but by reason of the advisor's will, the law is not a *counsel*, but a *command*, and is defined thus: *law is the command of that person, whether man or court, whose precept contains in it the reason of obedience.*"[32]

One of the salient and typical features of traditional natural law theory is the thesis that a positive law is valid only if it conforms to the law of nature. In St. Thomas's famous words: "There does not seem to be a law which is not just, for insofar as it participates in justice it also participates in virtue."[33] Hobbes's theses which we have illustrated above all appear to negate this theory. First: it pertains to the sovereign to establish what is good and what is evil, so that what is commanded is just, and what is prohibited is unjust. Therefore, the law is just not because it conforms to a law which is different and superior, but merely because it has been issued by the legitimate sovereign. Second: if no civil law can be contrary to the law of nature, there can be no disagreement between civil law and the law of nature. Only such disagreement would allow us to consider a civil law invalid, independently of whether it was issued legitimately or not. Third: if the subject must obey the sovereign's commands as commands, independently of their content, it follows that the sovereign's commands, that is his laws, are valid independently of their conformity to the law of nature. Should we therefore draw the conclusion that for Hobbes, once the state has been instituted, its laws are all valid, even those contrary to the laws of nature? And should

30. "For he who is obliged to obey the commands of any man before he knows what he will command him, is simply and without restriction tied to the performance of all commands whatsoever" (ibid., VIII, 1, p. 109).

31. "In that precept of not eating of the tree of *the knowledge of good and evil* . . . God did require a most simple obedience to his commands, without dispute whether that were *good* or *evil* which was commanded" (ibid., XVI, 2, p. 228).

32. Ibid., XIV, 1, pp. 182–83. See also *Leviathan*, XXV, p. 166.

33. *Summa Theologica*, I, II, q. 95, art. 2.

Hobbes and Natural Law Theory

we conclude that the subject is bound to obey all civil laws, even those contrary to the laws of nature? But if we can answer this question in the affirmative, can we still speak of Hobbes as a natural law theorist? Should we not count him among the most radical supporters of legal positivism, indeed of that radical form of legal positivism represented by ethical legalism?

I believe that we can give a direct answer to this question by pointing to the third version of natural law theory, and illustrating all its implications. This appears to be the version closest to Hobbes's thought. As already stated, the specific feature of this third version of natural law theory is to acknowledge that, once the state has been instituted, only one law of nature survives. This is the law that imposes on human beings the obligation to obey civil laws. The logic of this theory prompts us to conclude that the general law of nature, which founds the legitimacy of civil power, preemptively resolves any future conflict between the laws of nature and civil laws. And this is so independently of Hobbes's particular thesis that it pertains to the sovereign to determine the content of natural laws. If a conflict were possible between civil law and natural law, the citizen who obeyed the latter rather than the former would violate the general law of nature which prescribes obedience to civil laws. One could answer that the general law prescribes obedience only to those civil laws that are not in contrast with the laws of nature. But if this were the case, the general law of nature would be meaningless, for it would be enough to establish a duty of obedience to particular laws of nature. In other words: if the citizen had an obligation to obey only those civil laws that conform to the laws of nature, there would be no need to resort to the law of nature that establishes the duty to obey civil laws. It would be sufficient to assert the duty to obey the laws of nature, in order to obtain the obedience required by civil laws.

The interpretation offered here presents the third version of natural law theory as a theory which aims at ensuring the legal system as a whole against the disobedience of individuals, by formulating a law of nature which legitimates positive law. If this interpretation is correct, we can consider the third ver-

Hobbes and Natural Law Theory

sion of natural law theory as a transition between traditional natural law theory and legal positivism. This interpretation would also explain why some commentators can maintain that Hobbes is still a natural law theorist with the same confidence with which others maintain that he is already a legal positivist.[34] And they can hold these different interpretations, although they substantively agree in their interpretations of Hobbes's thought.

What prompts us to count Hobbes's system among natural law theories is that both conditions which we believe characterize every possible version of natural law theory are present in his thought: the existence of natural law besides positive law, and the superiority of the former to the latter. Vice versa, what suggests that we can consider Hobbes's theory close to positivistic theories is the way in which the attribute of superiority functions. In the first two versions of natural law theory, natural law is superior to positive law in the sense that a positive norm contrary to natural law is not valid. In other words, the conformity of norms to natural law is the criterion of validity for every single norm of positive law. This is so in both versions. In the first version, positive norms are deductively derived from the general principles of natural law, while in the second version, positive laws guarantee the effectiveness of the corresponding natural laws. In both cases, the consequence is that a positive norm is valid only if it conforms to natural law. In the third version of natural law theory, it is legitimate to say that the law of nature is superior to positive law, because the former founds the legitimacy of the latter and makes it obligatory. But the consequence of this position is that natural law founds the legitimacy of, and makes obligatory the positive legal order as a whole, not the individual norms

34. "It is interesting to note that one of Hobbes's theses—that is, the fact that the law of nature is merely the foundation and justification of positive law—prompts Bobbio, on the one hand, to identify Hobbes as the initiator of legal positivism, and prompts Kelsen, on the other hand, to consider Hobbes as a natural law theorist, and to confirm his [Kelsen's] conviction that the main aim of natural law theory is to attribute an absolute and sacred foundation to positive law" (Cattaneo, *Il positivismo giuridico inglese*, p. 49).

Hobbes and Natural Law Theory

which comprise it. Civil power is instituted on the basis of a law of nature. But once civil power is instituted, the individual norms of the system derive their validity from the authority of the sovereign, and no longer from particular laws of nature. Individual norms may thus be valid without conforming to the laws of nature. What holds for this principle of legitimation of the legal order also holds for the principle of efficacy in Kelsen's system. The principle of efficacy constitutes the criterion of validity of the legal order as a whole, not of its individual norms. There may thus be individual norms which continue to be valid without being effective. In the same way, Hobbes's principle of legitimation provides a criterion of validity for the whole legal order, not for individual norms. There may thus be norms which are valid even if they are contrary to the law of nature.

I mention the principle of efficacy because I wish to avoid any confusion between Hobbes's system and modern legal positivism. And I wish us to avoid mistaking it for contemporary positivism because of the closeness of his system to the theory of legal positivism. We may assign to legal positivism all theories that do not recognize that there exists natural law alongside positive law. For these theories there is no law other than positive law. As seen, Hobbes establishes the law of nature as the foundation of positive law. Therefore he is not a legal positivist. If a modern positivist retraces his steps to the fundamental norm of the positivist legal order, this law is not a law of nature, but a hypothesis or a conventional premise. If he seeks a principle legitimating the legal order, he does not look for it in a norm which transcends that order, but in the fact, which is empirically verifiable, that the legal order is de facto obeyed. Indeed, in a modern positivistic theory the principle of efficacy replaces Hobbes's general law of nature, and thus clears away even the last trace of natural law theory.

3.   This analysis, which places Hobbes's thought between natural law theory and legal positivism, would be incomplete if we did not remark that Hobbes is far away from drawing all possible consequences from his premises. We should not be

Hobbes and Natural Law Theory

more Hobbesian than Hobbes. Despite his intentions and his statements, which we have just analyzed, Hobbes admits in some cases the right to resist an unjust law. In discussing the slave's obedience toward his master he already noted: "By virtue therefore of this promise, there is an absolute service and obedience due from the vanquished to the vanquisher, as possibly can be, *excepting what repugns the divine laws.*"[35] At the beginning of the third part of *De Cive,* he briefly summarizes his thought and says: "They who have gotten the sovereign command, must be obeyed simply, that is to say, *in all things which repugn not the commandments of God.*"[36] Let us remember that laws of nature and divine commandments are for Hobbes one and the same thing. The difference between them does not regard their content, but only their source. In another passage, he writes: "That which is prohibited by the *divine law,* cannot be permitted by the *civil;* neither can that which is commanded by the *divine law,* be prohibited *by the civil.*"[37] Nonetheless, once he has conceded this principle, Hobbes tries to limit its effects as much as possible, by defining exactly the cases in which disobedience is legitimate, and recognizing the right of resistance only in extreme situations, so that these decisions are not left to the discretion of individuals.

As is well known, and has been illustrated several times, from the fundamental ethical maxim according to which life must be preserved, Hobbes draws the conclusion that the right to life is inalienable. But we do not always remember that Hobbes aims at protecting the right to eternal life, not only to this earthly life. The sovereign may command anything except that which jeopardizes earthly and eternal life. If he issues such a command, the right of resistance arises, or, to quote, "the right of disobedience."[38] Cattaneo has recently analyzed in detail the cases relating to the right to life.[39] But let us be careful. If we wish to draw all consequences from Hobbes's

35. *De Cive,* VIII, 1, pp. 109. Italics are mine.
36. Ibid., XV, 1, p. 204. Italics are mine. See *Leviathan,* XXXI, p. 232.
37. *De Cive,* XIV, 3, p. 185.
38. *Leviathan,* XXI, p. 142.
39. Cattaneo, *Il positivismo giuridico inglese,* pp. 88ff., 103ff.

Hobbes and Natural Law Theory

premises, we should recognize that here too the sovereign gets the upper hand. For we have seen that for Hobbes it is the sovereign who defines theft, homicide, and adultery. It is the sovereign who decides that to kill in self-defense, or to kill an enemy in war is not homicide. In the same way, he can decide that to kill a subject in other circumstances is not homicide, as in the case of capital punishment.

Hobbes makes extremely slender concessions to the freedom to disobey with respect to the right to eternal life. Divine laws are either laws of nature—which the state alone may interpret—or laws regarding worship. In relation to the latter, Hobbes analyzes the duties of human beings in the kingdom of God according to nature, the Old Testament, and the New Testament. The duties in the kingdom of God according to nature concern either conventional or natural ways of worshipping God. In the former case, it is the state which must determine these; in the latter, the state must also intervene to make public worship uniform, and to give one interpretation, valid for all subjects. "It may therefore be concluded, that the *interpretation* of all laws, as well *sacred* as *secular* (God ruling by the way of *nature* only), depends on the authority of the city. . . . Whatsoever God commands, he commands by his voice. And on the other side . . . whatsoever is commanded by them both concerning the manners of honouring God, and concerning secular affairs, is commanded by God himself."[40]

Hobbes admits only two exceptions to the duty of obedience: (1) when the sovereign commands subjects to offend God; (2) when he commands subjects to honor himself as if he were God.[41] In analyzing briefly duties toward God according to the Old Testament in chapter XVI of *De Cive,* Hobbes tries to show that the Hebrews were bound to obey their chiefs in all things unless a superior's command should imply the negation of divine providence or impose idolatry. Hobbes concludes: "In all other things they were to obey. And if a king or priest, having the sovereign authority, had commanded some-

---

40. *De Cive*, XV, 17, p. 222. See *Leviathan*, XXXI, p. 240.
41. But even this exception is eliminated in *Leviathan*, XLV, p. 427.

Hobbes and Natural Law Theory

what else to be done which was against the laws, that had been
his sin, and not his subject's; whose duty it is, not to dispute,
but to obey the commands of his superior."[42] And finally, in
discussing duties toward God according to the New Testament, Hobbes on the one hand concedes that "the subjects
ought to obey their princes and governors, excepting those
which are contrary to the commands of God." But on the other
hand he immediately takes it away: "The commands of God, in
a Christian city, concerning *temporal affairs* . . . are the laws
and sentence of the city derived from those who have received
authority from the city to make laws and judge of controversies; but concerning spiritual matters . . . are the laws and
sentence of the city, that is to say, the Church."[43] In conclusion:
"In a Christian commonweal obedience is due to the sovereign
in all things, as well as *spiritual* as *temporal*."[44]

As we can see, Hobbes was willing to leave some margin for
civil disobedience in order to guarantee the security of earthly
life. But he was much less liberal when the security of eternal
life was at stake. I look to my own life, for the state looks to my
eternal life. Once again, the crucial norm which Hobbes employs to reinforce the principle of obedience is the law of nature that prescribes obedience to civil laws. This law of nature
is also, like all laws of nature, a divine commandment; therefore it is a command, which must also be obeyed if one wishes
to save one's eternal life. How can we admit that the citizen dis-
obeys the state in order to ensure his own eternal life, when
one of the conditions for ensuring it is to obey the divine/
natural law that prescribes obedience to the state? By obeying
the state, the citizen thus kills two birds with one stone. He
gains peace both on earth and in heaven. The conclusion of
Hobbes's system further proves that Hobbes prefers the natural law theory of the third type. Among all the laws of nature,
the one prescribing obedience to civil laws takes over. It is the
essence of this law that, once it has been recognized and re-

42. *De Cive*, XVI, 18, p. 249. See *Leviathan*, XL.
43. *De Cive*, XVIII, 13, p. 315. See *Leviathan*, XLIII.
44. *De Cive*, XVIII, 13, p. 315.

Hobbes and Natural Law Theory

spected as the precondition for earthly security and eternal salvation, it makes all other laws of nature invalid, by founcing
the validity of all civil laws. "The law of Christ therefore concerning killing and consequently all manner of hurt done to
any man, and what penalties are to be set, commands us to
obey the city only."[45]

The starting point of this essay was the acknowledgment
that, through various paths, modern natural law theory begins
with Hobbes. Its point of arrival is the acknowledgment that
Hobbes's natural law theory is such as to pave the way to legal
positivism, more than to perfect the edifice of traditional natural law theory. However, it would be mistaken to conclude that
natural law theory falls into the arms of legal positivism. Quite
the contrary. The truth is that Hobbes invents, elaborates,
and refines the' most sophisticated ingredients of natural law
theory—the state of nature, the laws of nature, individual
rights, the social contract. But he ingeniously employs them to
build a gigantic obedience machine. We shall have to wait for
Locke if we wish to find the method of natural law theory,
which Hobbes handles so well, joined to and harmonized with
the typical ideology of natural law theory, which establishes
limits to the power of the state, and which Hobbes refutes
and rejects. Modern natural law theory comes to us through
Hobbes, but is affirmed only through Locke.

45. Ibid., XVII, 10, p. 266.

[6]

REVIEW ARTICLE

HOBBES'S 'LEVIATHAN'

Quentin Skinner

The Divine Politics of Thomas Hobbes: An Interpretation of 'Leviathan'. By F. C.
HOOD. Oxford: The Clarendon Press, 1964. Pp. 263. 45s.

The Hunting of Leviathan. By S. I. MINTZ. Cambridge University Press, 1962.
Pp. 189. 27s. 6d.

The *Leviathan* continues to suffer a sea change. The hindsight view of Hobbes's
system has recently been undergoing radical transformation. From being regarded
as the prototype of a Utilitarian, Hobbes has been converted into the prototype of
a Kantian deontologist. It used to be axiomatic that Hobbes's political theory
represented a deduction from an egoistic psychology: obligation was explained as
the enlightened calculation of individual self-interest. It is now suggested that the
grounds of obligation may need to be detached from the psychological observation:
an attempt is being made to anchor the politics of *Leviathan* firmly to the traditions
of Natural Law. The major source for this change has been the brilliant contribution
of Professor Warrender.[1] And now Professor F. C. Hood's book proclaims him the
latest recruit to the ranks of these revisionists.

The attempted transformation of *Leviathan* has already added a valuable insight,
but the revisions have also been damagingly criticized, notably by Professors Brown[2]
and Raphael.[3] A great deal of tidying-up has now got to be done. Professor Hood's
attempt, however, to elucidate *The Divine Politics of Thomas Hobbes* will not be
found to provide any help towards narrowing the range of legitimate debate. All
recent discussion is simply ignored. The most recent critical work mentioned was
published (in German) over thirty years ago. Neither Professor Warrender's work
nor any of his critics are cited at all. Professor Hood's own interpretation, moreover, by no means simply enlists him on Professor Warrender's side: he is concerned
also to introduce a perspective on Hobbes's text of almost self-conscious novelty.

The novelty of Professor Hood's approach consists of an attempt to 'make sense'
of Hobbes by considering all of his writings on morals and politics 'as a whole'
(p. vii).[4] He concludes that although *Leviathan* does contain a theory by which men
are said to be rationally obliged by a calculation of self-interest, this does not
represent Hobbes's 'real' system of obligation. Prudential obligation, according to
Professor Hood, is merely 'artificial', a device by which 'unjust men' can be turned
into decent citizens. Hobbes's real interest is said to lie in explaining the grounds,
apart from fear of sanctions, on which a 'just' man could 'naturally' be said to be
obliged. This true obligation is said to be grounded on a recognition that the Laws
of Nature are not only the dictates of reason, but also the commands of God.

---

[1] H. Warrender, *The Political Philosophy of Hobbes, His Theory of Obligation* (Oxford, 1957).
Hereafter cited by page only.
[2] Stuart M. Brown, Jr., 'Hobbes: The Taylor Thesis', *The Philosophical Review*, LXVIII
(1959), 303–23, an excellent survey of the debate.
[3] D. D. Raphael, 'Obligations and Rights in Hobbes', *Philosophy*, XXXVII (1962), 345–52,
an excellent traditionalist re-statement.
[4] I cite from Professor Hood's book hereafter by page only.

322   REVIEW ARTICLE

Hobbes's 'real' system is in short that of a traditional Christian moralist. Professor Hood adds that the 'artificial' concept of prudential obligation also found in *Leviathan* is there only as the result of a misguided attempt by Hobbes to detach some purely 'scientific part' of his system from the 'religious whole'. *Leviathan* represents Hobbes's 'failure' (p. viii) in his attempt to ground real obligation on any source other than on the authority of Scripture. Even within *Leviathan* Hobbes is said to have come to see that true obligation could only be a matter of conscience. The prudential obligation of the unjust might seem enough to ensure peace, but Hobbes saw that it was still wicked, for he 'accepted the ordinary Christian view that whenever a man acts against his conscience he sins' (p. 213). 'Therefore Hobbes did not succeed', Professor Hood concludes (p. 229), 'in converting any part of his Christian moral thought into science.' Its structure remained that of a theory of 'Divine Politics'.

This analysis places Professor Hood within a particular tradition in the study of intellectual history, by which it is taken to consist (both necessarily and sufficiently) of a type of philosophical exercise. The meaning of a writer is said to be elucidated (and elucidated fully) when all of his works are considered together on a level sufficiently abstract for discrepancies to disappear and for a 'doctrine' to emerge. *Leviathan* may appear to present an autonomous civil philosophy, but in Professor Hood's view 'Civil philosophy must, however, be compatible with a truth which lies beyond its ken' (p. 138). It has to be located within the still more general system of which it can only form one part. The precise form of a writer's system of thought may not itself become evident in any one work. But it is always possible 'to infer a good deal' (p. 143), and it is by inference from the 'artificial' parts to the 'real' whole that interpretation must proceed.

The view that 'meaning' has to be elucidated by the construction of the most coherent theory a writer can be made to yield is obviously central to the business of textual interpretation. Professor Hood's belief that a 'close examination of the relevant texts' should of itself still 'yield increasing understanding' (p. vii) echoes a protest, already made by Professor Warrender, that Hobbes has suffered misunderstanding because 'his works have been read by pages, when those of many smaller figures have been read by sentences' (p. 3). What is now needed to 'correct the effects of this treatment' is again seen to be simply 'a more detailed study of his theory'. This approach is shared, in fact, by all of the most sophisticated recent commentary on Hobbes: Professors Macpherson,[5] Warrender, and Hood are all concerned to reduce Hobbes to coherence in virtue of a theory about the 'real' assumptions of his thought.

None of these commentators, however, seems entirely candid about the difficulties raised by this approach itself. As the method is claimed to be necessary, its exponents appear also to regard it both as self-justifying and sufficient. It is my contention that neither of these assumptions is warranted. Professor Hood's analysis seems only the most colourful and least plausible contribution to a type of study which is itself misconceived. I want to try, in what follows, to demonstrate that this approach to the study of texts involves peculiarities of assumption which seem insufficiently explained; to show that in the particular case of Professor Hood's study the conclusions reached give a misleading impression of Hobbes's political system; and to suggest (and here Dr Mintz's new book is a valuable help) a different type

---

[5] C. B. Macpherson, *The Political Theory of Possessive Individualism, Hobbes to Locke* (Oxford, 1962).

of inquiry which seems necessary if confusions of this type are to be clarified or avoided.

All interpretation involving rationalizations of an author's own statements must depend in effect on textual suppressions. A theory about the author's intentions is constructed, which then allows the omission of alleged inconsistencies of presentation. But it is difficult to see how this equation of 'meaning' with abstracted coherence could ever be regarded as a self-evident conclusion, however necessary the procedure might seem. It must be essential first for the reader to be made aware of the type of evidence being discounted in the name of the higher truth. It must be essential also for the commentator to explain the grounds on which evidence is being dismissed as irrelevant to the writer's 'real' design.

It is this need for specific justification which the traditional approach seems expressly to ignore. It is true that there might be cases in which textual rationalizations could be virtually self-justifying, if concerned only with internal muddles. It is true, for example, that Professor Warrender assumes only an 'inner coherence' (p. viii) in Hobbes's text, which can only be revealed if certain vagaries of detail are eliminated. But where the concern is not merely with improving the author's presentation, but with invoking evidence apart from the text as a means of re-stating what the author must be doing, the problem of justification must become acute. And it is this much more ambitious undertaking which is in fact implied by the interpretations both of Professor Macpherson and of Professor Hood.

It is true that even in this type of case the thesis might still be readily accessible to verification. Professor Macpherson, for example, is concerned to re-state, in effect, the assumptions governing Hobbes's thinking. It is suggested that the validity of Hobbes's remarks may be limited by his conditioning to think in a particular way. The claim is still sufficiently empirical: as Mr Laslett[6] has shown, to be valid in principle it needs to be demonstrated that the social framework was of a type that could have determined Hobbes's assumptions in the ways assumed. But the re-statements proposed by Professor Hood seem both less plausible, and less readily open to any such verification. Professor Hood's concern is to re-state, in effect, Hobbes's own statements about his intentions. As Hobbes's statements of intention are so unequivocally given, the enterprise might be thought to stand in need of the most careful justification. To set against Professor Hood's treatment of *Leviathan* as the somewhat ineptly detached part of a larger whole is Hobbes's own view (p. 390)[7] that it represents a 'whole Doctrine'. To set against Professor Hood's exposition of this doctrine in transcendental terms is Hobbes's own claim that his intention was to assimilate politics to psychology, to 'ground the Civill Right of Soveraigns, and both the Duty and Liberty of Subjects, upon the known naturall Inclinations of Mankind' (p. 390).

Professor Hood's justification for his re-statement is based on his claims about the whole character of Hobbes's thought. Hobbes's intentions, both in the discussion of psychological principles and of political obligation, are said to be meaningful only when seen to be compatible with the implied theory of Divine politics. Professor Hood's main effort of interpretation thus centres on the attempt to prove that *Leviathan* must be located within this 'religious whole' of Hobbes's works.

---

[6] P. Laslett, 'Market Society and Political Theory', *The Historical Journal*, VII (1964), 150–4.

[7] In citing from *Leviathan*, I use (since Professor Hood uses) the *Everyman's Library* edition (London, 1914). Hereafter cited by page only.

The *Divine Politics* begins with a long Introduction, setting forth this perspective on the whole system to the still somewhat baffled reader. The detailed exposition which follows then closely paraphrases Hobbes's own presentation in *Leviathan*. Professor Hood begins with an elucidation of the nature of human nature; proceeds with a discussion of the Laws of Nature; and ends with a consideration of the validating grounds of men's obedience. The exposition is claimed to reveal in Hobbes's account a sequence of moral preferences, grounded on the psychological investigation, reflected in the theory of obligation, both of which are said in turn to reflect the Divine structure.

It can be shown, however, in the first place that Professor Hood gets betrayed by this approach into making unexamined assumptions of a marked peculiarity about Hobbes's work. The major assumption has to be that all of Hobbes's writings can be regarded as being in the same mode. This does lead to some fruitful reconsideration of the relations between *Leviathan* and the other incarnations of Hobbes's views on ethics and politics. But it also seems to lead Professor Hood to place the gravest weight on works which Hobbes himself regarded as incidental to his main design. On the central issue, for example, of the relations between ethics and politics, Hobbes regarded *Leviathan* as his last word. It was there that he claimed to have shown 'no such Inconsistence of Humane Nature, with Civill Duties, as some think' (p. 386). Yet Professor Hood is prepared to regard 'the later statements in the prose autobiography' as an exposition of 'Hobbes's final position' on this crucial point (p. 28). The assumption of some grander design infusing each of Hobbes's individual works seems, in fact, to leave no means of assessing relative significance, or of distinguishing the logically from the merely chronologically final. A further assumption, moreover, of Professor Hood's theory must be that in some sense Hobbes himself failed to understand what he was doing. It has to be assumed that Hobbes went to the trouble of attempting to present systematically, in *Leviathan*, a set of views in which he did not 'really' believe. It also has to be assumed that although he held other views apart from this, he would have been content to make no effort to explain systematically what these views were like at all.

It can also be shown in detail that the exposition of *Leviathan* which follows in Professor Hood's account is grounded not on a necessary perspective on the text, but on a sequence of textual misunderstanding. The difficulties begin with the opening account 'Of Man', which has to be presented in Professor Hood's interpretation not as an undifferentiated account of residues, but in effect as a distinction between the elect and the damned. 'The virtuous few', according to Professor Hood, 'read the law written in their hearts; the unjust majority act on their calculation of private natural good and evil' (p. 205). Hobbes is thus claimed in his psychological investigation to be making clear his own moral preferences. He is making 'moral judgements on most men' (p. 66), and 'the men whom Hobbes admired were the just, that is the morally good, minority' (p. 35). The fact that Hobbes himself never suggested that this was his intention, never himself elaborated any distinction between the just and the unjust, merely provokes Professor Hood into counter-assertion: 'in fact the inquiry into human nature falls into two parts, though Hobbes fails to make clear that it does so' (p. 64).

The view that Hobbes is concerned in his psychological theory with making moralistic discriminations seems, however, to rest on a failure to recognize the logical structure of his work.[8] Hobbes's essential claim in Part II of *Leviathan* was

---

[8] An excellent discussion of the logical structure of *Leviathan* is contained in D. Krook, Mr. Brown's Note Annotated', *Political Studies*, I (1953), 216–27.

to have proved a theorem, to have shown that the truth of his political conclusions was necessarily entailed by the truth of their psychological premiss. There can be no place in such a demonstration for making empirical distinctions, certainly not distinctions based on 'experience of seventeenth-century Englishmen' (p. 65). Hobbes's declared aim was to give an account of 'the natural propensities' of all men, entailed by the given definition of a man's felicity as 'continuall successe in obtaining those things which a man from time to time desireth' (p. 30). Moral distinctions are not merely irrelevant: they are logically excluded by the character of the inquiry.

Professor Hood's view, moreover, can be shown to have no sufficient textual warrant. It is never suggested, in Hobbes's deduction of the need for absolute power, that it is based on a recognition of the outweighing of a few just men by the majority of the wicked. Hobbes speaks of men in general as all 'continually in competition for Honour and Dignity' (p. 88). The need for the leviathan is deduced from the fact that 'Nature hath made men so equall' (p. 63) that the natural consequence must be war. This 'natural condition of Mankind' is itself seen not as the outweighing of a few, but as a condition in which 'every man is Enemy to every man' (p. 64), made unavoidable by the fact that it is in the nature of man to 'love Liberty, and Dominion over others' (p. 87), demonstrably true because 'necessarily consequent (as hath been shewn) to the naturall Passions of men' (p. 87).

When Professor Hood goes on to his interpretation of Hobbes's theory of obligation, he similarly represents the theory as being divided into two parts. In Civil Society, everyone becomes obliged, by fear of sanctions, to obey the commands of the state. This is, however, only the artificial form of obligation, the means of compulsion to the unjust. Hobbes is also represented as believing that 'a valid covenant without the sword has strength to hold a just man' (p. 130). It is this type of obligation, moreover, which is seen as the proper basis for the state: 'it was impossible for Hobbes to provide a psychology of the fulfilment of natural obligation on principles of nature only' (p. 123). Hobbes's theory of obligation is thus presented not as a deduction but as a problem in moral deliberation, so that '*Leviathan* must present difficulty to those who have no understanding of Divine justice' (p. 26).

The distinction claimed by Professor Hood between the two different types of obligation is made as strong as possible by much repetition. Many times the claim is re-iterated that civil philosophy is merely 'the science of an artificial body, an artificial man with an artificial right' (p. 147). It becomes difficult not to submit to these somewhat Hegelian distinctions, not to believe that such an artificial obligation must undoubtedly be of an inferior type, that such artificial unity 'is, and must be, grounded on a real unity' (p. 137). Hobbes himself, however, never speaks of this division which Professor Hood regards as so crucial, never uses the concept of artificial obligation at all. It might then seem a somewhat tendentious undertaking to base an account of Hobbes's theory on an invented terminology. But again, Hobbes's omission merely provokes Professor Hood into further counter-assertion. 'It would have been clearer', he claims (p. 116) if Hobbes had 'written in terms of moral and civil obligations, or of natural and artificial obligations', and his failure to think of this is 'misleading' (p. 117).

It is not immediately apparent where Professor Hood does find his evidence to justify making this distinction between two types of obligation. At the start of his book it seems to be based on an attempt to discover in Hobbes an active piety. 'My position is', he says in the opening chapter (p. 5), 'that the presumption that Hobbes was sincere in his Christian profession can be supported by arguments at

east as strong as any that have been advanced in favour of the contrary presumption.' But this irrelevance is fortunately not followed up. Professor Hood's conclusion seems subsequently to be based entirely on a suggested rationalizing of
Hobbes's text. It is still difficult to discover its precise source, but the conclusion
is none the less clear: what it amounts to is that a man can properly be said to be
obliged or forbidden, in Hobbes's theory, simply by the Laws of Nature, without
reference to any sanction. The attempt, however, to locate such a claim within
Hobbes's account seems in principle misconceived, quite apart from the problem
of textual verification: it seems to be expressly ruled out by the manner of Hobbes's
presentation.

Hobbes's presentation of his theory of obligation is in the form of proving a
theorem about conduct. As Hobbes's point of departure is his delineation of human
psychology, so the character of obligation is determined as a necessary deduction
from this point. When Hobbes states men's obligation, therefore, in the form of
obligation to obey the Laws of Nature, the command and the obligation are there
not in virtue of any authority, but as a part of the definition. While it is then no
doubt true to say, as Professor Hood does, that Hobbes 'defined a law of nature
decisively as a prohibition' (p. 85), it is to mistake Hobbes's procedure to assume
that such a command must imply any sort of external authority as commander.

These dictates of Reason', Hobbes points out (p. 83), 'men use to call by the name
of Lawes; but improperly: for they are but Conclusions, or Theoremes concerning
what conduceth to the conservation...of themselves.' To say then that a man is
obliged to obey the Laws of Nature is, in Hobbes's account, simply to say that he
fulfils the definition of being a man. To say, similarly, that a man is forbidden by
these Laws is simply to say that certain activities would logically exclude him from
Hobbes's definition. These 'precepts, by which men are guided', as Hobbes calls
them (p. 189) may still properly be referred to as Natural Laws: they are observed
frequencies of occurrence. There are Laws of a man's nature, in the sense of
habitual patterns of behaviour. There are prohibitions, in the sense that, on Hobbes's
definition, certain types of action would be psychological impossibilities. Hobbes's
'articles'—'which otherwise are called Laws of Nature'—represent a means of
showing what a man is like, as a way of demonstrating both the possibility and the
need for Hobbesian political obligation.

There is no place in such a sequence of definitions for any separate concept of
authority or of moral deliberation. Hobbes did not himself conclude (as does
Professor Hood) that he had contrived to raise a problem not soluble in its own
terms, but that he had 'sufficiently or probably proved all the Theoremes of Morall
doctrine' (p. 197) 'from the Principles of Nature onely' and 'from Definitions...
universally agreed on' (p. 199). To be obliged, in Hobbes's scheme, by the Laws of
Nature is not a factual but a logical matter. To be obliged by the Civil Laws is not
a question of prior morality, but only of a known sanction. To conflate these two
accounts is to ignore Hobbes's basic political axiom, that men can only be said to be
guided in the sense of recognizing ways of mediating a psychological situation which
is itself irreducible.

Hobbes's essential conclusion is that there can be no true obligation without a
known power to enforce it: in a famous phrase, 'Covenants, without the Sword, are
but Words, and of no strength to secure a man at all' (p. 87). Again, Professor
Hood's rationalization of this account seems to have no sufficient textual warrant.
It depends, first, on inverting Hobbes's own presentation of the relation between

Covenanting and the State. Hobbes speaks of men, as a result of a rational calculation, covenanting to 'conferre all their power and strength upon one Man' (p. 89), to whom they then owe total obedience. Professor Hood reverses this order, speaking of Covenanting after the institution of the State. His account thus certainly contrives to suggest an independent obligation to obey covenants; but it has ceased to be an exposition of Hobbes's own argument. Professor Hood's rationalization depends also on the straightforwardly mistaken impression that Hobbes 'distinguished between "words" and "empty words"' (p. 130), so that 'he did not say that covenants without the sword are of no strength to hold a man at all'. But this is exactly what Hobbes did say, and I know of no place where he makes this distinction—nor does Professor Hood cite one.

Professor Hood appears to misunderstand the *type* of obligation described by Hobbes. The *source* of this misunderstanding in turn seems to lie in his assumption that the theory requires some external validating conditions, some further guarantee of the conditions under which a man is obliged. Hobbes is said to believe in a prior source of moral authority, a belief which he is said to reveal when he 'goes behind his philosophic fiction of a command without a commander to the reality from which the fiction was derived, when he says that the second law of nature is the law of the gospel' (p. 97). The basis for Leviathan's 'unlimited artificial right' (p. 153) is thus seen to lie in the congruence of its actions with the prior natural obligation of both sovereign and subject to obey the Laws of Nature seen as the commands of God. The Commonwealth is properly the 'moral unity of natural persons bound together by God by His natural laws' (p. 137).

Part III of Professor Hood's book aims to give content to this division of authority, liberty and law in the Commonwealth into their artificial and natural parts. Again, Hobbes himself never makes any such division, never speaks of the obligation beyond power. He presents both the rights of the sovereign and the liberties of the subject as deductions from their rights of Nature. But again, this merely provokes Professor Hood into counter-assertion. Hobbes's retention of the rights of Nature introduces an 'unnecessary inconsistency' (p. 139). Hobbes 'should have seen' that what he was really trying to suggest was a 'naturalist representation of the Divine moral authority of the sovereign' (p. 142). 'The best explanation' for Hobbes's failure to point out this crucial distinction 'is that Hobbes made a mistake' (p. 156).

Professor Hood's further division, however, appears to depend on ignoring Hobbes's systematic presentation of his theory of obligation—a system which it has been Professor Warrender's great contribution to make clear. Man's primary obligation, in the state of Nature as much as in civil society, is to obey the Laws of Nature: all other obligations must be deduced from this point. The concept of an 'artificial' obligation, contingent on the setting up of the State, cannot have any place in this system. If men are then said to obey these laws because they are seen to be the commands of God, they cannot also be said to have other obligations which they respect for some other reason. This whole issue, moreover, of the grounds of obligation is quite separate from the exposition of the system itself. As Professor Warrender pointed out (though his critics have largely chosen to ignore the distinction) the system itself cannot represent a theory of moral obligation in any ordinary sense.[9] As he also pointed out, if there is then said to be some kind of

---

[9] Professor Warrender now seems, however, to have gone beyond this point. See 'Hobbes's Conception of Morality', *Rivista Critica di Storia della Filosofia*, XVII (1962), 434-49.

moral basis to this structure, grounded on a recognition that the Laws of Nature are also the commands of God, then this is 'to make a new departure' (p. 278), and to canvass a suggestion which has nothing to do with the character of the system itself.

It is true that this exposition would still leave it open to Professor Hood to conclude (as he does) that obligation does in fact derive from this equation of the Laws of Nature with the Laws of God. Professor Warrender himself also goes on, in the last part of his book, to canvass the same suggestion (though much more guardedly) as to the validating conditions of obligation. The aim, however, appears to be misconceived. To deduce obligation from Hobbes's equation is to introduce an evaluative concept into a purely logical exercise. Hobbes does speak—in a dozen places at least, in *Leviathan*—of the Laws of Nature as the Laws of God. But in none of these passages is he speaking of obligation. The equation simply recognizes a necessary entailment of the Hobbesian definition of a Law of Nature as a rule of a man's behaviour. Hobbes was also committed to believing that for all behaviour there must be a cause. The cause then must certainly be God, if you choose to define God (as Hobbes did) as the cause of everything. Hobbes's description is independent, however, of any suggestion that it is in virtue of their character as the commands of God that Natural Laws are said to *oblige*: such a claim, moreover, Hobbes himself never makes.

It can further be shown that where Hobbes does speak of the grounds of obligation, his account is explicitly concerned to refute any attempt to base civil law on its congruence with some unwritten natural law of God. It is an axiom with Hobbes that 'the Law is a Command' (p. 143), that 'all Lawes, written, and unwritten, have their Authority, and force, from the Will of the Common-wealth' (p. 142), so that 'it were a great errour, to call the Lawes of Nature unwritten Law' (p. 147). They are 'not properly Lawes' at all (p. 141), but 'precepts' of reason, 'by which men are guided' (p. 189). It is only possible, then, to speak of obligation to obey the law when it is known to be a command of the civil power. Obligation derives not from authority but from sanction. Even when a law may seem to have been created by the authority of long custom 'it is not the Length of Time that maketh the Authority, but the Will of the Sovereign signified by his silence' (p. 141). It is not possible, then, to speak of the Laws of Nature themselves as the grounds of obligation: they do not fulfil the necessary character of Law. The only sense in which a Natural Law could be said immediately to oblige would be if the Commonwealth decided to create such an obligation: 'when a Commonwealth is once settled', certain Natural Laws might properly become law, 'as being then the commands of the Commonwealth; and therefore also Civill Lawes: for it is the Soveraign power that obliges men to obey them' (p. 141).

Professor Hood's explanation of the conditions under which men are said to be obliged involves also the claim that Hobbes recognizes moral limitations on a man's proper obedience. These limitations are given by Professor Hood's division of obligation into its artificial and natural parts. The Sovereign is said to acquire an artificial right against the subject which is 'unlimited' (p. 153), and which might therefore extend even to authorizing 'the act by which the sovereign defeats his intention by killing him' (p. 153). The subject, however, is said to retain 'a part of his natural right which is inalienable' (p. 152), which might extend to the 'moral right to disobey the sovereign when his disobedience does not frustrate the end of the commonwealth' (p. 13).

The 'retention of natural right', however, cannot have any place in Hobbes's deduction of the need for absolutism. To Hobbes it is axiomatic that the only means of escape from 'that miserable condition of Warre, which is necessarily consequent...to the naturall Passions of men' (p. 87) is for every man to submit entirely to the power of Leviathan as King of the Proud. Anything less than total obedience is total destruction. Hobbes concludes without qualification that 'the only way' to avoid *Bellum omnium contra omnes* is for all men to 'conferre all their power and strength upon one Man, or upon one Assembly of men' (p. 89). It is precisely this recognition, essential to Hobbes's deduction of absolutism, which Professor Hood's concept of 'retained right' seems to deny. This deduction, however, involves one singular limitation, which Hobbes does not fail to notice. As a man obeys the State as the necessary means to his own preservation, he may refuse obedience on any occasion when the State appears to endanger his life. The exception is entailed by Hobbes's definition: 'the end of Obedience is Protection' (p. 116). A man cannot be made to covenant to put his life in danger, as his only reason for covenanting at all was to prevent danger to his life. Hobbes himself sums up the exception: 'the right men have by Nature to protect themselves, when none else can protect them, can by no Covenant be relinquished' (p. 116). It is precisely this exception, entailed by Hobbes's definition, which Professor Hood's concept of 'complete authorization' seems to deny.

The place within this scheme of rights and obligations of the rest of *Leviathan*—Parts III and IV—provides a puzzle which has much exercised the commentators. In the fourth part of his book, Professor Hood goes on to consider finally Hobbes's intentions at this point. The issue has provoked debate even among those who have agreed on the predominant rationalism of Hobbes's system. Professor Oakeshott[10] has seen the Books as an intrinsic part of the larger logical whole. But Mr Brown has preferred to speak of a 'masterly special application'[11] of a theory completed in Book II. Mr Brown's critique of Professor Oakeshott has, however, been criticized in turn by Mrs Krook, who agrees in seeing the last parts as intrinsic to Hobbes's design, 'because it is Christian men for whom he is designing the commonwealth'.[12] A further quite different interpretation is suggested by Professor Hood himself, who admits (before he found it incompatible with Hobbes's Christian moralism) to having held the very peculiar view that Hobbes's argument from scripture is 'ironical' (vii).

Professor Hood's treatment now, however, of this vexed question is extremely brief. The debate among commentators gets no acknowledgement; his own exposition of 'Christian Politics' occupies only twenty pages at the end of his book. The intention of this exposition is not always clear. Professor Hood writes in places as if it is the possible 'danger to the peace' of Christianity (p. 234) which Hobbes discusses. Hobbes himself is careful to discuss only the dangers of the Churches. But Professor Hood's conclusion is never in doubt. Hobbes's use of scriptural evidence is held to confirm the general thesis that it is 'reasonable to view Hobbes as a Christian thinker' (p. vii), whose civil philosophy was 'not theory, but doctrine' (p. 233), derived from Scripture, a source which is itself 'brighter than the light of

---

[10] M. Oakeshott, *Introduction* to *Leviathan* (Basil Blackwell, 1946), pp. xliv–l. The most sensitive discussion.

[11] J. M. Brown, 'A Note on Professor Oakeshott's Introduction to the *Leviathan*', *Political Studies*, I (1953), 63.

[12] D. Krook, loc. cit. p. 223.

fallible human reasonings' (p. 234). The view that Hobbes was concerned in his political philosophy to raise moral issues rather than to supply a political demonstration is claimed to be proved. The refusal to take account of the structure of Hobbes's philosophy, and Hobbes's own statements of intention, are regarded as vindicated. It is 'really' the Scripture which forms the 'grounds' of Hobbes's 'doctrine' (p. 236). Hobbes himself may claim that the place of the last two Books is to demonstrate the possibility of interpreting Scripture 'in confirmation of the Power of Civill Soveraigns, and the Duty of their Subjects' (p. 329), a power and duty which he had already independently grounded 'upon the known naturall Inclinations of Mankind' (p. 390). But Professor Hood still concludes that 'only laws oblige in conscience; and these dictates of reason are laws of God only as revealed in Scripture' (p. 253), so that the final position is that 'to Hobbes himself civil philosophy was the handmaid to Christian politics' (p. 233).

Professor Hood's completed investigation indicates precisely the manner in which expositions of political theories themselves tend to become philosophical exercises. The investigation proceeds exclusively by rationalizations of texts; it is concluded when the 'doctrine' is elucidated; it makes no pretence of considering the intellectual relations between Hobbes's work and other political discourse of the age. The presumption (and it is widespread) is that—as Professor Warrender has put it— the 'question of what his theory is' may fairly be regarded as 'prior' and quite separate from the question of its historical location (p. ix). It is this approach, however, which itself seems to be misconceived. The issue raised by Professor Hood's work is not merely textual; it involves also a general question of methodological adequacy. It can be shown that historical and exegetical consistency cannot fairly be regarded as separate issues.[13] It can be shown, in the particular case of Professor Hood's work, that if its thesis were correct, then much in both the manner and the content of political discourse in Hobbes's time would thereby be rendered either absurd or incredible.

The inadequacy of Professor Hood's approach is revealed, first, by its presumption that interpretation can only proceed by the closest analysis of the writer's actual words. Professor Hood takes his stand on the claim that it must be acknowledged 'historically more credible' that Hobbes 'believed what he wrote' rather than that he 'wrote with his tongue in his cheek' (p. 253). The force of his claim to have discovered in Hobbes a theory of Divine politics rests mainly on his insistence that Hobbes's remarks should be taken at their face value 'on the presumption that he was essentially a sincere writer' (p. vii). The demand implied for a closer adherence to the text is no doubt salutary; the attitude itself has the air of complete commonsense. Yet this is neither so necessarily valid nor so revealing as it is made to seem. For the approach depends in effect on ignoring any element of historical conditioning in Hobbes's manner of presenting his views.

It must still remain essential to consider this question of conditioning, to consider whether any alternative modes of discourse could possibly have been acceptable to Hobbes's audience. The question of usage cannot be simply a crude issue between sincerity or cynicism in a writer. It may be that Hobbes felt bound, by

---

[13] J. G. A. Pocock, 'The History of Political Thought: a Methodological Enquiry', *Philosophy, Politics and Society*, ed. P. Laslett and W. G. Runciman, Second Series (Basil Blackwell, 1962), pp. 183–202, gives an excellent account of both activities, but still seems to regard them as alternatives.

custom or audience, to make use of the traditionally available modes of discussion, the modes of Natural Law writings and of scriptural debate. But it may be that this usage could leave Hobbes's meaning still an open question. He might have felt on occasion unable to say anything other than what he did say, whatever he may have felt. Professor Hood remarks, for example, that 'Hobbes claimed that he was no heretic' (p. 235). But such a remark does not really reveal anything Whatever Hobbes's private views may have been, it is inconceivable that anyone in his situation would ever publicly have claimed anything else. As Hobbes himself intimated, in the account Aubrey gives of his remarks about Spinoza,[14] there were certain things he felt he could not prudently say.

It follows that it must remain essential, in assessing the seriousness of Hobbes's various passing remarks, to consider what place they could have within the general philosophical framework to which he is committed. It is a commonplace (though more readily demonstrable from the more refined debate of later periods) that to accept the bare words, without constant reference back to the writer's general commitments, may be to produce not just confusion but absurdity. We might conclude, say, that Bolingbroke was an admirer of Walpole, or that Junius was in the pay of the Ministry. Even with a writer so apparently forthright as Hobbes, the issue must remain crucial. Hobbes does, for example, make a number of remarks which seem to leave the status of his religious persuasions an open question. It is then essential to bear in mind that Hobbes is committed also to a rigorously nominalistic philosophical system, in which '*True* and *False* are attributes of Speech, not of Things' (p. 15),[15] in which all moral order is no more than a creation of the imagination. When Professor Hood claims then that although Hobbes 'never speaks of a moral absolute', yet 'there are clear indications that in his thought God is the Moral absolute' (p. 101), all that he does is to produce a conclusion which is procedurally improper according to Hobbes's own system. To bear in mind Hobbes's general commitment is to make it difficult to understand how so literal an approach as Professor Hood demands could ever be valid.

The inadequacy of Professor Hood's approach is revealed also by its presumption that discussion of Hobbes's philosophy is properly separate from discussion about the more general state of ethical and political thinking at the time. Professor Hood certainly makes no attempt to present his work as any sort of contribution to the understanding of Hobbes's place within the political spectrum of his age. If his interpretation were correct, however, it would be bound to imply interesting links between Hobbes as an intellectual and the intellectual society in which he moved. But this does not happen: if the exegesis is correct, both Hobbes's standing and the ethical and political discussions of his day become almost impossible to understand.

Hobbes himself would become guilty of a carelessness in the exposition of his thought amounting to stupidity. As a Christian moralist, he would have been bound to recognize the inevitability of 'a point', as Professor Hood puts it, 'at which he had to supplement scientific deduction with religious conviction' (p. 137). It then becomes almost impossible to understand why Hobbes should have gone on trying

---

[14] Professor Hood cites (p. 1) this passage, from Aubrey's *Life* of Hobbes, but seems to regard it as bearing on the question of Hobbes's sincerity. It is evident from the MS., however (Bodleian MSS. Aubrey, 9, fo. 7), that the note refers to Hobbes's prudence. Professor Hood is quoting a mis-transcription by Aubrey's editor, Andrew Clark (*Aubrey s Brief Lives* (Oxford, 2 vols., 1898), I, 357) in which the passage is reduced to nonsense.

[15] For full discussion of this doctrine as central to Hobbes's system, see D. Krook, 'Thomas Hobbes's Doctrine of Meaning and Truth', *Philosophy*, XXXI (1956), 3–22.

to 'detach' a 'philosophical part' from his 'religious whole'. The attempt cannot even be regarded simply as an unfortunate experiment, as Hobbes was perverse enough to persist in it in three works, over some fifteen years. It also becomes almost impossible to understand Hobbes's attitude to the contemporary reception of this enterprise. In spite of his well-known predilection for the quiet life, Hobbes presented his 'traditional doctrine of Divine Politics' (p. 253) so outrageously that it was everywhere taken for the work of a dangerous atheist. In spite of the alarm this caused him, moreover, Hobbes never took the trouble to exculpate himself by giving any systematic explanation of his 'real' system. But if it was really true that there was 'nothing that is original in Hobbes's moral thought' (p. 13), he had every cause to defend himself by pointing this out to all his excited critics. A further peculiarity, however, is that Hobbes himself—with what would have to be regarded as quite gratuitous folly—still insisted on pointing out instead (at the end of Book II of *Leviathan*) 'how different this Doctrine is, from the Practise of the greatest part of the world' (p. 197).

If Professor Hood's thesis were correct, it would also reduce the attitudes of Hobbes's contemporaries to unexplained paradox. Consider, first, the attitudes of those contemporary writers (though they have so far been largely ignored) who spoke of themselves in their writings as 'Hobbists'. When intellectuals like, for example, Sir William Petty admitted to agreement with certain of Hobbes's principles, it was never the principles of Christian moralism they had in mind. Petty was a nominalist in philosophy, an absolutist in politics, and something like a sceptic in religious matters. In each case, it was the authority of Hobbes that he cited. Men like Petty would then have to be regarded not only as totally misguided in their reading of Hobbes, but also of a much greater originality than Hobbes himself. And yet it was Hobbes, and not these apparently much more dangerous followers, who was to be arraigned for atheism.

We also have to consider the attitudes of those many contemporary writers whose stance was avowedly anti-Hobbist. Their reactions to Hobbes's alleged materialism and atheism can now be studied in detail in Dr Mintz's admirable book.[16] This contribution is both learned and stylish, and will be straightforwardly helpful to all students of Hobbes. It traces the reactions to Hobbes of the contemporary philosophical moralists: the attacks (especially by More and Cudworth) on Hobbes's materialism, and (especially by Bramhall) on his determinism. This location of Hobbes within contemporary ethical debate is a genuine contribution, the more valuable in view of the customary isolation of Hobbes from his intellectual milieu. The central contention of Dr Mintz's study is that Hobbes became 'the *bête noire* of his age' (p. vii), and that the charge 'to which all other differences between Hobbes and his contemporaries can be reduced' (p. 45) was that he was an atheist. Dr Mintz has compiled a check-list (pp. 157–60) of contemporary anti-Hobbist literature, which includes over two dozen pieces written between the publication of *Leviathan* and Hobbes's death in 1679 with the specific aim of pointing out the dangers of Hobbes's heterodoxy. It seems curious, then—if we assume Professor Hood's thesis to be correct—that not only did all of Hobbes's critics contrive to miss entirely the point of his work, but that they were all mistaken in exactly the same way. This is, moreover, historically as well as exegetically curious. Hobbes's readers would have been highly attuned to even the most intellectual presentation of Christian moralism in ethical theory. Cudworth's presentation, for example, was infinitely

[16] I cite by page only.

more convoluted than Hobbes's, and yet he was always recognized as being engaged on such an activity. None would have been attuned, however, to expect a completely nominalist system. What we eventually have to believe, then, of Hobbes's contemporary opponents, is so complex as to seem incredible: all of them entirely missed the point Hobbes was concerned to make, although it was a point they were highly attuned to see; all of them saw instead the opposite point, although none was attuned to do so, and although Hobbes was not in fact making such a point at all.

The price of assuming that Professor Hood's thesis could be correct seems too heavy: Hobbes is reduced to paradox, and his contemporaries to absurdity. Exegetical coherence is gained at the expense of any historical plausibility. This danger, moreover, seems inherent in the tendency to treat the study of intellectual history as ersatz philosophy. When inquiry proceeds exclusively by the analysis of a conventional number of classical texts, their relation to their contemporary philosophical undergrowth is bound to stop being visible. There is thus still no account of the intellectual relations, rather than merely reactions, implied either by Hobbes's philosophical or scientific interests. Even in Dr Mintz's historically-minded investigation, Hobbes's influence is still treated exclusively causally, and regarded as exclusively 'negative' (p. 147). Only one attempt is made by Dr Mintz to relate Hobbes to any more general contemporary attitudes: he is seen as part of the force behind the divorce of Wit from Virtue characteristic of Restoration *belles lettres*. This suggestion is Dr Mintz's one implausible contribution. The causal links are in fact incapable of being demonstrated. The implication of this situation, moreover, is that a great deal of matter is being neglected. For if the study of political theory is to be a properly historical investigation, it has got to include some account of political theory as a social activity, carried on at a number of interacting levels of abstraction at any given time. Hobbes's position still involves him in a tradition of discourse, even if he was to be the cause mainly of a re-assertion of a contrary tradition. The point, moreover, is not a suggestion merely of a different type of inquiry. To add an historical dimension is to add information relevant to any assessment of a classical text. The consequence of neglecting such location, in the case of *Leviathan*, has been that conclusions which are historically absurd are capable of being seriously canvassed. If there is to be any prospect of clearing up the confusions into which the study of Hobbes's work has fallen, it is less philosophy, and more history, which is needed.

QUENTIN SKINNER

[7]

THOMAS HOBBES AND HIS DISCIPLES IN FRANCE AND ENGLAND

Quentin Skinner

I

When Thomas Hobbes arrived in France at the end of 1640, "the first of all that fled"[1] from the growing threat of civil war in England, he began an exile which was to last eleven years, an exile which was moreover to prove the most intellectually fruitful period of his whole life. In Paris he was to reach the height of his polemical powers, conducting his debates with Descartes[2] on the existence of secondary qualities, and with Bishop Bramhall[3] on free will. In Paris he was also to bring to fruition a lifetime of speculation about the science of politics, completing the *De Cive* and writing the whole of *Leviathan*.[4] At the same time he was active in the circle of leading scientists and philosophers gathered round the figure of Marin Mersenne, and was to spend much of his time in optical experiments and mathematical speculation.[5]

It may not have been pure chance that Hobbes in exile was to reach the top of his creative powers. For it is an ironic but very revealing fact about his intellectual biography that he was to find in France all the brilliant and congenial intellectual company which in England he was always to miss. On his return to England in 1651 Hobbes was to become an isolated figure. He was isolated for much of his time in the remote wilds of Derbyshire, where he confessed to finding "the want of learned Conversation was a great inconvenience".[6] He was isolated too in much of his political and mathematical speculation, as he was to provoke only quarrels with the orthodox scientists

---

[1] Hobbes's own remark. See *The English Works,* ed. Sir William Molesworth, 11 vols. (London, 1839–45), IV, 414 (hereafter cited as *E.W.*).

[2] Hobbes discussed this dispute as early as 1641. See letter Hobbes à Mersenne pour Descartes, Paris, March 30th 1641, in *Œuvres de Descartes,* ed. C. Adam and P. Tannery, 13 vols. (Paris, 1897-1957), III, 341–348.

[3] For discussion, see G. C. Robertson, *Hobbes* (Edinburgh, 1886), pp. 163–167. For bibliography, H. Macdonald and M. Hargreaves, *Thomas Hobbes: a Bibliography* (London, 1952), pp. 37–41.

[4] Hobbes mentions and dates completion of the works in *Thomas Hobbes Malmesburiensis Vita Carmine Expressa,* his verse autobiography, in *The Latin Works,* ed. Sir William Molesworth, 5 vols. (London, 1839–45), I, xc–xcii (hereafter cited as *L.W.*).

[5] Mersenne and group fulsomely cited in *L.W.,* I, xc–xci.

[6] J. Aubrey, *Brief Lives,* ed. A. Clark, 2 vols. (Oxford, 1898), I, 338.

154   QUENTIN SKINNER

and divines.[7] He was to take no part in the scientific societies of the Restoration period, and he wrote no further works of political thought.

It is a mistake, nonetheless, to see in Hobbes a complete outcast from
intellectual society, a writer who was studied only to be refuted, whose impact was entirely "negative".[8] This is to ignore the significance of Hobbes's
links with the more sympathetic intellectual society which he had found in
Paris during his exile, and to ignore the fact that even after his return to
England Hobbes was to remain closely in touch with a number of these
scientific and philosophical friends. There is evidence that he continued to
exchange views with them about his own political works, and that they kept
him up to date with developments in the Academies of Paris which he had
known. It becomes clear, moreover, from their correspondence, that Hobbes
in exile left an abiding impact and an avowed following in French intellectual
society. The extent and the significance of these links have received no attention. A study of Hobbes's correspondence thus suggests some important implications about the types of interest prevailing in the "Republic of Letters"
at this time, and about the influence of Hobbes's own works on this intellectual society.

                                    II

It is now possible to reconstruct, from studying their correspondence, a list
of most of the members of Mersenne's circle whom Hobbes met in Paris and
got to know well. Some of this evidence can be found in the newsletters of
Samuel Sorbière, of Mersenne himself, and from other writers who made it
their business to keep the small circles of the learned in touch with each
other. But most of the evidence is contained in the archive of Hobbes's own
correspondence, which has remained unpublished and unexamined at Chatsworth. It is on this source that the ensuing discussion is mainly based.[9]

At Mersenne's meetings Hobbes is known to have met many of the most
important representatives of Continental scientific thought. He met Mersenne

---

[7] Robertson, *Hobbes*, pp. 167–185 (Mathematical disputes); S. I. Mintz, *The Hunting
of Leviathan* (Cambridge, 1962), pp. 63–109 (attacks on materialism).
[8] Mintz, p. 147.
[9] The MSS, formerly at Hardwick, previously made available to three scholars, none
of whom made any use of correspondence. Robertson, "Note on the Hardwick MSS", in
Hobbes, p. 236n., mentioned Du Verdus, but cited no letters and dismissed rest of correspondence as "of no account". F. Tönnies, *Thomas Hobbes, der Mann und der Denker*
(Stuttgart, 1912) cited MSS in sources, but quoted only one (p. 45), and again made no
use of correspondence. L. Strauss, *The Political Philosophy of Hobbes* (Oxford, 1936),
mentioned Chatsworth MSS (p. xiii), but again cited no correspondence. I am very
greatly indebted to His Grace the Duke of Devonshire, and to the Trustees of the Chatsworth Settlement, for permission to examine and to cite from the archive of correspondence. I am also much indebted to Mr. T. S. Wragg, the Librarian of Chatsworth, for
invaluable advice and help.

himself, with whom he had already corresponded about the study cf optics.[10] He met Fermat,[11] perhaps the leading French mathematician,[12] who was later to write observations about some of Hobbes's own mathematical views.[13] He met and corresponded with Gassendi,[14] one of the leading figures in Mersenne's circle, as well as in the later Academy *chez* Montmor. And he no doubt met many of the other great figures mentioned by De Coste as the friends of Mersenne — the Huygens, the Pascals, Roberval, Torricelli.[15]

Hobbes seems to have found his closest friends, however, and his closest intellectual links, among some of the lesser luminaries within this group. Among these were several of the other English expatriates who had settled into Parisian intellectual society.[16] He met Sir Kenelm Digby, a correspondent of Mersenne's,[17] and already an old friend of Hobbes's, who had written to him from Paris as early as 1637 to send a copy of Descartes's newly published *Discourse on Method*.[18] He met John Bramhall, the Laudian bishop in exile from the Puritan Revolution in England, who was later to be his most effective controversial opponent. He met the young William Petty, just qualified as a doctor at Leyden, and sent to Paris by John Pell with a letter of introduction to Hobbes. Petty "became acquainted with Father Mersen" and his circle of friends during 1645,[19] studied with Hobbes himself, and collaborated with him in producing the drawings for Hobbes's treatise on optics.[20] Among Hobbes's closest friends were also several of the French philosophers and scientists. He got to know Montmor, the rich "virtuoso" whose house became a chief meeting-place of the learned after Mersenne's death in 1648.[21] And he came closely in touch with several of the men who were to form the nucleus of this later Academy — in particular with Du Verdus, de Martel, and Sorbière.

[10] See Introduction to P. Marin Mersenne, *Correspondance*, ed. C. de Waard, 7 vols. (Paris, 1932–1962), I, xvi–xlviii.

[11] Pierre de Fermat (1595–1665), correspondent of Mersenne, knew several of Hobbes's friends. See R. Lenoble, *Mersenne ou la Naissance du Mechanisme* (Paris, 1943), p. xxxviii.

[12] The contemporary view. See M. Costar, "Mémoire des Gens de Lettres célèbres de France", *Continuation des Mémoires de Littérature et d'Histoire de Mr de Salèngre*, 11 vols. (Paris, 1726), II, 341. Also mentions most of Mersenne group.

[13] Samuel Sorbière, *A Voyage to England* (tr. 1709), p. 96.

[14] Pierre Gassendi, *Opera Omnia*, 6 vols. (Lugdini, 1658): Vol. VI, *Epistolæ* (e.g., VI, 522, Hobbes to Gassendi, 1649).

[15] F. Hilarion de Coste, *La Vie du R. P. Marin Mersenne* (Paris, 1649), p. 30 *et. seq.*, and p. 89 *et. seq.*, lists of Mersenne's friends. Also included Descartes, Gassendi, Fermat, Galileo, and Hobbes himself.

[16] H. Brown, *Scientific Organisations in Seventeenth Century France* (Baltimore, 1934), pp. 59–63 mentions Digby and Petty in this connection.

[17] According to de Coste, p. 92, though appears as D'lgbi.

[18] M. Nicolson, "The Early Stage of Cartesianism in England", *Studies in Philology*, XXVI (1929), p. 358.

[19] Petty to Pell, Paris, November 1645, printed in Lord Edmond Fitzmaurice, *The Life of Sir William Petty* (London, 1895), pp. 7–8.

[20] Fitzmaurice, pp 5–6. Cf. Aubrey, ed. Clark, I, 367–368.

[21] On Montmor academy, and relations to Mersenne's circle, see Brown, chs. III–V.

All of these later leaders of the Montmor Academy had also been members of Mersenne's circle during the 1640's. Du Verdus was a pupil of Roberval[22] (one of the leading members of the earlier group), and there is evidence to suggest he must have known Mersenne well.[23] De Martel was a nobleman and an amateur of science,[24] but was also a correspondent of Mersenne's[25] and friendly with a number of the leading mathematicians of the day, including both Fermat and Du Verdus himself.[26] Sorbière was another correspondent of Mersenne's[27] though he was himself less a constructive scientific writer than an organiser of scientific enquiry — one of a type in this phase of the Scientific Revolution, of which the most notable was to be Oldenburg. Sorbière knew everyone, and corresponded with nearly all of the group whom Hobbes got to know well — with Du Bosc and Du Prat as well as with De Martel and Du Verdus, and with Hobbes himself as well as with many others among the giant figures.[28]

These were the men who became Hobbes's closest intellectual contacts, and with whom he was always to retain his links. With De Martel Hobbes kept up a correspondence after returning to England,[29] and even while Hobbes was still in France we find De Martel writing specially for news about him, when absent from Paris.[30] With Du Verdus Hobbes seems to have been particularly close. When Hobbes came to write his autobiography it was addressed to "this candid friend, who knew his ways so well".[31] While in France he seems to have thought at one point of remaining permanently in exile and going to stay with Du Verdus in Languedoc.[32] Both men always professed the highest regard for each other: this was to lead Du Verdus to translate

---

[22]   Du Verdus: invariably so called, though real name François Bonneau, Sieur de Verdus. On relation to Roberval's work, see M. Cantor, *Vorlesungen über Geschichte der Mathematik,* 4 vols. (Leipzig, 1880–1908), II, 800–806.

[23]   Mersenne à Torricelli, December, 1644, discussed Du Verdus's work. See *Œuvres de Fermat,* ed. P. Tannery and C. Henry, 4 vols. (Paris, 1891–1912), IV, 85.

[24]   According to R. Pintard, *Le Libertinage Erudit* (Paris, 1943), p. 332, who takes most of this material from Samuel Sorbière, *Epistolae . . . ad illustres et eruditos viros scriptae* (Paris, 1673).

[25]   See below, n. 30.

[26]   Hobbes MSS (Chatsworth), Box 2, *Letters to Hobbes, unclassified* (bundled by name of correspondent). De Martel to Hobbes, April 1655: cites Du Verdus and Du Prat; April 1657: cites Fermat; August 1657: cites Du Bosc. All Hobbes MSS citation is from this source, hereafter cited as Hobbes MSS. Sources in Latin, French, English. All translations mine. Spelling and punctuation modernised, but dates old-style.

[27]   de Coste, *Mersenne,* p. 95.

[28]   Samuel Sorbière, *Lettres et Discours* (Paris, 1660). Letters to Du Prat, pp. 64–68 and 390–394; to Du Bosc, pp. 151–169; to De Martel, pp. 573–606; to Hobbes, pp 631–636, and in Hobbes MSS.

[29]   Hobbes MSS, Box 2, De Martel to Hobbes, 1656 and 1657.

[30]   MSS Bibliothèque Nationale, De Martel to Mersenne, July 1648, cited in Brown, p. 59.

[31]   Hobbes, *L.W.,* I, xcix.

[32]   Hobbes, *Thomas Hobbes Malmesburiensis Vita,* autobiography, *L.W.,* I, xv.

one of Hobbes's works, the *De Cive*;[33] it was to lead Hobbes to dedicate one of his own works to Du Verdus, the mathematical *Examinatio et Emendatio*.[34] With Sorbière too Hobbes was to keep up many contacts even apart from their correspondence. Sorbière was to be much concerned with the publication of several of Hobbes's later works,[35] and he was also to receive from Hobbes a dedication.[36] He was to act as Hobbes's translator,[37] and as his intermediary with the publishing-house of Bleau in Amsterdam when it handled the first collection of Hobbes's works in 1668.[38]

These friends were to provide Hobbes with his chief intellectual contacts after his retirement to England in 1651. It now becomes possible to establish from their correspondence the fact and the significance of these continued links. It is clear that their aim, first, was to keep Hobbes generally up to date with developments in scientific and philosophical thought. We find Du Verdus writing to Hobbes several times during 1656 to keep him informed about developments in the still inchoate Montmor Academy in which they had all become concerned.[39] And when the Academy eventually became incorporated in 1657, and took on a formal existence with Sorbière as its Secretary, we find Sorbière himself writing to Hobbes to explain how this had come about, and to give an account of the Constitution which he and Abraham Du Prat had drawn up for the Academy.[40] During the same period we also find letters from several other members of the group *chez* Montmor — from De Martel, giving news of Fermat and Du Verdus,[41] from Du Bosc,[42] and from Du Prat.[43]

The Academy was even more concerned, however, to keep Hobbes up to date with the progress of their own researches. An even larger circle of correspondents continued to keep Hobbes in his retirement in touch with the discussion of problems which were known to interest him in both philosophy

---

[33] The second translation, issued 1660. See Macdonald and Hargreaves, pp. 21–22.

[34] "Clarissimo viro domino Verdusio, nobili Aquitano", *L.W.*, IV, Preface.

[35] The re-issue of *De Cive* in 1647; the issue of the *Opera Philosophica* in 1668: both by Bleau, with Sorbière as intermediary. See Robertson, *Hobbes*, p. 62 and p. 197n.

[36] *Dialogus Physicus* — inscribed "Viro Clarissimo et Amicissimo Samueli Sorbiero", *L.W.*, IV, 235.

[37] Sorbière translated *De Cive*, 1649, as *Elemens Philosophique du Citoyen*. See Macdonald and Hargreaves, pp. 20–21.

[38] The Hobbes MSS include correspondence between Bleau and Hobbes: cf. n. 35, above.

[39] Hobbes MSS, Box 2, Du Verdus to Hobbes, May and October 1656, cited Mylon, De Martel, Peleau.

[40] Sorbière, *Lettres et Discours*, pp. 631–636. The only surviving account of the constitution.

[41] Cf. n. 26, above.

[42] Hobbes MSS, Box 2, Du Bosc to Hobbes, September 1659. Du Bosc seems to have stayed with Hobbes in England during the 1620's. See Pintard, p. 627.

[43] Hobbes MSS, Box 2, Du Prat to Hobbes, October 1655, September 1656. Hobbes evidently tried in 1646 to get Du Prat a job with the Cavendishes. See Pintard, p. 333. Du Verdus knew Du Prat and De Martel. See Michel de Marolles, *Mémoires*, and *Suite des Mémoires*, 2 vols. (Paris, 1656–57), I, 199.

and science. Hobbes was thus to continue hearing reverberations during the 1650's of the discussions he had held in Paris a full decade earlier. Sorbière wrote to ask his views on Boyle's treatise *De Naturae Aeris*;[44] a correspondent in 1656 was still writing to attack his views on free will;[45] another as late as 1659 was still discussing his views on optics.[46] Hobbes also continued to receive a number of letters about mathematics — the leading interest of the Montmor Academy.[47] Claude Mylon, Pierre Blacu, Oldenburg and Du Verdus all wrote about mathematical problems, Du Verdus continuing his inquiries as late as 1671.[48]

But Hobbes was never merely treated as an ordinary corresponding member of the Academy. He was also regarded by all of his correspondents with the special deference due to a "very great philosopher",[49] a "Master" from whom they hoped to learn. Letters from several strangers spoke of their wish to come to England specially to meet him. Paris was said to be "full of such people" (according to one letter of introduction to Hobbes) "who ask me the whole time what you are doing, and whether we may hope for some further product of your genius".[50] Another writer who proposed coming to England to meet Hobbes wrote that he had "seen everything that Des Cartes, Gassendi, Galileo, Mersenne have done", but that "none of it compares with what I can learn from your book [*Leviathan*] all the time".[51] Letters from members of the Montmor Academy expressed a similar deference — without the fatuity, but with no less seriousness. An introduction to Hobbes was clearly regarded as essential for any member visiting England. When Guisony (an occasional member, and regarded as an expert on "physical speculations")[52] came to Oxford in 1659 he had instructions from both Du Prat and Sorbière to get in touch with Hobbes, and in fact wrote to him immediately to discuss his researches.[53] When Sorbière himself came to England four years later Hobbes was to be the first man he sought out in his quest for instruction "in matters of Literature, and the Sciences".[54]

---

[44]   Hobbes MSS, Box 2, Sorbière to Hobbes, undated.
[45]   Hobbes MSS, Box 2, Tandy to Hobbes, 1656.
[46]   Hobbes MSS, Box 2, Guisony to Hobbes, May 1659.
[47]   Oldenburg wrote of Montmor group as mainly mathematical, 1659, and mentioned Du Prat and Mylon. See the Royal Society MSS, *Liber Epistolaris*, quoted in Brown, p. 99.
[48]   Hobbes MSS, Box 2, Mylon to Hobbes, 1657; Blacu to Hobbes, 1659; Du Verdus to Hobbes (total of 32 letters), 1656–1761; *Liber Epistolaris*, Oldenburg to Hobbes, June 1655. Letter about mathematics. Cites previous correspondence. (Information on Oldenburg kindly provided by Professor A. Rupert Hall.)
[49]   Hobbes MSS, Box 2, Du Verdus to Hobbes, April 1665.
[50]   Hobbes MSS, Box 2, Morny to Hobbes, May 1661.
[51]   Hobbes MSS, Box 2, Peleau to Hobbes, May 1656.
[52]   Chapelain to Huygens, August 20, 1659, speaks of Guisony and his work, *Œuvres Complètes de Christian Huygens*, 22 vols. (La Haye, 1888–1950), II, 468 and note.
[53]   Hobbes MSS, Box 2, Guisony to Hobbes, May 1659.
[54]   Sorbière, *Voyage*, p. 26. Montconys also seems to have visited Hobbes at the same time. See *ibid.*, p. 27.

III

Hobbes's connections, moreover, with the group he had known during his exile went much further than this exchange of intellectual and autobiographical detail. It is clear that Hobbes was also to create, as the author of *Leviathan,* a sensational impact and a real influence on their ways of thought. It is in the establishment of these intellectual links that the MSS evidence relating to Hobbes's disciples becomes of the most crucial importance. The MSS become particularly important partly because it happened that Hobbes's retirement to England coincided with the publication of *Leviathan.* The group with whom Hobbes had discussed his work in Paris were thus left to put in writing all of the questions which a reading of the book raised in their minds. They also become important because it happened that Hobbes's political works were to gain a sufficiently sinister reputation for any public or printed avowal of sympathy with their views to become very difficult. In this way the printed sources have contrived to suggest that Hobbes remained a figure in complete intellectual isolation. But in the privacy of memoranda and correspondence it can be seen that Hobbes's intellectual relations were often much closer than has been implied.

It becomes evident, in the first place, that the *Leviathan* in France gained an immediate popularity. Copies were circulated (according to Du Bosc's account) among most of Hobbes's own friends in the Montmor Academy.[55] There was also (according to both Du Prat and Sorbière) a widespread demand for a French translation.[56] The Parisian booksellers were even prepared at one point to raise a fund among themselves to finance a translator.[57] We find Du Prat writing to Hobbes in 1656 that "I have this very day spoken to a bookseller about the printing of your *Leviathan* here, who did open his ears to the proposition, and answered that your *De Cive* in French sold publicly, and that you were an author so well known, as he made no doubt but your book would sell away".[58] Du Bosc similarly wrote that "all the learned men I know desire that *Leviathan* were in French or Latin" and that he regarded the business of translating it as "a matter of the highest importance".[59] "Everyone who talks about the book", according to Du Verdus, "values it equally highly both for its soundness of doctrine and for its excellence of style".[60] And the translations were in fact to be supplied by Sorbière and by Du Verdus themselves. Sorbière produced the first French translation of *De*

[55] Hobbes MSS, Box 2, Du Bosc to Hobbes, September 1659, acknowledged receipt of *Leviathan* and *De Homine* from Hobbes's publisher. Circulated among De la Mote, Du Prat, Sorbière.
[56] Hobbes MSS, Box 2, Du Prat to Hobbes, October 1655; also September 1656, in reply to Hobbes to Sorbière.
[57] Hobbes MSS, Box 2, Du Prat to Hobbes, October 1655.
[58] Hobbes MSS, Box 2, Du Prat to Hobbes, in English, September 1656.
[59] Hobbes MSS, Box 2, Du Bosc to Hobbes, in English, September 1659.
[60] Hobbes MSS, Box 2, Du Verdus to Hobbes, August 1654.

Cive in 1649, and of the *De Corpore Politico* in 1652. Du Verdus produced another translation of the *De Cive* ten years later.[61] Both Du Verdus and Du Prat also offered to undertake the much larger task (which Hobbes himself was eventually to complete) of translating *Leviathan*.[62] Du Verdus got as far as sending a specimen French translation of one chapter to Hobbes before he evidently gave up the task.[63]

It also becomes evident that among the group whom Hobbes had known in Paris — both French and English — he began to be regarded during the 1650's as the complete expert on questions of political science. Du Verdus, for example, was to claim that Hobbes was "the one writer ever to have understood completely the nature of ethics, and hence to have constructed a true and proper political theory, and demonstrated the nature of every man's duties and obligations towards others, and hence also the duties of the subject to the Sovereign".[64] Du Verdus's pupil Peleau (who claimed in 1656 to have read the *De Cive* thirty times) similarly concluded that it was due to Hobbes alone that "we can now see clearly and without confusion through the obscurity of the sciences".[65] Hobbes's own pupil William Petty[66] was in the same way always to regard "clarissimus Hobbius"[67] as the one modern writer on politics to be taken entirely seriously, the one writer "who always examines everything he talks about with the most complete care".[68] Many of the political memoranda which Petty in later life was accustomed to write out to clear his own mind were in fact paraphrases or transcriptions from the *Leviathan*.[69] Many of his own formed views on "sovereignty" and on "Empire" similarly indicated his belief — as he confessed himself — that these concepts ought to "signify even as large a power as Mr. Hobbes attributes to his *Leviathan*".[70]

It is true that recognition of *Leviathan* as "the greatest, perhaps the sole, masterpiece" of English political philosophy[71] was mainly restricted, during Hobbes's lifetime, to this small and rather private circle of friends. It is

[61]   See Macdonald and Hargreaves, pp. 13 and 20–22.
[62]   Hobbes MSS, Box 2, Du Prat to Hobbes, October 1655, claimed to be thinking of making own translation.
[63]   Hobbes MSS, Box 2, Du Verdus to Hobbes, January 1657, enclosing complete draft of Chapter IV, *Of Speech (Du Langage)*.
[64]   Hobbes MSS, Box 2, Du Verdus to Hobbes, April 1665.
[65]   Hobbes MSS, Box 2, Peleau to Hobbes, May 1656 (fo. 2).
[66]   I am very greatly indebted to the Most Hon. the Marquis of Lansdowne for permission to examine and to cite from the Petty Papers (Bowood). I have tried here mainly to cite evidence in print, but chief evidence for Petty's debts to Hobbes is still in MSS, which I hope shortly to examine more fully.
[67]   *The Petty Papers,* ed. The Marquis of Lansdowne, 2 vols. (London, 1927), II, 34.
[68]   *Petty Papers,* II, 34. Translation mine.
[69]   Some evidence of this even in printed sources: see *Petty Papers,* I, 152-162 (general philosophy and definitions); I, 121–128 (religion); I, 16–21, 229 and 234 (political details, including discussion of "Normanism" and the "State of Nature").
[70]   *Petty Papers,* I, 219.
[71]   The judgment is from M. Oakeshott, "Introduction" to *Leviathan* (Oxford, 1946), p. x.

evident, nonetheless, that there was also some attempt on the part of these disciples to spread wider the word of Hobbes's creed. Montmor himself, for example, helped to spread word of Hobbes's special merit when Col. Tuke of the Royal Society visited his Academy in 1661. Montmor specifically mentioned Hobbes to him as one of the men they felt most capable of "the advancement of all sorts of learning in England" — a view which Tuke was himself to repeat to the Royal Society in London.[72] Sorbière, too, became one of Hobbes's leading popularisers. When he issued his translation of the *De Corpore Politico,* the reader was assured that every work produced by Hobbes meant a masterpiece, and that "in the study of politics there has never been anything so fine or so just" as Hobbes's own contribution.[73] Sir William Petty also was to remain true to his youthful enthusiasms in continuing to urge Hobbes to his friends,[74] correspondents,[75] and even children[76] as the only writer on political thought. If the popularity of Hobbes's system was to be stillborn, it was hardly for lack of enthusiasm among his own circle of friends.

It becomes evident, moreover, that although most of Hobbes's disciples spoke and wrote of his work mainly in this rather crude spirit of propaganda, there are nonetheless signs that some of them also studied Hobbes's political system in a much more critical and even creative spirit. Although no printed evidence has survived of sympathetic attempts to evaluate Hobbes's conception of a "geometry" of politics, there are several discussions among the unpublished letters and memoranda of both Du Verdus and of Petty which concern precisely this central theme of Hobbes's work. And although these remarks are scattered and few, they do provide the first evidence that has come to light of the direct influence of Hobbes's hopes and schemes for a Science of Politics.

Both Du Verdus and Petty agreed with Hobbes that his most epoch-making and fruitful suggestion had been the view that a political science might be constructed by a method analogous to "geometrical" demonstration. Both took up and agreed with Hobbes' remark in *Leviathan* that geometry was "the only science that it hath pleased God hitherto to bestow on Mankind".[77] "To be a philosopher", as Du Verdus remarked to Hobbes himself, "it is necessary to be a Geometer".[78] And Du Verdus went on to conclude that this combination had made Hobbes "the only writer ever to have constructed a true metaphysical system", since he was "the only writer to have designed

---

[72] Thomas Birch, *The History of the Royal Society,* 4 vols. (London, 1756), I, 26–27.
[73] Samuel Sorbière, "Le Libraire au Lecteur" in *Le Corps Politique* (n.p., 1652).
[74] Memoranda on reading, Petty Papers (Bowood). See also *Petty Papers,* II, 5.
[75] See Edward Southwell to Charles Petty, in *The Petty-Southwell Correspondence,* ed. The Marquis of Lansdowne (London, 1928), p. 311.
[76] See *Petty-Southwell Correspondence,* p. 305.
[77] Hobbes, *E.W.,* III, 23–24.
[78] Hobbes MSS, Box 2, Du Verdus to Hobbes, December, 1655 (fo. 3).

a philosophical system in a properly geometrical manner".[79] Petty was independently to make an almost identical comment: "I think that the best
Geometricians were the most sagacious men, or that the most Sagacious men
did ever make the Best Geometricians".[80] And it is clear that what Petty
had in mind here was not a specific mathematical skill so much as a capacity
for thought that (as he remarked elsewhere in speaking of "geometry"[81])
"takes in a great number of principles". For the list of men whom he believed embodied this capacity most notably were "Molière, Suarez, Galileo,
Sir Thomas More, Sir Francis Bacon, Dr. Donne, Mr. Hobbes, Descartes".[82]

Both Du Verdus and Petty also agreed with Hobbes about the manner in
which "geometrical" demonstration might be introduced into political speculation. As Du Verdus wrote to Hobbes, quoting from the Wisdom of Solo-
mon, the method is in fact natural, and is given by the fact that "God has
made everything in weight, in number, in measure", so that a correct account
of any sort of structure is sure to provide the key to all sorts of explanation.[83]
The same concept was to provide the centre-point of Petty's own attempts
at political demonstration. In the Preface, addressed to James II, of his unpublished *Political Pastimes and Paradoxes,* Petty remarked by way of explaining his work that "When I find out puzzling and perplexed matters that
may be brought to terms of Number, Weight, and Measure and consequently
be made demonstrable, and when I find things of vast and general concern-
ment, which may be discussed in a few words, I willingly engage upon such
undertakings, especially when they tend to your Majesty's glory and greatness, and the happiness of your people, being one of them myself".[84]

The hope that politics might be assimilated to an investigation of the
psychology or the sociology of the mass was to be as crucial in Petty's political schemes as Du Verdus saw it to be for Hobbes. In Hobbes's case it took
the form of an investigation into the observable nature of individual psychology, with the intention of deducing certain irreducibly necessary political
consequences. In Petty's case it was to take the form rather of a demand
for an investigation into the precise form of political and social commitments,
with the aim of making the control of states a matter for rational calculation.
But it is clear that the aims are strongly analogous, and that both Du Verdus
and Petty[85] shared with Hobbes the vision of a political science. As Petty

---

[79] *Ibid.* (fo. 7).
[80] *Petty-Southwell Correspondence,* p. 158.
[81] *Petty Papers,* II, 199.
[82] *Petty-Southwell Correspondence,* p. 158.
[83] Hobbes MSS, Box 2, Du Verdus to Hobbes, December 1655 (fo. 3).
[84] Petty Papers (Bowood), Vol. IV, item 36, fo. 1, MS dated 1687, in Petty's hand.
Items 1 and 21 are copies of same. Item 36 roughly set up for printer but never published.
For similar claim in print, see "Preface" to *Political Arithmetick* in *The Economic
Writings of Sir William Petty,* ed. C. H. Hull, 2 vols. (Cambridge, 1899), I, 244.
[85] Hull, "Introduction" to *Economic Writings,* pp. lxi–lxiii, noted Petty's affinities to
Hobbes.

was to put it to the Royal Society, "there is a Political Arithmetic, and a Geometrical Justice to be yet further cultivated in the World".[86] It is clear, finally, that both writers were quite aware of the debt which their vision owed to the example of Hobbes's own works.

IV

The evidence about Hobbes's personal and intellectual contacts suggests some important implications. The chief importance of the evidence lies perhaps in the account it suggests of Hobbes's impact and influence as a philosopher of politics. It is clear that the men whom Hobbes had moved among in Paris, both French and English, came to regard him in effect as their particular expert on matters of political science, came "to seek from your person" (as one of them put it) "the solution of all doubts".[87] This discovery is of particular historical importance because it so much runs counter to the accepted historiography. Both the leading studies of Hobbes's political influence have stressed that it can only be gauged by "the intense opposition" which his views provoked.[88] It has been assumed that Hobbes's only immediate effect was to cause a "widespread reassertion of the accepted principles" which single-handedly he had "tried to sweep away".[89] The discovery of an avowed contemporary following for Hobbes's view suggests the need for some re-appraisal of these assumptions. It becomes possible, and necessary, to recognise and to locate the place of Hobbes's system within the known spectrum of political discussion in the age.[90]

There are grounds for suggesting, moreover, not merely that this conventional account of Hobbes's total rejection is false, but that it has arisen from a partial view of the evidence, from excessive concentration on a parochial English reaction. Hobbes was widely denounced in England, but he seems to have been widely accepted abroad. We have to square his unthinking rejection by many English critics with the equally unthinking discipleship implied by many of his foreign correspondents. Hobbes's English critics also typically made no attempt to understand his aims. All their attacks, as has been pointed out,[91] were conveniently assimilated to the level at which Hobbes could be charged with "atheism" and totally condemned. But again this does not seem to have been typical of Hobbes's reception on the Continent. At least some

---

[86] Sir William Petty, *A Discourse ... Concerning the Use of Duplicate Proportion* (London, 1674). Epistle Dedicatory, Sig. A, 10b.
[87] Hobbes MSS, Box 2, Bagshawe to Hobbes, in English, March 1658.
[88] J. Laird, *Hobbes* (London, 1934), Pt. III, esp. ch. IX; John Bowle, *Hobbes and his Critics* (London, 1951), esp. ch. II.
[89] Bowle, p. 13 and p. 43.
[90] For further attempt at this see my "History and Ideology in the English Revolution", *The Historical Journal*, Vol. VIII (1965), pp. 151–178.
[91] Mintz, p. 45,

of his followers recognised and sympathised with his most ambitious hopes for a Science of Politics. And at least some of this enthusiasm seems to have been conveyed back even to England. The case of native genius failing to carry weight abroad is familiar; it may be that Hobbes to some extent provides an example of the converse case.

The sympathy with Hobbes's hopes for a Science of Politics suggests that his links with popular attempts to construct mechanistic explanations for every type of phenomenon may well have extended further than his obvious preoccupation with Matter and Motion. His hopes were based on the most popular scientific strategy of the time: when Du Verdus described Hobbes's achievement by invoking the familiar text on measure, number, and weight, this was to see it in effect as a part of the general attempt to explain by quantifying. It was simply to apply to Hobbes the motto of the age, the motto — it has even been suggested — "of all scientific effort since that time".[92] His particular hope of using mechanistic models in the study of human affairs was itself to become the chief focus of philosophical enquiry: the great quest of the next century was to be for the Newton of the Moral Sciences. Hobbes seems to have been animated by the same hope, the hope that "the science of man" might prove — as Hume was to put it — to be "the only solid foundation for the other sciences".[93]

Hobbes himself laid claim to a unique place in this development, his famous boast being that *De Cive* had been the first work to establish the possibility of treating politics as a science. But his procedure seems to have been no different from the most fashionable methodology of the New Science. And although Hobbes stood early in the tradition of attempting to apply the method to studying human affairs, he by no means stood alone. The *Delle Cause della grandezza delle città* of Botero, for example, translated into English in 1606, has been recognised as an even earlier attempt to apply similar methods of "genuine scientific empiricism" to the study of man and society.[94] It can scarcely have been chance that in the list of only ten authors on politics cited by Hobbes in his Library-list at Chatsworth, the first name mentioned was Botero.[95] It is also clear, finally, that Hobbes's disciples recognised the fashionable trend in his approach to politics almost as much as they felt influenced by his own particular conclusions.

The evidence on the relations between Hobbes and his disciples is also of interest for the implications it suggests about Hobbes's own reactions to avowed followers. It is clear that he was not only aware of the reverent spirit in which his pronouncements were accepted, but that he also regarded his disciples' affinities, and his own oracular role, with some seriousness. This

[92]   Carl J. Friedrich, *The Age of the Baroque* (New York, 1952), p. 93.
[93]   David Hume, *A Treatise of Human Nature* (London, 1738), vol. 1, Introduction.
[94]   Friedrich, p. 119.
[95]   Hobbes MSS, Box 2, item E 2, *Catalogues*, in Hobbes's hand, 40 pp. "Polit." entries on fo. 9.

attitude of tolerance and interest is the more remarkable in view of Hobbes's habitual refusal to comment on his own political system for the benefit of anyone who criticised or failed to understand it. The correspondence of these disciples, with their demands for comment and elucidation, was in fact to draw from Hobbes his only known comments offered to students of his political works.[96]

The affinities, for example, of Petty's work to Hobbes's views was to draw from Hobbes one of his very rare acknowledgments of the value of a contemporary writer. When Petty published his essay on *Duplicate Proportion,* with its "new hypothesis of springing or elastic motions" as well as its promise of a "geometrical justice", Hobbes was to write of it to Aubrey that "if I had seen his book before it went to the press I would not (as he thinks) have hindered it, but done as the Society did, that is, urged him to print it. For the doctrine is easy to be demonstrated. The last Chapter which is of Elasticity is different from the Principle which I have taken for Natural Philosophy; but I am of opinion that his supposition is very true, and will go a great way".[97] When other disciples wrote to Hobbes about his work, Hobbes was to show similar interest and encouragement. When Du Verdus wrote some five pages of detailed questions about doctrines in the *Leviathan,* at the time when he was first reading and interleaving it, he evidently received a full set of answers from Hobbes.[98] And When Du Verdus decided a year or two later that he might try to translate the book, he sent and received replies to a further eleven pages of questions about Hobbes's language and doctrines.[99] There are even signs that Hobbes submitted to having points of his doctrine debated by his correspondents. Peleau wrote for example to query Hobbes's view that Man could be regarded as basically anti-social. He later wrote again to thank Hobbes for the trouble he had taken to explain his views further and to assure him that all doubts had been resolved.[100]

These glimpses into the nature of Hobbes's contemporary influence undoubtedly provide the correspondence with its chief historical importance. It is also important, however, for providing an incidental but very revealing insight into the sociology of science at the time. The extent of active interest in Hobbes's political works among even the scientists seems very much to

[96] Hobbes's comments can only be implied from correspondence of disciples: Robertson (p. 236n.) tried and failed to discover Hobbes's answers. I have published Hobbes's only known reply to questioning about his politics in "Hobbes on Sovereignty: an Unknown Discussion", *Political Studies,* Vol. XIII (1965), pp. 213–218.
[97] Hobbes to Aubrey, February 1674, Petty Papers (Bowood), Vol. VI, Pt. 11, item 17. For explanation of how this MS. got into the Bowood archive, see Aubrey, ed. Clark, 1, 368.
[98] Hobbes MSS, Box 2, Du Verdus to Hobbes, August 1654. Queries 4th August. Thanks for reply 20th August.
[99] Hobbes MSS, Box 2, Du Verdus to Hobbes, Queries December 1656. Thanks January 1657.
[100] Hobbes MSS, Box 2, Peleau to Hobbes, Letter with queries undated. Thanks October 1656.

endorse the view that despite the trend towards specialised scientific enquiry, the "natural philosopher" still "clung to his old name and status",[101] still remained interested in the broadest possible strategy for scientific enquiry.

It has been said, and no doubt correctly, that both the Mersenne and Montmor groups confined their attentions almost exclusively to mathematical and experimental science.[102] The scientists of Mersenne's group certainly gained their chief notoriety from publicising Galileo's discoveries, their chief following from studying the system of Descartes. The Montmor Academy similarly gained its chief fame from the fact that it was to be the first group to hear the news of Huygens' discovery of Saturn's rings.[103] It was perhaps not surprising that when the official French Academy of Science was incorporated in 1666, the same interests — and to a large extent the same men — were to gain a complete ascendency.

The original suggestions for an Academy, however, had tried to allow for a much wider and more humanistic approach to scientific studies. The original plan was to include "not just those interested in geometry and physics, but also those learned in political, literary and historical matters".[104] The interests of the Montmor Academy suggest, moreover, that the original scheme for official incorporation was intended to recognise the fact of a prevailing eclecticism among the scientists. Sorbière's constitution for the Montmor Academy had particularly mentioned "the liberal arts" among the types of study they wished to encourage.[105] And when Sorbière wrote to Colbert in 1663 to ask for official patronage, he specifically mentioned that their meetings had been disrupted by "a group of men" who had "preached experiments only".[106]

All the evidence on the contacts between Hobbes and the members of the Montmor Academy endorses this view: they continued to stand for the most liberal approach to scientific studies. None of the members who corresponded with Hobbes about the details of his system were themselves engaged in the study of political philosophy. Fermat and Du Verdus were both prominent mathematicians, active in specialised controversy and research.[107] Sorbière, De Martel, and Du Prat had all originally trained as physicians, and the latter

---

[101] The conclusion of the study by A. R. Hall, *Ballistics in the Seventeenth Century* (Cambridge, 1952), p. 163.

[102] A. R. Hall, *The Scientific Revolution,* 2nd ed. (London, 1962). Ch. VII provides best introduction to Scientific Societies.

[103] Huygens also corresponded with several of Hobbes's friends, including Mylon (see Huygens, *Œuvres,* II, 373) and Guisony (*ibid.,* XXII, 66–67).

[104] J-B. du Hamel, *Regiae Scientiarium Academiae Historia* (Paris, 1698), p. 3. Translation mine.

[105] Sorbière to Hobbes, *Lettres et Discours,* p. 634.

[106] Sorbière to Colbert, quoted in Brown, p. 126.

[107] For Fermat's work, see Cantor, *Vorlesungen,* II, 798. For Du Verdus's, see letter on mathematical dispute quoted in P. Tannery, "Sur le Mathématicien François Chauveau", *Bulletin des Sciences Mathématiques,* XIX (1895), 34-37.

two evidently continued to practice,[108] while De Martel had in addition a career in public life.[109] Yet it still seemed relevant to Gassendi and Mersenne to encourage them to translate and study Hobbes's schemes for a political science.[110] It still seemed worthwhile to Du Verdus and Sorbière to spend much of their time in making the translations. And it still seemed relevant to all these scientists to study and correspond about Hobbes's political works as soon as they appeared.[111]

The concern to establish a philosophy of politics had not yet lost its place in the general strategy of enquiry into the philosophy of nature. Although the specialised researches of the Academy of Science were to replace the eclecticism of the earlier Academies within the decade, this seems to have reflected not the prevailing mood among scientists, but rather a conscious attempt to limit their range of studies. Although the major achievements of the earlier Academies were already in the field of specialised research, this had not yet come to claim their exclusive attention. It is here that Hobbes seems to belong. In his contacts with the Scientific Academies, as much as in his own systematic enquiries into the nature of Man and Society, he can be seen to fit into that phase of the Scientific Revolution which had not yet relinquished its hope of taking all knowledge to be its province.

QUENTIN SKINNER
Cambridge University

[108] Du Prat addressed by Sorbière 1659 as "medicin du Roy". *Lettres et Discours*, p. 64. De Martel spoken of as doctor, 1659, when Oldenburg visited Montmor Academy. Brown, p. 141.
[109] Samuel Sorbière, "Praefatio in qua de Vita, et Moribus Petri Gassendi disseritur", in Gassendi, *Opera Omnia*, 1, Sig. ĩ, 2b., referred to De Martel as a man whose "concern with public affairs has not prevented him from taking an active part in philosophical study". Translation mine.
[110] Mersenne to Sorbière, 1646, MSS Bibliothèque Nationale, cited in Lenoble, p. 577.
[111] De Martel was "one of the first men to read" *De Cive*, according to Pintard, p. 332. Fermat read it within a month or two of its first appearance. See Fermat to Mersenne, 1642, in *Œuvres de Fermat*, II, 243–44.

[8]

Grotius, Carneades and Hobbes*

RICHARD TUCK*

In the course of the philosophical reflections which constitute the *Prolegomena* to his *De Iure Belli ac Pacis*, Grotius singled out two figures of antiquity for particular attack. One was Aristotle, and the anti-Aristotelian character of his work was well-known to contemporaries and has been obvious to most subsequent commentators.[1] But the other was Carneades, the head of the sceptical Academy, and the anti-sceptical thrust of the Grotian enterprise has been less frequently remarked on (though it too was obvious to the early-eighteenth-century 'historians of morality' such as Barbeyrac). In this paper I shall argue that it was this aspect of Grotius's theory which gave it a central importance, and which furthermore linked his programme with Hobbes's: the similarities between their views, which Grotius himself seems to have been uneasily conscious of are genuine, and vital for a full understanding of what Hobbes thought he was doing.[2]

The centrality of the attack on Carneades in the *Prolegomena* is made quite clear by Grotius himself. As he said,

> since it would be a vain Undertaking to treat of Right, if there is really no such thing; it will be necessary, in order to shew the Usefulness of our Work, and to establish it on solid Foundations, to confute here in a few Words so dangerous an Error. And that we may not engage with a Multitude at once, let us assign them an Advocate. And who more proper for this purpose than Carneades...? This Man having undertaken to dispute against Justice, that kind of it, especially, which is the Subject of this Treatise, found no Argument stronger than this. Laws (says he) were

* This paper is a revised version of one delivered at a Symposium on Grotius at the University of St. Andrews, May 1983.

* Jesus College, Cambridge.

[1] See Grotius's remark in the Prolegomena to *De Iure Belli ac Pacis* XLIII — "Truth, for the Discovery of which *Aristotle* took so great Pains, is now oppressed by nothing more than the very name of *Aristotle*". This quotation, and all subsequent quotations from the work, comes from the great English translation of Jean Barbeyrac's edition of *De Iure belli ac Pacis, The Right of War and Peace* (London 1738) p. xxviii. For the reaction of contemporaries, see Barbeyrac's notes in ibid, or J. Felden, *Annotata in Hug. Grotium, De Iure Belli ac Pacis* (Amsterdam 1653).

[2] I have enlarged on this aspect of the matter in my paper "Optics and Sceptics: The Philosophical Foundations of Hobbes's Political Thought".

instituted by Men for the sake of Interest; and hence it is that they are different, not only in different Countries, according to the Diversity of their Manners; but often in the same Country, according to the Times. As to that which is called NATURAL RIGHT, *it is a mere Chimera. Nature prompts all Men, and in general all Animals, to seek their own particular Advantage: So that either there is no Justice at all, or if there is any, it is extreme Folly, because it engages us to procure the Good of others, to our own Prejudice.*[3]

Like the confrontation with Aristotle in the same work, Grotius here spelt out in detail a confrontation which had already been present at a central point in his astonishing early work the *De Indis* (known misleadingly to modern historians as the *De Iure Praedae*). Already in 1604/5 Grotius concluded his fundamental discussion of the law of nature by remarking,

the foregoing observations show how erroneously the Academics — those masters of ignorance — have argued in refutation of justice, that the kind derived from nature looks solely to personal advantage, while civil justice is based not upon nature but merely upon opinion; for they have overlooked that intermediate aspect of justice which is characteristic of human-kind. What Grotius meant by this last remark we shall see presently.[4]

To attack Carneades in 1604 or 1625 was not of course simply to attack a long-dead classical philosopher. It was primarily to attack the modern sceptics whose appeal to contemporary intellectuals was profound — and with whom the youthful Grotius himself seems to have had some sympathy. This modern scepticism was embodied in such works as Pierre Charron's *Of Wisdom*, which first appeared in French in 1601, and was re-issued at least twelve times between 1601 and 1663; it was soon translated into English, and ran through eight editions between 1608 and 1670. There had been elements of scepticism present in humanism from its very beginnings; the repudiation of medieval *a priori* and demonstrative arguments in all fields, but especially that of ethics, had at times (for instance in the writings of Valla) a highly sceptical tinge. But earlier humanists had been saved from true scepticism by their rediscovery of the classical Aristotle. Aristotelian ethics assumed that there are real moral properties to be perceived and an intersubjectivity of morals, despite the fact that there can be no *a priori* and demonstrative arguments about

---

[3] *The Rights of War and Peace* pp xiv/xv (Prolegomena V).
[4] *De Iure Praedae Commentarius* I, A translation by G. L. Williams (Oxford 1950) p. 13. Grotius in his letters about this work always refers to it as e.g. his "De rebus Indicis opusculum" (*Briefwisseling* I ed. Molhuysen, 's-Gravenhage 1928, p. 72).

ethical matters — Aristotle had no less of a belief in objective moral standards than a driving instructor has in objective standards of good driving, though both would deny that their subject can be taught through *a priori* and deductive argument. Aristotelian physics was based on a similar realism — in fact (in modern philosophical terms) a 'naive' realism, for it assumed that the world is at least roughly as it is perceived, and that there are real properties of objects which can be perceived veridically by a human observer. Unlike ethics, however, physics was for Aristotle a demonstrative science.[5]

What was new about late sixteenth-century scepticism was its avowedly anti-Aristotelian character. As Charron said, Aristotle 'hath uttered more grodse absurdities than [all philosophers], and is at no agreement with himelf, neither doth he know many times where he is'.[6] The sceptical attack on Aristotle's physics concentrated on the uncertainty of sense-perception; as Charron again said,

> the eie pressed downe and shut, seeth otherwise than in ordinary state; the eare stopt, receiveth the obiects otherwise than when it is open; an infant seeth, knoweth, tasteth, otherwise than a man; a man than an olde man; a sound than a sicke; a wise than a foole. In this great diversitie and contrarietie what shall we hold for certain?

There might be properties of objects of the kind which the Aristotelian talked about, but the sceptic believed that there is no secure criterion for distinguishing, veridical perceptions from illusory ones. The wise man simply has to suspend judgement in physical matters. This was the conclusion the sceptics reached also in ethics, but on rather different grounds. Here, they emphasised the variety of human moral and legal beliefs and practices — 'there is no opinion held by all, or currant in all places, none that is not debated and disputed, that hath not another held and maintained quite contrarie unto it'.[7] Since there is no criterion for determining what is correct in this multiplicity of beliefs, the wise man will not choose his actions according to some universal canon of rectitude but will use a lower-level principle — primarily, obedience to the customs and laws of his own society.

---

[5] The best account of this aspect of Aristotle's ethics is R. Sorabji, *Necessity, Cause and Blame* (London 1980); for a short account of Aristotle's naive realism in physics see W. K. C. Guthrie, *A History of Greek philosophy* VI (Cambridge 1981) pp. 294-5.

[6] P. Charron, *Of Wisdome*, London n.d. (before 1612) sig. a7v. What I say here is based on my discussion of the same topic in my paper on "Optics and Sceptics" referred to above, n.2.

[7] Ibid p. 42.

In politics this attitude was usually linked to an enthusiasm for the works of Machiavelli or the theorists of a quasi-Machiavellian 'political science' such as Lipsius. The impossibility of a true and definite moral knowledge put a great weight on the avowedly uncertain and non-theoretical maxims which made up this prudential tradition of political science, since they constituted an appropriate set of principles by which a sceptic could live. Thus a sceptical prince, at least in Charron's eyes, turned out to be very close to a Machiavellian prince: for example, discussing the rule of law he remarked,

> to dispatch and secretly to put to death, or otherwise without forme of iustice, some certaine man that is troublesome and dangerous to the state, and who well deserveth death, but they cannot without trouble and danger be enterprised and repressed by an ordinarie course; herin there is nothing violated but the forme. And the prince, is he not above formes?[9]

In theology, to consider the last feature of late-sixteenth-century scepticism which will be relevant to my theme, the sceptic was led naturally to what is usually termed a "fideistic" position, namely that there are no rational grounds for a belief in any religion. As Charron said in one of his most famous phrases, "all religions have this in them, that they are strange and horrible to the common sense".[10] But just as the wise man was not free to pick any moral belies he chose, so he was not free to pick any religious beliefs; in another work Charron argued that there were important political and prudential reasons for maintaining religious beliefs in a community, and that in general Christianity (and specifically *Catholic* Christianity) was the best bet. But there could be no rational proof of the existence of God: "every deity who can be proved and established by reason . . . is a false and not a true deity.'" This view became surprisingly popular among Catholics, and Popkin has argued that even Bellarmine endorsed it.[12]

This complex of beliefs became plausible wherever men had to cope with the state structures thrown up in the aftermath of the sixteenth-century wars of religion. Those powerful states, resting on an open and deep-

---

[8] Ibid p. 238.

[9] Ibid p. 362.

[10] Ibid p. 277.

[11] "Toute Deité, qui se prouve & s'establit par raison, . . . est false & non vraye Deite". P. Charron, *Les Trois Veritez* (2nd ed. Bordeaux 1595) sig. B2 (my translation).

[12] R. Popkin, *Te History of Scepticism from Erasmus to Spinoza* (Berkeley 1979) pp. 68-73. This work is of course the major guide to this whole area.

ly-entrenched military force, had come into being to secure a balance between irreconcilable confessional groups; their legitimacy could not be that of the pre-Reformation monarchy, since they each now contained fundamentally opposed ideologies in an uneasy relationship. For the men involved in running these states, a strong commitment to one of these ideologies would have represented a betrayal of their function: their job was to keep the society going, and to suspend judgement over the issues in dispute within it. The classic illustration of this is early-seventeenth-century France; modern scepticism found its major exponents there, and the career of someone like Richelieu (who protected and advanced many of the sceptics and *libertins erudits*) shows how a disengagement from traditional moral and political theories went along with a clear-headed use of the techniques of a manipulative political science. "In matters of state, the weakest are always wrong" observed Richelieu to Grotius in 1625[13] — a remark which could have come straight from Carneades (or even Thrasymachus). But even in the United Provinces the same attitudes could be found: Oldenbarnevelt was a man in many ways cast in the same mould as Richelieu or Olivares, running a pluralist state like theirs, and it is not surprising that the should have held that "to know nothing is the safest faith".[14]

For most of the interesting philosophers of early-seventeenth-century Europe, the sceptics' attack on traditional Aristotelianism was definitive. There could be no easy rejection of scepticism in favour of a simple dogmatism. But equally, most of them seem to have come to feel that scepticism needed some kind of refutation — a refutation that took its arguments seriously but transcended them. This became a self-conscious and fully-developed programme for the first time only in France in the 1620s and 1630s, when a group of philosophers round Marin Mersenne set out to try to put all the sciences on a modern, post-sceptical foundation (a group whose most famous members were Descartes, Gassendi and Hobbes, but that programme seemed plausible only because there already existed examples of modern sciences which met the requirements, though without the explicit and general philosophical underpinning which could now be given to them. The first significant modern refutations of scepticism had come from people working in narrower fields than these philo-

---

[13] In materie van staet de swackste altijdt ongelijck moet en hebben. Grotius' rather feeble reply was, "God and Time would bring the truth to light" (Godt ende de tijdt de waerheyt souden ontdecken). Grotius *Briefwisseling,* II p. 448.

[14] J. den Tex, *Oldenbarnevelt*, I (Cambridge 1973) p. 7.

sophers: from men like Galileo in the case of physics, and like Grotius in the case of ethics and politics. But, before either the new post-sceptical sciences or the post-sceptical philosophies had been developed, former sympathisers of the sceptics had begun to feel troubled. A good illustration of this is provided by a book published in the year in which Grotius began work on the *De Iure Praedae* — Lipsius's *Manductio ad Stoicam philosophiam*. In his famous *De Constantia* of 1584, Lipsius had depicted the wise man as disengaged from passionate political involvement: patriotism was a dangerous emotion and political communities existed purely for the selfish interests of individuals. Although he produced copious citations from Stoics to support this, the picture he drew was one which had great appeal to sceptics such as Charron, who in turn quoted extensively from the work in his *De la Sagesse*. Twenty years later, however, in his *Manductio*, Lipsius crisply distinguished between the various ancient schools of philosophy (itself a rather unusual move at this date) and made clear the incompatibility between Stoicism and Scepticism. Seneca had attacked the sceptics for holding that "the whole universe is a vain and deceptive shadow" — "I cannot readily say whether I am more vexed at those who would have it that we know nothing, or with those who would not leave us even this privilege" — and Lipsius endorsed his criticisms.[15] But he could go no further: the ancient sources upon which he relied did not contain any systematic and high-level critique of scepticism by a Stoic. The two principal works on scepticism in antiquity, the treatises of Sextus Empiricus and Cicero's *Academica*, both represent the sceptics' arguments against their opponents and not (or at least not as fully) *vice versa*. What Lipsius did was to point to the possibility that a refutation of scepticism could come from a broadly Stoic direction. and Grotius almost immediately made that possibility actual.

Grotius's first exercise in moral and political theory, in his astonishingly precocious career, was by no means opposed to the intellectual culture of Montaigne, Charron and the early Lipsius. We possess only one book of his *Parallela Rerumpublicarum*, on which he was working in 1602, and a few letters relating to it. But its general character is clear: it was an elaborate discussion of the dissimilarities in institutions and moral outlook between different societies (in the book which we possess, the Athenians, the Romans and the Dutch, though in an earlier book he seems to have

---

[15] J. Lipsius, *Manductionis ad Stoicam Philosophiam Libri Tres* (2nd ed. Antwerp 1610) p. 76, quoting Seneca, *Epistulae Morales* LXXXVIII (I have quoted the Loeb translation).

discussed the Cretans, the Spartans and the Carthaginians).[16] The dis-similarities are explained in terms of a kind of Bodinian climatics, the history of the various societies and (perhaps most originally, and a sign of what was to be a consistent feature of Grotius's historical writings) their different economies. If, as Grotius argued, our moral outlook is so tightly conditioned by the material circumstances of our society, then the prospect for traditional moral realism is poor indeed: the wise man will inevitably do what the sceptic recommended, and stick closely to the local customs and beliefs of his community. At the beginning of his twenties, it would have been safe to predict that Grotius would turn out to be the Dutch equivalent of one of the French *libertins erudits*.

But in March 1605 Grotius could write to his German admirer Lingels-heim, to whom he had lent part of the *Parallela* when he visited The Hague in the spring of 1603 that now "it begins to displease its author".[17] He had begun work on a very different kind of treatise which exposed the inadequacy of the views contained in the *Parallela*. This was his treatise *De Indis*, christened by its modern editors *De Iure Praedae*, written both to persuade Dutch public opinion that the sizure of Portugese ships in the East Indies by ships of the Dutch East India Company was legitimate, and to demonstrate to an international audience (particularly the Spaniards) that the Dutch activity was legitimate. It is significant that it was the problem of colonial competition, of the clash between states, that prompted Grotius to think in a new way: if moral relativism was true, then there was a sharp disjunction between how the wise lived within his community and how he lived outside it. The sceptic could explain and defend adherence to the conventions of a particular society, but he could offer no such advice to the man obliged to navigate not just the oceans of the world but all its different moralities as well. The familiar response to the sceptic, that no one can actually *live* their scepticism, took on a new force in this context.[18]

---

[16] Grotius, *Parallelon Rerumpublicarum Liber Tertius* I ed. J. Meerman (Haarlem 1801) p. 15; see also his letter to Bertius comparing the Roman constitution with that of Athens and Sparta, September 4 1602 (*Briefwisseling* I p. 29). Lingelsheim, who borrowed part of the complete work (probably Liber Tertius) and had discussed the whole enterprise with Grotius, described it in April 1603 as a work "de patria sua Hollandia" — so it is possible that some of what later appeared in the *De Antiquitate Reipublicae Batavicae* was originally incorporated in it. A. Reifferscheid ed., *Briefe G. M. Lingelsheims, M. Berneggers und ihrer freunde* (Heilbronn 1889) p. 10.

[17] "Parallela . . . quae sane auctori suo displicere coeperunt". *Briefwisseling* I p. 52.

[18] See M. F. Burnyeat, "Can the Sceptic Live his Scepticism?" in *Doubt and Dogmatism. Studies in Hellenistic Epistemology* ed. M. Schofield et al. (Oxford 1980) pp. 20-53.

Superficially, what Grotius did in the *De Iure Praedae* was to reinstate a pre-Renaissance way of talking about ethics and politics. He quotes extensively from scholastic writers, and it was easy for modern commentators on Grotius to fall into the error of assuming that he was simply reviving their views. In fact, as we shall see, he was producing a very different kind of theory. But the references to scholastic writers signal two things. One is simply that he was writing in part for a Spanish audience, and therefore chose to use as authorities figures who were still influential in the Spanish universities.[19] But the other is that he was once again introducing into European political thought the idea of a demonstrative and *a priori* science — the continual goal of late-medieval writers on the law of nature and the main casualty of the Renaissance. He outlined his own methodology, and made clear its fundamentally anti-Aristotelian character (at least, as Aristotle was understood by humanists), as follows.

> *First, let us see what is true universally and as a general proposition; then, let us gradually narrow this generalization, adapting it to the special nature of the case under consideration. Just as the mathematicians customarily prefix to any concrete demonstration a preliminary statement of certain broad axioms on which all persons are easily agreed, in order that there may be some fixed point from which to trace the proof of what follows, so shall we point out certain rules and laws of the most general nature, presenting them as preliminary assumptions which need to be recalled rather than learned for the first time, with the purpose of laying a foundation upon which our other conclusions may safely rest.*[20]

And indeed, the whole work is tightly organised as a series of discussions round nine fundamental Rules and thirteen associated Laws. In the writings of the scholastics, their concentration on the law of nature as a foundation for their arguments had led them to blur the distinction between the "practical" sciences such as ethics and the "theoretical" sciences

---

[19] Grotius said later of his *Mare Liberum* (which was of course extracted from the *De Iure Praedae*) that it was designed "to give us courage, in case anyone resigned a manifestly just cause, and to see if we could get the Spaniards to modify their pursuit of a case which had been weakened not just by cogent arguments but by the authority of their own people" (partem eius commentarii, . . . seorsim edere statui *Maris Liberi* nomine, hoc animo ac spe, ut et nostris animum adderem ne quid de manifestissimo iure decederent, et experirer an ab Hispanis obtineri posset ut causam non tantum validissimis argumentis sæ et popularium suorum auctoritate jugulatam agerent paulo remissius". Grotius, *Defensio Capitis Quinti* in S. Muller, *Mare Clausum. Bijdrage tot de Geschiedenis der Rivaliteit van Engeland en Nederland in de Zeventiende Eeuw* (Amsterdam 1872) p. 332, my translation.

[20] Grotius, *De Iure Praedae* I p. 7.

such as physics or mathematics — according to Aquinas, the distinction was merely that in the practical sciences deductions from the fundamental and *a priori* axioms were more difficult and contentious than in the theoretical sciences.[21] Grotius's return to the law of nature as the basis for his discussion led him to make the same move, and to instate mathematics as the methodological model for the human sciences — a development which was to determine more than anything else the character of seventeenth-century European political thought.

But though he shared this broad objective with the scholastics, his manner of securing it was quite different. No medieval writer had had to confront scepticism — even Ockhamism was not the same kind of challenge to ethical theories as Pyrrhonism was to be in the sixteenth century. Consequently, they had simply not been pushed on the question of ethical relativism. Thus Aquinas in his *Secunda Secundae* could account for all the standard moral virtues as aspects of the law of nature without being in any way troubled by the obvious acceptability of such vices as greed (or even more idolatry) in many human societies.[22] The apparatus of the Aristotelian vices and virtues was accepted by most scholastic writers as an accurate account of a universal morality, even though they wished to put it on a theoretical and not a practical basis. Merely to restate the scholastic theories (as late-sixteenth-century Iberian scholastics themselves found) was thus not sufficient to cope with the sceptical challenge that the Aristotelian virutes were local and not obvious to non-Europeans.

Grotius's answer was first to make a number of what seemed self-evident and uncontentious propositions about the nature of law, what he termed his "Rules":

I. What God has shown to be his will, that is law.

II. What the common consent of mankind has shown to be the will of all, that is law.

III. What each individual has indicated to be his will, that is law with respect to him.

IV. What the commonwealth has indicated to be its will, that is law for the whole body of citizens. . . (etc.)[23]

These propositions avoided talking (for example) about reason as a source of law, and thus could reasonably play the role of uncontentious primary

---

[21] Aquinas, *Summa Theologiae* 1a2æ94.4 (Blackfriars ed. xxviii pp. 86-7).

[22] See *ibid.* 2a2æ47-170 (Blackfriars ed. xxxvi-xliv).

[23] Grotius, *De Iure Praedae* I p. 369.

principles. The problem was going to be their content, for the sceptic had hitherto denied that any universal promulgations of the first two kinds could actually be detected in the world. The crucial move which Grotius made was to accept at this point the force of the sceptical argument, and to concede that indeed the only genuinely universal human trait, and therefore the only one which a God could legitimately be thought of as instilling in all men, was self-interest.

> *Since God fashioned creation and willed its existence, every individual part thereof has received from Him certain natural properties whereby that existence may be preserved and each part may be guided for its own good, in conformity, one might say, with the fundamental law inherent in its origin. From this fact the old poets and philosophers have rightly deduced that love, whose primary force and action are directed to self-interest, is the first principle of the whole natural order. Consequently, Horace should not be censured for saying, in imitation of the Academics, that expediency might perhaps be called the mother of justice and equity.*[24]

Upon this basic principle of self-interest, he argued, were grounded the first two principles of the law of nature (and hence the first two Laws which he set out as corollaries to his Rules): "It shall be permissible to defend one's own life and to shun that which threatens to prove injurious" and "It shall be permissible to acquire for oneself, and to retain, those things which are useful for life." As he said, "on this point the Stoics, the Epicureans and the Peripatetics are in complete agreement, and apparently even the Academics have entertained no doubt.[25]

What they *had* entertained doubts about was the extension of this self-love to the love of others. Grotius went on to argue that indeed men do have a universal desire for a social life; but he interpreted this desire in what was by traditional standards an extremely minimalist manner. We all find in society a degree of protection and comfort, which leads to the third and fourth laws of nature being respectively "Let no one inflict injury upon his fellow" and "Let no one seize possession of that which has been taken into the possession of another." Grotius was quite clear, however, that self-interest is the primary and over-riding principle, and that altruism must in some way be explicable in terms of self-interest.

> *The order of presentation of the first set of laws and of those following immediately thereafter has indicated that one's own good takes precedence over the good of another person's — or, let us say, it indicates that by nature's ordinance each*

---

[24] Ibid p. 9.
[25] Ibid p. 11.

individual should be desirous of his own good fortune in preference to that of another... Nevertheless, in questions involving a comparison between the good of single individuals and the good of all ..., the more general concept should take precedence on the ground that it includes the good of individuals as well. In other words, the cargo cannot be saved unless the ship is preserved... Livy summed up this view in the following concise statement: "While the state remains unharmed, it will easily answer for the safety of private property too. In nowise will you be able to protect your own interests by betraying the public interest".[26]

It is important also to stress that according to Grotius this natural sense of society with all other men does not entail any obligation to *help* them, or to foster the kind of moral life which Aristotle envisaged for his ζῷον πολιτικόν. It merely entails an obligation to refrain from harming them. Only in organised states does something more emerge:

There are laws peculiar to the civil covenant, ... which extend beyond the laws already set forth, as follows: Individual citizens should not only refrain injuring other citizens, but should furthermore protect them, both as a whole and as individuals; secondly, Citizens should not only refrain from seizing one another's possessions, ... but should furthermore contribute individually both that which is necessary to other individuals and that which is necessary to the whole.[27]

The natural society of men is one in which individuals pursue their own interests up to the point at which such a pursuit actually deprives another of something which they possess; it is not one of benevolence, as we would customarily understand the term.

It is this minimalist character of the principle of sociability which made it in Grotius's eyes a principle which the moral relativist could accept, and which could therefore underpin the "intermediate" kind of justice, "characteristic of human-kind", which he sought to establish in opposition to the sceptics. We can put it more clearly by asking if we can genuinely conceive of a society in which its members' lives, and the "things useful for life" which they have acquired, are under threat. These basic commodities are the things possession of which is guaranteed by the "sociable" laws of nature, and it is indeed hard to imagine a society in which they are not secure. Grotius could therefore reply convincingly to the relativist that there are indeed some moral universals, for there has been and could be no society in which these minimum requirements are not met. He could of

[26] Ibid pp 21/22.
[27] Ibid p. 21.

course not reply in this way to a more sophisticated sceptic (of, say, the Human type), for whom the observed fact of ethical variety was not a particularly important argument; but moral relativism as we have seen was at the heart of late-sixteenth and early seventeenth-century ethical scepticism, and Grotius's argument is reasonably effective in that context.

It is important, moreover, to stress that his was an argument which *transcended* but did not straightforwardly *refute* the sceptic. The sceptical argument against traditional moral theories still stood: there *was* an enormous variety in human moral and political practices, and, outside an extremely slim core, what people believed and did in their societies was up to them. Whatever was possible within a society was *ipso facto* legitimate, and Grotius was able to use empirical evidence drawn from his enormous knowledge of world history to show that all kinds of surprising practices were compatible with social life. It was because of this minimalist moral theory that such evidence (the use of which some writers on Grotius have found puzzling) was relevant, and it remained an important way of arguing for all writers in the seventeenth-century natural law tradition.

As a consequence of this fundamental theoretical position, Grotius was led straightforwardly to construct a new and distinctive account of civil society. If there were no basic natural laws other than the ones we have surveyed (for all the other ones in the *De Iure Praedae* derive from those four), then the world which men inhabited by nature was one without civil institutions. They possessed property in themselves and in possessions necessary for life, but anything more complex had to be understood as the result of men bargaining in various ways with these possessions. A central claim of the work was thus that the rights enjoyed by a state or its government could not be different in kind from the rights enjoyed by an individual in the state of nature. "Just as every right of the magistrate comes to him from the state, so has the same right come to the state from private individuals".[28] One of the reasons why this had seemed implausible to earlier writers was that princes or supreme magistrates possess the power to punish offenders, and this seemed to be a special right which no individual could possess; but Grotius was quite clear that this was not so. The first four laws of nature together entailed a right to exact restitution for wrongs committed against oneself, and since as he said "an injury inflicted upon one individual is the concern of all ... primarily because of the example set", each person in a state of nature had an interest in restraining or

[28] Ibid. p. 92.

punishing anyone who infringed another's rights and deprived them of their possessions. He supported this claim with the identical argument that John Locke was later to use in the same context, namely that modern states claim the right to punish foreigners for their transgressions, and that such a right must arise from the law of nature and not from civil law.[29]

Grotius thus drew the blueprint according to which most of the interesting political theories of the next century were constructed. A state of nature was first to be described, in which men would enjoy the same kind of moral status that they would subsequently enjoy in civil society – the "rights" or "property" which they possessed were the *same kind of things* as the "right" or "property" possessed in a city, and not (as Rousseau most famously later, and in direct opposition to Grotius, claimed[30]) *categorically* different. Out of this state of nature, a civil society would then emerge to protect and benefit natural men. There were various general constraints upon what kind of civil society was possible, but a far greater variety of social forms was possible than had ever occurred to Aristotelian writers. This was the modern political science, attacked by all the opponents of the modern world such as Robert Filmer – who saw clearly enough how his patriarchalism was supported by Aristotle but threatened by Grotius, Selden and Hobbes (for what could be more local than a patriarchal monarch?)[31] And its modernity consisted precisely in its transcendence of scepticism, so that it could appear not narrowly dogmatic but (once its implications were grasped) a genuinely universal way of thinking about politics.

Although Grotius published only part of this remarkable work, in the form of *Mare Liberum* (1609), the basic arguments as I have depicted them are presented unchanged, and indeed greatly clarified, in *De Iure Belli ac Pacis*. In one respect they now appeared even more unassailable from the sceptic, for Grotius argued in a notorious phrase that the laws of nature would be valid "though we should even grant, what without the greatest Wickedness cannot be granted, that there is no God, or that he takes no Care of human Affairs".[32] The point of this was that if it is true that the minimalist law of nature represents what is *necessary* for the existence of a

---

[29] Ibid.

[30] This is of course the burden of *The Social Contract*, which opens with an eloquent attack on Grotius.

[31] See Filmer's *Patriarcha*, chapters VIII and IX for his attack on Grotius and Chapter XII for his use of Aristotle (in *Patriarcha and Other Political Works of Sir Robert Filmer*, ed. P. Laslett, Oxford 1949).

[32] *The Rights or War and Peace* p. xix (Prolegomena XI).

society, that is, as we have seen, that we cannot conceive of a society in which it does not operate, then equally we cannot conceive of God creating such a society. All beliefs about God's existence or character, of the kind which the sceptic might question, were thus irrelevant to ethics. Some Ockhamists had argued the same about the necessity of the natural law, but Grotius gave a very different content to the argument.

This issue has been, I suppose, the most discussed of all matters in Grotian scholarship, and it is worth a brief examination. His developed view appears first in his theological writings of the second decade of the century, and particularly in his *Defensio Fidei Catholicae* of 1617; there, he argued that

> *As in physics, so in moral matters, something is called "natural" either properly or less properly. "Natural" in physics is properly used about the necessary essence of anything — as when we say that a living creature must have sensations. It is less properly used about something which is convenient or suitable, as when we say that it is natural for a man to use his right hand. Similarly in morality, those things are properly natural which necessarily follow from the relationship of the things themselves to a rational nature — such as the immorality of lying. Other uses, as when we say that a son should succeed his father, are less proper.*[33]

Much of what God did could be described as "natural" only in this improper sense, and Grotius preferred to describe such non-necessary acts (including such things as the punishment of sinners) as part of God's *positive* law. These were after all precisely the acts of God around which theological disputes of the kind he was arguing against, had tended to cluster — once again, Grotius was proposing that the possibility of genuine dispute showed *ipso facto* that the matter under dispute was not part of the law of nature, since if it was, disagreement would be strictly inconceivable.

So clear-headed was Grotius about this, that he abandoned vast areas of traditional theology. First, the Decalogue could not be an account of natural law. None of his scholastic predecessors could have gone so far, but Grotius was prepared to assert in *De Iure Belli ac Pacis* that the

---

[33] Naturale autem aliquid, ut in physicis, ita in moralibus aut proprie aut minus proprie dicitur. Naturale in physicis proprie est, quod rei cuique essentiae necessario coheret, ut animanti sentire: minus proprie vero, quod alicui naturae conveniens & quasi accommodatum est, ut homini dextra uti. Sic ergo in moralibus sunt quaedam proprie naturalia, quae necessario sequuntur ex rerum ipsarum relatione ad naturas rationales, ut perjurium esse illicitum: quaedam vero improprie, ut filium patri succedere. Grotius, *Opera Theologica* III (London 1679) p. 311 (*Defensio Fidei Catholicae de Satisfactione Christi* cap. III), my translation.

Commandments were given by God solely to the Jews, and that they did not differ in any formal respect from the mass of Mosaic ceremonial and judicial law.[34] Only an independent comparison of the Decalogue with the law of nature as elucidated by Grotius could show which of its precepts were natural; Grotius eventually concluded that the prohibition on idolatry and the command to keep the Sabbath could not be seen as part of law of nature, since plenty of societies has worshipped idols and worked seven days a week.[34a] His Dutch contemporaries were fully aware of the novelty and danger of this view: when Grotius's friend the Remonstrant J. A. Corvinus described the Decalogue as divine positive law and not the law of nature in a tract of 1622 defending the Remonstrants' theology, the orthodox Antonius Walaeus (who had been the minister at Oldenbarnevelt's execution) exploded that this was doctrine "hitherto unheard of among Christians" — and he was probably right.[35]

Second, even a belief in a Judaeo-Christian God was not entailed by the law of nature. The only propositions about God to which all men would assent, and whose denial was fundamentally incompatible with life, were "that there is a deity, (one or more I shall not now consider) and that this deity has the care of human affairs." "Those who first attempt to destroy these Notions ought, on the Account of human Society in general, which they thus, without any just Grounds, injure, to be restrained".[36] Christians believed more than this, and were justified in acting on their beliefs, but they could not claim that their Christianity was founded on the law of nature — that was a local error, once agan. They might claim that it was founded on some positive law of God given to a particular community (as had been the positive law of the Jews), but nothing more.[37] Grotius was of course not consistent here in his minimalism, since it is clear at least to us that an irreligious society is conceivable, but the idea that a religious belief is necessary to sustain social life was so widespread in the early seventeenth century that it is not surprising that Grotius endorsed it. The first person to

---

[34] *The Rights of War and Peace* pp. 17-23 (I.1.16 and 17).

[34a] See his later *Explicatio Decalogi, opera Neologica* I pp. 34-51.

[35] Legem vero moralem esse legem positivam ... inauditum est hactenus inter Christanos. A. Walaeus, *Responsio ad Censuram Ioannis Arnoldi Corvini*, in *Opera Omnia* II (Leyden 1643) p. 168. Corvinus's remark was in his reply to Du Moulin's *Anatomy of Arminanism*, his *Petri Molinaei Novi Anatomici Mala Encheiresis* (Frankfurt 1622) p. 160.

[36] *The Rights Of War and Peace* pp. 444 and 445 (II.20.46).

[37] See ibid p. 31 — "I shall not suppose that, which others do, that there is nothing in the Gospel (except Points of Faith, and the Sacraments) but what is injoyned by the Law of Nature; for that, in the Sense that most Divines take it, I cannot think true." (I.2.6).

question it seems in fact to have been his contemporary Paolo Sarpi.[38]

Grotius's controversial claim that the law of nature was in some sense independent of God's will, while it resembled the Ockhamist theory, was thus used to make a very different point from any which his medieval predecessors had made — and it was this different point which was the most controversial aspect of his argument. His intention was not so much to provide a particular philosophical account of the epistemological status of the law of nature, as to make a strong distinction between God's natural and positive laws, and to place in the second category much of what traditional theology had rather loosely left in the first. Anything which the sceptic might question about religion or God's will was positive law, to be defended on the avowedly low-level basis of history or authority (as Grotius defended much of Christianity in his *De Veritate Religionis Christianae*); only the unquestionable was the law of nature.

It is clear from what I have said that Grotius's political philosophy was indeed a plausible candidate from the role of the modern political science which the post-sceptical philosophers of Europe sought. In the last part of this paper I want to sketch one, surprising, way in which it received the general philosophical underpinning with which Grotius himself had not provided it (nor, it seems, had sought to do so).

The process of providing philosophical foundations for this modern political science did not, of course, leave the science itself unaltered. We are not to expect an immaculately Grotian theory erected on some suitable post-sceptical metaphysics. The analogy is with the philosophers' approach to Galilei; universally praised, at least by the members of the Mersenne circle such as Gassendi, Descartes and Hobbes, he seemed to provide a new physics that was clearly correct in its broad outlines. But he philosophers were not above proposing new physical theories or correcting aspects of Galilean physics, if doing so permitted them to put forward a coherent and comprehensive metaphysics.

The first surprising fact is that only Hobbes, in this generation of philosophers, was able to provide a post-sceptical ethics and politics *at all* (Gassendi did so only after reading Hobbes). The revealing contrast is with Descartes: both claimed to have put human knowledge as a whole on a new and "scientific" foundation, but Descartes utterly failed to deliver on his promise to produce an ethics to match his physics. He remained one of the only two major philosophers in history not to have written systematically

---

[38] See D. Wootton, *Paolo Sarpi. Between Renaissance and Enlightenment* (Cambridge 1983).

on ethics or politics (the other, interestingly, being Wittgestein). The difference between Descartes and Hobbes in this area is largely due to Descartes's concentration on the solution to what he took to be the fundamental sceptical problem, namely the existence of a material world. The prominence he gave to this issue was unparalleled in any ancient or sixteenth-century sceptical text — as Burnyeat has pointed out, the ancient sceptics did not in general doubt that there *was* a material world, they merely doubted that we could know the *truth* about it.[39] In his *Discourse on the Method* Descartes set out a familiar set of sceptical doubts, and a familiar set of sceptical answers as his provisional epistemology and morality — in particular, to suspend judgement in the physical sciences, and to live as a loyal but fundamentally disengaged citizen of his commonwealth — but he implied that all these doubts could be resolved if the fundamental issue of the material existence of the world was established. In fact, of course, *ancient* scepticism remained unrefuted by Descartes: the material existence of the world does not entail that moral relativism is untrue. So Descartes despite his intentions remained a pretty pure sceptic in these matters — a point underlined by the fact that the only political philosopher he was at all drawn to was Machiavelli.[40]

Hobbes had a much wider enterprise in view. After reading the *Discourse,* he too became interested in the hyperbolical doubt, but it never assumed the overwhelming importance for him that it had for Descartes. Hobbes remained anxious to provide a post-sceptical science for each area of human concern. He provided it in physics through an *a priori* demonstration of the reality of moving material objects and the validity of the Galilean laws of motion; in ethics, he sought to provide a similarly *a priori* basis for a broadly Grotian theory, through showing how his own account of the way in which men's mind work confirmed answer of the Grotian kind to the sceptic.

This is, I know, a contentious and surprising claim. But we can see one central and obvious way in which Hobbes was influenced by the Grotian inheritance if we consider the most distinctive feature of his theory (present in all three statements of it, *The Elements of Law* (1640), *De Cive* (1642) and *Leviathan* itself). This is a distinction between a state of nature in which men possess natural rights, and a state of civil society which they construct using those rights. As Spinoza later perceived, in terms of Hobbes's own

---

[39] See M. Burnyeat, "Idealism and Greek Philosophy: What Descartes Saw and Berkeley Missed" in G. Vesey ed., *Idealism Past and Present* (Cambridge 1982), pp. 19-50.
[40] See G. Rodis-Lewis, *La Morale de Descartes* (Paris 1957) pp. 100-5.

59

theory this is an unnecessary apparatus: for what Hobbes argues, as we all know, is that it is in men's interest to submit to a sovereign and to allow it to govern them (up to the point at which it actually threatens their life). If this is in men's interest, then that is all that needs to be said: there is simply no point in depicting a state of nature which is then superseded in some way.[41] But if Hobbes believed that the modern political science had to take this form, and that his task was to provide it with a philosophical underpinning, then we can see why he argued in this way.

Moreover the specific arguments upon which Hobbes based his transcendence of scepticism are close to the arguments which Grotius had employed. Like Grotius, Hobbes accepted the force of the sceptical case: human societies do exhibit radically different moral beliefs and practices, and for most of our moral beliefs the only justification which we can give for holding them is that they are the beliefs current in our own society. Moreover there is indeed a terrifying degree of self-interest in human affairs. Grotius's paraphrase of Carneades, that "Nature prompts all Men, and in general all Animals, to seek their own Particular Advantage" could also be an accurate paraphrase of one of Hobbes's most famous assumptions. But, like Grotius, Hobbes believed that the very fact of human self-interest could be used as the foundation for a genuine ethical science: since (as he believed) it was a true universal, its universality confirmed by the psychological arguments that unlike Grotius he was able to deploy, and since it was possible to show that certain principles and practices followed from it, a reasonably complex (though still minimal, in comparison with traditional moralities) ethical theory was possible.

Furthermore, if we interpret Grotius's claim about human sociability in the sense in which I interpreted it earlier in this paper, namely that as an answer to the sceptical moral relativist Grotius's point is that all societies must exhibit the minimal principles of respect for life and legitimate possession, then Hobbes's whole theory emerges as an *explanation* of why that should be so, rather than as a *denial* of it. The difference between them is then that Hobbes's explanation, because of the character of his fundamental theory, and in ways I do not wish to enlarge on here, turned on the creation of a civil sovereign to ensure that the society came into being as an effective guarantor of these principles, while Grotius believed that even in the absence of such a civil society the principles would be respected — and hence could be used to handle problems of war between sovereigns. It was this which Grotius singled out as his primary criticism of *De Cive* when

---

[41] See B. de Spinoza, *The Political Works* ed. A. G. Wernham (Oxford 1958) pp. 25-7.

he read it in 1643, though he was aware that it was reasonable to criticise the book for not being fully "in accordance with my principles" — i.e. that it was indeed the same kind of enterprise as his own.[42]

But even so, the difference between them is still not all that great. Hobbes in fact argued that in a state of nature men will only attack one another if they believe that by doing so they are protecting themselves — i.e. protecting their lives or their possession of the things they judge necessary for life. And Grotius also of course believed that this was a legitimate basis for war. The difference between them in this area then narrows down to the fact that Hobbes believed that an individual's assessment of what is necessary for his protection is inherently unstable and subjective, while Grotius did not.[43] Grotius in fact conceded that it is possible for people to be mistaken in their view of what they are entitled to do, and that they cannot be blamed or punished for their mistake — so there are elements in the *De Iure Belli ac Pacis* which point straightforwardly even in the direction of this most un-Grotian side of Hobbes.[44]

Leviathan is of course a very different work from *De Iure Belli ac Pacis*, and Hobbes would make an unlikely tutelary god for a Peace Palace. But if what I have been saying is correct, the difference between the two works is more that Hobbes made theoretically coherent and explicit certain things that were implicit in Grotius, than that he *fundamentally* challenged him. The disturbing features of Hobbes' foundational enterprise were sufficient to prompt his successors in this genre — notably Cumberland, Pufendorf and Locke — to seek other ways of underpinning the modern political science. But when at the turn of the seventeenth and eighteenth centuries political philosophers looked back in an attempt to place their enterprise historically, they were all in no doubt that Grotius and Hobbes had had a common programme (though equally they were in no doubt that Hobbes had failed to make the modern science coherent). They all saw that Grotius had provided them with a political theory with which men could live in a post-sceptical world, without losing sight of the force of the sceptics' challenge to their predecessors, though they also saw that the theory was not sufficiently well-founded for the more philosophically sophisticated

---

[42] Grotius, *Epistolae* (Amsterdam 1687) pp. 951-2.

[43] Contrast Hobbes's remarks on the right of a criminal to struggle against the executioner (e.g. in his *De Cive* II.18) with Grotius's denial of precisely this right, *De Iure Belli ac Pacis* II.1.17. I enlarge on this matter in my article "Optics and Sceptics" referred to above n.2.

[44] *The Rights of War and Peace* p. 490 (II.23.13).

audience of the late seventeenth century.[45] Als Le Clerc said, in remarks well this side of idolatry, but with much force to them,

> *If he was not thoroughly acquainted with the Art of thinking justly, the Philosophy of his Time being still very obscure, he has supply'd, in a great Measure, that Defect, by the Force of his good Sense. If, without the help of Art, he has shewn so much delicacy of Taste, and true Discernment; what would he not have done, had he been more intire Master of that Art of reasoning justly, and of rightly methodizing his Thoughts, which has since prevail'd?*[46]

---

[45] This history is first outlined by Samuel Pufendorf in his *Specimen Controversiarum circa Jus Naturale ipsi nuper Motarum* (Lund 1678). The best statement of it is by Jean Barbeyrac, in the form of a preface to his French translation of Pufendorf's *De Iure Naturae et Gentium* (Paris 1709), which was translated into English as *A Historical and Critical Account of the Science of Morality* and prefaced to the fifth English language edition of Pufendorf (London 1749).

[46] [J. Le Clerc], *Parrhasiana* (Amsterdam 1699) pp. 346/7. I quote from the translation in Barbeyrac's *Historical and Critical Account* p. 67.

Part III
Fragmented Hobbesian Scholarship

[9]

THUCYDIDES AND HOBBES'S STATE OF NATURE

George Klosko and Daryl Rice

Scholars have long been aware of Thucydides' influence on Thomas Hobbes's political thought. In 1628 Hobbes published a translation of Thucydides' *History of the Pelopponsian War*.[1] In his prefatory address 'To the Readers', Hobbes discusses the value of reading Thucydides, especially the historian's vivid description of past events. By reading them, an intelligent man is able to add to his own experience.[2] It seems that Hobbes himself profited from his reading, which undoubtedly helped to shape his ideas. Scholars have noted that Hobbes's distrust of democracy was influenced by the lessons of Thucydides, [3] while his generally unsentimental view of politics no doubt bears a similar stamp. In fact, as Richard Schlatter says in his valuable article on the subject, many of Hobbes's reflections on how human beings behave 'read like generalizations from Thucydides' examples'.[4] The clearest instance is the fact that Hobbes's account of the three major sources of strife in the state of nature—competition, diffidence, and glory—is probably based on the analysis of human motives presented by the Athenians in Book I of Thucydides, who attribute their actions to 'fear, honor, and profit'.[5]

The purpose of this brief paper is to point out one particular instance of Thucydides' influence on Hobbes that has gone unnoticed. We believe it can be seen that the specific elements in Hobbes's classic description of human life in the state of nature are heavily influenced by a brief description of life among the earliest inhabitants of Hellas in Book 1 of Thucydides' *History*. We think this is worth pointing out here, not only because the description in question is one of the best known in all of political thought, but because it

---

[1] This occupies Volumes VIII and IX of *The English Works of Thomas Hobbes*, collected and edited by W. Molesworth (11 vols., London, 1839–45) (all references to Hobbes are to this edition, abbreviated *E.W.*) Hobbes's translation was reprinted in 1959, edited by David Grene, with an Introduction by B. de Jouvenal (Ann Arbor, 1959)

[2] *E.W.*, VIII, viii.

[3] See, e.g. de Jouvenal, 'Introduction', xii; R. Schlatter, 'Thomas Hobbes and Thucydides', *Journal of the History of Ideas*, 6 (1945), pp. 358–60. In his verse autobiography, Hobbes relates that he garnered an anti-democratic message from Thucydides, the propagation of which was one of his reasons for translating the work; also see *E.W.* VIII, xvi–xvii.

[4] Schlatter, 'Thomas Hobbes and Thucydides', p. 357.

[5] Schlatter, loc, cit.; Hobbes, *Leviathan*, Ch.13 (*E.W.*, III, 113); Thucydides I, 75. (Here and throughout, we use Hobbes's translation of Thucydides).

G. KLOSKO & D. RICE

affords additional evidence of Thucydides' continuing influence upon his translator.[6]

Hobbes's language in the paragraph in question is well-known. We reproduce it here, with numbered divisions for convenience of reference:

(H 1) In such condition there is no place for industry, (H 2) because the fruit thereof is uncertain: (H 3) and consequently no culture of the earth; (H 4) no navigation nor use of the commodities that may be imported by sea; (H 5) no commodious building; (H 6) no instruments of moving and removing such things as require much force; (H 7) no knowledge of the face of the earth; (H 8) no account of time; (H 9) no arts; (H 10) no letters; (H 11) no society; (H 12) and, which is worst of all, continual fear and danger of violent death; (H 13) and the life of man solitary, poor, nasty, brutish and short.[7]

As we shall see, there are no parallels in Thucydides for the details in (H 7–12), nor for the rhetoric in (H 13), but the other six details can in varying degrees be traced back to a passage early in Book I.

We reproduce the passage from Thucydides' description of the earliest Hellenes, with similar numerical divisions. The translation is Hobbes's, though it should be borne in mind that Thucydides' language is extremely dense and impossible to render literally in English.[8] Since Hobbes was of course acquainted with the original Greek, specific verbal parallels or non-parallels between this passage and the one in *Leviathan* are not as significant as they might otherwise be. The parallels are seen much more clearly by looking at Thucydides' original Greek.[9]

---

[6] Approximately twenty-three years elapsed between the publication of *Leviathan* (1651) and the translation of Thucydides.

[7] *E.W.*, III, 113.

[8] Thucydides uses some 65 Greek words, Hobbes some one hundred and seven English words. Hobbes is not alone in this expansion. All the translations checked were in a similar range: Rex Warner (Penguin edition: Baltimore, 1954): 112 words; C.F. Smith (Loeb Classics Library edition: Cambridge, Mass., 1919): 109 words; B. Jowett (Boston, 1883): 97 words; R. Crawley (used in Modern Library edition: New York, 1951): 96 words.

[9] τῆς γὰρ ἐμπορίας οὐκ οὔσης οὐδ' ἐπιμειγνύντες ἀδεῶς ἀλλήλοις
οὔτε κατὰ γῆν οὔτε διὰ θαλάσσης, νεμόμενοί τε τὰ αὐτῶν ἕκαστοι ὅσον
ἀποξῆν καὶ περιουσίαν χρημάτων
οὐκ ἔχοντες οὐδὲ γῆν φυτεύοντες, ἄδηλον ὂν ὁπότε τις ἐπελθὼν καὶ
ἀτειχίστων ἅμα ὄντων ἄλλος ἀφαιρήσεται,
τῆς τε καθ ἡμέραν ἀναγκαίου τροφῆς πανταχοῦ ἂν
ἡγούμενοι ἐπικρατεῖν οὐ χαλεπῶς ἀπανίσταντο, καὶ δι'
αὐτὸ οὔτε μεγέθει πόλεων ἴσχυον οὔτε τῇ ἄλλῃ παρασκευῇ

(T 1) For whilst traffic was not, (T 2) nor mutual intercourse but with fear, neither by sea nor land, (T 3) and every man so husbanded the ground as but barely to live upon it, (T 4) without any stock of riches, (T 5) and planted nothing; (T 6) (because it was uncertain when another should invade them and carry all away, especially not having the defence of walls); (T 7) but made account to be masters, in any place, of such necessary sustenance as might serve them from day to day: (T 8) they made little difficulty to change their habitations. (T 9) And for this cause were of no ability at all, either for greatness of cities (T 10) or other provision.[10]

We think it can be seen that the contents of the two passages are similar. Each describes the effects of overall social conditions upon a series of factors which can be distinguished: (A) work in general; (B) agriculture; (C) travel and trade; (D) construction of buildings; (E) related powers. There is also a sixth factor, (F) a brief causal explanation. These six items are taken up in the two passages respectively as follows.

(A) is cited in (H 1). The sense of 'industry' here seems to be either 'systematic work or labor', the fourth definition found in the O.E.D, a sense in which it was used (by Shakespeare, in Act III of *Cymbeline*) at least since 1611, or simply connoting application and exertion, which is the O.E.D.'s third definition, examples of which usage can be found as far back as 1531. If 'industry' is used with either sense (or with something of both senses), the thrust of (H 1) is similar to a combination of (T 3) and (T 4), i.e. that the early Hellenes scratched out a subsistence existence, and nothing more.

(B), that Hobbes's natural men and Thucydides' early Greeks did not plant crops is stated in (H 3) and (T 5).

(F), similar causal explanations for (A) and (B) are found in (H 2) and (T 6). In both cases general insecurity is to blame. Apparently, Hobbes also directly attributes all other features to this insecurity.

(C), a lack of navigation and trade, is cited in (H 4) and (T 1) and (T 2), though it should be noted that Thucydides' account is more inclusive, as there is no traffic or trade by land or sea.

(D), the lack of commodious buildings, is cited in (H 5) and (T 9), though the latter speaks of great cities rather than buildings.

The parallel in regard to (E) is a bit looser than these others. In (H 6) Hobbes speaks of a specific weakness, the inability to move and remove objects. What Thucydides has in mind in (T 10) is not clear, but the weakness is not specific. Thucydides seems to mean that, as the early Hellenes were

---

[10] Thucydides, I, 2; Hobbes, *E.W.*, VIII, 2.

unable to create great cities, they could not create anything else great either. C.F. Smith's translation more clearly captures the sense of the Greek: the Hellenes 'were not strong as regards either the size of their cities or their resources in general (*oute megethei poleon ischuon oute te alle paraskeue*)'. But however the clause is translated, the parallel is not exact.

Let us review the evidence. It seems that there are strong similarities between two passages in regard to (A), (B), (C), (D), and (F). And while the parallel concerning (E) is less strong, the two passages are similar in referring to an additional inability related to construction. In addition to this series of parallels, (F) is particularly striking, in that both Hobbes and Thucydides explain *both* a lack of economic effort in general and of agriculture in particular because of insecurity. Also in regard to (C), both thinkers mention an absense of *both* traffic and trade. Though the overall insecurity mentioned by Thucydides in (T 7) and (T 8) is not taken up by Hobbes, it seems that the rest of his description generally is. Thus, given the overall similarity of the two passages and the two striking parallels mentioned in this paragraph, it seems reasonable to conclude that Hobbes based this classic description of man in the state of nature upon this passage in Thucydides.[11]

And so we have additional evidence that, as Schlatter says, Hobbes's reading of Thucydides helped to shape 'the broad outlines and many of the

---

[11] In both *The Elements of Law* (1640) and *De Cive* (1642), there are passages that anticipate the description of the state of nature in *Leviathan*. We reproduce these: 'The estate of hostility and war being such, as thereby nature itself is destroyed, and men kill one another, (as we know also that it is, both by the experience of savage nations that live at this day, and by the histories of our ancestors the old inhabitants of Germany, and other now civil countries, where we find the people few, and short lived, and without the ornaments and comforts of life, which by peace and society are usually invented and procured) . . .' (*The Elements of Law*, I, 1, 12; *E.W.*, IV, 84–5); 'But it is easily judged how disagreeable a thing to the preservation either of mankind, or of each single man, a perpetual war is. But it is perpetual in its own nature; because in regard of the equality of those that strive, it cannot be ended by victory. For in this state the conqueror is subject to so much danger, as it were to be accounted a miracle, if any, even the most strong, should close up his life with many years and old age. They of America are examples hereof, even in this present age: other nations have been in former ages; which now indeed are become civil and flourishing, but were then few, fierce, short-lived, poor, nasty, and deprived of all that pleasure and beauty of life, which peace and society are wont to bring with them.' (*De Cive*, I, 13 *E.W.*, II, 12). The second passage clearly prefigures the description of the state of nature in *Leviathan*.

It is notable that, although Hobbes cites the experiences of various peoples in both passages, he does not mention the early Greeks. It appears, then, that in writing *Leviathan* he returned to Thucydides, in order to flesh out the brief accounts in his earlier works.

We are grateful to Maurice Goldsmith for calling our attention to these passages.

details of his own thought'.[12] To the list of details brought forward by previous scholars, we would add Hobbes's view of what life would be like under conditions of extreme vulnerability, subject to invasion at any time.

George Klosko   UNIVERSITY OF VIRGINIA
Daryl Rice   TEXAS A & I UNIVERSITY

[12] Schlatter, 'Thomas Hobbes and Thucydides', p. 362. Leo Strauss should be mentioned as a scholar who devotes significant attention to the relationship between Hobbes and Thucydides: *The Political Philosophy of Hobbes* (Oxford, 1936), while Peter Pouncey discusses it in some detail in his recent work, *The Necessities of War* (New York, 1980), though without noting the parallels in their descriptions of the state of nature (see esp. the Appendix, 'Human Nature in Hobbes').

[10]

HOBBES AND RATIONAL CHOICE THEORY

PATRICK NEAL

University of Vermont

THE depiction of the natural condition of mankind by Thomas Hobbes (Hobbes 1968) has long been a source of fascination to students of political theory. In the past two decades, the concepts and categories of rational choice theory have been increasingly employed as one means of interpreting, illuminating, and understanding Hobbes' teaching (Hampton 1986; Brams 1985: 139-46; Kavka 1983; Laver 1981: 17-18, 43-47; McLean 1981: 339-51; Taylor 1976; Gauthier 1969). The issue I propose to explore herein is that of determining the extent to which this approach does indeed succeed in bringing clearly into focus the essence of that teaching. I shall suggest that though not without value, the appropriation of Hobbes' teaching to the terms of rational choice theory reaps a good deal less than Hobbes attempted to sow.

There are a number of mundane senses in which this conclusion is at once obvious and trivial, all rooted in the fact that Hobbes, seminal thinker that he was, planted widely. To take the extreme, no one employing the conceptual framework of rational choice or game theory attempts to use this framework to say anything about Parts III ("Of a Christian Commonwealth") or IV ("Of the Kingdome of Darknesse") of *Leviathan*.[1] If the conclusion that rational choice theory fails to illuminate fully Hobbes' lessons amounted to no more than this, we would be wasting our time. But the conclusion would be significant if it turned out that aspects of Hobbes' theory which rational choice theorists themselves choose to discuss purport to illuminate resisted assimilation. I shall argue that this is just the case, especially in regard to attempts to treat Hobbes' state of nature as an exemplar of a prisoners' dilemma situation. More importantly, the conclusion would take on even greater significance if it turned out that insofar as one specified and reflected upon the *differences* (underlying the, admitted, similarities) between Hobbes' understanding of the sociopolitical world and that offered by rational choice theory, one were led to question the coherence, cogency, and ultimately the adequacy, of rational choice theory itself as an attempt to make sense of that world.

This essay suggests that this too is the case, and at the very least aims to show that the question of whether it might be is worth serious reflection, and ought not be dismissed out of hand. It is not claimed, however, that Hobbes' theory itself is sufficient to generate a fully negative

Received: April 16, 1987
First Revision Received: November 3, 1987
Second Revision Received: February 9. 1988
Accepted for Publication: February 10, 1988

[1] An excellent recent discussion of these sections is Johnston (1986).

conclusion regarding the adequacy of rational choice theory. Indeed, were
this so, it would be hard to account for the *similarities* between Hobbes'
account of the world and that offered by rational choice theory. Certain
of Hobbes' departures from rational choice theory *point toward,* but do
not themselves fully *constitute,* a negative judgment regarding the adequacy of rational choice theory. There is, in my judgment, *within* Hobbes'
theory a tension between those elements which are and are not amenable to interpretation along the lines of rational choice theory, for if reflection upon Hobbes' teaching gives us reason to question the adequacy of
rational choice theory, it must also give us reason to question the similar
elements of his own. The question then arises as to how we are to understand these "tensions."

Two possibilities will be considered: (1) these tensions constitute a
contradiction in Hobbes' theory such that we must conclude that Hobbes'
theory is inconsistent and hence flawed, or (2) these tensions accurately
reflect permanent, paradoxical features of the reality of the human condition, such that Hobbes' theory, far from being flawed, is indeed all the
more plausible insofar as its internal tensions give theoretical expression
to practical tensions inherent in politics. If (1) were correct, and if we
accept for the moment the hypothesis that the rational choice elements
of Hobbes' theory were the ones we would jettison in order to (a) render his theory consistent and (b) render it more accurate as a description
of the human political condition (i.e., we proceed on the assumption that
Hobbes' departures from rational choice theory *do* lead us both toward
the rejection of rational choice theory as an account of political reality
and toward the rejection of those elements of his own theory inconsistent with his departures), then we would conclude (1¹) that the tenets
of rational choice theory are neither necessary nor sufficient for giving
an account of human reality, i.e., that they ought be abandoned altogether. A corollary of (1¹) would be that Hobbes has little more to teach
us about how to understand man and society, than showing us how not
to. On the other hand, if (2) were correct, then me might conclude
(2²) that the tenets of rational choice theory are necessary, though not
sufficient, to the giving of an accurate account of human reality. They
would have to be supplemented by those elements of Hobbes' theory (the
"departures") not amenable to interpretation in terms of the tenets of
rational choice theory. A corollary of (2²) would be that Hobbes has a
great deal, perhaps everything, to teach us about how to understand man
and society.

Which are closer to the truth, (1) and (1¹) or (2) and (2²)? Answering
that question is the ultimate aim of an inquiry upon which this paper only
embarks. Let us begin, then, by considering the tenets of rational choice
theory and Hobbes' account of man and society with an eye to exploring their similarities and differences.

The Tenets of Rational Choice Theory

It is exceedingly difficult to give a denotative definition of "rational
choice theory." The term has become common within the lexicon of po-

litical science, yet no clear and distinct set of criteria for delimiting the axiomatic tenets of this theory are accepted as canonical, not least because not all of those conventionally referred to as practitioners of rational choice theory agree about how to properly describe or utilize "it." Perhaps it is only those concerned, for whatever reasons, to criticize "rational choice theory" who insist upon seeing it as a unified whole, and perhaps it would be best to say that there is no rational choice theory, only rational choice theories. But since I too come to bury rather than praise, I shall speak of rational choice *theory* or *the* rational choice approach to understanding politics, and leave it to the reader to judge whether what I create thereby is a straw man. And if it is no more than that, I will plead only that I have found it a particularly interesting one, and will happily take credit for it.

The essence of rational choice theory resides in (1) its instrumentalism, (2) its individualism, and (3) its subjectivism. These three aspects, when combined, result in the fundamental aim of rational choice theory, which is to understand sociopolitical relations and institutions as the instruments created and used by mutually disinterested and rationally self-interested agents in the attempt to maximize the degree to which they can successfully pursue their particular ends and satisfy their particular preferences, whatever those might be. Rational choice theory as here defined does not necessarily presuppose the thesis that the substance of individual preferences is unaffected by one's social or historical context. This thesis seems clearly untenable, but many who would agree also often suppose that rational choice theory is flawed because it is intimately tied to this thesis.

(1) *Instrumentalism*

Instrumentalism means the methodological decision to view sociopolitical relations and institutions as dependent variables, their nature and existence to be explained and understood with reference to (hypothetical or real) actions undertaken by antecedently defined individual selves. Such a view is to be distinguished from any approach to understanding sociopolitical reality which takes either relations or institutions to be independent variables, the actions and identities of individual selves thence being seen as parts with reference to these wholes. Instrumentalism, then, must deny that human beings are in any inherent or intrinsic sense social beings, for to accept such a thesis would be to presuppose what instrumentalism purports to explain — the *social relations* between individual selves. Instrumentalism seeks to understand relations in terms of selves, not selves in terms of relations.

(2) *Individualism*

Because antecedently defined selves are the foundation, the independent variables, in explanation on the instrumentalist approach to relations and institutions, "individualism" is a second aspect of rational choice theory. Further, these separate selves are "antecedently defined" insofar as they are understood to be rationally self-interested maximizers of utility. Hence "individualism" refers to both a specification of individual action as the fundamental term in social explanations *and* to a motivational theory about individuals sufficient to generate such explanations. That motivational theory is contained in the view that individuals are to be understood as rationally self-interested maximizers of utility. Though often referred to as "rational agents," I shall call such selves "Economic-rational (E-rational) agents," in an attempt to avoid begging the question of whether activity proceeding from such motivation is "really" rational (Green 1981). More specifically, "E-rational agency" is defined by:

E:1 — Agents having reflexive, transitive, and complete orderings over alternative actions available to them, these orderings called preferences.

E:2 — Agents preferring more to less and hence seeking the maximal and efficient satisfaction of their own preferences.

E:3 — Agents aware that all other agents are also E-rational. E-rationality thus gives to each agent the following aim: "Seek the maximal and efficient satisfaction of your own preferences, given that everyone else does the same" (Green 1981: 14-15).

(3) *Subjectivism*

By subjectivism, I mean that rational choice theory treats the problem of value in a way consistent with the tenets of instrumentalism and individualism, that is, the good for an individual is constituted by the content of his or her preferences, the object of his or her desires. Value is subjective in a double sense; it is defined relative to the individual subject and there is no objective order or standard to serve as a basis for assessing the intrinsic moral worth of alternative definitions. On this subjective account of the good, there can be a "common good," insofar as each separate self happens, as a contingent matter of fact, to hold a preference in common. The common good would then be an aggregate of similar individual goods. What there cannot be, on the subjective account of the good, is a common good understood as an end which it is morally incumbent upon all men and women to pursue, regardless of their particular preferences or desires. Were this so, the good would not be defined relative to particular subjects.

THE PRISONER'S DILEMMA AND PUBLIC GOODS

E-rational agents often find themselves between a rock and a hard place. These are "prisoner's dilemma" (PD) situations, the formal structure of which is given below in Figure 1.

Figure 1

	Column Player	
	Cooperation	*Non-Cooperation*
Cooperation	R-10, C-10	R-1, C-20
Row Player		
Non-cooperation	R-20, C-1	R-5, C-5

Assuming the numbers refer to units of utility, the dilemma consists in the fact that R and C, insofar as they are E-rational, will each choose the non-cooperative strategy with the result of each receiving 5, where they could have received 10 each had they both chosen the cooperative strategy.

For purposes of discussion, it will be useful to present the situation in the following format.[2] Taking 1 to constitute the "sucker's payoff" (S), 5 to constitute the "punishment payoff" (P), 10 to constitute the "reward payoff" (R), and 20 to constitute the "temptation payoff" (T), the situation may be represented as below in Figure 2.

Figure 2

		Column Player	
		Cooperation	Non-Cooperation
Row Player	Cooperation	R, R, [1]	S, T [2]
	Non-cooperation	T, S [4]	P, P [3]

Whenever $S < P < R < T$, E-rational agents find themselves confronted with a PD situation. The preference orderings for R and C in such situations are as follows, where the numbers refer to the quadrants of the matrix above.

PD PREFERENCES

	Row	Column
First	4	2
Second	1	1
Third	3	3
Fourth	2	4

Each agent, acting either from the desire to maximize (non-cooperation in pursuit of T) or from the fear that the other will do so (non-cooperation to prevent S), chooses the non-cooperative strategy and both wind up with P though both could have received R had they each cooperated.

This game is often said to illustrate the problem E-rational agents face when the production of a public good is at stake, that is, a good such that no one can be excluded from enjoying its benefits. As a citizen, I enjoy the protection of a system of national defense, a benefit I would enjoy whether I paid taxes to support that system or not. My not paying my taxes will not result in the dissolution of that institution, and my paying taxes will not be sufficient to provide for that institution unless mil-

---

[2] I draw here upon the classic work of Rapaport and Chammah (1965). Other more recent works which lay out clearly the fundamental tenets of rational choice theory and the logic of the Prisoner's dilemma are Abrams (1980) and Hardin (1982).

lions of others do so as well. But as long as they do, I need not. As an
E-rational agent, my first preference is to not pay taxes, have everyone
else do so, and enjoy the benefits of national defense as a free-rider. Insofar as everyone were E-rational, no one would pay taxes, institutions
providing public goods would collapse, and all would be left without
goods each would find it useful to have. Hence a rationale for the state
to punish those who do not pay taxes to a degree sufficient to make free-
riding an unattractive alternative for E-rational agents. The state itself can
thus be understood as that institution which, possessing a monopoly on
the legitimate use of force, undertakes to provide a range of "public
goods" for its E-rational citizens, goods which each has an E-rational reason to desire but would not undertake to support in the absence of the
coercive power of the state. Analysts employing this framework disagree
as to which institutions in contemporary political societies can be correctly said to fall under this criterion, some maintaining that many goods
presently generated under the auspices of the state are not inherently public goods and would be better left to private productive arrangements
amongst consenting agents. It does seem, however, that at least one public
good is necessary for the production of any other public or private goods,
and this is the system of social order secured by the state itself. (Communitarian anarchists might disagree about the necessity of such a state,
but they would also deny the strictly E-rational character of individual
agents, and so we shall leave this issue aside.) However, the explanation
of the state in terms of rational choice theory is no easy matter, and it
is here we begin to see clearly the similarities with Hobbes.

Assuming the tenets of rational choice theory, we can imagine a pre-
sociopolitical condition composed of mutually disinterested E-rational
agents, and call it a state of nature.[3] Any relationships or institutions would
have to be explained as arising from the actions of such E-rational agents.
The catch is that the possible existence of any conceivable relation or
institution will be undermined because of the logic of E-rationality. Mutually disinterested E-rational agents, by definition, lack what we can call
the internal or external "forces" necessary to create or generate the institution which, if it existed, would result in raising the utility satisfaction of each. The simplest way to see this is to think in hypothetical terms
of a postulated agreement or contract between E-rational agents to create the institution of the state. The problem is that of explaining why
any such agent would live up to the terms of the postulated agreement
instead of pursuing the ideal E-rational contract, one where everyone except X agrees to cooperate in upholding the agreement, and X rides freely.
But Y, Z and all other E-rational agents have the same strategy, and so
the "agreement" withers away. By lack of "internal forces," I mean the
absence of any relation between the agents sufficient to generate the

---

[3] It is perhaps worth noting that "state of nature" is a term used in rational choice theory
simply analytically to denote a pre-political condition of E-rational agents. For the classical contract theorists, the concept is used because that condition is taken to tell us
something substantive about human nature.

cooperation necessary to insure the upholding of the postulated agreement. For example, if the agents trusted one another they could establish the agreement, but trust *is* a relation between individuals, and cannot be presupposed without violating the tenets of rational choice theory, for therein relations are to be explained, not presupposed. And if we try to imagine E-rational agents creating the relation of trust because it would be useful for each, we are back in the same dilemma as above. E-rational agents need some relation to underwrite the possibility of other relations — but this is their dilemma. By lack of "external forces," I mean the absence of any body sufficient to make the agents keep their agreement. If such a body existed, however, the agents would not need to create one. To suppose such an external force would be to dissolve, not resolve, the dilemma facing E-rational agents in the state of nature.

I take it then, that a rational choice theorist concerned to explain the *generation* of either internal relations between agents or the generation of an external institution such as the state, must either appeal to factors outside the strict logic of E-rationality, or relax, at least for a moment, the requirements of that logic. Otherwise, E-rational agents would seem stuck in the PD dilemma of the state of nature and could not get about their business.

HOBBES AND THE PRISONER'S DILEMMA

It is this "moment" which will be of interest as we turn to Hobbes. It is clearly possible to read significant aspects of Hobbes' argument in *Leviathan* along the lines of rational choice theory, and, specifically, to understand Hobbes' depiction of the natural condition of mankind as an exemplar of a PD situation. The agents in Hobbes' state of nature, living (hypothetically) under condition's of ". . . continual fear, and danger of violent death . . ." (Hobbes 1968: 186), would each be better off under the conditions of security for life and property provided by a sovereign political authority. Yet in the state of nature, any move toward cooperation aimed at instituting sovereign authority would also be a move toward leaving oneself open to exploitation at the hands of one's "apparent" cooperators. Assuming that agents in Hobbes' state of nature can conceptually distinguish (i) "offers of cooperation" from (ii) "threats disguised as offers of cooperation," it is nevertheless the case that as a *practical* matter, (i) and (ii) are indistinguishable under the conditions of the state of nature, for as Hobbes puts it, under those conditions ". . . there is no way for any man to secure himself, so reasonable, as anticipation; that is, by force, or wiles, to master the persons of all men he can, so long, till he sees no other power great enough to endanger him . . ." (1968: 184). Of course, given the fundamental equality of men, which means that ". . . the weakest has strength enough to kill the strongest . . ." (1968: 183), no man can have reasonable hope of successfully subduing others to the point that no power is left great enough to endanger him. But even if the agents realize this, and let us assume they do, they still lack the internal or external resources necessary to institute the sovereign with which each would be better off. For while each can see that (R, R) leaves each better off than (P, P), each also knows that cooperating in pursuit of (R, R) leaves one open to receiving (S) should another exploit one's cooperation in pursuit of (T). And such exploitation is simply nature's way. To make the first cooperative move in the attempt to institute sovereignty and leave the state of nature would amount simply to ". . . expose oneself to prey, (which no man is bound to) . . ." (1968: 190), and hence Hobbesian agents in the state of nature seem doomed to remain there.

The formal structure of the PD thus seems to give us a nice "visual" representation of the logical form of the dilemma facing men in Hobbes' state of nature. Moreover, it seems to bring out clearly the precise nature of that dilemma; just as there is no way out of a prisoner's dilemma, there seems to be no way out of Hobbes' state of nature.

Yet upon a closer look, it can be seen that Hobbes' state of nature is not actually a PD situation at all. That "closer look" entails a consideration of the substantive payoffs available to human beings in the state of nature. The wages of mutual non-cooperation are not merely a collective outcome which leaves each worse off than they would be under a sovereign, but an outcome which leaves each *as bad off as he can possibly be* — that is, facing certain death under the uncertain conditions of the state of nature. Moreover, once we think in substantive rather than formal terms, we see that the strategy of pursuing T (temptation) through non-cooperation is not actually very tempting. Whether it brings momentary success or not, it leaves one in the state of nature, which is to say that success could only be momentary, and hence no success at all. The only way for human beings to secure their existence is through mutual cooperation aimed at instituting sovereignty (R, R). All other collective outcomes reduce to the same — death in the state of nature. Even those able to exploit cooperation for their own benefit in the short run must know that, in the long run, we're all dead.

Hence a graphic portrayal of Hobbes' state of nature, taking account of the substance of his teaching, would appear as in Figure 3.

Figure 3

		Column Player	
		Cooperation	Non-Cooperation
	Cooperation	Life	Death
Row Player			
	Non-cooperation	Death	Death

It can thus be seen that even as regards the formal structure of the situation facing individuals in Hobbes' state of nature, that situation is not a PD, but a "coordination game" in which there is a stable and optimal collective outcome, the problem being that of cooperating to institute it. In PD situations, on the other hand, the stable collective outcome

(P, P) is not optimal, and the optimal collective outcome (R, R) is not stable.

Of course, even if Figure 3 is accepted as the correct rendering of Hobbes' state of nature, the problem of getting out of it still remains, and that question is an old one for students of Hobbes. Let us consider two approaches which have been taken toward this question, approaches which differ not so much in terms of providing different answers to the issue, but rather in terms of how they frame and conceptualize the issue. The first approach would be to take the question at face value, and to suppose that Hobbes, if his theory is to be judged consistent and coherent, must provide some explanation of how, hypothetically, human beings might exit the state of nature, or at least must provide the theoretical materials from which such an explanation could be constructed, even if Hobbes himself did not bother explicitly to construct it. Plamenatz's treatment of Hobbes in *Man and Society* is an example of such an approach (1963: 132-38). A more recent statement of this position, which we shall take up momentarily, has been advanced by Jean Hampton (1986).

The second approach takes the question itself as misguided, and, pointing out that the *Leviathan* is addressed to civilized human beings who enjoy the benefits of social and political order, takes Hobbes' point to be one of explaining to them how they can keep themselves from winding up in the state of nature, not one of explaining to uncivilized beings how to get out of it. On this approach, the question of how, or whether, individuals would exit the state of nature is simply otiose; indeed one might suppose that Hobbes' teaching would be more persuasive just to the extent that his readers concluded that exits from the state of nature *are* inexplicable. Hence, rather than constituting a weakness or flaw in his theory, Hobbes' "failure" to explain how individuals could hypothetically exit the state of nature would be seen from this approach as one further "positive" component of his practical teaching that those fortunate enough to live under sovereign authority ought obey it: the alternative is the horrible dilemma of the state of nature.

Again, these are not so much competing answers to the same question as they are different ways of approaching and understanding the question itself. At the same time, they embody different conceptions of how to read and understand Hobbes. Without claiming that they need be entirely incompatible with one another, it seems clear that the second approach will tend more than the first to highlight and indeed to illuminate the rhetorical, symbolic, and persuasive aspects of Hobbes' theoretical formulations, for on that approach it is the practical aim of Hobbes' teaching which is treated as the unifying thread by means of which one might unravel and understand his teaching as an integrated set of symbols aimed at *influencing* his reader's cognitive processes.

The contrasts between the two approaches can be specified more precisely by considering Hampton's critical analysis of Hobbes' argument from the perspective of the first approach.

Hampton takes up the issue of whether Hobbesian agents in a state of nature could institute an absolute sovereign, and argues that they could not. The crux of her argument is to point to the tension between (a) the requirement of a sovereign who is absolute in the sense of deciding all questions in the commonwealth and (b) the fact that Hobbesian agents empower such a sovereign by obeying its punishment commands "whenever *they decide* such obedience is conducive to their best interests" (206). Hobbes' argument, thus understood, is said to fall prey to a problem of "regress," since the condition in (b) which is necessary to empower sovereignty (individual decision) undermines the requirement for sovereignty (making all decisions) specified in (a). Later, Hampton considers a modified and "rehabilitated" account of Hobbes' position (the "fallback" position) designed to make it more tenable. Before doing so, however, she pauses to take up the possibility that Hobbes' argument in *Leviathan* might be salvaged on its own terms by understanding it as what she calls a "conversion argument," and it is her treatment of this possibility we need to consider, for it may appear similar to the interpretation proposed herein.

The "conversion" referred to here is that of converting E-rational agents into obedient citizens, a conversion seen as necessary given the consequences of E-rationality on the part of individuals (failure to institute effective sovereignty, death in the absence of such). Hampton summarizes the idea as follows:

> Suppose it is possible and rational for each subject to convert to a different standard of rationality: Whereas in the state of nature an individual would use an expected-utility calculation to evaluate the extent to which any action would be best for him, given his self-regarding desires, in the commonwealth he would convert to using the *sovereign's* expected-utility calculation to evaluate the rationality of any action. . . . If this conversion were possible, creating an absolute sovereign would be accomplished by becoming *a new kind of reasoner*. the action of authorization, understood figuratively as a kind of surrender to the sovereign, would literally mean giving up one's own judgement of the rationality of an action and instead adopting the sovereign's judgement of an action's rationality as one's standard for evaluating which actions to perform. (209)

Having laid out the interpretation, and citing scattered passages from Hobbes' text which seem to suggest it, Hampton nevertheless rejects it as a plausible reading of Hobbes. However, it is my contention that the force of her critical argument rests ultimately upon reading *Leviathan* as a set of theoretical arguments detached from any practical attempt to effect the very conversion being argued for at a theoretical level. To put it another way, she treats the conversion argument as a possible Hobbesian answer to the question of how Hobbesian agents might exit the state of nature through the institution of sovereignty, and finds it wanting in this regard. I suggest that it should be understood not as a proposed solution to this theoretical problem, but as outlining a program of practical educational activity aimed at maintaining and enhancing obedient citizenship in an existent commonwealth. What determines our assessment of the conversion argument, then, is our conception of Hobbes' *audience* and our conception of how he is trying to influence that audience.

Hampton finds the conversion argument implausible because it asks agents who are defined as "hard-wired" with the desire to preserve their own lives to put their preservation effectively in jeopardy by converting to a desire which makes the sovereign's preservation, and not their own, their ultimate goal (211). This, however, seems to misunderstand the sort of conversion Hobbes is attempting to effect, which is one of *identification* of one's ultimate goal with that of the sovereign upon the realization that failure to do so imperils one's preservation insofar as it generates a regress to the state of nature. A Hobbesian agent torn between maintaining a right of personal judgment against sovereignty or accepting the judgments of a sovereign conceived as an external force is an agent who has simply failed to convert. "Conversion," then, would amount not simply to accepting the sovereign's judgments regarding action as authoritative, but also to doing this because one now identifies oneself, and one's judgment, with the sovereign. Successful conversion would be constituted by the (previously) external sovereign being internalized through a relationship of identity.

Hampton later sees this when she remarks that such conversion would in effect dissolve the problem of Hobbesian agents instituting sovereignty: if agents in the state of nature were to convert in *this* way, there would simply be no problem of how to institute sovereignty. She thus rejects the conversion account on the grounds that it does not solve, but rather wishes away, the problem of how Hobbesian agents in the state of nature could institute sovereignty. This is, in a sense, true. Conversion is seen in a different light, however, once one remembers that Hobbes is writing not to agents in the state of nature, but to citizens removed from it. It is my contention that Hobbes is himself trying to effect (or buttress) this sort of conversion through the writing of *Leviathan;* it may be understood as the practical aim of Hobbes' therapeutic teaching, rather than as a proposed solution to the philosopher's problem of how Hobbesian agents might exit a state of nature.

Conceiving it as a proposed response to the latter problem, Hampton finds the conversion argument far-fetched: ". . . it seems at best unlikely and at worst ridiculous to think that Hobbesian people could 'will' to make this (sovereign's preservation) their new goal" (211). Yet one can imagine Hobbes agreeing, and remarking that it is for just this reason that his teaching is necessary and beneficial — it is a means of "educating" these recalcitrant wills. Until E-rational agents convert to identifying with their sovereign, and hence conceive their preservation and the preservation of sovereignty as one, their calculations persist as a threat to the preservation of both. The conversion argument, then, is indeed implausible if one takes it as an explanation of how Hobbesian agents might exit the state of nature. If, however, one conceives Hobbes' purpose and audience along the lines argued for here, it is seen not as an argument that fails, but as an account of the practical aim Hobbes desires to see implemented, and is trying to implement.

What are the implications for Hobbes' teaching in relation to rational choice theory if one reads and understands Hobbes along the lines of the second approach above, that is, an approach focusing upon the practical meaning and import of Hobbes' teaching? One immediate virtue of such an approach has already been sketched; we need not conclude that Hobbes committed a "howler" in failing to explain how individuals could have exited the state of nature. Further, we could see why Hobbes' practical teaching would be obscured, perhaps even vitiated, by any attempt to abstract from its substance and present it in formal terms. For if Hobbes' lessons are to be understood, it is of the essence that citizens realize that in matters of obligation regarding sovereign authority, the ultimate and underlying issue is, literally, one of life and death. Hobbes' teaching requires that these "payoffs" be both (a) understood in terms of their substance and (b) understood as the only *two* ultimate consequences of obedience and disobedience respectively. Only then might Hobbes be successful in frightening his readers into the realization that obedience to sovereignty is at once rational and necessary.

One might object that Hobbes' purpose is not to frighten, but rather to lay before us the rational grounds of obedience to sovereign authority. It is true that Hobbes does this in *Leviathan,* for therein he shows the E-rational agent that the successful pursuit of his or her particular ends is dependent upon a system of social order guaranteed by sovereign power, and further that this system of social order is itself dependent upon constraints being imposed upon the maximizing behavior of E-rational agents. Yet if reason alone were sufficient to comprehend Hobbes' teaching, and result in the self-imposition of these restraints, one would be moved to wonder why that teaching remains necessary. His teaching remains necessary because humans' passions too often cloud their reason, and because, as Hobbes says, "The passion to be reckoned upon, is fear" (1968: 200). It is Leviathan, the state, which imposes constraints upon the maximizing behavior of E-rational agents in the only sure and effective way; that is, by appealing not to their reason but by making them *afraid* of the punishment which attends free-riding and disobedience. Similarly, it is *Leviathan,* the text, which would, if read and understood, save such agents the trouble and pain of learning these lessons the hard way. And if one considers that text not only as a formal argument but as a sustained piece of persuasive rhetoric, then one sees that therein too the passion reckoned upon is fear, more precisely the fear of death. Hobbes, through the metaphorical rhetoric of the *Leviathan,* attempts no less than to provide his readers with an imaginative and vicarious experience of their own death, with the aim of thereby impressing upon their minds in the most vivid way possible the necessity of obedience. That "impressing" proceeds as much, if not more so, by the way of the passionate fear of death as by the way of a cool and calculating reason. Hobbes' readers must realize something more than simply the lesson that actions based upon E-rationality can, under certain circumstances, leave everyone worse off then they could have been. They must be brought to the realization that "worse off" is equivalent to death, if they are effectively to be persuaded of the virtues of obedience. Hobbes, then, attempts to scare citizens to death, in order that they might secure their lives.

HOBBES AS CRITIC OF RATIONAL CHOICE THEORY

But even should this be so, does it really give us reason to call Hobbes a *critic* of rational choice theory? I want to suggest that it does, though it is admittedly criticism in a special sense. Insofar as a reading of Hobbes along the lines of rational choice theory abstracts from the substance of his formulations in order to present his theory in its formal structure, the symbolic force of Hobbes' rhetoric is lost, and with it goes a good portion of the persuasive power of his appeal. But does this really matter? Taking the point of view of Hobbes, it would not matter a great deal if there were grounds for supposing that the lessons he aims to teach are *only obscured* by the purely formal reading. For one might suppose that the "formalization" of Hobbes' substantive account of the state of nature which renders it as a prisoner's dilemma situation would by itself by enough rationally to convince E-rational agents that it is sometimes in their own long-term interests to constrain their maximizing behavior and cooperate with others. If, however, there were grounds for supposing that the formalization of Hobbes' argument not only *obscures* but actually *undermines* the lessons he wishes to teach, then it would matter a great deal, and one might reasonably call Hobbes a critic of rational choice theory.

Are there any grounds for thinking that a formalization of Hobbes' account along the lines of rational choice theory goes so far as to *undermine* his teaching? A case in support of the conclusion that there are can be sketched by first stating the grounds generally and then by applying them to the specific case of "The Foole," whom Hobbes addresses in Chapter 15 of *Leviathan*.

The general grounds are constituted simply by the fact that Hobbes treats reason as subservient to the passions, and hence any attempt to affect the way human beings act must acknowledge this and aim its appeal at those passions. Hobbes' appeal is aimed at what he takes to be the most fundamental of those passions, the desire for self-preservation and a corresponding fear of death. Since this presupposes a substantive conception of human nature, and because like all such conceptions it is bound to be controversial and force us to open up discussions at the level of fundamental ontology, rational choice readings of Hobbes which abstract from these substantive suppositions seem to provide a way of avoiding these controversial issues while retaining something of value in Hobbes' theory. They give us E-rational agents with a desire to maximize the satisfaction of their interests, while Hobbes gives us similar E-rational agents, but with a substantive conception of certain fundamental interests. Yet just because Hobbes' teaching proceeds from and attempts to work upon those substantive passions, the formalization of his account turns out not to "retain" so much as to undermine the force of his argument. Consider the case of "The Foole":

> The Foole hath sayd in his heart, there is no such thing as justice; and sometimes also with his tongue; seriously alleging, that every man's conservation, and contentment, being comitted to his own care, there could be no reason, why every man might not do what he thought conduced thereunto: and therefore also to make, or not make; keep or not keep covenants, was not against reason, when it conduced to one's benefit. He does not therein deny, that there be covenants; and that they are sometimes broken, sometimes kept; and that such breach of them may be called injustice, and the observance of them justice: but he questioneth, whether injustice, taking away the feare of God (for the same Foole hath said in his heart there is no God), may not sometimes stand with reason, which dictateth to every man his own good; and particularly then, when it conduceth to such a benefit, as shall put a man in a condition, to neglect not onely the dispraise, and revilings, but also the power of other men. (Hobbes 1968: 203)

The Foole is the quintessential E-rational agent, who would free-ride when he determined that he could get away with it. Hobbes might tell the Foole that if everyone reasoned similarly, social order would collapse, and all, the Foole included, would be thrown back into the state of nature. The Foole, however, is apparently aware of this. He maintains that injustice might *"sometimes* stand with Reason, which dictateth to every man his own good." And it is clear that these times (and only these times) are those wherein the Foole will have calculated that he will be able to get away with it, that is, put himself "in a position . . . to neglect the power of other men."

Now it is quite likely that situations giving rise to the temptations which attract the Foole are bound to exist in any society. The only way to prevent them from arising would be the existence of a sovereign so powerful that each and every act of injustice could be found out and punished, and every citizen would know this, and hence never consider such activity. Orwell lays down the necessary condition for such a regime in *1984;* at the extreme, subjects would have to be rendered incapable of even conceptualizing the possibility of injustice. Whether such a condition is possible, we may safely take it that Hobbes himself does not entertain it,[4] for the very fact that he is moved to argue with the Foole indicates that he does not envision this condition as being necessary for social order.

Hobbes presents two arguments against the Foole. Insofar as each appeals to reason, they are bound to fall short of persuading the Foole of the error of his ways. The arguments would be potentially persuasive only

---

[4] Actually, I remain unsure about this. Insofar as the sovereign is responsible for "the right ordering of speech," the logic of Hobbes' argument does seem to point in the direction of Orwell.

insofar as they were to affect his passions, by playing upon his fear of death. Hobbes' first argument is;

> First, that when a man doth a thing, which notwithstanding any thing can be foreseen, and reckoned on, tendeth to his own destruction, howsoever some accident which he could not expect, arriving may turne it to his benefit; yet such events do not make it reasonably or wisely done. (1968: 204)

This does no more than tell the Foole that he ought not calculate the probability of getting away with injustice under a given set of empirical circumstances. Hobbes is urging that since there will always be *some* probability of being caught and punished (no matter how miniscule) the Foole is unreasonable in not pursuing a risk-averse strategy which makes *any* such probability (no matter how miniscule) decisive in his calculations. But if the Foole would accept this, there would be no problem in the first place, that is, he would not be a "Foole" to begin with. The Foole's foolishness consists in the fact that for him, it is an open and empirical question as to whether one ought, E-rationally, to perform just or unjust acts. The Foole is always willing to entertain the thought of acting unjustly, and where the expected utility of injustice exceeds by some determinate degree the expected costs, he is willing to act unjustly.

In his first counter-argument, Hobbes simply maintains that a reasonable person would see that expected costs always and necessarily exceed expected benefits, and hence would never treat the question as an empirical one. But if the Foole were persuaded by this, he would not be foolish. What then, would persuade him? If we rule out the possibility of an Orwellian sovereign capable of doing the job, then we are left with an appeal to the Foole's fear of death, and hence with the necessity of adding a passionate dimension, based upon Hobbes' substantive beliefs about human motivation, to the rational dimension of the counter-argument. That is to say, the one thing that might persuade the Foole of the error of his ways would be some grounds for making him believe that the expected costs of disobedience *necessarily* outweigh the expected benefits. And this ground would be the realization that expected costs = death, for then the Foole might be frightened into pursuing the risk-averse strategy of obedience, for no degree of expected benefits could ever outweigh the disutility of death, and as long as there is even a miniscule probability of death, that will be enough to tip the balance of the equation toward obedience, for nothing could be worse than death. But Hobbes' readers, foolish or otherwise, cannot be expected to learn this lesson unless the substance of his teaching is considered. If Hobbes is to have any chance of saving Fooles from themselves, they must be made to see that questions of just vs. unjust behavior are all reducible to the single question of life vs. death.

Formalization of his account not only obscures this lesson in abstracting from the substance of his teaching, but undermines that teaching insofar as formalization encourages "Foolish" behavior by turning men's minds away from the fear of death and in the opposite direction toward the possibilities of gain. Forgetting that the issue is life vs. death, amnesiac Fooles look at social order along the lines of the formal account of the N-person prisoner's dilemma, and seek to determine the values of T, R, P, and S and the probability of achieving T, R, P, and S in a given situation. They imagine that where T is great and S is small, and where the probability of achieving T is great and the probability of achieving S is small, they might wisely practice injustice. The formalization of the situation leads them to look at this as an open question, and in that sense undermines Hobbes' ability to teach his lessons. If he is to succeed at awakening Fooles from their dangerous amnesia, he must appeal to their deepest passion, and bring them to the conscious realization that the price of non-cooperation is death, and hence to the realization that pursuit of T can never be rational. Men who see only the form of Hobbes' teaching cannot receive his therapy.

Hobbes' second argument against the Foole is as follows:

> Secondly, that in a condition of warre, wherein every man to every man, for want of a common power to keep them all in awe, is an enemy, thare is no man can hope by his own strength, or wit, to defend himself from destruction, without the help of confederates; where every one expects the same defence by the confederation, that any one else does: and therefore he which declares he thinks it reason to deceive those that help him, can in reason expect no other means of safety, than what can be had from his own single power. He therefore that breaketh his covenant, and consequently declareth that he thinks he may with reason do so, cannot be received into any society, that unite themselves for peace and defence, but by the errour of them that receive him; nor when he is received, be retayned in it, without seeing the danger of their errour; which errours a man cannot reasonably recken upon as the means of his security: and therefore, if he be left, or cast out of society, he perisheth; and if he live in society, it is by the errours of other men, which he could not foresee, nor recken upon; and consequently against the reason of his preservation; and so, as all men that contribute not to his destruction, forebear him onely out of ignorance of what is good for themselves. (1968: 205)

Here, more emphatically than in the first counter-argument, Hobbes seeks to "remind" the Foole that the wages of injustice are death, that practicing injustice in the name of self-interest can lead him to "perisheth." Whether these arguments are successful in turning men's eyes toward the possibility of death is, and must be, an open question. Therapy is not always successful. But at the least, it seems fair to say that any persuasive power they might have for foolish readers is dependent upon those readers realizing that the issue *is* one of life and death — and this is possible only insofar as one attends to the substance as well as the form of Hobbes' account of the state of nature. Hobbes notes that "all men are by nature provided of notable multiplying glasses, (that is their Passions and self-love,) through which every little payment appeareth a great grievance; but are destitute of those prospective glasses, (Namely Morall and Civill Science) to see a farre off the miseries that hang over them, and cannot without such payments by avoyded" (1968: 239). To replace the "multiplying glasses" requires, quite requires, quite literally, a change in the angle of vision through which society is viewed. The Foole lacks the lenses which would enable him to envision "a farre off the miseries that hang over" him. Hobbes could enable him to see these miseries in the distance, and hence change his ways, by making him look inward, and come face to face with that which he has foolishly repressed and forgotten: the fear of his own death. Hobbes, then, turns out to be something of an existentialist cum psychoanalyst, concerned to bring men's death before their eyes so that they might undergo a kind of cognitive transformation which would, by leading them away from the maximizing reason of E-rationality, cure the commonwealth of one source of its hitherto perennial discontents.

CONCLUSION

Near the end of her critical account of the plausibility of Hobbes' "conversion" argument, Hampton speculates on what would be necessary to make his argument work. The crucial condition would be that just outlined; the Hobbesian citizen would have to see only two possibilities open to him, those of (1) obeying sovereignty through conversion or (2) dying, to the exclusion of the third possibility entertained by the Foole (3) of giving the appearance of converting while maintaining in reality the right of private judgment to be judiciously employed in potentially advantageous free-riding situations. Hampton argues that in order to exclude (3) and make (1) and (2) the only possible choices, the sovereign would have to possess some sort of device capable of penetrating and knowing the citizen's consciousness to a degree which made it impossible for the citizen to trick the sovereign by giving the appearance of converting while not actually doing do. Considering an episode of *Star Trek* which imagined such a device, she remarks:

> But should we take *Leviathan* to be an implicit plea for the development of such devices? The suggestion seems ridiculous. We have made Hobbes' argument valid in a way that amounts to a reductio ad absurdum of the argument. (219)

One could summarize the reading the Hobbes proposed in this essay by saying that it endorses this "ridiculous suggestion" as the appropriate way to understand Hobbes, and even goes it one better. Not only is *Leviathan* a plea for such a device, it *is* such a device itself. It is created by an author who realizes that psychological conversion, not technological coercion, is the most efficacious means of establishing a secure commonwealth. Hobbes' attempt to secure perpetual civil peace does not await the development of devices now only imagined in the realm of science fiction; to the contrary, it makes use of the oldest practice in politics itself, that of effecting a relationship of identity between ruler and ruled, which, to the degree it is successful, renders direct coercion unnecessary. It is worth recalling, in this vein, the remarks concerning *Leviathan* with which Hobbes concludes:

652   *Western Political Quarterly*

Therefore, I think it may be profitably printed, and more profitably taught in the Universities, in case they also think so, to whom the judgements of the same belongeth. For seeing the Universities are the Fountains of Civill, and Morall Doctrine, from whence the Preachers, and the Gentry, drawing such water as they find, use to sprinkle the same (both from the Pulpit, and in their conversation) upon the People, there ought certainly to be great care taken, to have it pure, both from the Venime of Heathen Politicians, and from the Incantation of Deceiving Spirits. And by that means the most men, knowing their Duties, will be less subject to serve the Ambition of a few discontented persons, in their purposes against the state; and be the lesse grieved with the contributions necessary for their Peace, and Defence; and the Governours themselves have the lesse cause, to maintain at the Common charge any greater Army, than is necessary to make good the Publique Liberty, against the Invasions and Encroachments of forraign Enemies. (728)

REFERENCES

Abrams, Robert. 1980. *Foundations of Political Analysis*. New York: Columbia University Press.

Brams, Steven. 1985. *Rational Politics*. Washington: Congressional Quarterly Press.

Gauthier, David. 1969. *The Logic of Leviathan*. Oxford: Clarendon Press.

Green, Leslie. 1981. "Authority and Public Goods," paper presented at the Annual Meeting of the Canadian Political Science Association.

Hampton, Jean. 1986. *Hobbes and the Social Contract Tradition*. Cambridge: Cambridge University Press.

Hardin, Russell. 1982. *Collective Action*. Baltimore: Johns Hopkins University Press.

Hobbes, Thomas. 1968. *Leviathan* (ed. C. B. Macpherson). Harmondsworth: Penguin Books.

Johnston, David. 1986. *The Rhetoric of Leviathan*. Princeton, NJ: Princeton University Press.

Kavka, Gregory. 1983. "Hobbes' War of All Against All." *Ethics* 93: 291-310.

Laver, Michael. 1981. *The Politics of Private Desires*. Harmondsworth: Penguin Books.

McLean, Ian. 1981. "The Social Contract in Leviathan and the Prisoner's Dilemma Supergame." *Political Studies* 29: 339-51.

Olson, Mancur. 1965. *The Logic of Collective Action*. Cambridge, MA: Harvard University Press.

Plamenatz, John. 1963. *Man and Society*. 2 vols. New York: McGraw Hill.

Rapaport, Anatol, and Albert M. Chammah. 1965. *Prisoner's Dilemma: A Study in Conflict and Cooperation*. Ann Arbor: University of Michigan Press.

Taylor, Michael. 1976. *Anarchy and Cooperation*. London: Wiley.

[11]

'God Hath Ordained to Man a Helper': Hobbes, Patriarchy and Conjugal Right

CAROLE PATEMAN

There are two conflicting and equally misleading interpretations of Hobbes: either he is a patriarchalist like Filmer – but the premise of Hobbes's theory is that political right originates in maternal not paternal lordship; or he is an anti-patriarchalist – but he endorses the subjection of wives to husbands in civil society. To appreciate how Hobbes turns mother right into a specifically modern, non-paternal form of patriarchy, an understanding is required of his peculiar view of the family as a protective association of master and servants that originates in conquest (contract). Secondly, a conjectural history of the defeat of women by men in the natural condition and their incorporation into 'families' has to be provided. The overthrow of mother right enables men to enter the original contract, to create Leviathan in their own image, and to secure the fruits of their conquest by establishing patriarchal political right, exercised in large part as conjugal right.

'The decisive moment in the conjuring trick has been made, and it was the very one we thought quite innocent.'

L. Wittgenstein, *Philosophical Investigations*

Most studies of Hobbes have nothing to say about the relation of his political theory to seventeenth-century patriarchalism. Writers who have thought it worthwhile to consider the question have almost all agreed that Hobbes's argument is patriarchal, although more recently the claim has been made that, for example, Hobbes's views were subversive of 'patriarchal attitudes', or that his theory is free from patriarchal assumptions.[1] More strongly, in a rational choice interpretation of Hobbes (which shares Hobbes's radical individualism) the implicit assumption is that Hobbes's theory is so far opposed to patriarchalism that his sovereign can be referred to as 'she'.[2] Despite such differences, political theorists are united on one point; they agree that to argue about patriarchy is to argue about the family and paternal power. Hobbes is assumed to be a patriarchal theorist in the same sense that his adversary Sir Robert Filmer is a

Department of Government, University of Sydney. This article will appear as a chapter in Mary L. Shanley and Carole Pateman, eds, *Feminist Interpretations and Political Theory* (Cambridge: Polity Press, forthcoming).

[1] The arguments are those, respectively, of Richard A. Chapman, '*Leviathan* Writ Small: Thomas Hobbes on the Family', *American Political Science Review*, 69 (1975), 76–90, at p. 77; and John Zvesper, 'Hobbes' Individualistic Analysis of the Family', *Politics* (UK), 5 (1985), 28–33 at p. 33. For references to other discussions of Hobbes and patriarchy see Chapman, '*Leviathan* Writ Small', p. 76, fns 2–14.

[2] Jean Hampton, *Hobbes and the Social Contract Tradition* (Cambridge: Cambridge University Press, 1986).

patriarchalist; or, conversely, Hobbes is assumed to be opposed to patri-archalism because his theory is antithetical to Filmer's on some crucial issues.

The major debates about patriarchy over the past two decades have been con-ducted by feminists, not mainstream political theorists, but feminists have paid remarkably little attention to political theory in the controversy over the mean-ing and usefulness of the term 'patriarchy'. None the less, the predominant assumption among feminists, or, at least, among those engaged in the theoretic-ally informed controversies over patriarchy, is also that patriarchal relations are familial relations and that patriarchal political right is paternal right.[3] To be sure, many feminists also use 'patriarchy' to mean the power that men exercise over women more generally – what I shall call masculine right – but, notwith-standing the copious empirical evidence available to support this interpretation, the usage has not yet been given a great deal of theoretical substance. A major reason for this lack of theoretical robustness is the feminist neglect of the argu-ments among political theorists about patriarchy in the seventeenth century. Feminist scholars have undertaken some very revealing and exciting work on the classic texts of political theory, but little attention has been paid to Hobbes, whose writings are of fundamental importance for an understanding of patriarchy as masculine right. Hobbes is a patriarchal theorist – but the possibil-ity that is considered by neither conventional political theorists nor feminists is that he is a patriarchalist who rejects paternal right.

Both feminism and political theory are dogged by an anachronistic, although literal, interpretation of patriarchy as father-right. Patriarchy is assumed to be about fathers and mothers. For example, Di Stephano has argued that Hobbes is a masculinist theorist, but her reading of Hobbes is that his arguments rest on a denial of the mother. His picture of natural, atomized individuals, who spring up like mushrooms – 'consider men as if but even now sprung out of the earth, and suddenly, like mushrooms, come to full maturity, without all kind of en-gagement to each other'[4] – denies any significance to the mother–child relation-ship and the dependence on the mother that provides the first intersubjective context for the development of human capacities. Di Stephano claims that there is no room for nurture within the family in Hobbes's state of nature; 'men are not born of, much less nurtured by, women, or anyone else for that matter'.[5] Hobbes's family is certainly very peculiar, but the problem with Di Stephano's argument is that, in the state of nature, mothers, far from being denied, are en-throned. For Hobbes, political right in the natural condition is mother-right. Hobbes goes to great lengths to deny that father-right is the origin of political right, yet he is still seen as a patriarchalist in the same sense as Filmer for whom political and paternal power were one and the same. A different problem con-

[3] Contemporary feminist arguments about patriarchy are discussed in Carole Pateman, *The Sexual Contract* (Cambridge: Polity Press; Stanford: Stanford University Press, 1988), chap. 2.

[4] Thomas Hobbes, *Philosophical Rudiments Concerning Government and Society* [the English ver-sion of *De Cive*], in *The English Works of Thomas Hobbes of Malmesbury* [hereafter *EW*] (London: John Bohn, 1841), vol. II, chap. VIII, p. 109.

[5] Christine di Stephano, 'Masculinity as Ideology in Political Theory: Hobbesian Man Con-sidered', *Women's Studies International Forum*, 6 (1983), 633–44, at p. 638.

fronts the writers who argue that Hobbes subverts patriarchalism, or merely tacitly assume that the terms 'men' and 'individual' in Hobbes's texts are used generically; they fail to explain why Hobbes's writings contain so many references to the rightful power of fathers – or why he endorses the subjection of wives to husbands.

Commentators on Hobbes, like almost all political theorists of the recent past, see no problems of political interest arising from the subordination of wives to husbands. Conjugal right, the right exercised by men, as husbands, over their wives, is not a matter that falls within their scholarly purview. The standard interpretations of the theoretical battle between the classic contract theorists, including Hobbes, and the patriarchalists of the seventeenth century is that the engagement concerned the political right of fathers and the natural liberty of sons. That the father was also a master, exercising jurisdiction over servants and apprentices, is acknowledged, but another inhabitant of the family is usually ignored. The father is also a husband, and as a husband is a master over his wife. In discussions of Hobbes and patriarchy, the position of the *wife* in the family is rarely mentioned. She appears, if at all, in another capacity, as a *mother*. When a problem about women is admitted to exist, it is taken to be that of maternal jurisdiction over children; patriarchy is familial and about fathers and mothers.

The failure to distinguish marriage from the family and to recognize the existence of conjugal right means that the most distinctive aspect of Hobbes's political theory is disregarded. Hobbes is the only contract theorist (and almost the only writer admitted into the 'tradition' of Western political theory) who begins from the premise that there is no natural dominion of men over women. In his natural condition female individuals are as free as, and equal to, male individuals. The remarkable starting point of his political theory is usually passed over extremely quickly. Even in discussions that focus on patriarchy no questions are asked or explanations offered about why and how it is, in the absence of sexual dominion in the state of nature, that marriage and the family take a patriarchal form. Nor is anything odd seen in the fact that Hobbes argues both that women are naturally free and always subject to men through (the marriage) contract.

There are also other problems about Hobbes, patriarchy and contract when 'patriarchy' is interpreted literally. Some commentators have noted certain tensions in Hobbes's arguments between contract and patriarchy; one earlier scholar, for instance, took the logical position that if Hobbes is interpreted as a patriarchalist then the original contract is superfluous.[6] Another commentator has attributed a consensual form of patriarchy to Hobbes and argued that his patriarchalism is, therefore, the strongest form – and even a more typically English variety.[7] Hobbes would not have been the only seventeenth-century writer to try to combine patriarchy (i.e. father-right) and consent, but to ride

[6] Leslie Stephen in 1904; cited by Gordon Schochet, *Patriarchalism in Political Thought* (Oxford: Basil Blackwell, 1975), p. 234.

[7] R. W. K. Hinton, 'Husbands, Fathers and Conquerors', *Political Studies*, 16 (1968), 55–67, at p. 57.

both horses is to perform a clever trick indeed. The trick is all the more noteworthy in Hobbes's case since he took contract much further than most other
classic contract theorists and claimed that even infants could be said to have
contracted themselves into subjection to mothers. Since the fundamental presupposition of Sir Robert Filmer's patriarchalism was that all political right derived from the natural procreative power of fathers and that sons were naturally
subject from birth, there is, to say the least, some explanation required of why
and how Hobbes constructs a consensual patriarchal theory from the premise of
mother-right and infantile contracts.

To posit a contract by an infant is to reject outright any suggestion that political subjection is natural and to confirm in the most emphatic possible manner
that all dominion is conventional in origin. Yet it was precisely the doctrine of
the natural freedom of mankind and its corollary, contract and consent, that Sir
Robert saw as the major cause of sedition and political disorder. Why, then,
should a purported advocate of patriarchy as paternal right, and a writer who,
in his own way, was as absolutist as his opponent, take so many pains to deny
the assumptions of Filmer's theory? More generally, if political right has a
natural origin in fatherhood and contract is thus superfluous – and, according to
Filmer, politically dangerous – why should Hobbes argue that civil society was
created through an original contract? To find answers to these questions requires that the discussion of Hobbes's theory is placed on a new footing.

To remain within the standard, patriarchal interpretation of 'patriarchy' as
fatherly power is also to remain within a patriarchal reading of Hobbes's texts, a
reading that ignores the subjection of women. Hobbes's patriarchalism is a new,
specifically modern form, that is conventional, contractual and originates in conjugal right, or, more accurately, sex-right; that is, in men's right of sexual access
to women, which, in its major institutional form in modern society, is exercised
as conjugal right (a term also providing a polite locution in, say, a discussion of
Adam and Eve). To appreciate the character of Hobbes's patriarchal theory
a new reading is also required of two other aspects of his arguments. Firstly,
the distinctive features of his natural condition – mother-right and the absence
of natural dominion of male over female individuals – have to be taken seriously
as fundamental premises of his political theory. Secondly, Hobbes's extraordinary conception of the family needs to be emphasized. Hobbes did not
merely leave no room for nurture or argue that the family was conventional, a
political rather than a natural social form. For Hobbes, a 'family' was solely
composed of a master and servants of various kinds and had its origins in conquest.

I

Before looking in greater detail at Hobbes's arguments it is necessary to say
something more about patriarchy and to look again at Filmer's patriarchalism.[8]

---

[8] This section draws on Pateman, *The Sexual Contract*, chap. 4.

A good deal of confusion over the term 'patriarchy' has arisen because of the failure to distinguish between three different historical forms of patriarchal theory: traditional, classic and modern. Traditional patriarchal argument assimilates all power relations to paternal rule. For centuries the family and the authority of the father at its head provided the model and metaphor for political society and political right. The traditional form is also full of stories, of conjectural histories, about the emergence or creation of political society from the family or the coming together of many families. Such stories are also to be found in the writings of the classic contract theorists, even though they defeated and eliminated the second, short-lived form of classic patriarchalism. Classic patriarchy was formulated and died in the seventeenth century and is exemplified by Sir Robert Filmer's arguments. Schochet shows in *Patriarchalism in Political Thought* that Sir Robert broke with the traditional form by insisting that paternal and political rule were not merely analogous but identical. In the 1680s and 1690s, 'the Filmerian position very nearly became the official state ideology'.[9] The classic form was a fully developed theory of political right and political obedience and was the first of its kind; 'there was no patriarchal theory of obligation prior to 1603'.[10] The standard claim in political theory is that patriarchalism was dead and buried by 1700 – but the form that passed away was Filmer's classic patriarchy.

Filmer wrote in response to the challenge posed by the doctrine of the natural freedom of mankind. If men were born free and equal then, necessarily, political right or the dominion of one man over another could be established in one way only; through an agreement (contract) between those concerned that such a relation should be brought into being. According to Filmer, acknowledgement that Adam had been granted monarchical power by God by virtue of his fatherhood cut the ground from under the feet of the contract theorists. At the birth of his first son, Adam became the first king and his political right passed to all subsequent fathers and kings, who were one and the same: all kings ruled as fathers in consequence of their procreative power, and all fathers were monarchs in their families. Sons were born into political subjection to their fathers and hence to the monarch: no such political nonsense as talk of contracts was required to justify political subjection. Filmer's account of the natural origin of political right appears straightforward enough, and no hint is given in discussions of the relation between the theories of Hobbes and Filmer that patriarchy is more complicated.

Paternal right is only one dimension of patriarchy – as Filmer himself reveals. Filmer's apparently straightforward statements obscure the original foundation of political right. Paternal power is not the origin of political right. Father-right is established only after political right has been brought into being. Another act of political genesis is required before a man can acquire the natural right of fatherhood. Sons do not spring up like mushrooms, as Filmer was quick to

---

[9] Schochet, *Patriarchalism in Political Thought*, p. 193.
[10] Schochet, *Patriarchalism in Political Thought*, p. 16.

450   PATEMAN

remind Hobbes. Adam's political title is granted *before* he becomes a father. If he is to be a father, Eve has to become a mother. In other words, *sex-right or conjugal right must necessarily precede the right of fatherhood*. The genesis of political dominion lies in Adam's sex-right, *not* in his fatherhood.

Filmer makes clear that Adam's political right is originally established in his right as a husband over Eve: 'God gave to Adam ... the dominion over the woman', and, citing *Genesis* 3:16, 'God ordained Adam to rule over his wife, and her desires were to be subject to his'.[11] (*Genesis* states that Eve's 'desire shall be to thy husband, and he shall rule over thee'). Adam's desire is to become a father, but in no ordinary sense of 'father'. He desires to obtain the remarkable powers of a patriarchal father. Filmer briefly mentions Adam's original, Divine grant of political right over Eve at various points, but it has a shadowy presence in his writings. In recent (patriarchal) commentaries on his texts, sex-right has completely disappeared. And, to be sure, when reading Filmer from the perspective of only one dimension of patriarchalism, conjugal right is not easy to discern under the cloak of Adam's fatherhood.

The biblical patriarchal image (here in Locke's words) is of 'nursing Fathers tender and carefull of the publick weale'.[12] The patriarchal story is about the procreative power of a father who is complete in himself, who embodies the creative power of both female and male. His procreative power both gives and animates physical life and creates and maintains political right. Filmer is able to refer to Adam's power over Eve so casually because classic patriarchalism declares women to be procreatively and politically irrelevant. The reason that Adam has dominion over 'the woman' is, according to Filmer (here following the patriarchal idea of fatherhood, which is very ancient), that 'the man ... [is] the nobler and principal agent in generation'.[13] Women are merely empty vessels for the exercise of men's sexual and procreative power. The original political right that God gives to Adam is the right, so to speak, to fill the empty vessel. Adam, and all men, must do this if they are to become fathers. But men's generative power has a dual aspect. The genesis of new physical life belongs in their hands, not in the empty vessel. Men are the 'principal agents in generation', and 'generation' includes political creativity. Men's generative power includes the ability to create new political life, or to give birth to political right.

In view of the character of the extraordinary powers that classic patriarchalism arrogates to men, it is appropriate that the powers are contained in the

---

[11] Sir Robert Filmer, *Patriarcha, or the Natural Powers of the Kings of England Asserted and Other Political Works*, ed. Peter Laslett (Oxford: Basil Blackwell, 1949), p. 241; p. 283. *Genesis*, too, can be interpreted in more than one way, and equality of men and women in the sight of God is not incompatible with male supremacy in human affairs; e.g. Calvin argued from both the perspective of *cognitio dei* (the eternal, Divine perspective in which all things are equal) and the perspective of *cognitio hominis* (the worldly perspective in which humans are hierarchically ordered). See Mary Potter, 'Gender Equality and Gender Hierarchy in Calvin's Theology', *Signs*, 11 (1986), 725–39.

[12] John Locke, *Two Treatises of Government*, 2nd edn, Peter Laslett, ed. (Cambridge: Cambridge University Press, 1967), Bk II, 2.

[13] Filmer, *Patriarcha*, p. 245.

name of 'father' and encompassed under the writ of 'fatherhood'. The presence of conjugal right is very faint in Filmer's writings because (although at one level he must acknowledge it) Adam's original political right is subsumed under the power of fatherhood. For instance, after stating that Eve and her desires are subject to Adam, Filmer continues in the next sentence, 'here we have the original grant of government, and the fountain of all power placed in the Father of all mankind'. Moreover, Adam is also Eve's father. In the story in the book of *Genesis*, Eve is created only after Adam and the animals have been placed on earth. God creates and names the animals and Adam but, we are told in *Genesis* 2:20, 'for Adam there was not found an help meet for him'. Eve is then created, but she is not created *ab initio* but *from* Adam, who is, in a sense, her parent, and Adam, not God, gives Eve her name. Filmer is therefore able to treat all political right as the right of a father. Eve is not only under the dominion of Adam, but he is (with God's help) the 'principal agent' in her generation. The father in classic patriarchal theory is not just one of two parents – he is *the* parent, and the being able to generate political right.

The greatest story of masculine political birth is the story of an original contract that creates civil freedom and civil society. The classic patriarchalists lost the battle over fathers and sons and the natural origin of political right. Patriarchalism, in the sense of paternal right, ceased to be politically relevant by the end of the seventeenth century. Civil society is constituted by the (ostensibly) universal, conventional bonds of contract not the particular, natural bonds of kinship and fatherhood. However, the standard account of the defeat of patriarchy ignores the fact that the contract theorists had no quarrel with classic patriarchism over the true origin of political right; they fought against paternal right but had no wish to disturb the other dimension of patriarchy, conjugal right.

The 'freedom of mankind' in contract argument means what it says, the freedom of *men*. The victory of contract doctrine over the classic form of patriarchal argument was, rather, the *transformation* of classic patriarchy into a new form. The contract theorists constructed their own, modern patriarchal argument – the third of the historical forms. Modern patriarchy is contractual not natural and embodies masculine right not the right of fatherhood. Hobbes, the most brilliant and bold of contract theorists, is a patriarchal theorist in the modern sense, but his arguments differ in some significant respects from those of his fellow contract theorists and, in the end, it was they, not Hobbes, who provided the necessary theoretical framework for patriarchal civil society.

II

On the face of it, Hobbes's writings seem unequivocally opposed to both dimensions of classic patriarchy. Hobbes's theory rests on mother-right and the absence of natural sexual dominion; how, then, does Hobbes transform natural maternal power and women's natural freedom into patriarchal right, and why have scholars been able to identify so many passages in Hobbes's writings where

452   PATEMAN

he apparently falls back on the traditional form of patriarchal argument? The appropriate place to begin to consider the conjuring tricks is with Hobbes's picture of the natural condition. Hobbes's imaginative resolution of civil society into its most fundamental ('natural') parts was much more rigorous than the similar undertakings of the other contract theorists. Hobbes was willing to take the logic of individualism to its most radical conclusions in this as in other respects. When Hobbes reconstitutes natural entities in perpetual motion into something recognizably human, the result is that humans interact in a natural condition that can barely be recognized as social. Hobbes's state of nature is the famous war of all against all, and, in a statement which is rarely seen as of political significance, Hobbes writes that in the natural condition there are 'no matrimonial laws'.[14] Marriage – that is to say, a long-term relation between the sexes – must be brought about in exactly the same way as any other relation between the inhabitants of the state of nature where there is no natural order of dominion, nor any politically significant difference in strength or prudence between individuals. Relations can arise in two ways only; either individuals contract themselves into a given relationship; or one, by some stratagem, is able to coerce another into the desired arrangement. This is also true of relations between a man and a woman. In the natural condition women face men as free equals; Hobbes writes that,

whereas some have attributed the dominion to the man only, as being of the more excellent sex; they misreckon in it. For there is not always that difference of strength or prudence between the man and the woman, as that the right can be determined without war.[15]

In the state of nature there is no law to regulate marriage – and no marriage. Marriage does not exist because marriage is a long-term arrangement, and long-term sexual relationships, like other such relationships, are very difficult to establish and maintain in Hobbes's natural condition. The boundaries separating the inhabitants one from another are so tightly drawn by Hobbes that each one can judge the rest only from a subjective perspective, or from the perspective of pure self-interest. Natural individuals will, therefore, always break an agreement, or refuse to play their part in a contract, if it appears in their interest to do so. To enter a contract or to signify agreement to do so is to leave oneself open to betrayal. Hobbes's natural state suffers from an endemic problem of keeping contracts and of 'performing second'; 'If a covenant be made, wherein neither of the parties perform presently, but trust one another; ... upon any reasonable suspicion, it is void: ... And ... he which performeth first, does but betray himself to his enemy'.[16] The only contract that an individual, of his or her own volition, can enter into in safety is one in which agreement and performance take place at the same time. An agreement to perform an act of coitus provides an example of a contract that comes close to meeting this criterion, but an agree-

[14] Hobbes, *Leviathan*, in *EW*, vol. III, chap. XX, p. 187.
[15] Hobbes, *Leviathan*, pp. 186–7.
[16] Hobbes, *Leviathan*, chap. XIV, pp. 124–5.

ment to marry, to enter into a long-term sexual relationship, would founder in the same manner as contracts to create other relations that endure over time.

The women and men in Hobbes's state of nature can engage in sexual intercourse and, therefore, children can be born. A child, however, is born a long time after any act of intercourse. As Hobbes notes, in the absence of matrimonial laws proof of fatherhood rests on the testimony of the mother. Since there is no way of establishing paternity with any certainty, the child belongs to the mother. Hobbes's argument is all the more striking since he, too, suggests that men are the 'principal agents' in generation. Echoing the classic patriarchal view of fatherhood, Hobbes writes that 'as to the generation, God hath ordained to man a helper'[17] – but the female 'helper' in the state of nature becomes much more than an auxiliary once the birth takes place. Hobbes insists that no man can have two masters and so only one parent can have dominion over the child. In the natural condition the mother, not the father, enjoys this right. In direct contradiction of Sir Robert Filmer and the patriarchal doctrine that political right originates in the father's generative power, Hobbes proclaims that, 'every woman that bears children, becomes both a *mother* and a *lord'*.[18] At birth, the infant is in the mother's power. She makes the decision whether to expose or to nourish the child. To have the power to preserve life is, according to Hobbes, to exercise rightful dominion, whether the subject is a newly born infant or a vanquished adult. If the mother preserves the infant, she thereby becomes a lord; 'because preservation of life being the end, for which one man [or infant] becomes subject to another, every man is supposed to promise obedience, to him [or her], in whose power it is to save, or destroy him'.[19]

From 1861 for a half century or more (following the publication of Sir Henry Maine's *Ancient Law* and Johann Bachofen's *Mother Right*) another controversy raged about political origins, matriarchy and patriarchy. The proponents were all reluctant to admit that matriarchy in the literal sense – rule by women as mothers – ever existed, even hypothetically.[20] Similarly, some contemporary theorists still find it necessary to take issue with Hobbes's logic on mother-right. The rather amusing objection has been raised that Hobbes is mistaken; a mother 'simply does not wield' the power Hobbes ascribes to her.[21] The 'helper' herself always requires another helper. In Hobbes's day, the objection continues, the mother was attended by a midwife or male physician, and it is the latter who, at the moment of birth, has power over the child in her or his hands. Hobbes should have concluded that neither fathers nor mothers possessed an original political power in the natural condition, but then his argument against natural paternal right would have been 'more absurd still'. In his eagerness to combat Filmer, Hobbes 'overlooked the defects attached to an argument which would

---

[17] Hobbes, *Leviathan*, chap. XX, p. 186.

[18] Hobbes, *Philosophical Rudiments*, chap. IX, p. 116.

[19] Hobbes, *Leviathan*, p. 188.

[20] For an account of the controversy, see Rosalind Coward, *Patriarchal Precedents* (London: Routledge & Kegan Paul, 1983), chap. 2. See also Pateman, *The Sexual Contract*, chap 2.

[21] Preston King, *The Ideology of Order* (London: Allen & Unwin, 1974), p. 203.

transfer this power to a party – the mother – whom no one supposed ever had a proper right or even opportunity to exercise it (given the establishment of a civil society)'.[22] Precisely; in patriarchal civil society, past or present, political theorists rarely are willing to contemplate that mothers (women) could legitimately exercise political right, even in an hypothetical state of nature or as a matter of mere logic. The other social contract theorists, unlike Hobbes, built masculine sexual dominion as a natural fact of human existence into their political theories and so demonstrated in a straightforward fashion that, for all that their arguments are couched in universal terms, equality, freedom and contract are a male privilege – although contemporary political theorists still manage to avoid noticing the fact.[23] Hobbes's logic is impeccable. In his natural condition (whatever the facts of childbirth in the seventeenth century), a pregnant woman would not give herself up as a hostage to fortune by enlisting helpers in her labours; no free, strong woman would place her right of dominion at risk with such assistance.

By nature, a mother is a lord who can do as she wills with her infant. If she decides to 'breed him', the condition on which she does so, Hobbes states, is that, 'being grown to full age he become not her enemy'.[24] That is to say, the infant must contract to obey her. The mother's political right over her child originates in contract, and gives her absolute power. A woman can contract away her right over her child to the father, but, when the premise of Hobbes's argument is that women naturally stand as equals to men, there is no reason why a woman should do this, and, least of all, why she should *always* do so. To argue that a tiny infant can contract, or should be regarded as if it had contracted, with its mother is, as Filmer insisted, anthropological nonsense. In terms of Hobbes's understanding of 'contract', however, this agreement is as convincing an example of a contract as any other in Hobbes's writings. Scholars have drawn attention to Hobbes's claim that the reasons and circumstances under which agreement is given are irrelevant to the validity of the contract; for Hobbes, it makes no difference whether a contract is entered into after due deliberation or with the conqueror's sword at one's breast. Submission to overwhelming power in return for protection, whether the power is that of the conqueror's sword or the mother's power over her newly born infant, is always a valid sign of agreement for Hobbes. Hobbes's assimilation of conquest to contract, enforced sub-

---

[22] King, *The Ideology of Order*, p. 206; p. 205. Hobbes's most recent biographer suggests that his argument about mother-right derives from his own experience as a child. Hobbes's views perhaps owed much to that occasion during those years when the curate [Hobbes's father], possibly long before his disappearance, was forced by his character and circumstances to yield the government to Hobbes' mother' (Arnold A. Rogow, *Thomas Hobbes: Radical in the Service of Reaction* (New York and London: W.W. Norton and Co., 1986), p. 132). Hobbes's father, rather fond of drink and neglectful of his parish, fled after being accused of assaulting a rector of a neighbouring parish. Ironically Rogow was unable to find any new information about Hobbes's mother. Even her maiden name remains uncertain.

[23] The other classic contract theorists are discussed in Pateman, *The Sexual Contract*, chaps 3 and 4.

[24] Hobbes, *Philosophical Rudiments*, chap. IX, p. 116.

mission to consent, is often remarked upon, but the political significance of his peculiar notion of contract for the origin of the family in the state of nature and for the making of the original pact is less often appreciated.

III

The logical conclusion of Hobbes's resolution of civil society into its natural parts of rational entities in motion, and his reconstitution of the natural condition, is that the sexes come together only fleetingly and that the original political right is mother-right. Yet Hobbes also writes in a passage (cited by Chapman and Schochet, for example), 'that the beginning of all dominion amongst men was in families. In which, ... the father of the family by the law of nature was absolute lord of his wife and children: [and] made what laws amongst them he pleased'.[25] And he also refers to familial government or a 'patrimonial kingdom' in which the family,

if it grows by multiplication of children, either by generation, or adoption; or of servants, either by generation, conquest, or voluntary submission, to be so great and numerous, as in probability it may protect itself, then is that family called a *patrimonial kingdom*, or monarchy by acquisition, wherein the sovereignty is in one man, as it is in a monarch made by *political institution*. So that whatsoever rights be in the one, the same also be in the other.[26]

Moreover, Hobbes also makes statements such as 'cities and kingdoms ... are but greater families',[27] and 'a great family is a kingdom, and a little kingdom a family'.[28] He also remarks that Germany, like other countries 'in their beginnings', was divided between a number of masters of families, all at war with each other.[29] Such statements have been treated as evidence that Hobbes was a patriarchalist like Filmer and that his natural condition was composed of families not individuals. Such an interpretation leaves unanswered the questions of how the transformation comes about from mother-right to the patriarchal family in the state of nature and how the family is generated.

Chapman has stressed that Hobbes's family is an artificial, political institution rather than a natural social form, but its extraordinary character consists in more than a conventional, political origin. No attention is paid to the most bizarre aspect of Hobbes's account of the family because conjugal right and the position of a wife are ignored. Indeed, the scholars involved in the debate about Hobbes and the family have not paused to wonder how there can be wives in the state of nature where there is no law of matrimony. Nor have they asked how

---

[25] Thomas Hobbes, *A Dialogue between a Philosopher and a Student of the Common Laws of England*, *EW*, vol. VI, p. 147.

[26] Thomas Hobbes, *De Corpore Politico, or The Elements of Law*, *EW*, vol. IV, chap. IV, pp. 158–9.

[27] Hobbes, *Leviathan*, chap. XVII, p. 154.

[28] Hobbes, *Philosophical Rudiments*, chap. VIII, p. 108.

[29] Hobbes, *Leviathan*, chap. X, p. 82.

families can come into existence when marriage does not exist and yet marriage is the 'origin' of the family. Hobbes's 'family' is very curious and has nothing in common with the families of Filmer's pages, the family as found in the writings of the other classic social contract theorists, or as popularly understood today. Consider Hobbes's definitions: in *Leviathan* he states that a family 'consist[s] of a man and his children; or of a man and his servants; or of a man, and his children, and servants together; wherein the father or master is the sovereign'.[30] In *De Cive* we find, 'a *father* with his *sons* and *servants*, grown into a civil person by virtue of his paternal jurisdiction, is called a *family*'.[31] What has happened to the wife and mother? Only in *Elements of Law* does he write that 'the father or mother of the family is sovereign of the same'.[32] But the sovereign cannot be the mother, given the conjectural history of the origin of the family implicit in Hobbes's argument.

The 'natural' characteristics postulated by Hobbes mean that long-term relationships are very unlikely in his state of nature. However, Hobbes states in *Leviathan* that, in the war of all against all, 'there is no man who can hope by his own strength, or wit, to defend himself from destruction, without the help of confederates'.[33] But how can such a protective confederation be formed in the natural condition when there is an acute problem of keeping agreements? The answer is that confederations are formed by conquest. If one male individual manages to conquer another in the state of nature the conqueror will have obtained a servant. Hobbes assumes that no one would wilfully give up his life, so, faced with the conqueror's sword, the defeated man will make a (valid) contract to obey his victor. Hobbes defines dominion or political right acquired through force as 'the dominion of the master over his servant'.[34] Conqueror and conquered then constitute 'a little body politic, which consisteth of two persons, the one sovereign, which is called the *master*, or lord; the other subject, which is called the *servant*'.[35] Hobbes distinguishes a servant from a slave, but his definition of a servant makes it hard to maintain the distinction: 'the master of the servant, is master also of all he hath: and may exact the use thereof; that is to say, of his goods, of his labour, of his servants, and of his children, as often as he shall think fit'.[36]

The master and his slave-servant form the little body politic of a defensive confederation against the rest of the inhabitants of the state of nature. That is to say, according to Hobbes's definition of a 'family', the master and his servant form a family. For Hobbes, the origin of the family is entirely conventional. A 'family' is created not through procreation but by conquest, and a family consists of a master and his servants, i.e. all those, whatever their age or sex who fall

[30] Hobbes, *Leviathan*, chap. XX, p. 191.
[31] Hobbes, *Philosophical Rudiments*, chap. IX, p. 121.
[32] Hobbes, *De Corpore Politico*, chap. IV, p. 158.
[33] Hobbes, *Leviathan*, chap. XV, p. 133.
[34] Hobbes, *Leviathan*, chap. XX, p. 189.
[35] Hobbes, *De Corpore Politico*, chap. III, pp. 149–50.
[36] Hobbes, *Leviathan*, chap. XX, p. 190.

under his absolute jurisdiction. A 'family' composed only of a master and his male servants is a singular institution and it becomes more singular still if this male household contains children. Hobbes remarks at one point that sovereignty can be established 'by natural force; as when a man maketh his children, to submit themselves, and their children to his government'.[37] Children have again sprung up like mushrooms, ready to submit to (contract with) their fathers. And what of their mothers; how are they included in the 'family'? In the natural condition there are two ways only in which sexual relations between free, equal women and men can take place. Either a woman freely contracts to engage in intercourse or she is outwitted and taken by force. There is no reason why a woman should contract of her own free will to enter into a long-term sexual relationship and become a 'wife', that is, to be in servitude to – to become the servant (slave) of – a man. In the state of nature a woman is as able as a man to defend herself or to conquer another to form a protective confederation of master and servant. Why then does Hobbes assume that only men become masters of servants?

The answer is that, by the time the original contract is entered into, *all* the women in the natural condition have been conquered by men and become servants. Hobbes is explicit that 'dominion amongst men' begins in the defensive confederation or small body politic he calls a family, but he does not spell out that men also gain dominion over women by creating 'families'. A conjectural history of how this comes about might run as follows: at first, women, who are as strong and capable as men, are able to ensure that sexual relations are consensual. When a woman becomes a mother and decides to become a lord and raise her child, her position changes; she is put at a slight disadvantage against men, since now she has her infant to defend too. Conversely, a man obtains a slight advantage over her and is then able to defeat the woman he had initially to treat with as an equal. Mothers are lords in Hobbes's state of nature, but, paradoxically, for a woman to become a mother and a lord is her downfall. She then has given an opening for a male enemy to outwit and vanquish her in the ceaseless natural conflict. Mother-right can never be more than fleeting.

The original political dominion of maternal lordship is quickly overcome and replaced by masculine right. Each man can obtain a 'family' of a woman servant and her child. Thus mother-right is overturned and the state of nature becomes filled with patriarchal 'families'. All the women in the natural condition are forcibly incorporated (which for Hobbes, is to say contract themselves) into 'families' and become the permanent servants of male masters. The 'help' given by women to men in procreation then becomes the unending help of domestic servitude. The 'wife' is relegated to the status of a helper too politically insignificant to be worthy of listing as a member of this peculiar protective association. A story along these lines is necessary to explain the existence of patriarchal 'families' in the state of nature, and also to explain why a patriarchal law of matrimony is instituted through the original contract.

---

[37] Hobbes, *Leviathan*, chap. XVII, p. 159.

But it is hard to tell a consistent and convincing story about women's subjection when beginning from the postulate of natural freedom and equality between women and men.[38] The conquest of women would surely take more than one generation. Some women, either by choice or the accident of nature, would be childless and so would remain free. Indeed, once childless women saw the fate of women who decided to exercise maternal lordship they would, as rational beings, choose to remain childless and conserve their natural freedom. Free women would, however, be found only in the first generation in the natural condition. Childless women would die, and all subsequent generations of women would be born into servitude (and so, according to Hobbes's definition of servitude, would be under the jurisdiction of the master). The problem with this version of the conjectural history is that, if there are free childless women in the first generation in the natural condition, there is no reason why they should not form protective confederations of their own by conquering men, or each other, and so obtaining servants. Women and men would then wage the war of all against all as masters of 'families' – and who knows who might win in the end? But, in Hobbes's theory we do know who wins, and thus there is only one story that can be told. Women must all be conquered in the first generation; there can be no female masters in the state of nature or there will be no original contract and no law of matrimony.

IV

The method through which Hobbes constructed his picture of the state of nature meant that, as a ruthlessly consistent theorist, he had to begin from the logical but shocking premise of an absence of sexual dominion and original mother-right. But Hobbes was well aware, as indicated in the passages that I cited above, that, historically, paternal right and the subjection of wives was the established custom. In the *logical* beginning, all political right is maternal right. In the *historical* beginning, masculine or 'paternal' right holds sway. The story of the defeat of women in the state of nature explains how patriarchal 'families', incorporating all the women, are formed through conquest and ruled by 'fathers'. This stage of the history of the natural condition must be reached if men are to enter the original contract, exercise their political creativity and create a new phase of history in the form of modern patriarchal society. Commentators on contract theory generally take it for granted that there are no problems in referring to 'individuals' entering into the original contract, so implying that any or all of the inhabitants of the state of nature can participate. Some commentators are more careful, and Schochet, for example, notes that in the seventeenth century fathers of families were assumed to have sealed the original pact. He argues that Hobbes shared this assumption. Despite Hobbes's use of traditional patriarchal language, his 'families' are not ruled by men as fathers but by men as

---

[38] I am grateful to Peter Morriss for raising the question of generations and for other helpful criticisms.

masters. Masters of families rule by virtue of contract (conquest) not their paternal, procreative capacity. Men as masters – or as free and equal men – enter into the original contract that constitutes civil society. Women, now in subjection, no longer have the necessary standing (they are no longer free and equal or 'individuals') to take part in creating a new civil society.

The civil law of matrimony, which upholds conjugal right, is created through the original pact. Political theorists consistently omit to mention one of the most remarkable features of Hobbes's political theory. Hobbes makes it quite clear that conjugal right is not natural. Conjugal right is created through the original contract and so is a *political* right. The right is deliberately created by the men who bring civil society into being. The other classic contract theorists presuppose that the institution of marriage exists naturally and that conjugal relations are non-political relations, carried over into civil society. In Hobbes's theory, the law of matrimony is created as part of the civil law. Contemporary political theorists, too, take for granted that the structure of the institution of marriage is non-political and so they pay no attention to conjugal right. Hobbes's political theory makes clear what the other classic contract stories, and contemporary commentaries on contract theory, leave implicit: that the original contract is not only a *social* contract that constitutes the civil law and political right in the sense of (state) government; it is also a *sexual* contract that institutes political right in the form of patriarchal – masculine – power, or government by men, a power exercised in large part as conjugal right.

Hobbes states that in civil society the husband has dominion 'because for the most part commonwealths have been erected by the fathers, not by the mothers of families'.[39] Or again, 'in all cities ... constituted of *fathers*, not *mothers* governing their families, the domestical command belongs to the man; and such a contract, if it be made according to the civil laws, is called matrimony'.[40] If free and equal women could enter the original contract there is no reason whatsoever why they would agree to create a civil law that secures their permanent subjection as wives. Matrimonial law takes a patriarchal form because *men* have made the original contract. The fact that the law of matrimony is part of the civil law provides another reason for self-interested individual men to make a collective agreement. In addition to securing their natural liberty, *men as a sex* have an interest in a political mechanism which secures for them collectively the fruits of the conquests made severally by each man in the natural condition. Through the civil institution of marriage they can all lawfully obtain the familiar 'helpmeet' and gain the sexual and domestic services of a wife, whose permanent servitude is now guaranteed by the law and sword of Leviathan.

Hobbes had no wish to challenge the law of matrimony of his own day, embodied in the common law doctrine of coverture. The law of coverture was given classic expression by Sir William Blackstone in his *Commentaries on the Laws of England* in the eighteenth century. Under coverture, a wife had no

---

[39] Hobbes, *Leviathan*, chap. XV, p. 187.
[40] Hobbes, *Philosophical Rudiments*, chap. IX, p. 118.

independent juridical existence; she was a civilly dead being, absorbed into the person of her husband. No one, it would seem, could fail to be struck by the legal powers given to husbands, whether in Blackstone's gloss on the law or in marital practice – powers that can only be compared, as they were regularly compared by feminists in the nineteenth century, to those of slave-masters.[41] Yet patriarchy runs so deeply in the contemporary theoretical consciousness that Chapman comments (echoing Blackstone) that 'the most striking feature of the common law family is the liabilities attached to the man, particularly regarding the acts of his wife and servants'.[42] Now, if women had made the original contract, civil law might well reflect the fact and attach all manner of 'liabilities' to men. But we did not make it, and could not have made it, and so 'the most striking feature' of coverture is the juridical non-existence of a wife (just as she disappears in Hobbes's definition of the 'family' in the state of nature). The liabilities of the husband that impress Chapman are the other side of the wife's subjection. 'Liabilities' are the price the husband pays for being a master, that is, a protector. The most fundamental premise of Hobbes's political theory is that no individual will give up the right of self-protection.[43] In the state of nature women too have this right, but in civil society women as wives have given up (been forced to give up) this right in favour of the 'protection' of their husband – and husbands are now protected by the sword of Leviathan.

Students of Hobbes do not usually make a connection between the original overthrow of mother-right and the establishment of Leviathan. The crucial political significance of the conquest of women in the natural condition is that, unless the defeat occurs, Leviathan is impossible to envisage. The conjuror Hobbes is far too clever a wizard for his patriarchal successors and the trick is never remarked upon in discussions of his theory. If women took part in the original contract the awesome figure of the mortal god Leviathan could not be created. Leviathan can be brought into being only if participation in his generation is confined to men. The creation of civil society is an act of masculine political birth; men have no need of a 'helper' in *political* generation. In the state of nature, individuals are differentiated only by their sex; that is to say, by their bodily form (in strength, rationality and prudence there is no politically significant difference between individuals with female bodies and individuals with male bodies). Hobbes's account of the institution of Leviathan makes sense only if the participants in the original contract all have the same bodily form.

The creation of Leviathan, Hobbes tells us, involves 'more than consent, or concord; it is a real unity of them all, in one and the same person'.[44] When men cease to be a mere natural multitude and transform themselves through the act

---

[41] On the implications of coverture, see Pateman, *The Sexual Contract*, chaps 5 and 6.

[42] Chapman, '*Leviathan* Writ Small', p. 84, fn. 90.

[43] Hampton, *Hobbes and the Social Contract Tradition*, pp. 197–207, argues that his deduction of absolute sovereignty fails precisely because Hobbes makes self-protection an absolute right. But because she takes no account of Hobbes's patriarchalism, she fails to mention that, if the argument about sovereignty in the state is correct, then conjugal sovereignty fails too.

[44] Hobbes, *Leviathan*, chap. XVII, p. 158.

of contract into a unified body, or body politic, bound together through the conventional bonds of contract and civil law, their unity is represented in a very literal sense by the person of their (absolute) master and ruler, Leviathan. They create him 'to bear their person', and, Hobbes states, 'it is the *unity* of the representer, not the *unity* of the represented, that maketh the person *one*'.[45] No such unity would be possible if both sexes took part in the constitution of Leviathan – there could be no representative figure who could represent the 'person', the bodily form, of both sexes. Men must be represented and their civil unity given literal symbolic personification by one of their own kind. Similarly, 'private bodies' are also represented by one person, and Hobbes uses the example of 'all families, in which the father, or master ordereth the whole family'. Husband and wife cannot govern jointly in the family; there can be one master only, and the husband is the necessary 'one person representative' of the family in civil society.[46] An act of masculine political birth creates civil beings and their sovereign in the image of their makers (only Adam, the first man, through the hand of God, could generate a woman). If the representer is to be unified, he must be *he*. To attempt to represent both sexes within the figure of one master would be to dissolve his unity and oneness and to shatter political order.

V

Hobbes turned classic into modern patriarchy but several features of his argument worked against him becoming a founding father of modern patriarchal theory. For example, Hobbes negated Filmer's arguments but that was not sufficient to create the theory required for civil patriarchy. Hobbes turned Filmer's social bonds into their opposite. Filmer saw families and kingdoms as homologous and bound together through the natural, procreative power of the father. Hobbes saw families and kingdoms as homologous, but as bound together through the conventional tie of contract, or, what for Hobbes is the same thing, the force of the sword. Hobbes also agreed with Filmer that sovereignty must be absolute – but sovereignty in the state, not in private bodies. Civil fathers and masters are not miniature Leviathans. Their powers run only so far as permitted by Leviathan's laws and his sword. Leviathan thus enabled Hobbes to offer a solution to the problem that dogged Filmer's classic patriarchalism. Hinton has noted that if fathers were kings then there could be no king with true monarchical power.[47] Hobbes's civil masters cannot detract from the absolute mastery of Leviathan. Hobbes's solution, however, retained absolutism in the state, the form of political right that, as Locke argued, had to be replaced by limited, constitutional government in a properly *civil* order.

---

[45] Hobbes, *Leviathan*, chap. XVI, p. 151.

[46] Hobbes, *Leviathan*, chap. XXII, pp. 221–2.

[47] R. W. K. Hinton, 'Husbands, Fathers and Conquerors', *Political Studies*, 15 (1967), 291–300 at pp. 294, 299.

The absolute power of Leviathan's sword was not the only problem with Hobbes's patriarchalism. Hobbes was too revealing about civil society. The political character of conjugal right was expertly concealed in Locke's separation of what he called 'paternal' power from political power and, ever since, most political theorists, whatever their views about other forms of subordination, have accepted that the powers of husbands derive from nature and, hence, are not political. Not only are a range of important questions about domination and subjection in our own society thus suppressed, but some other important questions about the 'origin' of civil society are also neatly avoided. In the past two decades, individualism of a radical, Hobbesian kind has become very influential, although the absolutist conclusions that Hobbes drew from his individualist premises are rejected in favour of a view of the state as a minimal, protective association.[48] The association is held to have a legitimate origin in voluntary transactions between individuals in the state of nature. In the final chapter of *Leviathan*, Hobbes writes that, 'there is scarce a commonwealth in the world, whose beginnings can in conscience be justified'.[49] Hobbes's 'beginning' of the original contract between men can only be justified if, as he believed, political order depended upon the erection of Leviathan. Without Leviathan, and from Hobbes's starting point of free and equal women and men, a voluntary beginning might be possible. Such a story could not be told by political theorists who acknowledge only half the original contract (the social contract) and thus endorse patriarchal right. The origin of the patriarchal protective state in Hobbes's theory lies in the conquest and servitude of women in the state of nature and in their civil subjection and domestication as wives.

Hobbes's theory is an early version of the argument, presented in the later nineteenth and early twentieth centuries in elaborate detail and with reference to much ethnographic data, that civilization and political society resulted from the overthrow of mother-right and the triumph of patriarchy. The silences and omissions of contemporary political theory and the standard readings of Hobbes's texts do nothing to question that argument. Scholars do not mention the problems about women and the civil order arising from Hobbes's theory and the subsequent development of contract theory: for example, why has conjugal right never been seen as political when every other form of power has been subjected to the closest scrutiny and judgement? Why is women's exclusion from the original pact not mentioned in most discussions of contract theory? If women can take no part in the original contract what is their status as parties to the marriage contract? Has Hobbes's identification of enforced submission with consent (contract) any relevance to present-day sexual relations? By the beginning of the eighteenth century, when, according to political theorists today,

---

[48] For an argument that absolutist conclusions are ultimately unavoidable, see Carole Pateman, *The Problem of Political Obligation*, 2nd edn (Cambridge: Polity Press; Berkeley and Los Angeles: University of California Press, 1985), chap. 3. Hampton, *Hobbes and the Social Contract Tradition*, interprets Hobbes's commonwealth as a union of slaves within the will of a master.

[49] Hobbes, *Leviathan*, Part IV, p. 706.

patriarchalism had come to an end, Mary Astell asked, 'if *all Men are born Free, how is it that all Women are born Slaves?*'[50] Most political theorists have yet to recognize the existence or relevance of Astell's question – or the political significance of the fact that Hobbes did not think that we were so born.

[50] Mary Astell, *Some Reflections Upon Marriage*, 4th edn (New York: Source Book Press, 1970; originally published 1730), p. 107.

[12]

HOBBESIAN POLITICAL ORDER

RUSSELL HARDIN
University of Chicago

READING HOBBES IN OTHER WORDS:
CONTRACTARIAN, UTILITARIAN, GAME THEORIST

The political theory of Hobbes is variously seen as a forerunner of both utilitarianism and contractarianism. The transparent oddity of these views is that today's contractarians view utilitarianism with hostility, frequently treating it as the theory that must be defeated if contractarianism is to stand. The core value in contractarianism is consent, which is taken to be right-making. If a people consent to rule by ayatollahs, such rule is right no matter how abhorrent others elsewhere may find it. The core value in utilitarianism is utility or welfare somehow defined. As applied to politics, utilitarians judge that government best which most conduces to the benefit of its people. The particularity of the example for contractarianism and the abstractness of the case for utilitarianism are indicative of their different thrusts.

As a practical matter, Hobbes need not be inconsistent in holding both contractarian and utilitarian views of government. It may happen that we consent to what produces greatest welfare. In fact, it was Hobbes's greatest genius to fit these together in a striking way. He argued convincingly that universal egoism, which is merely welfarism at the individual level, could be channeled by strong government to produce universal welfare and that egoists, for their own benefit, would want such government.[1] He also claimed that most people are egoists, so that his prescription should apply to real societies. It would not apply if insufficiently many people were motivated by

AUTHOR'S NOTE: *I wish to thank Paul Bullen, Thomas Christiano, Judge Richard Posner, the informal Tuesday evening theory seminar at the University of Chicago, the Departments of Political Science at Duke University and Washington University of St. Louis, and participants in the symposium of the Central Division meetings of the American Philosophical Association, April 1989, for comments on an earlier draft of this essay.*

egoism, if too many were concerned to promote particular religious views or to promote their honor or glory as defined by success in warlike endeavors.

But as a strictly theoretical matter, commitment to consent and commitment to welfare are not equivalent and may be contrary. Hence, at base, Hobbes's theory is ambivalent.

Hobbes is also ambivalent about what problem he wishes to resolve. His discussion is more or less equally about the creation and the maintenance of sovereign government. His overriding actual concern at the time of writing, even his likely motivation for writing, was surely the maintenance of sovereign government in the face of revolutionary fervor and turmoil. But his discussion of creation has provoked more commentary by far. Again, a theory of creation need not conflict with a theory of maintenance, but it need not be the same theory either.

As it happens, Hobbes's two ambivalences are overlapping in the following sense. His theory of maintenance of a sovereign is primarily welfarist while his theory of creation is primarily contractarian. (Hence, in Hobbes's case at least, the claim that utilitarianism is inherently conservative seems to fit.) However, even in his concern with creation, his background view is often utilitarian and in his discussions even of maintenance he often invokes consent or at least tacit consent. Indeed, in some contexts he asserts that silence can imply consent (*Leviathan*, chap. 14, 193[167]; chap. 26, 313 [138]).[2]

Part of the confusion in Hobbes is ours. Our central categories for reading him are, unfortunately, not his categories. For example, C. B. Macpherson says that Hobbes introduced, "in other words," the notion of the social contract.[3] When we read Hobbes, we tend to read him almost entirely in other words, it seems. Yet we read Hobbes not simply as literature but as social theory because we want to understand politics in our own categories. Hence we are stuck with the burden of not merely reading Hobbes but of re-reading him.

Over the past two decades or so we have taken to re-reading Hobbes in yet another contemporary vocabulary, that of game theory. In particular, there is a newly established consensus that in Hobbes's vision, the state of nature is plagued with Prisoner's Dilemmas. It is sometimes further supposed that the problem of escaping from the state of nature by creating government is itself a large Prisoner's Dilemma. The Prisoner's Dilemma is the centerpiece of discursive game theory. Since its discovery around 1950, it seems to have gone on, slowly at first but then with alarming rapidity, to have swallowed all of sociology and much of social theory, including normative theory.[4] The claims that Hobbes is a contractarian and that his problem is the resolution of a grand Prisoner's Dilemma are seen essentially as a single thesis in different vocabularies. If so, they stand or fall together. Alas, they fall separately. Hobbes is, in some respects, wrong to invoke contractarian arguments and, as Gregory Kavka and Jean Hampton persuasively argue,[5] the modern game-theoretic re-readers are wrong to think that Hobbes's account of the problem of creating government is a Prisoner's Dilemma.

The rise of the Prisoner's Dilemma is a distant result of the invention of game theory, one of the greatest intellectual advances in our understanding of social and political theory, by Neumann and Morgenstern nearly half a century ago.[6] "Game theory" is not the best of names for that advance because the understanding of games per se is of little moment in social theory and because the chief contribution of Neumann and Morgenstern is hardly a theory in any case. Rather, their contribution is a framework for analyzing social interactions. The beauty of the framework is the way in which it forces us to keep various interactions clear to ourselves as we reason about them. Often, keeping them persistently clear seems nearly sufficient to understand very much about the ways they work.

Naturally, there were forerunners of so central a discovery as the framework of game theory. Many of the great political philosophers have at one point or another in their analysis had some grasp of the structure of relevant strategic interactions. Apart from Hume,[7] however, none seems to have so pervasive a strategic sense as Hobbes, as in his *Leviathan*. Indeed, his strategic grasp is so clear that contemporary readers regularly associate game theoretic categories and ideas with Hobbes's arguments. In particular, he spells out the structure of the Prisoner's Dilemma with eloquent clarity in the failure of beneficial exchanges in the state of nature. I therefore think the contemporary urge to remake Hobbes in our own vocabulary is constructive and enlightening. The first major effort in this urge is David Gauthier's *The Logic of Leviathan* twenty years ago.[8] The most assiduous and instructive effort to make Hobbes a modern game theorist is that of Gregory Kavka in his recent *Hobbesian Moral and Political Theory*.[9] From Gauthier to Kavka, our understanding of Hobbes has been remade and clarified.

I wish to join the enterprise of re-reading Hobbes as a proto-game theorist. With Kavka and Hampton, I wish to argue that Hobbes's central problem of political order is not the problem of the Prisoner's Dilemma. We need political order, in Hobbes's view, in part to help us overcome the logic of the Prisoner's Dilemma in our quotidian relations. But the task of creating or maintaining political order is not itself a Prisoner's Dilemma but, rather, a coordination problem. Hence its resolution is not contractarian in the straightforward sense of that term but is conventional. It depends far less (if at all) on what people consent to than on what will work. Insofar as he recognizes

and even argues this, Hobbes is more nearly a social scientist than a normative theorist.[10] Against Kavka and Hampton, however, I also wish to argue
that the central problem that Hobbes mastered is not the creation of government from the state of nature but the maintenance of government. The
problem of the instant creation or elevation of a sovereign from the state of
nature is not an interesting problem either normatively or social scientifically,
and concentration on it distorts the greater value that Hobbes's analysis has
for us.

It is common, of course, to re-read classical writers in contemporary terms.
This has often been done to Hobbes. Such re-reading can be misleading
because we may tend not merely to translate but to transmute, to recast not
only the vocabulary but the arguments of the earlier work. To some extent
this is plausibly unavoidable, especially if the earlier vocabulary and hence
arguments were vague. For example, in part because of Hobbes's own
vagueness, readers often impose willy-nilly on his arguments the contractarian vision of government to the neglect of other elements of his odd view.
Hobbes is a forerunner of that vision, as articulated later by Locke and others
but partly in a negative or provocative sense, as Euclidian geometry is a
forerunner of non-Euclidian geometries such as Riemannian geometry. It is
partly in reaction to Hobbes that the contractarian enterprise flourished. That
enterprise was not merely an elaboration of Hobbes but was an alternative to
what are often seen as the worst parts of Hobbes, especially the pervasive
egoism. Or at best it was a very partial elaboration of Hobbes, because
although he creates government by covenant (which is merely a contract that
is not immediately fulfilled), he often defies the central elements of early
contractarian thinking. He is not concerned to substitute consent for religious
bases of obligation. (Indeed, he could generally do without a notion of
political obligation, but that is here a side issue.) In any case, he frequently
denies that we do in any meaningful sense consent to rule by our sovereign.
Moreover, most of us do not even understand the issue. All that we need do
is submit to a powerful sovereign who has devices for coercing us. This
gunman view of the sovereign, who is not idly called *Leviathan* in Hobbes's
greatest work, makes a mockery of contemporary contractarian paeans to the
beauty of consent.

In defending these claims, I will first demonstrate Hobbes's understanding of the Prisoner's Dilemma structure of contracting and exchange. I will
then lay out the structure of Hobbes's theory with its potentially misleading
dual focus on the laws of nature and the laws of a sovereign. Getting the
arguments of these two sections clear is important because they are the source
of the common understanding of Hobbes as the contractarian resolver of the

grand Prisoner's Dilemma of social order. With the sketch of these arguments in place, I will turn to the role of the Prisoner's Dilemma in Hobbes's state of nature and the range of strategic devices available for escaping from the state of nature, including the role of social contract thinking in Hobbes. These two issues are rightly seen as closely related in that contractarian arguments are most persuasive when applied to Prisoner's Dilemmas from which all can benefit through regulation of their cooperative behavior by a contract. It is evidence of the power of Hobbes's strategic sense that, in contemporary language, he implicitly rejects the Prisoner's Dilemma description of the state of nature, which he could clearly understand, even if in other words.

CONTRACT AND THE PRISONER'S DILEMMA

To see that Hobbes fully understands the Prisoner's Dilemma but does not make it the central problem of *achieving* political order, consider his lengthy discussion of contract, which takes up most of chapter 14 and much of chapter 15 of *Leviathan*. A contract involves mutual transferring of rights. Such transfers are accomplished by "Bonds, that have their strength, not from their own Nature, (for nothing is more easily broken than a mans word,) but from Feare of some evill consequence upon the rupture" (chap. 14, 192 [65]). A contract in the state of nature is void. Indeed, to perform one's side of a contract first in the state of nature is wrong because "he which performeth first, does but betray himselfe to his enemy; contrary to the Right (he can never abandon) of defending his life, and means of living." But "if there be a common Power set over [the contractors], with right and force sufficient to compell performance, it is not Voyd" (chap. 14, 196 [68]).

It should be clear that Hobbes sees the strategic structure of exchange by contracting as a Prisoner's Dilemma because his ordering of the payoffs of the possible outcomes is that of the Prisoner's Dilemma. We both prefer the state in which we have exchanged to the status quo. To either of these states, we each prefer to be the recipient of the other's half of our contract without having to fulfill our half. And it is obvious that Hobbes thinks the worst outcome for each of us is to fulfill first and then not to have the other fulfill — so much so, indeed, that he thinks it wrong of one of us to fulfill first as doing oneself too great harm. In addition to recognizing the payoff structure of the Prisoner's Dilemma in his account of contracting, Hobbes also recognizes the individual incentive to defect on one's fellow contractor, an incentive that he supposes can only be overcome in general through enforcement by government, so that without government enforcement we cannot rely on contracting. This is, of course, the central problem of the single-play Prisoner's Dilemma.

Hobbes concludes that, in essence, the very notion of contract is empty where there is no civil power to enforce contracts because virtually all would defect. It follows that there can be no contract prior to the creation of government. It is both a practical and a moral point that "the *Validity* of Covenants begins not but with the Constitution of a Civill Power, sufficient to compell men to keep them" (chap. 15, 203 [72]; emphasis added). Oddly for the view of many contemporary readers of him, then, Hobbes seems in one breath to give license to the Prisoner's Dilemma model of the establishment of government and — misanthrope that he is — in the next to take it away. Yet it is clear that Hobbes sees the Prisoner's Dilemma problem as the central ground for the creation of government with coercive power. It is also clear that he cannot consistently resolve the problem by simply invoking contract or covenant, either practically or morally. He has ruled them out of the state of nature.

THE STRUCTURE OF HOBBES'S THEORY

In *Leviathan*, Hobbes begins his strategic account of the possibilities for political order in the context of his discussions of contract and covenant. Any major philosopher's account of such a significant and difficult issue is likely to allow for varied interpretations. Hobbes's account here virtually generates varied interpretations because it is driven by what are in many ways two separate discussions going at once. One discussion is of the laws of nature. This is a quasi-Kantian account of how one would want or could rationally will everyone to behave. The second discussion is of the difficulties one must have in acting according to the apparent dictates of the laws of nature in the actual world, or rather of the unreasonable costs one would bear if one were to act according to them.

To distinguish the two discussions, Hobbes notes that the laws of nature apply *in foro interno*, in the mind, whereas our fundamental political problem is how to motivate people *in foro externo*, in public:

> The Lawes of Nature oblige *in foro interno*; that is to say, *they bind to a desire they should take place*: but *in foro externo*; that is, to the putting them in act, not alwayes. For he that should be modest, and tractable, and performe all he promises, in such time, and place, where no man els should do so, should but make himselfe a prey to others, and procure

> his own certain ruine, contrary to the ground of all Lawes of Nature, which tend to
> Natures preservation. (Chap. 15, 215 [79]; emphasis added)

The Kantian tone of Hobbes's Lawes of Nature is expressed clearly here in his variant of a categorical imperative in his "desire they should take place."[11] The laws of nature are all derivable, Hobbes thinks, from the ground principle that nature tends to its own well-being. Hence the laws of nature are such as, if they were universally followed, would conduce to the well-being of all. They are generally laws governing interactions to enable all to prosper individually by leaving each other free from fear of attack on person or property.[12]

The derivation of the laws of nature is, again, a matter of supposed logic to Hobbes, as derivations of physical or geometrical laws are. In fact, of course, they also depend on many empirical claims, many of which are dubious. But the laws are not themselves subject to bargaining or agreement in any sense other than intellectual agreement from anyone who has "sifted to the bottom, and with exact reason weighed the causes, and nature of Common-wealths" (chap. 20, 261 [107]). They are strictly rationalist, as are the central moral principles of Kant or of such contemporary thinkers as Alan Gewirth, David Gauthier, and John Rawls.[13] Just as Rawls's derivation of his principles of justice can be done by a single representative person behind the veil of ignorance, so Hobbes's laws of nature could be derived by Hobbes sitting at his desk and thinking carefully and hard, more carefully and harder, he supposes, than anyone before him on this subject (chap. 20, 261 [107]).[14]

The comparison with Rawls is apt in another important respect. From a grasp of Hobbes's laws of nature, *nothing immediately follows for our behavior*. We can fully understand the laws or Rawls's principles of justice and still act as though they did not govern our behavior. Indeed, in both cases, it is not even generally clear what it would mean for a single individual to act according to the derived laws or principles. Hobbes goes so far as to say that it would be wrong for a single person to follow the laws of nature in the actual world if no one else were following them because to do so would make one a prey to others and procure one's own certain ruin, "contrary to the ground of all Lawes of Nature, which tend to Natures preservation" (quoted earlier). Recall Hume's similar concern: "I should be the cully of my integrity, if I alone shou'd impose on myself a severe restraint amidst the licentiousness of others."[15] That would be too much to expect, especially of a rational, self-interested person. One can be obliged to follow the dictates of the laws of nature only in the context of a political society ruled firmly by a sovereign who will enforce them as *legal* laws. Similarly, Rawls's principles should lead to the design of institutions that will produce just distributions, in part by giving people incentives for relevant behavior.

Hobbes uses the term "law" in two different ways that he expressly distinguishes. Laws can be theorems, as in mathematics or physics, hence absolute and eternal (chap. 15, 215 [79]). The "Lawes of Nature" are laws in this sense; they are merely "Theoremes concerning what conduceth to the conservation and defence of [men]" (chap. 15, 217 [80]). One might rather say these are not absolute but merely functionalist in the sense that they depend on human nature. If humans were otherwise, perhaps especially if they were less self-seeking, the laws of nature might be different.

In their second meaning, laws can be the commands of a sovereign, hence legal and contingent. There can be no laws in this sense without a sovereign; that is, there can be no laws in the state of nature. Moreover, notions of right and wrong, justice and injustice have no place in the state of nature, nor are they inherent faculties of the body or mind. If they were they might be in anyone who was alone in the world, just as one's senses or passions would be. Justice and injustice are, rather, qualities "that relate to men in Society, not in Solitude" (chap. 13, 188 [63]). Such notions as justice are defined by law in the second sense of that term. In Hume's terminology, justice and its relatives are artificial virtues. In both Hobbes and Hume, the whole point of such qualities or virtues is strategic: They are valued not per se but rather for their beneficial regulation of social interaction.

What is the relationship between the two kinds of law? It is the office of the sovereign to impose legal laws to accomplish the ends of the laws of nature:

> The Office of the Soveraign . . . consisteth in the end, for which he was trusted with the Soveraign Power, namely the procuration of *the safety of the people.* . . . But by Safety here, is not meant a bare Preservation, but also all other Contentments of life, which every man by lawfull Industry, without danger, or hurt to the Common-wealth, shall acquire to himselfe. (Chap. 30, 376 [175])[16]

But this just means, if Hobbes's derivation of the laws of nature is correct, that the sovereign should essentially see to their fulfillment. (It is ironic that, against those who see Hobbes as the architect of American bourgeois government in many respects, the U.S. Supreme Court recently ruled that American state governments do *not* have a constitutional duty to protect people against each other. A sovereign power could hardly be less Hobbesian.[17]) Once such a sovereign is there to enforce law, thereby making the creation of law possible, then everyone may finally bring actions in foro externo in line with prescriptions in foro interno.

In passing, note the difference between Hobbes's rationalist derivation of his laws of nature and recent rationalist derivations of moral principles. Gauthier and Gewirth seem to think it a matter of logic or self-consistency that we act according to their rationally derived principles once these are understood. Hobbes clearly does not think anything of the sort for his laws of nature. He thinks we require the sovereign to motivate us to act in foro externo as we would want in foro interno for all to act. However, he seemingly gives license to Gauthier's claim that Gauthier's program is really Hobbes's as well.[18] Hobbes says that injustice in the controversies of the world is "somewhat like to that, which in the disputations of Scholers is called *Absurdity*" (chap. 14, 191 [65]). Hobbes means that such an injustice as the violation of one's contract or promise in civil society is a contradiction with one's original agreement. As such a contradiction, it is vaguely like a logical contradiction. He does not go on to deduce the obligation to keep a promise, as John Searle[19] and others do, from the apparent contradiction of not keeping it after having made it. And he certainly does not go on to suppose, as Gauthier seems to do,[20] that such a contradiction would motivate me to keep my promise even though it might be in my immediate interest not to. Hobbes's rationalism goes only to the point of deducing what general practices would be in our interest. It does not entail any purely rational motivation then to abide by those practices.

THE STATE OF NATURE

Again, the Prisoner's Dilemma that Hobbes recognizes is at the level of individual interactions in the state of nature. It does not follow from this that the state of nature and its potential resolution constitute a grander Prisoner's Dilemma. There is, however, some license in his words and in a casual view of his problem for supposing that his social contract is to resolve such a grand dilemma. The Hobbesian state of nature is analogous to the usual large-number Prisoner's Dilemma analysis in the following sense. The outcome that one wishes to improve in a Prisoner's Dilemma is the status quo in which no one is cooperating. This outcome is strongly Pareto inferior to that outcome in which all are cooperating. That is to say, *all* are better off in the all-cooperate than in the none-cooperate or all-defect outcome. Similarly, in Hobbes's state of nature, all could be better off if all followed the laws of nature in foro externo. That is, of course, why they are laws at least in foro interno.

There are two main differences between the state of nature and the usual Prisoner's Dilemma.[21] The first difference is in the relative nastiness of the state-of-nature and the Prisoner's Dilemma all-defect outcomes. In the state of nature, we all have incentive not merely not to cooperate with but even preemptively to kill one another. In the usual Prisoner's Dilemma, we merely have an incentive not to cooperate. The condition of settlers on an otherwise uninhabited frontier is like the usual Prisoner's Dilemma, not like the state of nature. I work my land, you work yours, and neither of us benefits from the cooperative gains from specialization and trade. This is a sanguine if impoverished state of affairs. It is not the sanguinary state of nature. The difference here may be important for Hobbes, but it is not central for the present claim against the received Prisoner's Dilemma account of his theory.

The fundamentally important strategic difference between the Prisoner's Dilemma and the state of nature is that the latter can be characterized neither as a single interaction nor even as a simple iterated interaction. It involves a messy jumble of many interactions, some iterated, others not. Many of these interactions, both actual and potential, must be Prisoner's Dilemmas, both iterated and not. Apart from preemptive murder, it is especially the potential Prisoner's Dilemma interactions of mutual cooperation through contracting and promising that most interest Hobbes. The loss of benefits from such interactions as well as the constant threat of death characterize the pain of the state of nature. Our problem is therefore not how to resolve one interaction but how to regulate this messy jumble. *This* problem is not simply a large Prisoner's Dilemma, iterated or otherwise. It does not have a two-person analog of a 2 × 2 payoff matrix with strategies of cooperating and defecting. It is virtually all or nothing in two senses. First, we find a system for regulating our quotidian Prisoner's Dilemma interactions or we do not. Second, *we all* find such a system or we all fail together. The payoff structure of this problem is dreadful payoffs to all if we do not regulate and very good payoffs to all if we do. There will be no mixture of cooperators and defectors; therefore, there is no analog of the cooperate-defect and defect-cooperate outcomes of the usual Prisoner's Dilemma.

One might ask what it would even mean to defect while others cooperate in moving from the state of nature to creation of government. It would not be like free riding in a large-number Prisoner's Dilemma or collective action interaction in which the defector receives extra benefits or avoids costs while receiving all benefits available to others. Because the common interest on which we all would want to coordinate in creating a sovereign is the interest in having a sovereign capable of coercing any defectors, defection would likely entail either being suppressed by the government or going into exile.

Neither of these would be a preferred option for most people. Hence defection is not a dominant strategy in the game of creating and maintaining government, as it is in single-play or large-number Prisoner's Dilemmas.[22]

This problem requires collective resolution of a kind very different from the spontaneous voluntarist acts of all individuals that can resolve many coordination games. For example, we could — and, indeed, evidently did — establish a convention for driving either on the left or on the right by spontaneously falling into one pattern or the other.[23] We might similarly suppose Hobbes's problem could be resolved by convention.[24] At the stage of the state of nature and the initial creation of government, however, our problem is not one of adapting a regular response to a *recurring* coordination interaction. For Hobbes's problem of political order, that is, of the regulation of manifold Prisoner's Dilemma and other interactions, it is not merely a pattern of coordinated actions, taken repeatedly, that we require but, rather, a sanctioning mechanism created to regulate our quotidian interactions. Our problem is to create once and — we might hope — for all a government that resolves our ongoing potential Prisoner's Dilemma interactions. We wish to coordinate now, not by convention.

As an explanatory theory of how an actual state works, however, an argument from convention is essentially correct.[25] Our government stays in power because citizens daily follow the convention of obedience defined by our particular sovereign. This is a convention in the clear, technical sense of the term as used by David Lewis.[26] It is in everyone's interest to be obedient if everyone else is but not if most others are not. I cannot generally gain by being disobedient. Moreover, maintenance of an extant government may, after all, be the principal concern of Hobbes and the central focus of most of his arguments. The state of nature is not an origin but a possible destination of society. We can get to it all too readily by revolution. We can avoid it by convention. We may even go further to argue that the growth and development of institutions of government proceed by convention. This would be eminently consistent with Hobbes's views, as will be discussed, on the desirability of democracy or popular rule.[27]

How might we coordinate to create a sovereign? If it is true, as Hobbes thinks it very nearly is,[28] that all share in the preference for a strong mechanism, we could all simply get together one time to create it as we might finally meet to resolve contrary practices of driving left and right. If so, then there is a sense in which Hobbes could be called contractarian despite the fact that his problem is not Prisoner's Dilemma. Against this possibility, Hobbes regularly says that this very understanding of the situation is one that has come only to him and hence only late in the history of societies, and he seems to think most people are never going to understand it (chap. 20, 261 [107]). Even independently of a failure of understanding of the situation, however, there are two plausible objections to this contractarian move, both consistent with most of Hobbes's text but neither — I think — explicitly stated by Hobbes.

First, the grim conditions of the state of nature make it essentially impractical for us all to get together to do anything. Indeed, they make it impractical for us even to coordinate on a time and place for meeting by undercutting the possibility of credible discussion. This is one point in the analysis at which Hobbes's particularly nasty picture of the state of nature may play a significant theoretical role. (It may also play a role in Hobbes's apparent sense that once the problem of political order is understood, the resolution is easy because the perceived universal benefits are enormous.) Hobbes's own discussion of voting as a mechanism for choosing the sovereign seems contrary to his own characterization of the problems of dealing with each other in the state of nature.

Second, our problem is not a pure coordination interaction. There is no one single possible resolution of the state of nature. Rather, there are varied possible forms of government on which we could coordinate. Hobbes mentions monarchy, aristocracy, and democracy. Hence there is potential conflict on how to resolve our problem even if we could overcome our fear of death long enough to meet and establish government.[29]

The only plausible way out of the state of nature is to change the game by changing the incentives to each individual. This is also generally true for any Prisoner's Dilemma in which the costs of risking cooperation far outweigh the benefits of it. And it is commonly true for very large-number Prisoner's Dilemma interactions. But the players in a game cannot pull themselves up by their own bootstraps to change the incentives they face. They require some kind of external intervention. Again, this aspect of the Prisoner's Dilemma analysis is analogous to Hobbes's central problem. The external intervention that many political philosophers of his time invoked was intervention by God to sanction individuals for their antisocial behavior. Hobbes lived in a time in which the invocation of different gods was arguably the chief political problem. That was a problem that could not be resolved by bringing in a particular god. Hobbes therefore required a new solution.[30]

One should not go very far toward thinking there is an actual problem in Hobbes's analysis here. There is nothing more than the kind of conceptual analysis that stands behind his account of the laws of nature. He is canvassing conceptual not practical possibilities. The nearest thing to a state of nature that we are likely to find in historical records or known experience is in brief periods of the breakdown of social order. Apart from such moments, the

nearest thing may be analogous to life among the Yanomamö, an aceph-
alous society along the Brazilian-Venezuelan border, as described by C. R.
Hallpike. The Yanomamö and other such societies, he says,

> engage in warfare because among other reasons they cannot stop, not because they
> necessarily as a culture derive any benefit from fighting. In the absence of any central
> authority they are condemned to fight for ever, other conditions remaining the same,
> since for any group to cease defending itself would be suicidal. In some cases of this
> type the people have no real desire to continue fighting, and may welcome outside
> pacification.[31]

This is almost a picture of the state of nature as conceived by Hobbes. The
chief difference is that the fighting is not randomly individual by individual
but community by community. Hence there is substantial social organization
with genuine control over individuals. In a similar case, among the Fore of
Highland New Guinea, external intervention that was not very forceful, that
played little more than a signaling role was sufficient to bring peace. "The
warfare was not liked, and the distant presence of but a single patrol officer
and a handful of native police was grasped as an excuse to cease."[32] The
problem could be reduced to a signaling problem because there was immediately a single plausible resolution of it when the colonial power arrived on
the scene.

CONTRACTING OUT

A common reading of Hobbes is that his solution was virtually to forget
or ignore the very problem he saw and to trick up government by contract or
mutual agreement. Yet there is a general consensus among contemporary
social theorists that we cannot get cooperation in large-scale Prisoner's
Dilemmas from narrowly self-interested choices on the part of all the relevant
individuals. By implication, Hobbes is a dismal failure.

Consider first the relative consensus on the irresolvability of large-number
Prisoner's Dilemmas.[33] It is generally agreed that small-number Prisoner's
Dilemmas that are iterated are resolvable by spontaneous action that is only
self-interested. Moreover, such resolutions may govern large populations
who frequently engage in small-number Prisoner's Dilemma interactions,
such as person-to-person promise keeping or truth telling.[34] But these accounts do not generalize to cover large-number interactions,[35] for which
self-interest seems inadequate to produce cooperation. Someone may yet
devise a convincing argument for why, even from narrowly self-interested

considerations, we should cooperate, but the most convincing arguments so far are clearly against a self-interest resolution of large-number Prisoner's Dilemmas.

If Hobbes has not merely failed to understand this point, how then does he resolve the collective problem we face in creating beneficial government? He does not have the vocabulary to put it this way, but I think it clear that he himself sees the problem as a coordination problem in the following sense. As compared to the state of nature, many forms of government would be generally preferred by all. Government based on monarchy, aristocracy, or even broad democracy would all be better than no government for virtually all of us.[36] Our task in the state of nature is to coordinate in putting one or another form of government into place so that it might then coerce us to act as though we are motivated by the cooperative spirit of the laws of nature. This is a view that could be reached clearly enough in foro interno. The solution is coordination, coordination indeed that need not be intentional. All that need be intentional is submission out of self-interest once there is a government that works well enough to force submission.

Hobbes implicitly goes further than this in the assumptions of his account. He thinks we should rationally all agree that the best form of government would be absolute monarchy. Hence the coordination problem we face is not in choosing a form of government but rather in choosing an embodiment of it. The wonderfully metaphorical engraving that decorated the title page of the first edition of *Leviathan* and that has been widely reprinted expresses Hobbes's coordination vision succinctly. In that engraving, the sovereign's body is either made up of or clothed by the people of the commonwealth. Those people are not engaged in interactions with one another, as contractors would be. They are all uniformly engaged in coordinating their gazes on the face of the sovereign. Hobbes gave license to the artist, saying, "This is more than consent, or Concord; it is a reall Unitie of them all, in one and the same person" (chap. 17, 227 [87]). Of course, at the point of this metaphorical representation there already exists a sovereign. How do we get to that point?

Since we are all relatively equal in any sense that matters, many of us would be plausible candidates for sovereignty, so our coordination problem is a complicated one.[37] But it is also therefore a relatively simple one in that it hardly matters whom we finally get as our sovereign. What matters is that we finally succeed in coordinating. If someone comes to power through self-seeking and cunning, still we have the benefits of a sovereign. But if it is up to us to make a choice of one of us over others, we have a difficult problem. "Thus," because we are all equal, Leo Strauss writes, "the *problem of sovereignty* arises."[38] We cannot select from simple reason — there is none — but only from arbitrary will. Bertolt Brecht's Mack the Knife says first comes food and then morality. Hobbes says first comes victory over hunger and cold and then politics.[39] Hobbes has the better insight.

Hobbes offers two routes to a sovereign from the state of nature. The first is by covenant. We all agree to lay down our arms on condition that all others do likewise and we transfer our right to self-defense to our chosen sovereign (chap. 18, 228-29 [88]). The second is that we suffer conquest and we acquiesce in the rule of our conqueror because it is not in our interest individually to oppose him (chap. 20, 255 [103-4]). The grand consent of the first resolution is missing from the second. But note that the power available to the conqueror, as demonstrated by the conquest, must be substantial. What could be the power of our newly chosen sovereign under our mutual covenant? That newly elevated leviathan cannot have had great power before our choice or he could simply have established himself as sovereign without our gracious consent.

The central explanatory concern in this creation of a powerful coercive sovereign out of the state of nature by covenant is how can the new sovereign have the power to sanction those who are not obedient? We know from occasionally overwhelming experience that extant sovereigns have such power. The most troubling point in Hobbes's account is one that seems to trouble him most. At least we might suppose it troubles him from the fact that he raises it and then passes it by with overt sleight of hand. Let us follow him in that account.

Hobbes describes as a covenant the consensual creation of a sovereign from the state of nature in which, we may recall, all are effectively equal in power of coercion: I lay down my arms if you and all others lay down yours. He has forcefully argued (and even convinced us) that a covenant in the state of nature where it cannot be enforced is invalid, both practically and morally. What will make this one valid is, after it is entered, the coercive power of the sovereign, either a person or a council, it establishes. Hobbes recognizes great difficulties in this transition and wavers between saying we transfer rights to the sovereign and saying we transfer power. What is the form of that power? In the English edition of *De Cive*,[40] which is a more or less literal translation of the original's Latin, Hobbes writes of the power of a newly elected sovereign, "which *power* and *Right of commanding*, consists in this, that each Citizen hath conveighed all his strength and power to that man, or Counsell; which to have done (because no man can transferre his power in a naturall manner) is nothing else then to have parted with his Right of resisting."[41]

Here, Hobbes falters. We can consent all we want to, but, as a matter of actual fact, we cannot simply hand our power over to anyone if it is constituted primarily of our human capacities. I consent to the movement of the mountain before us out of our path, but it will not happen therefore. And our new sovereign cannot enter office with any power worth having for the awesome tasks ahead.[42] In *Leviathan*, published the same year as the English *De Cive*, the parallel passage avoids the difficulty. Hobbes here says of the sovereign upon election that "by this Authoritie, given him by every particular man in the Common-Wealth, he hath the use of so much Power and Strength conferred on him, that by terror thereof, he is inabled to forme the wills of them all, to Peace at home, and mutuall ayd against their enemies abroad" (chap. 17, 227-28 [87-88]). The problem of how right turns to power has been magically left out of discussion. Yet only a paragraph earlier, Hobbes says of the inhabitants of the state of nature that "it is no wonder if there be somewhat else required (besides covenant) to make their Agreement constant and lasting" (chap. 17, 226 [87]).

In sum, Hobbes knows that power is necessary for order and that power cannot be conjured up by mere consent. But he does not know how to resolve this dilemma to get a state in place.

POWER AND THE MAINTENANCE OF RULE

Hobbes's other focus throughout his political works is on keeping a present government safe from revolution. An extant government is likely to have substantial power that may take two forms. First, it may have resources, such as wealth and weapons, that can be put to general use to achieve varied ends, especially including the coercion of those insufficiently obedient to the laws. Various revolutionary leaders have been backed by very little of such resources and yet have defeated governments that had substantial resources available. Their power generally has taken the form of substantial popular following, the coordination of many people behind their purposes. In many primitive states, this may be the principal form of central power. The collapse of a sovereign's power, as in Hobbes's own time, can come quickly when there is coordination of many citizens behind an opposing Cromwell.

Unfortunately, one cannot simply plan and achieve coordination with much hope of success. If it happens, it does so through many independent choices or commitments. Hobbes's excessively defensive inhabitants of the state of nature could not simply agree to coordinate on my elevation to sovereign and then stick by that commitment. Recall that Hobbes thinks it nonsense to suppose the sovereign could bind himself by mere act of will. This is nothing special about the sovereign. It is the central problem of everyone in the state of nature as well, because we cannot bind ourselves by act of will to fulfill our contracts. If we could, we would have no need of a sovereign to coerce us.

What Hobbes needs here is one of the major insights of the Scottish Enlightenment: that social institutions can be the unintended consequences of a pattern of human actions taken for reasons other than the creation of the institutions.[43] Writing at the height of the Scottish Enlightenment, Hume is much better on the issue of how we happen to coordinate on some one of many possibilities.[44] He clearly recognizes the issue's significance as an independent problem and offers compelling, often clever resolutions of it, many of them in the long footnotes of his *Treatise*.[45] Surely, Hobbes would have appreciated such resolutions and would have adopted them, even if perhaps egoistically without citation.

But clearly, there are many passages in his accounts of extant government and its value in which Hobbes seems, yet again, to be a forerunner of the later way of seeing things. Perhaps every major theorist concerned with actual as well as theoretical societies must have had some sense of the role of unintended consequences in the larger social order. Hobbes is basically historicist in his understanding and even in his evaluation. What is is good. Therefore, he wishes to give us a justification for our allegiance to what is. He knows where he wants to go but does not know how to get there. Even without a sense of how to get there, however, he can give very strong arguments for why it is not in our interest to let our government collapse. His arguments depend on certain factual claims that may be wrong. In particular, he seems to have a very grim view of the possibilities of destruction in a revolution. Anyone who contemplates the Lebanons and El Salvadors of history will not immediately think Hobbes entirely wrong.

What force does the state of nature argument have if Hobbes can only explain and justify continuation but not creation of government? It helps to explicate what the natural interests of people are and how they can be served only by the artificial device of government. The role is strictly to show why government is good, not to explain how it could come to be. But that is, oddly, enough for Hobbes's normative project of justification. He does not require a connection between origin and actuality to justify actuality. Against this view, Kavka defends his focus on creation of a sovereign by covenant rather than by conquest:

> The reason for this is that we wish to construct a normative as well as descriptive Hobbesian political theory. We are concerned with whether the State can be *justified*, on what grounds, and with what limitations or restrictions. And we want our arguments to be persuasive to . . . individuals who conceive themselves as morally independent be-

ings. Therefore it is of more interest to us in what manner and form a State might be founded by agreement among independent rational individuals, than how they have actually originated via family ties and conquest.[46]

But on any account — Hobbes's, or the variants of Kavka and Hampton — the origin of sovereignty in a covenant in the state of nature is incredible, not plausible. What is not possible cannot justify anything. Yet Hobbes gives, assuming his facts are roughly right, compelling justifications for maintenance of government and for the general existence of government. Moreover, these justifications have normative appeal that the covenant theory does not have. In the face of actual histories of the rise of governments, a contractarian justification of an extant state requires a theory of rectification or an implausible theory of current consent. Hobbes's maintenance justification requires no such theory.

POPULAR RULE

Consider a major side issue in Hobbes's accounts of political order: his apparent dislike of popular rule. This issue provides a good case for working through Hobbes's analysis. It is instructive to see how, if one makes certain factual assumptions that Hobbes seems to have made, his apparent dislike of democracy fits his general analysis for explanatory or social scientific reasons rather than for moral or other more direct reasons.

Hobbes clearly seems to prefer monarchy and aristocracy to democratic or popular rule. Indeed, although perhaps unjustly, his *The Elements of Law*, a forerunner of *Leviathan*, was read as a defense of monarchy at the time the king was under siege from the Long Parliament.[47] Leslie Stephen suggests that "Hobbes's dislike to popular rule may be due in part to a certain intellectual difficulty. . . . [He] is not comfortable with abstractions."[48] That is an odd, even startling, explanation for one who avowed himself to be the abstract geometer of political thought and who elaborated the abstract, not to say absurd, notion of the state of nature. It seems more likely that Hobbes was uncomfortable with the particular kind of "abstraction" involved in leaping to popular rule in his time. To put the issue in stodgy terms, popular rule was untried and therefore unknown in Hobbes's time. One who preferred the status quo to change must have preferred the known to the unknown even more. If not the king, then at least a Cromwell.

To give Hobbes the greatest possible credit in his view of popular rule, note that it is clearly consistent with his general view of the rightness of a particular form of government. A form of government is right for a given society and time if it is currently working. Alternatives have against them the very high costs of transition: "And they that go about by disobedience, to doe no more than reforme the Common-wealth, shall find they do thereby destroy it" (chap. 30, 380 [177]). We learn what works by hard experience and our experience contributes to the value of what we have. The credibility of popular rule requires some experience of it and the development of requisite institutions, conventions, and so forth that cannot simply be conjured into place because we want popular rule. They have to grow. It is plausible that popular rule in Hobbes's time would have brought chaos, that the transition to popular rule had to be relatively slow rather than immediate. Of course, Hobbes may also have had a substantive objection to popular rule in his time because he may have feared the distribution of destructive and coercive religious beliefs that may have driven much of the agitation for popular rule and other reforms. But even such a substantive objection is in keeping with his conventional conception of the value of government per se and of a particular extant government.

Could Hobbes consistently object to popular rule as it works in contemporary democratic societies such as England and the United States? No. His conventional understanding implies that these governments are the right governments now. As long as there is relative concord among their subjects, these governments conduce to prosperity (chap. 30, 380 [177]). Hobbes's problem is not that he is inherently antidemocratic in the sense of wanting to block or override the interests of the masses. Indeed, he is among the most egalitarian of all political philosophers. In the great Anglo-Saxon tradition, he is arguably more egalitarian than Mill and certainly more egalitarian than Locke and Hume. He is antichaos. He thinks, perhaps wrongly as it turns out, that participation is likely to be chaotic. Hence he is antiparticipation and in that sense antidemocratic.

CONCLUDING REMARKS

Hobbes is perhaps the original discoverer of the fact that ordinary exchange relations are, in other words, a Prisoner's Dilemma problem unless there is some coercive power to back them up.[49] Therefore, we need a powerful government. This is an exaggeration of the plausible case in any context that we actually know because we can often motivate cooperative exchange relations among those who interact repeatedly and who can come to recognize the benefits of continuing their exchange interactions.[50] But if our exchange relations are restricted to the small numbers with whom we can repeatedly interact, we still face a serious loss of opportunities that we could enjoy if we could guarantee reciprocal fulfillment of even isolated exchanges. Moreover, even in ongoing relationships, we cannot trust one another to abide by exchanges that involve very large values, so that our relationships will still be restricted. For example, to whom would you sell your house on a legally unenforceable contract to pay you a large monthly sum for the next twenty years?[51] Hence even if we do not go all the way with Hobbes in thinking unregulated social interactions would be constantly murderous, we must agree with him that they would be radically poorer than what we could have under a properly functioning government.

It is precisely because he understands the Prisoner's Dilemma that Hobbes finds government both necessary and problematic. But his understanding does not go so far as to cast the problem of creating or maintaining government as itself a Prisoner's Dilemma. Creating and maintaining government is an important problem because it is the key to resolving quotidian Prisoner's Dilemmas, not because it is itself a Prisoner's Dilemma.

Consider one final objection to counting Hobbes a contractarian. The fundamental urge of contractarian political philosophers is to give a particular justification of the state, generally, indeed, to give a justification of a particular kind of state, the kind that the philosopher of the moment thinks we would have agreed to. The absolutist implications of the state of nature — that any extant working government is the best government for us now just because it avoids revolution and its costs — guts any government's claim to legitimacy or rightness on any other basis than the facts of historical accident.[52] It also guts contractarianism.[53] Any need for consent to the *kind* of government, *on the merits of that kind*, is violated by Hobbes's historicist justification of the rightness of any extant government. In actual practice, on Hobbes's view, we today should want democracy not because it is especially good but primarily because we already have it. To borrow his distinction, we might also want it in foro interno because it is ideally good if it can be made to work. But it does not follow that if we do not already have democracy, we should therefore strive to put it in place in foro externo where, collectively, we lead our lives.

On this understanding, the commonplace claim that Hobbes is a proto-utilitarian is compelling. Hobbes justifies a government according to the benefits it offers relative to alternative governments. Other grounds for justification are irrelevant to him. Indeed, even the judgments of those subject to a government are irrelevant to him so long as their judgments do not lead them to disharmony. What is possibly left of contractarian thinking when one has such a view? And what contemporary contractarians would claim such Hobbesian parentage for their views?

NOTES

1. As Stephen Holmes argues, egoism was a healthy tonic to other, more divisive commitments, many of them in some sense communitarian. See Stephen Holmes, "The Secret History of Self-Interest," in *Beyond Self-Interest*, edited by Jane Mansbridge (Chicago: University of Chicago Press, 1990).

2. I will cite *Leviathan* in parentheses in the text by chapter and page number. The first page number is for Hobbes, *Leviathan*, edited by C. B. Macpherson (Harmondsworth, Middlesex: Penguin, 1968). The second number [in brackets] is that of the original edition of *Leviathan* in 1651. Unless stated otherwise, all Hobbes quotations and thoughts are from *Leviathan*. See a similar claim for silence as consent in Thomas Hobbes, *Human Nature* in *The English Works of Thomas Hobbes*, edited by William Molesworth (London: Bohn, 1860), vol. 4; passage in chap. 13, §11, 76.

3. C. B. Macpherson, "Introduction" to Hobbes, *Leviathan*, 40; also see 43-44. Macpherson notes, however, that "Hobbes's case does not rest on the possibility of men in a state of nature making a contract to establish political society" (p. 61). And he generally argues for a hypothetical, rather than an actual, interpretation of Hobbes's supposed contractarian position (pp. 43-45). There is wide consensus on Macpherson's view of Hobbes as a contractarian. See Don Herzog's brief "story" on this consensus in Herzog, *Happy Slaves* (Chicago: University of Chicago Press, 1989), chap. 3. As noted later, Jean Hampton and Gregory Kavka do not fully join in the consensus.

4. Hence the title of Arthur Stinchcombe's review of works by Jon Elster: "Is the Prisoner's Dilemma All of Sociology?" *Inquiry* 23 (1980): 187-92.

5. Gregory Kavka, *Hobbesian Moral and Political Theory* (Princeton, NJ: Princeton University Press, 1986), 179-88, and Jean Hampton, *Hobbes and the Social Contract Tradition* (Cambridge: Cambridge University Press, 1986), 138-47.

6. John von Neumann and Oskar Morgenstern, *Theory of Games and Economic Behavior* (Princeton, NJ: Princeton University Press, 1953, 3d ed.; originally published 1944).

7. I spell out the strategic structure of Hume's moral and political theory in *Morality within the Limits of Reason* (Chicago: University of Chicago Press, 1988), esp. chap. 2.

8. David Gauthier, *The Logic of Leviathan* (Oxford: Oxford University Press, 1969). Gauthier calls the Prisoner's Dilemma by name only in a footnote (p. 79n), perhaps because, on his own account, Gauthier seems to have discovered the Prisoner's Dilemma only late in the writing of this book. See the preface to his *Morals by Agreement* (Oxford: Clarendon, 1986), v.

9. Kavka, *Hobbesian Moral and Political Theory*.

10. Kavka implicitly supports this view in the preponderance he gives to explicating Hobbes's "descriptive theory" over his moral theory.

11. A. E. Taylor argues that Hobbes's ethical theory is independent of his psychological doctrines and that it is not based on self-interest. "Hobbes's ethical doctrine proper . . . is a very strict deontology, curiously suggestive, though with interesting differences, of some of the characteristic theses of Kant" ("The Ethical Doctrine of Hobbes," *Philosophy* 13 [1938]: 406-424, at 407-8). I think Taylor's central thesis is wrong but that his Kantian associations have some license in Hobbes. The Taylor thesis has been soundly criticized. See, for example, Stuart M. Brown, Jr., "Hobbes: The Taylor Thesis," *Philosophical Review* 68 (July 1959): 303-23.

12. One's person is, indeed, counted as part of one's property by Hobbes (chap. 30, 382-83 [179]).

13. Alan Gewirth, *Reason and Morality* (Chicago: University of Chicago Press, 1978); David Gauthier, *Morals by Agreement* (Oxford: Clarendon, 1986); and John Rawls, *A Theory of Justice* (Cambridge, MA: Harvard University Press, 1971).

14. In an apt metaphor, Hobbes attributes part of the success of his understanding to the slow process of historical learning from experience, as we learn over the centuries how to build better, more lasting houses. "So, long time after men have begun to constitute Common-wealths, imperfect, and apt to relapse into disorder, there may, Principles of Reason be found out, by industrious meditation, to make their constitution (except by externall violence) everlasting" (chap. 30, 378 [176]).

15. David Hume, *A Treatise of Human Nature*, edited by L. A. Selby-Bigge and P. H. Nidditch (Oxford: Clarendon, 1978, 2d ed. [1739-40]), bk. 3, pt. 2, sec. 7, 535.

16. To be consistent, Hobbes must suppose his sovereign will find it in his own interest to serve the people well, as he does suppose (chap. 18, 238-39 [94]).

17. The decision, by a 6 to 3 vote rendered February 22, 1989, exonerated Wisconsin state officials of personal liability for ignoring pleas to protect a child from child abuse. Chief Justice Rehnquist's majority opinion argued that the intent of the relevant constitutional clause was not to force the state to protect citizens from each other but to protect citizens from the state (*New York Times*, February 23, 1989, 1).

18. Gauthier, *Morals by Agreement*, 162.

19. John Searle, "Deriving 'Ought' from 'Is,'" in Searle, *Speech Acts: An Essay in the Philosophy of Language* (Cambridge: Cambridge University Press, 1969), 175-98.

20. Gauthier argues that it is rational to adopt a disposition to cooperate with others who have adopted a like disposition. Gauthier calls this disposition "constrained maximization" (*Morals by Agreement*, chap. 6). This is to suppose one could simply will to bind oneself to the laws of nature. That would have been a remarkably easy solution for Hobbes because it would have let him end *Leviathan* soon after establishing the laws of nature. "Constrained maximization" was not in Hobbes's vocabulary, but it seems not grossly tendentious to say he rejects it outright.

21. "Usual" in the sense that they are the Prisoner's Dilemmas analyzed by most game theorists and played by most experimental games subjects.

22. Defection might be a dominant strategy for an individual who wants revolutionary change but wants to avoid the potential costs that revolutionary action might bring to individual participants. But these costs are what the extant regime can inflict, not the costs of creating a government de novo.

23. For further discussion of the establishment of such a convention, see Hardin, *Morality within the Limits of Reason*, 47-53.

24. In an earlier variant of part of his *Morals by Agreement*, Gauthier reconstructs Hobbes on an argument from convention (David Gauthier, "Thomas Hobbes: Moral Theorist," *Journal of Philosophy* 76 [October 1979]: 547-59). However, Gauthier is concerned with Hobbes's supposed moral theory rather than his political theory: He wishes to make of Hobbes's laws of nature a moral rather than a legal code. He also bases his account on an odd reading of Hobbes's admittedly vexed response to the Foole who queries whether it would not, in fact, be rational to violate one's covenants (chap. 15, 203-5 [72-73]).

25. There are elements of a convention theory of the maintenance of government in various past philosophers, most extensively in Hume and Adam Smith and, with clumsy missteps, in Austin.

26. David K. Lewis, *Convention* (Cambridge, MA: Harvard University Press, 1969).

27. One should not overstate the extent of Hobbes's understanding of the convention argument for the *maintenance* of political order. If the argument is sound, it suggests that power need not be so absolute as Hobbes insists it be. He says, "And whosoever thinking Soveraign Power too great, will seek to make it lesse; must subject himselfe, to the Power, that can limit

it; that is to say, to a greater" (chap. 20, 260 [107]). Against Hobbes's apparent logic, we can, through devices of convention, restrain one another, and varied parts of a government may do so as well. Indeed, contemporary democratic governments are strategically designed to separate powers in order to reduce overall power, especially capricious power.

28. See later note 36 for discussion of his exception of some of the nobility of his time.

29. Kavka and Hampton discuss the impure coordination problem that Hobbes faces. See Kavka, *Hobbesian Moral and Political Theory*, 184-88; Hampton, *Hobbes*, 150-53.

30. Moreover, Hobbes implicitly rejects the invocation of God to give one an incentive to act properly in the state of nature, as for example, by fulfilling one's promise or covenant. He says that an oath makes no difference to one's obligation: "For a Covenant, if lawfull, binds in the sight of God, without the oath, as much as with it: if unlawfull, bindeth not at all: though it be confirmed with an oath" (chap. 14, 201 [71]). Since covenants are generally not lawful in the state of nature, they do not bind there in God's eyes even though sworn before God. By implication, God cannot be tricked into service to bring order to the state of nature by ruling over each individual there.

31. C. R. Hallpike, "Functionalist Interpretations of Primitive Warfare," *Man* 8 (September 1973): 451-70.

32. E. R. Sorrenson, "Socio-ecological Change among the Fore of New Guinea," *Current Anthropology* 13 (1972): 349-84. See further, Elizabeth Colson, *Tradition and Contract: The Problem of Order* (Chicago: Aldine, 1974), 62-69.

33. Among moral theorists, Gauthier is probably the major dissenter from this view. His *Morals by Agreement* is primarily a theory of why we would self-interestedly choose to act cooperatively in Prisoner's Dilemmas. However, his generalization of his theory of constrained maximization from two-person to large-number Prisoner's Dilemmas is by assertion rather than by demonstration (see Gauthier, *Morals by Agreement*, 130n).

34. See, e.g., Russell Hardin, *Collective Action* (Baltimore: Johns Hopkins University Press, 1982), esp. 218, and Robert Axelrod, *The Evolution of Cooperation* (New York: Basic Books, 1984).

35. For criticisms of several tentative generalizations from two-person to large-number iterated Prisoner's Dilemma, see Russell Hardin, "Individual Sanctions, Collective Benefits," in *Paradoxes of Rationality and Cooperation: Prisoner's Dilemma and Newcomb's Problem*, edited by Richmond Campbell and Lanning Sowden (Vancouver: University of British Columbia Press, 1985), 339-54.

36. The "virtually" covers an exception that seems to have bothered Hobbes. Under his fifth law of nature, Compleasance, "a man that by asperity of Nature, will strive to retain those things which to himselfe are superfluous, and to others necessary; and for the stubbornness of his Passions, cannot be corrected, is to be left, or cast out of Society, as combersome thereto" (chap. 15, 209 [76]). Herzog supposes that the nobility were the target of this worry because, contrary to Hobbes's ground principle for his laws of nature, they were not interested in seeking or enjoying peace but actually preferred strife in which they could achieve glory and honor (*Happy Slaves*, chap. 3).

37. See Hampton's extended discussion, *Hobbes*, 150-66.

38. Leo Strauss, *The Political Philosophy of Hobbes: Its Basis and Its Genesis* (Chicago: University of Chicago Press, 1952; first published 1936), 159.

39. Thomas Hobbes, *De Cive*, edited by Howard Warrender (Oxford: Clarendon, 1983 [1651]), 2.5.5.

40. The English title was *Philosophicall Rudiments Concerning Government and Society*.

41. Hobbes, *De Cive*, 2.5.11.

42. Hampton supposes power can be more or less instantly created because the newly elected sovereign can call on a small number of citizens to capture any lawbreaker, say, a contract breaker. This small group, or posse, faces, she says, not a Prisoner's Dilemma but rather a "step good" problem in which everyone must cooperate or the endeavor fails. But each member of the posse would rather bear the expected cost of her participation in the posse than have the sovereign falter and return everyone to the state of nature. Hence each will cooperate and the lawbreaker will be captured and brought for punishment (Hampton, *Hobbes*, 176-86). This is a too labored story that, like Hobbes's very problem of creating a sovereign out of the state of nature, sounds more like a story than a real problem or prospect. Kavka seems only somewhat less confident (*Hobbesian Moral and Political Theory*, 243-44, 254-66), but see David Braybrooke, "The Insoluble Problem of the Social Contract," *Dialogue* 15 (March 1976): 3-37.

43. Herzog ruefully notes that this insight was not available to Hobbes (Herzog, *Happy Slaves*, chap. 3).

44. So good that he rightly merits the credit David Lewis gives him for discovering a proto-game-theoretic account of convention (Lewis, *Convention*, 3-4).

45. Hume, *Treatise*, bk. 3, pt. 2, sec. 3, 504-13 (especially the footnotes) and sec. 10, 553-67. Hume specifically labels the resolution a convention: "And this may properly enough be call'd a convention or agreement betwixt us, tho' without the interposition of a promise; since the actions of each of us have a reference to those of the other, and are perform'd upon the supposition, that something is to be perform'd on the other part" (*Treatise* 3.2.2, 490).

46. Kavka, *Hobbesian Moral and Political Theory*, 181. This is an odd argument: that part of what makes our form of government right is that it originates in a right way. There was once an analogous view of what makes humans subject to morality: that they originate by the creation of and in the likeness of god. If we originated from some primordial slime, we apparently could not be subject to morality. Surely, any such argument from origins is eventually wrong, both for humans and for forms of government.

47. The injustice in this reading is that Hobbes was arguably merely defending whatever government was firmly in place against what he saw as the chaos of revolutionary fervor. He asserts, "That you will esteeme it better to enjoy your selves in the present state though perhaps not the best, then by waging Warre, indeavour to procure a reformation for other men in another age, your selves in the meane while either kill'd, or consumed with age" (Thomas Hobbes, *De Cive*, "Preface," 36). Similarly, he notes "that the estate of Man can never be without some incommodity or other; and that the greatest, that in any forme of Government can possibly happen to the people in generall, is scarce sensible, in respect of the miseries, and horrible calamities, that accompany a Civill Warre" (*Leviathan*, chap. 18, 238 [94]). Unfortunately, therefore, as Macpherson notes, "in immediate application [Hobbes's work] supported the King against Parliament" (Macpherson, "Introduction," 20).

48. Leslie Stephen, *Hobbes* (London: Macmillan, 1904), 203.

49. For the general argument, see Russell Hardin, "Exchange Theory on Strategic Bases," *Social Science Information* 2 (1982): 251-72.

50. Hardin, *Collective Action*, esp. chaps. 9 through 14; Axelrod, *The Evolution of Cooperation*.

51. See further, Hardin, *Collective Action*, 200-5.

52. Macpherson, "Introduction," 13.

53. Hampton presents a compelling Hobbesian account of why contractarianism cannot work as a general theory of the state and why Hobbes's theory is not contractarian on usual meanings of that term. She then oddly concludes that we should nevertheless call her Hobbesian resolution a variant of contractarianism, as she chooses to do (Hampton, *Hobbes*, 279). It would contribute more to understanding to assert that it is not contractarian.

Russell Hardin is Mellon Foundation Professor of Political Science, Philosophy, and Public Policy Studies at the University of Chicago. He is currently working on issues in ethics and public life and on the foundations of rational choice and social order. He is author of Morality within the Limits of Reason *(University of Chicago Press, 1988) and the immediate past editor of* Ethics: An International Journal of Social, Political and Legal Philosophy.

[13]

HOBBES AND THE FOOLE[1]

KINCH HOEKSTRA
Oxford University

Answere not a foole according to his folly, lest thou also be like unto him.
Answere a foole according to his folly, lest hee be wise in his owne conceit.
— Proverbs 26:4-5

I

A focal point of twentieth-century commentary on Hobbes has been the few paragraphs in chapter 15 of *Leviathan* where Hobbes presents the objections of someone he calls the "Foole" and then sets out to meet these objections. The Foole maintains that it is reasonable to break covenants, or act unjustly, when it is advantageous for one to do so. According to the usual interpretation, Hobbes's answer is that it is never reasonable to act unjustly, for it is never reasonable to think that doing so will be advantageous. The primary reason that this short section has drawn so much ink, I suppose, is that this answer seems unrealistic and simply wrong, and critics have hurried to worry the chink in Hobbes's argumentative armor. A supplementary reason for the critical attention has been that Hobbes's perceived debility, if the standard interpretation is followed, has meant that Hobbes's reply to the Foole has been a battle line between that interpretation and an alternative (according to which Hobbes bases his political philosophy on the primacy of our obligation to obey an independent standard such as divine command).

I will propose an interpretation of the argument that would minimize Hobbes's vulnerability at this point. If my interpretation is correct, the

AUTHOR'S NOTE: For close scrutiny of previous drafts, I am indebted to Edwin Curley, Al Martinich, David Peritz, Rosamond Rhodes, Russ Shafer-Landau, Quentin Skinner, Ralph Walker, and Bernard Williams. I am especially grateful to Marina Galanti for critical suggestions.

argument with the Foole would lose the sort of importance it has had—but that is to the good, as it is now widely seen as a crucial weakness in Hobbes's theory.[2] I hope the following considerations will at least help to subdue the critical readiness to seize on the reply to the Foole as a way of dismissing Hobbes or what he is taken to represent (theories of justice as mutual advantage, for example).

It is generally agreed that the Foole's position is that sometimes the dictates of self-interest demand that we break covenants. (Note, though, that the Foole's words are open to the richer interpretation that it will also be reasonable to *make* a covenant solely for the benefit that the making of it will confer, even without the initial intention of keeping the covenant.)[3] There is disagreement about how best to characterize Hobbes's response. Let c stand for the dictate to keep covenants and s for the dictate of self-interest, understanding the possibility of diverging dictates as the possibility that one dictate can prescribe different actions from the other. We are concerned with two possibilities:

(D) c and s can diverge, or
(~D) c and s cannot diverge.

Most interpreters of Hobbes—including David Gauthier and Jean Hampton—have read Hobbes in his reply to the Foole as endorsing (~D).[4] The striking (but not only) drawback of this reading is that it attributes to Hobbes a view widely recognized as mistaken and in evident tension with Hobbes's own precepts.[5]

A few interpreters[6] have instead read Hobbes as endorsing (D) in his reply to the Foole and, more precisely, the following version thereof:

(D.1) c and s can diverge: in case of divergence, c overrides s.

This interpretation apparently countenances an inconsistency with Hobbes's fundamental psychological assumption that a person necessarily pursues his or her own apparent good. Additionally, it would seem to leave us with an inconsistent deontology rather than an intrepid attempt to develop a theory of obligation that begins from basic assumptions of predominantly self-interested behavior.[7] Even proponents of the so-called Taylor-Warrender thesis usually emphasize that for Hobbes, it is always in one's interest to obey God, thus subscribing to a version of (~D).[8]

There is, however, another possible permutation within this framework, namely:

(D.2) c and s can diverge: in case of divergence, s overrides c.

The reason that this has lacked expositors as an interpretation of Hobbes's reply is probably that *the Foole himself adduces this position*. I will argue that

Hobbes nonetheless also endorses it. That is, Hobbes does not disagree with the Foole about the fact that the dictate to keep covenants can diverge from the dictate of self-interest or about which takes priority in case of divergence. Rather, Hobbes disagrees with the Foole about the extent and the nature of the divergence, and he views the divergence from a fundamentally opposed position. Not least, Hobbes regards the way the Foole maintains his doctrine to be self-contradicting. If either of the other interpretations (D.1 or ~D) is followed, Hobbes comes across as having unrealistic fundamental premises. Showing the plausibility of the third alternative would support the view that Hobbes proceeds with exemplary pragmatism.

II

The Foole says that when it conduces to one's benefit, it is reasonable to break covenants; in the case where the end of one's covenant breaking is sufficiently valuable—for example, the control of a kingdom—then "you may call it Injustice, or by what other name you will; yet it can never be against Reason, seeing all voluntary actions of men tend to the benefit of themselves; and those actions are most Reasonable, that conduce most to their ends" (L xv.4). Hobbes disagrees somewhat with the Foole's belief that all one's voluntary actions tend to one's own benefit. Hobbes thinks one pursues one's own apparent good in one's voluntary actions. This is different from the Foole's position, as (1) one may fail in the pursuit, and (2) what appears to one to be good or beneficial may in fact be bad or detrimental. In addition, Hobbes objects to the Foole's claim that "those actions are most Reasonable, that conduce most to their ends." Hobbes rightly points out that the reasonableness of an action is to be gauged not by actual outcome but by reasonably expected outcome. Further, it is not clear that Hobbes subscribes to the utility maximization model of reason implied in the Foole's claim.[9] Yet, Hobbes seems to tax his opponent with more than these remonstrations and abuses him as a Foole from more pressing motives.

What is the nature of the folly that gives the Foole his name?[10] The most obvious answer is that he contradicts himself, that he pursues his own destruction in the name of his own advantage.[11] This folly, however, can only be understood to apply if the Foole is necessarily discovered; that is, if his doctrine does not remain private. A related possibility is that Hobbes is referring to the folly that he identifies especially with lack of discretion (L viii.1-3). A person's private thoughts are not subject to the charge of folly, for these "run over all things, holy, prophane, clean, obscene, grave, and light, without shame, or blame; which verball discourse cannot do, farther than the Judgement of the Time, Place, and Persons." It is the public manifestation of lack of wit that is accounted folly; want of discretion is specifically a defect of discourse.[12]

If he proclaims his doctrine, the Foole, who holds that reason demands that one act only for one's own benefit, is foolish indeed. He thereby gives notice that he is not to be trusted in covenants, and so diminishes the benefit he can reap therefrom. He also risks converting others to his position, which will allow him to depend less on others' being in good faith when they covenant with him and may lead to less surrounding peace and productivity; again, his benefits are likely to be diminished.[13] Is Hobbes's Foole so stupid?

There is strong evidence that he is. Hobbes introduces the indirect speech of the Foole as follows: "The Foole hath sayd in his heart, there is no such thing as Justice; and sometimes also with his tongue; seriously alleaging . . ." (L xv.4). A strict reading of this sentence would take the Foole as a singular example, though such an example may be typical. The Foole who sometimes denies justice with his tongue can represent only those individuals who sometimes deny justice with their tongues. His position does not embrace people who deny justice only in their hearts.[14] Also, the Foole's doctrine is presented as something that the Foole *seriously alleges*. The only things that the Foole specifically says in his heart are that there is no such thing as justice (which he also says sometimes with his tongue) and that there is no God. All the rest—that is, the substance of the doctrine—is seriously alleged by him (i.e., declared to be the case). Further, Hobbes makes this counterargument in his reply to the Foole: "he which *declares* he thinks it reason to deceive those that help him, can in reason expect no other means of safety, than what can be had from his own single Power."[15] If Hobbes's refutation of the Foole depends on the fact of the Foole's declaration, then such declaration is integral to the Foole's position. It may readily be doubted that it is always foolish to deceive those who help one or might help one, but Hobbes is certainly right if what he means is that it is foolish for one who needs help to announce that he thinks it reasonable to deceive one's helpers. Hobbes's target here may not be, as is assumed in the usual interpretation, a Silent Foole, but an Explicit Foole.[16]

The Foole may be explicit by word or example. In the first case, which I will call that of the Loud Foole, he expressly and publicly declares that he thinks that injustice or lawbreaking may sometimes be reasonable.[17] The alternative, which I will dub the Flagrant Foole, flouts justice so blatantly that his actions themselves speak loudly, serving as a declaration that he believes that one can reasonably act unjustly.[18] Injustice may be flagrant not only by its openness but also by its visibility: holders of high positions of public trust, for example, are prone to flagrancy even when their infraction would in other circumstances be discreet. Both kinds of Explicit Foole will tend to incite others to contravene contracts and (therefore) laws, or at least will have the effect of eroding respect for contracts and laws.

Hobbes is preoccupied with those who foment rebellion more than with ordinary criminals, but he does have a particular concern with flagrant crime, as it too can incite disobedience. The degree of crime is exacerbated by "the contagion of the Example" and "the mischiefe of the Effect" (L xxvii.29): "And generally all Crimes are the greater, by the scandall they give; that is to say, by becomming stumbling-blocks to the weak, that look not so much upon the way they go in, as upon the light that other men carry before them" (L xxvii.36). In discussing crime, Hobbes consistently emphasizes the example, the public crime over the private. Even within the realm of private crimes, he focuses on those "where the dammage in the common opinion of men, is most sensible,"[19] for what ensues when common opinion is swept away by bad example or bad precept is civil war, the political *summum malum*.

"He therefore that breaketh his Covenant," Hobbes continues, "and consequently *declareth* that he thinks he may with reason do so, cannot be received into any Society . . . but by the errour of them that receive him" (L xv.5, emphasis added). In the mid-seventeenth century, it was common to use *consequently* either to indicate a logical or causal link, or to indicate mere temporal succession, without implication of a logical or causal link.[20] If it is taken to mean he declares *thereafter*, we are dealing here with a Loud Foole; even if it is understood as meaning that he declares *thereby*, Hobbes's Foole is a Flagrant Foole.[21] Either way, he is an Explicit Foole.

That Hobbes in his response to the Foole means to highlight the Foole's declaration rather than simply the Foole's belief is given further plausibility by the fact that this is how William Lucy interpreted this passage in 1663: "his answer is drawn from a *declaration* that that man should make, *that he think's it fit to deceive*. . . . He speak's onely of such who manifest and declare they will *deceive*." Thus, it was readily feasible for a mid-seventeenth-century reader to understand Hobbes's talk of the Foole's declaration quite literally.[22] Lucy joins most modern commentators, however, in arguing that the Foole gets the better of Hobbes. He regards the challenge of the Foole to be the challenge of the Silent Foole, and so when Hobbes provides an answer to the Loud Foole, Lucy complains that "he attempt's one proposition, and, by shuffling and changing the Tearmes, prove's another."[23] We can accept Lucy's reading of Hobbes's answer and yet save Hobbes from this charge by upholding the interpretation that the challenge itself is that of the Explicit Foole, which is why it is to the Explicit Foole that Hobbes replies.

Hobbes is appropriating Psalm 14:1, according to which "The foole hath sayd in his heart, There is no God."[24] Even when quoting the Bible inexactly, Hobbes almost invariably employed italics: whatever its inspiration, he marks the Foole as his own creation by leaving the introduction of the Foole unitalicized both in the 1651 and the 1668 editions. Hobbes elsewhere quotes the psalmist's verse exactly when discussing atheism, a belief;[25] in choosing here to replace God with justice and to add the Foole's tongue, Hobbes clearly signals his transformation of the verse. It is the more striking, therefore, that many commentators have tended to ignore Hobbes's amplification, thereby cutting out the Foole's tongue. Curley stands with most critics when he sums up the position as "The fool says in his heart that there is no such thing as justice, meaning by that that it is rational for me to break my covenants whenever that will conduce to my benefit,"[26] and Boonin-Vail inverts the matter when he maintains that "Hobbes emphasizes that the Foole has said this 'in his heart,' not merely with his tongue."[27] Hobbes's emphasis is brought out not only by his emendation of the Bible but also by the fact that he regards the tongue as making the difference between war and peace. As he says in DC v.5, "the tongue of man is a trumpet of warre, and sedition."[28]

Hobbes is keenly aware of the significance of his emendation, for he repeatedly demarcates the ambit of political intervention in these terms. In *The Elements of Law*, he insists that

> no human law is intended to oblige the conscience of a man, but the actions only. For seeing no man (but God alone) knoweth the heart or conscience of a man, unless it break out into action, either of the tongue, or other part of the body; the law made thereupon would be of none effect, because no man is able to discern, but by word or other action whether such law be kept or broken.[29]

And in *Leviathan*, Hobbes maintains that "Beleef, and Unbeleef never follow mens Commands" because they cannot be induced by promised rewards or threatened punishments, but we are bound to follow the sovereign's command "to say with our tongue, what wee beleeve not."[30] Hobbes, who was so sensitive to the crucial difference between thinking something and publicly proclaiming it, is not likely to have been careless or haphazard when specifying that the Foole says with his tongue and alleges and declares his doctrine.

In his argument against the Foole, Hobbes aims to get citizens to obey by arguing for the imprudence of proclaiming injustice. This strategy has two possible audiences: the Explicit Foole is encouraged not to be an Explicit Foole, and the people are encouraged to treat the Explicit Foole as a fool and a menace. Hobbes employs another strategy, reflected in other parts of the work, that is aimed at influencing those who govern. The thrust of this strategy is to argue that it is imprudent to allow such proclamation and to provide a justification for commanding that certain doctrines be proclaimed or not proclaimed. Both strategies are centrally concerned with bridling the tongue.

Hobbes reworks the argument with the Foole when he reconsiders it for the Latin edition of *Leviathan*, first published in 1668.[31] There, Hobbes clarifies his meaning by excluding any possibility that he is discussing the Silent Foole. Both occasions where we are told in the English edition that the Foole has said something in his heart are excised in the Latin edition. Thus, Hobbes pointedly truncates the then-familiar verse from the Vulgate. The psalmist's "Dixit insipiens in corde suo: non est Deus" (accurately quoted by Hobbes in the 1647 annotation to DC xiv.19 and in the 1668 appendix to *Leviathan*) becomes Hobbes's "Dixit Insipiens, Non est Iustitia."[32]

III

A major reason to adopt the Explicit Foole interpretation is that otherwise we risk making Hobbes the foolish one, who has constructed an objection that he doesn't understand and fails to meet.[33] So A. Zaitchik says,

> The problems with this reply are so astoundingly obvious that one must wonder how Hobbes dared to give it. . . . Hobbes seems to miss the point of the Fool's objection, which was not that unilateral violation of covenant is *generally* advantageous or rational but rather that it might *sometimes* be.[34]

The Explicit Foole interpretation would not run into this problem. The Explicit Foole announces that he sometimes will break contracts; Hobbes responds that his position—that is, being an Explicit Foole—is *always unreasonable* (though it may sometimes turn out to be profitable, against reasonable expectation). Any interpreter who regards Hobbes as replying to the Silent Foole has to ascribe to Hobbes the bold naïveté that it is *always unreasonable to break contracts*; that is, that one can *never* reasonably calculate that the risks of breaking a contract or a law are outweighed by the advantages of breaking it.[35]

Hobbes does not subscribe to this unrealistic simplification. "It is of it selfe manifest, that the actions of men proceed from the will, and the will from hope, and feare, insomuch as when they shall see a *greater good*, or *lesse evill*, likely to happen to them by the breach, then observation of the Lawes, they'l wittingly violate them."[36] Nonetheless, Hobbes does think that such a breach is unlikely to be reasonable: people seldom consider the full ramifications of contract breaking and tend to overestimate their ability to elude detection. Thus, they often act without calculating sufficiently or make mistakes in their calculations. Hobbes is eager to emphasize the unlikelihood that violation will be reasonable and the high risk that is run. Certain actions, such as initiating rebellion, are extremely risky (the probability of payoff is low, the probability of punishment is high, the probability of discovery is high, and the magnitude of punishment is great), and therefore it is practically impossible that they will be reasonable. Citizens are also liable to underestimate the risk of more quotidian violations, either by not accurately figuring the possible price or the probability that they will be caught. But this does not make reasonable violation impossible in principle, for there could be a very low or nonexistent sanction for a particular breach or a low-to-moderate sanction with a very low probability of discovery or enforcement.

When it appears reasonable to a citizen to act unjustly, it may be that the mistake in calculation is not the citizen's but the sovereign's, for setting up a punishment schedule that encourages violation or for allowing the impression that observation or enforcement is unlikely. (Even when the sovereign is imprudent in this way, however, it will not be reasonable for a citizen to *advocate* violation.) So, for example, Hobbes observes that "those that deceive upon hope of not being observed do *commonly* deceive themselves" (L xxvii.16, emphasis added) and yet admits that if a penalty is not sufficient, people will reasonably choose the crime (L xxvii.8). Hobbes specifies in his answer to the Foole that an agent's action is against reason if it is against the benefit of the agent (L xv.5). If it appears to a person that breaking a law will lead to profit or pleasure, the only thing (other than a rare generosity) that can restrain him or her is fear (L xxvii.19). So, if the fear is not sufficient (which it is up to the sovereign to ensure, especially via education and the reward and punishment schedules), that person will break the law.[37] The setting of a punishment that is

> not great enough to deterre men from the action, is an invitement to it: because when men compare the benefit of their Injustice, with the harm of their punishment, by necessity of Nature they choose that which appeareth best for themselves: and therefore . . . it is the Law that tempted . . . them.[38]

According to Hobbesian psychology, people will always consider breaking covenants if they see profit therein. Silent Fooles will be with us always, but Explicit Fooles will tend to swell their number and audacity. The thing to be done is to alter the payoff scale to ensure as far as possible that covenant breaking will not be reasonable and to silence the Fooles who foment such covenant breaking. Hobbes devotes several sections of *Leviathan* to advising the sovereign to structure the payoff scale to deter injustice most effectively. He devotes the reply to the Foole to silencing those who encourage injustice.

Hobbes may well regard as relatively futile or even counterproductive the argument that people can never reasonably break a contract. He is certainly right to see that the public espousal of the reasonableness of contract breaking and illegal behavior poses a grave threat to the precious peace he so assiduously seeks. Occasional low-risk, low-publicity, silent infringements are for a commonwealth survivable, if not always innocuous; the incitement of infringement, however, is deadly to the commonwealth. In the latter category fall the many books, pamphlets, sermons, and speeches of the 1630s and 1640s that justified disobedience to government or outright rebellion against it on the basis of disadvantages the people suffered at the hands of the sovereign. In 1620, Hobbes might have written of "Those . . . (if any such insensible creatures be) that dislike the restraint, & striue, & declaime against obedience to *Lawes*" that "they make themselues so contemptible. as no obiection of theirs can be worthy the answering" (HS 516). As it became evident in subsequent decades that even one or two Loud Fooles could plunge a country into civil war, such declamation demanded an answer.[39] Far from missing the point of the Foole's doctrine, Hobbes sees that the point to be addressed is its propagation as doctrine.

It has sometimes been remarked that the reply to the Foole is isolated and aberrant, contradicting even proximate passages in *Leviathan*. When read as a reply to the Explicit Foole, however, it turns out to be consistent with Hobbes's attempt in *Leviathan* to combat (and also to harness) the forces of rhetoric[40] and the influence of powerful position. Portraits of the Loud Foole are plentiful in *Leviathan*, as are those of the Flagrant Foole.[41] It is sometimes observed, however, that the reply to the Foole is "a passage which seems to have no parallels in Hobbes' earlier expositions of his theory."[42] Again, when we read this reply as addressed to the Explicit Foole, we can recognize echoes throughout Hobbes's works. As Hobbes puts it in *De Cive*,

> It is also manifest, that all voluntary actions have their beginning from, and necessarily depend on the will, and that the will of doing, or omitting ought, depends on the opinion of the *good* and *evill* of the *reward*, or *punishment*, which a man conceives he shall receive by the act, or omission; so as the actions of all men are ruled by the opinions of each; wherefore by evident and necessary inference, we may understand that it very much concerns the interest of Peace [*pacis communis interesse plurimum*], that no opinions or doctrines be delivered to Citizens, by which they may imagine, that either by Right they may not obey the *Lawes* of the City . . . or that it is lawfull for to resist him [viz., the sovereign], or that a lesse punishment remaines for him that denies, then him that yeelds obedience.[43]

In *The Elements of Law*, Hobbes adopts Sallust's judgment of Catiline from *De coniuratione Catilinae* 5.4 ("*satis eloquentiae, sapientiae parum*," which he quotes—albeit uncrossing the chiasmus—in EL xxvii.13 and again in DC xii.12): "there can be no author of rebellion, that is not an eloquent and powerful speaker, and withal . . . a man of little wisdom"[44]; in *De Cive*, he remarks that it is precisely eloquent folly that results in seditiousness.[45] Additionally, the Explicit Foole plays a role in Hobbes's later works and could plausibly be called the main character of *Behemoth*.[46] Thus, the Explicit Foole interpretation has the further virtue of consistency with the rest of Hobbes's thought.

IV

Hobbes's response to the Foole relies in great measure on the idea that, although such an error can happen, it is not reasonable to expect others to commit the error of allowing a Foole to enter or remain in their society (L xv.5). It may be objected, therefore, that the error involved in allowing an Explicit Foole in one's society would be too palpable to be plausible; that is, that it would *not* happen.[47] Many people in Hobbes's day, however, did suffer the continued company of those who recommended lawbreaking and even esteemed them and sustained them in positions of influence.[48] By sounding the alarm to these people and urging them to ostracize any such exponent, Hobbes gives an Explicit Foole a further reason (i.e., beyond pointing out to him the unreasonableness of his activity) consonant with his declared principle of self-interest to be silent and discreet.

Further, remember that the error of a Foole being allowed into society, though possible, is supposed to be unlikely enough that it is unsafe for the Foole to rely on it. On the usual interpretation, such error is harder to explain. If I think it reasonable to break contracts when doing so is beneficial, keeping this view to myself, I will tend to break contracts when discovery of my violation is impossible or unlikely despite the reasonable suspicion of others. And if others are reasonably vigilant but nonetheless cannot detect my violation, it seems idiosyncratic to say that they are in *error*.[49] The position that we entrust with power only those who deal fairly is dismissed by Hobbes as a paralogism, on the basis that we may well not *know* whether our expectation of fair play will correspond to the facts (DM xxxviii.17-18). According to Hobbes's own principle in his reply to the Foole, a course of action is to be judged reasonable based on its expected rather than its actual result; therefore, those who let the Silent Foole into their confederation act *with* reason[50]—the ones who act against reason are those who allow the Loud Foole or the Flagrant Foole in their confederation.

It is worth recalling that Hobbes hardly considers error an unusual phenomenon. All mankind is highly prone to "errour, and misreckorning" (L xxii.5); "Errour, [is] commonly incident to humane Nature" (L xxii.11); moreover, "such is the ignorance, and aptitude to error generally of all men . . . as by innumerable and easie tricks to be abused" (L xxxvii.12). Does a stealthy deceiver not therefore have reason to feel confident of success? As Hobbes says of the common deceivers who pretend to work miracles, "the Impostors need not the study so much as of naturall causes, but the ordinary ignorance, stupidity, and superstition of mankind" (L xxxvii.10; cf. HS 375-7). If ignorance and error are so widespread and so easy to exploit, the fact that the Foole cannot reasonably expect others to make the error of allowing him in their confederation indicates that his conduct must be more egregious than that of the Silent Foole.

The most generalized passage about reasonable expectation in Hobbes's reply is rather contorted: "when a man doth a thing, which notwithstanding any thing can be foreseen, and reckoned on, tendeth to his own destruction, howsoever some accident which he could not expect, arriving, may turne it to his benefit; yet such events do not make it reasonably or wisely done."[51] An important ambiguity lurks in the notion of an action that tends to one's own destruction. Often, Hobbes opposes the idea of that which tends to the destruction of one's own nature to the idea of that which tends to the preservation of one's own nature. He sometimes employs the tendency to destruction or preservation as tantamount to the tendency toward death or survival and sometimes—perhaps because he holds that one's nature is to choose the apparently more advantageous over the less—as corresponding to loss and profit more generally. This ambiguity seems to trouble Hobbes in his discussion of the laws of nature, particularly in his discussion of the Foole. In the 1651 *Leviathan* (xiv.3), Hobbes defines a law of nature as a precept that forbids a man to do that "which is destructive of his life, or taketh away the means of preserving the same; and to omit, that, by which he thinketh it may be best preserved." In the 1668 *Leviathan*, Hobbes makes an important alteration or clarification here, defining a law of nature as a precept that forbids a man to do that "which appears to him to tend to his own loss."[52]

This modification is important in ways that cannot be pursued here. It is relevant to the present argument because it highlights that Hobbes might mean one of two things: that the Foole is unreasonable according to the criterion of reasonably expected gain (where that is understood as determining only the question of whether the contemplated action is likely to be profitable overall) or of reasonable risk (where the question is whether the magnitude of potential profit, multiplied by the probability of its being realized, is greater than the magnitude multiplied by the probability of loss).

Consider the first criterion, which Hobbes probably employs if by something that "tendeth to his own destruction," he merely means that it will probably bring loss rather than gain. (Hobbes seems to imply no more when he says later in the paragraph [L xv.5] that an action is unreasonable, the favorable result of which one "could not foresee, nor reckon upon"; nor when, two paragraphs later, he says that the favorable result "cannot reasonably be expected, but rather the contrary.") A Silent Foole can sometimes reasonably expect to gain from breaking a covenant. The Explicit Foole, however, cannot even reasonably expect an overall gain from his actions.[53] The judgment that one is foolish who chooses a course of action from which he can expect net damage is fitting only if it is the Explicit Foole who is being judged. The Silent Foole may sometimes reasonably expect a net benefit from injustice (it is likely that he will profit), but generally would not be reasonable to act on or rely on this expectation (though profit is probable, the risk is too great). Someone who cheats on an examination (or shoplifts, or plagiarizes this article) may reasonably expect to profit, but, because of the magnitude of the repercussions in case of discovery, such an action would be unwise. If Hobbes were here judging the Silent Foole, we could at least expect him to mount an argument that one may be foolish even when choosing a course of action that can be expected to be profitable.

If by *destruction* Hobbes instead means to indicate the magnitude of risk, the judgment of the Foole as unreasonable still seems much more appropriate to the Explicit Foole. By this criterion, it is unreasonable to take the risk of the action (i.e., it is not just an unreasonable expectation but an unreasonable action). One will sometimes be able to calculate that the probability *and* magnitude of costs and benefits will favor silent violation. On both the criterion of reasonable action and that of reasonable expectation of gain, therefore, it is blatant rather than silent behavior that is foolish.

V

Other parts of the argument may seem to tell against the Explicit Foole interpretation. It may be objected that when Hobbes discusses gaining the kingdom of heaven by violence, or when he discusses rebellion, he is not talking about proponents of covenant breaking but simply about covenant breakers.

The scenario of assaulting heaven does not put into question the interpretation defended above because the judge of such violations is omniscient. Where the judge is God ("that taketh the will for the deed" [EL xxv.10]), Hobbes can happily include both Silent and Explicit Fooles, for the violations of the former, however irrelevant politically, will be as readily detectable as the activities of the latter. Put differently: in the eyes of God, every act of injustice (and, indeed, every attempted or intended act of injustice) is an act of explicit foolishness.[54]

The other scenario is that of breaking the covenant of obedience to the earthly sovereign by rebellion. Hobbes says that some people who disallow injustice for everything else allow it "when it is for the getting of a Kingdome." These people presumably make this exception because "it conduceth to such a benefit, as shall put a man in a condition, to neglect not onely the dispraise, and revilings, but also the power of other men" (xv.4). Ostensibly, that is, not only is the benefit unusually great, it is such that it would ensure against punishment effects and negative reputation effects, thereby annulling or dramatically decreasing the usual magnitude of loss.

Hobbes considers two illustrations of this scenario from which he thinks a person will be tempted to conclude that one who gains sovereignty by killing the sovereign will have acted reasonably. The first illustration is drawn from the ancients who believed "that *Saturn* was deposed by his son *Jupiter*," and yet who "believed neverthelesse the same *Jupiter* to be the avenger of Injustice." In the preface to *De Cive*, Hobbes indicates what is at stake in this ancient example:

> They kept their Empire entire, not by arguments, but by punishing the wicked, and protecting the good; likewise Subjects did not measure what was just by the sayings and judgements of private men, but by the Lawes of the Realme; nor were they kept in peace by disputations, but by power and authority: . . . therefore they little used as in our dayes, to joyn themselves with ambitious, and hellish spirits, to the utter ruine of their State; . . . in truth, the simplicity of those times was not yet capable of so learned a piece of folly. Wherefore it was peace, and a golden age, which ended not before that Saturn being expelled, it was taught lawfull to take up arms against Kings.

Thereafter, however, Jupiter had to contend with private citizens who attacked justice by insisting on their own judgments, thereby ushering in an era of war. Hobbes takes the golden age as ending not simply with the expulsion of Saturn but with the lesson of rebellion taught thereby.[55] Rebellion is clearly Hobbes's central concern, but he sees himself as particularly engaged in combating the *teaching* of rebellion. Hobbes also wants to challenge the idea that someone can be acting justly when acting rebelliously. The idea of Jupiter avenging injustice in overthrowing Saturn is particularly an anathema to

Hobbes because it depends on the idea that the sovereign acted unjustly and that a subject rightly took it upon himself to punish this injustice. As in the widely misconstrued "A Review, and Conclusion" of the English *Leviathan*, Hobbes endeavors to take a position that condemns the rebels for their rebellion but nonetheless recognizes the successful rebel as the legitimate sovereign, thereby condemning further warfare as rebellion. Rebellion is unjust, but it does not disqualify someone from being the sovereign, and nobody can justly complain of a sovereign's injustice. That is, a sovereign cannot as sovereign act unjustly, but he or she may have acted unjustly before becoming the sovereign.

Such a position brings Hobbes to his second illustration, for it resembles a position he finds in Sir Edward Coke. "Somewhat like to a piece of Law in *Cokes* Commentaries on *Litleton*; where he sayes, If the right Heire of the Crown be attainted of Treason; yet the Crown shall descend to him, and *eo instante* the Atteynder be voyd."[56] Johann Sommerville reports that "Hobbes observed that Coke's reasoning constituted an invitation to heirs to kill monarchs";[57] what Hobbes observes, however, is that "From which instances a man will be very prone to inferre" that it can never be against reason for the heir to kill the sovereign, as those actions are most reasonable that are most beneficial to oneself. Hobbes concludes that this inference is what is mistaken: "This specious reasoning is neverthelesse false" (L xv.4). The inference is invalid for a number of reasons. Most notably, such an outcome is not reasonably to be expected, so it is not reasonably pursued.[58] It is not Coke's premise that is singled out as false but the inference drawn therefrom. Coke's premise, together with the further (almost Hobbesian) premise that "all the voluntary actions of men tend to the benefit of themselves," may even be why Hobbes considers the reasoning to be "specious" (i.e., attractive).[59] It is a dangerous premise, however, for it can be taken to imply that the regicide was not unjust, and therefore to sanction the idea of reasonable and just rebellion.

Hobbes wants to maintain that although this person, now sovereign, can determine justice and injustice, his or her becoming sovereign was nonetheless unjust. It is a particularly delicate issue for Hobbes, who endeavors to evade the diametrical dangers of allowing the sovereign's attainment of sovereignty to be characterized as unjust and of insisting that the current sovereign's rebellious attainment of sovereignty was just. Hobbes tries to negotiate this difficulty by identifying the source of the obligation of subjects to the sovereign as simply the sovereign's possession of sovereignty rather than the legitimacy of the way in which the sovereign ultimately acquired it. "Therefore I put down for one of the most effectuall seeds of the Death of any State, that the Conquerors require not onely a Submission of mens actions to them for the future, but also an Approbation of all their actions past." Hobbes insists that a sovereign who teaches that his title is justly acquired unwittingly sanctions his own overthrow (R&C 8).

Hobbes more clearly disagrees with Coke when the question is about treasonous declaration. Hobbes argues against Coke's use of the common saying that bare words cannot make a traitor.[60] According to Coke's principles thus stated, treason cannot consist of mere words, and successful treason is no treason, so only those who have attempted to kill the sovereign and failed can be tried for high treason. Not surprisingly, Hobbes finds this insufficient. Also unsurprisingly, Hobbes is particularly eager to squelch treasonous *declaration*. Hobbes argues that if a man "declares . . . with his own mouth" his treasonous intent, that constitutes a far better proof of treason than the provision of weapons or poison (DCL 99), and he even implies that there can be no silent high treason: "Seeing then the Crime is the Design and Purpose to kill the King, or cause him to be killed, and lyeth hidden in the Breast of him that is Accused; what other Proof can there be had of it than words Spoken or Written."[61]

Hobbes is able to maintain that rebellion is foolish in part because it will integrally require public advocacy and flagrant action. Not only does this make the rebel a vulnerable target for punishment, it is likely to result in what Hobbes sometimes calls an absurdity of action, for the rebel incites his or her own downfall. The possible exception to this would be an heir apparent who kills the sovereign. It is noteworthy that Hobbes judges even that action as unreasonable not only because one cannot expect to succeed but also in terms of the attendant advocacy of such action precisely in the case of success: "because by gaining it so, others are *taught* to gain the same in like manner, the attempt thereof is against reason" (L xv.7, emphasis added). An heir will generally be a prime suspect if a hereditary sovereign dies in questionable circumstances.[62] One might nonetheless insist that there could be cases where an heir runs a very low risk of detection. Whether or not such a point is allowed, it does not affect the fact that what Hobbes is discussing is an heir who is likely to be denied the enjoyment of his unlikely success by someone who has learned the lesson of disobedience.

In replying to the Foole, Hobbes relies primarily on a refutation in terms of reason, but he might have shored up his argument in terms of prudence.[63] To exemplify the likelihood that an heir's actions will be flagrant, that a treasonous heir can reasonably expect to inherit a treasonous end, he could have multiplied instances from English and Continental history of deposers being deposed. In the last paragraph of the Latin *Leviathan*, Hobbes refers to the recent civil wars as one such example:

The democrats won, and they established a democracy; but they paid the price of their great crimes by losing it in no time at all. A single tyrant seized control. . . . When their legitimate king was finally restored, they asked for pardon (i.e., acknowledged their foolishness) [*stultitiam suam agnoverunt*].[64]

VI

It is time to consider three central objections.[65] (1) The first objection stems from the fact that I have focused on rebutting the usual interpretation that Hobbes fails to meet the challenge of the Silent Foole. There are other interpretations, however, according to which Hobbes argues against the Silent Foole and (in some way) *succeeds*; if some such interpretation is valid, it would at least avoid the problem of attributing a notoriously weak position to Hobbes. I will, therefore, try to deal very briefly with the best exponents of different types of such a view.

First, there are interpretations that are close to the traditional view of Hobbes's reply. According to one interpretation, Hobbes makes a plausible argument for the point that it is usually foolish to break contracts in conditions of security. Kavka concludes, "Hobbes's reply succeeds generally, but fails in special cases in which the risks due to violation are both low (compared to the potential gains) and calculable."[66] This is to say, however, that it completely fails, for the Foole—according to the Silent Foole interpretation followed by Kavka—believes just that violation is reasonable in some cases, which are presumably those where risks are calculably low. A disparate interpretation, put forth by Nunan, is that Hobbes makes a plausible argument (or at least finds the argument plausible) that keeping contracts is *always* in one's best earthly interest. Evidence has been provided above that Hobbes does not believe this, and it is revealing that Nunan's argument hinges on an implicit reliance on the Explicit Foole interpretation.[67]

An alternative reading is suggested by David Boonin-Vail, who regards other construals of Hobbes's reply to the Foole (including Kavka's) as falling to the charge of rule worship. He thinks that his interpretation of Hobbes as a virtue theorist provides Hobbes with "a substantially more cogent reply to the Foole": according to this reading, Hobbes is arguing that the *disposition* to justice is more profitable than the *disposition* to maximize advantage.[68] But this interpretation is susceptible to the same objection that Boonin-Vail finds so devastating to other theories, for it too involves a kind of rule worship. If the person with the just disposition maximizes his or her advantage by keeping contracts even when short-term benefit calls for violation (because, say, the immediately profitable course risks the person's security or survival), then the Foole will also follow that policy, though possibly from a different disposition. Similarly, if the Foole is foolish for sometimes acting against his long-term interest in keeping covenants, the person with the just disposition is also foolish for doing so. Without an adequate account of relevant psychological differences, justifying an uncompromising disposition in terms of overall or long-term advantage is no more acceptable than justifying a rigid rule in these terms. It is not clear that the relevant disanalogy between a maximizing rule and a maximizing disposition can be maintained. A clearer matter is that Hobbes does not try to defend such a disanalogy; he is not concerned to argue that a rule-oriented disposition is more profitable than other dispositions and other forms of rule following. In his answer to the Foole, at any rate, he focuses on just and unjust *actions*.

A. P. Martinich provides an importantly different exposition. Martinich says that Hobbes gives three reasons why a person should keep covenants, even when to do so seems not to be in his or her self-interest.[69] First, contract breakers are discovered and suffer for it. Second, people in the state of nature need confederates to survive, and no one wants to help a known deceiver. Third, "Hobbes says that people should keep their promises in the state of nature because that is the only sure way 'of gaining the secure and perpetual felicity of heaven.' "[70] Even when taken together, the first two reasons provide a very weak rejoinder to the Silent Foole who only violates when the risks are calculably low. If Hobbes is to have an adequate answer, according to this scheme, he must rely heavily on the third reason (which is also the one in which Martinich is most interested). But if Hobbes regards this as a legitimate reason, why does he even offer the others? A rational and self-interested calculator who finds the third reason convincing would find it sufficient in itself, whereas such an agent who is not persuaded by this reason will not regard the other two reasons as sufficient. Even more of a puzzle: as Martinich insists, Hobbes is replying to someone who does not believe in God, so how can *any* theological reason convince someone who thinks like the Foole? These difficulties dwindle when we see that the possibility of gaining the kingdom of God by unjust violence is given as a hypothetical example ("what if it could be gotten by unjust violence?") in a paragraph where the Foole is arguing that the prospect of a great enough good, such as the one contested in cases of rebellion, will always make the act reasonable. Hobbes provides his general answer (roughly corresponding to Martinich's first two reasons) to the Foole's general argument and then disputes examples from reputed authorities that would bolster the Foole's attempt to justify rebellion—the getting of the kingdom of heaven by violence (Matthew 11:12), the gaining of an earthly kingdom by violence (Coke's commentaries on Littleton), and an ancient example somewhere between the two (the tale of Jupiter's ascent to the throne; cf. Note 55)—clearly marking that he understands them as illustrations of the Foole's doctrine: "As for the Instance of gaining . . . Heaven" (L xv.6); "And for the other Instance of attaining Soveraignty by Rebellion" (L xv.7). The story from Matthew is assimilated to the Foole's position in the same way as the story from Greek mythology: not as something he personally believes, but as an illustration that people frequently believe that rebellion can be reasonable or trust alleged authorities who would propagate such belief. Hobbes's argument against the Foole here is not that one who keeps contracts in the state of nature is assured of going to heaven, but that one cannot expect to conquer any kingdom, including that of God, by rebellion.

Hobbes's relevant theological argument comes after he has addressed the Foole's general argument and examples, as a kind of appendix to the reply to the Foole. He goes on to address a position that is somewhat different from the Foole's (L xv.8):

> There be some that proceed further; and will not have the Law of Nature, to be those Rules which conduce to the preservation of mans life on earth; but to the attaining of an eternall felicity after death; to which they think the breach of Covenant may conduce; and consequently be just and reasonable. . . . But because there is no naturall knowledge of mans estate after death; much lesse of the reward that is then to be given to breach of Faith; but onely a beliefe grounded upon other mens saying, that they know it supernaturally, or that they know those, that knew them, that knew others, that knew it supernaturally; Breach of Faith cannot be called a Precept of Reason, or Nature.

The Foole, who does not consider extraworldly costs and benefits relevant, is answered on his own terms. Then Hobbes considers those who go further than the Foole, those who say not only that breach of covenant will not be punished in the afterlife but that it will be rewarded. Hobbes does not respond to these people that the third law of nature applies to otherworldly calculations; indeed, he seems to object to their notion that a law of nature can ensure anything at all in the afterlife. Instead, Hobbes says that any such assurance is based on attenuated hearsay of supernatural revelation. It is hard to see how such a dismissal would not also apply to a claim that the keeping of covenants, rather than the breaking of them, is rewarded in heaven. In sum, Hobbes regards theological argument as marginal to the problem of the Foole; when he puts forward a theological argument in a related case, it seems to amount to the point that theological considerations should play no part in one's calculations.[71]

(2) Another objection arises from considering the argument with the Foole in its textual context, which is a defense of Hobbes's individuation of the

638   POLITICAL THEORY / October 1997

third law of nature as *"That men performe their Covenants made,"* within a chapter titled "Of other Lawes of Nature." The argument with the Foole is meant to support the law of nature that people keep the covenants they make—not that they proclaim to do so or refrain from exhorting people not to do so. One might object, therefore, that the Silent Foole interpretation fits better with Hobbes's purpose in this place.

Hobbes concludes that "The keeping of covenants, therefore, is a precept of reason, i.e., a natural law."[72] This does not mean that it is always reasonable to keep covenants, for sometimes (most notably, in the state of nature) it is not reasonable to *act* on the law of nature to keep covenants: "The Lawes of Nature oblige *in foro interno*; that is to say, they bind to a desire they should take place: but *in foro externo*; that is, to the putting them in act, not alwayes" (L xv.36). (In concluding *De Homine* [xv.4], Hobbes maintains generally that the laws of nature cannot be observed in the absence of civil laws and a power of coercion.) It might be pressed that this exception does not apply to the Foole, for "he that having sufficient Security, that others shall observe the same Lawes towards him, observes them not himselfe, seeketh not Peace, but War; & consequently the destruction of his Nature by Violence" (L xv.36), and the Foole is in just such conditions of security. It is unclear, however, that others will be observing a law that requires them to keep contracts regardless of the profit or loss of doing so. For example, an agent in the state of nature who is faced with someone who has performed his or her part of an agreement first cannot safely assume that such performance indicates that person is following a law; at least, such an agent does not have sufficient security that the other will act according to the relevant law of nature thereafter. Also, it is hard to see how one will be encouraging war and ensuring one's own destruction if one is a cautious and silent Foole.

Hobbes argues that the laws of nature are good because they are the means to "peaceable, sociable, and comfortable living" (L xv.40). But he is not talking here about all laws of nature. He is concerned only with the laws of nature dictating peace, which aim at "the conservation of men in multitudes; and which onely concern the doctrine of Civill Society." The beliefs of the Silent Foole and, to a great extent, his actions, will be among those things that concern particular individuals that "are not necessary to be mentioned, nor are pertinent enough to this place" (L xv.34). It may be that one reason why such things are not to be mentioned is that Hobbes is not eager to emphasize that he shares certain premises with the Silent Foole, for to write in defense of the Silent Foole is to be an Explicit Foole. Hobbes chooses to write explicitly against the Explicit Foole and to be relatively silent about the Silent Foole (while recommending policy to limit his disobedience). It is the Explicit Foole who encourages war and brings about his own destruction, so it is to be expected that Hobbes's discussion of the third law of nature revolves around him. At any rate, it is not unreasonable for Hobbes to defend a law of nature in large part by denouncing and confuting those who publicly undermine it. According to Hobbes, people will generally *not* "performe their covenants made" if they think that breaking them will be more beneficial. Ensuring against this is partly a matter for the sovereign's policy, but that policy will be ineffective unless Explicit Fooles are silenced.

(3) A related objection would be that if we know from Hobbes's writings that he shares premises with the Foole (e.g., proposition D.2 from section I, above), Hobbes himself would thus far be a Loud Foole. In section II, we saw that Hobbes's premises are significantly different from the Foole's, but this objection may require further comment.[73] To the extent that Hobbes does regard the Foole's premises as true, does Hobbes not to that extent recommend that the truth be suppressed? It should first be observed that what Hobbes objects to is the doctrine of the Foole being publicized. Certain individual premises, like given individual words, may not by themselves imply the doctrine or its dangers. Further, Hobbes has no general objection to muffling any doctrine that threatens to disturb the peace. If the doctrine made public has been prohibited, then it is simply a case of disobedience, which "may lawfully be punished in them, that against the Laws teach even true Philosophy."[74] In the case of those who broadcast a doctrine that has not been specifically prohibited, if it be a doctrine (such as that of the Foole) that would "tend to disorder in Government, as countenancing Rebellion, or Sedition," Hobbes is adamant: "let them be silenced, and the Teachers punished by vertue of his Power to whom the care of the Publique quiet is committed" (L xlvi.42; cf. L xviii.9, xlii.67).

Although Hobbes and the Foole may agree that the dictate of self-interest can diverge from the dictate to keep covenants, Hobbes thinks the Foole is mistaken about the nature and extent of the divergence. For Hobbes, this by itself is enough to distinguish wisdom from folly and enough to make one promote peace and another war. The Foole seems to think of profitable injustice as a relatively common possibility and regards certain actions (such as attempting to seize a kingdom) as always reasonable. Hobbes regards profitable injustice as a rarity and the unjust actions favored by the Foole—especially rebellion—as the most unreasonable of all; he also considers the Foole's pronouncement of his doctrine to be the height of witlessness. Moreover, Hobbes views occasions of divergence as occasions to be minimized if at all possible, whereas the Foole views them as great opportunities. As Hobbes observes, one should interpret not according to isolated passages but by the main design and scope of the writer (L xliii.24). Hobbes consistently seeks to buttress civil peace and cauterize seditious doctrine, and he is therefore confident in offering his work to the scrutiny of "the Publique Judge of Doctrine" as containing nothing contrary to the disturbance of public tranquillity (R&C 17, 16).

Leviathan is meant to govern the proud (L xxviii.27; note that pride is identified with self-conceit at L viii.18). In expounding the law of nature against pride, Hobbes alludes to Proverbs 26:5 to make the point that one would not only be wrong to be proud but would be foolish; that is, pride tends to thwart the objectives of the proud.[75] "Nor when the wise in their own conceit, contend by force, with them who distrust their owne wisdome, do they alwaies, or often, or almost at any time, get the Victory" (L xv.21). At the beginning of his dialogue on the causes of the civil wars (B 2^r = p. 1), Hobbes deplores the "double folly" of self-conceit. Far from doubling the Foole's folly by openly rebuffing his conceit of wisdom, Hobbes aims thereby at a double wisdom and the correlate deflection of a double folly. Although Milton would undoubtedly be ranked by Hobbes with the fomenters of civil war who make "a false presumption of their own wisdom" (L xxvii.16), he puts the point deftly: "If you are wise, and silent, you are a foole: if you are a foole and silent; you are wise."[76]

In concluding part II of the *Leviathan*, Hobbes announces that he wants the doctrines of that work taught publicly, so that "men may learn thereby, both how to govern, and how to obey" (L xxxi.41). In the answer to the Foole, Hobbes shows that his greatest enemies—the greater for sharing the principle that it is reasonable to seek one's own advantage—are those who publicly teach disobedience or governance that will induce disobedience.[77] From his first writings to his last, Hobbes has a consuming preoccupation with those who publicly incite disobedience.[78] If these can be controlled, civil war may be avoided, although the rest of Hobbes's political program be ignored. Even if the citizens are "much wounded and torne with affronts, and calumnies, by them who are in Authority," and even if "there be as many men as you wil, infected with opinions repugnant to Peace, and civill Government," unless they have hope, one prerequisite of which is leaders, "there will no sedition follow; every man will dissemble his thoughts, and rather content himself with the present burthen, then hazard an heavier weight [*grauia potius ferent quam grauiora*]."[79]

The Explicit Foole interpretation would not have languished for over three centuries were there not much to recommend the Silent Foole interpretation; I am sure that it will still find defenders. According to the criteria of textual, logical, and historical coherence, however, I think that we should recognize the Foole who so provokes Hobbes as an unquiet one, an advocate of private self-interest over civic duty. If we do so, we have one more reason to take Hobbes seriously.

NOTES

1. Seventeenth-century spelling and punctuation are ordinarily retained as a rule without the "[sic]" notation. I have modernized some typographical conventions, such as superscripts, the long *s*, ligatures, and Latin diacritical marks. Italicization in quotations is in the original unless noted. The following abbreviations of Hobbes's works are employed: EL—*The Elements of Law*, reference to continuous chapter numbers, as in J.C.A. Gaskin's edition (Oxford, UK: Oxford University Press, 1994); DC—*De Cive*, citations in English follow Howard Warrender's edition (Oxford, UK: Oxford University Press, 1983) of the 1651 translation unless noted; citations from the Latin follow Warrender's edition (Oxford, UK: Oxford University Press, 1983) of *Elementorum Philosophiae Sectio Tertia De Cive*; DM—Bibliothèque Nationale (Paris) MS fonds latin 6566A, reference to *Critique du* De Mundo *de Thomas White*, ed. Jean Jacquot and Harold Whitmore Jones (Paris: Vrin, 1973); L—*Leviathan*, ed. Richard Tuck (Cambridge, UK: Cambridge University Press, 1991), R&C—"A Review, and Conclusion" of that edition; LL—the Latin *Leviathan* of 1668, App.—Appendix thereto; DH—*De Homine*. All references to the foregoing works are to chapter and section or paragraph. In addition, HS—*Horae Subsecivae* (London, 1620: reference to page of this edition): note that although three discourses from this work have been attributed to Hobbes, the attribution is dubitable; cf. *Three Discourses*, ed. Noel B. Reynolds and Arlene W. Saxonhouse (Chicago: University of Chicago Press, 1995). T—*Eight Bookes of the Peloponnesian Warre*, reference to page number of *Hobbes's Thucydides*, ed. Richard Schlatter (New Brunswick, NJ: Rutgers University Press, 1975); DCL—*A Dialogue between a Phylosopher and a Student, of the Common-Laws of England*, reference to pagination of first edition, as given in Joseph Cropsey's edition (Chicago: University of Chicago Press, 1971); B—*Behemoth or The Long Parliament*, reference to folio number of St. John's College (Oxford) MS 13 and to corresponding page of the Tönnies edition, reprinted, with an introduction by Stephen Holmes (Chicago: University of Chicago Press, 1990); EW—*The English Works of Thomas Hobbes of Malmesbury*, ed. Sir William Molesworth (London: John Bohn, 1839-45: reference to volume and page number). Hobbes consistently refers to the Foole as "he"; to avoid awkwardness, I follow this usage.

2. Kurt Baier, for example, remarking that "Hobbes's argument to rebut [the Foole] . . . is, notoriously, feeble," asserts that Hobbes's failure at this point is "the main flaw" or "the crucial flaw in Hobbes's position." David Copp and David Zimmerman, eds., *Morality, Reason and Truth: New Essays on the Foundations of Ethics* (Totowa, NJ: Rowman & Allanheld, 1985), 206, 207.

3. The Foole maintains that "to make or not make, keep or not keep, covenants was not against reason, when it conduced to one's benefit" (L xv.4). According to the usual interpretation, an agent A promises an agent B that she will do x if B does y, thinking it a beneficial exchange; if A comes to regard the exchange as deleterious, she may reasonably renege on doing x. According to the richer interpretation, A may reasonably promise B that she will do x if B does y, *thinking it beneficial so to promise, regardless of whether she thinks it beneficial to exchange x for y*. However implausibly, Hobbes himself sometimes rejects this idea (see, e.g., DC iii.2).

4. In Jean Hampton's words, Hobbes concludes that "it is always rational (i.e., in one's self-interest) to keep covenants." Jean Hampton, *Hobbes and the Social Contract Tradition*

(Cambridge, UK: Cambridge University Press, 1986), 65. See also, for example, David Gauthier, *The Logic of Leviathan: The Moral and Political Theory of Thomas Hobbes* (Oxford, UK: Clarendon, 1969), 89, and Jonathan Kemp, *Ethical Naturalism: Hobbes and Hume* (London: Macmillan, 1970), 17. Others subscribe to (~D) with the added specification *in the long run.* See K. R. Minogue, "Hobbes and the Just Man," *Hobbes-Forschungen,* ed. Reinhart Koselleck and Roman Schnur (Berlin: Duncker & Humblot, 1969), reprinted in Maurice Cranston and Richard S. Peters, eds., *Hobbes and Rousseau: A Collection of Critical Essays* (Garden City, NY: Doubleday, 1972); D. D. Raphael, *Hobbes: Morals and Politics* (London: George Allen & Unwin, 1977); R. A. Grover, "The Legal Origins of Thomas Hobbes's Doctrine of Contract," *Journal of the History of Philosophy* 18 (1980): 177-94; Daniel M. Farrell, "Reason and Right in Hobbes' *Leviathan,*" *History of Philosophy Quarterly* 1, no. 3 (1984): 297-314; and Richard Nunan, "Hobbes on Morality, Rationality, and Foolishness," *Hobbes Studies* 2 (1989): 40-64. A. P. Martinich, the most recent defender of a divine-command interpretation of Hobbes's theory, seems to fall into this last camp; cf. *The Two Gods of Leviathan: Thomas Hobbes on Religion and Politics* (Cambridge, UK: Cambridge University Press, 1992), 118-19, 135.

5. Hampton notices this tension: "Hobbes's answer to the fool is remarkable, because it directly contradicts the position taken in the chapters we have previously discussed in which Hobbes appears to adopt the fool's position to explain the failure of contracts in the state of nature." Hampton, *Hobbes and the Social Contract Tradition,* 65; cf. pp. 78-79.

6. See Howard Warrender, "Hobbes and Macroethics: The Thoery of Peace and Natural Justice," *Hobbes's "Science of Natural Justice,"* ed. C. Walton and P. J. Johnson (Dordrecht: Martinus Nijhoff, 1987), 306: "Hobbes then goes on to indicate [in the argument with the Foole] that in the keeping of covenants there is more involved than simple calculation of self-interest. . . . I am not allowed to make and break covenants as self-interest or expediency might dictate, and Hobbes is very firm on this point." For a kindred claim, see William E. Connolly, *Political Theory and Modernity* (Oxford, UK: Basil Blackwell, 1988), 26.

7. Note Leibniz's characterization: "I posit together with Carneades (and Hobbes agrees) that justice without one's own utility (either present or future) is the greatest folly, for the proud boastings about the cultivation of virtue for its own sake given by the Stoics and Sadducees are far distant from human nature" (letter to Hermann Conring, 13/23 January 1670).

8. See Howard Warrender, *The Political Philosophy of Hobbes: His Theory of Obligation* (Oxford, UK: Clarendon, 1957), 272-77. See also pp. 636-37, below.

9. Most rational-choice or game-theoretic interpreters of Hobbes (e.g., Gauthier and Tito Magri) have accepted this model of reason as Hobbes's. The most convincing challenge to this view is Gregory S. Kavka's suggestion that Hobbesian agents are disaster avoiders rather than utility maximizers. See his *Hobbesian Moral and Political Theory* (Princeton, NJ: Princeton University Press, 1986).

10. *Foole* comes from the Latin *follis,* meaning a bellows or a windbag. ("Etymologies are no Definitions," Hobbes remarks [DCL 103], "and yet when they are true they give much light towards the finding out of a Definition.")

11. Cf. George Sandys, *Ovid's Metamorphosis Englished, Mythologized, and Represented in Figures* (Oxford, 1632), Book 13, line 137: "O foole, that thus thy owne vndoing seekes!"

12. L viii.9-10; cf. 23. Note that Hobbes opens his "Preface Concerning the Vertues of an Heroique Poem," saying that "in all Writings published, the Vertues required . . . are comprehended all in this one word *Discretion*"; *Homer's Odysses* (London, 1675), sig. B1^r = EW 10, p. iii.

13. This is a paradox, for example, of Thrasymachus's doctrine in the first book of the *Republic.* It is one reason for the difficulty of presenting the immoralist position without ringing a false note.

14. The passage is nonetheless often read this way. To do so, however, is to treat "Agent A has said x to himself and sometimes to others, seriously alleging . . ." as tantamount to "All A-like agents, both those who say x only to themselves and those who say x to others, believe. . . ." Such an equation requires more justification than it has received.

15. L xv.5, emphasis added. The Foole's proclaiming of his doctrine does not, of course, preclude his believing it. That he denies justice in his heart and with his tongue indicates that he believes what he goes on to assert; this suggestion may be reinforced somewhat by the fact that the Foole *seriously* alleges and declares *he thinks it reasonable* to deceive. Elsewhere, Hobbes claims that people will more happily and forcefully profess that which they are convinced is true (DC xiii.9), and he specifically maintains that orators could not be so foolish as to poison the people with seditious opinions unless they themselves believed them (DC xii.12).

16. By "Silent Foole," I mean a silent violator who breaks contracts when it seems advantageous to do so: that is, the Silent Foole refers to someone who silently endorses or acts consistently with the doctrine of the Foole. As will become clear, I do not think that Hobbes sees such a silent violator as necessarily or always foolish, and I do not think Hobbes's target in his reply to the Foole is such a violator.

17. Hobbes sometimes suggests that the paradigmatic case of public proclamation is an act of speech. Raia Prokhovnik observes, "It is speech, spoken language in a public context, that represents the real watershed, for Hobbes, between the natural and artificial, between private and public. . . . It is the *spoken* word which is crucial"; *Rhetoric and Philosophy in Hobbes' Leviathan* (New York: Garland, 1991), 115. Compare Quentin Skinner, *Reason and Rhetoric in the Philosophy of Hobbes* (Cambridge, UK: Cambridge University Press, 1996), 108-10. Hobbes at one point indicates that the words of the sovereign do not constitute sovereign command if they are merely spoken (DCL 197), but this is not his prevailing view (cf., e.g., DC xiv.14 and the last sentence of LL xv).

Robert Payne, in a letter written to Gilbert Sheldon shortly after the publication of *Leviathan*, seems to consider Hobbes's work a "private tract," probably because it is a private citizen's writing (September 16, 1651), in *Theologian and Ecclesiastic* 6 (1848): 224. The contemporary political importance of broadsides, pamphlets, and published sermons ensured, however, that Hobbes did not ultimately regard printed matter distributed beyond the circle of the author's friends as private; he certainly regarded *Leviathan* as a public act (cf. *An Answer to Bishop Bramhall*, EW 4, 317).

18. On Bracton, Coke, and Hobbes on declaration by deed versus by word, see DCL 95-100, and Cropsey's note 16, pp. 106-7 of his edition of DCL. Hobbes distinguishes and delineates traitorous declaration by deed and traitorous declaration by word at DC xiv.20. He uses *declaration* to encompass both words and deeds at, for example, EL xv.11, DC i.12, and B 52^v = p. 108.

19. L xxvii.41; cf. L xxvii.37-49. On the relative importance of example versus precept, note also HS 403-7; T 4, 18; L xii.26, xxvii.35; *De Corpore* I.v.13; DH, xiii.7, xiv.13; B 10^r = 18, 26^v = 54; and *An Answer to Bishop Bramhall*, EW 4, 346.

20. For an example of Hobbes using the word to mean merely following in succession, see EL iv.1.

21. If it remains ambiguous, the possibilities remain open that he means either or both. The examples Hobbes uses lend themselves to ambiguity, so he may have been lumping both sorts of Foole together for the purposes of his argument.

22. Therefore, the interpretation cannot be considered impossible on the ground of anachronism. And Lucy's corroboration contributes to its plausibility more strongly than this, as such possibility exists whenever the interpretation is not *im*possible. The fact that the only contemporary to analyze this passage in detail—who is also the only critic whose responses to *Leviathan*

Hobbes ever commends (*Six Lessons to the Professors of the Mathematiques* ... [London, 1656], p. 64 = EW 7, p. 356)—provides an interpretation that is eminently defensible on other grounds indicates more than that such an interpretation is merely possible.

23. William Lucy, Bishop of St. David's, *Observations, Censures and Confutations of Notorious Errours in Mr. Hobbes His Leviathan and Other His Bookes* (London, 1663), 221-22; cf. pp. 215-23.

Lucy is the only commentator I have read who interprets Hobbes's answer according to the Loud Foole interpretation. The only commentator (as far as I know) who seems to endorse a version of the Flagrant Foole interpretation—though by attributing to Hobbes an appeal to religious belief and by assuming that his argument need only succeed in certain cases, without explaining how such an interpretation is to be justified textually—is S. A. Lloyd, *Ideals as Interests in Hobbes's Leviathan: The Power of Mind over Matter* (Cambridge, UK: Cambridge University Press, 1992), 95-98.

24. This verse is equivalent to Psalm 53:1. In the Vulgate, the corresponding verses are Psalms 13:1 and 52:1.

25. Cf. the note to DC xiv.19; EW 4, pp. 293 and 384 (*An Answer to Bishop Bramhall*); and the Appendix to the Latin *Leviathan*, iii.10. Compare these with the employment of this verse in the Rome essay of *Horae Subsecivae* (361), Robert Burton's use of it in *The Anatomy of Melancholy* 3.4.2.1, and Bacon's discussion of it in his essay "Of Atheism." The fool of the verse had long since been ascribed a position and defended or criticized on its basis: Anselm in his *Proslogion* had attacked the fool, which inspired the defense of Gaunilo, son of Gauthier (*Gaunilonis Liber Pro Insipiente*), which in turn was met by Anselm's *Contra Insipientem*. (Anselm's argument, which has come to be known as "ontological," is that the fool cannot both have an idea of God and deny his existence. The ontological argument was taken up again by Descartes and criticized by Hobbes in the third set of objections to the *Meditations*.) In the eleventh-century debate, as in several biblical commentaries of the seventeenth century, it is emphasized that the fool's position is one of thought and not of words or actions.

26. Edwin Curley, "Reflections on Hobbes: Recent Work on His Moral and Political Philosophy," *Journal of Philosophical Research* 15 (1989-90): 183.

27. David Boonin-Vail, *Thomas Hobbes and the Science of Moral Virtue* (Cambridge, UK: Cambridge University Press, 1994), 149.

28. "*hominis autem lingua tuba quaedam belli est & seditionis.*" See also L xxix.8. This phrase is incorporated into the 1667 Dutch translation of *Leviathan* xvii (p. 173: "*Soo dat de tonge van den mensch een regte trompet is, om oorlog ende oproer wt te blasen*"). The textual warrant for such inclusion is uncertain; it may be that the translator consulted *De Cive* to assist comprehension and simply inserted this passage accidentally or because of its rhetorical appeal.

29. EL xxv.3. Cf. DC xviii.6 and the 1647 annotation thereto.

30. L xlii.11. See also L xxvii.2; xxxvii.13; xl.2; xlii.19, 43, 80, 106, 107; xliii.22, 23; xlv.12-13, 27; xlvi.37, 42; and App. ii.60-64. The position that belief cannot be legislated was widely disputed in Hobbes's England; it was most commonly maintained by anti-absolutists. The Leveller Richard Overton, for example, wrote in 1647, "The inward man is God's prerogative; the outward man is man's prerogative. . . . And God, who only knoweth the heart and searcheth the reins, hath reserved the gubernation thereof to himself as his own prerogative. . . . For the sword pierceth but the flesh; it toucheth but the outward man; it cannot touch the inward," quoted from A.S.P. Woodhouse, ed., *Puritanism and Liberty*, 2d ed. (London: J. M. Dent & Sons, 1974), 332. The notion that only God can govern the heart or the thoughts (which occurs frequently in both Old and New Testaments) was a commonplace of literary, religious, and political writing before and during Hobbes's time. For examples, see Richard Hooker, *Of the*

Laws of Ecclesiastical Polity, i.12, and Hugo Grotius, *De Imperio Summarum Potestatum circa Sacra*, iii.1, 9.

31. I assume here the insufficiency of François Tricaud's contention, in *Léviathan* (Paris: Sirey, 1971), xvi-xxix, that much of the Latin *Leviathan* was composed before the English, but nothing fundamental to my interpretation depends on this assumption. In any case, Tricaud admits (and Hobbes insists, in *An Answer to Bramhall*, EW 4, 317) that the Latin redaction incorporated significant later changes, and he makes no particular claim that the Latin version of the argument with the Foole predates the English.

32. British and American scholars have tended to treat the 1651 *Leviathan* as the culmination of Hobbes's political philosophy. For an important recent work that begins to give the 1668 edition its due, see Edwin Curley, ed., *Leviathan, with Selected Variants from the Latin Edition of 1668* (Indianapolis, IN: Hackett, 1994). For example, Quentin Skinner remarked in an early article: "The *Leviathan* was to provoke the publication of a dozen full-scale attacks within Hobbes's lifetime. But Hobbes himself produced no glosses for those who had misunderstood, and no replies to those who had attacked him. The *Leviathan* was simply abandoned"; see "Hobbes on Sovereignty: An Unknown Discussion," *Political Studies* 13 (1965): 213-18; the citation is from the version reprinted in Preston King, ed., *Thomas Hobbes: Critical Assessments*, vol. 3 (London: Routledge Kegan Paul, 1993), 760; but now see Skinner, *Reason and Rhetoric*. Hobbes *did* reply to some criticisms of *Leviathan*, most extensively to those of Bishop Bramhall and John Wallis. His usual method of clarifying and amending his political theory, however, was to produce new versions thereof (witness the succession EL, DC, L). Far from abandoning the *Leviathan*, Hobbes labored over a careful translation and extensive redrafting of the work and added an appendix that included responses to objections (particularly by theologians) against the English edition.

It is worth remarking that only a few full-scale attacks on *Leviathan* were published in the seventeen years between the English and Latin versions, and Lucy's work is likely to have been the last of these that Hobbes read before giving his Latin manuscript to the printers. In a later work, in which he considers differences between the English and Latin editions of *Leviathan*, Lucy writes as if Hobbes intended the alterations to address Lucy's 1663 criticisms; see *An Answer to Mr. Hobbs His Leviathan: With Observations, Censures, and Confutations of Divers Errours, Beginning at the Seventeenth Chapter of That Book* (London, 1673), especially page 15 of the postscript and "The Epistle to the Reader." If Hobbes revised his argument with the Foole with Bishop Lucy's objection in mind, it is revealing that he met the charge of equivocation and elucidated his purpose not by providing a reply that is more relevant to the challenge of a Silent Foole but by underscoring that he is replying to the Explicit Foole.

33. Gauthier, for example, says that Hobbes's response to the Foole is "rather lame" (p. 12) and "tends to miss the point of the objection" (p. 136); see David Gauthier, *Moral Dealing: Contract, Ethics, and Reason* (Ithaca, NY: Cornell University Press, 1990). "Hobbes's reply to 'the fool' is not very convincing. It seems simply false to maintain that a man can never expect breach of covenant to be conducive to his preservation": the Foole "is, after all, no fool" (*Logic*, pp. 87, 88). Cf. Gauthier, "Why Ought One Obey God? Reflections on Hobbes and Locke," *Canadian Journal of Philosophy* 7, no. 3 (1977): 437 and Gauthier, "Hobbes's Social Contract," *Perspectives on Thomas Hobbes*, ed. G.A.J. Rogers and Alan Ryan (Oxford, UK: Clarendon, 1988), 131. Indeed, Gauthier (*Logic*, pp. 62, 87, 94), maintaining that at this point Hobbes's moral theory collapses into inconsistency, felt compelled to modify and reformulate Hobbes's reply to try to save him from himself. Among others who endorse the Silent Foole interpretation and then conclude that Hobbes's answer to the Foole is a failure are the following: E. F. Carritt, *Morals and Politics: Theories of Their Relation from Hobbes and Spinoza to Marx and*

Bosanquet (Oxford, UK: Clarendon, 1935), 43; Minogue, "Hobbes and the Just Man," 169; Farrell, "Reason and Right in Hobbes's *Leviathan*"; Gregory Kavka, "The Reconciliation Project," *Morality, Reason and Truth,* ed. David Copp and David Zimmerman (Totowa, NJ: Rowman & Allanheld, 1985), 304-5; Andrzej Rapaczynski, *Nature and Politics: Liberalism in the Philosophies of Hobbes, Locke, and Rousseau* (Ithaca, NY: Cornell University Press, 1987), 93-94; Johann P. Sommerville, *Thomas Hobbes: Political Ideas in Historical Context* (London: Macmillan, 1992), 183 n. 76; and Tito Magri, *Contratto e convenzione: Razionalità, obbligo e imparzialità in Hobbes e Hume* (Contract and Convention: Rationality, Obligation, and Impartiality in Hobbes and Hume) (Milan, Italy: Feltrinelli, 1994), 140-49.

34. "Hobbes's Reply to the Fool: The Problem of Consent and Obligation," *Political Theory* 10, no. 2 (1982): 246-47.

35. As mentioned below at the end of section IV, such interpreters may have to attribute an even more extreme thesis to Hobbes: that one can never reasonably expect contract breaking to be advantageous. Incidentally, note that even according to the Silent Foole interpretation, Hobbes does allow for the reasonableness of not keeping mutual agreements in the state of nature.

36. DC v.1. Cf. HS 507-8, EL xii.6, DM xxxiii.3 (fol. 372r), EW 5 (p. 272), and L xlii.67: "For it is evident to the meanest capacity, that mens actions are derived from the opinions they have of the Good, or Evill, which from those actions redound unto themselves; and consequently, men that are once possessed of an opinion, that their obedience to the Soveraign Power, will bee more hurtfull to them, than their disobedience, will disobey the Laws, and thereby overthrow the Common-wealth, and introduce confusion, and Civill war; for the avoiding whereof, all Civill Government was ordained." Note that this is given as a reason why the sovereign must judge which doctrines are sufficiently irenic to be allowed to be taught publicly.

37. Note, too, that Hobbes recognizes that fear can *cause* crime (L xxvii.19). Thus, the sovereign may be culpable not only for there being not enough fear in a given situation but also for there being too much.

38. L xxvii.8. Cf. L xxviii.9: "If the harm inflicted be lesse than the benefit, or contentment that naturally followeth the crime committed, that harm is not within the definition [of punishment]; and is rather the Price, or Redemption, than the Punishment of a Crime: Because it is of the nature of Punishment, to have for end, the disposing of men to obey the Law; which end (if it be lesse than the benefit of the transgression) it attaineth not, but worketh a contrary effect." Cf. also L xxi.5, xxvii.32 and 35, and xiv.7: "the Bonds, by which men are bound, and obliged . . . have their strength, not from their own Nature, . . . but from Feare of some evill consequence upon the rupture." In the paragraph that sets the stage for the Foole's entrance, Hobbes insists that people must be compelled to act justly "by the terrour of some punishment, greater than the benefit they expect by the breach of their Covenant" (L xv.3).

39. Compare the observation in B 9^r = 16 that "a few such orators would be able to make a great sedition." In *The Serpent Salve, or, A Remedie For the Biting of an Aspe* . . . (n.p., 1643), a contemporary (John Bramhall) observes that though treason had hitherto been cloaked, to be judged only by the rebels' deeds, recent times have seen "seditious Oratours" and "seditious Authors" whose "tongues are . . . Trumpets," who defy rule "nakedly and professedly . . . without any Mask" (sig. D3 and pp. 1-2, 40, 55, 86).

40. For illuminating interpretations of this project, see David Johnston, *The Rhetoric of Leviathan: Thomas Hobbes and the Politics of Cultural Transformation* (Princeton, NJ: Princeton University Press, 1986); Prokhovnik, *Rhetoric and Philosophy*; Lloyd, *Ideals as Interests*; and Skinner, *Reason and Rhetoric*.

41. An example of the former—"And that such as have a great, and false opinion of their own Wisedome, take upon them to reprehend the actions, and call in question the Authority of them that govern, and so to unsettle the Lawes with their publique discourse" (xxvii.16)—and

of the latter—"Also in a man that hath such reputation for wisedome, as that his counsells are followed, or his actions imitated by many, his fact against the Law, is a greater Crime. . . : For such men not onely commit Crime, but teach it for Law to all other men" (xxvii.36). An example of their collocation: "But for those that by Writing, or Publique Discourse, or by their eminent actions, have already engaged themselves to the maintaining of contrary opinions [i.e., contrary to 'the whole Doctrine' of *Leviathan*], they will not bee so easily satisfied" (R&C.13).

42. Curley, "Reflections on Hobbes," 217 n. 37. Cf. Gauthier, *Logic*, 83: "And in *Leviathan*, though not in Hobbes's earlier political writings, he proceeds to deny that men judge correctly in supposing that they will benefit from breach of covenant."

43. DC vi.11. Note that in the 1647 annotation of this section, Hobbes explains that dissension arises not because the principle is false but because it is publicized: "*There is scarce any Principle . . . from whence there may not spring dissentions, discords, reproaches, and by degrees war it selfe; neither doth this happen by reason of the falshood of the Principle, but of the disposition* [ingenium] *of men, who seeming wise to themselves, will needs appear such to all others: . . . yet they may be restrained by the exercise of the supreme power, that they prove no hinderance to the publique peace. Of these kind of opinions therefore I have not spoken of in this place.*" In the preface, Hobbes justifies his publication of this work as being "*for your sakes Readers, who I perswaded my selfe, when you should rightly apprehend and throughly understand this Doctrine I here present you with, would rather chuse to brooke with patience some inconveniences under government . . . then selfe opiniatedly disturb the quiet of the publique.*"

44. EL xxvii.14; cf. 12-15, xxviii.7; DC xii.12-13; and L R&C.13. Skinner has argued, "We find no reference in *Leviathan* to Sallust's portrait of Catiline . . . and above all no suggestion that eloquence may be a treasonous art"; see Quentin Skinner, " 'Scientia civilis' in Classical Rhetoric and in the Early Hobbes," *Political Discourse in Early Modern Britain*, ed. Nicholas Phillipson and Quentin Skinner (Cambridge, UK: Cambridge University Press, 1993), 93. In the argument with the Foole, however, we can hear a loud echo of Hobbes's reading of Sallust on Catiline. Hobbes insists in his argument against the Foole that treason is always likely to depend on or constitute proclamation; also, the Foole's declaration would constitute treason according to Hobbes's conception (cf. DC xiv.20, L xxvii.37, L xxviii.13).

45. Cf. DC xii.12-13 and xiii.9. Although, as specified below in note 79, Hobbes in DC xii.11 lists several factors necessary for sedition, he immediately thereafter (in the marginal note to xii.12) indicates that a persuasive fool would suffice: "*Eloquence alone without wisdom is the onely faculty needfull to raise seditions*" ("*Virtus qua opus est ad seditiones excitandas, sola eloquentia est sine sapientia*").

46. In his useful introduction to *Behemoth*, Stephen Holmes characterizes a primary theme as follows: "The rebellion was driven by ideas that vexed the mind and distorted people's perception of their own advantage. . . . Seditious opinions . . . crept into English heads by way of books and public speech. . . . England's problems were wrought by a joint looseness of pen and tongue" (pp. xxv-xxvi). Consider, for instance, the "ambitious ignorant orators," with whose help "Parliament destroyed the peace of the kingdom; and . . . reduced this government into anarchy" (p. 109).

47. Cf. Lucy, *Observations, Censures and Confutations*, 221-22.

48. See, for example, L xxx.8: "by the flattery of Popular men," the people have often been seduced from their loyalty, "not onely secretly, but openly." In the first dialogue of *Behemoth* ($18^r = 36$, amplified in the second dialogue [31^v-$32^r = 64$]; cf. also $34^r = 69$ and $24^v = 50$), Hobbes describes how "certain persons, having endeavoured by books and sermons to raise sedition, and committed other crimes of high nature," upon their release from prison were met "with great applause of the people, that flocked about them in London, in manner of a triumph."

49. Certainly, such lack of knowledge is not generally attributable to "defect in Reasoning," which Hobbes equates with error at L xxvii.10 (compare with *De Corpore* I.v.1). It would conceivably be attributable to error as he describes it in L v.5 but would amount to what he usually distinguishes from error as ignorance (as in L xxvii.4-12; cf. L iv.13, v.19, xi.18, xliv.3; compare also Hobbes's twelfth objection to Descartes's *Meditations* in *The Philosophical Writings of Descartes*, vol. 2, trans. John Cottingham, Robert Stoothoff, and Dugald Murdoch (Cambridge, UK: Cambridge University Press, 1984), 133; EL v.13; DM xxxvii.2 (fol. 409r); *Six Lessons to the Professors of the Mathematiques* . . . (London, 1656), 30 = EW 7, 268; and *The Questions Concerning Liberty, Necessity, and Chance*, EW 5, 186.

50. And therefore a Silent Foole would reasonably expect to be allowed into a confederation, other things being equal. M. M. Goldsmith, *Hobbes's Science of Politics* (New York: Columbia University Press, 1966), 114, glossing the reply to the Foole according to the Silent Foole interpretation, says: "No one who thinks that he is right in breaking his contractual obligations to others can expect anyone to treat him (except by accident, mistake, stupidity, or ignorance) as anything but an enemy." This would be true of someone who declares that violating contracts is justifiable, but not of someone who thinks it but does not declare it, for the "ignorance" of the others in such a case is predictable, being only the lack of omniscience. (In Hobbes's words, cited above, it is "he which declares he thinks it reason to deceive those that help him, [who] can in reason expect no other means of safety, than . . . his own single Power.") A calculating Silent Foole can expect others *not* to treat him as an enemy, except in case of *his* accident, mistake, stupidity, or ignorance.

51. L xv.5. The Latin version, as translated by Curley in his edition of the *Leviathan*, runs: "anyone who does what, as far as can be foreseen and understood by reason, tends to his own destruction, even though something unforeseen happens which makes the outcome fortunate, has nevertheless acted imprudently, because what happens is unforeseen." Curley believes that "in calling the fortunate outcome 'unforeseen' Hobbes does not mean that it is (necessarily) improbable, but merely that it is not predictable with (tolerable) certainty" (p. 91 n.6). Hobbes, however, suggests more than that the fortunate outcome is not predictable with tolerable certainty. He specifies that as far as the actor can reasonably predict, the action will promote his ruin: thus, the actor can reasonably predict that the fortunate outcome will *not* occur ("*si quis id faciat, quod, quantum prospici et ratione intelligi potest, ad suam ipsius tendit destructionem, quanquam improvisum aliquod accidat quod eventum felicem efficiat, factum nihilominus fuisse imprudenter, quia improvisum*").

52. "*. . . quod ad damnum suum sibi tendere videbitur.*" I think a similar shift or explanation may take place in the concluding sentence of the reply to the Foole. "Justice, therefore, that is to say, Keeping of Covenant, is a Rule of Reason, by which we are forbidden to do any thing destructive to our life; and consequently a Law of Nature" (L xv.7) becomes: "*Pactorum ergo observatio rationis praeceptum est, id est, lex naturalis*" (LL xv.6: "Therefore keeping of covenant is a precept of reason, that is, a natural law"). Note that even in the English version of L xv.5, Hobbes contrasts destruction with benefit.

53. Hypothetical scenarios where this would not hold could be concocted, but Hobbes is concerned here with politically relevant situations.

54. See also pp. 636-37, below.

55. Hobbes could have drawn on any of a number of sources for this tale, but the most likely is probably Hesiod or Ovid, perhaps in conjunction with Bacon. There is evidence that Hobbes may have made a close study of Hesiod, as du Verdus reports in his letter to Hobbes of July 24/August 3, 1664, Letter 168 of *The Correspondence*, ed. Noel Malcolm, vol. 2 (Oxford, UK: Clarendon Press, 1994), 622. Hesiod says that the time of Kronos was a golden age (*Works and Days*, lines 109-26) and that Justice is the daughter of Zeus, siding with him against wrongdoers

(*Works and Days*, lines 256-60). Like Hesiod, Plato characterizes life under the rule of Kronos as "happy, without civil war" (*Laws*, 713e; cf. *Statesman*, 269a-274c) and links the absoluteness of the rule to its peace and prosperity. In the Platonic *Hipparchus*, that notorious Athenian symbol of the enemy of democracy enjoys a rehabilitative comparison to Kronos; the supposed tyrannicides and democratic heroes Harmodius and Aristogeiton thus brought Athens only misery (229b-d; cf. the Aristotelian *Constitution of Athens* xvi.7, and Thucydides vi.53-9). In the *Metamorphoses*, Ovid marks the end of the Golden Age with the expulsion of Saturn and Jupiter's subsequent unjust reign. "But when that into Lymbo once Saturnus being thrust,/The rule and charge of all the worlde was under Jove unjust" (Book I, lines 129-30 of Arthur Golding's 1567 translation).

Hobbes was thoroughly familiar with Bacon's *De Sapientia Veterum*; see the letters to Hobbes from du Verdus of August 20, 1654, September 23, 1654, October 5, 1665 (encl.), and the letters from Fulgenzio Micanzio to Cavendish, translated by Hobbes (e.g., of June 17, 1616, February 24, 1617, and January 12, 1618); a copy of the work was in the Hardwick library, according to the catalogue from the late 1620s. Bacon recounts and interprets Typhon's rebellion against Jupiter in the second tale, "Typhon, or a Rebel," and traces Jupiter's own patrimony of rebellion in the twelfth tale, "Coelum, or Beginnings." In the latter, we are told that Coelum, the most ancient of the gods, had his generative parts severed by his son Saturn, who in turn had his genitals cut off—with the same knife he had used to dismember his father—by his son Jupiter, who drove Saturn into Tartarus and usurped the kingdom (cf., e.g., Hesiod, *Theogony*; Plato, *Euthyphro*, 5e-6a). See also Pierre Bayle, *Dictionaire Historique et Critique* (Rotterdam, 1697) *sub* "Jupiter," especially note A on pp. 226-27 of volume 2, part 1.

56. *Attainder* is roughly equivalent to a conviction of felony or treason. For some seventeenth-century distinctions, see John Cowell, *The Interpreter: or Booke, Containing the Signification of Words . . .* (London, 1637; first printed in 1607), *sub* "Attaine," "Attainted," and "Attainder."

Tricaud notes (*Léviathan*, p. 145 n. 26) that this is a quotation from *The First Part of the Institvtes of England or, A Commentarie vpon Littleton, not the name of a Lawyer onely, but of the Law it selfe*; he further notes that Coke concludes the phrase by citing a precedent ("as it fell out in the case of *Henrie* the seuenth"), which Hobbes silently drops. I quote from I.i.8 (folio 16r) of the first edition of the *Institutes* (London, 1628), but—despite the claim made by Tricaud, Tuck, and Curley in their respective editions of *Leviathan* that Hobbes follows the second edition—it cannot be reliably determined from the minor differences at the points where Hobbes quotes Coke in *Leviathan* whether he relied on the edition of 1628, 1629, 1633, or 1639.

Coke interprets the settlement as determining both that attainder of treason does not preclude coronation and that coronation cancels attaint. In the Latin *Leviathan*, Hobbes elides the latter aspect, which is the one that Coke's great rival Francis Bacon underscored in *The Historie of the Raigne of King Henry The Seuenth* (published in London in 1622, around the time when Hobbes was in his occasional employ): "It was at that time incidently moued amongst the *Iudges* in their Consultation, what should be done for the King himselfe, who likewise was attainted? But it was with vnanimous consent resolued, *That the Crowne takes away all defects and stops in bloud: and that from the time the King did assume the Crowne, the fountaine was cleared, and all Attaindors and Corruption of bloud discharged*. But neuerthelesse for *Honours* sake it was ordained by *Parliament*, that all *Records* wherein there was any memorie, or mention of the Kings *Attaindor*, should be defaced, cancelled, and taken of[f] the *File*" (p. 13).

In harmony with what is reported in these passages (though arguably not with its being reported), Hobbes may have good reason to remain silent about the case of Henry VII (cf. Thomas Tenison, *The Creed of Mr Hobbes Examined* [London, 1670], 148)—especially given the prevailing interpretation that Henry's usurpation was justified by Richard III's tyranny. Bacon's history opens: "After that Richard the third of that name, King in fact only, but Tyrant both in

Title and Regiment, and so commonly termed and reputed in all times since, was by the *Diuine Reuenge*, . . . ouerthrone and slaine at *Bosworth*-field: There succeeded in the Kingdome the Earle of *Richmond*, thence-forth stiled Henry the Seuenth" (p. 1). This work was pointedly republished after the surrender and imprisonment of Charles I, to whom (when Prince of Wales) it had been dedicated by Bacon as providing a model for kingship; *Historia Regni Henrici septimi Angliae Regis, Opus vere politicum* (Leiden, 1647).

57. Sommerville, *Thomas Hobbes*, 183 n. 76.

58. It might be objected that when the payoff is sufficiently high, as in the case of a kingdom, it might be reasonable to pursue something that it is not reasonable to expect. For example, it is not reasonable to expect that my ticket will be the one randomly drawn out of the pile of one hundred tickets, but if given the chance to pay one dollar for one of one hundred tickets for a prize of one million dollars, it is reasonable to proceed. In answering, Hobbes can introduce the counter to that payoff (e.g., by pointing out that the situation needs to be modified such that most ticket buyers are likely to be executed). Further, in the case of sovereignty, it is important to clarify what is expected: a rebel will have a better chance of overthrowing the sovereign, say, than of doing so and ruling peacefully thereafter in his place.

59. We cannot understand specious as meaning false here, for Hobbes is saying, however specious this is, it is *nonetheless* false. Cf. the Latin version: "*Verumtamen ratiocinatio haec, utcunque speciosa, falsa est.*" Note, for example, that Hobbes, in the preface to DC, says that the opinions of the moral philosophers are "*partim recta & speciosa, partim bruta & ferina*" (which the translator makes "*partly right and comely, partly brutall and wilde*"). And where Hobbes has *specious* in L xxi.9, he renders it *dulci* in the Latin translation.

60. DCL 97. Hobbes goes on to argue that "If a Man should Publickly Preach, that the King were an Usurper . . . there is no doubt but it were Treason" (DCL 98), and it should be mentioned that Coke may have agreed with this view. A search of the house of Edmond Peacham turned up papers inveighing against the King and warning of an uprising of the people, the King's sudden death, and the murder of his officers. A central question in the infamous trial that followed was whether there was an intent to preach from these documents or have them printed. In Francis Bacon's letter to the king of January 31, 1614, he sets forth the issue as follows:

That there be four means or manners, whereby the death of the king is compassed and imagined.

The first by some particular fact or plot.

The second by disabling his title; as by affirming that he is not lawful king, or that another ought to be king, or that he is an usurper, or a bastard, or the like.

The third by subjecting his title; as either to pope or people; and thereby making him of an absolute king a conditional king.

The fourth, by disabling his regiment, and making him appear to be incapable or indign to reign.

See James Spedding, ed., *The Letters and the Life of Francis Bacon* . . ., vol. 5 (London: Longmans, Green, Reader, and Dyer, 1869), 109. Bacon argued that Peacham's case was of the last type. Against the prosecution, Coke argued that no words of scandal or defamation—even to the effect that the King was utterly unworthy to govern—count as treasonous unless they disable his title. In the end, Peacham admitted authorship of the writings and denied any intention to publish or preach them (p. 128), but this did not save him from torture and death in prison.

61. DCL 97. The Philosopher, the more Hobbesian interlocutor in this dialogue, takes a harsher view of any utterances that might tend toward popular disobedience. His position seems more consonant than the Lawyer's with the judgment during the time of Henry the Sixth that

condemned a man for treason for saying that "the King was a Natural Fool, and unfit to Govern" (DCL 98). Note the broad definition of treason in *De Cive*: "it is a *word* or *deed* whereby the Citizen, or Subject, *declares* [*est factum vel dictum quo ciuis, seu subditus, declarat*] that he will no longer obey that man or Court to whom the supreme power of the City is entrusted" (xiv.20, emphases added; cf. L xxvii.37, xxviii.13; App. ii.32). Hobbes's view of treason stands out, on one hand, for its focus on a very broad range of verbal declaration and, on the other hand, for its dismissal of the pertinence of silent intention or doctrine. He thereby repudiates, among others, Jean Bodin, who had written that "the subiect is not only guiltie of treason in the highest degree, who hath slaine his soueraigne prince, but even he also which hath attempted the same; who hath giuen councell or consent thereunto; yea if he haue concealed the same, or but so much as thought it." *The Six Bookes of a Commonweale*, trans. Richard Knolles (London: G. Bishop, 1606), II.v, 222. Cf. John Cowell, *The Interpreter*, *sub* "Treason," still followed in Thomas Blount's *Nomo-Lexikon: A Law-Dictionary* . . . (London, 1670): "High treason . . . [is] an offence done against the securitie of the Commonwealth, or of the Kings most excellent Majestie: whether it be by imagination, word, or deed."

Don Herzog, *Happy Slaves: A Critique of Consent Theory* (Chicago: University of Chicago Press, 1989), 107-8, attributes to Hobbes the view that thought is public, as well as the view that thought is private. He thereupon announces, "The contradiction is blatant," and accuses Hobbes of flat negation of his own key positions, inconsistency, "self-contradiction," and "absurd speech." But Hobbes simply regarded thought as private. Its manifestations are for Hobbes public, and the attempt to influence thought is a public activity, but thought itself is unequivocally private. There is a political dimension to persuasion (the project of external influence of the internal) and a political dimension to expression (the project of making the internal external), but Hobbes regarded thought itself as conceptually independent of these projects.

Incidentally, Hobbes does not think that the Foole is a "natural fool," for natural fools are incapable of justice and injustice, there is no law over them, and they are unable to make contracts (L xxvi.12; cf. DCL 34). Like the "excellently foolish" lettered men of L iv.13, who "abound in copiousnesse of language," the Foole's folly is more learned and more dangerous. Cyril Tourneur, in *The Atheist's Tragedie* (London, 1611) provides a fit portrait (Act V, scene i):

With all thy wisedome th'art a foole.
Not like those fooles that we term innocents,
But a most wretched miserable foole,
Which instantly, to the confusion of
Thy proiects with despaire thou shalt behold.

62. Hobbes holds it to be a rule that "amongst Praesumptions, there is none that so evidently declareth the Author, as doth the Benefit of the Action" (L xlvii.1, stated more forcefully in the Latin: "*Nam inter praesumpta nullum majus est, neque quod authorem criminis ita manifeste arguit, ut a crimine utilitas*"). See the explanation in HS 288-89 that Livia was suspected of the murder of heirs of Augustus, especially because of "the benefit which thereby accrewed vnto her owne sonnes. This last is of much importance in the iudgement of men: for to whomsoeuer comes the profit of strange and vnexpected accidents, to him also, for the most part, is imputed the contriuing, and effecting of them, if they be thought able. To *Liuia* appertaineth the suspicion of their death, because it was good for her that they should dye when they did."

63. For present purposes, I follow the somewhat simplified view that reason is the reckoning of consequences of names, acquired by industry and method, and that it is distinguished from prudence, which is had by experience (EL iv.10, DM xxxviii.9 [fol. 432^{r-v}], L v.17 and ix.1), which history collects (cf. T 6). (Note, however, that in EL vi.1, experience is also claimed to

underpin science; in DH xi.10, history is said to provide the evidence on which science rests; and in EL v.12, EL ix.18, and EW 5, p. 398, Hobbes indicates that reason depends on experience.) Considerations of prudence could be relevant in replying to the Foole, especially given that government involves prudence (L viii.11), and the Foole would do well to reason with the prudent man of L iii.7 (cf. EL iv.7): "he that foresees what wil become of a Criminal, re-cons what he has seen follow on the like Crime before; having this order of thoughts, The Crime, the Officer, the Prison, the Judge, and the Gallowes." Insofar as Hobbes bases his answer on reason rather than prudence, he may aspire to provide a more reliable answer that is less susceptible to altering with circumstances. (Note, however, that Hobbes adds an appeal to prudence in the Latin edition). For an analysis of reason versus prudence in the thought of Hobbes and some of his predecessors, see Gianfranco Borrelli, *Ragion di stato e Leviatano: Conservazione e scambio alle origini della modernità politica* (Reason of State and Leviathan: Continuity and Change at the Roots of Political Modernity) (Bologna, Italy: Il Mulino, 1993).

A. P. Martinich and Rosamond Rhodes have suggested to me that the distinction between reason and prudence is at the core of the reply to the Foole: the Foole proceeds according to prudence, which relies on particular experience and is thus fallible, whereas Hobbes responds in terms of reason, which depends only on general truths and is thus not susceptible to error—cf. Rosamond Rhodes, "Hobbes's unReasonable Fool," *The Southern Journal of Philosophy* 30, no. 2 (1992) and Richard Tuck, "Hobbes's Moral Philosophy," *The Cambridge Companion to Hobbes*, ed. Tom Sorell (Cambridge, UK: Cambridge University Press, 1996), 193-95. Were this the case, however, we would expect Hobbes to make much of the distinction here, but he does not even mention it. If Hobbes's target were prudence, he would have made his point more forcefully had he said as much, pointing out that the prudent person can still make important errors. But his target is folly rather than prudence, and when Hobbes distinguishes reason or wisdom from prudence, he also distinguishes prudence from folly—which he equates with forsaking one's natural judgment to follow the "generall sentences" of others that are "subject to many exceptions" (L v.21-2). And Hobbes understands the folly of the fool who hath said in his heart that there is no God as *imprudence* (annotation to DC xiv.19).

Further, Hobbes's use of "reason" in the reply to the Foole (as elsewhere) is not clearly distinguishable from prudence. Hobbes states in xv.5 that an outcome that turns out to be beneficial contrary to reasonable expectation does not render the action leading to that outcome reasonable. If the "reason" in question were tantamount to the infallible method of science, then there could be no possibility of actual result diverging from predicted result.

64. LL xlvii.29 (Curley's translation from his ed., p. 488). In the *Dialogue* (DCL 196), the Philosopher maintains that rebellion brings about a perpetual chain of usurpations. A refrain of *Behemoth* is that rebels are adept at pulling down government and inept at setting up a stable substitute. Disobedience and rebellion lead to competing factions, struggles for sovereignty, and a succession of overthrows. Hobbes's narrative of the events in England from 1640 to 1660 is not a portrait of pure Brownian anarchy but a history of the "revolution," the cycle of usurpations. A précis of the dozen shifts of sovereignty during the war is given at B 93^r = 195-96.

65. Although commentators have seized on Hobbes's reply to the Foole as the exclusive evidence that Hobbes held that any act of injustice is bound to be unreasonable, another central objection (which I do not here have space to develop) would build on other places where Hobbes seems to endorse that position. I have found no passages that seriously undermine the Explicit Foole interpretation, but some of the more challenging are EL xxvii.13; L xxvii.10, xxvii.16, and xxx.5; LL xlvii.28; and B 22^r = 44.

66. Kavka, *Hobbesian Moral and Political Theory*, 378; see Richard E. Flathman's similar argument in *Political Obligation* (New York: Atheneum, 1972), 303-5. In a recent article, "The Rationality of Rule-Following: Hobbes's Dispute with the Foole," *Law and Philosophy* 14

(1995), Kavka argues that Hobbes successfully answers the Foole, but his concluding question—"is uncertainty really so widespread, and error so likely, that we cannot reliably determine potential rule violations ahead of time 'when ... [they] conduced to ones benefit'?"—undermines the crux of his argument (on pp. 26-28).

67. See Nunan, "Hobbes on Morality, Rationality, and Foolishness," 59; cf. Edna Ullmann-Margalit, *The Emergence of Norms* (Oxford, UK: Clarendon, 1977), 71-72.

68. "To insist that the Foole keep his covenants, even when reneging is in his long-term interest, because doing so is generally in his interest does seem to constitute an irrational form of rule worship. . . . If the Foole's choice is between framing his will by justice and framing it by the apparent benefits of his actions, the defense of justice may proceed without succumbing to the folly of rule worship. The Foole's disposition must be rejected because even though it may allow him to exploit a few opportunities for gain that the just person cannot exploit, it exposes him to the unacceptable risk of being found out. . . . When we ask why the just person is not practicing an irrational form of rule worship when she refuses to exploit a clear opportunity to renege with impunity, we have a satisfactory answer: She is acting from a disposition justified in terms of its ability to maximize her prospects for security. Were she to alter her disposition to take advantage of short-term benefits, she would render herself the sort of person who would in the long run be exposed and killed" (Boonin-Vail, *Thomas Hobbes and the Science of Moral Virtue*, 150). Boonin-Vail's argument here seems to depend first on taking the Foole as one who will follow his long-term interest and then on considering him to be someone who pursues his short-term interest even when that frustrates his long-term interest. More important, although the hub of the Foole's problem is his failure properly to identify his interest, Hobbes does not propose—*pace* Minogue, Raphael, et al. (cf. n.4, above)—that this consists in an inability to distinguish short-term from long-term interest.

69. What Martinich actually says is that these are the three reasons Hobbes gives for why one should observe the laws of nature, even when it is not seemingly in one's self-interest (*The Two Gods of Leviathan*, 118). These are not generally applicable reasons for why one should follow all the laws of nature, however (they do not apply, for example, to the law of nature stipulating primogeniture or to that mandating that a judge should depend on witnesses in controversies of fact): they are specifically related to the third law of nature, that covenants be kept. This point affects Martinich's way of reconciling self-interest and the laws of nature, but I am here interested in his argument only as it applies to the third law of nature.

70. Martinich, *The Two Gods of Leviathan*, 118.

71. These considerations also weigh against the exposition of the reply to the Foole given by Howard Warrender. "It is evident," believes Warrender (*The Political Philosophy of Hobbes*, 276), "that only the last of these reasons [viz., that the subject risks his or her eternal salvation] is conclusive; the rest is merely cautionary advice." Opposed to this sort of exegesis is Bishop Bramhall's reading of the reply. Bramhall insists that Hobbes does *not* adduce forfeiture of the kingdom of heaven as reason not to rebel; see *The Catching of Leviathan, or the Great Whale* (London, 1658), 515-16; cf. Seth Ward, *Against Resistance of Lawful Powers: A Sermon Preached at White-Hall, Novemb. Vth 1661* (London, 1661), 35 and Lucy, *Observations, Censures and Confutations*, chap. 28.

72. Curley's translation of the Latin, 92 n.8, of his edition of *Leviathan*.

73. The extent of similarity between what Hobbes holds and the Foole announces may nonetheless explain why Hobbes lapses into unwonted opacity when the matter is explicitly raised. In introducing the distinction of thoughts hidden in our hearts and external words and actions, Hobbes indicates in a private tract (which was later published, contrary to Hobbes's wishes, as *Of Liberty and Necessity*) that certain truths, such as that of the necessity of all events, are likely to have a bad effect on most people and should thus be kept private (EW 4, 256-57;

cf. EW 5, 2, 23-26, 151, 198-99, 433-35). He also observes that "uncivill words" can be "hainous, and hazardous. . . , whether that which is said in disgrace be true or false" (*Six Lessons to the Professors*, 55 = EW 7, 332).

74. L xlvi.42; cf. *An Answer to Bishop Bramhall*, EW 4, 329. Hobbes is sometimes tempted to deny that the requirements for peace may lead to suppressing or inhibiting the truth, but, as here, he admits it on consideration. Hobbes thinks that the sovereign should become involved in doctrinal questions primarily with a view to doctrinal uniformity and peace rather than truth (cf. *An Historical Narration Concerning Heresy, and the Punishment Thereof*, EW 4, 391-93).

75. Recall that for Hobbes, a law of nature is a precept of reason that forbids one to do that which is destructive of one's life and requires that which will best preserve it (L xiv.3).

76. Milton's note in the margin of Sir Richard Baker's translation of Virgilio Malvezzi, *Discovrses upon Cornelius Tacitus* (London, 1642), 218, as given in Thomas Ollive Mabbott and J. Milton French, eds., *The Uncollected Writings of John Milton*, vol. 18 of *The Works of John Milton* (New York: Columbia University Press, 1938), 495. Compare John Donne's "The triple Foole," which opens: "I am two fooles, I know,/For loving, and for saying so"; when this is published in verse, then "I, which was two fooles, do so grow three;/ Who are a little wise, the best fooles bee"; see Herbert J. C. Grierson, ed., *The Poems of John Donne*, vol. 1 (London: Oxford University Press, 1912), 16.

77. See the conclusion of the Latin *Leviathan*: "Who will believe that those seditious principles are not now completely destroyed, or that there is anyone (except the democrats) who wishes the suppression of a doctrine whose tendency toward peace is as great as that of my teaching? So that this would not happen, I wanted it to be available in Latin. For I see that men's disagreements about opinions . . . cannot be eliminated by arms. In whatever way evils of this kind arise, they must be destroyed in the same way. . . . So that democratic ink is to be washed away by preaching, writing, and disputing" (xlvii.29: Curley's translation, p. 488).

78. Deborah Baumgold, *Hobbes's Political Theory* (Cambridge, UK: Cambridge University Press, 1988), usefully emphasizes Hobbes's concern with ambitious elites but constructs a false dichotomy by claiming that this concern eclipses any anxiety about uncivil ordinary subjects. For Hobbes, ambitious leaders are particularly dangerous insofar as they make ordinary subjects uncivil. "Political ambition," maintains Baumgold (p. 122), "as opposed to political obligation, is the central problem of the political theory." Although Hobbes usually condemns ambition, he sometimes suggests that it is not necessarily deleterious to the commonwealth (cf. DC xiii.12, L x.47, L xxix.20, and the epistle dedicatory of EL). His condemnation is unambiguous *insofar as* ambition threatens peace. The prevalent way that happens is via the erosion of political obligation. The vexed question of obligation cannot therefore be bypassed, but it must be coupled with the challenge of the ambitious who lead the people to disobey.

79. DC xii.11. For sedition to follow, the discontented need not only leaders (i.e., commanders and someone to "*stirre up* and *quicken them*") but also arms, numbers, and mutual trust. Hobbes cannot do much to withhold arms, but without the other factors, these are no threat. The argument with the Foole can be seen as aspiring to dissuade or discredit the leaders, minimize the discontent, and decrease the number and the mutual trust of the seditious. (Compare this enumeration to that of EL xxvii.1: "Without these three: discontent, pretence, and hope, there can be no rebellion; and when the same are all together, there wanteth nothing thereto, but a man of credit to set up the standard, and to blow the trumpet.")

Kinch Hoekstra is a Fellow in Philosophy at Balliol College, Oxford. His current research interests are in ancient and early modern political philosophy.

[14]

Time, History and Eschatology

in the Thought of

Thomas Hobbes

J.G.A. Pocock

The change from the medieval interpreta-
tive gloss on a passage of Scripture to the
new grammatical analysis of the passage
brought forth an entirely new question in
theology. The rhetorical commentaries of
the earlier period, generally concerned with
delineating the intention of a phrase and
never questioning any matter of textual
integrity, gave way to the disquisitiones
philologicae *in which all instances of textual*
corruption were investigated, and the whole
emphasis placed upon exact rendition. The
older query, so to speak, of "What does
God mean here?" became the far more ar-
resting question, "What has God said
here?" Allegory, mystic paraphrase, trop-
ology and the whole formal literature of
interpretation were uncompromisingly at-
tacked as doctrinal irrelevancies by syntax
and lexicography. Grammar, not specula-
tion, became the greatest heresy of the

> *Christian world, and unhappily no fires could be kindled to consume the* rudimenta linguae *of Hebrew and Greek.*
>
> George Newton Conklin, Biblical Criticism and Heresy in Milton (*New York: King's Crown Press, Columbia University, 1949*), *pp. 1–2*

THE ASSERTION that Hobbes's political philosophy is "unhistorical," though often made and in some senses correct, is neither economical nor elegant. There are simply too many ways in which a man's thought can be said to be "historical," and too many ways of negating each one of these statements, for the epithet alone to have any very obvious meaning. Hobbes, as is generally known, declared that you could not ground a philosophy of politics on the study of human experience as recorded in history because, as he put it, "experience concludeth nothing universally." [1] But this did not prevent his being interested in history; the thought even of his later years can be observed keeping pace with some of the sharpest and most advanced historical perception of his time.[2] On matters of English tenurial and Parliamentary history, he profited by his friendship with Selden [3] and went beyond that great but elusive scholar in some respects. Again, his famous characterization of the papacy as "the ghost of the deceased Roman Empire, sitting crowned upon the grave thereof," [4] like his interpretation of the Cluniac campaign for clerical celibacy,[5] could only have come from a

---

[1] Hobbes, *Elements of Law*, I, iv, 10 (ed. Tonnies, repr. ed. London, 1969, p. 16).

[2] Pocock, *The Ancient Constitution and the Feudal Law*, ch. vii.

[3] Selden's *Titles of Honour* (1614 and 1631) is almost the only contemporary work mentioned with respect in *Leviathan* (i, 10; Oakeshott edition, Oxford: Basil Blackwell, p. 62).

[4] *Leviathan*, iv, 47 (Oakeshott, p. 457).

[5] In *Behemoth*; Hobbes argues that this was designed to separate the kingly office from the priesthood (*English Works*, VI, 180–1). The interpretation may not be correct; what matters is the quality of the thought that produced it.

vivid and freely ranging historical imagination. The epithet "unhistorical," then, is not immediately justified and needs clarification; and this has been sensibly and acceptably provided by, for instance, M. M. Goldsmith.[6] But it should be observed that what has happened illustrates the lack of economy arising from historians' use of the rhetoric of common speech. An appropriate-seeming term occurs to someone and is used; it wins enough acceptance to become part of the conventional wisdom. But in conventional use it is discovered to bear too many possible meanings to be uniformly applicable to the evidence, and the community of historians is saddled with the necessity of discovering the sense or senses in which it can be used so as to mean something.[7] Professor Goldsmith has shown that there are indeed ways in which Hobbes's thinking may accurately be termed "unhistorical," but the very success with which he does so inevitably if unintentionally carries the implication that he has vindicated the original adoption of the term and its use by his predecessors; and the way in which it has come into use remains uneconomical and has involved an excessive deployment of what Hobbes himself memorably termed "insignificant speech." [8]

Historians are condemned to this sort of thing, and it is not intended to suggest that they have any alternative to using common speech first and refining it afterwards.[9] But specialized techniques may be developed as means of cutting corners in this process and rendering it more economical, and it is part of

---

[6] M. M. Goldsmith, *Hobbes's Science of Politics* (New York: Columbia University Press, 1966), pp. 232–42, 251–52.

[7] The language used here is intended to give some indication of my debt to Kuhn's *The Structure of Scientific Revolutions*.

[8] "I say not this as disproving the use of universities; but because I am to speak hereafter of their office in a commonwealth, I must let you see, on all occasions by the way, what things would be amended in them; amongst which the frequency of insignificant speech is one." *Leviathan*, i, 1 (Oakeshott, p. 8). See also i, 8 (Oakeshott, pp. 51–52).

[9] On this see J. H. Hexter, *Reappraisals in History* (London, 1961), and my review article in *History and Theory*, III, 1 (1963).

the intention of this essay [10] to assert that one technique exists
which may be applied to the question whether or not a man's
thought is "historical." Instead of applying an epithet and then
debating its use until some precise meaning for it is discovered,
it should be possible to institute a critical enquiry aimed at discovering what, if any, elements that may be termed "historical"
a man's thought contained. There is, of course, one obvious difficulty in the way of such a proceeding. It may seem necessary
to establish in advance canons of what constitutes "historical"
thinking, and this can all too easily lead to the sort of academic
high-jump contest beloved of Hegelian and Crocean scholars, in
which the bar of true historicity is raised again and again until
only the fortunate candidate succeeds in leaping it. But we are
not obliged to engage in such sterile olympiads. It can be shown
that the language even of pre-historicist social and political
thinkers carries a constant tissue of statements, explicit and implicit, about the time-structures in which society and the political order were thought of as existing, and that these consisted
mainly of statements about the occurrence, recurrence and continuity of the modes of human action and cognition held to
constitute social and political behaviour, as well as the divine
actions and utterances which in monotheist contexts were indispensable to its understanding. Time so conceived differed
from the time of the physicist or the metaphysician in being
filled with—indeed, composed of—a rich texture of the acts,
words and thoughts of personal and social beings; and in stating
the continuities, recurrences and occurrences of which it consisted theorists frequently encountered problems which com-

[10] An earlier version was read to the Midwest Conference on British
Studies, at the University of Kansas on 26 October 1968, and at a Uni-
versity of Wales colloquium at Gregynog Hall on 14 March 1969. M. M.
Goldsmith, Steven Schwarzschild, Quentin Skinner and William M. La-
mont have helped me by criticism at various stages in its preparation; and
I owe a special debt to discussion and correspondence with Patricia Spring-
borg during the preparation of her unpublished master's thesis (Patricia
M. McIntyre, "Authority, Ecclesiastical and Civil, in Hobbes's *Leviathan*,"
University of Canterbury Library).

pelled them to recast their thoughts in terms of process, change and discontinuity.[11]

At this stage in the analysis, it becomes in principle possible to show how specific thinkers and traditions of thought have encountered problems of this kind, how they have dealt with them and what further problems have arisen in consequence of their responses; and in doing so, modes of thought may be met with which approximate to what we mean when we use such terms as "historical." At the cost of some looseness, we may employ such terms in exploring these intellectual developments, and to do so has the great advantage of being positive instead of evaluatory. Instead of trying to determine whether a man's thought was or was not "historical" according to some preconceived criterion, we can trace the ways in which—rather than the extent to which—his thought had become involved in questions and answers of the kind to which such a term may possibly be illuminatingly applied; and we can concern ourselves with the substance rather than the epithet, with what his thought was rather than with what it may not have been.

The problem, then, becomes that of discerning the languages, explicit or implicit, concerning time of which Hobbes made use, what he did with them and in what ways he turned them to his characteristic purposes. There were a number of modes in which it was possible for men of his day to conceptualize society's existence in time and time itself as the dimension of social existence,[12] and of two of these at least Hobbes made significant use. It must be remembered, not only that these modes of conceptualization seem remote and primitive to minds of the twentieth century, but that they imposed cramping limi-

---

[11] For two attempts to state the theory of this kind of time-awareness, see "The Origins of Study of the Past: a Comparative Approach," *Comparative Studies in Society and History*, IV, 2 (1962), and essay 7 in this volume.

[12] I have tried to particularize them more fully in "The Onely Politician: Machiavelli, Harrington and Felix Raab," *Historical Studies: Australia and New Zealand*, XII (1966), 46. See also above, pp. 80–85.

tations against which minds of the seventeenth can be seen struggling, often in vain. It was, that is to say, difficult for the contemporary intellect to conceive of the sequence of events and problems in time except in terms which suggested that these were accidental and irrational, that few and limited means existed whereby the human mind could understand and control them and that the means of maintaining a political system as a structure of intelligent behaviour existing in time, foreseeing its emergencies and maintaining its own stability, were correspondingly limited and the prospects of success small. One entire rhetoric, of Greco-Roman and Florentine origin—that of fortune and innovation, cycle and equilibrium—was available for the dual purpose of stressing the instability of politics in time and suggesting means by which recurrent disorder might after all be controlled; but Hobbes made little or no use of it. Instead, his thought stresses in the first place—in order to reject or minimize later—that very ancient doctrine of man's ability to understand and control the accidents of time, which was based on the concept of experience. The human mind, it was held, dealt with secular happenings by recollecting one's previous encounters, and those of other men, with phenomena resembling them and by trading on the assumption that likes recurred in like circumstances, so that responses appropriate on former occasions would prove appropriate on what appeared to be occasions of recurrence. Only further experience could test this presumption, and of that experience, even if the test were passed, only the memory would remain, so that the whole procedure would have to be gone through again on the next encounter with a similar phenomenon; [13] but a sufficiently lengthy accumulation of similar experiences would equip us with a tradition of usage looking

---

[13] A classical statement of this position was coined in reply to Hobbes's *Dialogue of the Common Laws*, by Sir Matthew Hale. See Holdsworth, *History of English Law* (London and Boston, 1924), V, 499–513: and Pocock, *The Ancient Constitution and the Feudal Law*, pp. 170–81, and the next essay in this book.

back to its own antiquity—the doctrine of custom evolved by English common lawyers is the classic instance of this—while the individual, operating on his own experience and that which he shared with other men, might at least develop in the present the quality called "prudence," which was in the individual and his moment what custom was in institutionalized antiquity.

It was of this Hobbes declared "experience concludeth nothing universally." He was not being particularly striking or original when he used those words; his philosophical radicalism lay in his ideas about how memory did operate to point to universal conclusions. It was a commonplace that since experience and use were based on nothing but presumption, they could never provide rational demonstration that the consequences they predicted would follow, or explanation of why they did so; and to all but the most drastic innovators, the demonstrable and the universal were interchangeable terms. But it is worth studying attentively the language in which Hobbes points out the limitations of experience and prudence, both because it indicates clearly how far secular political understanding was seen as the understanding of events in time and because it demonstrates how closely Hobbes's own views on this matter were still tied to the medieval trinity of reason, experience and faith:

But this is certain: by how much one man has more experience of things past than another, by so much also he is more prudent and his expectations the seldomer fail him. The present only has a being in nature; things past have a being in the memory only; but things to come have no being at all, the future being but a fiction of the mind, applying the sequels of actions past to the actions that are present, which with most certainty is done by him that has most experience, but not with certainty enough. And though it be called prudence when the event answereth our expectation, yet in its own nature it is but presumption. For the foresight of things to come, which is called providence, belongs only to him by whose will they are to come. From him only, and supernaturally, proceeds prophecy. The best prophet naturally is the best guesser, and the best guesser he that is most versed and studied in the matters he guesses at, for he hath most signs to guess by. . . .

As prudence is a presumption of the future, contracted from the experience of time past, so there is a presumption of things past, taken from other things, not future but past also. For he that hath seen by what courses and degrees a flourishing state hath first come into civil war and then to ruin, upon the sight of the ruins of any other state will guess the like war and the like courses have been there also. But this conjecture hath the same uncertainty almost with the conjecture of the future, both being grounded only upon experience.[14]

Particular events, Hobbes is saying, take place in time and we have only sense and memory to tell us of their occurrence. If we attempt to think diachronically, to reason from occurrence at one point in time to occurrence at another, we shall be compelled to rely on the presumption that one event will be attended with circumstances like those attending another which resembles it. This presumption can only be tested by experience, and we can draw no general conclusions from it. Therefore the most we can do, so long as we continue to think in this manner, is to accumulate more remembered data and more cases in which the event has confirmed the presumption. In this way the individual acquires prudence and—Hobbes could have added—society builds up traditions and customs; but the process is a quantitative and actuarial one, in which the probabilities of successful prediction grow ever greater while never attaining certainty. Certainty of prediction, or prophecy, or providence—the

---

[14] *Leviathan*, i, 3 (Oakeshott, p. 16). In extended quotations, I have sometimes modified Hobbes's punctuation in ways that seem to me to make the sequence of ideas plainer to a modern eye.

terms are used interchangeably—belongs only to God, because he is not an observer of events, but the author of them.

It is the time-bound nature of human intelligence which renders it incapable of predicting occurrences and events with any certainty. "Signs of prudence are all uncertain, because to observe by experience, and remember all circumstances that may alter the success, is impossible." [15] We inhabit a flux in which there is more going on than can be observed at one moment, and too much change to permit of our recollections remaining valid for long; it is an indication that Hobbes took a relatively stable, customary society for granted that he dealt with this problem in terms of the limitations of experience, where Machiavelli had seen it in terms of the difficulty of innovation in a world controlled by chance.[16] But we can escape from the flux, and enter a world of scientific certainties, if we abandon our insistence on thinking diachronically and, instead of seeking to argue from moment to moment, occurrence to recurrence, reason from premise to consequence. This will liberate us from Plato's cave, from the world of phenomenal time:

> No discourse whatsoever can end in absolute knowledge of fact, past or to come. For as for the knowledge of fact, it is originally sense and ever after memory. And for the knowledge of consequence, which I have said before is called science,[17] it is not absolute but conditional. No man can know by discourse that this or that is, has been or will be, which is to know absolutely; but only that if this be, that is; if this has been, that has been; if this shall be, that shall be; which is to know conditionally, and that not the consequence of one thing to another, but of one name of a thing to another name of the same thing.[18]

---

[15] *Ibid.*, i, 5 (Oakeshott, p. 30).
[16] See in particular chs. ii, vi and xxiv–xxv of *The Prince*.
[17] *Leviathan*, i, 5 (Oakeshott, pp. 29–30).
[18] *Ibid.*, i, 7 (Oakeshott, p. 40).

Hobbes does not even mention the possibility of knowing that if this is, that shall be; so determined is he to separate the world of logical from that of temporal consequence, the world of rationally perceived necessary consequence from the world of facts observed by sense and memory as they occur in time. Knowledge of the former world he terms "science" or "philosophy," knowledge of the latter "history." [19] From this point in the analysis we are constructing, he may be seen going on to show how knowledge of premise and consequence brings knowledge of cause and effect, knowledge of the universe of consequences knowledge of the universe of motions. Through extension of this kind of knowledge, we discover the laws of nature that bind our consciences; we discover the necessity for a representative sovereign and are led to perform the acts which set him up; we conclude that God exists and is all-powerful, and that the normative laws which our reason discovers must be also his commands. This complex process of making discoveries and acting upon them takes place in time—there is no action or motion in Hobbes's world which does not—but has no history; it is synchronic, observable as taking place at any and every moment, and does not necessitate that any civil society, or mankind at large, possess a past, present or future in which the stages of its development may be observed. Hobbes has followed the pattern, very common in the history of Western philosophy, of removing from the domain of political time into that of political space,[20] a removal usually carried out for precisely the reason which he gives: the sequence of events in time cannot be known with certainty sufficient to be termed "philosophical."

---

[19] *Ibid*, i, 9 (Oakeshott, p. 53). Professor Oakeshott, arguing that a distinction between science and philosophy is emergent in Hobbes's thought, agrees (Introduction, p. xxi) that he uses the terms synonymously.

[20] The very valuable terminology is that of Sheldon S. Wolin, *Politics and Vision* (New York and London, 1961), *passim*. See also John W. Gunnell, *Political Philosophy and Time* (Wesleyan University Press, 1968).

Only by abandoning diachronic for philosophical thinking can we understand scientifically how political authority must come into being, or erect a system of authority on a foundation of rational certainty.

We have now uncovered and clarified a sense in which it can very properly be said that Hobbes's political philosophy is unhistorical. He distinguished between philosophy and history as two modes of knowledge and ascribed scientific or rational demonstrability only to the former. But we must be careful not to suppose we have proved too much, or to fall into this error by using the words "philosophy" and "history" loosely and anachronistically. Since Hobbes uses "philosophy" as the name of one of two modes of knowledge, it clearly does not follow that phenomena which are known historically do not exist or have no relevance to politics. A more subtle error would be to suppose that "history," which Hobbes uses to denote the world of phenomena sensed and remembered as occurring in time, denotes each and every way in which human existence in time is known or important. It may seem natural to suppose that the temporal sequential phenomena which become apparent to our perceptions embrace the totality of human history, though a philosopher of history would probably find this supposition naïve; but even the debate which we might hold with him would not save us from the anachronism of supposing that what Hobbes meant by "history" embraced every way in which the seventeenth-century intellect saw human existence as carried on in time and marked by its stages. All that we have considered so far consists of Hobbes's responses to the assertion that man's temporal existence was known to him through experience; yet it is quite certain that contemporary thought saw man as having another history, known in another way. The anachronism of refusing to recognize this accounts for the extraordinary neglect and inattention paid to Hobbes's text by the whole tradition of modern scholarship.

Leviathan consists of four books, with an introduction and a

conclusion. Books I and II contain the doctrine to which attention has already been given and the rest of Hobbes's political
philosophy, properly so called; and the interest of philosophers
and historians of philosophy has quite rightly been focused
upon them. But at midpoint in the whole work, at the end of
book II and the outset of book III, Hobbes embarks on a new
course. He states quite plainly [21] that human existence, knowledge, morality and politics must be thought of as going on in
two distinct but simultaneous contexts: the one of nature,
known to us through our philosophic reasoning on the consequences of our affirmations, the other of divine activity, known
to us through prophecy, the revealed and transmitted words of
God.

> . . . there may be attributed to God a twofold kingdom,
> *natural* and *prophetic:* natural, wherein he governeth as
> many of mankind as acknowledge his providence, by the
> natural dictates of right reason; and prophetic, wherein hav-
> ing chosen out one particular nation, the Jews, for his sub-
> jects, he governed them, and none but them, not only by
> natural reason, but by positive laws, which he gave them
> by the mouths of his holy prophets.[22]

The change in mid-sentence from present to past tense indicates
the major and significant alteration that has begun to occur.
The Christian God operates in time, and our knowledge of
prophecy is our knowledge of the time-frame and scheme of
events within which he does so. There are two ways in which
this comes to be the case: first, God performs acts, including
acts of revelation to prophets, at various points in time; second,
the words by which we have knowledge of his acts are revealed

---

[21] *Leviathan,* ii, 31 (Oakeshott, pp. 232–34) and iii, 32 (Oakeshott,
pp. 242–43).
[22] *Ibid.,* ii, 31 (Oakeshott, pp. 233–34). The formal link is that men
must hear God commanding them directly before they can in the full
sense be obliged to obey him. This kind of obligation is not universal, but
peculiar to the chosen or elect.

to prophets at specific moments in time, and are subsequently transmitted through tracts of time by the authority, religious or civil, on which the prophets and their words are taken to be authentically God's. Actions and words, both divine and human, prophetic and civil, join to constitute a time-scheme which is not only that within which Christian thought is inescapably conducted, but is actually that of which the Christian has knowledge. Our knowledge of God is knowledge of his acts, gained through his words, both of which are performed in time and schematize it. Hobbes therefore affirms the existence of a sacred history, which does not appear in the scheme of philosophical and historical knowledge set out in book i, chapter 9, but which does constitute virtually the whole of the subject-matter of books iii and iv. In these books Hobbes sets forth his perceptions of the Christian religion, or as he significantly calls it "the prophetic kingdom of God," as a system of belief in past acts and utterances of the deity, and of expectation of future acts which those utterances foretell. Following the orthodox scheme, in short, his exposition of the Christian faith concluded with an eschatology; following certain less orthodox schemes, it is very nearly reducible to one.

The two books in which Hobbes expounds Christian faith and its sacred history are almost exactly equal in length to books i and ii;[23] yet the attitude of far too many scholars towards them has traditionally been,[24] first, that they aren't really there, second, that Hobbes didn't really mean them. For this obviously unsatisfactory state of affairs various reasons can be

[23] In the first edition of *Leviathan*, the Introduction plus bks. i and ii total 193 pages, bks. iii and iv minus the Review and Conclusion 192. I am indebted to Professor Goldsmith for pointing this out.

[24] Exceptions to this all too general rule may be found in the writings of A. E. Taylor (Keith C. Brown, ed., *Hobbes Studies*, Harvard University Press, 1965, pp. 35, 50, 54n.), Willis B. Glover (Brown, *op. cit.*, pp. 141–68), Oakeshott (Introduction, pp. xliv–l, lxi–lxiv) and Goldsmith (*op. cit.*, pp. 217–27, and "A Case of Identity" in King and Parekh, eds., *Politics and Experience: Essays Presented to Michael Oakeshott* [Cambridge University Press, 1968]).

suggested. In the first place, the history of thought has been too much left in the hands of philosophers, historians of philosophy and scholars who have assumed that the history of thought can be subsumed under the history of successive philosophic systems. Since Hobbes was a major philosopher, and books III and IV of *Leviathan* are manifestly not philosophy, it has seemed simplest to leave them out; and on grounds like these scholars feel justified in producing students' editions of *Leviathan* from which books III and IV, and of *De Cive* from which chapters XVI and XVII, are simply omitted. In the second place, for historical reasons inclusive of that just given, scholarship has suffered until recently from a fixed unwillingness to give the Hebrew and eschatological elements in seventeenth-century thought the enormous significance which they possessed for contemporaries. In the third place, Hobbes's readers since his own lifetime have found reason to doubt if he was a man of deep personal piety and even to affirm that he was an atheist; and even the recent revival of interest in the possible role of God in his thought [25] has focused upon the theory of natural law, which forms part of his philosophy, and not upon his doctrines of prophecy and eschatology, which do not.[26] It has thus come to be a near-orthodoxy that he did not believe what he wrote in the unread half of *Leviathan*, and that consequently these books have no meaning, though the fallacy should be evident of affirming that the sincerity of a man's belief in what he

---

[25] See Brown, *op. cit.*, *passim*; Howard Warrender, *The Political Philosophy of Hobbes: His Theory of Obligation* (Oxford, 1957), F. C. Hood, *The Divine Politics of Thomas Hobbes* (Oxford, 1964) and Quentin Skinner, "Hobbes's *Leviathan*," *The Historical Journal*, VII (1964), 321–33. Some of these writings—notably Hood's—make a serious attempt to show that the thought of bks. iii and iv is implicit in i and ii, but do not focus on the analysis of prophetic content.

[26] Prophecy cannot, of course, be the object of philosophical knowledge as Hobbes understands the latter; nor does he include sacred history in his classification of the modes of that branch of knowledge (i, 9), presumably because it is not an object of sense-knowledge. His theory of knowledge determines the status of our belief in prophecy, but cannot determine the content of what we believe.

says suffices to determine the content of what he says or its impact upon others. Although esoteric reasons have been suggested why Hobbes should have written what he did not believe,[27] the difficulty remains of imagining why a notoriously arrogant thinker, vehement in his dislike of "insignificant speech," should have written and afterwards defended sixteen chapters of what he held to be nonsense, and exposed them to the scrutiny of a public which did not consider this kind of thing nonsense at all. The only recourse open to the historian is to examine, not Hobbes's sincerity of conviction, but the effects which his words seem designed to produce, reconstructing the meanings which their contents would appear to have borne, first, in the thought-patterns characteristic of the time, secondly, in the thought-patterns characteristic of their author. If the effect or the intention of books III and IV was to reduce the Christian revelation to insignificance, this will be discovered not by making prior assumptions about Hobbes's beliefs when he wrote them, but by paying attention to what he actually wrote. And, further, if we are to conclude that he esoterically intimated that Christian eschatology was nonsense, we must begin by ascertaining the ways in which it was conventionally held to make sense.

Prophecy and eschatology—to which Hobbes in effect reduces the whole body of revealed religion—were not merely a system of dogmas for believers, but a highly important component of the conceptual equipment possessed by Christian Europe. They constituted an intellectual scheme of a distinctive kind, known by an intellectual faculty unlike any we have so far considered. The greater part of their content consisted of acts which God was said to have performed in the past, or which it had been promised that he would perform in the future; and

---

[27] The classic instance is that of Leo Strauss (Brown, *op. cit.*, p. 27, n. 43). It is odd that Strauss seems to speak of the view that Hobbes meant what he said as constituting a "prevalent practice"; belief in his theistic sincerity has surely been a minority opinion.

each statement of which prophecy consisted had itself been uttered by God or his prophets at a distinctive moment in time. In
two ways, therefore, prophecy constituted a sacred history, and
if "prophecy" and "revelation" were taken as interchangeable
terms, it must follow that knowledge of the Christian revelation
was in a sense historical knowledge. But the question must arise
of how the events of this history were to be known. It would be
common ground to Hobbes and a scholastic thinker that they
were not accessible to reason, since they were not consequences
to be inferred or deduced from a premise, and that they were
equally inaccessible to experience, since their content (as distinct from their verbal utterance) did not belong to the realm
of phenomena which the individual sensed and remembered for
himself. They were statements, made on specific occasions and
transmitted through subsequent time, which we accepted either
as true or as authoritative—it was on this point that the schools
divided—by means of a faculty of the mind known as faith.
Faith was distinct from either reason or experience, and this
must be why sacred history, to which so large a part of *Leviathan* is devoted, does not figure in the scheme of knowledge set
out in chapter 9 and divided into modes of philosophy and
modes of history. Experience and prudence, forms of thought
appropriate to the study of natural and civil history, have no
part to play in the study of revealed history.

Books III and IV, then, form in a sense Hobbes's contribution
to the study of faith, both as a system of revealed truth and as a
faculty of the mind. But at a much earlier point in *Leviathan*,
immediately after drawing his distinction between experiential
knowledge of facts and logical knowledge of the consequences
of verbal affirmations, he had turned his attention to the question of what faith was; and it will aid our study of his eschatology if we keep in mind what he there said:

When a man's discourse beginneth not at definitions, it
beginneth either at some other contemplation of his own,

and then it is still called opinion; or it beginneth at some saying of another, of whose ability to know the truth and of whose honesty in not deceiving he doubteth not; and then the discourse is not so much concerning the thing as the person, and the resolution is called BELIEF and FAITH: *faith* in the man, *belief* both *of* the man and *of* the truth of what he says. So that in belief are two opinions, one of the saying of the man, the other of his virtue. . . . But we are to observe that this phrase, *I believe in* [and its Greek and Latin equivalents] are never used but in the writings of divines. Instead of them in other writings are put, *I believe him* [etc.] . . . [and] this singularity of the ecclesiastic use of the word hath raised many disputes about the right object of the Christian faith.

But by *believing in,* as it is in the creed, is meant not trust in the person, but confession and acknowledgement of the doctrine. For not only Christians, but all manner of men do so believe in God as to hold all for truth they hear him say, whether they understand it or not; which is all the faith and trust can possibly be had in any person whatsoever; but they do not all believe the doctrine of the creed.

From whence we may infer that when we believe any saying, whatsoever it be, to be true from arguments taken not from the thing itself or from the principles of natural reason, but from the authority and good opinion we have of him that hath said it, then is the speaker or person we believe in or trust in, and whose word we take, the object of our faith; and the honour done in believing is done to him only. And consequently, when we believe that the Scriptures are the word of God, having no immediate revelation from God himself, our belief, faith and trust is in the church, whose word we take and acquiesce therein. And they that believe that which a prophet relates unto them in the name of God, take the word of the prophet, do honour to him and in him trust and believe touching the truth of what he relateth, whether he be a true or a false prophet. And so it is also with all other history. . . . If Livy say the Gods made once a cow speak and we believe it not, we distrust not God therein, but Livy. So that it is evident that whatsoever we believe, upon no other reason than what is drawn from authority of men only and their writings, whether they be sent from God or not, is faith in men only.[28]

The last conclusion that we should draw from this passage is that Hobbes is declaring God to be non-existent or irrelevant. If we can only believe that God spoke on the authority of men who speak to us subsequently, we believe that he spoke once we accept their authority, and in so believing we invest him as well as them with the authority that comes with speaking. What Hobbes is doing is historizing faith in a new way, one of the highest relevance to politics. Faith is reposed in a system of statements and in the authors who transmit them through time, and whether we stress the statement or the author as the object of our faith, a large part of the content of the statements made and transmitted by every author, saving God himself, consists of statements about previous authors. Since once we accept that an author spoke, whether directly or on the authority of another, we invest that speaker with an authority of divine origin, it follows that the whole body of our faith is reducible to the construction of a system of authors and of authority, existing through time and resting on the statements they transmit, our opinion of the authority they have as transmitters, and the authority of the previous speakers, back to God himself, whom we accept as authors in the act of accepting any one of them. This system of authority constituted by faith differs from the system of authority constituted in the erection of the civil sovereign in that historicity is of its essence; it rests upon the transmission of words through time, words which constantly reiterate

[28] *Leviathan*, i, 7 (Oakeshott, pp. 41–42).

statements about previous utterances of the same words; and the individual believer becomes involved in this history as he validates and perpetuates it through faith.

There exist then in *Leviathan* two structures of authority, one as a-historical as the other is historical, and they will come into direct and potentially competitive coexistence once the commonwealth constituted in books I and II becomes "a Christian Commonwealth"—words which, including the article, form the title of book III. The civil sovereign is set up by the a-historical processes of civil philosophy and natural reason, which among other things declare that God exists and commands obedience to the laws of nature which the sovereign also enjoins. He now finds himself faced by a new system of authority, resting upon what are accepted to be utterances of the same God, made in a past and concerning a future, but in no way deducible by the reason which set him up and validates his authority. The sovereign, and the student of civil government, must pay urgent attention to the content as well as the transmission—which, again, forms a large part of the content—of the body of revelation on which rests the structure of religious authority; the inhabitants of the a-historical world of reason must enter the historical world of faith. Since faith is reposed in the content of revelation as well as in its authors and transmitters, and since on the other hand the content of the statement transmitted affects in many ways the sort of authority possessed by those involved in its transmission, the whole content of revealed religion is potentially of concern to the civil magistrate. We shall see that this is particularly true of revelation's eschatological component.

The one thing which scholars do generally know concerning Hobbes's doctrine of prophecy is that God does not speak to us direct but mediately, through the utterances of men—the prophets and Christ in his human nature—to whom or in whom he reveals himself; and that whether God has indeed spoken direct to any man is a thing past any man's capacity to determine,[29] so that the belief we repose and publicly own in the prophets is grounded either on our opinion—which is never our knowledge—of their authenticity, or on the command of the civil sovereign once he is constituted and requires us in the name of civil peace to accept this man as prophet or this doctrine as the word of God.[30] And on the supposition, which there is no need to contest here, that Hobbes did not show that anything except the needs of civil peace bound the will of the sovereign in decreeing matters of this sort, it is usual to drop the subject, leaving it to be inferred that the revealed prophetic word means nothing but what the sovereign ordains that it shall mean, and that the domain of prophecy has been successfully reabsorbed by that of nature, by the unhistoric rationality of the civil order and its sovereign.

But that is not how Hobbes proceeds, and if it is what he really meant then he meant something other than what he said. The history of God's prophetic word, and the future prophesied by that word, constitute the sacred history of mankind, and if Hobbes had meant that sacred history had no meaning of itself and that the sovereign might rewrite it to suit the permanent or passing needs of society, he would hardly have written chapter after chapter of exegesis with the proclaimed intention of arriving at the truth about it. Yet this is what he did, and hav-

---

[29] *Ibid*, i, 7 (Oakeshott, p. 42); i, 12 (Oakeshott, pp. 77–80); i, 14 Oakeshott, p. 90); ii, 26 (Oakeshott, pp. 186–88); iii, 32 (Oakeshott, pp. 243–46); iii, 34 (Oakeshott, pp. 254–55); iii, 36 (Oakehott, pp. 277–85); iii, 37 (Oakeshott, pp. 286–91); Review and Conclusion (Oakeshott, p. 465).

[30] *Ibid.*, ii, 26 (Oakeshott, p. 188); iii, 32 (Oakeshott, p. 246); iii, 34 (Oakeshott, pp. 254–55); iii, 38 (Oakeshott, pp. 290–91); iii, 42 (generally, but in particular Oakeshott, pp. 327–30 and 340–41). Since some Jewish and all Christian kings have ruled in times when direct prophetic inspiration was in suspension or at an end, their opportunities for sitting in judgment upon true prophets have been limited. The interesting case, with which Hobbes does not deal, is that of Elisha, who conveyed the Lord's command to Jehu, authorizing him to overthrow King Joram and take his throne (in 2 Kings ix). Jehu must have exercised his own judgment as to the authenticity of this revelation by one who was already an accredited prophet.

ing once acknowledged the existence of prophecy he could
hardly have done less or more. The magistrate may be the supreme and unchallenged interpreter of God's word, but that is
not at all the same as being its author—either in the sense of
being God himself or of being one of those acknowledged as
uttering that word at God's direct or even mediated command.
The authority by which the sovereign interprets the prophetic
word is clearly distinct from the authority by which the word
is uttered; and since the word, its content, its transmission and
its authors constitute a history, the secular ruler finds himself
inhabiting a history which he did not make—it does not owe
its being to the natural reason which produced him—and which
indeed looks forward to a time when his authority will be exercised by the risen Christ. The word and the history it connotes
are given him, and his authority as interpreter begins only from
acceptance of it as *datum*. Hobbes therefore, as a private man,
a subject and (so he tells us) a Christian, inhabiting the same
history, finds it desirable to pursue an accurate interpretation
of the same data, and does not wait in mindless quiet for the
sovereign to interpret it to him.

The prophetic word of God constitutes the past, present and
future of mankind. At moments in the past, God spoke to
prophets, who relayed his word to his peculiar people—the Jews
first and the Christian elect later; it was his word commanding
them, and their acceptance of him and his prophets as uttering
it, which constituted the peculiar kingdom of God over them,
and a peculiar kingdom thus differs in kind from a natural civil
kingdom. After the deaths of the various prophets, there were
—as there still are—periods of time in which the people continued to accept their word as God's and to remember them as
having received and given it.[31] Sacred time, thus far, consists
of moments of divine revelation and continua of human transmission. But a prophet may be a *prolocutor* who speaks in

[31] *Ibid.*, i, 7 (Oakeshott, p. 40); i, 12 (Oakeshott, p. 78); iii, 36 (Oakeshott, pp. 282–85); iii, 40 (Oakeshott, p. 312).

God's name—all revelation is prophecy in the sense that it is
mediated through such men—or a *predictor* who foretells what
is to come.[32] Some part of the content of prophecy is prediction
in that it foretells a future, composed of divine actions, including the action of foretelling it, in which we believe and which
we expect. The present, consequently, is a time of remembering past prophecies and expecting the future which they
foretell.

But all these subdivisions of sacred history, including the future, are also subdivisions of the history of political authority.
In the synchronic, a-historical world of natural civil authority,
there is movement from a phase in which we know by reason
what are the laws of nature and that they are also the commands of God, but are obliged by this knowledge only in conscience and *in foro interno*,[33] to a phase in which our wills and
actions are lawfully obliged because there is now one Leviathan
whom we have constituted with power to command us. But in
the diachronic world inhabited by God's peculiar people, this
purely natural movement does not take place, because God is
active from the time of Abraham,[34] commanding men directly,
not only through reason and experience, but through his word
which is spoken by the prophets. Political authority is present
from certain moments and it has a history—including a recorded commencement—because the prophetic word has a past,
present and future and entails different modes of authority at
different times.

For two reasons, the authority which God exercises over his
peculiar people is a civil or political authority in the full sense
of the term: first, because God is literally present and commanding the people through positive laws, peculiar to themselves, issued through his prophets; second, because the people

[32] *Ibid.*, iii, 36 (Oakeshott, pp. 275–76).
[33] *Ibid*, i, 15 (Oakeshott, p. 103).
[34] *Ibid.*, ii, 26 (Oakeshott, pp. 187–88); iii, 35 (Oakeshott, pp. 266–
67); iii, 40 (Oakeshott, pp. 307–8). The covenant with Abraham is
relatively little emphasized as compared with that with Moses.

have covenanted, at Sinai and on other occasions,[35] to obey him through his prophets, acknowledged as uttering his laws. The term "covenant" is used here in a variant of the full Hobbesian sense. In the natural world the covenant sets up Leviathan, the mortal god, a man or men bearing the person of all other men composing the community. In the prophetic world the people covenanted with Moses to speak with God for them, and so obliged themselves to accept as God's word all that Moses told them for such.[36] Does this mean that Moses as representative sovereign constituted Israel a people in a manner no different from that of other Leviathans? Not if we accept, as there is no sign that Hobbes did not, that God spoke to Moses, for then Moses was in the prophetic world and not simply in the natural. We cannot know that God spoke to him; the authority on which we accept this must be largely his own; the faith by which we acknowledge it must be largely faith in Moses; but once we accept it Moses becomes the lieutenant of God in a way in which the civil sovereign can never be, since in the natural world God rules through reason and not through positive and peculiar command.

God exercised direct political authority—that is to say, he was king—over Israel from the time of Moses to that of Samuel. He ruled, it is true, through lieutenants of two kinds: a constituted succession of priest-kings in the line of the heirs of Aaron, and—given the people's frowardness and constant demands for signs of his will—an extraordinary and occasional succession of judges and other prophets, recognized by a far from infallible popular opinion as speaking with his voice.[37] But with the death of Eli the line of the ruling high priests ended, and the misdeeds of the children of Samuel caused the people to lose faith

---

[35] A renewal of the covenant took place under Esdras, at the return from the Captivity, but did not constitute a new civil sovereignty. *Leviathan*, iii, 40 (Oakeshott, p. 315) and iii, 42 (Oakeshott, p. 342).

[36] *Ibid.*, ii, 20 (Oakeshott, p. 134); ii, 26 (Oakeshott, p. 188); iii, 35 (Oakeshott, pp. 267–78, 270); iii, 40 (Oakeshott, pp. 308–11); iii, 42 (Oakeshott, pp. 340–41).

[37] *Ibid.*, iii, 40 (Oakeshott, pp. 311–12).

in the prophetic succession in a way that proved irrevocable.[38] Samuel—who was soon to pronounce the old law at an end [39]— presided over that most controversial moment in pre-Exilic history as seen through seventeenth-century Christian eyes, the election of Saul to be king in the manner of the Gentiles. Innumerable were the emphases which could be selected in interpreting this event, and Hobbes's treatment can be seen as it were suspended between two of them: emphasis that it constituted a "rejection" and "deposition" of God from his direct kingship over Israel, and insistence that this nevertheless occurred with his permission and consent, so that the authority of the kings was not merely natural, but had his express and positive sanction.[40] But if we compare the works on politics

[38] *Ibid.*, i, 12 (Oakeshott, pp. 78–79); iii, 35 (Oakeshott, p. 268); iii, 39 (Oakeshott, p. 314).

[39] *De Cive* (*English Works*, II, 245). Hobbes gives St Jerome as authority for this.

[40] *Elements of Law* (Cambridge University Press, 1928), Pt. I, ch. 7, sec. 5, pp. 127–28: no distinction drawn between high-priests and kings. *De Cive*, xvi (*English Works*, II, 245): "the kingdom of God by way of priesthood (God consenting to the request of the Israelites) was ended"; "new priesthood and new sovereignty . . . founded in the very concession of the people." *Leviathan*, i, 12 (Oakeshott, p. 79): "faith also failed; insomuch as they deposed their God from reigning over them." ii, 20 (Oakeshott, p. 134): "when the people heard what power their king was to have, yet they consented thereto, and say thus . . . *we will be as all other nations*. . . . Here is confirmed the right that sovereigns have. . . ." ii, 29 (Oakeshott, p. 213—passage deals with "the infirmities of a commonwealth"): "And as false doctrine, so oftentimes the example of different government in a neighbouring nation disposeth men to alteration. . . . So the people of the Jews were stirred up to reject God, and to call upon the prophet Samuel for a king after the manner of the nations." iii, 35 (Oakeshott, pp. 268–69): "after the Israelites had rejected God, the prophets did foretell his restitution; as . . . I will reign over you, and make you to stand to that covenant which you made with me by Moses, and brake in your rebellion against me in the days of Samuel and in your election of another king . . . it were superfluous to say in our prayer, *Thy kingdom come*, unless it be meant of the restoration of that kingdom of God by Christ, which by revolt of the Israelites had been interrupted in the election of Saul." iii, 38 (Oakeshott, p. 294): "they rebelled." iii, 40 (Oakeshott, pp. 313–14): "cast off by the people, with the consent of God himself. . . . And yet God consented to it. . . . Having therefore rejected God, in whose right the priests governed, there was no authority left to the priests, but such as the king was pleased to allow

which Hobbes is known to have composed before the outbreak
of the Civil War—the *Elements of Law,* written in 1640, and
De Cive, published in 1642—with the language published in
Leviathan in 1651, we shall notice an important difference of
emphasis and an extension of the argument into new fields of
relevance.[41] The stress in *Leviathan* falls very heavily indeed, in
ways not paralleled in the earlier works, upon the idea that the
supreme purpose of Christ's mission is to restore the literal and
political kingdom of God upon earth that existed from Moses
to Samuel; that, since the Jews have rejected Christ's invitation
to re-enter this kingdom, it is now to be exercised over a new
peculiar people, the Christian elect; and that through the death,
ascension and promised return of Christ, the second kingdom
of God is to begin only at his return and at the resurrection of

---

them; which was more or less, according as the kings were good or evil.
. . . (p. 314) And afterwards, when they demanded a king after the
manner of the nations, yet it was not with a design to depart from the
worship of God their king . . . they would have a king to judge them in
civil actions, but not that they would allow their king to change the
religion which they thought was recommended to them by Moses. So
that they always kept in store a pretext, either of justice or religion, to
discharge themselves of their obedience, whensoever they had hope to
prevail" [!]. There follows on p. 315 a confused account of the dealings
of the later kings with the prophets after Samuel; Elijah and Elisha are
not mentioned. iii, 41 (Oakeshott, pp. 318–19): Christ to restore the
kingdom "cut off by rebellion," but only to proclaim its future coming;
Pilate accepts his claim to be king of the Jews as not contrary to the laws
of Caesar. iii, 42 (Oakeshott, p. 376): "Before the people of Israel had,
by the commandment of God to Samuel, set over themselves a king, after
the manner of other nations, the high-priest had the civil government,
and none but he could make or depose an inferior priest. But that power
was afterwards in the king. . . . Kings therefore may in like manner ordain and deprive bishops, as they shall think fit for the well-governing of
their subjects." It would on the whole appear that a kingdom of men
legitimized by nature exists only in an interlude of sin and rebellion against
God. The king reigns in God's absence, but that absence is caused by the
king's election.

[41] Chs. xvi and xvii of *De Cive* should be carefully compared with bk.
iii of *Leviathan,* and the relation between the two texts considered. If we
conclude that Hobbes's interest in eschatology sharply increased between
1642 and 1651, this must have occurred during his residence at Paris, in
a *milieu* not usually considered eschatologically minded.

the saints, which is to end this world and inaugurate a new one.
Where in the first kingdom God reigned in his representatives
Moses and the prophets, he will reign in the second kingdom in
the person of Christ risen in his human nature and his human
body; and the identity of Christ's kingship with that of Moses
is insisted on so strongly that it impels Hobbes to one of the
only two occasions in *Leviathan* on which he resorts to the
typological mode of argument, in which Christ and his precursors are presented as reiterating and perfecting a common figurative pattern.[42] If the sole purpose of Christ's mission is to restore the immediate civil rule of God over his peculiar people
which ended with the election of Saul, it might almost seem
as if that event constituted a second fall of man, something
which the whole process of redemption exists to undo. Hobbes
does not go to these lengths, since he wishes to maintain the
legitimacy of Davidic kingship over the peculiar people; though
in common with the general trend of Christian interpretation
of later Jewish history, he does not attempt to assign post-Exilic
forms of political power a distinctive role in the history of
prophetic authority, and the emphasis falls by default on the
utterances of the Exilic prophets in foretelling Jesus as the
Messiah.[43] But the fact remains that his history of prophetic
authority has been projected into an eschatological future. His

[42] *Leviathan*, iii, 41 (Oakeshott, pp. 316–17): the sacrificed goat and
the scapegoat both "types" of Christ; pp. 320–21: the "similitude with
Moses"—twelve princes and twelve apostles; seventy elders and seventy
disciples; circumcision and baptism; the washing of lepers a "type" of
baptism. "Seeing therefore the authority of Moses was but subordinate,
and he but a lieutenant of God, it followeth that Christ, whose authority
as man was to be like that of Moses, was no more but subordinate to the
authority of his Father."

[43] *De Cive* (*English Works*, II, 248) and *Leviathan*, iii, 40 (Oakeshott,
p. 315) make the point that post-Exilic history is too confused to be of
authority. iii, 36 (Oakeshott, p. 280): "after the people of the Jews had
rejected God, that he should no longer reign over them, those kings which
submitted themselves to God's government were also his chief prophets,"
in the *prolocutor* sense presumably. iii, 42 (Oakeshott, pp. 341–42): the
problem of when the Exile prophecies became canonical.

politics have taken on a messianic dimension, just as the messianism they entail is almost brutally political.

As Hobbes's thought enters the domain of eschatology, it begins to make use of apocalyptic: both that part of the content of acknowledged revelation which had to do with the acts of God promised for a future, and the doctrines and speculations, for historical reasons largely heterodox or heretical, which had been built up around it. He insists unremittingly on the literal and physical nature of Christ's return, the literal, physical and political character of his kingdom after the resurrection of the saints. It is to be exercised on earth,[44] and indeed from Jerusalem,[45] since "salvation is of the Jews (*ex Judaeis*, that is, begins at the Jews)"; the speculation is of the same order as that which represented the conversion of the Jews as a necessary preliminary to a millennial *regnum Christi*. Formally, Hobbes is not a millennialist, or at least a pre-millennialist, since his kingdom of Christ follows and does not precede the end of this world;[46] but as the allusion to Jerusalem shows, his "world to come" so closely replicates this world that the distinction tends to disappear. On an earth indistinguishable from this one, Christ in his risen human body is to reign for ever over the elect in theirs, and "for ever" has no other meaning than that time as we know it in this life is prolonged *ad infinitum*.[47] The risen saints will neither beget nor die; since Hobbes refuses to accept eternal torment, or any evil greater than personal death, he has the damned resurrected to face the certainty of a second and eternal death, not to be suffered before they have begotten children in the state of damnation, who will continue to all

---

[44] *Leviathan*, iii, 38 (Oakeshott, pp. 292–96).

[45] *Ibid.* (Oakeshott, pp. 301–3). On p. 294 it seems that the conversion of the Jews must precede the second kingdom.

[46] *Ibid.*, p. 303; also p. 295.

[47] *Ibid.*, iv, 44 (Oakeshott, pp. 411–12); the damned to be renewed "as long as the kind of man by propagation shall endure, which is eternally," *Answer to Bishop Bramhall* (*English Works*, IV, 299): "*God's mercy endureth for ever*, and surely God endureth as long as his mercy; consequently there is duration in God, and consequently endless succession of time."

eternity the generations of men doomed to perish utterly without help from the God who visibly and humanly reigns over
them.[48] Since Hobbes could as well have extinguished the
damned without allowing them to breed, his theory of damnation is gratuitous; and since he knew more clearly than most
men that damnation consists in the deprivation of hope, it
appears more than usually abominable. Its importance, however, is that it underlines both the material and the temporal
nature of his hereafter. Salvation and damnation both happen
in the world of matter and of time. As Hobbes denies that eternity is a *nunc-stans* or "eternal now," and will permit it only
to be an infinite prolongation of the time we know,[49] so his
"heaven" is located in no spiritual and (until we ask where God
is now) hardly any spatial realm, but essentially in time—in the
infinite future of the material world.[50] It is this which links his
hereafter to the millennium of the Protestant sects; Gerrard
Winstanley had already shown that Christ's resurrection could
be described exclusively in terms of a transformation of this
world's conditions. Again, Hobbes's determination to acknowledge no processes outside the world of matter, space and time
led him to follow many radical sectarians and much contemporary higher criticism [51] in propounding the doctrine of mortalism, according to which the soul could have no existence
apart from the body, but must perish with it at death and enjoy
immortality only with it on resurrection.[52] This too was an
apocalyptic heresy: immortality did not consist in the soul's

[48] *Leviathan*, iii, 38 (Oakeshott, pp. 296–300); iv, 44 (Oakeshott, pp.
410–12).

[49] *Ibid.*, iv, 46 (Oakeshott, p. 443). *Of Liberty and Necessity* (*English
Works*, IV, 271). *Answer to Bishop Bramhall* (*English Works*, IV, 298–
300).

[50] *Leviathan*, iii, 38 (Oakeshott, p. 294–95).

[51] G. H. Williams, *The Radical Reformation* (London, 1962), *passim*.
George Newton Conklin, *Biblical Criticism and Heresy in Milton* (New
York: King's Crown Press, Columbia University, 1949). Nathaniel H.
Henry, "Milton and Hobbes: Mortalism and the Intermediate State,"
Studies in Philology, XLVIII (1951), 234–50.

[52] *Leviathan*, iii, 38 (Oakeshott, p. 292); iv, 44 (Oakeshott, pp. 407–
12).

existence outside time, but was a gift to be received by the elect in an infinite future. Clearly, what is going on is a conjunction of some kind between Hobbes's philosophical materialism and the apocalyptic and millennialist speculation reaching a high-water mark in England about the time that *Leviathan* was published, a conjunction occurring at the point where salvation could be presented as a temporal, a historical and even a millennial process; and we have to understand this conjunction if we are to understand Hobbes's political eschatology.

Among the radical sects—one has only to mention *Man's Mortalitie,* usually ascribed to the Leveller Richard Overton [53] —such a heresy as mortalism could go hand-in-hand with chiliasm and enthusiasm; the paradox of the doctrine is that it could flourish among mystics whose belief in the primacy of the spirit was so absolute that they saw spirit as immanent in matter to the point where it could by no means be separated from it. Man's spirit was his body and his body his spirit; the resurrection of the one was the resurrection of the other, and it was blasphemy to try to separate the two. Along these lines it was perfectly possible for a devout and even mystical Christian to be a systematic materialist. A hundred years after Hobbes, Joseph Priestley was to combine materialism with millennialism,[54] and in his own day one has but to think of Gerrard Winstanley to be reminded of a cluster of sects subscribing to varieties of materialist pantheism. Hobbes does not share the outlook of these men; it can quite conclusively be shown that his thought does not rest on belief in the primacy of the spirit, but on denial of this belief, but he has to be understood as living in the same

[53] John Canne's edition, giving the author as "R.O.," was dated from Amsterdam in 1649. See W. Haller, *Liberty and Reformation in the Puritan Revolution* (New York, 1955), pp. 175–78; and for doubts about the authorship, Henry, *loc. cit.,* n. 51, above.

[54] See, as introductory to an extensive literature, "Institutes of Natural and Revealed Religion" and "Disquisitions Relating to Matter and Spirit," in *Theological and Miscellaneous Works of Joseph Priestley,* ed. J. T. Rutt (London, 1825), II and III. For the relations of science and millennialism in the eighteenth century, see Ernest Tuveson, *Millennium and Utopia* (Berkeley and Los Angeles, 1949).

world and belonging to the same context in intellectual history. We do not profit by treating him in isolation or by treating him in the light of ideas about materialism and atheism which belong properly to the nineteenth century.

Christianity is a prophetic religion, which cannot wholly escape from depicting the salvation of men as an event taking place in the future; and its insistence on the resurrection of the body imparts a bias towards depicting this event as taking place in the material and even social environment of human life, and therefore in the future of that environment. But these tendencies have always been combated, for reasons which are of vast importance to political thought because they have affected the views men hold of the nature and authority of the Church. St Augustine, and Catholic tradition after him, discouraged thought focused on the idea of a future collective redemption of mankind in time or at its end, and stressed that we were not told much of these things and that what we did know was better interpreted as figurative of the individual soul's redemption and ascent to God. The effect was to divert attention from the diachronic to the synchronic presentation of God's relation to men; instead of human salvation being brought about by a succession of acts performed by the eternal upon the world in time, it appeared rather in terms of the passage of numbers of souls through time to eternity—a passage performed through the actions of pure grace upon the individual's spirit, which however were usually thought of as institutionalized in the sacramental and other channels provided by the organizational Church, exercising in the world of time an authority derived from the eternal. The medieval Church thus rested largely upon the minimization of the eschatological perspective and the diversion of attention from the historical to the institutional; its philosophy correspondingly dealt in terms of the intelligibility of timeless universals in which part of God's reality was accessible to human reason.

As a tactical consequence of this, late-medieval heresy and both the magisterial and the radical Reformations, all bent on undermining the foundations of the institutional Church, commonly adopted arguments which pressed Christian thought back towards the eschatological perspective and its apocalyptic and millenarian forms. (That Calvin himself is an exception is a momentous fact in the history of English Puritanism.) If salvation came through grace, not reason, or through faith, not works, the Christian community might appear not a body of pilgrims ascending the Church's institutional ladder through time into eternity, but a body of faithful situated in time, reading God's word given in the past, commemorating Christ's passion suffered in the past, and reposing faith in a promise which was very largely an undertaking that he would return in the future. Salvation came through this expectation and not through Christ's real presence in the immediate now of the sacramental union; but it followed both that salvation could only come about in time and that Christ himself was seen as operating diachronically. He had come in the past and would return in the future; and salvation itself might be seen as a historical process. Joachim of Calabria, or perhaps rather the Spiritual Franciscans who had adapted his teachings,[55] had depicted the three persons of the Trinity as operating through successive ages to make history a process of the reunion of man with God. In this and other ways, it happened that every statement to the effect that salvation was to be expected in time became a blow struck at the sacerdotal enemy. Eschatology, prophecy and even millennialism became weapons in the armoury of Protestantism, whether the Protestant community was seen as a secular nation organized under its prince or as a gathered congregation separated from his obedience; and scholars have remarked [56] that several sixteenth-century princes took a deep—and, remotely and vaguely, Joachite—interest in the

---

[55] Gordon Leff, *Late Medieval Heresy* (2 vols., Manchester, 1967), I, 68–83.

[56] Frances A. Yates, "Queen Elizabeth as Astraea," *Journal of the Warburg and Courtauld Institute*, X (1947), 27–82, esp. 78–79.

idea that the authority of the Holy Spirit differed somehow from that of the Vicar of Christ. Certainly, a secular prince who had encouraged his subjects to believe that the Kingdom of God or the Age of the Spirit was at hand might live to regret it; such an expectation, especially when couched in millennial terms, might inconveniently underline the transitoriness of his authority, and his divines might make haste to preach that the Son of Man came as a thief in the night and none knew the hour of his coming. But it was the temporal (and so the transitory) nature of his authority which had led him to encourage such ideas in the first place. Prophecy and eschatology formed a device for drawing the process of salvation more fully within the world of time, and so subjecting its outward organization to temporal authority; history (and especially sacred history) was the instrument of the secular power. The adjectives "secular" and "temporal" themselves indicate the primacy of time, and even the apocalyptic of Patmos or Calabria was to a surprising degree a means to secularization.

We are now in a better position to see what Hobbes was about when he made use of the rhetoric of eschatology and apocalyptic. He does not employ the language of Patmos— there are only five references to the Book of Revelation in *Leviathan* and three to the Book of Daniel, none of them very important [57]—but he is engaging in traditional anti-Papal strategy when he reduces the Christian religion to a system of prophecy. All that has happened is that God has pronounced, through the mouths of prophets, certain words in time; the occasions of these pronouncements, together with other happenings to which they refer, constitute a series of divine acts in past time; we believe that these acts were performed by believing the authors and the words which they have relayed to us; these words include foretellings and promises of a resurrection

---

[57] Oakeshott, pp. 275, 278, 293, 297 (2), Revelation; 263, 299, 365, Daniel.

and a world to come; by believing these among other words, we ensure to ourselves a reward which will be only then, in that future. All is *logos*, and *logos* is a system of communications through time. Since salvation and even eternity are entirely temporal, there can be no Church in the sense of a spiritual institution communicating between time and an eternal now; and Hobbes denies not only purgatory, to do which was orthodox Protestantism, but the separate existence of the soul between the death and resurrection of the body, to do which was less orthodox though intellectually somewhat fashionable, in order to deny that there is a process of salvation occurring outside historical and political time, over which the Church exercises a separate authority that must be obeyed in the here and now.

Neither the use of apocalyptic in *Leviathan*, nor its mortalism and materialist literalism, suffice to place Hobbes outside the mainstream of Protestant thinking. Protestantism was the religion of the word, and the word not only consisted in large measure of a system of prophecies concerning future time, but in its character as a series of utterances required men to think in terms of a time-scheme which it was necessary to express in an eschatological language.[58] But Hobbes's thought is antisectarian as well as anti-Papal, and it is here that his role in the Protestant tradition becomes visibly enigmatic. He set himself to counter the sin of Korah, Dathan and Abiram, who had rebelled against Moses on the ground that "all the congregation are holy, every one of them." [59] If Protestantism was the religion of the word, it was also the religion that exalted the primacy of faith, and the story need not be rehearsed here of how in Puritan thinking the life of faith had become a realm of direct spiritual experience, in which the individual might, and regularly

---

[58] For the classical modern study of this, see W. Haller, *Foxe's Book of Martyrs and the Elect Nation* (London, 1963). Michael Fixler, *Milton and the Kingdoms of God* (London, 1964), should also be consulted.

[59] *Leviathan*, iii, 40 (Oakeshott, p. 310).

sought to, feel himself the subject of direct action by the will and redemptive mercy of God; or how the word became the vehicle of the spirit, and the spirit—moving rather in the individual than in the congregation or the church—the means of interpreting the word. By 1651, when *Leviathan* appeared, every possible challenge implicit in this development was being publicly articulated and the collision between private inspiration and the authority of the civil magistrate had become a staple of political debate. The far greater attention paid to apocalyptic in *Leviathan* than in *De Cive* may perhaps be a consequence of this. Puritan millennialism was essentially spiritualist: a Joachite Third Age, a Fifth Monarchist thousand-year reign of Christ and his saints were, however literally intended, modes of envisaging a day in which all the elect should be immediately and permanently possessed by the Holy Spirit. But the paradox was that this primacy of the spirit operated against the tendency of apocalyptic to draw salvation back into time and tended rather to restore the eternal now of an earlier Christian tradition. It placed the individual saint where the Church had once been, in an immediate relation to the eternal, and gave him authority originating outside time for his actions within it. There is a relationship between Hobbes's insistence that covenants must be kept[60] and the debates at Putney as to whether men might find authority in their spiritual experience for regarding engagements as superseded;[61] and William Prynne's discovery that Quakers were Franciscans in disguise is only a somewhat idiosyncratic expression of a widespread Erastian realization that the struggle against sectaries was a second front of the war against papists.[62]

---

[60] *Ibid.*, i, 15 (Oakeshott, pp. 93–94).
[61] A. S. P. Woodhouse, *Puritanism and Liberty* (London, 1948), pp. 9–13, 25–36, 45–52, 86–95.
[62] William M. Lamont, *Marginal Prynne* (London, 1963), explains the curious but contemporary relation between apocalyptic and Erastianism in Prynne's thinking. See also his *Godly Rule: Politics and Religion, 1603–60* (London, 1969).

Hobbes, then, set out to destroy "enthusiasm," [63] which he considered a form of madness,[64] the sin of Korah, Dathan and Abiram, a doctrine that must place the authority of prophetic utterance at the disposal of any man who might claim it on grounds that could not be evaluated by his fellows. In attacking Bishop Butler's "very horrid thing" he stood at the outset of a century and a half's Anglican orthodoxy, but the manner of his attack does much to explain why that orthodoxy devoted much of its energy to attacking him. He denies the reality of "enthusiasm" or "inspiration"—defined as the infusion of God's spirit into that of a man—by ruthlessly denying both the reality of "spirit" in the ordinarily accepted sense of the term and the possibility of the individual's directly experiencing God except on the rarest of historic occasions. This denial was conducted by means, and we may be tempted to explain it as the consequence, of Hobbes's philosophical materialism. In a universe consisting of matter and motion "spirit" may be the name of an extremely subtle corporeal substance, or a metaphor helping to express the state of a man's thoughts and feelings, notably— but conventionally—on such occasions as he has heard God's word directly or indirectly; [65] there can be no justification for using it as a nonsense-word to express the ubiquity of a non-substance. Nor can we intelligibly use it to describe any medium of communication between God and man. When God communicates with men he does not enter their bodies himself— the only man in whom "the Godhead dwelt bodily" was Jesus [66] —or blow an extremely subtle wind into their nostrils; [67] nor,

---

[63] The word is used in *Leviathan*, i, 8 (Oakeshott, p. 49) and ii, 33 (Oakeshott, p. 246). The terms "inspiration" and "infusion" are, however, far more common: i, 3 (Oakeshott, p. 13); i, 8 (Oakeshott, pp. 47–50); iii, 32 (Oakeshott, p. 244); iii, 34 (Oakeshott, pp. 259, 264–65); iii, 36 (Oakeshott, pp. 280–82); iv, 45 (Oakeshott, p. 429); iv, 46 (Oakeshott, p. 445).

[64] *Ibid.*, i, 8 (Oakeshott, pp. 47–50).

[65] *Ibid.*, iii, 34 (Oakeshott, pp. 255–60).

[66] *Ibid.*, iii, 36 (Oakeshott, p. 280); iv, 45 (Oakeshott, p. 429).

[67] *Ibid.*, iii, 34 (Oakeshott, p. 264). When Christ breathed on his disciples, this was a sign (p. 429).

certainly, does he communicate with them through a shared non-substantial being. He speaks to them either mediately, through words, which are systems of motions transmitted through space and time to the senses—in a phrase of St Paul's which Hobbes quotes, "faith comes by hearing" [68]—or by supernatural revelations, of which we do not know very much, but may ask whether they are made by affecting the senses of men or, as in the case of Moses, by means altogether beyond our understanding. The men who receive these revelations—of which there have been none since the deaths of the first apostles—cannot communicate to other men the experiences by which they receive them, and it is only by opinion, faith and public authority—all of which involve the transmission of words—that others believe they were made. It is to such verbal, material, social and historical processes that a man who claims a direct "spiritual" revelation must appeal if he wishes others to accept his claim; he cannot invoke the word "spirit" in order to give himself authority and would do better to avoid its use altogether.

The argument has implications far beyond what can be discussed by elucidating the workings of a system of philosophical materialism. If God cannot be known to us through the operation of his spirit upon ours, he can be known to us, and can work upon us, only through his words, and knowledge of these words is historical knowledge; they were given to us in past time, and both their content and the faith we repose in them have been transmitted through complex social processes taking place in time and involving awareness of their earlier stages. It can be said, furthermore, that the God of revelation and faith acts upon men only through history and is present to them only in history. The God of nature and reason is known to all men through processes which involve no history; but if there have been no revelations and no miracles since the lifetimes of the

---

[68] *Ibid.*, iii, 29 (Oakeshott, p. 212); iii, 43 (Oakeshott, p. 387).

Christians who knew Jesus as a man,[69] then the God who acts positively to rule and redeem his peculiar people is not immediately present to us now. We have nothing of him except his word, and these prophetic and revealed utterances were given in past time and are acting upon us only through the modes of their transmission through subsequent time. Hobbes's God—of whom Bramhall asserted, and Hobbes did not deny, that he existed wholly in time [70]—begins to resemble the *deus absconditus* of modern radical theologians and, as has been the case with some of them, his operations are entirely eschatological. He was in direct relationship with us only when he spoke to us directly; that relationship will be restored only when he speaks to us directly again, which will be—the elect know through their faith in his given word—in his second kingdom which is to come.

Hobbes's nominalism, as well as his materialism, is at work here. By nominalism may be understood—if only for elucidation of the present context—a philosophy which asserts that our knowledge is of words, denoting things that are not to be understood in themselves, so that words are at once all-important to knowledge and imperfect in the knowledge they supply. Hobbes added, of course, that philosophy was a knowledge of the relation between ideas, arrived at by reflection on the content of words and logically certain in itself; but his system of prophecy is not a mere extension of his system of philosophy, and can be discussed without committing us to deciding how far the latter is consistent with the nominalist language which he undeniably uses. Now, a consequence of nominalism in this sense is that God is not to be known through understanding of

---

[69] *Ibid.*, iii, 37, contains Hobbes's doctrine concerning miracles, which are extraordinary works of God designed to procure credit to an extraordinary minister speaking directly from him. Cf. *Leviathan*, iii, 32 (Oakeshott, p. 246), marginal note: "Miracles ceasing, prophets cease, and the Scripture supplies their place."

[70] Bramhall, *Works*, IV (Oxford, 1844), 523–24; Hobbes, *English Works*, IV (n. 49, above).

his nature, but rather as will or power and through the revelations or prophecies—themselves words—which he wills to make known to us; and a further consequence is that these words may not be fully intelligible, and that what matters is rather the faith by which we acknowledge them to be God's words than the reason by which we apprehend their meaning.

Hobbes's God is one of whom we can know by reason only that he must exist and must be all-powerful. His nature is incomprehensible, and anything we may say about it is no more than language designed to honour his power.[71] When therefore such a God speaks to us, what is required is that we believe and acknowledge the words to be his rather than that our understanding be enriched by their contents; they can communicate to us, and their function is to communicate, primarily a reminder of his power and an injunction to obey him; and Hobbes indicates that nearly all religious and prophetic teaching is reducible to this form, including the injunction to obey and expect the kingdom of God that was and shall be over his peculiar elect. Faith in God's word is little more than acknowledgment of his power; the Ten Commandments,[72] the Old and New Testaments[73] convey little more than reminders and injunctions of that power; and, conversely, it is by the faith we repose in his word that his civil power over us, the subjection of our wills to his, is constituted. His civil and prophetic kingdom rests on a voluntary submission by the elect; we may refuse him that kingdom, or reject him after acceptance as the Jews did, by refusing or withdrawing the measure of faith necessary to constitute it. His word to the elect, given on peculiar occasions, is that his power is; the elect constitute his civil kingdom by believing that he spoke this word on peculiar occasions, through the mouths of peculiar men, and addressed it peculiarly to them. Such a civil kingdom was, from Moses to Samuel,

---

[71] *Ibid.*, ii, 31, *passim*; iii, 34 (Oakeshott, p. 257).
[72] *Ibid.*, iii, 42 (Oakeshott, pp. 339–40); iv, 45 (Oakeshott, p. 424).
[73] *Ibid.*, iii, 33 (Oakeshott, p. 253).

but it ceased to be; Christ, in whom we repose faith as God himself, promised the elect a restoration of that kingdom, but since it visibly does not exist at present, our faith in Christ must be our acceptance that he was God in person, restoring God's kingdom by uttering his word, but that he spoke the word and restored the kingdom in a future tense, by promising that he would come and rule again. Our relation to God is one of civil obedience. God is not here now in such a way that he can be so obeyed, but we ensure ourselves a place in his future obedience by believing that Christ was sent to promise that his kingdom would come again. God's word is invariably command, and our faith in it invariably acknowledgment of a kingdom; but at present we are acknowledging and constituting a future kingdom by believing the author of words uttered in a future tense. By believing that God, who has the power to rule, will come and rule again, we ensure ourselves a place in his kingdom. The whole structure of faith and salvation has been reduced to a system of statements in and about time. This is the inner meaning of Hobbes's premise that the one article of faith necessary to salvation is "Jesus is the Christ." [74]

This radical temporalization of salvation is the consequence of the sharpness of the distinctions Hobbes draws between the traditional trinity of experience, reason and faith; for this alone is sufficient to indicate that statements concerning God's relation to his peculiar people, since they cannot be universals, must be made not a-historically, but at particular times; and if faith is defined both as that by which statements of this order are accepted, and as that by which salvation is effected, then salvation becomes a matter of acceptance of a historical scheme. The content of the statements is of significance mainly as providing the scheme with a future, expectation of which becomes the principal means of salvation; but we are to be saved less because we have faith that God will save us than because we

---

[74] *Ibid.*, iii, 43 (Oakeshott, pp. 388–93).

acknowledge—and thus actualize—his power to do so. In Hobbes's theology, God's power is known to us far more certainly than his mercy or goodness, and we do not so much receive his grace as help to reconstitute his civil kingdom. This is not merely to temporalize Christian salvation, but to politicize it. Faith in and knowledge of God are mere acknowledgments of power; but that power is committed by words it has used, and we are committed by our faith that those words were spoken, to a scheme of its action in time.

The tactical thrust of Hobbes's argument is now clear. It is directed against new presbyter as well as old priest, and against new saint as well as old scholastic—against anyone, that is, who may claim that the process of salvation authorizes his civil actions or power in the present. The tactic of combining apocalyptic with mortalism served, as it always had, to destroy the claim that the Church possessed the keys to an individual's salvation at the hour of his death; he could be saved or damned only by an action which God was to take in the future, and the Church was merely a community of faithful expectant of that future act. Hobbes furthermore directed his radical nominalism against the claim of the schoolmen that there existed a structure of essences through which the character of the eternal might be apprehended by men in time and its actions upon time rendered accessible to reason; we shall see that he regarded the erection of this philosophy as the chief event in the history of the false church or "kingdom of darkness." But he also turned his nominalism against the saints with a systematic demolition of the claims of the spirit, as opposed to the temporal word, to act as the vehicle of salvation in time. The Joachite Spirituals had in their day sought to historize salvation by declaring that the Age of the Son was being superseded by the Age of the Spirit, in which God would be manifest in all men—a belief not unknown among Hobbes's contemporaries,[75] and, despite its revo-

[75] Gerrard Winstanley, James Nayler.

188   TIME, HISTORY AND ESCHATOLOGY

lutionary possibilities, capable of vesting the hierarchies of
human society with sacerdotal authority. There is one point at
which Hobbes's doctrine seems to echo Joachism: he suggests
that God's Trinity may be known from his having been personated on earth three times—by Moses and the prophets as
the Father, by Jesus as the Son, by the apostles and their successors as the Spirit.[76] But not only does his drastic handling of
the term "spirit" render it more than usually difficult for him
to give a satisfactory account of the Third Person of the Trinity; [77] the apostolic mission is little more than to represent the
Son in his absence, or rather—since we should avoid using the
word "represent" in its properly Hobbesian sense—to transmit
through time the word that the Son came, redeemed us [78] and
promised to return. The Christian present—the time now elaps-
ing between the apostles and the general resurrection—is less a
Kingdom of the Spirit than an era in which God is known to
his peculiar people through the Word.

It follows that the apostles and their successors are not
strictly prophets in either sense of the term. From Moses to
Samuel there were, intermittently but frequently, prophets in
the sense of *prolocutores*—men to whom God spoke and who
relayed his words to the people, and through whom as well as
the high priests God exercised his civil kingdom. The prophets
of the Exile were *predictores*, men who exercised no civil authority, but were inspired (a metaphor, of course) to foretell
the birth of Christ, by whom the kingdom would be restored.
When Christ came, he did not restore the kingdom in this
world but left words constituting his promise to do so in a
future world; and once these words had been spoken by God

---

[76] *Leviathan*, i, 16 (Oakeshott, p. 107); iii, 33 (Oakeshott, p. 253);
iii, 41 (Oakeshott, p. 322); iii, 42 (Oakeshott, pp. 323–24). Bramhall,
Works, IV, 526–27; Hobbes, *English Works*, IV, 306, 310–12, 315–17.

[77] E.g. *Leviathan*, iii, 34 (Oakeshott, p. 265).

[78] For Hobbes's account of the redemption see *Leviathan*, iii, 41 (Oakeshott, pp. 316–17). Christ's three functions, those of a redeemer, a pastor
and a ruler, are to be exercised sequentially in time.

himself in human form, there was no need for special revelations to other men which could merely repeat their substance.
The apostles themselves, as men who had walked with God,
would seem to have possessed extraordinary powers, but these
were not transmissible; [79] and God ceased to perform miracles
as signs of the authenticity of his word. Now that he had spoken words concerning his return, faith became a simple matter
of accepting those words as spoken by him, and this was not to
be done on the authority of other men's having received a special commission to speak for him. The age of prophets ended
with that of miracles. The word was no longer spoken through
chosen men; it had been spoken once and for all—since its
content was essentially a promise concerning a future time—
and faith was now to be reposed in it as spoken, recorded and
transmitted. The business of the faithful was to expect the
return (and very little more). They expected that Christ would
return through believing that he had said he would, and the
church was that organization through which they transmitted
his words, and belief in them, to one another. Faith came by
hearing.

But Christ, unlike Moses, had left no Tables of the Law,
civilly promulgated to the people on a public occasion; since his
kingdom was not of this world, i.e. was not then or now, but to
come, he could not have done so. Hobbes emphasized, what the
scholarship of his age could see well enough, that the New
Testament was the result of a process, through which its various
books had been written, assembled and recognized as canonical,
taking place over time.[80] This brought us back to the problem,
with which he had dealt early in *Leviathan,* of the mechanisms
of belief and faith. It was not possible altogether to separate
belief in the thing spoken from belief in the person speaking—
the God of Jews and Christians was therefore especially *logos,*

---

[79] *Ibid.,* iii, 42 (Oakeshott, p. 351).
[80] *Ibid.,* iii, 33 (Oakeshott, pp. 252–53); iii, 42 (Oakeshott, pp. 338–
39, 342, 345).

a God who had spoken [81]—and in the world of human continuity this raised the question of the human transmitter of words formerly spoken. Hobbes's famous remark that the cause of all religious change was "unpleasing priests" [82] was not a mere secularist's joke; he meant that loss of faith necessarily involved loss of credence in persons authorized to transmit belief-systems through social time. But this sort of credence, he had emphasized, meant our continued good opinion of the transmitters; the line of the ruling high priests had ended with the sons of Eli, that of the ruling prophets with the sons of Samuel, precisely because this opinion had been forfeited. It might seem, then, that faith, necessarily a historical and a social phenomenon, rested on no other foundation than the faithful's continued good opinion of the authorized speakers and transmitters of the word; and if the Christian communities had continued as voluntary congregations of believers, this would in fact have been the case. But a great historical transformation had prevented it. Instead, it had happened, either accidentally or providentially (but Hobbes does not state how), that entire civil societies had become Christian and that civil sovereigns had been converted to Christian belief, and this had brought the entire process of the transmission and determination of faith into the domain of public acts performed by civil authority as constituting public corporations. The task of deciding what words were to be believed, what writings regarded as canonical and what authors and doctors considered authentic and authoritative, now ceased to be performed by unincorporated opinion and fell instead to the civil sovereign; faith itself, always a decision, [83] became a public act, only to be performed by one whose authority rested on neither opinion nor faith.

[81] For Christ as the word made flesh see *Leviathan* iii, 36 (Oakeshott, pp. 274–75).

[82] *Ibid.*, i, 12 (Oakeshott, p. 80).

[83] *Ibid.*, i, 7 (Oakeshott, p. 40): "so the last opinion in search of the truth of past and future is called the JUDGMENT, or *resolute* and *final sentence* of him that *discourseth*."

The sovereign's authority comes into being through the processes of natural civil reason, at least to the extent that reason makes us aware that natural laws exist, have to be obeyed and can be obeyed only in certain conditions, though Hobbes may never have made it plain how men became capable of the acts of fiction and personation by means of which the sovereign was created. At all events, he was not set up by, nor did his authority rest on, either opinion or faith, and we have already seen that there is no chapter of history which we need understand in order to understand this process. If we now ask by what kinds of intelligence the sovereign exercises his functions, that is, of course, a separate question from asking what authorizes him to perform them, and tends to divert our attention from the truth that his *raison d'être* is less to exert intelligence than to perform acts of will; but evidence can no doubt be found to indicate that Hobbes saw the sovereign's intelligence as consisting in civil philosophy rather than civil experience.[84] When we learn therefore that the sovereign, who owes his existence neither to faith nor to history, acquires an unlimited right to take the decisions of which faith consists, in the history which faith constitutes and acknowledges, it is tempting to conclude—something was said of this earlier—that the a-historical has somehow annexed and annulled the historical, and that the sovereign's decisions in matters of faith and observance will be taken with an eye to the needs of civil society and none to the imperatives of Christian belief. But this does not seem to be correct. Reason and nature command—reason indeed tells us that God commands—that we will the existence of civil society and will to give up to the sovereign our power of privately determining our social or public actions; and when the decisions of faith become public actions of public concern, reason commands that they be taken by the sovereign, since to do otherwise would be to erect other authorities, other than civil in their origins, but now

[84] This has been the usual interpretation of his *Dialogue of the Common Laws.*

capable of challenging him on his own grounds, which the nature of civil society commands must not be done. But it does not follow that the sovereign's decisions in matters of faith will be determined solely by considerations of the well-being of society. The situation which we are studying has arisen because civil societies and their sovereigns have become involved in the historical world of faith. Since they are so involved they have brought with them the considerations and the forms of intelligence which dictate their own self-perpetuation; but all that has happened is that the mechanisms of faith, the decisions to accept certain words as spoken by God and certain men as authoritatively transmitting them, have left the sphere of opinion and entered that of public obligation. The objects on which the mind is focused in belief—the words and acts said to be those of God, the writings and teachings of men—have not altered and cannot be the objects of rational knowledge. Hobbes may perhaps be shown to have cared too little about the possibility that the sovereign would take his decisions in the field of faith for reasons of civil prudence, but he cannot be shown to have substituted either prudence or philosophy for belief. The distinction he had formally drawn between these three modes of knowledge remained as sharp as ever.

We can now see that Hobbes's religious heterodoxy [85] is of a fideist-sceptical kind, very characteristic of its age, but not to be confused with the deist rationalism of the next century. He found himself faced by scholastics who invested both God and reality with timeless attributes or essences which could be rationally known, and by saints and enthusiasts who affirmed the existence of a world of spirit, operating within time, but giving the time-dwelling individual opportunity of direct contact with the eternal. Both positions seemed to him philosophically absurd because they intruded unreal entities upon the understanding, and politically dangerous because they intruded unreal

---

[85] Glover (in Brown, *Hobbes Studies*, n. 24, above) has argued the case for a good deal of orthodoxy in his thought as well.

forms of authority upon the government. In reply he asserted a
radically nominalist theology, entailing a God of whom nothing
could be known except his existence and his infinite power, and
rehearsed the great rhythms of the Way of Negation [86] in order
to dismiss the God of Greek and scholastic philosophy in favour
of a purely Hebrew I AM. It may be that such a God, however
much we may stress his simplicity and eternity, is condemned
to exist within time, since if we can know nothing of his attributes we can apprehend him solely through his acts; when
Bramhall reaffirmed the scholastic doctrine of the *nunc-stans*
or eternal now, Hobbes replied that he could attach no meaning whatever to this concept. But in addition there was available, and was just then at the peak of its importance in English
thought, an alternative rhetoric of God, in which affirmations
concerning him were made not as philosophical attributions,
but as historical statements, and he was shown not as exerting a
timeless intelligibility, but as affirming his relation to a peculiar
people, who could be located only in history, with the result
that his acts concerning them must be located there too.
Hobbes embraced the concept of the Judeo-Christian elect with
the effect of confining the known and positive God within
history and still more drastically separating the spheres of reason and faith; a consequence was that when the "mortal god"
of political science entered the domain of faith and history, the
power he exercised did not amount to a power to change or an-
nul it.

If a God of history could be effectively employed in answer
to the God of the schoolmen, he had become a paradigm for
the saints and enthusiasts, who employed revelation and apocalypse as means of asserting their immediate spiritual links with
him. Hobbes employed both materialist and nominalist weapons
to destroy the concept of spirit altogether and leave our contact
with God confined to knowledge of his words, and the content

---

[86] *Leviathan,* ii, 31 (Oakeshott, pp. 237-38).

of those words virtually confined to acts and affirmations cf his power. Experience of God was conceivable only in the past and the future, the two times of the existence of his civil kingdom. To orthodox Christians this seemed, understandably and perhaps rightly, incompatible both with Christian faith as they had received it and with the existence of God as they considered they believed in him. But we cannot conclude that it was Hobbes's intention to affirm God's non-existence. He was simply denying that faith could affirm the existence of any but a God of history, and the more he repeated that denial the more he affirmed that God's reality; he was left with the irreducible concept of a God whose being was power, who was believed to have exerted power in the past and to have promised that he would return to exert power in the future, and with a conceptual system that included belief and historical authorities and from which he made no attempt to eliminate them. Having used apocalyptic against the scholastics, he could not eliminate it by further secularization; for if apocalyptic is a device for drawing God back into time, and if secularization is defined as the affirmation of the supremacy of time, then we need more than secularization to destroy apocalyptic. We need the replacement of belief by something else. Hobbes made no attempt to effect such a substitution. He treated belief with epistemological and brutal literalness, but the result was to leave intact the structure of historical authority towards which belief was directed. That structure included a future and an eschatology, and so Hobbes remained—inescapably but with no sign of a will to escape on his part—the author of two prophetic books.

The scheme of God's words and acts in time constitutes sacred history, but the stages by which the word and belief in it have been transmitted through time constitute what may be termed Christian history. This is a history of social communications and social structures, and the sensitivity to the variety of verbal and linguistic communication, characteristic both of late-Renaissance scholarship and of Hobbes's philosophy, makes him sharply aware of it. The history of belief includes both the processes by which the books of Scripture were written, disseminated, authorized and made canonical, and the processes by which Christian communities became coterminous with civil societies and the mechanisms of belief coterminous with the mechanisms of public law. There is another branch of history to which Hobbes's discoursing of religion commits him, and this is a history of error and perversion. He adopted what was long to remain the standard Protestant position that the greater part of the history of the Church consisted of Papal usurpation and its accompanying superstitions. Any polemicist who desires to reject as illegitimate the greater part of an existing and traditional order faces two simultaneous necessities, one for a necessarily somewhat anti-historical account of how things ought to be, the other for a necessarily non-normative account of how they came to be as they deplorably are; and this should warn us against being naïvely surprised when we find historical and unhistorical thinking together in such a man's works.[87] To Hobbes the Papal Church, and in no small measure the Anglican and Presbyterian Churches, all of which seemed to claim a civil authority apart from that of the civil sovereign, were prime examples of that which ought not to be but nevertheless was; and he set himself to explain the divagations from the norm which alone could account for their existence. As regards the Papal Church, there was available a well-established means of doing so. The apocalyptic history prevalent in most Protestant countries, and developed in England chiefly by John Foxe, confidently explained the rise and predicted the downfall of Roman authority by attributing it to the operations of Antichrist, a malign spiritual being operating through time and involved in the eschatology of the Book of Revelation and the subsequent commentaries thereon. This mode of explanation involved intensive reliance on allegory, typology, numerology and the rest of the

[87] I have tried to state this in greater theoretical completeness in essay 7 in this volume.

apparatus of prophetic interpretation. Hobbes had no liking for such intellectual pursuits; he preferred to take his metaphors singly; and, what was of far greater significance, he had carried his antipathy to talk of "spirit" and "spirits" to the point of denying the Devil and all his angels.[88] Apocalyptic for him was a verbal, not a spiritual mystery: not a matter of unveiling the esoteric history of the universe, but one of discovering what God had said he would do. It could therefore contain no account of what might have been done contrary to God's revealed will for mankind; and Hobbes's account of "the kingdom of darkness," the matter of the fourth book of *Leviathan*, rests formally on his express denial that the Pope is to be in any sense identified with Antichrist. This being is indeed mentioned in Scripture, but as one who shall come claiming falsely to be the returning Christ; and however many and various the false claims of the Pope, he has never asserted anything like that.[89] Exegesis is used to destroy mystical interpretation, and the illegitimate authority of Rome is reduced at one blow from the status of spiritual iniquity to that of intellectual error and deception. But the causes of error can be discovered where the mysteries of iniquity cannot, and the way is now open for Hobbes to study the Papal usurpation as a historical phenomenon. It is plain, however, that the explanations he provides originate in the need to provide alternatives for the mystical interpretations of traditional Protestant apocalyptic. The elaborate witticisms in which the Papacy is presented as a "kingdom of fairies" [90]—of unreal essences and authorities—do no more than erect substitutes for the rhetoric in which it appeared the kingdom of Satan and Antichrist, the Beast and the Whore;

---

[88] *Leviathan*, i, 8 (Oakeshott, pp. 50–51); iii, 34 (Oakeshott, p. 263); iii, 38 (Oakeshott, pp. 298–99); iv, 44 (Oakeshott, p. 397); iv, 45 (Oakeshott, pp. 421–22).

[89] *Ibid.*, iii, 42 (Oakeshott, pp. 364–65). Hobbes's point helps to explain the savagery of the punishments inflicted on James Nayler, who did apparently claim to be Christ.

[90] *Ibid.*, iv, 47 (Oakeshott, pp. 457–58).

and the description of the Church as the "ghost" of the Empire, "sitting crowned upon the grave thereof," is both a superb historical image and a piece of secularized apocalyptic—the new Babylon arisen in place of the old and sitting upon seven hills.

The history of error, which in Hobbes takes the place of Protestant apocalyptic history, records the temporary triumph [91] of priestcraft and Gentilism. The former rests on the false assertion that the Church, in some presently constituted form, is or represents the kingdom of God spoken in the Scriptures; on this are based the claims of presbyters, bishops, and above all the Pope, to exercise authority *jure divino* or *Dei gratia*—that is, to derive it from God without the intervention of the civil sovereign. While Hobbes consistently regards Papalism as the paradigmatic and most dangerous instance of this claim, and spends more time refuting it than any other,[92] he includes in his condemnation Laudian bishops,[93] Geneva presbyters [94] and, though only by implication, self-appointed prophets and visible saints; and out of all these he builds up a history of spiritual usurpation that cannot have been read with any pleasure by the dispossessed bishops of the Interregnum. First presbyters, then bishops and finally the Bishop of Rome asserted in the first Christian centuries claims to exercise authority direct from God; and in recent English history these "knots" upon Christian "liberty" [95] have been untied in the reverse order to that in

---

[91] *Ibid.*, iv, 46 (Oakeshott, p. 435): "old empty bottles of Gentilism, which the doctors of the Roman Church, either by negligence or ambition, have filled up again with the new wine of Christianity, that will not fail in time to break them."

[92] There is no Protestant counterpart to the two long refutations of Bellarmine: *Leviathan*, iii, 42 (Oakeshott, pp. 361–83); iv, 44 (Oakeshott, pp. 405–18).

[93] The references are not specific, but are to bishops claiming *jure divino* authority. E.g., *Leviathan*, iii, 42 (Oakeshott, p. 357). Hobbes's thinking here may be compared with that of Prynne; Lamont, *op. cit.*

[94] See the critique of Beza in *Leviathan*, iv, 44 (Oakeshott, pp. 406–7).

[95] Hobbes is speaking of "Christian liberty" in the severely orthodox Protestant sense.

which they were tied up—the Papal power having been destroyed by Queen Elizabeth, that of the bishops who still claimed authority *jure divino* by the presbyterians, and lastly that of the presbyterians by an agency Hobbes does not identify:

> . . . and so we are reduced to the independency of the primitive Christians, to follow Paul, or Cephas, or Apollos, every man as he liketh best; which, if it be without contention, and without measuring the doctrine of Christ by our affection to the person of his minister (the fault which the apostle reprehended in the Corinthians), is perhaps the best . . . there ought to be no power over the consciences of men but of the Word itself, working faith in every one, not always according to the purpose of them that plant and water, but of God himself that giveth the increase.[96]

Hobbes at this moment would have been content—as one suspects the majority of Englishmen would in 1651—with a system of independent congregations under civil rule, no less than with bishops who claimed only a *jure humano* authority, and there is a relationship between this ecclesiological position and the heightening of interest in apocalyptic observable in *Leviathan*. He would not feel that this progressive undoing of the chains of spiritual usurpation presaged the imminent return of Christ, because he did not hold that even faith enabled one to predict one event from another; prophecy enjoined us to expect, but did not empower us to presage. But he had written at length about apocalyptic because this was a necessary means of destroying the spiritual usurpations that England seemed to be overcoming at the end of the Civil Wars; and he was now in a position to argue that the fallacy of spiritual jurisdiction rested on a confusion of the timeless with time. He could not accuse the ecclesiastics (even the saints) of contending that Christ in

---

[96] *Leviathan*, iv, 47 (Oakeshott, pp. 455–56).

his kingdom had come again; the Papacy was not Antichrist; but he could accuse them of confounding, in his terms, the "kingdom of grace" with the "kingdom of glory," [97] of supposing that because a kingdom was promised for the future they could exercise in the present an authority which could only exist when the kingdom was restored. To make such a claim was to contend that the kingdom existed outside time and that they were its lieutenants within time—to repeat in another form the error of the *nunc-stans*. There was a considerable affinity between this and the error of believing in the doctrine of separated essences, which provides the second theme of the history of the Kingdom of Darkness.

This theme is the history of the importation into the revelation of the true God of the errors of the "Gentiles"—a term to all intents and purposes interchangeable with "Greeks and Romans." [98] The Gentiles, being ignorant of the physical processes of vision, took things which they imagined they saw for gods and disembodied spirits; [99] and later, being equally ignorant of the mental processes of the formation of ideas, took the words which they coined in excessive profusion for the names of real entities. [100] In this way was built up the kingdom of darkness, an empire of "insignificant speech" in which men were ruled by imaginary entities, bodiless and independent of space and time, manipulated by ecclesiastics to provide themselves with spiritual authority: a kingdom of spirits, then, maintained by superstition and scholasticism; a kingdom of ghosts which could only be compared to the kingdom of fairies supposed by folk-imagination to exist as an invisible double of our world, coterminous with it. All this was the result of the importation of Greek thought and mental habit into the revelation made by

---

[97] *Ibid.*, iii, 35 (Oakeshott, p. 270); iii, 42 (Oakeshott, p. 329); iv, 44 (Oakeshott, p. 399); iv, 47 (Oakeshott, p. 451).

[98] See the account of "Gentile" religion in *Leviathan*, i, 12 (Oakeshott, pp. 73–76).

[99] *Ibid.*, i, 12 (Oakeshott, p. 71); iv, 45 (Oakeshott, pp. 418–19).

[100] *Ibid.*, iv, 46 (Oakeshott, pp. 435–37).

God to the Jews and Christians. Hobbes's hatred of the contemporary universities is very largely a hatred of the Greek heritage which he saw them as carrying on, and which he saw as the foundation of the ecclesiastical conspiracy against civil authority and society.

Set in a different context, of course, this feature of Hobbes's thought appears as the "new philosophy" in revolt against the old, a Galilean and Cartesian rejection of Aristotelianism. But in the context in which it occurs, it depicts Hellenic superstition in opposition to, and as encroaching upon, the prophetic religion of Moses and Christ. One would like to know more about Hobbes's ideas of the historic relation between false philosophy, prophecy and true philosophy. Did the fact that God had revealed himself to the Jews and first Christians as acting and speaking words in time help save them from conceiving the erroneous belief in separated essences, which was only communicated to them by "contagion" from the Hellenized Jews of the Diaspora, the Hellenic and Hellenistic converts of the post-Pauline era? [101] Or was the true revelation helpless to resist false philosophy until the true philosophy had been independently arrived at? Hobbes's need to construct a historical dimension to his thought does not carry him to the construction of answers to these questions. It is plain, however, that he most rigorously separated the Hellenic from the Hebraic components of his cultural tradition and went further than any major philosopher since Augustine in rejecting the former and relying upon the latter. In this he must be most sharply separated from the English and French political deists of the next century, the lineage of Toland and Voltaire—classicists to a man, who sought to reduce the God of prophecy to a theorem in

---

[101] *Ibid.* (Oakeshott, pp. 419–20, 423, 430–35). Cf. Frances A. Yates, *Giordano Bruno and the Hermetic Tradition* (London, Chicago and Toronto, 1964), p. 437: "Thus it may be suggested, the true unifying principle of Mersenne's work [*Quaestiones in Genesim*, 1623] is Moses, an orthodox Moses, who, turning his face against magic, ushers in the new science." Hobbes had known Mersenne and his circle in Paris.

philosophy and, as Hobbes would certainly have predicted, put forward predominantly republican theories of politics in so doing. Hobbes was not of the opinion that Christianity was "reasonable" or "not mysterious," though he defined "mystery" with a razor as sharp as Ockham's and a good deal more recklessly wielded. The Christian mystery to him was the belief that God had spoken in history and had said that he would return in time. The God of prophecy and history was the only God of whom Hobbes would speak; the God of faith was the only God compatible with his political system.

[15]

*Some Guidelines into Hobbes's Theology**

As it is well known, Hobbes states in *Concerning Body* that "The subject of philosophy... excludes theology" as well as "the doctrine of angels, and all such things as are thought to be neither bodies nor properties of bodies", because "where there is no generation or property, there is no philosophy."[1]

These utterances induced many scholars to conclude that the references Hobbes made to religion and theology are only opportunistic ones, and that he had no real interest in these matters. This opinion is strengthened by a very long tradition, beginning with Hobbes's very contemporaries: they suspected Hobbes of atheism, because of the anti-ecclesiastical character of his thought, and this opinion has been shared by a large number of modern critics. But the main argument for Hobbes's disinterest in theology is based on this sharp distinction between philosophy and theology. The recent book on Hobbes by Polin[2] – a really good book, however, – is a shining example of this way of considering the question.

Today, however, an increasingly large number of scholars takes Hobbes's concern with theology very seriously: for, it is a matter of fact that Hobbes wrote more than one theological tract, developing a very unorthodox and original doctrine about God and the human soul. This does not imply that he was an apologist of Christian religion, nor that his politics were theological-

---

* This is a paper read at the 'Hobbes Fourth Centenary Conference' (Hertford College, Oxford, 2nd–4th September, 1988). For Hobbes's works, the following abbreviations will be used:

OL: *Opera philosophica quae latine scripsit omnia*, W. Molesworth (ed.) 5 vols., London, 1839–1845, reprint Scientia, Aalen, 1961.

EW: *The English Works*, W. Molesworth (ed.) 11 vols., London, 1839–1845, reprint Scientia, Aalen, 1962.

L: *Leviathan*, C.B. Macpherson (ed.) Penguin Books, Harmondsworth, 1968.

HE: *Historia ecclesiastica carmine elegiaco concinnata*.

CH: *Concerning Heresy, and the Punishment Thereof*.

AB: *An Answer to a Book Published by Dr. Bramhall... Called the 'Catching of the Leviathan'*.

[1] *Elements of Philosophy, The First Section, Concerning Body*, I.i.8, *EW* I, p. 10.

[2] R. Polin, *Hobbes, Dieu et les hommes*, Paris, PUF, 1981 (see esp. 5–72).

ly founded. Certainly, Hobbes's political system cannot be defined as a kind of a 'theology of history', as Kodalle maintains in his book;[3] nevertheless we can reasonably state that Hobbes investigated both into God's nature and God's relations to mankind, paying attention to the advantages he could derive from it, to support and strengthen his ideas and proposals.

In any case, distinguishing theology from philosophy, for Hobbes, does not mean refusing to discuss the object of theology, nor avoiding a theological confrontation: it only means stating that these two discourses do not allow reciprocal interferences, and that the application of demonstrative and philosophically rigorous methods to the object of theology gives rise to misleading and contradictory results.[4]

This is perhaps a too clear and simplified description of Hobbes's methodological intent: it does not reflect the real complexity of Hobbes's attitude to theology. We can admit that in his works Hobbes scattered many suggestions of this project, but he did not observe it constantly: sometimes he gives the impression that he devaluates all kinds of theology, sometimes he seems to allow himself to discuss typically theological matters by a language and an arguing manner that it would be very hard not to define a philosophical one. If on the one hand he declares that he adheres to a fideistic ideal that seems to exclude all rational analysis of the revealed dogma, on the other hand he is one of the first scholars who endeavoured to take the Bible's narration and the Biblical way of thinking into a rational, very critical consideration.

How can we resolve these antinomies? It is clear enough that we cannot require an absolute coherence of a philosopher, not even a rationalistic one, and in any case, often the supposed contradiction depends only on the inadequacy of our parameters. An answer reasonably satisfying can be given, however, by the theological writings I will speak of; for they give us a perspective that mediates between rationalism and fideism, and at the same time clarifies the very complex question about the distinction between philosophy and theology. By these writings, Hobbes rejects and refutes *a particular kind of theology,* while keeping his discourse on a level that, following his own definition, cannot but be said a theological one; in the same way, he criticizes *a particular kind of rhetoric,* while making a strong and reiterated use of rhetorical patterns. If anybody desires a confirmation of this last,

---

[3] K.M. Kodalle, *Thomas Hobbes − Logik der Herrschaft und Vernunft des Friedens,* München, Beck, 1972.

[4] I enlarge on this topic in my essay: *Hobbes and the Problem of God,* in *Perspectives on Thomas Hobbes,* G.A.J. Rogers and A. Ryan (eds.) Oxford, Clarendon Press, 1988, pp. 171−187.

apparent paradox, he has only to look at that famous page of *De cive*, where Hobbes distinguishes between good and bad eloquence, by a discourse literally framed by the rhetorical figure of antithesis.[5]

The structural analogy we can point out in the manner Hobbes treats two cultural fields so dissimilar as theology and rhetoric, is implicitly confirmed by another consideration: in both cases, Hobbes's criticism of the bad use of these disciplines is strictly connected with a hard polemic against the classical heritage affecting the culture of the modern age.

As it is well known, Hobbes holds a great part of the classical culture responsible for handing an extremely effective tool of social and political subversion to the demagogues of his time. Hobbes's polemic is aimed at the demagogic use of rhetoric to make people feel strong emotions, but it also strikes at those Greek historians and philosophers who praised democratic ideals, and at those Roman historians who cultivated republican ideals in the imperial age: for they branded any absolute sovereign as a tyrant, and spoke emphatically in praise of tyrannicide.

That does not mean that Hobbes should feel himself not involved in this classical culture, some aspects of which he criticized. Besides the fact that he used rhetoric in his philosophical discourse, we cannot forget that he was deeply influenced by Aristotelian *Rhetorics*, as it clearly emerges from some versions of his theory of passions. Of Aristotelian *Rhetorics* Hobbes made also a concise translation, and in any case he translated *Iliad* and *Odyssey* in his eighties. He then was a humanist, though of a particular kind, and an heir of the great Erasmian tradition: but he strongly opposed himself to the political implications developing from an excessive admiration for the classical way of life: a very dangerous attitude, shared by the uneasier highbrows of his time.

In Hobbes's eyes, however, ancient thought has a subtler and more indirect responsibility for the evils troubling the modern age: it gave rise to theology. Hobbes regards theology as being the hybrid and disastrous result of an illicit union between the tradition of Hebraic and early-Christian religion, and Greek philosophy. As Hobbes points out in *Leviathan*, this process started when Hellenism began to affect the Hebraic culture, but it grew in Patristics, and continued, with more and more devastating effects, in Scholastics.

Following in that his master Francis Bacon, Hobbes expresses in *Leviathan* his dislike for Greek philosophy: he places Plato himself, while avow-

---

[5] Cfr. *Philosophical Rudiments Concerning Government and Society*, xii.12. Critical Ed. by H. Warrender (*De Cive — The English Version*, Oxford, Clarendon Press, 1983), p. 154.

ing that he is "the best philosopher of the Greeks"[6], alongside Aristotle, Cicero, Seneca and Plutarch among 'Sophists' and "maintainers of the Greek and Roman anarchies".[7] In any case, going beyond this unfavourable opinion, grounded on political interests, Hobbes condemns the whole of ancient philosophy without appeal: ancient physics "was rather a dream than science", the moral philosophy of the Greeks was only "a description of their own passions", their logic "nothing else but captions of words, and inventions how to puzzle such as should go about to pose them"[8]. As for Aristotle, Hobbes goes so far as to attribute to him other people's faults, like the paternity of the theory of separated substances. Hobbes could not be unaware that this theory was Platonic, much more than Aristotelian: why did he charge Aristotle with it? Probably because he aimed, more than at the historical person, at the symbolic object of his generalized polemic against Greek spiritualism and its following scholastic issues.

As it is well known, a vivid example of Hobbes's polemical genius can be drawn from the fourth part of *Leviathan*, devoted to the 'Kingdome of Darknesse', where he discusses some fundamental features of Aristotelian and Scholastic metaphysics, putting them in connection with the general ideology of the Catholic church. In Hobbes's view, Hebraic culture, such as it expresses itself in the Old Testament, had a substantially earthly and materialistic nature, and New Testament itself does not testify to an explicitly spiritualistic attitude. Greek religion had transmitted to the Hebraic one the notion of a 'demon', but this notion had still a corporeal connotation, albeit of a very subtle matter. Troubles began – Hobbes says – when, within the late Hebrew and early Christian thought, doctrines inspired to Aristotelianism acquired more and more strength.

We have already outlined the relative strangeness of Hobbes's charge against Aristotle: this charge takes form mainly in *Leviathan*, where the Greek thinker is held responsible for having formulated the theory regarding the substance as an essence. We will give further details of this discussion when speaking of Hobbes's theological tracts: here suffice it to say that for Hobbes equating essence and substance is a self-contradictory operation, because the essence is an intellectual abstraction, while the substance is a real, and therefore corporeal, being. Nevertheless, according to Hobbes, this theory made people believe that something *real* exists, that cannot be placed anywhere, something that is only contained in the intellect, or that is similar to things that are contained in the intellect. That is to say that people would

---

[6] *L*, 46, p. 686.

[7] *Philosophical Rudiments* cit., xii. 3, p. 148.

[8] *L*, 46, p. 686.

be brought to believe that real but not corporeal things, like essences or substantial forms, exist, and therefore things exist of a purely spiritual character, such as to upset even the original notion of spirit, which had been worked out both by archaic Greek thought and by Hebraic thought.

Thus a wholly 'spiritual' nature is attributed to man's soul, which is conceived as a substantial form, albeit separable from the body; of a similar quality are the natures of demons and of angels, that become themselves something like substantial forms, with the only difference that they have no body on which to be inherent. In this way the grafting of Aristotelian philosophy on the Hebraic-Christian religious tradition generates a belief in the existence of a large number of beings that, although immaterial, people the world, scaring men and nations: an extremely effective ideological tool, of which the Church makes use, in order to keep and expand its power at the expense of the civil sovereign.

Given these premises, the whole display of doctrines and ceremonies in the Church takes on an ideological hue: for it is described by Hobbes in terms of an ideology meant to exert the Church's power on consciences. Such theological doctrines as those regarding the existence and description of Purgatory and Hell, when they undergo Hobbes's merciless examination and critical analysis, show their instrumental nature and their subordination to a design of the subjection of nations and the humiliation of princes. So do ecclesiastical regulations and sanctions such as priests celibacy and excommunication. The same holds true for liturgical forms of worship, such as exorcisms and the invoking of saints, which Hobbes considers as a decay of primitive Christian piety due to a contamination from Greek demonology and philosophy, which had already partially spread into late-Hebraic culture.

Thus a theology spoiled in its premises by its links with a bad philosophy enters the service of an ideology obnoxious to established order. How can this be mended? In the first place, it would be necessary to free the genuine matter of faith of the Hebraic-Christian religious tradition from the Greek spiritualistic superstructure which is foreign to it; which will imply a careful philological and historical analysis of the causes and procedures of this contamination. In this way, not only the careful philological analyses of the Biblical text to be found in *Leviathan* become clear, but also the fact that in *Historia ecclesiastica* the history of Christianity is meditated anew. So a theoretical support of the whole procedure is insured by a repeated stressing of a voluntaristic notion of God and by a fideistic notion of religion that in their turn easily fit into the general 'artificialistic' structuring of the relationship between man and world which constitutes the peculiar character of Hobbes's thought, to be found as well in his voluntaristic and conventionalistic conception of law and science.

But Hobbes goes beyond this. For the way he deals with this fideism and voluntarism, full as they are of Pauline features and Lutheran and Calvinistic echoes, holds already a theological form, so as theological is the tracing of the genuine meaning of Biblical terms, as well as the interpretation in an earthly meaning of Old Testament or Gospel narrations. Moreover, if we adopt Hobbes's polemical definition of the term 'theology' as a philosophical restatement of a revealed item, then his discussion of the figure of Christ, of his relationship with the Father, of God's corporeal nature, is a theological one. In discussing these issues it is clear that Hobbes is trying to reconsider the object of faith within a non-spiritualistic philosophical attitude, but rather a decidedly materialistic one; an attitude which is based on the assumption that what is real is corporeal and that nothing real exists unless it be a body. In this way, Greek spiritualism ends up by being substituted by an opposite trend, and exactly when a yoking of religion and Aristotelianism is defined as unacceptable, an integration of Christian dogma and philosophy is nevertheless enacted, except that this is now Hobbes's materialistic rationalism. The fact that Hobbes would call 'theology' only the one influenced by bad philosophy is after all not so meaningful: what should be stressed at this point is the impact of such a strictly and absolutely rationalistic approach on religious tradition, which will imply a heterodox and perturbing outcome.

Nevertheless, Hobbes's suggestion of such a personal and subversive theology does not estrange him from the religious outlook of his own time. On the one hand, in the restless melting pot of Protestantism, forever kept on the boil by the temptation of individual interpretation, even quite heterodox stands find their place, and this is even more true of England in the Interregnum. On the other hand, in spite of the obvious peculiarity of such an approach, Hobbes would end by restating, paradoxically, his inability to cut the links with contemporary religious tradition, while at the same time trying to free it of century-old ambiguities and inconsistencies by a rigidly discriminating analytical attitude. In other words, he was trying to save Christianity from absurdity, although the resulting doctrine could meet but little attention on the part of those whose religious attitude was inspired by the doctrines suggested by the vast number of reformed churches and sects.

As for forms of worship, Hobbes appears to stand by the most advanced Puritan standards, even to a defence of iconoclasty, which may appear as a contradiction in a man who was Church of England, at least by political choice. It is undeniable that his doctrine of God's corporeity takes him very far from an Anglican outlook, as well as his maintaining the fact that the human soul dies with the body, although envisaging the resurrection of both on Doomsday. But on this last point, thanks to the deeply torn doctrinal

92

situation of English Protestantism, he could find himself on common ground with an unknown fanatic like Richard Overton, as well as with Thomas Browne and John Milton.[9] On the contrary, it was easy for him to go directly back to the great Protestant thinkers when he was fighting for a definite denial of human freewill and when he was stressing the incomprehensible and unforeseeable divine will.

To make things more intricate, the difficulty could be thrown in, of conciliating a God deduced in a purely natural and rational way (who is absolutely unknowable by the rules of a negative theology that only allows the attribute of existence to be spoken) and the personal and revealed God of Biblical tradition, all too human and knowable in his utterances, emotions and decisions. But, apart from the fact that medieval thought, from Augustine onwards, already had to a large extent defined an albeit unsafe compatibility between the 'God of the philosophers' and the 'God of the Bible', it must be said that Hobbes does not attempt to mediate between the two images; he merely records the historical fact of the pact with Abraham, so that the undefined God of reason shall from that time be called 'the God of Abraham', and later 'of Isaac' and 'of Jacob'.[10] The determination of this infinite God is not explained, because it is not rationally explicable (in this sense, Biblical God is as inexplicable as the other one in his reasons and resolutions): this determination is simply *a fact* that enacts the breaking of history into an area up to this point dominated by natural reason. Of history, that cannot be reduced to science, but that keeps all its links with prudence.

In any case, in Hobbes's thought, the two versions of God hold two specific and sufficiently peculiar functions: for the God that is the outcome of a purely rational process is not really a personal God, but the final – or first – cause of the necessary link of natural events. From the materialistic point of view from which Hobbes moves, this universal determination covers down to the slightest details of human actions: in this way God sustains the necessary determination governing man's will and cuts out any form of free will. But in a wider sense, God, the efficient cause of any motion, stands as a warrant to the mechanical working of a material universe and of its rational comprehensibleness: it stands warrant, finally, to the metaphysical

---

[9] Cfr. Richard Overton's *Mans Mortallitie*, only published with the author's initials and a false placename (Amsterdam) in 1643. This pamphlet had further editions up to 1675. As for Thomas Browne, see *The Religio Medici and Other Writings*, Everyman's Library 92, London and New York, Dent and Dutton, 1962, p. 8. For Milton, see *De doctrina christiana*, I, xiii. (In *The Works of John Milton*, New York, Columbia U.P., vol. XV, 1933, pp. 218–251). For a general view of the problem, see: N.T. Burns, *Christian Mortalism From Tyndale to Milton*, Cambridge Mass., Harvard University Press, 1972.
[10] *Philosophical Rudiments* cit., XVI.viii, p. 204.

grounding of a mechanistic materialistic interpretation of nature, which is typical of Hobbes's philosophy.

On the other hand, the personal and revealed God of Scripture, by the expression of his will, sanctions the foundation of the law governing human relations, and stands therefore warrant to the unlawfulness of any social behaviour protected and regulated by the State, that is, by the civil sovereign. If, therefore, the philosophical God stands warrant to the consistency and plausibility of physics, the Biblical God sanctions one of the general reasons for obligation to obedience (the other one being of an empirical-factual sort) and stands therefore warrant to the solid ground on which Hobbes's political philosophy rests. Was Hobbes sincere in his revaluation of revealed religion, albeit within the limit of the severe earthly reduction discussed above? It would be hard to prove it, and not very relevant either, for the purposes of an analysis of a philosophy; what matters is rather the evaluation of the significance of a theological fact in Hobbes's thought taken altogether, of the consistency and usefulness of such a grafting; finally, of the ideological and doctrinal reasons, as well as of the theoretical consequences connected with such a grafting.

* * *

Hobbes wrote rather extensively on theology: apart from the so-called *Anti-White*[11] (that would be rather defined as a book on the impossibility of theology), some chapters in *Elements of Law* and *De cive* and most of all the third and fourth parts of *Leviathan*, one should take into account his writings on the issue of free will, the short treatise *Of Liberty and Necessity* and the *Questions Concerning Liberty, Necessity and Chance,* addressed to John Bramhall, the *Historia ecclesiastica,* the little, but very important treatise *Concerning Heresy,* the Answer to Bramhall's *Catching of Leviathan,* the *Appendix* to the Latin edition of *Leviathan*; not to speak of the short discussion on heresy from a political-juridical point of view contained in the *Dialogue* about the *Common Laws.* Obviously enough, all these works deserve attention, but I think that three or four of them in particular, such as the *Historia ecclesiastica,* the tract on *Heresy,* the *Answer* and the *Appendix,* are the most meaningful for the purpose of going deeper into the matter now in hand, leaving the Biblical interpretation aside, which deserves a specific kind of consideration. The works here considered are rather late in Hobbes's

---

[11] *Anti-White* refers to the manuscript published by J. Jacquot and H.W. Jones under the title *Critique du De mundo de Thomas White* (Paris, Vrin, 1973), in the third part of which is contained a lengthy discussion of the theoretical impossibility of theology.

career (they were written between 1659 and 1671, the approximate term of the *Historia ecclesiastica's* drawing up), and have the common characteristic of developing the natural sequel to the theories put forward in *Leviathan*. They are often more radical than Hobbes's previous writings: for example, not one of Hobbes's works ever reached polemical violence to be found in vast parts of the *Historia ecclesiastica*,[12] a verse pamphlet, whose purpose was to expose the growth of papal power by means of a history of the expansion of the power of the Church in its different aspects up to the beginnings of Reformation.

The poem is thus structured according to a scheme that follows chronologically, albeit by wide strokes of the brush, the history of the development of the Church, beginning with the Pauline spreading of the Christian word; the first 468 lines, nevertheless, make up a sort of introduction which outlines in general terms the relationship between an astronomical competence, its arrangement into an astrological doctrine and the establishment of

---

[12] *Historia ecclesiastica* has hardly been taken into consideration by Hobbes's scholars. It is almost never mentioned even in the most recent studies; moreover, little is known of its origin, of the exact date of composition, of Hobbes's purpose in writing it. Almost everything we know about it comes from Aubrey, whom we shall be quoting from the edition of the *Life of Thomas Hobbes of Malmesburie* (in *Letters Written by Eminent Persons in the Seventeenth and Eighteenth Centuries*, London and Oxford, Longman *et al.*, Munday and Slatter, 1813, second part of the second volume, pp. 593–637) which Molesworth himself made use of in his brief introduction (*OL*, V, p. 342). Aubrey says that in 1659 Hobbes was living in London, "where he wrote, among other things, a poem in Latin hexameter and pentameter, on the Encroachment of the Clergie (both Roman and Reformed) on the Civil Power. I remember I saw there five hundred verses and more." (*Letters* cit., p. 612). Five hundred out of the total 2242 lines had therefore already been written in 1659. Molesworth also quotes a passage from the prose *Life* in which Hobbes says he wrote both *Behemoth* and *HE* (although for the latter he is obviously talking about the completion of the work) 'circa annum aetatis suae octogesimum', and that his poem was numbered about 2000 lines (*Vita*, in *OL*, I, p.xx). Later a record was found in the Chatsworth House Archives, of a payment by Hobbes to James Weldon, Hobbes's usual copyist, who had received the sum of one pound for a transcription of *HE* (Cfr. M.M. Reik, *The Golden Lands of Thomas Hobbes*, Detroit, Wayne State University Press, 1977, p. 225 n. 3). Since the record is dated 'September–October 1671', we can conclude that the poem had been definitely finished by that date, and that therefore, if in 1659 it had reached about 500 lines, the further 1700 had been added in the decade between 1660 and 1670. The work will remain unpublished in Hobbes's lifetime because of its blasphemous and violent character. Possibly, when the work was not yet finished, Hobbes went so far as to think of burning his own copy, again according to Aubrey's *Life*, for fear of ecclesiastical persecution (*Letters* cit., pp. 612–613). In this sense Hobbes likens *HE* to *Behemoth*, in his prose *Life*, just because 'non sinebant tempora ut publicarentur' (*Vita* cit., p. xx.)

the power of priesthood in the most ancient civilizations, such as the Ethiopian and Egyptian. This introduction ends with a plea against Greek thought, itself deemed guilty of undermining the authority of the State by ideological sophisms, foreshadowing the attacks that Hobbes will launch in the pages immediately following.

The rest of the work can be summarized as a history of the creeping of Greek philosophy into the sound tissues of original Christianity, which ends by taking up its theoretical divisions generating even more pernicious dogmatical divisions, resulting in the so-called heresies. The poem becomes therefore also a history of councils (the Nicene one in particular) and of the way in which temporal authorities, beginning with Constantine, would open up wider and wider gaps to the interference of the ecclesiastical power, the enacting of whose designs was made easier by outside issues, such as the decline of Roman Empire and barbaric pressure and the appearance of the danger of Islam; as well as by a thoughtful cultural policy, such as for instance the Church's care in setting up university teaching.

Within this scheme, the usual Hobbesian tenets of a voluntaristic-Reformed origin are set, the ones on God's unknowableness and ineffability and on necessity of only referring to Scripture (therefore not to tradition), in order to acquire a genuine Christian attitude; this in open contrast to the pretension of theologians of knowing "what, when and why, and in which way God wills and acts".[13] The responsibility obviously belongs to 'false philosophers', those 'good-for-nothing' who infiltrated into Christ's fold because 'food was there' and then mounted to the highest degrees of hierarchy because they were good "at throwing sour confutations" and at "twisting an uncertain dilemma at their pleasure", while 'saintly and pious' men, stunned and frightened off by such self-assured dialectics, out of candor dare not step in.[14]

Out of the encroaching presence of philosophers among the Fathers, Hobbes, as I mentioned above, makes heresies stem, in the sense that the grafting of theories foreign to the original doctrinal wealth of Christianity, produces those contrasts which Councils are called to bring to an end, by condemning one of the two contending issues: thus, "conquering meant being a Catholic, being conquered, a heretic".[15] This line contains a completely lay vision of Christianity, and a striking one for its modern broad-mindedness, which wholly upsets the terms of the matter from a traditional Catholic notion, where a deployment of theological thought and dogmatics

[13] *HE*, 1.22, *OL*, V, p. 349.
[14] *HE*, 11.470 and ff., *OL*, V, p. 362.
[15] *HE*, 1.514, *OL*, V, p. 363.

96

brings out a larger and larger emerging of truth, against which the error of the other positions in its mistakenness stands out.

It is a sort of notion, this one of heresy, into which Hobbes will be going deeper in other works too, fearing to be prosecuted himself for this crime.[16] In a wider speculative panorama, he will also go back to analyzing the Nicene argument about Christ's nature, in relationship to the Father's. Hobbes is deeply interested in the Nicene Council, not only because of its doctrinal aspects (and from this point of view Hobbes shows a certain amount of understanding towards Arianism), but also for the significance of Constantine's resolution to set up a Council, to whose conclusions he could not nevertheless avoid submitting himself. The Fathers wrapped the Revelation "in thick darkness", in order to "govern Scripture at their pleasure", that Scripture which in its turn "would govern kings";[17] this is how the foundations of spiritual supremacy over temporal power were first set, so that at the end "both Leviathan and Behemoth had had a ring set into their nose: both king and people became slaves."[18]

But this is not all. *Historia ecclesiastica* does not simply sketch out the growth of ecclesiastical power, but it also goes into a myriad of political, exegetical and strictly religious themes, endlessly pouring out moral anger and showing a feeling for irony and grotesque possibly unexpected in an author like Hobbes, whose readers were rather used to the unforgiving logic of his rational analysis. One could view his most delicate and penetrating psychological observations on the genuine Fathers, on the pious saintly men with a simple heart, who "nothing else had learnt,/ but that Christ had died on the Cross for them", but who "dared not contradict the learned", because they "feared, in worrying about words,/ some learned men might say they were ignorant".[19] A simplemindedness on whose side the most learned Hobbes set himself, satisfied himself to proclaim Christ's divinity taken from "sola Scriptura", against all foggy and devious subtleties, all the verbal vainglory of Scholastic theologians.

The whole poem, in any case, is spread over with a humanistically religious attitude, which bridges Hobbes's anti-intellectual attitude derived from his aversion to Scholasticism, and his aspiration to a conduct of life regulating relations among men in the sign of humility and meekness. Something which had already been coming through, among the tight trammels of his naturalistic analysis of man, in his inability to hide his hostility to the overbearing and arrogant behaviour of the 'vainglorious' towards the 'moderate'.

[16] For example, in *Concerning Heresy.*
[17] *HE*, 11.771 and ff., *OL*, V, p. 370.
[18] *HE*, 11.1229–30, *OL*, V, p. 381.
[19] *HE*, 11.707 and ff., *OL*, V, p. 368.

In this sense, the sketching of a Christian ideal of life, set forth by Hobbes in the final lines of this poem, appears – as P.J. Johnson has outlined very acutely – to be particularly meaningful, in the way in which he presents, in Erasmian accents, the principles of what could become a lay moral of brotherhood, by suggesting that they altogether represent the practical virtues required by Christ of his followers, in order to give them happiness: the Christian here ideally painted is meek and far from wrathful, is not ambitious and does not therefore aspire to supremacy upon other men; he is moderate and tries to live justly, can be critical of his deficiencies, and is vastly understanding to others, and 'bears ungrudgingly his own evils'.[20] On the background of a stoical-sounding declaration both in faith and in habits, Job's Biblical figure stands out once again, a figure forever attracting the attention of Hobbes's religious and political thought.

Thus *Historia ecclesiastica* clarifies the meaning of Hobbes's criticism of theology as being influenced by Greek philosophy, by means of a vast historical design that provides a practical background to a theoretical analysis of the matter. In other writings, Hobbes will go deeper into his confutation of the spiritualistic character of Christian religion and theology, analyzing what appears to him to be a great theoretical mistake and misunderstanding of Greek and Latin Fathers. Naturally, Hobbes's discussion of the question is spoiled – so to say – at its beginnings by a previous materialistic attitude that is justified only in assertive terms: as it is well known, Hobbesian materialism has very questionable foundations, in *Anti-White* as in *Leviathan;* and also in the *Objections* to the Cartesian *Meditations* Hobbes gives us the impression that he simply sets his materialistic conception against Cartesian dualism, without either really motivating his position, or demolishing the other one.[21]

The only real foundation of Hobbes's materialism – but not a real denial of spiritualism – is to be found in *Concerning Body,* where he comes to a sort of an onthological proof of the existence of the body: curiously enough, it is a question of a subjective deduction of it from the idea of space we have in our mind,[22] in a Cartesian-tasting way, except for the non-innatistic feature of Hobbes's gnoseology. But this is another problem, a very complex one, not included in my present aims. I only want to underline the fact that Hobbes, in his discussion of spiritualism in *Leviathan,* gives no reasons, but only

---

[20] *HE*, 11.2229–42, *OL*, V, p. 408. On these lines P.J. Johnson appropriately drew attention, in the conclusion to his essay *Hobbes's Anglican Doctrine of Salvation*, in *Thomas Hobbes in His Time*, R. Ross, H.W. Schneider and T. Waldman (eds.) Minneapolis, University of Minnesota Press, 1974, pp. 102–125.

[21] See *Objectiones ad Cartesii Meditationes*, Ob. II, *OL*, V, pp. 252–253.

[22] Cfr. *Elementorum philosophiae sectio prima De corpore*, II.i, *OL*, I, pp. 90–91.

definitions, and in the same way he behaves in that short treatise he wrote *Concerning Heresy,* where the demonstration of the thesis that God is corporeal is advanced in the same assertive terms which Hobbes employs in *Leviathan* to state that body is the only substance one can talk of.[23]

Hobbes's argument in favour of God's corporeity is simple and plain, consistent with the principles of Hobbes's materialistic metaphysics: if God exists, he is a substance, that is to say a real being, independent of any other thing. But the peculiar feature of real beings, of substances, is that they are placed in space, that they are extended: and whatever is extended is a body. All real things, being 'somewhere', are corporeal, either visible or invisible, either finite or infinite, and God does not escape this connotation.[24] This conclusion risks involving Hobbes in a pantheistic perspective, which he would still deny in *Leviathan*: in any case, Hobbes does not obviously find many Christian authorities he could cite in support of his doctrine, save for Tertullian, to whom he refers on many occasions; but he supports his thesis passionately and pointedly, always referring it to sacred texts, and comparing it with more traditional theological interpretations.

It is clear that the heresy of which Hobbes feared to be accused mainly consists in this doctrine of God's corporeity; a doctrine that could already be evinced from his statements about the inconsistency of the concept of 'spirit' as 'incorporeal substance' in *Leviathan*. But in that regard he was always very cautious, and reticent: in fact, he never published *Concerning Heresy* in his life, and the same can be said of the *Answer* to Bramhall, where the same doctrine is expounded. Only in 1668 he decided to make his thought clear, in the *Appendix* to the Latin *Leviathan*.[25] In any case, in *Concerning Heresy* Hobbes endeavours to prevent any possible charge by theologians, aiming at demonstrating that the traditional theory of God's incorporeity is the result of a terminological confusion.

In fact, the matter is much more complex than Hobbes seems to show, in his already intricate discussion: in his simplified scheme, Greek and Latin philosophers were aware that 'substance' is an individual being, that is to say, a body, while 'essence' is a general abstraction, a mere product of the intellect. Once more, Aristotle is the villain of the piece, although the direct responsibility of the misunderstanding was ascribed to the aristotelically minded Fathers: in Hobbes's opinion, some Greek Fathers equated in the word 'οὐσία' the concept of 'essence' with the concept of 'substance', and

---

[23] *L*, 34, pp. 428–429; 46, p. 689.

[24] Cfr. *CH, EW*, IV, p. 393.

[25] 'Affirmat quidem Deum esse corpus' (Hobbes is here speaking of himself): *Leviathan, Appendix, OL*, III, p. 561.

this mistake was strengthened by the Latin Fathers, who translated the word
'οὐσία' by 'substantia', but referring to the meaning of 'essence'.[26]

In any case, Hobbes, by a bit crudely superimposing his own philosophy's
materialistic grid to this argument, maintains – as I was remarking above –
that God is a real, concrete being and, as such, a body: an 'ὑποκείμηνον' or
'ὑπόστασιζ', (in the sense of 'subject', individual reality) not an 'οὐσία',
that is an abstract essence. Hobbes also maintains that when, in sacred or
synodal texts, God is defined by means of an abstract term (such as when he
is called 'wisdom', or 'deity') this is a metonymical use of the term, and
therefore a simply rhetorical one, not because he should be thought of as
having an incorporeal nature, such as the one of abstractions, that are
nothing real.[27]

In the *Answer* to Bramhall, the doctrine of God's corporeity is stated in a
definite way and supported by an argument similar to, but also more articulate than the one to be found in the tract on heresy, with some elements
smacking of Pantheism, such as when he says that God "is either the whole
universe, or part of it".[28] In this context, God is defined as a "most pure,
simple, invisible spirit corporeal", who pervades the universe following a
hypothesis Hobbes puts forward very cautiously in the *Answer* – like mineral water, when mixed to river water, pervades it, producing a new, milk-
seeming, composite. In the same way, God "who is an infinitely fine Spirit,
and withal intelligent, can make and change all species and kinds of body as
he pleaseth",[29] by a way that reminds us of stoical solutions, but that it would
be very hard not to refer also to Henry More's 'Spirit of Nature'.

It is true that there is a difference between Hobbes's pervading God and
More's Spirit of Nature: the first is God, the second is a subordinated, plastic
power of God; Hobbes's God is 'intelligent', while More's Spirit works as
an instrument, 'devoid of all sense and perception'.[30] But, in any case, both
these solutions satisfy the requirement of allowing God to have a dimensioned relationship to the world. The real difference, rather, lies elsewhere:
despite his pureness and simpleness, and unlike More's, Hobbes's God is not
an incorporeal, though dimensioned, spirit: he cannot *penetrate* bodies,
because he is a body, like all other bodies: like mineral water, he cannot be
really 'every where', in the sense that "every part of the one... be in every

---

[26] Besides the well known pages of ch. 46 of *Leviathan*, see *CH, EW*, IV pp. 394–5; *AB,
EW*, IV, pp. 302–312; *Appendix* to *Leviathan* cit., pp. 528–533.

[27] Cfr. *CH, OL*, IV, p. 395.

[28] *AB, OL*, IV p. 349.

[29] *AB, EW*, IV, p. 310.

[30] Henry More, *The Immortality of the Soul*, A. Jacob (ed.) Dordrecht/Boston/Lancaster,
M. Nijhoff, 1987, p. 18.

part of the other",[31] he mixes himself with all the smallest parts of the universe, thus producing all the modifications and changes in the matter, that give rise to its differentiation. In this sense, God may be 'a part' of the universe: if he is conceived as the universe itself, that seems to move Hobbes over, from a flavour of Cantabrigian mechanistic mysticism, to a more structured atmosphere, reminiscent of Spinoza.

The *Answer* also deals with other hot issues, such as the doctrine of the soul's dying with the body and of their joint resurrection on Doomsday, as well as a denial of eternal torment for the damned, who would undergo a second and final death after Judgement, as Hobbes had already advanced in *Leviathan*. About this assumption, it should be remarked that in the *Answer* Hobbes makes its outline somewhat vaguer, although its substance stands:[32] in the same way, he slightly changes his view of Trinity as expounded in *Leviathan* in terms of juridical representation, as if God in his relation with man was represented by the three 'persons' of Moses, Christ and the Apostles.[33] Here, as well as in the *Appendix,* which is coeval, Moses is taken out of the triad, in which God the Father directly puts himself.

It can be said that this is only a matter of shades of the same hue; which is true, except that the shades manifest the real and lively interest Hobbes had in this sort of matter. In fact, he was brought to change ever so slightly his doctrines, as he says in the *Answer,* after discussing them with theologians friends of his:[34] what he did not change and rather publicly stated in *Appendix* is the doctrine of God's corporeity, which holds the same – if not a larger – degree of heterodoxy and dangerousness.

One can surmise that in 1668 Hobbes would have no more reason to fear a violent reaction from the Church, or that in any case he would feel strong enough to face it. But, in this case, the changes to his doctrine of the second death of the damned and of the juridical interpretation of the mystery of Trinity would not be the product of a prudential retreat, but rather of a real rethinking that brings down the radical quality of some of the *Leviathan*'s tenets.

[31] *AB, EW,* IV, p. 310.

[32] What is meant here is, that in *Leviathan* Hobbes had gone so far as to suggest that the damned would die forever after Judgement and that the eternity of torments could be understood as regarding the species rather than single beings, who would have lived exactly the way we live today on earth (*L*, 44, pp. 647–648); in *AB*, on the contrary, he increases the hypothetical quality of the latter assumption, without denying the 'second death' of the wicked. See *AB, OL,* IV, pp. 350–356.

[33] Cfr. *L*, 16, p. 220; 42, pp. 522–523.

[34] In *AB* Hobbes refers explicitly to Dr. John Cosin, bishop of Durham, whom he had met during his exile in Paris. Cosin was, so to say, a right-wing Anglican. See *AB, EW,* IV, p. 317. Hobbes also refers to Dr. Joseph Mede as one of his sources, cfr. *AB, EW,* IV, p. 327.

On the other hand, an intellectual only superficially interested in theological problems would not have brought all this energy and this amount of learning to bear on such a binding subject – from whichever point considered – as God's corporeity: he goes so far as to state – by deftly interpreting one of Athanasius utterances – that God was in Christ "in such manner as body is in body";[35] a phrase that is not casually dropped, but that rather aims at transposing the controversial issue of the relation between Father and Son into a materialistic key. In this sense, the Father would have generated a Son, Christ, who has God within himself, and is therefore God in so much that there would be, between Father and Son, a consubstantiality to be understood in corporeal terms. A rather crude statement, which can appear a simplistic one, if it is referred to all the difficulties connected with the numberless discussions on Christ's double nature, human and divine, sent down by tradition. Nevertheless, a statement showing lively and direct participation on Hobbes's part in the debate on this issue, which confirms Hobbes's interest in transposing into a materialistic key (and therefore into *his own* philosophical terms) a number of issues and problems that Patristical and Scholastical theology had dealt with in an 'Aristotelian' key.

* * *

Although the matter in hand be so complex and intricate, and keeping in mind the point at which studies on it have arrived, I ·feel a number of conclusive remarks can be made. To begin with, that this body of writing qualifies the idea that Hobbes had a more participatory attitude to theology than was admitted in the past; after all, the reaction itself of his contemporaries shows how seriously involved he was in this sort of issues. On the other hand, if one keeps in mind the fact that all the writings referred to are late ones, and if one compares them with Hobbes's early works (for example *Elements, De cive* and *Anti-White*), one is brought to believe that his theological interest has been growing richer over the years, along with, and after, the growth of his interest in the Bible. Hobbes moved from a position in which he would simply make use of a religious attitude to political ends, up to a point in which he would try to operate upon Christian theology, in order to bring it back to an appreciation of its most genuine roots, which would be

---

[35] *AB, EW*, IV, p. 307.

found to coincide with the worldly and materialistic attitude of his philosophy.[36]

Università degli Studi di Milano

[36] On our side is the comment by D. Johnston (*The Rhetoric of Leviathan – Thomas Hobbes and the Politics of Cultural Transformation*. Princeton University Press, 1986, p. 130) according to which, if the purpose of Hobbes in his earlier works "had been to show that there could be little or no conflict between a man's duties to God and his obligations to his earthly sovereign", his "new aim was to expose the superstitious and magical elements in Christianity so that these could be expelled from Christian doctrine".

[16]

Calvin and Hobbes, or, Hobbes as an Orthodox Christian

Edwin Curley

Three years ago, in the proceedings of an Italian conference on Hobbes and Spinoza, I published an article arguing that Hobbes was at best a deist, and most likely an atheist.[1] In a recent book on Hobbes, A. P. Martinich devoted an appendix to criticizing that article, as part of his case that Hobbes is not merely a theist, but an orthodox Christian, and specifically, that he had "a strong commitment" to the Calvinist branch of the Church of England.[2] It has been suggested that I respond to Martinich's rebuttal, and I think I should. Martinich's work is arguably the best available book of its kind.[3] Pursuing the issues this book raises may help us to see why it is worth our while to be curious about the differences between the English text of *Leviathan*, first published in 1651, and the Latin text of that work, first published in 1668. This is a topic generally ignored in English-language discussions of Hobbes and one in which I have a special interest.[4]

The great virtue of Martinich's book is that he is very precise about what his thesis

---

[1] See "'I Durst Not Write So Boldly' or, How to Read Hobbes' *Theological-Political Treatise*," in *Hobbes e Spinoza, Atti del Convegno Internazionale, Urbino, 14–17 ottobre, 1988*, ed. by Daniela Bostrenghi, intro. by Emilia Giancotti (Napoli: Bibliopolis, 1992). By 'deist' I understand someone who believes in a personal God, but rejects divine revelation as a basis for religious belief. By an 'atheist' I understand someone who rejects the existence of any God.

[2] *The Two Gods of "Leviathan"* (Cambridge University Press, 1992), 1–2. Subsequent references to this book will cite page numbers in parentheses in the text.

[3] I know no other sustained attempt to argue for such a bold thesis about Hobbes's religious views. Sharon Lloyd's *Ideals as Interests in Hobbes's "Leviathan"* (Cambridge University Press, 1992) is similar in certain respects: she assumes, as Martinich does, that Hobbes was a sincere Christian, who wished to make Christianity more acceptable to a modern age, and she argues that taking his Christian commitments seriously is essential to understanding his political philosophy. But she does not claim that Hobbes is orthodox (17, 112, and 345–46) or attempt to deal with the full range of Hobbes's positions on religious issues.

[4] The edition of *Leviathan* I recently published with Hackett is the first in English to systematically translate variant passages from the Latin edition. In referring to *Leviathan* I cite passages by chapter and paragraph number, as given in my edition, which also has other material I believe will be useful (e.g., Hobbes's verse autobiography, excerpts from his prose autobiography and from Aubrey's biography, a glossary, annotation, and extensive indices). It was François Tricaud who paved the way here, by publishing a French translation which gave a very careful account of the differences between the English and Latin versions (Paris: Sirey, 1971). It is an embarrassment to English-language scholarship that we should need the French to show us how to treat one of our greatest philosophers.

258   JOURNAL OF THE HISTORY OF PHILOSOPHY 34:2 APRIL 1996

entails. A writer will count as an orthodox Christian if and only if he adheres to "the authoritative Christian creeds of the first four church councils," by which he means the Apostles' Creed and the Nicene Creed.[5] There are some obviously good reasons for focussing on those creeds: they probably have wider acceptance among Christian churches than any others; the Church of England, to which Hobbes proclaimed his allegiance, requires acceptance of those creeds;[6] and Hobbes himself would certainly have liked this definition of orthodoxy.[7]

There are also some less obviously good reasons for focussing on those creeds. One of the Hobbesian doctrines most apt to lead to charges of atheism is his materialism. He holds that the notion of an incorporeal substance is a contradiction (L iv, 21), and this leads him—not to deny the existence of God and the human soul—but to say that they are material beings (L xii, 7, xliv, 15, Latin Appendix iii, 6). By the seventeenth century a tradition had developed within Christianity of holding that God and the soul are immaterial beings.[8] But the early church councils were primarily concerned with defining the church's position on the trinity, and they are silent on these metaphysical issues. As far as they are concerned, a Christian can be a materialist about both God and the soul (and some Christians have been).

Similarly with respect to the doctrine of immortality. One reason Christian theologians have often felt it necessary to insist on the immateriality of the soul has been that otherwise it might seem to be destructible.[9] In *Leviathan* Hobbes holds that in itself the

---

[5] Those are the creeds he mentions (2, 6, 61). Queen Elizabeth gave these councils special status when she established the High Commission, which was not to pronounce as heretical any doctrine not condemned by one of them. (Cf. *Leviathan*, Latin App. ii, 30.) Perhaps the Apostles' Creed shouldn't count as the work of those councils; parts of it probably date as early as the second century; the present text probably dates from the eighth century (see Gordon Melton, *Religious Creeds* [Gale Research Co., 1988], 1). This description does, however, fit the Nicene Creed, whose earliest form dates from the first general council, held at Nicaea in 325 C.E., and whose present form was adopted somewhat later (according to Hobbes [*English Works*, IV, 400–401], at the fourth council, held at Chalcedon in 451).

[6] For example, the Thirty-Nine Articles of the Church of England identify those creeds as ones which "ought thoroughly to be received and believed, for they may be proved by most certain warrants of Holy Scripture" (Melton, *Religious Creeds*, 23). For Hobbes's declarations of allegiance to the Church of England, see my edition of *Leviathan*, lxiv–lxv, lxvii–lxviii.

[7] Cf. his various discussions of heresy (e.g., in *Leviathan*, Latin App. ii, 30, 52; in *Behemoth*, EW VI, 174–76; and in the "Historical Narration concerning Heresy," IV, 405–406).

[8] See Calvin, *Institutes of the Christian Religion*, I, xi, 2, on the immateriality of God, and I, xv, 2, 6, on the immateriality of the soul. This is also the doctrine of Aquinas (cf. *Summa theologiae*, I, qu. 3, art. 1, and qu. 75, art. 1).

[9] Aquinas holds that the soul would be incorruptible even if it were composed of matter and form (I, qu. 75, art. 6). But Calvin seems to have thought the immateriality of the soul was essential to its immortality. Cf. *Institutes*, I, xv, 2. It's worth noting that Calvin's early theological treatise, *Psychopannychia*, was a defense of the immortality of the soul against the doctrine that the soul sleeps between the death of the body and the last judgment. Calvin associated this doctrine (wrongly, it seems) with the Anabaptists, and deferred publication of his treatise when friends pointed out that the position he was attacking was quite similar to one Luther held. See Willem Balke, *Calvin and the Anabaptist Radicals* (Grand Rapids: Eerdmans, 1981), 25–34, and Calvin, *Opera quae supersunt omnia*, V, 165–232, 1866 ed. (*Corpus reformatorum*, vol. XXXIII).

soul *is* destructible; it is not naturally immortal (L xxxviii, 4). Of course the God who made a living creature out of the dust by his word can, if he chooses, bring a dead carcass back to life and make the creature thus restored live forever (L xliv, 15, 32). But immortality is a possible consequence of divine grace, not a necessary consequence of man's nature. The early creeds, however, are not concerned to pronounce on the immortality of the soul. As far as they are concerned, a Christian can be a mortalist (and some Christians have been).

This theory leads naturally to a certain asymmetry in Hobbes's treatment of the fates of the saved and the damned. Our term 'grace' is derived from the Latin *gratia*, which signifies what is pleasing, or a favor or kindness done to someone, or a gift (cf. L xiv, 12). It seems reasonable enough to think of the immortality enjoyed by the elect in heaven as a gift, a kindness done them. Even if you believe that we are saved by works rather than faith, how could anyone, in a finite lifetime, behave well enough to deserve an eternal reward (cf. L xiv, 17)? It does not seem equally reasonable to say that it is by divine grace that the damned suffer eternal torment in hell. Some kindness! Perhaps as a result, Hobbes, so tough-minded on so many topics, is rather tender-minded on the punishment of the reprobate. Calvin had held that the wicked will suffer eternally, that they will "find no rest from being troubled and tossed by a terrible whirlwind, from feeling that they are being torn asunder by a hostile Deity, pierced and lanced by deadly darts, quaking at God's lightning bolt, and being crushed by the weight of his hand."[10] Hobbes, however, contends that the wicked will get some rest, that God will keep them in hell for a while, suffering excruciating agonies, and then annihilate them in a second death:

It seemeth [OL: too] hard to say that God, who is the father of mercies, that doth in heaven and earth all that he will, that hath the hearts of all men in his disposing, that worketh in men both to do and to will, and without whose free gift a man hath neither inclination to good nor repentance of evil, should [OL: will to] punish men's transgressions without any end of time, and with all the extremity of torture that men can imagine, and more. (L xliv, 26; "OL" indicates an interpolation based on the Latin version of this passage.)

Hobbes does not deny that hell itself exists eternally as a place of punishment; he does deny that any particular wicked person will suffer there till eternity. And he recognizes that this implies that the human race must continue to propagate till eternity, in order to keep up the supply of sinners.[11] By the seventeenth century a tradition had devel-

---

Hobbes' position in *Leviathan* is in some respects like Luther's, and Christian interpreters of Hobbes sometimes appeal to this fact to support reading his mortalism as acceptable Christian doctrine. But so far as I can see Hobbes does not attribute any existence to the soul between the death of the body and its resurrection, not even a sleeping one. Assuming that some continuity of substance is essential to personal identity, it is obscure why, on his view, we should identify the man who is resurrected with any previously existing person.

[10] *Institutes,* III, xxv, 12. I cite the Battles translation (Westminster Press, 1960).

[11] Cf. L xliv, 29. Martinich suggests that Hobbes is trying to come up with a "plausible, relatively humane and biblically based doctrine of hell" to compete with the view which had become standard in the seventeenth century. But he thinks the attempt a failure: "The idea of an infinite number of wicked people tortured for a finite period of time is not much more satisfying

oped within Christianity of holding that the punishment of individual sinners is eternal.[12] But the early creeds are in fact silent on this subject. So as far as they are concerned, a Christian can reject the doctrine of eternal punishment for the damned (and some Christians have).

Again, some readers of *Leviathan* have wondered whether Hobbes's moral views are really consistent with Christian teachings. Suppose we take Hobbes's enumeration of 19 laws of nature in chapters xiv and xv of *Leviathan* as an attempt to provide new foundations for an old morality. Martinich takes them that way (119), and I agree. The new foundation is a definition of 'law of nature' which makes it essential to a law of nature that it prescribe the means to self-preservation (L xiv, 3; xv, 41). Martinich makes the point that, though this might sound "offensive to pious ears," there is "nothing inherently non-Christian" about it. The gospels frequently offer the hope of heaven and the fear of hell as reasons for complying with their prescriptions (117–18). The real question, though, is whether the old morality Hobbes seeks to found is the morality of the gospels. Hobbes identifies his second law of nature with the Golden Rule (L xiv, 5); some have called this a bold act of appropriation, since the Golden Rule is normally thought to prescribe that we love our enemies and do good even to those who hate us, whereas Hobbes's second law prescribes that we be willing to lay down our right to all things, *when others are so too*. Perhaps Hobbes's insistence on reciprocity is incompatible with the spirit of the Golden Rule.[13] Still, the early creeds have nothing to say about these issues; they make no prescriptions about conduct. So far as they are concerned, a Christian can do as she pleases to her enemies (and many Christians have).

Martinich has hit upon an ingenious argumentative strategy here, one whose potential even he does not seem to fully realize. For example, in L xxv, 2–3, Hobbes distinguishes between counsels and commands in the following way: both involve imperatives; in a command the only reason the commander offers for obedience is his own will; so the object of the command is some good to the commander; a counsellor will offer reasons based on the good of the person counselled. Now Martinich interprets Hobbes as a divine command theorist; the laws of nature oblige because they are divine commands (87–99). In this respect he continues a line of interpretation begun by Taylor and Warrender. But he notices a problem with this view, one which I do not recall Taylor or Warrender addressing. If the laws of nature oblige because they are divine commands, and if a command is an imperative justified by the fact that obedience to it will benefit the commander, we seem to be driven to the conclusion that God

---

than the idea of a finite number tortured for an infinite period of time" (259–60). That seems right. It also seems doubtful that Hobbes's doctrine is consistent with the Christian doctrine of the last judgment. There was considerable discussion of (and discomfort with) the doctrine of hell in the seventeenth century. The classic study is D. P. Walker's *The Decline of Hell* (University of Chicago Press, 1974), which finds that Hobbes's views were beyond the pale.

[12] That this is Calvin's view is evident from the passage cited in the text. It was also Aquinas's view (*Summa contra gentiles*, III, ch. 144).

[13] Cf. *The Elements of Law*, I, xvii, 15: "The sum of virtue is to be sociable with them that will be sociable, and formidable to them that will not."

commands obedience to the laws of nature because our obedience will benefit him. Martinich maintains that an orthodox Christian will find this conclusion "obviously absurd" (132). And it would, perhaps, be an awkward conclusion for Hobbes to reach, given his contention that God has no ends (L xxxi, 13). But there is no reason, on Martinich's definition of orthodoxy, why drawing this conclusion would mark Hobbes as an unorthodox Christian. The early creeds are quite silent on the question whether God benefits from our obedience to his commands. So far as they are concerned, a Christian is free to believe what he likes on that subject.

The same holds for the question whether the imperatives of the gospel are commands or merely counsels. The reformers had tended to insist, against the authority of Aquinas, that they were commands.[14] Hobbes, atypically, sides with Aquinas (L xxv, 10; xliii, 5). But clearly this is an issue on which Christians may agree to differ. The early creeds are quite silent on the question whether the imperatives of Jesus impose a moral obligation on us or are merely good advice about the way to get to heaven. So far as they are concerned, a Christian is free to believe what she pleases about those imperatives.

What should we conclude from this? I think Professor Martinich has demonstrated, as fully as the nature of the case permits, that if we adopt his plausible definition of "orthodoxy," and if we take Hobbes at his word, Hobbes must have been an orthodox Christian.[15] That is no small accomplishment. But perhaps it will be just as well to emphasize the exact wording of the concession just made. There will be some question, of course, about what the nature of the case permits. The more important question, though, is whether we should take Hobbes at his word. I had thought, when I wrote the article Martinich criticizes, that Hobbes was frequently ironic in his treatment of religion in *Leviathan*. Martinich contends that there are no undertones of irony in what Hobbes says about religion (27–28), and that I am operating "with a defective idea of how to recognize irony" (351). He thinks I am inclined to see irony where none is intended.

I had attributed to Hobbes a particular form of irony which I called "suggestion by

---

[14] Cf. Calvin, *Institutes*, II, viii, 56–57, and Luther, *On Secular Authority*, ed. Harro Höpfl (Cambridge University Press), 4, 8, with Aquinas, *Summa theologiae*, I-II, qu. 108, art. 4, II-II, qu. 184, art. 3, qu. 186.

[15] Cautious readers, however, might wish to suspend judgment about Martinich's more specific claim that Hobbes was a Calvinist. Apart from the differences already noted between Calvin and Hobbes—regarding the nature of God and of the soul, the immortality of the soul, the eternal punishment of the damned, and the status of Jesus's commands—there are several other areas of presumptive disagreement: on conscience (vii, 4), on sin (xxvii, 1), on the authority of sovereigns to determine, within their dominions, which books contain the word of God (xxxiii, 1), on Jesus's belief in possession by demons (viii, 26), on the universality of the desire for power over others as an end in itself (xi, 2), on the reliability of the transmission of the law of Moses (xxxiii, 5), on the meaning of "the Kingdom of God" and the place in which the elect will enjoy eternal life (xxxv, 1, 11; xxxvii, 3; xliv, 4), on whether Mark 6:5 implies that Jesus was unable to perform miracles in his own country (xxxvii, 6), on whether the Pope is the Antichrist (xlii, 87–88), and on the necessity of works for salvation (xliii, 3). (For the contrasting passages in Calvin, see the annotation in my edition of *Leviathan*.) But perhaps these differences are unimportant by comparison with the similarities Martinich notes.

252   JOURNAL OF THE HISTORY OF PHILOSOPHY 34:2 APRIL 1996

disavowal." In this rhetorical device a writer presents a series of considerations which might reasonably lead his reader to draw a certain conclusion, but then denies that that conclusion follows. Consider, for example, Hobbes's treatment of prophecy, miracles, and scripture in L xxxii, xxxiii, xxxvi, and xxxvii. What he says on these matters might fairly be summarized as follows: miracles are important because they are a criterion of true prophecy (where a prophet is understood to be a messenger of God); one way you tell whether someone who claims to be a prophet is really a prophet is by seeing whether he (or she) can perform miracles (that's a necessary but not a sufficient condition); there is some difficulty, though, about applying this criterion; the crafty can easily persuade the gullible that they have performed a miracle when they have merely used their cunning (and perhaps confederates) to deceive; since being thought to be a prophet gives you great power over those who believe you to be a prophet, the unscrupulous have a strong incentive to try to deceive us; there *are*, of course, genuine miracles and genuine prophets; or at least, there *were* a long time ago (a time we know about only from ancient documents); but miracles don't happen any more; so nowadays we should be very wary of anyone who claims to perform miracles, and claims, on the basis of that performance, to be a messenger of God.

Now, does Hobbes intend his readers to draw a stronger conclusion than the one he in fact draws? Does he mean to cast doubt not only on present miracles, but also on those of the past (and, by implication, on the prophecy to which they testify and on the claim of scripture to be a divine revelation)? Martinich says no. Hobbes's intent is merely to discourage his contemporaries from accepting seventeenth-century claimants to prophecy, who might try to use the authority thus gained to disturb the political order (236). We should take Hobbes at his word when he says he accepts the occurrence of miracles and prophecies in the past. Literal interpretation is the default mode for the interpretation of texts; ironic interpretation is acceptable only when literal interpretation makes no sense (43). There is nothing in what he says on these subjects which has not been said by some Christian whose loyalty to the faith is unimpeachable (241–46). Martinich concedes that Hobbes's treatment of these issues did in fact contribute to a decline of belief in revealed religion. But he takes this to be an unintended consequence of Hobbes's writing as he did (345). Hobbes is neither a coward nor a liar, and it would have been a cowardly deception for him to have denied conclusions he really wanted people to draw, when he could have maintained his integrity by keeping silent (30–32).

I had not thought, of course, that Hobbes was a coward, for all that he likes to boast of his fearful nature. If he really held the views my article attributed to him, it would have been decidedly risky for him to publish them openly, given the penalties for dissent operating at the time.[16] I had thought that he was rather daring to publish what he did. Nor had I thought that Hobbes was a liar. I didn't think that the use of irony quite constituted lying. The kind of irony I claimed to find in *Leviathan* places the responsibility for drawing the right conclusion on the reader. Only those will be de-

---

[16] I cited W. K. Jordan, *The Development of Religious Toleration in England, from the Convention of the Long Parliament to the Restoration, 1640–1660* (Harvard University Press, 1938).

ceived who don't have a good sense of where an argument ought to lead. Neither had I thought that Hobbes was a fool, who could not anticipate what the likely consequences of his actions would be. Silence on a subject so important, I thought, was not an attractive option to him, since he believed revealed religion to be dangerous, not only to the political order, but also to the progress of science.

Still, I think Martinich has raised a very significant issue here how do you tell whether or not a text is ironic? I would grant that in interpreting texts we must operate with some kind of presumption in favor of literal interpretation. Does Martinich go too far when he says that an ironic interpretation is acceptable only if the literal interpretation makes no sense? I had held that Hobbes wrote with deliberate ambiguity, intending one set of readers to see the irreligious implications of his text, and another set to credit the disavowals of heterodox intent,[17] so as to undermine religion without incurring punishment by the defenders of the faith. This strategy can work only if the literal interpretation makes *some* sense. So Martinich's rule will automatically exclude an ironic interpretation of any work seeking that complex effect. It might also exclude an ironic interpretation of Swift's "A Modest Proposal." Swift certainly took some pains to see that his proposal to market the children of the Irish poor as table delicacies made sense, not only from an economic, but even from a moral point of view. (The lives of the poor were so wretched that they themselves, when grown, would count it a blessing to have been sold for food at the age of one year!) As a result, some of his first readers took it to be a serious proposal and were horrified. But if we reject Martinich's rule, and if we wish to avoid reading modern unbelief into old books, which may be quite innocent of our corruption, what rule can we follow?

Some readers of Hobbes might reply by alleging that Hobbes frequently contradicts himself on religious topics, and that this is a marker of our need to be alert to hints of heresy. E.g.:

(1) in *De cive* xv, 14, and in *Leviathan* xxxi, 14, Hobbes affirms that it is manifest by natural reason that existence is to be attributed to God; in his *Examination of Thomas White's "De Mundo,"* xxvi, 6, he contends that the authorities ought not to permit attempts to demonstrate the existence of God, because when ordinary men see that people who wish to believe in God's existence are unable to prove it, they will infer that God does not exist.[18]

(2) In *Leviathan* iii, 12, xxxi, 28, Hobbes affirms God's incomprehensibility; later in *Leviathan* (xlvi, 12) he criticizes the Jews for succumbing to the influence of Greek philosophy by incorporating the doctrine of God's incomprehensibility into their teaching.

(3) In the Appendix to the Latin *Leviathan* (i, 95) Hobbes acknowledges that the doctrine of God's incorporeality is affirmed in the articles of religion which define the Anglican faith, and that it must not be denied on pain of excommunication; in the same

---

[17] "'I Durst Not Write So Boldly'," 589–93.

[18] Hobbes wrote his *Examination of Thomas White's "De Mundo"* in 1642, but it lay, unrecognized as a Hobbesian work, in the Bibliothèque nationale in Paris until after the Second World War. Jean Jacquot and Harold Whitmore Jones published an edition of the original Latin text in 1973 (Paris: Vrin), and Jones published an English translation in 1976 (Bradford University Press).

264   JOURNAL OF THE HISTORY OF PHILOSOPHY 34:2 APRIL 1996

Appendix (iii, 6) he affirms God's corporeality and defends the orthodoxy of that position by citing the authority of Tertullian.

(4) In *Leviathan* xxxviii, 4, Hobbes denies that the soul is naturally immortal, and contends that its immortality is a matter of divine grace; in *The Elements of Law* (II, vi, 6) and *De cive* (xvii, 13) he affirms without qualification that the soul is immortal.

(5) In *Leviathan* xxxii, 5, Hobbes says that if someone claims to have had a direct revelation from God, and I question the claim, it's hard to see what argument he could give which would oblige me to believe him; in L xxvi, 40, he had taken a stronger position: that no one can be sure that someone else has received a direct revelation from God unless he himself has received directly from God a revelation that the other person has had a direct revelation from God.

(6) In *Leviathan* xiv, 23, Hobbes claims that the only way to make a covenant with God is by the mediation of someone to whom God has spoken "either by revelation supernatural or by his lieutenants that govern under him and in his name"; in L xviii, 5, he takes the stronger position that only the sovereign can mediate a covenant with God.[19]

Perhaps not all of these are strict contradictions. And certainly not all of them come from *Leviathan* itself. But collectively they do seem to demonstrate a tendency to vacillate on important religious issues, and some would say that this should make us suspicious.

To this Martinich can certainly reply, with justice, that authors often contradict themselves without being aware of it, and that Hobbes could not have intended all of these contradictions as hints about how to read *Leviathan*. Some of them are contradictions between *Leviathan* and works Hobbes never published (such as the *Examination of Thomas White's "De Mundo"*); some are contradictions between *Leviathan* and works Hobbes wrote many years earlier, when he may not even have planned to write *Leviathan*, and after which he may have changed his mind. Moreover, he might say, even where the contradiction occurs within *Leviathan* itself, Hobbes would not have expected his readers to notice contradictions which occur in passages from different chapters, which may be many pages apart.[20]

---

[19] Of course there is a quite general question in Hobbes as to whether it is possible for man to covenant with God, with or without a mediator. A covenant is a kind of contract (xiv, 11), and hence involves a transfer of rights (xiv, 9). But God's rights are supposed to be a consequence of his omnipotence (xxxi, 5). So it is unclear how he can either acquire or lay aside rights (cf. my annotation at xiv, 23).

Martinich is aware of this problem (cf. his 181–82, 291–94), though he does not define it in quite the way I have. He thinks Hobbes too was aware of the "tension" between God's sovereignty and his entering into covenants. But he apparently does not think Hobbes intended to suggest that tension to his readers. L xiv, 17, and xl, 1, are interesting here.

[20] In fact, this is what Martinich does say (55) about a contradiction Berman had alleged between L vi, 36 (which implies that God is capable of being imagined) and L xi, 25 (which implies that he is not). Of course Alexander Ross had noticed a similar difficulty about reconciling vi, 36, with iii, 12 (in *Leviathan Drawn Out with a Hook* [London, 1653], 10). But in his case the contradictory passages were only 15 pages apart, not 25; so perhaps they are within the attention span Hobbes would have presumed. It is difficult to give a precise rule here. Clarendon showed

Perhaps we ought not to put too much emphasis on Hobbes's vacillations regarding religious issues. What would really be helpful here would be more examples of suggestion by disavowal. Martinich (351) complains that I offer only a few examples of this technique.[21] Clearly the numbers matter in such cases, since the more evidence we have, the further we go towards establishing what the lawyers call a pattern of behavior. If we had more examples of the technique at work, particularly if some of them were quite clear cases, then it might be more reasonable to judge that Hobbes is using the technique in cases where there would otherwise be legitimate doubt about his intentions.

We might suppose we had such an example in Hobbes's discussion of angels in L xxxiv, 23–24, where the issue is whether or not we should regard angels as incorporeal substances. After an extended discussion of various Old and New Testament passages which tend to support a negative answer, Hobbes concludes by reporting that, though philosophical and theological considerations had inclined him to reject angels as "apparitions of the fancy," numerous (unspecified) passages in the New Testament had extorted from him a confession of the weakness of his reason and an admission of their reality. On the literal reading xxxiv, 24, is inconsistent with xlv, 31, and App. iii, 15– 18. And the attitude Hobbes displays toward reason in xxxiv, 24, comes somewhat oddly from an author who could write that men set themselves against reason as often as reason is against them (xi, 21). Still, Martinich takes what Hobbes says at face value here (250–52); so I suppose this must be counted as a doubtful case.

But what about Hobbes's treatment of the trinity? Given the centrality of the early creeds to Martinich's definition of orthodoxy, and the centrality of the doctrine of the trinity to those creeds, this is a case of more than incidental interest. The basic facts about Hobbes's way of dealing with the trinity will be well enough known to Hobbes scholars. But the topic has not been at the forefront of recent discussions, so a brief review may be in order. In L, xvi, Hobbes defines a person as one "whose words or actions are considered either as his own, or as representing the words or actions of another man, or of any other thing to whom they are attributed, whether truly or by fiction" (xvi, 1). The primary application of this doctrine is political: a multitude of men become one person when, by the consent of all, some man or assembly represents them (xvi, 13). But Hobbes also uses his theory to explain how one God can be three persons: God is said to be one person when represented by Moses, another when represented by Jesus, and a third when represented by the apostles.[22]

---

remarkable alertness in noting the contradiction between xxxii, 7 (the Egyptian sorcerers performed great miracles) and xxxvii, 9–10 (no created spirit can perform a miracle). These passages were no fewer than 38 pages apart.

[21] Martinich does not actually challenge any of the Hobbesian examples I discussed, though he does discuss and reject an example I had drawn from Elizabeth Anscombe, as (I foolishly imagined) a clear illustration of the technique at work. Perhaps I might have chosen other examples. Descartes's discussion of appeals to scripture in the letter he wrote dedicating his *Meditations* to the Faculty of Theology at the Sorbonne comes to mind (Adam and Tannery, VII, 1–2). But I suspect that any historical example I used might be open to challenge, since part of the point of this rhetorical device is to permit doubt about the author's intentions.

[22] In point of fact, Hobbes gives different accounts of who God's representatives on earth are. The least generous mentions only Moses, Jesus, and the apostles. Cf. xvi, 12. But in other places

266   JOURNAL OF THE HISTORY OF PHILOSOPHY 34:2 APRIL 1996

From an orthodox Christian standpoint, this theory has certain disadvantages. It apparently makes Moses and the apostles (and all the rest) coequal with Jesus as persons of the trinity, whereas the intent of the doctrine of the trinity would seem to be to give Jesus a status greater than that possessed by any mere human. Prima facie, Hobbes's theory denies the eternity of the three persons of the trinity. And since the third representative (and in some versions of the theory, the first also) is a multitude with no collective decision-making procedure, it is hard to see why there are only three persons in this trinity. These problems did not go unnoticed by Hobbes's contemporaries, and they seem sufficiently obvious that you would think a theologically sophisticated author would have anticipated the negative reaction of the orthodox.[23] Martinich acknowledges that Hobbes's interpretation of the trinity is not free from problems (207). But he thinks they are problems inherent in any sincere attempt to explain a doctrine which may be inconsistent (and which, if consistent, is hard to show to be consistent). Hobbes was trying, in good faith, to make the doctrine of the trinity both coherent and orthodox. He failed, but he could hardly have succeeded. His failure is not to be read as an indication of underhanded motives, as if he were saying "the only way you can make this doctrine coherent is to make it radically unorthodox."

Some readers may find it disappointing that Martinich does not say more about what happened to Hobbes's theory of the trinity in the Latin edition of *Leviathan*. Most scholars are aware that Hobbes acknowledged defects in the theory of the English edition and dropped it from the Latin editions.[24] But many students of Hobbes are not aware of what replaced it. It is a pity that Martinich does not discuss the way Hobbes responded to criticism on this point. In some places, of course, Hobbes just deleted the theory of the English *Leviathan* without putting anything in its place (xlii, 3). Sometimes he just replaced the discarded theory with the treatment of the trinity in the Anglican catechism (xvi, 12; Appendix iii, 11–14). But in ch. i of the Latin Appendix, which has no analogue in the English *Leviathan*, Hobbes engages in an extended analysis of the Nicene Creed, with particular emphasis on its formulation of the doctrine of the trinity. I will not suggest, as some might wish to do, that Professor Martinich has not done his homework here. But it does seem plausible to think that a conscientious

---

he adds the successors of Moses (the high priests and kings of Judah) and the successors of the apostles "to this day" (cf. xxxiii, 20). I assume that the successors of the apostles include the popes (cf. xliv, 32) and I suppose they also include the kings and queens of England from the time of Henry VIII, since they are the heads of the church in their domains.

[23] For Bramhall, see Hobbes, EW IV, 314–15. For Clarendon, see *A Brief View and Survey of the dangerous and pernicious errors to Church and State, in Mr. Hobbes' Book Entitled "Leviathan"* (Oxford, 1676), 246. Martinich does not attach much weight to the criticisms of Hobbes's religious views made by his contemporaries, on the grounds that most of Hobbes's contemporary critics were Arminian Anglicans, who would use any stick to beat a Calvinist, or uncompromising royalists, who didn't like Hobbes's contractarian rejection of divine right theory (35). This makes it rather important for him to establish Hobbes's Calvinism.

[24] See his answer to Bramhall, EW IV, 316–17. Alterations in response to criticism of his treatment of the trinity occur not only in xvi, 12 and xlii, 3, but also in xxix, 16; xxxiii, 20; xl, 14; xli, 9; xlii, 18; xliv, 32.

scholar, defending the thesis Martinich defends, might have felt an obligation to say *something* about this text.

We might suppose that Martinich thought he had covered the matter by what he said about Hobbes's analysis of the Nicene Creed in the "Historical Narration concerning Heresy" (EW IV, 392–402). But it seems that in fact he didn't think that. Here's what he says, omitting only the page references: "The chief theological purpose of the early creeds was to insist that there is only one God, who is three persons. And the chief political purpose of them was peace. . . . After delivering a learned disquisition on the meaning of the Apostles' Creed [sic] relative to the various heresies it was meant to counteract, Hobbes discusses the history of heresy in England" (60–61). There seems to be an unfortunate confusion here about just which creed is up for discussion in the "Historical Narration": the Apostles' Creed or the Nicene.[25] The two creeds are quite similar, of course, and Hobbes does *mention* the Apostles' Creed as he is introducing his discussion of the Nicene Creed. But the two creeds do have differences which appear to have been important to Hobbes, and in the "Historical Narration" it is the Nicene Creed, not that attributed to the Apostles, on which Hobbes focuses. A brief consideration of the Latin Appendix may help to explain why.

The Appendix is written as a dialogue between two parties, designated as "A" and "B." In ch. i A starts matters off abruptly by asking B to explain the Nicene Creed to him, "not so that I may grasp these matters in my mind, but so that I may understand the words of the faith in such a way that they are consistent [*consentanea*] with Sacred Scripture" (App. i, 1). This is the translation I gave in my recent edition of *Leviathan*. Perhaps the translation of *consentanea* is tendentious. The point of A's question, it might be said, is not to demand explanation of a prima facie inconsistency between the creed and scripture, but to demand a proof that the creed follows from scripture, in accordance with article 20 of the Anglican Church.[26] Arguably, a better translation would be "that they agree with Sacred Scripture," suggesting simply a need to show that there is good scriptural authority for each element of the creed.[27]

Suppose this is right.[28] It will be sufficient here if we assume that the prima facie problem with the creed is merely that there is not good scriptural authority for all of it. Twice in the Latin *Leviathan* Hobbes says otherwise. In the Latin version of ch. xlvi Hobbes adds several paragraphs to the English version, giving a brief account of early church history. In this section he writes that the Nicene Council condemned "not only

---

[25] This is evidently not a casual slip, since it also occurs on p. 2, where Martinich says that in the "Historical Narration" Hobbes "approvingly explicates the Apostles' Creed."

[26] Cf. Appendix, i, 96: "In article 20 it is said that the church ought not to ordain anything to be believed which cannot be deduced from Sacred Scriptures." (Actually, Hobbes's version of article 20 would be more apt as a paraphrase of article 6.)

[27] Cf. the translation of the Appendix by George Wright, published (with extensive annotation and commentary) in *Interpretation* 18 (1991): 323–413.

[28] I'm not sure it is. Cf. A's comment in i, 63: "So far you have explained the doctrine of the Nicene Creed in such a way that it does not seem to me that you have shaken the Christian faith at all; instead you have strengthened it, though in your own way." A curious reader might wonder why A seems to think there is a prima facie conflict between the creed and the Christian faith, and whether B has really explained that conflict in a way which ought to satisfy A.

Arius, but also all heresies which had arisen since the birth of Christ, summing up briefly the orthodox faith in the creed called Nicene, taken from Scripture itself, with no admixture of Greek philosophy at all" (xlvi [OL], 10). Similarly, in the Appendix, A notes that "almost all those theologians who published explanations of the Nicene creed use definitions taken from the logic and metaphysics of Aristotle, when they ought to have proven the holy Trinity from Sacred Scripture alone . . . ," and then expresses his amazement that "the Nicene Fathers, so many of whom were philosophers, did not bring into the creed itself those terms of art which they used in their explanations" (i, 90). Is there any ground to regard these statements as ironic? It *is* false—manifestly false, I would have thought—that the Nicene Creed contains no terms of art derived from Greek philosophy. Specifically, in defining the relation between God the Son and God the Father, it says that Jesus was "of the substance [*ex tes ousias*] of the Father," and "of one substance [*homoousion*] with the Father." When someone says something manifestly false, we often take that as a sign of an ironic utterance.[29] There may be a special danger in reading historical texts, that we will project our own ideas about truth and falsity onto an earlier author, inferring irony where all that is present is error. But it seems unlikely, in this instance, that Hobbes did not know what we know. The use of the term *homoousios* (one feature which distinguishes the Nicene from the less metaphysical Apostles' Creed) was also one of the most controversial features of that creed.[30] The council majority had wanted to adhere only to scriptural language, but embraced the term *homoousios* when it became apparent that they could not distinguish themselves from the Arians without departing from scriptural language.[31] Hobbes seems to be well-informed about that history. Here's what he says about it in the "Historical Narration":

> For this word, *of one substance*, in Latin *consubstantialis*, but in Greek *homoousios*, that is, of one essence, was put as a touchstone to discern an Arian from a Catholic; and much ado there was about it. Constantine himself, at the passing of this creed, took notice of it for a hard word, but yet approved of it, saying that in a divine mystery it was fit to use *divina et arcana verba*, that is, divine words and hidden from human understanding— calling that word *homoousios* divine, not because it was in the divine Scripture (for it is not there), but because it was to him *arcanum*, that is, not sufficiently understood. *And in this again[32] appeared the indifferency of the Emperor, and that he had for his end, in the*

---

[29] See, for example, the analysis of irony in Robert Fogelin's *Figuratively Speaking* (Yale University Press, 1988), 5–23.

[30] In Appendix i, 17, A calls it "that great article which in the ancient church produced so many disturbances, exiles and killings."

[31] See Jaroslav Pelikan, *The Christian Tradition, Vol. I: The Emergence of the Catholic Tradition (100–600)* (University of Chicago Press, 1971), 202.

[32] Hobbes also accuses Constantine of "a greater indifferency than would in these days be approved of" for having agreed to enforce adherence to whatever articles of faith the bishops assembled at the Council of Nicaea agreed on (EW IV, 392). As Hobbes notes in the Latin Appendix (ii, 30), the situation of the Anglican Church under Elizabeth was like that of the Roman Church under Constantine. (William Haugaard's *Elizabeth and the English Reformation* [Cambridge University Press, 1968], which generally defends Elizabeth against charges of indifference in matters of religion, is interesting here. See 236–37.)

calling of the Synod, not so much the truth, as the uniformity of doctrine, and peace of his people that depended on it. The cause of the obscurity of this word, *homoousios,* proceeded chiefly from the difference between the Greek and Roman dialect in the philosophy of the Peripatetics. (EW IV, 393, Hobbes's emphasis)

It might be suggested that when Hobbes wrote the Latin Appendix, which was published in 1668, he was not aware that *homoousios* was not a scriptural term, and that he discovered this between the composition of that work and that of the "Historical Narration," which was not published until 1680. But in the Latin *Leviathan* Hobbes does seem to be generally well-informed about the history of the early church councils (see, for example, xlvi, 9–11, App. i, 14; ii, 20, 24, 52; iii, 6); and to explain the orthodox doctrine of the trinity, he apparently thinks it necessary to engage in an extended discourse on the technical terms of Greek philosophy (i, 59–91).

If we read as ironic Hobbes's denials that the Nicene Creed contains an admixture of Greek philosophy, what follows? Hobbes regularly professes adherence to the Reformation principle that Scripture alone is the test of what a Christian must believe. Here's a nice passage from the Latin Appendix:

> I shall really say nothing about this [the immortality of the soul], except what I find said clearly and without any ambiguity in Scripture, which no other text plainly contradicts. You, of course, along with nearly everyone else, take from the philosophers the doctrine that the human soul cannot perish. But I, having now the Sacred Scriptures, do not desire the philosophers as my masters. Nevertheless, if you show me some passage from Sacred Scripture where another immortality is attributed to the human soul besides that which is given to men under the name of eternal life, I too shall think with the philosophers. (i, 46)

Martinich appeals to similar passages in the English *Leviathan* to support his contention that Hobbes is a good reformed theologian (e.g., on 66). But suppose Hobbes's insistence on the *sola Scriptura* principle, combined with his repeated affirmations (of the manifestly false claim) that the Nicene Creed is untainted by Greek philosophy, is a way of calling our attention to the fact that the Creed itself fails the fundamental test of reformation theology. If he is serious about his adherence to the *sola Scriptura* principle, he could not be, by Martinich's definition of orthodoxy, an orthodox Christian. On this hypothesis he would be raising, delicately, a dilemma for reformed Christians generally: if you permit Church tradition and the decisions of Church councils to define the Christian faith, it may be difficult to reject such Roman Catholic extravagances as the doctrine of purgatory; if you insist that Christian doctrine is limited to what can be read in scripture or proven from scripture, you may have to sacrifice a doctrine as dear to your hearts as the trinity. And he would be suggesting a particular problem for the Anglican "middle way," which (in what might appear to be a spirit of unprincipled political compromise) accepted exactly four general church councils as valid: the Thirty-Nine Articles which define the basic teaching of the Anglican Church are inconsistent, requiring believers to accept the Nicene Creed, and at the same time denying the Church permission to require any doctrine for which there is not adequate scriptural authority.

270   JOURNAL OF THE HISTORY OF PHILOSOPHY 34:2 APRIL 1996

Hobbes comes back to this issue in the third chapter of the Latin Appendix, where he is replying to objections made against the English *Leviathan*, among them one which challenges him to explain how his denial of incorporeal substances is compatible with his affirmation of the existence of God. He takes the opportunity to argue for the orthodoxy of his view that God is corporeal: "Not even the Nicene Council defined it as an article of faith that God is incorporeal. The fathers who were present, however, thought that God was incorporeal (whether they all thought this I don't know). And Constantine himself approved the term *homoousios*, i.e., coessential, because it seemed to him to follow from that term that God is incorporeal. Nevertheless, they did not want to introduce the term *incorporeal*, which is not in Sacred Scripture, into the creed" (iii, 6). There is more at stake here than just the question of God's corporeality. Specifically, this passage does raise the question: how, if the fathers rejected the term *incorporeal* because it was nonscriptural, could they in consistency approve the equally nonscriptural term *homoousios?*

I presume Martinich would reply that an ironic reading of Hobbes on the trinity attributes too much subtlety to him. It may be reasonable for us to draw these conclusions from what Hobbes says. But it does not follow that Hobbes intended us to draw them. To suppose that Hobbes could see that these conclusions followed from what he said, or could see that readers might reasonably think they did, is to suppose that Hobbes was as perceptive as we are. As Martinich says, "A general problem with Straussian interpretations is that they overestimate the abilities of philosophers."[33] We have no right to suppose that Hobbes could see what we see, particularly when doing so implies attributing to Hobbes the moral flaw of pretending to be an orthodox Christian when he was not. Hobbes is as entitled to a presumption of innocence as anyone else accused of unorthodoxy. Unless it is proven beyond a reasonable doubt that Hobbes is guilty, we must acquit him.

What shall we conclude from all of this? I believe that in that earlier essay of mine I was, as Philo might say, less cautious on the subject of Hobbes's religion than I am accustomed to be, and than the subject deserves. Perhaps I was unduly influenced by a comment Aubrey reports Edmund Waller[34] as having made, when Aubrey asked him, after Hobbes's death, to write some verses in praise of their friend. Waller declined, saying that he was afraid of the churchmen, and that "what was chiefly to be taken notice of in his elegy was that he, being but one, and a private person, pulled down all the churches, dispelled the mists of ignorance, and laid open their priestcraft" (lxxi in

---

[33] I acknowledge that my interpretation of Hobbes is Straussian (as is my interpretation of Spinoza). But I am not a Straussian *in general*. Regarding Descartes, see my exchange with Hiram Caton ("The Problem of Professor Caton's Sincerity," *Independent Journal of Philosophy* 5/6: 10–15). Regarding Leibniz, see "The Root of Contingency," in *Leibniz, A Collection of Critical Essays*, ed. Harry Frankfurt (Anchor, 1972), 69–97.

[34] For an account of the relationship between Hobbes and Waller, see *The Correspondence of Thomas Hobbes*, ed. Noel Malcolm (Oxford University Press, 1994), II: 913–15. In his life of Hobbes, Aubrey reports that it was Waller who sent Spinoza's *Theological-Political Treatise* to Lord Devonshire, asking him to solicit Hobbes's opinion of it, thereby prompting Hobbes to make the remark which was the subject of the essay Martinich criticizes: "He has outthrown me a bar's length; I durst not write so boldly." Cf. my edition of *Leviathan*, lxviii.

my edition of *Leviathan*). Martinich's book has persuaded me that it is not only Hobbes's professed enemies who have misunderstood his philosophy, but that even those who think themselves his friends are capable of profoundly misreading his intentions. But which of Hobbes's friends has him right, Martinich or Waller?[35]

EDWIN CURLEY

University of Michigan, Ann Arbor

---

[35] For helpful suggestions about the earlier drafts of this paper I am indebted to Stephen Darwall, Louis Loeb, and Quentin Skinner. I pursue the issues of this paper further in an article entitled "Religion and Morality in Hobbes," which I believe will appear in the proceedings of the conference held in memory of Greg Kavka, in Irvine, February 1995.

[17]

THE ARTIST OF THE *LEVIATHAN* TITLE-PAGE

KEITH BROWN

FEW title-page designs, if any, can rival the success of that bluntly eloquent engraving which prefaces the first edition (1651) of Thomas Hobbes's *Leviathan* (fig. 1). Though it was re-used for two further editions in the author's own lifetime, successive reproductions have given it far wider currency since its reappearance in the great Molesworth edition of Hobbes's collected works of 1839-45.[1] Today it is still quite commonly invoked in expositions of Hobbes's thought: even if there have also been murmurs that it must take part of the blame at least, for certain persistent misunderstandings or oversimplifications of key elements in his theory. It is a remarkable record, and the plate has attracted scholarly attention and a certain amount of debate, not just as a trailer to *Leviathan* but also in its own right. In 1852, Whewell inadvertently launched the notion that the face of Leviathan was first so drawn as to resemble that of Charles I[2] and then, in the next two editions, altered to resemble Cromwell: a persistent myth, still amazingly accepted as fact even in a work published as late as 1971.[3] Meanwhile the question of attribution has been sporadically canvassed; and for a while appeared to be closed. In 1898, F. A. Borovský, in his supplement to Gustav Parthey's descriptive catalogue of the works of Wenceslas Hollar, credited the *Leviathan* title-page engraving to this artist; and it is still mounted with the Hollar title-pages in the volumes devoted to Hollar's work in the Department of Prints and Drawings in the British Museum. In A. F. Johnson's *Catalogue of English Engraved and Etched Title-Pages* (Oxford, 1934) the engraver is recorded as unknown: Major H. Howard (whose own card-catalogue of Hollar's work is now also in the British Museum) having satisfied Johnson that small details of the lettering were inconsistent with Hollar's work. Without impugning either Borovský or Howard, it may be added that other details too ought to have raised doubts about the Hollar attribution, particularly the architecture of some of the buildings depicted. Hollar was a man with an evident interest in buildings, who understood—and accurately observed—architecture. It is unlikely that such a man would plant a ridge-roof upon a fortification that is plainly of the Bastille type (small left-hand panel), and the crudity of some of the little churches depicted seems out of character too. The work is also a little unworthy of Hollar in other ways. Despite its proven effectiveness, and the very high degree of technical skill shown in the way in which a sharp separateness is given to the individual figures within the outline of the Mortal God, without losing a sense of weight and mass in the figure as a whole, there is a slight deadness about the

Fig. 1. T. Hobbes, *Leviathan* (London, 1651), title-page. 240 × 155 mm

design, as well as perhaps a slight old-fashionedness. In part, no doubt, this may be due to the artist fleshing-out someone else's idea: originally planned perhaps in fairly precise detail by a man in his sixties whose younger years had coincided with the heyday of the Emblem Book in England, and who had never shown any special practical talent for the visual arts.[4] For in fact no one but Hobbes himself is likely to have been familiar enough with his vast manuscript, prior to publication, to have dared to reduce the nub of its argument to this confident emblem; and both its slightly bullying didacticism and its imaginative quality seem to have very much the stamp of his mind: a purely *verbal* image such as his splendid Gothic figure of the Papacy as the ghost of the deceased Roman Empire 'sitting crowned upon the grave thereof', has obvious kinship with the picture of the great Leviathan, towering up over its engraved landscape. The fact that Hobbes also prefixed a drawn version of the same emblem to the handsome manuscript copy of *Leviathan* which he gave to Charles II (now in the British Library, fig. 2) is surely another pointer to the degree of his own engagement in the design.

None the less, the slight 'deadness' of the printed title-page, referred to above, so uncharacteristic of Hollar, cannot simply be referred back to the original conception of the design; it is there in the execution of the engraving. Moreover, 'deadness' is not in this case a merely subjective term of abuse: it is an objectively demonstrable characteristic of the engraving—a kind of slackness of thought, or failure of attention—which shows up clearly when comparison is made with the drawn version presented to Charles. The most important difference between the two versions, as far as their relation to Hobbes's system of ideas is concerned, is of course in the composition of Leviathan's body. I will discuss below the separate issues this raises. The differences in relatively small details of execution are of special interest in the present case. Take, for example, the uppermost pair of the two columns of small panels. In the drawing, the ridge-roof the engraver planted on the Bastille-like castle turns into two gables, at right angles to each other, of a separate building within the circuit of the curtain-wall; and the castle is crowned, not just by a domestic chimney-stack but by some sort of turret or watch-tower: a logical culmination to the placing of the castle itself upon a height, emphasizing the idea of overriding control. The gateway of the engraver's castle is almost cyclopean, yet refuses to look us squarely in the eye, and no very obvious roadway leads away from it towards us. Here again the drawing is superior. It is remarkable how much is lost too, in a minor way, by the engraver shifting the roof-top figure of Christ away from the arched western pediment of the drawn church (for which he substitutes a lumpy gable), thus destroying a neat sculptural echo of the common presentation in church art of both Christ and the Almighty standing or seated enthroned above the cosmic arch: an echo which makes a transitional link to the superior figure of Leviathan in the panel above, rising over the arched landscape in a manner reminiscent of precisely the same tradition of Christian iconography. The engraver's handling of the main upper panel is no better. The layout of his little town is much less well integrated with its citadel, and gives the impression of houses jammed down to fill empty spaces at points where the drawn version has a much more definite sense of a street plan. The drawing avoids also the military oddity of letting a tall house almost lean into the main gateway

26

Fig. 2. T. Hobbes, *Leviathan* (1651), drawn title-page. Eg.1910. 248 × 173 mm

of the fortifications. Worse, however, is the deadening of verticals and lines of perspective in the panel as a whole. This does not merely weaken the focus of the whole image upon the figure of Leviathan: it also results in an image which less well expresses the general sense of the book. In the engraving, apart from the sprinkling of tin-tacks which make Leviathan afraid to rest his elbows on the far horizon, and the uncomfortable line of spiky spires aimed just outside his right armpit, the overwhelming upthrust comes from the large twin-towered church. In the drawing, the upthrust of the big church is echoed by a scattering of very prominent trees and some particularly sharply pointed tower roofs on the right of the church itself, all of which disappear in the engraved version. The resultant loss is not simply æsthetic: an emblem prefacing a highly rationalistic, anti-ecclesiastical work has been simplified into a picture in which it is only the church which points with any force to higher things, rather than a whole world directing our attention upwards, or rather, Leviathan-wards, while in the drawing there is a great deal that serves to take us into the picture, towards the heart as it were of Leviathan; all of which is absent in the engraved plate. It is worth giving attention to such details, for it will be seen that they may prove a larger point than the one which I set out to make.

Howard showed forty years ago that details of the lettering of the engraved title-page were unlike Hollar's work. The above comparisons show a slackness of attention, failure of intelligence, insensitivity to architecture, and indifference to possibilities of perspective, all of which seem equally un-Hollar-like. Exultant mastery of perspective depth in particular is a marked Hollar attribute. But the absence of such virtues in the engraving is demonstrated by contrast with their presence in the drawing, which shows other characteristic attributes of Hollar's style. The peculiarly 'soft' quality of the drawing, especially noticeable in the representation of Leviathan's face, is almost a Hollar trade-mark in itself, for instance, and his slight clumsiness with the human figure might be thought to be reflected in Leviathan's somewhat nerveless wrists. A stronger indication, however, is to be found in the treatment of Leviathan's eyes: this can be matched elsewhere in Hollar's work.[5] Moreover, the original attribution of the engraving to Hollar was not simply absurd: one has only to look at a print such as his *Einnahme der Stadt Oppenheim durch die Schweden* to see its point; and all such pointers of course apply *a fortiori* to the drawing. This is suggestive enough in itself. But the suggestion becomes positively insistent when two further points are taken into account. In the first place, the implication of the comparisons made above is clearly that the drawing is antecedent to the engraving. It is not necessarily the drawing from which the engraved title-page was taken; but at the very least it represents a second copy or alternative state of the original design, by the hand of the same artist. The way in which it repeatedly gives a clearer expression, even in quite small details, to points blurred by the engraver puts this beyond serious doubt. Secondly, Howard's grounds for denying the attribution of the engraving to Hollar do not seem to apply to the drawn version. On this point it is impossible to speak absolutely categorically, since the details of Howard's case do not seem to have been recorded; but it seems obvious that he must have been thinking particularly of the inscription 'Non est potestas' which heads the engraved page, where both the slope of the lettering and the form of the letter p do not look like Hollar's work, despite the immense variety of his lettering styles. Significantly, this inscription does not appear in the drawing, where there are also various small differences in the style of the lettering of the title-panel. It appears to be possible to match all the little divergences in lettering style in the drawn version of the title-panel elsewhere in Hollar's work, and the general style of the title-panel lettering in both versions is certainly one he used.[6] The conclusion seems inescapable: Wenzel Hollar is the artist of the drawn title-page presented to Charles II, and the engraved title-page was made in England from a Hollar drawing sent over by Hobbes along with his manuscript. The cutting of the engraving in England seems implied by its omission of the big sharply pointed trees in the large panel, and of the extremely tall spire-like roofs on the right-hand towers of the town fortifications, since both silhouettes were alien to the southern English landscape; while the engraving's slightly reduced degree of effectiveness in expressing the sense of the book also might be thought to suggest a craftsman not in touch with either the original artist or the author.

The fact that he took the trouble to procure the presentation manuscript he gave to Charles II proves its importance to Hobbes. His full motives for the gift were clearly quite complex, but he knew in advance that the Royalists were unlikely to approve the book, and simple self-defence must have been one powerful factor. He needed to show that this was not a book that he felt ashamed of in Royalist company: that it was a work of science, presenting permanently valid principles, which only an accident of the times made apt to 'frame the minds of a thousand gentlemen' to conscientious obedience to Cromwell. In addition, the missionary urge natural to every political philosopher from Plato onwards must also have moved him as he presented the manuscript to Charles: the claims his book makes for itself are sufficient proof of that. It follows from this that Hobbes is unlikely to have been too casual about the presentation of his gift, of which the drawn title-page doubling the functions of today's blurb and dust-jacket design, was the most important part. This in itself would be sufficient to explain his turning to Hollar: probably one of the greatest graphic artists whose name would have been familiar to Hobbes, and also Charles's old tutor in drawing, whose style could be expected to suit the royal taste. In this connection it is of interest that for a period running at least from the execution of Charles I to his son's defeat at Worcester, Hollar is thought to have been consciously courting the favour of the Prince. Although he had made his home in Holland during the Civil War years, it has been asserted that he joined the Royalists in the Channel Islands for a while around 1650, and the most recently published study of his work accepts that there are reasons for suspecting that when he later returned to England he did so as a clandestine Royalist courier.[7] Hollar, in touch with Royalist circles, thus may have passed through France at a suitable time, and Hobbes could in any case have easily enough made contact with him even when in Holland, either by a personal visit or via intermediaries. For although Hobbes himself was living among the English exiles in Paris, his admirer Sorbière, for example, seems to have brought out editions of his master's work indifferently in Holland or Paris as convenience served, and there was always ample communication between the English Royalists in both countries. In short, there seems to be no practical obstacle to postulating that Hobbes was making use of Hollar's services some time around 1650-1, and it appears that Hollar would have had reasons of his own for taking particular interest at that time in any commission destined for the young Charles II. He would also have been well placed, had Hobbes so wished, to borrow the features of the young Prince for his representation of the Mortal God: a point to which we must return.

This brings us back in a different way to the question of attribution. To what extent do we face here a work of Wenzel Hollar, and to what extent are we facing a work of Thomas Hobbes himself? To a puzzling degree, the general co-ordination of the details of the design can be read either in straightforward aesthetic terms, or else as a further embodiment of the ideas of the book. From the first point of view, it exhibits finesses unlikely to have been within Hobbes's compass; from the second point of view it seems to exhibit a familiarity with Hobbes's work that one might have thought would have been beyond Hollar. Which is the correct way to read it? If the answer is an Empsonian *why not both?* then what seems to be implied is a degree of collaboration between artist and author so close as to be of interest even on those grounds alone. A concrete example will make the point clearer. Take for instance the visual progression which links the two columns of small panels to the large panel above them. On the left it is simple enough. From the collisions of the battle scene we rise to the crowded trophy of weapons, in which the drum and flag (which unite many men and bring them into step) are most prominent and are placed between crossed muskets. The hint of the muskets is picked up in the next panel, in the image of the cannon (force directed to a single end), with the symbol of sovereignty aptly floating above it, which is then transformed into the crown of towers on their commanding high place. From the multiple disorder of the battlefield (for Hobbes the State of Nature is the state of war of all against all) we are thus led upwards through images of controlled force, authority, and command, in a sequence the natural culmination of which is the great crowned figure of Leviathan rising commandingly over its own hilltop: a reasonably uncomplicated transition, quite as likely to stem from Hollar as from Hobbes. Even so, some questions suggest themselves. One neat point about the drawing is the conspicuous inconspicuousness of the citadel of the little town, symmetrical with the big church, yet so flattened and unemphatic that it noticeably fails to provide a rung on the visual ladder we have been climbing towards Leviathan. In terms of Hobbes's ideas in the book that is perfectly correct; to have given more prominence to the citadel would have been to commit a tautology, since what it stands for is better represented by the over-riding figure of the Mortal God. Yet is this a point that one would have expected Hollar to have taken unprompted? On the other hand, there is no sign that Hobbes possessed the talent or inclination for the purely visual game-with-a-hoop that goes on in the left-hand panels: taking a plain circle, making it into the rim of a drum, turning the drum into a cannon-wheel, then laying the circle flat, so that the heavily notched and ridged rim of the wheel becomes the cresting of a crown—this is the sport of a draughtsman, not of a philosopher. It is the same in the parallel column: a visual progression links the right-hand sequence of binary images via the emphasized division of the mitre, and the repeated double church towers to Leviathan's twin weapons of sword and pastoral staff, thus helping to tie the big panel in with the rest of the plate in a way which does not seem to have much to do with its ideas content. Within the smaller sequence itself, the draughtsman can again be seen playing his games. It is delightful to see how the Disputation can be read, in relation to the panel above it, as a trident—with the central body of Church opinion topped by the authority of the President—or as a fork; and delightful too to see how the trophy of theological weapons focuses upon the diagonally placed fork whose shape is picked up not only by the mitre but also by Leviathan's sword and staff. Again one wonders whether this is all. Consider for instance the curious design of the two churches. The flanking of a church by high thin towers half way down its length is rare in European architecture, and is primarily associated with southern Germany, Bohemia, and Switzerland. This is an area in which Hollar had travelled and worked during an important phase in his career. So it is perhaps not surprising that the church in the small panel is very reminiscent of the Neupfarrkirche in Regensburg, where Hollar stayed in the train of the Earl of Arundel and where he received his Patent of Nobility from the Emperor; or that the general silhouette of the larger church should suggest that of Augsburg Cathedral as it appeared in Hollar's day (except for the hanging pepperpot turrets on the tower tops, which are a characteristic feature of the Gothic of Hollar's native Bohemia); or that we should find much the same arrangement of central twin towers and spires in a Hollar drawing of the Swiss convent of Einsiedeln.[8] None the less, despite these reminiscences, the two structures Hollar presents to us do not seem to be quite like any actual building. Both are interesting in their cross-breeding of classical and Gothic forms and the smaller church particularly, is imaginative, original, and creative. But would it have been created purely for the sake of filling out a tidy visual pattern? Is it merely coincidental that *Leviathan* is an anti-ecclesiastical book, attacking Church authority as a divisive force, and offering a clear, simple, and conclusive new intellectual method to replace the unsatisfactory tools of traditional styles of theologico-philosophical discussion, which so often prove to strike equally well in opposite directions? The idea of a church spire as a finger pointing the way to God was not new in Hobbes's day; and in his day too the Church was very markedly pointing the way to God with two rival, competitive fingers, Protestant and Catholic. In a highly number-conscious age, when even Hobbes himself thought it worth noting that his great work had been produced in the year of his Grand Climacteric,[9] is it possible that the twin spires of the church in the large panel, firmly placed where the expectation would be to find one single central spire, have a conscious significance? Considering the detailed reading which the Emblem books invite, it is not necessarily a sign of a too curious mind to consider this. Did Hobbes positively want a twin-spired church, or did Hollar just wish to avoid the weightiness of a large single tower that might detract visually from the predominance of the Mortal God? It is worth raising such considerations, however inconclusively, if only as a useful way of establishing the background against which the largest discrepancy between the drawn and the engraved versions has to be seen: the alteration of the face and of the composition of the body of the Mortal God. This is the only substantial change for which the will of the artist (or the author) rather than the ineptness of the engraver seems clearly to be responsible and Hollar might be thought to

31

be neatly combining, in the general strategy of the large panel, two traditions. The echoes of the frequent representations in religious art of Christ or the Almighty standing or seated enthroned above the Cosmic Arch (often holding sword and scales) are of course obvious, and were clearly recognized, since the rather crudely designed title-page of the French translation of the *Elements of Law* (1652)[10] borrows the figure of Leviathan and re-equips him with the traditional sword and scales. This allusion is strengthened in the drawing by the curvature and the blurring of the landscape beyond the first skyline, which can be seen to be land but has almost the effect of an arch of cloud. On the other hand, there was also a tradition of depicting an earth-goddess, under various names, as springing up from a bulge of ground, sometimes with some appropriate symbol in each hand.[11] Here too is an apposite parallel to the image of the Mortal and hence terrestrial God. Seen in this perspective, the superiority of the engraved body of Leviathan to the drawn version seems quite obvious. The drawn version seems unquestionably the better expression of Hobbes's ideas, as most people would understand them today, since the outward-looking faces make the point, important to him, that what Leviathan wills is what we will. Unhappily the image that conveys this notion also tends to raise visual memories of depictions of that devil whose name is Legion.[12] Therefore the neat wit by which the engraved design simply moves the adoringly contemplative host of the saved and blessed, familiar from the traditional paintings, into the silhouette of the Deity, seems preferable even while being less Hobbesian, and giving some encouragement to misunderstandings. If the presentation drawing does represent the earlier state of the design, then this appears to be an interesting instance of the draughtsman overruling the philosopher. By contrast, the alteration of the face of Leviathan seems to have no particular aesthetic significance, but may well have significance of another sort. There has been a myth among writers on Hobbes that the first version of the engraved title-page of *Leviathan* showed the features of Charles I, which was then changed to a portrait of Cromwell in the alleged second and third editions of the work. In fact this is untrue, for it has now been shown that the 'Charles I' edition is the real third edition (issued *c.* 1680), for which the same plate was used as for the two genuine editions of 1651, and consequently it carries the wrong date. But the plate was too worn to be used without retouching, and the retouching produced changes in Leviathan's face, thus giving rise to the myth.[13] None the less, the fact remains that it seems always to have been accepted that the face of Leviathan in the two genuine editions of 1651, though too hairy to be a precise photographic likeness, is unmistakably suggestive of the features of Oliver Cromwell. Some have seen this as an attempt at self-protection by Hobbes's London publisher, others have seen it as a piece of prudence, cowardice, or sycophancy by Hobbes himself at a time when, like Hollar, 'the truth was he had a mind to go home'. Others again have seen it as an act of simple common sense: Hobbes, a political philosopher seeking practical results by enunciating universal truths, was not necessarily either a coward or a renegade because he could see that Cromwell came closer than any other Englishman in 1651 to embodying the figure of Leviathan. In this connection it is therefore interesting that the face on the drawn title-page, again if one reduces its luxuriance of facial hair, is in fact strongly suggestive, not of Cromwell

Fig. 3. J. Dee, *A Letter* (London, 1599). 1608/657. 190 × 137 mm

nor even Charles I (for a beheaded Leviathan is a contradiction in terms) but of Charles II himself. As a child, the younger Charles seems to have been extremely good-looking, in a rather pudgy-faced juvenile way. Then, in his later teens and early twenties, his beak of a nose began to push its way up through his softly rounded youthful features. The process can be enjoyably followed through successive portrayals of Charles at various ages;[14] but in this case we need only turn to Hollar's own acknowledged engraving of Charles, dating from 1650 (fig. 4), in which appear the same pouched eyes as in the drawing—unusual in so young a man—and the same rather heavy strong nose, in an otherwise somewhat suety face, marked by thick eyebrows, which arch more than in the 'Cromwell' face. In both versions of the title-page the only real difference between the face depicted (which had to be generalized a little for iconic purposes) and that of the person alluded to, lies in the addition of a beard too small to conceal the features being portrayed, and a fuller moustache. If this has never stopped the face on the engraved title from being seen as that of Cromwell, then the face on the drawn title can be seen as Charles II. It may be said that this is no more than might be expected. All the same it does throw a useful sidelight on Hobbes's state of mind at this time. It is true that the Charles who received Hobbes's presentation was the apparently ruined refugee from the Battle of Worcester, but the manuscript must already have been in preparation before that catastrophe, when Charles looked a much larger political figure; and even after the battle the impressive fact remained that Charles had been crowned King of Scots. That both potential leaders of Great Britain should thus have been enabled to see their own image in that of Leviathan, certainly helps to dispose of any notion that the London publication of Hobbes's great work, with its engraved title, was a mere piece of fawning by a tired, frightened, and elderly fugitive. The author of *Leviathan* was a man exasperated and distressed by the splintering fabric of the state to which he belonged, who believed he knew the answer to his country's problems. To ensure that both men who might assume the mantle of Leviathan should understand their role, he was prepared to present it to them by visual as well as verbal hints, and he employed the services of the best artist he knew of for this purpose.

The wider context in which that artist did his work may be worth noting in conclusion. I have mentioned echoes of traditions of religious painting and of Emblem books in the *Leviathan* design. It may also be relevant that Hollar grew up in Prague, where he is known to have taken a close interest in the Imperial art collections, in which the work of Mannerist artists, notably Arcimboldo, had a modestly prominent place. The composition of figures whose outlines are made up of, often symbolically significant, smaller figures was a favourite Mannerist device, with which Hollar himself had experimented. In Holland there was a vogue for Oriental art, including the Chinese and Indian 'caprices' which used precisely the same device, and may in fact have inspired this particular European Mannerist convention.[15] All this is as much a part of the general climate in which the figure of Leviathan was created, as the European tradition of metaphors about the body politic. The packing together of the heads within the drawn version of Leviathan's body[16] seems confirmation that Hollar himself was not unaware of the fact.

34

Fig. 4. Hollar's engraved portrait of King Charles II (1650), after Diepenbeecke. Reproduced from E. Dostàl, *Václav Hollar* (Prague, 1924), pl. 30

1 The engraved title-page of *Leviathan* is the only original Hobbes title-page Molesworth found it necessary to reproduce.

2 W. Whewell, *Lectures on the History of Moral Philosophy in England* (London, 1852), 21: 'In the common editions, the face has a manifest resemblance to Cromwell . . . But in the copy belonging to Trinity College Library, the face appears to be intended for Charles the First . . . and the text of the book is a separate and worse impression, although the errata are the same with the other copies, as well as the date.' (Quoted in the prefatory Note to A. R. Waller's edition of *Leviathan* (Cambridge, 1904).)

3 D. G. Hale, *The Body Politic* (The Hague, 1971), 128, cites Waller's prefatory Note as the authority for this story.

4 The maps which Hobbes provided for his translation of Thucydides, and his prefatory comment on them, show this clearly enough.

5 See, for example, the large plate which Hollar dedicated to Alethea Howard. (I am indebted to Mrs. M. Corbett for drawing my attention to this, as well as for much other invaluable counsel.) A rather rounded drawing of the eyes can be observed in both cases.

6 The authorities of the National Gallery of Prague, which now incorporates the Hollareum, are of the opinion that the British Library drawing, about which I have consulted them, can be ascribed to Hollar. They make the reservation that this judgement is only based upon the study of a photograph, but consider that 'the softness of the drawing, the modellation of the face, and the artist's hand-writing' can all be related 'to Hollar's best drawings' (19 July 1974). My thanks are due to the National Gallery of Prague for their ready assistance in this matter.

7 Katherine S. Van Eerde, *Wenceslaus Hollar: Delineator of his time* (Charlottesville, 1970), 41–4.

8 F. Sprinzels, *Hollar Handzeichnungen* (Vienna–Prague, 1938), pl. 255. Compare also the massed small figures on pl. 165, 'Hinrichtung in Linz', with the engraved Leviathan title-page.

9 The point is made, rather casually, in his Latin verse autobiography. The symbolism traditionally attached to the number Two was division, sin: 'God hates the Duall Number, being knowne the luckless number of division' (Herrick, *Noble Numbers*).

10 *Le Corps Politique ou les Elements de la Loy Morale et Civile* (Paris, 1652).

11 See under 'Erde' in Otto Schmitt, *Reallexikon Zur deutschen Kunstgeschichte* (Stuttgart, 1967), vol. v.

12 See the engraved title-page to John Dee's *A Letter Containing a most briefe Discourse Apologeticall* (London, 1599). (Fig. 3.)

13 The confusion over the history of the early editions of *Leviathan* was finally cleared up in Hugh Macdonald and Mary Hargreaves, *Thomas Hobbes, A Bibliography* (London, 1952), 27–37.

14 See, for example, some of the numerous representations of Charles and his contemporaries inserted into the grangerized Rylands Library copy of E. Hyde, 1st Earl of Clarendon's *History of the Rebellion and Civil Wars of England* (Oxford, 1807).

15 See F. Legrand and F. Sluys, *Arcimboldo et les Arcimboldesques* (Aalter, 1955), 73.

16 A cloak the lining of which is composed of women's heads or faces, in a satirical engraved portrait of the Restoration wit Tom Killigrew (catalogued as by Hollar in the British Museum collection) seems to show a clear recollection of the drawn *Leviathan* title-page, of which indeed it might almost be considered a quiet parody. Killigrew's face and 'crown', in this portrait, are also distinctly reminiscent of Leviathan.

Acknowledgement. I owe a special debt to Mr. H. Neville Davies, of the Shakespeare Institute, Birmingham University.

[18]

Hobbes' Linguistic Turn*

Terence Ball
University of Minnesota

Thomas Hobbes has often been regarded as a "protopositivist" precursor of the scientific study of politics. Terence Ball argues here that it may be more appropriate to consider him as a thinker acutely aware that social and political reality is linguistically made. However, Hobbes was inclined to treat the distortion or breakdown of communication as a technical problem to be met by the sovereign's imposition of "shared" meanings.

Terence Ball is Professor of Political Science at the University of Minnesota. He is the author of Civil Disobedience and Civil Deviance *(1973), editor of* Political Theory and Praxis *(1977), co-editor of* After Marx *(1984), and numerous articles in professional journals. He is currently writing a book to be called* Reappraisals in Political Theory.

> The elementary political process is the action of mind upon mind through speech . . . Even as people belong to the same culture by the use of the same language, so they belong to the same society by the understanding of the same moral language. As this common moral language extends, so does society; as it breaks up, so does society.
>
> —Bertrand de Jouvenel

The history of momentous events and movements is almost invariably written by the winners rather than by the losers and also-rans, and this is as true of philosophical as of political movements. The winners who have written the history of the social sciences, and of political science in particular, have heretofore been the proponents of a positivistically conceived science of society. And, as one might expect, their version contains several significant omissions. Looking at Thucydides, ostensibly the first "scientific" historian, or Hobbes, the first self-consciously

* For criticizing an earlier version of this paper I thank Peter Euben and M. M. Goldsmith. Neither, of course, should be held responsible for the final result.

740   Hobbes' Linguistic Turn

"scientific" political theorist, or Hume, or Marx, or Mill, we find that certain aspects of their thinking are systematically neglected or ignored because they cannot be grasped by the canons of comprehension available to the methodological naturalist (or "positivist," if you prefer). The positivists are inclined to take as much of Thucydides and Hobbes as will fit their particular methodological mold and to discard the rest as irrelevant. Our predecessors are thereby shown to have been proto-positivists. This procrustean process of reinterpretation is not necessarily illegitimate. We do often interpret and understand our forbears not wholly in their terms, but partially in our own. In this sense all history is present history, and interpretation amounts (in Gadamer's phrase) to a fusion of horizons—our own and that of our predecessors.

I propose to reexamine several aspects of Hobbes' political philosophy from a perspective that may be called conceptual or linguistic. Used as a lens through which to view our predecessors and our relation to them, it enables us to restore previously ignored or discarded aspects of our intellectual ancestry. To reconsider our past is also to consider our present predicaments and future possibilities in a new light. My argument begins with a brief account of what the linguistic turn does, and does not, imply. I then go on to suggest that this turn was taken in political theory long before it was taken in philosophy, and that the first to take it in political theory was none other than the first self-consciously scientific thinker, Thomas Hobbes, who in turn grounds his science of politics at least partly upon the conceptual-*cum*-political insights of the first supposedly scientific historian, Thucydides. Viewed in this way, Hobbes emerges as a richer, more interesting—and methodologically more ambivalent—thinker than the protopositivist precursor of a naturalistic political science that he is generally presumed to be. I conclude by considering some of the political implications of Hobbes' linguistically grounded science of politics.

I. The Linguistic Turn

When we say that modern philosophy generally, and political philosophy in particular, has taken a linguistic turn,[1] we do not mean merely that philosophers are nowadays interested in investigating the nature and functions of language, for that has been a perennial concern (*vide* Plato's *Cratylus*). Roughly, we might say that the linguistic turn began with the realization that our language does not merely mirror the world but is instead partially constitutive of it. Our concepts and categories

1. The phrase comes originally, I believe, from Richard Rorty, ed., *The Linguistic Turn* (Chicago: University of Chicago Press, 1967).

are not ultimately reducible to names or labels to be affixed to independently existing phenomena or forms of life. On the contrary, reality —particularly political reality—is to a very considerable degree linguistically or conceptually constructed.[2] The materials out of which our common world is made are the concepts, categories, discriminations, divisions, designations and differentiations to be found in the language we speak. More than the lens through which we view the world, language is the medium through which we continually constitute and reconstitute it. And this we do by acting with, upon, and through our language. With language we perform actions and create worlds.

In hindsight, the linguistic turn appears almost as an instance of uncoordinated simultaneous discovery. Philosophers as different as Dewey and Wittgenstein, Peirce and Heidegger argued—albeit in markedly different idioms—that our world is conceptually and communicatively constituted. Heidegger put the point most strongly (and with uncharacteristic clarity) when he suggested that we do not have our language so much as it has us.[3] Not only philosophers, but linguists and anthropologists—Whorf and Sapir most notably—advanced and illustrated the claim that the social world is conceptually and communicatively constituted. As Dewey put it:

> Society not only continues to exist ... by communication, but it may be fairly said to exist in ... communication. There is more than a verbal tie between the words common, community, and communication. Men live in a community in virtue of the things which they have in common; and communication is the way in which they come to possess things in common.[4]

This, as we shall see, is a claim that Thucydides and Hobbes could have accepted.

II. Hobbes' New Science of Politics

Among Thomas Hobbes' many boasts, none was prouder than his claim to be the first truly scientific political thinker. Placing himself in some

2. See, e.g., Michael J. Shapiro, *Language and Political Understanding* (New Haven: Yale University Press, 1981); William E. Connolly, *The Terms of Political Discourse,* 2nd ed. (Princeton: Princeton University Press, 1983); Fred Dallmayr, *Language and Politics* (Notre Dame: University of Notre Dame University Press, 1984).

3. Martin Heidegger, *The Piety of Thinking* (Bloomington: Indiana University Press, 1976), p. 28.

4. John Dewey, *Democracy and Education* (New York: Macmillan, 1916), p. 4.

742   Hobbes' Linguistic Turn

very impressive company, he compared his achievement with those of
Galileo and Harvey. Physical science or "natural philosophy," he continues, "is therefore but young; but Civil Philosophy is yet much
younger, as being no older than my own book *De Cive.*" [5] Hobbes' own
assessment of his achievement has been widely accepted at face value.
Mill's remark that Hobbes was the first to view "the methods of physical
science as the proper models for the political" anticipates the claims of
later commentators.[6] According to this view, Hobbes attempted to apply
the methodological canons and criteria of the natural sciences to the
study of social and political phenomena. And being both a materialist
and a determinist, Hobbes conceived human actions to be ultimately
describable as physical matter in motion, and explainable via general
laws governing the motion of all matter.

Although there is no shortage of evidence to support such an interpretation, almost all of it comes from his boasts and his programmatic
pronouncements and little, if any, from his actual practice. As if to
underscore his contention that humans are apt to use language to mislead their unwary fellows, Hobbes often says one thing while doing
something else entirely. On the one hand, he compares his science to
Galileo's; but, on the other, he avers that it is the use and abuse of
speech that characterizes the sentient subject-matter of civil philosophy, and this makes his science quite unlike that of Galileo or Harvey.
Yet this tension goes almost wholly unrecognized because of our inclination to ransack the past in search of like-minded precursors. This results in text-book history of the simplest sort. The history of our discipline is supposedly the story of the forward march of science, as it
progressively discards the excess baggage of philosophy and assumes a
surer scientific aspect. Thus, for example, Plato's "preference for imaginative and somewhat rigid theoretical notions drawn from brilliant
fancy rather than hard fact" gives way to the "solid good sense" of
Aristotle, "the first great behavioral scientist." [7]

5. Thomas Hobbes, *English Works* [*E.W.*], ed. Sir William Molesworth (London: John Bohn, 1839), Vol. I, p. viii.

6. John Stuart Mill, *Autobiography* (New York: Columbia University Press,
1924), p. 116. In somewhat different ways and with different emphases, Mill's lead
is followed by, *inter alia*, Richard S. Peters, *Hobbes* (Harmondsworth: Penguin,
1967); J. W. N. Watkins, *Hobbes's System of Ideas* (London: Hutchinson, 1965);
and M. M. Goldsmith, *Hobbes's Science of Politics* (New York: Columbia University Press, 1966).

7. See, respectively, Robert A. Dahl, *Modern Political Analysis* (Englewood
Cliffs, N.J.: Prentice-Hall, 1963), p. 24; and Bernard Berelson and Gary Steiner,
Human Behavior: An Inventory of Scientific Findings (New York: Harcourt, Brace
& World, 1964), p. 13.

In Hobbes' case this "progressive" move is effected by dividing his life and work into two stages. The divide is marked by Hobbes' discovery of geometry. As Aubrey relates the story:

> He was ... 40 yeares old before he looked on geometry; which happened accidently. Being in a gentleman's library ..., Euclid's Elements lay open, and 'twas the 47 *El libri* I. He read the proposition. 'By G—,' sayd he (He would now and then sweare, by way of emphasis), 'this is impossible!' So he reads the demonstration of it, which referred him back to such a proposition; which proposition he read. That referred him back to another, which he also read. *Et sic deinceps,* that at last was demonstrably convinced of that trueth. This made him in love with geometry.[8]

After discovering Euclid, Hobbes discarded Thucydides; he ceased being the historically minded humanist who translated Thucydides and became the mathematically-minded social scientist who wrote the *Leviathan.*[9] Against the two-Hobbes thesis I shall suggest that he incorporated a central Thucydidean theme into his science, which thereby fails to prefigure later positivist conceptions.[10]

Hobbes' translation of Thucydides' *History* in 1629 (his first published work) contains an illuminating preface in which he calls special attention to the constitutive role of speech in political affairs. It is through the medium of language that societies exist and through their speech that men reason, rule, lie, command, calculate, dissimulate, deceive, justify, persuade and dissuade, accuse and excuse, commend and condemn. It is therefore no accident that a series of speeches should occupy pride of place in Thucydides' *History.* These speeches were not verbatim reports but were instead imaginative reconstructions in which Thucydides "make[s] the speakers say what was in [his] opinion demanded of them by the various occasions." [11] This practice has been dismissed or downplayed by some modern critics as so much window-

---

8. John Aubrey, *Brief Lives,* ed. O. L. Dick (Harmondsworth: Penguin, 1972), p. 230.

9. See, *inter alia,* Peters, *Hobbes,* ch. 1; Watkins, *Hobbes's System,* ch. 2; Goldsmith, *Hobbes's Science,* esp. ch. 7.

10. Although I find myself in partial agreement with the late Leo Strauss, who stressed the continuing importance of Hobbes' "humanist" phase I cannot agree with his version of the two-Hobbeses thesis, which seems to me to take insufficient account of Hobbes' understanding of science. See Strauss, *The Political Philosophy of Hobbes* (Chicago: University of Chicago Press, 1963).

11. Thucydides, *History of the Peloponnesian War,* trans. Crawley (New York: Modern Library, 1951), p. 14. For Hobbes' translation, see *E.W.,* VIII, p. 25.

744   Hobbes' Linguistic Turn

dressing, mere literary interruptions in an ongoing causal narrative.[12]

Not so Hobbes. Thucydides' use of "deliberative orations" is not peripheral but is in fact essential to his account. For it is through their speech that the actors reveal, and occasionally conceal, their real reasons for acting:

> The grounds and motives of every action [Thucydides] setteth down before the action itself, either narratively, or else contriveth them into the form of deliberative orations. . . . Digressions for instruction's cause, and other such conveyance of precepts, (which is the philosopher's part), he never useth; as having so clearly set before men's eyes the ways and events of good and evil counsels, that the narration itself doth secretly instruct the reader, and more effectually than can possibly be done by precept.

"In sum," Hobbes concludes, "if the truth of history did ever appear in the manner of relating, it doth so in this history: so coherent, perspicuous and persuasive is the whole narration, and every part thereof." [13] As we shall see, Hobbes' method and style are similarly inseparable; he too seeks to instruct without having recourse to explicit precepts— the political prescriptions being built, as it were, into the very structure and style of "scientific" argumentation.

From the conventional positivist perspective, Hobbes' admiration for Thucydides is at least partially clear if not wholly transparent. For Thucydides, like his translator, allegedly aspired to supply scientific explanations of political phenomena. Taking Hippocratic medicine as his model, Thucydides was in effect the Dr. Harvey of Hellenic politics. Distinguishing symptoms from causes, he traces the natural course of the political disease which, like the plague at Athens, has afflicted his countrymen and must now run its natural course. Thucydides' history accordingly takes the form of a naturalistic narrative in which causes precede effects in accordance with general laws.[14] In this narrative talk is cheap; words are irrelevant; and reasons are apt to be mere rationalizations masking underlying causal processes of which the agents are

---

12. See, e.g., Charles Norris Cochrane, *Thucydides and the Science of History* (London: Oxford University Press, 1929), esp. pp. 25–26; William T. Bluhm, *Theories of the Political System* (Englewood Cliffs, N.J.: Prentice-Hall, 1965), ch. 2.

13. Hobbes, *E.W.*, VIII, p. xxi.

14. Cochrane, *Thucydides*, chs. 3 and 9; Bluhm, *Theories*, ch. 2. In *The Idea of History* (New York: Oxford University Press, 1956), R. G. Collingwood— that most astute critic of "scientific" history—nevertheless accepts uncritically Cochrane's "scientific" reading of Thucydides' intentions (see p. 29).

unaware and over which they have little or no control. Thus the speeches of the actors are irrelevant distractions, inserted to provide literary relief from an otherwise relentless causal narrative. Thucydides' aim is supposedly to supply nomological knowledge of the appropriate causal connections, so as to enable the reader to recognize in future the symptoms of political disorder, the better to stem the most grievous excesses of the disease as it runs its natural, necessary, and inevitable course. This interpretation would seem to rely, perhaps too heavily, on Thucydides' account of the plague that afflicted Athens in the second year of the war.[15] Perhaps it is better understood as a dramatic device rather than as a scientific model of a natural process.

We find in Thucydides' *History* a foreshadowing of a theme and a tension that has, in our day, become a matter for theoretical reflection. On the one side, he appears to offer a straightforwardly naturalistic account of the etiology of one war, subsumed under a more general schema for analyzing subsequent conflicts. By understanding the causes of human conflict, we can in principle predict and perhaps control its course. Theoretical knowledge answers to the technical interest in prediction and control. This is the "scientific" Thucydides who is much admired by writers in the "realist" tradition.

Yet, Thucydides can be read in a different and arguably more illuminating light. What might at first appear to be natural and inevitable processes and events are themselves revealed, upon closer inspection, to be the creations—or, rather, the miscreations—of men talking past one another, failing, because of unperceived though potentially remediable distortions and misunderstandings, to communicate and thus to speak in the fraternal "tone of expostulation" that Pericles believed to be the proper mode of address between equals and allies.[16] Note, in this connection, the contrast between the Athenians' earlier eloquence and the spare monotone of the later speeches, the Melian dialogue in particular. The speech of the Athenians—formerly so eloquent and reasonable—is, in the sixteenth year of the war, reduced to the terse formulas and ritual banalities not only of their Spartan enemies but of their earlier "barbaric" Persian foes. All the arguments of the ill-fated Melians fall on deaf ears. Appeals to justice, and to the memory of past alliances against the Persian invaders, are summarily shrugged off. In this

15. Thucydides, *History,* Bk. II, ch. 7, pp. 110–115; *E.W.,* VIII, pp. 201–212. Cochrane (*Thucydides,* pp. 27–32), Collingwood (*Idea of History,* pp. 29–30), and Bluhm (*Theories,* pp. 26–30) are agreed that Thucydides' description of the plague reveals his deep methodological debt to the Hippocratic school. For a critique, see my *Reappraisals in Political Theory,* ch. 2 (forthcoming).

16. Ibid., Bk. I, ch. 5, p. 79; *E.W.,* VIII, p. 145.

746   Hobbes' Linguistic Turn

world, says the Athenian envoy, "the strong do what they can and the weak suffer what they must." [17] The Melian men are slaughtered and their women and children sold into slavery.

Even more pertinent is Thucydides' account of the revolution at Corcyra, in which the conceptual and communicative basis of political order is most fully and dramatically exemplified. When words lose their meaning, communication—and therefore community—is impossible. Conceptual confusion and political chaos are one and the same:

> Words had to change their ordinary meaning and to take that which was now given them. Reckless audacity came to be considered the courage of a loyal ally; prudent hesitation, specious cowardice; moderation was held to be a cloak for unmanliness; ability to see all sides of a question inaptness to act on any. Frantic violence became the attribute of manliness; cautious plotting, a justifiable means of self-defense. . . . To succeed in a plot was to have a shrewd head, to divine a plot a still shrewder [one]. . . . Oaths of reconciliation, being only proffered on either side to meet an immediate difficulty, only held good so long as no other weapon was at hand; but when opportunity offered, he who first ventured to seize it and to take his enemy off his guard, thought this perfidious vengeance sweeter than an open one, since . . . success by treachery won him the palm of superior intelligence. . . . The cause of all these evils was the lust for power arising from greed and ambition; and from these passions proceeded the violence of the parties. . . . [T]he use of fair phrases to arrive at guilty ends was in high reputation. . . .
>
> The ancient simplicity into which honor so largely entered was laughed down and disappeared; and society became divided into camps in which no man trusted his fellow. To put an end to this, there was neither promise to be depended upon, nor oath that could command respect; but all parties dwelling rather in their calculation upon the hopelessness of a permanent state of things, were more intent upon self-defense than capable of confidence. [18]

17. Ibid., Bk. V, ch 17, p 331; *E.W.*, IX, p. 99.

18. Ibid., Bk. III, ch. 10, pp. 189–191; *E.W.*, VIII, pp. 348–349. While revising the present essay for publication I discovered James Boyd White's *When Words Lose Their Meaning* (Chicago: University of Chicago Press, 1984), the third chapter of which approaches Thycydides' *History* in much the same way I do (and, I believe, as Hobbes did), viz. as an account of the political implications of conceptual confusion and communicative breakdown. I am grateful to Peter Euben for calling White's fine study to my attention.

Point for point, feature for feature, Hobbes' state of nature parallels Thucydides' description of the Corcyraean revolution. More striking still, Hobbes follows Thucydides' account of the essentially *conceptual* character of political conflict.

Hobbes and Thucydides, in effect, agree that polities are the collective communicative creations of their members. The role of Thucydides' theory is to expose, criticize, and attempt to remove the sources of blocked or systematically distorted communication. Political theory therefore answers to a "practical" interest in human understanding rather than to a "technical" interest in control. This is to speak in the idiom of Habermas and not of Thucydides and Hobbes, who say nothing at all about distorted communication, technical and practical knowledge, constitutive interests, and the like. And yet the hermeneutical risk seems worth taking. For it allows us to see features of their thought that are obscured by an interpretation which assumes that any science worthy of the name must necessarily yield nomological knowledge and answer to a technical interest in prediction and control. An alternative reading of Hobbes suggests that the choice need not be between science and nonscience but between two differently grounded conceptions of science.

Hobbes is hardly a closet critical theorist; nor does he reject the standard protopositivist account of explanation via general laws. But if he sometimes seems to profess one thing while actually practicing another that is because he does not distinguish between different levels of description. Although trying his hardest to remain a reductionist, he fails miserably and magnificently. His account, like that of Thucydides, is too richly suggestive, too pregnant with multiple possibilities, to be confined within any austerely reductionist framework. This may be because the linguistic turn, once taken, will not permit him to take the reductionist route that he apparently wished to follow. Once viewed as speaking subjects, and not merely as material objects, human beings become self-defining creatures of convention, not of nature.

If man *qua* body is an object amenable to natural-scientific explanation, man *qua* citizen is not: "What is to be understood about men insofar as they are *men,* is not applicable insofar as they are *citizens.*" [19] Man in the state of nature is scarcely more than a body bent upon preserving itself from annihilation; the instinct for self-preservation is natural, and shared with all other animals. "Every man," says Hobbes, "is

19. Hobbes, *De Homine,* in *Latin Works* [*L.W.*], ed. Molesworth (London: John Bohn, 1839), vol. II, ch. 13, p. 116; English translation in *Man and Citizen* [*M.C.*], ed. Bernard Gert (Garden City, N.Y.: Anchor Books, 1972), p. 68.

748   Hobbes' Linguistic Turn

desirous of what is good for him and shuns what is evil, but chiefly the
chiefest of natural evils, which is death; and this he doth by a certain
impulsion of nature no less than that whereby a stone moves downward." [20] Falling stones and man *qua* body are both subject to the laws
governing matter in motion. To explain a particular instance of either
is merely to subsume a description of it under the appropriate general
law. In this respect Hobbes does indeed appear to be the protopositivist
that he is reputed to be. Yet this apparently clear picture is quickly
clouded by several further considerations. For one, Hobbes is amply
aware that there are numerous and frequent counterinstances to the ostensibly general law that people act always to preserve themselves. Although their fear of violent death "encline[s] men to Peace," they repeatedly risk death for the sake of "honor" and other "trifles." [21] Thus
the natural instinct of self-preservation is occasionally overridden by
vain and prideful men. At the very least this general law would then
have to be restricted to the explanation of *rational* behavior.

The difficulty with this move is, however, immediately apparent. For
to be rational, says Hobbes, is to have the use of speech: "in reasoning,
a man must take heed of words." Since without language there is no
reason, only humans can be said to be fully rational.[22] But ironically it
is language—the medium of reason itself—which feeds vanity and in-
flames the passions. To reason with loose and imprecisely defined concepts just *is* to act in inflammatory, irrational and self-destructive ways.
That we are language-using and abusing creatures makes us, unlike
stones, ill-suited to be subjects of a natural science. And this difference
in subject-matter dictates a difference in method.

The "most notable and profitable invention of all others," Hobbes
says, "was that of SPEECH, . . . without which, there had been amongst
men, neither Commonwealth, nor Society, nor Contract, nor Peace, no
more than amongst Lyons, Bears, and Wolves." [23] Language is a blessing, in that it is the medium that makes reason and science possible; but
also a bane, because of our penchant for using words loosely and according to our own momentary appetites and inclinations. For every
good use of language there is a corresponding abuse; and it is our abuse
of language—making false statements, lying, making insincere prom-

20. Hobbes, *De Cive*, in *E.W.*, II, p. 8.
21. Hobbes, *Leviathan* [*Lev.*], ed. C. B. Macpherson (Harmondsworth: Penguin, 1968), ch. 13, p. 188; cf. also ch. 11, p. 164.
22. Ibid., ch. 4, p. 109 and ch. 5 *passim;* cf. *De Homine*, ch. 10, sec. 1, *L.W.*,
II, pp. 88–89; *M.C.*, pp. 37–38.
23. *Lev.*, ch. 4, p. 100.

ises, speaking metaphorically, boasting, insulting our fellows, and the like—that makes us wary and distrustful and that puts us, in short, in that "state of Warre" that is the state of nature.

The state of nature is for Hobbes both a description of dire political possibility and an ingenious methodological device according to which "we feign the world to be annihilated." The world thus methodologically dissolved is the common world of mutual meanings and shared significations. The state of nature is a condition of complete communicative breakdown, a veritable Babel of mutually incomprehensible voices and tongues. Or, to speak in a more modern idiom, the tragedy of the state of nature is that although its inhabitants are linguistically competent (in Chomsky's sense) they are not yet communicatively competent (in Habermas' sense). They have the capacity to speak, to construct and utter well-formed sentences but they are still apt to speak insincerely, self-interestedly, untruthfully.[24] Each attempts the impossible feat of speaking a private language; each tries, in Humpty-Dumpty fashion, to make words mean whatever he wishes them to mean. The upshot is that the concepts constitutive of civil order—"right" and "justice," for example—are meaningless sounds, signifying nothing. "To this warre of every man against every man, this also is consequent; that nothing can be Unjust. The notions of Right and Wrong, Justice and Injustice have there no place." In this natural state there is "no Propriety, no Dominion, no *Mine* and *Thine* distinct; but onely that to be every mans that he can get; and for so long, as he can keep it." [25]

The natural state of humankind is, however, quite unlike the natural condition in which the other animals find themselves. And this difference is again due to our being language-using creatures. "It is true," Hobbes acknowledges, "that certain living creatures, as Bees and Ants, live sociably with one another . . . and yet have no other direction, than their particular judgements and appetites; nor speech, whereby one of them can signifie to another, what he thinks expedient for the common benefit: and therefore some men may perhaps desire to know, why Man-kind cannot do the same." Hobbes has several answers. For one, the concepts of honor, dignity and envy are not available to ants and bees; for another, "they want that art of words, by which some men can represent to others, that which is Good, in the likenesse of Evil; and

24. See Jürgen Habermas, "Toward a Theory of Communicative Competence," *Inquiry* 13 (1970): 360–375; *Communication and the Evolution of Society,* trans. Thomas McCarthy (Boston: Beacon Press, 1979), ch. 1.

25. Hobbes, *Lev.,* ch. 13, p. 188.

750   Hobbes' Linguistic Turn

Evill, in the likenesse of Good." [26] Because we can speak, we can communicate our false beliefs, thereby deceiving others and, no less often,
ourselves: "man, alone among the animals . . . can devise errors and
pass them on for the use of others. Therefore man errs more widely and
dangerously than can other animals." Moreover, "because of the ease of
speech, the man who truly doth not think, speaks; and since what he
says, he believes to be true, he, unlike a beast, can deceive himself.
Therefore by speech man is not made better but merely given greater
possibilities." [27] Thus the task of the zoologist, and indeed the natural
philosopher generally, is easier and more straightforward than that of
the civil philosopher or political scientist. The former need not concern
himself with the linguistic and conceptual preconstitution of his science's object-domain; his subjects cannot lie, dissimulate and mislead,
for they lack the use of language altogether. The civil philosopher, by
contrast, deals with a wily subject made the more canny by his capacity
to acquire, to use—and above all to abuse—language. Thus civil philosophy necessarily takes a sharp turn—a linguistic turn—*away* from
natural philosophy.

Hobbes' civil philosophy differs from natural philosophy in several
significant respects. Natural philosophy deals in probabilities, civil philosophy in certainties; natural philosophy studies nature—the art of
God—whereas civil philosophy studies "the art of man." [28] "Since the
causes of natural things are not in our power, but in [God's] . . . [we]
cannot deduce their qualities from their causes." We can only "demonstrate that such and such *could* have been their causes. This kind of
demonstration is called *a posteriori,* and its science physics." By contrast, "politics and ethics (that is, the sciences of *just* and *unjust,* of
equity and *inequity*) can be demonstrated *a priori;* because we ourselves
make the principles—that is, the causes of justice (namely laws and
covenants)—whereby it is known what *justice* and *equity* and their op-
posites *injustice* and *inequity,* are." [29] Civil philosophy, in other words,
deals with the commonwealth, that most human of creations. Our
knowledge of matters political is more certain than our knowledge of
natural phenomena, for we have made the former but not the latter. The
creator's knowledge of his own creation is unique and privileged. And
just as God has perfect knowledge of his own creation, so may man have
perfect and certain knowledge of his.

26. Ibid., ch. 17, pp. 225–226.
27. *L.W.,* II, pp. 90–91; *M.C.,* pp. 40–41 (I have slightly altered the English
translation).
28. *Lev.,* Introduction, p. 81.
29. *L.W.,* II, pp. 93–94; *M.C.,* pp. 42–43.

It is ironic that Hobbes, who was so keenly critical of his medieval forbears, relies so heavily upon their doctrine that knowledge and creation are one. But he gives the medieval doctrine of *verum et factum convertuntur* a distinctly conventionalist twist. For unlike (say) Aquinas, who applies the doctrine to God's creation of the material world, Hobbes, the self-proclaimed materialist, applies it exclusively to the nonmaterial "artificial" world of concepts and ideas. The language devised by Adam was lost after Babel and must now be created anew.[30] Words and concepts are our inventions and have only such meaning as we give to them. Because the world of mutual meanings and shared significations—our world—is our own creation, we can know it in a way that we can never know the world of nature.[31]

Hobbes' new science of politics takes geometry as its model, not out of a Cartesian conviction that mathematics mirrors the underlying structure of the natural world, but because it does *not*. The civil philosopher's knowledge of matters political is every bit as certain as the geometer's, and for precisely the same reason: geometry is, in Hobbes' view, the product—indeed, the very paradigm—of human art and artifice. "Geometry, therefore is demonstrable, for the lines and figures from which we reason, are drawn and described by ourselves; and civil philosophy is demonstrable because we make the commonwealth ourselves." [32] Because the commonwealth is created by its members, they alone can have perfect knowledge of its structure and operation.

Any science worthy of the name, Hobbes suggests, must yield perfect, and not merely provisional or contingent knowledge.[33] Until Hobbes bestowed civil philosophy on us, geometry was "the onely Science that it hath pleased God hitherto to bestow on mankind." [34] The striking oddity of this claim is lessened somewhat by attending to Hobbes' distinction between two kinds of knowledge—roughly, that which we acquire through observation of "fact" and that which we gain through deduction. And this distinction is in turn tied to the claim

30. Ibid., ch. 4, p. 101. Hobbes' "brisk wit" is especially evident in his amusing and logically astute analysis of Adam's language. "How," he asks, "could Adam have understood the serpent speaking of 'death,' whereof he, the first mortal, could have had no acquaintance and therefore no idea?" See *L.W.,* II, p. 95; *M.C.,* pp. 38–39 (again I have altered the translation slightly).

31. In this respect, at least, Hobbes' new science resembles that of his erstwhile critic, Vico. See my "On 'Making' History in Vico and Marx," in Giorgio Tagliacozzo, ed., *Vico and Marx: Affinities and Contrasts* (Atlantic Highlands, N.J.: Humanities Press, 1983), pp. 77–93.

32. *E.W.,* VII, p. 184.

33. *L.W.,* II, p. 92; *M.C.,* p. 41.

34. *Lev.,* ch. 4, p. 105.

752   Hobbes' Linguistic Turn

that we have a special sort of knowledge of what we ourselves have made:

> There are of knowledge two kinds; whereof one is *Knowledge of Fact;* the other *Knowledge of the Consequence of one Affirmation to another.* The former is nothing else, but Sense and Memory, and is Absolute Knowledge; as when we see a Fact doing, or remember it done: And this is the Knowledge required in a Witnesse. The later is called *Science;* and is Conditionall; as when we know, that, if the figure showne be a circle, then any straight line through the Center shall divide it into two equal parts. And this is the Knowledge required in a Philosopher; that is to say, of him that pretends to Reasoning.[35]

Thus natural philosophy and civil philosophy are scientific in different senses. For civil philosophy can follow, as physics cannot, the lead of the geometer. True philosophy consists of reasoning, which Hobbes contrasts with empirical observation:

> Reason is not as Sense, and Memory, borne with us; nor gotten by Experience onely; as Prudence is; but attayned by Industry; first in apt imposing of Names; and secondly by getting a good and orderly Method in proceeding from the Elements, which are Names, to Assertions made by Connexion of one of them to another; and so to Syllogismes, which are the Connexions of one Assertion to another, till we come to a knowledge of all the Consequences of names appertaining to the subject in hand; and that is it, men call SCIENCE.[36]

What has heretofore passed for moral or civil philosophy has not, however, been genuinely scientific. "What hath hitherto been written by moral philosophers, hath not made any progress in the knowledge of the truth," says Hobbes, because they have not defined their terms precisely and deduced their conclusions accordingly. "For were the nature of human actions as distinctly known, as the nature of quantity in geometrical figures, the strength of avarice and ambition, which is sustained by the erroneous opinions of the vulgar, as touching the nature of right and wrong, would presently faint and languish; and mankind should enjoy such an immortal peace, that ... there would hardly be left any pretence for war." [37] But the pretense for civil war stems less

35. Ibid., ch. 9, pp. 147–148.
36. Ibid., ch. 5, p. 115.
37. *De Cive*, Epistle Dedicatory, *E.W.*, II, pp. 3–4.

from the crude views of the vulgar than from the pretentious and ostensibly learned opinions of the philosophers. And it is their failure to be "scientific" that is, in Hobbes' view, the root of almost all political evils. Loose concepts, imprecisely defined terms, metaphors, tropes, and figurative speech of all sorts are the sources of sedition. And these are all the more pernicious because they purportedly derive their authority from philosophy itself. Man alone, says Hobbes, has

> the privilege of Absurdity. . . . And of men, those are of all most subject to it, that professe Philosophy. For . . . there can be nothing so absurd, but may be found in the books of Philosophers. And the reason is manifest. For there is not one of them that begins his ratiocination from the Definitions, or Explications of the names they are to use; which is a method that hath been used only in Geometry; whose Conclusions have thereby been made indisputable.[38]

Hobbes' complaint is not merely methodological but political. The concepts bandied about by earlier philosophers—law, justice, right—pose a political danger of the first magnitude. In the conceptual confusions, contentions and disagreements of the philosophers we find the first stirrings of sedition and discord. Philosophers have heretofore lived in a world of words whose meanings they refuse to define; "and as men abound in copiousnesse of language, so they become more wise, or more mad than ordinary." [39] Such learned madness must sooner or later affect the multitude of the vulgar who further fuel and legitimize their private appetites by appealing to ill-defined notions of justice and right. Anyone doing this "will find himselfe entangled in words, as a bird in limetwiggs; the more he struggles, the more belimed." Traditional or unscientific philosophy is not the solution but is, politically speaking, the problem itself. Hence modern men are well-advised not to "spend time in fluttering over their bookes; as birds that entring by the chimney, and finding themselves inclosed in a chamber, flutter at the false light of a glasse window, for want of wit to consider which way they came in." Abandon Aristotle, and Cicero, and all previous philosophers so-called, counsels Hobbes, and takes the rigorous road of science. For "in the right Definition of Names, lyes the first use of Speech; which is the Acquisition of Science: And in wrong, or no Definitions, lyes the first abuse; from which proceed all false and senseless tenets." [40] From conceptual confusion comes political chaos.

38. *Lev.*, ch. 5, pp. 113–114.
39. Ibid., ch. 4, p. 106.
40. Ibid., ch. 4, pp. 105–106.

754   Hobbes' Linguistic Turn

Hobbes' fulminations against earlier philosophers predate and resemble Keynes' oft-quoted complaint that "madmen in authority, who
hear voices in the air," are more than likely "distilling their frenzy from
some academic scribbler of a few years back." [41] The England of
Hobbes' day, like his hypothetical state of nature, was populated by
madmen, each hearing his own particular voice distilled from one academic scribbler or another. The only cure for conceptual-*cum*-political
chaos was to be found, Hobbes thought, in civil philosophy of a more
surely scientific stripe. A veritable conceptual purge, amounting to nothing less than the complete scientization of the political vocabulary,
seemed the only solution. Just as geometers could not calculate without
first agreeing on definitions, so citizens cannot live together without
sharing a common vocabulary of concepts whose meanings are fixed in
advance. To the civil philosopher, and to the sovereign who follows his
lead, falls the task of purging the political and moral vocabulary of the
citizenry. By fixing once and for all the meanings of the concepts constitutive of the commonwealth itself, he dampens political conflict. By
linguistic art and artifice is created the great Leviathan.
   The first step to be taken by Hobbes' "mortall God" is to undo the
damage done at Babel, when the immortal God decreed that "every man
[be] stricken for his rebellion, with an oblivion of his former language." [42] The damage is to be undone by creating a new language, its
concepts strictly and "scientifically" defined. Thus the sovereign must
purge the philosophically tainted vocabulary of his subjects. For "the
Common-peoples minds, unless they be tainted with dependance on
the Potent, or scribbled over with the opinions of their Doctors [that
is, philosophers], are like clean paper, fit to receive whatsoever by
Publique Authority shall be imprinted in them." [43] The conceptual con-
tests fomented by all previous philosophers must be terminated by sovereign fiat, and true philosophy or "science" sent to rule Leviathan-like
over the children of pride. But this conceptual-*cum*-political purge does
not end here. Besides ridding our vocabulary of the last vestiges of
philosophy, Hobbes would purge it of poetry and literature as well.
Hobbes, no mean poet himself (he composed his autobiography in
Latin verse), vents his wrath upon metaphor and other "abuses of

41. Quoted in Robert L. Heilbroner, *The Worldly Philosophers* (New York:
Simon and Schuster, 1961), p. 2. For Hobbes' version, see *Lev.*, chs. 21 (esp. pp.
267–268), 26 (esp. pp. 315–317), and 29 (pp. 369–370); and *L.W.*, II, pp. 91–92;
M.C., pp. 40–41.
   42. *Lev.*, ch. 4, p. 101.
   43. Ibid., ch. 30, p. 379.

speech." [44] Into the fire go "obscure, confused, and ambiguous Expressions, also all metaphoricall Speeches, tending to the stirring up of Passion." [45] Political science or civil philosophy offers nothing less than a political purgative.

This purge cannot be politically neutral, for science itself has an intrinsic interest in social stability and political pacification. There is indeed a symbiotic relationship between Hobbes' science of politics and the pacific polity envisioned in *Leviathan*. There can be no science, Hobbes insists, where there is no safety, and conversely no lasting security without the aid of science, rightly understood and applied. Science promotes, and is itself part of, commodious living.[46] Without a thorough cleansing of the Augean stables of philosophy men cannot live commodiously.

Hobbes' claim that we must first agree upon definitions before we can come to agreement in moral and political judgments might at first sight seem, if not normatively neutral, then at least politically innocuous. But there are several reasons for thinking otherwise. For it is not only Hobbes' explicitly stated premises and his often painstakingly precise show of definitional rigor that are themselves politically charged; it is, more fundamentally, the "scientific" mode of argument itself that, like Thucydides' exquisitely crafted narrative, "doth secretly instruct the reader, and more effectually than can possibly be done by precept." [47] Hobbes appeals, after all, to precision: and who but an obscurantist can doubt that precision is a virtue? Yet this virtue is not its own reward. For to constrain language, to purge it of tropes and metaphors, to define its constitutive concepts tightly and precisely, just *is* to contain conflict. A sober language for a sober citizenry.

Hobbes' defense of linguistic austerity must be viewed against the background of an older rhetorical tradition in which the aim of political speech is to kindle the passions and direct the interests of the audience. Hobbes is as critical as Plato of appeals to the passions and mere "opinions" of the masses.[48] But, of course, Hobbes' approach and his appeals are no less "rhetorical." He relies upon—indeed he virtually invents—a new rhetorical form. He appeals not to the panoply of the passions but to our fear of death and our corresponding interest in physical safety and self-preservation. This rhetoric of sobriety is not so

44. Ibid., ch. 4, p. 102.
45. Ibid., ch. 25, p. 307.
46. *E.W.*, I, pp. 7–8.
47. *E.W.*, VIII, p. xxii.
48. *Lev.*, ch. 7, p. 131.

much a result of Hobbes' civil philosophy as it is a *requirement* for it. For it is only by assuming certain sorts of interests to be "natural" that his science acquires its intelligibility. It is by first assuming and then appealing to these natural interests that Hobbes is able to cast his arguments in ostensibly "scientific" form. But his explicit epistemological and methodological presuppositions matter less than his own covertly rhetorical strategy. The persuasiveness of Hobbes' science relies a good deal less upon his definitions and deductions than upon his metaphors. What after all is his state of nature if not an extended metaphor in which men are beasts, life is war, war is hell, and so on? And who is the sovereign if not a secular savior, a "mortall god" sent not from heaven but sprung, Athena-like, from the head of the civil philosopher himself? Hobbes was always more adept at detecting the mote of metaphor in another's eye than the beam in his own.[49]

Leaving aside Hobbes' reliance upon metaphor, analogy, allegory and other rhetorical stratagems, there are still other reasons for viewing his science with a skeptical eye. Consider again his contention that political science must proceed by defining the concepts constitutive of political discourse. These will characteristically be what we would nowadays call operational definitions. Consider, for example, his definitions of "law" and allied concepts like "justice." "Law in generall," Hobbes says, "is not Counsell, but Command; nor a Command of any man to any man; but only of him whose Command is addressed to one formerly obliged to obey him." [50] Thus no law, provided that it has been duly promulgated and pronounced by the sovereign, can *ever* be *un*just. To speak of an "unjust law" would be to contradict oneself. For sovereigns, says Hobbes, "*make* the things they command just, by commanding them, and those which they forbid, unjust, by forbidding them." [51] "By a good law," he says elsewhere,

> I mean not a Just Law: for no Law can be Unjust. The Law is made by the Sovereign Power, and all that is done by such a Power, is warranted, and owned by every one of the people; and that which

---

49. See Sheldon S. Wolin, *Hobbes and the Epic Tradition in Political Theory* (Los Angeles: William Andrews Clark Memorial Library, 1970); Norman Jacobson, *Pride and Solace* (Berkeley and Los Angeles: University of California Press, 1978), ch. 3; and Frederick G. Whelan, "Language and Its Abuses in Hobbes' Political Philosophy," *American Political Science Review* 75 (March, 1981): 59–75.

50. *Lev.*, ch. 26, p. 312.

51. *E.W.*, II, p. 151. Hobbes devises not only a "command theory" of law but of *justice* as well. See *L.W.*, II, pp. 117–118; *M.C.*, p. 69.

every man will have so, no man can say is unjust. It is in the Lawes
of a Commonwealth, as in the Lawes of Gaming: whatsoever the
Gamesters all agree on, is Injustice to none of them.[52]

From this it follows that the only operation or test by which we can
determine whether a particular command is indeed a law, and therefore just, is to see whether it in fact issues from the sovereign. If it
does, it is. *Q.E.D.*

This kind of conceptual clarification through operational definition is
not merely a verbal or semantic move having no substantive political
import. By implication and inclination, Hobbes' science of politics allies
itself with, and serves to legitimize, the alignment of power in the society
within which it is institutionally embedded. His science is not a neutral
broom for sweeping semantic rubbish into the dust-bin, but is, on the
contrary, clearly prescriptive, and pregnant with a peculiar vision of the
good society.

III. Objections and Answers

A critic might object that I am wrong in suggesting that Hobbes took a
linguistic turn three centuries ago. For one of the key features of the
linguistic turn in modern philosophy resides in its recognition that languages, or at any rate natural languages, enable speakers to perform
such speech-acts as making promises, excuses, agreements, and so on.
But Hobbes did not take, and could not have taken, anything like a
linguistic turn in our modern sense, for two reasons. The first is that he
was the crudest kind of nominalist. He subscribed, that is, to a word-
and-object conception of language, according to which words are names
or labels that we, by convention, attach to independently existing objects.[53] "All other Names, are but insignificant sounds." [54] And secondly,
Hobbes was an emotivist who held that moral and political concepts—
for example, "good" or "right"—are, strictly speaking, meaningless;
they serve, at most, to signal to others the speaker's state of mind. Thus
to say that something is good means merely that one approves of it;
conversely, to call something bad means only that one dislikes or dis-
approves of it. These are important objections. If they are valid, then
much of my argument is undercut if not defeated outright.

Consider first the claim that Hobbes was a nominalist for whom

---

52. *Lev.,* ch. 30, p. 388.
53. See John W. Danford, *Wittgenstein and Political Philosophy* (Chicago: University of Chicago Press, 1976), ch. 2, and pp. 43–48.
54. *Lev.,* ch. 4, p. 108.

758   Hobbes' Linguistic Turn

words were but names and who, therefore, would not consider the "performative" functions of language. This objection requires that we take at full face value Hobbes' own pronouncements about language, truth, and meaning. This we cannot do. For in his actual practice Hobbes implicitly but clearly recognizes that language is the medium through which human beings conceive, communicate, and perform any number of linguistic actions—swearing oaths, boasting, insulting, authorizing, accusing, excusing, recalling, inciting, lying, and so on *ad infinitum*.[55] Although obscured by his earlier nominalist pronouncements, this "performative" perspective comes clearly to the fore in *De Homine* (1658). The ostensibly "scientific" Hobbes of 1658 rather resembles the "historical" Hobbes of 1629. His discussion of speech in the tenth chapter of *De Homine* marks a turn—or rather a return—to an earlier Thucydidean theme. There Hobbes virtually abandons the crude label-and-object theory of meaning in favor of a richer and more variegated view about the ways in which language actually functions. That view, roughly speaking, focuses less upon language as a system of signs than upon *speech,* understood as the medium through which we *do* things with words. Or, to borrow a distinction from Saussure, we might say that Hobbes became progressively less interested in *langue* and more in *parole,* or language-in-use.

Three uses of speech are, Hobbes thinks, especially noteworthy. The first is that since speech enables men to *measure, count* and *number,* it makes navigation, timekeeping, and architecture possible. Secondly, "one may *teach* another, that is, communicate his knowledge . . . he can *warn,* he can *advise,* all these he hath from speech also; so that a good, great in itself, through communication becomes even greater." Thirdly and most importantly, "that we can *command* and understand commands is a benefit of speech, and truly the greatest. For without this there would be no society among men, no peace, and consequently no disciplines; but first savagery, then solitude, and for dwelling, caves." [56] These three benefits derive directly from the performative character of human speech. An unalloyed nominalist Hobbes was not.

Consider next the objection that Hobbes was a metaethical emotivist for whom moral and political terms had no meaning other than to signify

55. Geraint Parry argues that Hobbes' account of obligation anticipates J. L. Austin's notion of performative utterances. See Parry, "Performative Utterances and Obligation in Hobbes," *Philosophical Quarterly* 17 (1967): 246–253; and the critique by David R. Bell, "What Hobbes Does With Words," *Philosophical Quarterly* 19 (1969): 155–158. Unfortunately, both Bell and Parry focus almost exclusively upon the *Leviathan* and take no notice of the later *De Homine* (1658).

56. *L.W.,* II, pp. 90–91; *M.C.,* pp. 39–40; my italics.

the feelings of the speaker. This objection rests upon a misunderstanding. In the Babel of the state of nature, the emotive theory of meaning is indeed valid—and this is precisely what Hobbes thinks is *wrong* with the state of nature. In that precivil state words like "good" and "evil," "just" and "unjust," have no agreed-upon meaning, other than that of signaling approval or disapproval:

> But whatsoever is the object of any mans Appetite or Desire; that is it, which he for his part calleth Good: And the object of his Hate, and Aversion, Evill; And of his Contempt, Vile, and Inconsiderable. For these words of Good, Evill, and Contemptible, are ever used with relation to the person that useth them: There being nothing simply and absolutely so; nor any common Rule of Good and Evill, to be taken from the nature of the objects themselves; but from the Person of the man *(where there is no Commonwealth)*.[57]

Where there *is* a commonwealth, by contrast, moral concepts do have a single fixed, agreed-upon meaning. "What the legislator commands, must be held for *good,* and what he forbids for *evil.*"[58] In the commonwealth, therefore, the emotivist theory no longer holds true; each moral agent speaks the same moral language. By definitional fiat the sovereign ensures communication, secures consent, and guarantees conceptual continuity of meaning from person to person and from generation to generation. The sovereign supplies nothing less than the common coin of political communication, the conceptual currency that makes civil society possible. His primary function is to create and preserve order. And this he does by creating and maintaining meanings. Or, in a more Thucydidean idiom, his function is to ensure that words have meanings that they do not lose. Word and sword are two sides of the coin of civility. Without both there can be no lasting peace.

But civil peace comes at a price. There can, in Hobbes' commonwealth, be no fundamental dissent. There can be no criticism to the effect that, for example, the sovereign is acting illegally or that the laws he has enacted are unjust, because there is no vocabulary in which dissent is intelligible and criticism communicable. Hobbes' commonwealth is a conceptually closed society. Reason having been defined in terms of discourse duly scientized, political dissent—as distinguished from complaints about individual injury—is indicative of irrationality or insanity. His vision is not of an imaginary nightmare world but of a technocratic

---

57. *Lev.,* ch. 6, p. 120; my italics.
58. *E.W.,* II, p. 150.

760   Hobbes' Linguistic Turn

dream capable of coming all too true in our own time. The precursor of a conceptually sanitized and scientized society largely immune from internal criticism and deaf to dissent, Hobbes has proved to be a prescient prophet. The scientistic appropriation of the linguistic turn was, for Hobbes, an act of hope.[59] For us it stands as a warning.

59. Compare Hobbes' high hopes for linguistic austerity with another Englishman's worst fears: "Don't you see that the whole aim of Newspeak is to narrow the range of thought? In the end we shall make thoughtcrime literally impossible, because there will be no words in which to express it. Every concept . . . will be expressed by exactly *one* word, with its meaning rigidly defined and all its subsidiary meanings rubbed out and forgotten." George Orwell, *1984* (New York: New American Library, 1981), p. 46.

[19]

HOBBES'S PERSUASIVE CIVIL SCIENCE*

By Tom Sorell

Hobbes wrote about politics at a time of great political controversy in England, and he intended his treatises to have an effect on public opinion and behaviour. In the dedication to *The Elements of Law*, the earliest of his full-scale works, he claimed that 'it would be an incomparable benefit to commonwealth, if every man held the opinions concerning law and policy here delivered'. And he hoped that through the intervention of friendly aristocrats his views would reach a wide audience. Later, in *De Cive*, he said that when moral philosophy was 'derived from true principles by evident connection', as his was, it would prove an antidote to a wide range of popular prejudices about politics that had led to bloodshed (*E*, II, xi). *De Cive* was supposed to change people's minds. As for *Leviathan*, its Review and Conclusion says that if Hobbes's doctrine is taught in its pure form, 'most men, knowing their duties, will be 'ess subject to serve the amibition of a few discontented persons, in their purposes against the state'. The book was intended to win round a section of the public preyed upon by, as Hobbes called them, the movers and authors of sedition. All three of the political treatises, in short, were supposed to be persuasive.

They were also supposed to be scientific. In particular, they were intended to exhibit the rigorous argumentation of books of philosophy that Hobbes had encountered on the Continent during his travels there in the 1630s. To bear out his claim that he had something conclusive to say about matters of policy and justice, Hobbes presented his theory deductively, in the manner of teaching true science. He was proud of the demonstrative character of his doctrine but he was not confident that it would help to get his message across. The syllogistic presentation that he thought appropriate to science was not well suited to a general audience, and he worried about capturing and holding the attention of his readers.[1]

Lacking the gripping style of popular tracts and broadsheets, Hobbes's writings derived much of their impact from the timeliness of the questions

---

* All references are by volume and page number to the *English Works*, edited by Sir William Molesworth (1839–45).
[1] David Johnston, *The Rhetoric of Leviathan* (Princeton, N.J.: Princeton University Press, 1986), ch. 2.

TOM SORELL   343

they raised. In all three of his treatises on civil philosophy he outlined a doctrine with clear application to many of the disputed questions of the day. For example, it was a disputed question in the late 1630s whether King or Parliament ought to have the power to reorganize the Church of England. It was a disputed question whether Parliament or the Crown should control the armed force. It was a disputed question whether there should be Crown-controlled courts with procedures not in the common-law tradition. It was a disputed question, too, whether bishops should have a share of the local political power that had once been exclusively in the hands of the gentry. Hobbes's doctrine had something to say about all of these matters. It implied that it was bad for the sovereign power to be shared or watered down, and so it pronounced against the bishops, the common lawyers, and, where Parliament sought to take over Crown powers, against Parliament.

In 1640 Hobbes's doctrine told in favour of obedience to Charles I, in 1651 Cromwell. It supported any *de facto* holder of the sovereign power. And yet the doctrine was supposed to be able to persuade *anyone*, whether a partisan of the sovereign power or not. It was supposed to have persuasive power because it started from principles that, as Hobbes put it in the dedication to *The Elements of Law*, the passions of his readers would not seek to displace. Later, in *De Cive*, Hobbes said that the principles were known by experience to be true. In *Leviathan* and *De Corpore* he said that a certain kind of self-knowledge would confirm the doctrine based on his principles. In this paper I look into such claims, asking how an argument as dependent as Hobbes's is on very unflattering assumptions about human nature could have been expected to convince readers who would not like its conclusion.

I shall concentrate on Hobbes's inference from the passions to the inevitability of war in the state of nature, asking how this could be expected to persuade. After giving reasons why the inference can be considered unpersuasive, I shall suggest that Hobbes's precepts for avoiding war are compelling quite apart from the inference. I shall suggest also that in Hobbes's sense of 'scientific' the precepts form a scientific system. In fact, the precepts amount to a persuasive civil science. There is a difficulty for Hobbes in the idea of a science that fuses reason and eloquence; but at the end I indicate how Hobbes might have solved this problem.

I

One of the most distinctive and often discussed elements of Hobbes's political philosophy is his description of the condition of human beings in the state of nature. Hobbes paints a picture of human behaviour unconstrained by coercive law, and, officially at least, he expects that his readers will find what he depicts so fearful that they will prefer life under even a harsh system of law to life under no law at all.

Chapter 14 of Part I of *The Elements of Law* contains Hobbes's earliest description of the state of nature. Raising the question how secure men are by nature, that is, how secure they are when one considers their faculties of physical strength, reason, experience and passion, Hobbes answers, 'Not secure at all.' For while they are in fact equal to one another in most respects, not all of them are willing to admit it and satisfy themselves with a share of goods commensurate with their equality. A vainglorious few are bound to deny their equality and try to get by force a bigger share of available goods than others, who, wanting only their fair share, will resist and fight in turn. Independently of the encroachments of the vainglorious few, self-love, the desire to be pre-eminent and the relative scarcity of goods in general demand, make a conflict between people inevitable in the state of nature. What is more, according to *The Elements of Law*, there is a natural right of each to whatever goods there are, a natural right that leaves the means of getting what is wanted up to each individual. Whatever action looks as if it will succeed in securing desired goods is permissible, even if the action involves depriving potential competitors of their goods. So in the state of nature, according to *The Elements of Law*, hostility and war can be expected to prevail.

In *De Cive* and *Leviathan* Hobbes alters the details somewhat, but the general account remains pretty settled. Natural equality, vainglory, comparison and self-love are still identified as the causes in human nature of war (*De Cive*, ch. 1 ; *L*, ch. 13), and Hobbes continues to hold that in the state of nature each has a right to all.

Though the essentials remain the same in all three political treatises, the presentation changes in *De Cive* and *Leviathan*. Hobbes inserts material showing that the principles that inform his political philosophy are already present in the experienced person's understanding of other people's behaviour. One of his principles, the one made vivid by his account of the state of nature, is that men are naturally unsociable. In *De Cive* Hobbes identifies this principle as the negation of a tenet of Aristotle's and to convince his readers that he and not Aristotle is right, and that he and his readers are in agreement, Hobbes invites them to consider how they behave when they are in one another's company. He speaks of shallow market-friendships, the love of ridicule, the tendency to criticize people behind their backs (*E*, II, 3–6). This semi-anecdotal way of describing the unfortunate truth about human nature, though it is not entirely foreign to *The Elements of Law*, is uncharacteristic of the earlier book, where Hobbes prefers to stick to a more nearly syllogistic presentation. The standard sub-section of *The Elements of Law* starts with a definition of a term, moves on to the cause of the conception defined by the term, and perhaps draws a consequence from a definition, or shows how the term has been misdefined by other authors. Chapter 14 of Part I of *The Elements of Law*, which contains the argument for the inevitability of war in the state of nature, does not conform precisely to this pattern. Its starting points are principles drawn from the preceding thirteen chapters. But it exhibits the unadorned syllogistic style that the book associates with rigorous teaching.

The corresponding chapters of *De Cive* and *Leviathan* are written rather differently. In *Leviathan* this seems to be due to Hobbes's altering somewhat the standards for exact teaching or good demonstration. Whereas Chapter 13 of *The Elements of Law* requires for good demonstration that one put together unequivocal terms into evident affirmations, and evident affirmations into syllogisms, with all adornments avoided, in *Leviathan* the apt similitude (for 'opening the understanding') is admitted sometimes to be necessary for demonstration, counsel, and 'all rigorous search of truth' (*L*, ch. 6). Again by contrast with *The Elements of Law*, *Leviathan* not only strings together definitions and consequences of definitions; it states and answers objections.

Chapter 13 of *Leviathan*, on the inevitability of war in the state of nature, illustrates the more relaxed style. Chapter 13 starts with the standard argument for the inevitability of war, given human nature, this being called an inference from the passions. Then (*E*, III, 114) Hobbes adds a confirming line of thought for the reader who doubts his conclusion that men are naturally warlike.

> It may seem strange to some man, that has not well weighed these things; that nature should thus dissociate, and render men apt to invade, and destroy one another: and he may therefore, not trusting to this inference, made from the passions, desire perhaps to have the same confirmed by experience. Let him therefore consider with himself, when taking a journey, he arms himself, and seeks to go well accompanied; when going to sleep, he locks his doors; when even in his house he locks his chests; and this when he knows there be laws, and public officers, armed, to revenge all injuries shall be done to him; what opinion he has of his fellow subjects, when he rides armed; of his fellow citizens, when he locks his doors; and of his children, and servants, when he locks his chests. Does he not there as much accuse mankind by his actions, as I do by my words?

There is a parallel passage in the Preface to the 1647 edition of *De Cive* (*E*, II, xv). In both *Leviathan* and *De Cive* Hobbes anticipates the objection that he is questionably, perhaps even blasphemously, attributing evil to nature. To defuse this objection he first points out that he is not alone in holding that men are badly disposed to one another by nature, and then he adds that in any case he is not blaming nature for what is wrong with men.

Whether he meets the anticipated objections is a question I shall return to presently. What matters now is that Hobbes acknowledges that his account will strike some people as strange, and hence, presumably, as unconvincing. Since the main argument of the political treatises – the argument that it is necessary to obey the sovereign and keep the peace even though it is inconvenient – depends on the assumption that the alternative to obedience is general conflict, the concession that there is room for doubt about the basis in human nature for conflict is of some importance. Hobbes in fact entertains several possible objections to the claim that the seeds of war are in human nature. If his answers are compelling, then they reinforce his inference from the passions. If the answers are unconvincing, then no matter how sound the inference, the claim about the inevitability of war is compromised.

Now I believe that Hobbes's answers to objections can be faulted, and that the inference from the passions is questionable, and so I doubt that the main argument of Hobbes's political treatises is soundly based. To take the inference from the passions first, it trades on at least one principle about human nature that Hobbes never demonstrates, and on one principle about right that is controversial.

The principle about human nature that Hobbes never demonstrates is to the effect that men are conceited or in love with themselves, which makes them consider their individual talents and accomplishments to be far greater than those of others. The principle of right that is controversial, even in the natural-law framework in which Hobbes works, is that 'naturally every man has a right to every thing, even another person's body'. Traditional natural-law doctrine makes the right over another's body, that is over another's life, conditional on prior attack, and in general it forbids harming others.

Hobbes revises traditional natural-law doctrine to include a right to everything, but without providing a good reason for believing in this right. He might have said with some plausibility that in the state of nature each person is likely to be attacked and deprived of goods, even deprived of his life, and that, this being so, the end of self-preservation justifies one in striking out first. But characteristically he does not produce this defence either of the right of pre-emptive attack in particular or the right of unlimited appropriation in general. What he usually says is that one person may judge it useful to kill another or take his belongings, and that whether or not this judgement is wrong or baseless or rash, each person has only his standards of judgement to go by, it being a case in the state of nature of every man having to fend for himself. Now since Hobbes concedes that in the state of nature people can be very bad judges of what will benefit them, he must also admit that often killings in the state of nature are unnecessary for the well-being of

TOM SORELL   347

the people who carry them out. And this seems to conflict with the right of nature, which says that it is always all right for people who think it will benefit them to kill.[2] It cannot be all right if objectively no benefit accrues from a killing.

These problems with the principles Hobbes uses in his inference from the passions cast doubt on the indisputability of this inference. There are problems also with the way he answers objections to this inference. Let us return to the objection that his account is strange, since it implies that nature itself sets men against one another. Hobbes's answer to this objection is that this implication cannot really seem strange to his readers, since they take it for granted in the way they themselves behave toward their fellow men. They ride armed, they lock their chests and so on. This answer, however, is not to the point. Someone who takes the precautions Hobbes describes does not show by his actions that he has a certain view about human nature, for the thoughts behind the precautions need not be about mankind, or every human being or most human beings. The man who locks his doors and chests need only live in fear that some people or other – perhaps only a troublesome few – are disposed to attack and rob him. He need not believe it is characteristically human to be disposed to attack and rob, and yet this belief is at issue. It is true that the locks on the cautious man's doors and chests present an obstacle to everyone indifferently; it is not necessarily true that the cautious man locks his doors and chests against everyone.

Consider now another objection that Hobbes tries to answer in *Leviathan*, that there never was a war of all against all such as he describes. Strictly speaking, it is neither here nor there whether there ever was a war of all against all. Hobbes's argument is to do with how such a war would come about or could come about *if* it came about: there is no necessity to assume that it ever has come about. Hobbes, however, does not shrug off the objection as irrelevant. He says that he does not believe either that there has been a war of all against all. All he thinks there have been are local, relatively short-lived versions of this war of all against all. He gives the example of conflicts among the Indians in America. And in *Leviathan* he refers to national civil wars as indicators of what life in the state of nature would be like. To many of his readers the experience of the English Civil War would have been still very vivid. Hobbes expects these readers to look back on their experience and find it so ghastly that they are prepared to avoid it if there is any means of doing so safely. And he expects those who have not experienced civil war to be able to imagine it and act on the fear that the picture of it conjures up. He is evidently pretty confident about people's reactions to the thought of civil war, for in the opening chapter of *De Corpore* he claims that it is the worst calamity that can

---

[2] In general, a 'right' for Hobbes is a liberty to do a thing.

befall mankind, and he does not bother to back this up with an argument or allow for the possibility that anyone would disagree.

But how good a specimen of the supreme calamity or even of the most fearful general conflict *is* a civil war? Can't there be relatively peaceful places in a war zone and long periods of relief from open all-out fighting in the course of a civil war? Parts of even a Belfast or a Beirut are out of the way of violent conflict, and even the Green Line and the Shankhill Road must sometimes be quiet. What is more, and not necessarily against all reason, strong feelings of solidarity and community seem to spring up in areas that are otherwise torn apart by civil war, partly no doubt from a sense of shared ordeal. It would not be surprising if the English Civil War had comparable aspects. The claim that there is an end to the good things in life when security lapses does not seem to be true, though it has a great deal of initial plausibility.

Both Hobbes's description of the quality of war, then, and his argument that war is inevitable in the state of nature seem questionable. But if these elements of Hobbes's doctrine are uncompelling, must we not say that ingredients are lacking for a scientifically-based argument for keeping the peace and obeying a sovereign power? Must we not say that if the inference fails there is no sound basis for a persuasive civil science capable of keeping discontented people from breaking the law and rebelling? Since many commentators take the strictly scientific content of Hobbes's politics to be contributed by the inference from the passions, and its links with Hobbes's mechanistic psychology, it may seem that, if this inference does not go through, Hobbes is left without a persuasive civil science. I do not accept this conclusion, because I do not believe that the scientific status of Hobbes's politics depends particularly on the inference from the passions. I think that Hobbes's politics is scientific because it consists of a *deduction* of the so-called laws of nature or moral precepts calculated to avoid war, and because this deduction has the sort of evident starting point called for in Hobbes's philosophy of science.

It is true that if war is neither inevitable in the state of nature nor as horrible as Hobbes claims, then following the precepts is not rationally compulsory in order to preserve one's life. But it may still make a lot of sense to obey the laws of nature, for the quality of life is likely to be better if the laws of nature are obeyed than if they are broken. Even if the alternative to peace is not as bad as the life that is nasty, brutish and short, it is very likely to be worse than life conducted according to the laws of nature. So the precepts could have appealed on grounds of rational self-interest irrespective of the soundness of Hobbes's inference from the passions. The precepts could have appealed for other reasons, too; for they were carefully shown by Hobbes to recapitulate a Biblical moral code.

Not only can Hobbes's precepts be understood to be persuasive whether or not the inference from the passions is sound; they can also be seen to amount to a science whether or not the inference is sound. For given the two fundamental laws of nature – those enjoining one to seek peace if it can be done safely and to lay down rights for the sake of peace – all of the rest of the laws of nature can be deduced, and for Hobbes it is deductive structure that is crucial for the scientific status of a doctrine. Hobbes's system of precepts has another claim to scientific status, for it is supposed to uncover what the various patterns of behaviour enjoined by moral precepts – what the various virtues – have in common. What they have in common, according to Hobbes, is that they promote peace, and with that, self-preservation.

II

I am saying that Hobbes's system of the laws of nature, the precepts about seeking peace, laying down rights, keeping covenants, being complaisant, being grateful and the rest, amount to a moral philosophy that is both persuasive and scientific. When it was expounded by Hobbes it could be expected to be acknowledged by many people to give good reasons for action and omission and it had certain important things in common with other specimens of science developed at about the time it was developed. Hobbes's persuasive civil science, nevertheless, is a kind of embarrassment for Hobbes's philosophy of science, because he many times insisted that science was one thing and rhetoric or methodical persuasion another.

It is easy to exaggerate the tension between science and rhetoric to be found in Hobbes's writings.[3] The truth is, I think, that Hobbes's politics always combined rhetoric and science, but that it took some time for his philosophy of science to acknowledge this fact and recognize that science and rhetoric were reconcilable. In *The Elements of Law* Hobbes insists on a firm distinction, not wishing to tar his own writings with the brush he applies to the speeches of the movers and authors of sedition, and in *De Cive* and *Leviathan* he moves toward a reconciliation.

In *The Elements of Law* Hobbes claims that since it is by eloquence that the breeders of sedition try to foment rebellion they must be lacking in wisdom. For eloquence is only the power to persuade, not the power to show people the truth. It wins belief by trading on what people think already and by

---

[3] Johnston is guilty of exaggeration when he claims, in his recent book on the rhetoric of *Leviathan* (op. cit., p. 61), that Hobbes chose a scientific presentation of his politics in *The Elements of Law* and was only converted to the uses of rhetoric in *Leviathan*. At times, however, even Johnston finds himself reluctant to deny that *Leviathan* is a work of science or that *The Elements of Law* has flashes of eloquence. This undercuts his claim that a fundamental dilemma faced Hobbes's political philosophy and that a choice had to be made between rhetoric and science.

350 HOBBES'S PERSUASIVE CIVIL SCIENCE

manipulating the passions. It owes none of its force to evidence, which it has to do if it is to convey knowledge and so stand a chance of expressing wisdom or sciencu.

In *De Cive* (ch. 12, xii; *E*, II, 161–2), a similar line of thought is to be found. Hobbes distinguishes between eloquence bent only on persuasion, and eloquence used to demonstrate truth. The art of the former sort of eloquence is 'rhetoric', of the latter, 'logic'. One kind of eloquence, the kind whose art is logic, 'is never disjoined from wisdom' but the other kind 'almost ever'. And the reason? Rhetorical eloquence is 'a commotion of the passions of the mind, such as hope, fear, anger, pity' and derives from a metaphorical use of words fitted to the passions (*E*, II, 161). Logical eloquence, on the other hand, is 'an elegant and clear expression of the conceptions of the mind and riseth partly from the contemplation of the things themselves, and partly from an understanding of words taken in their own proper and definite signification' (*E*, II, 161). It is suitable, then, to the expression of truth and knowledge, while rhetorical eloquence is not.

By the time of *Leviathan*, Hobbes was prepared to give up his claim in *Elements of Law* and *De Cive* that science and rhetoric, eloquence and reason, had to be at odds. His considered opinion was that 'reason and eloquence, though not perhaps in the natural sciences, yet, in the moral, may stand very well together'. Nevertheless, it is a question whether the marriage of reason and eloquence in moral philosophy is really catered for in Hobbes's philosophy of science. The problem is not that Hobbes's philosophy of science positively excludes such a thing as a persuasive civil science; rather, it leaves such a thing undefined. Hobbes's idea of science, together with the cognate ideas of knowledge, logic and teaching, are better adapted to speculative than to practical matters, and it is the same for reason or ratiocination. In its primary sense, Hobbes's term 'ratiocination' means theoretical, not practical, reasoning. Similarly, 'speech' usually means propositional speech – the sort designed to state what is the case – and not the speech that expresses what ought to be done. When Hobbes tries to make room for an alternative to passion-stirring speech that is still prescriptive but also rational, scientific, and material for deductive reasoning, it is not immediately clear that he has the resources to do so.

Whether or not he was aware of it, a solution to this problem is available in *Leviathan*.[4] In Chapter 25 of the book Hobbes introduces the concept of counsel, which he proceeds to distinguish from both command and exhortation. Command is defined as imperative speech addressed to someone by a person who expects that his will to have something done is sufficient

---

[4] The next few paragraphs enlarge on a suggestion made in passing in the concluding chapter of my *Hobbes* (London: Routledge, 1986).

reason for the thing to *be* done. Hobbes adds that commands are issued for the benefit of the ones doing the commanding. Counsel, by contrast, is imperative speech accompanied by reasons why acting on the speech is for the benefit of the one *addressed*. Finally, exhortation is a perverted kind of counsel, counsel that is vehemently pressed for the honour or glory of having one's advice followed. Since it is imperative speech, counsel is essentially action-guiding or prescriptive; but since it can also be backed by reasons or reasoning it has something in common with scientific speech.

Now although Hobbes never identifies the precepts for sovereigns and subjects in his political treatises as pieces of counsel, they seem to meet the specifications given in Chapter 25 of *Leviathan*. When Hobbes tells rulers to exercise to the full the rights of sovereigns, when he names reluctance to exercise sovereignty as one of the causes of the dissolution of the state, he can certainly be understood to be issuing the imperative 'Exercise no less power than peace requires!' The imperative is not issued by Hobbes merely for his own benefit, and the reasons given for it do establish the benefit to the commonwealth which the sovereign personifies. So the reasons given are the kind that are supposed to accompany a piece of counsel. On the other hand, the counsel is not vehemently pressed. It is put to the ruler in a book largely composed of passionless, syllogistic speeches or demonstrations. Much the same goes for the imperative, namely 'Obey the law!' that Hobbes addresses to subjects or citizens. That, too, was put to his readers in books of cool, impersonal demonstrations. That, too, was accompanied by reasons why it was beneficial for subjects or citizens to follow the law.

Classifying the advice in Hobbes's political treatises as counsel enables one to resolve the tension that otherwise exists in his writings between the concepts of reason and eloquence. It fits in another way as well. What else but counsel could have come more naturally from a man who throughout his life earned his keep as a personal and political counsellor?[5]

The Open University

---

[5] Earlier versions of this paper were read to an Anglo-French conference on Rhetoric and Philosophy in April, 1987; a Hobbes conference held in Castleton, Derbyshire in September, 1987; and the University of Illinois at Chicago in April, 1988. I am grateful to all three audiences for helpful discussions. This paper is one of a sequence of three that I have published on the relation between politics and rhetoric in Hobbes. The others are 'The Science in Hobbes's Politics', in G. A. J. Rogers and A. Ryan, (eds), *Perspectives on Thomas Hobbes* (Oxford: Clarendon Press, 1988), and 'Hobbes's unAristotelian Political Rhetoric', *Philosophy and Rhetoric* (1990).

[20]

HOBBES'S BIBLICAL BEASTS
Leviathan and *Behemoth*

PATRICIA SPRINGBORG
University of Sydney

Beyond the actual works of nature a poet may now go; but beyond the conceived possibility of nature, never. I can allow a Geographer to make in the Sea, a Fish or a Ship, which by the scale of his map would be two or three hundred mile long, and think it done for ornament, because it is done without the precincts of his undertaking; but when he paints an *Elephant* so, I presently apprehend it as ignorance and a plain confession of *Terra incognita*.

Hobbes's Answer to Sir William Davenant's
Dedicatory Preface to Gondibert, 1651, 81.

(1) HOBBES'S BEAST,
THE BIBLICAL LEVIATHAN

In Hobbes's little discussed published response to Davenant's preface to *Gondibert*, dedicated to him, Hobbes reproves Davenant, the rigorous acolyte who claims to have learned his epistemology from Hobbes. Ghosts and spooks are one thing, Hobbes suggests, but to abandon the entire Western fabulous tradition of rhetoric and poesy was to abandon what distinguished civilization from the rude culture of the Americas. Civilization is the work of the imagination, "fancy," and the only restrictions on its exercise were those of appropriateness. There is, as we shall show, symptomatic irony in Hobbes's choice of the metaphor of the elephant. In the seventeenth century, Leviathan was taken for a great ship, a crocodile, or a whale, and Behemoth for an elephant. The *Oxford English Dictionary* credits Hobbes with lexical innovation, as the first to use the term Leviathan—the biblical serpent or sea monster, a huge ship or person of immense power and the "great Satan" of Isaiah 27:1—as the synonym for a commonwealth.[1] Hobbes's Leviathan is indeed a work of the imagination, a creature of artifice rather than nature, a *mortal* God, and scripture vouches for it.

Commentators have focused considerable attention on the iconography of the engraved frontispiece to *Leviathan*, believed to have been produced by the printer Andrew Crooke, under Hobbes's supervision, and perhaps the work of Hobbes's acquaintance and Charles's former tutor in drawing, the engraver Wenceslaus Holler.[2] The frontispiece depicts an image of Leviathan, a kinglike figure wielding sword and crozier, his gigantic body composed of the small bodies of the people of his realm. Overhead flies the banner headline from the Book of Job 41:33-4, "There is no power over earth than compares to him," the conclusion of which is reserved for the text: "a creature without fear . . . king over all the sons of pride." Much less attention has been focused on the significance of the biblical names *Leviathan* and *Behemoth,* in what would, in the seventeenth century, have been a most startling usage. Hobbes, in choosing *Leviathan* and *Behemoth* as his titles, drops enough hints to make it clear to his audience that he refers to none other than the beasts of the Apocrypha, familiar from the Hebrew Theogony and associated in chiliastic thought with the Second Coming. How does he mean the names then?[3] And what is their significance for his religious doctrine?

In a recent article, Tracy Strong argues, correctly I believe, that "God-given geometry is [Hobbes's] model of and for power to which none on earth compare," because men cannot only read it but *see* it. He cites Job 38:1-7, the beginning of the passage that leads to Hobbes's headline epigraph:

> Then the Lord answered Job out of the tempest: who is this whose ignorant words cloud my design in darkness? Brace yourself and stand up like a man; I will ask questions, and you shall answer. Where were you when I laid the earth's foundations? Tell me, if you know and understand. Who settled its dimensions? Surely you should know. Who stretched this measuring-line over it? On what do its supporting pillars rest? Who set its corner-stone in place, when the morning stars sang together and all the sons of God shouted aloud? (Job 38:1-7)[4]

The invention of geometry is credited to the ancient Egyptians as a rapid method to recalculate property boundaries washed away by the annual innundation of the Nile. It was appropriate that God should have used the language of geometry in the Hebrew theogony to establish his proprietorship in an antediluvian world—and trump the Egyptians. It was equally appropriate that Hobbes should have taken geometry as proof of his epistemology. If geometry, which laid the foundations of the world, belonged to the designs of God that could be *seen*, the Bible belonged to a dispensation of sacred texts that could be *read*, rendering superfluous the interventions of philosophers and theologians. So even Job 41:9-11 can be given a more optimistic reading. The divine show of strength is a show and tell:[5]

> Behold, the hope of him is in vain: shall not *one* be cast down even in the sight of him? None *is so* fierce that dare stir him up: who then is able to stand before me? Who hath prevented me, that I should repay *him? whatsoever is* under the whole heaven is mine.

Leviathan may be an image of the absolutist state, projected as a necessary, almost natural, work of creation. But as a work of creation it is not self-generating and, like Job, we must turn to its author for the source of its power. Absolute governments, the Leviathans of this world, from their archetypes in ancient Egypt and Babylon to their early modern types in the papacy, Spain, and France, were also constructed. Let us see how they were built, Hobbes says, and then ask the question whence their power derives. Leviathan and Behemoth, as perhaps God's answer to Job was intended to imply, are *mortal* Gods who have a role in the scheme of the *immortal* God. They have their own cycles of generation and decay and their maintenance is also a work of art.

Leviathan is the state, created by man in his image as man is created in the image of God, with divine sanction, indirectly as a continuation of the work of creation, or directly as an extension of the original *Fiat*, by which the world was made. Hobbes embroidered the metaphor, focusing on the "artificiality" of the state by creating a figure for the state as a species of *Automata*, with a spring, string, and wheels as heart, nerves, and joints, and *Soveraignty* as the "Artificiall *Soul*," "giving life and motion to the whole body."[6] In the important first chapter of part 2 of *Leviathan*, chapter 17, "*Of the Causes, Generation and Definition of a* COMMON-WEALTH," Hobbes noted of the covenants by which the artificial unity of the state is created and its sovereign authorized: "the Multitude so united in one Person, is called a COMMON-WEALTH, in latine CIVITAS. This is the generation of that great LEVIATHAN, or rather (to speake more reverently) of that *Mortall God*, to which wee owe under the *Immortal God*, our peace and defence."[7] At this point, *Leviathan* is no longer the body politic but the sovereign who personifies it. Returning in chapter 28 to the image of the automaton and "the nature of Punishment, and Reward; which are, as it were, the Nerves and Tendons, that move the limbes and joynts of a Common-wealth,"[8] Hobbes concluded:

> Hitherto I have set forth the nature of Man . . . together with the great power of his Governour, whom I compared to *Leviathan*, taking that comparison out of the two last verses of the one and fortieth of *Job*; where God having set forth the great power of *Leviathan*, calleth him King of the Proud. *There is nothing*, saith he, *on earth to be*

compared with him. He is made so as not to be afraid. Hee seeth every high thing below him; and is King of all the children of pride. But because he is mortall, and subject to decay, as all other Earthly creatures are; and because there is that in heaven, (though not on earth) that he should stand in fear of, and whose Lawes he ought to obey; I shall in the next following Chapters speak of his Diseases, and the causes of his Mortality; and of what Lawes of Nature he is bound to obey.[9]

This is a startling innovation in the reading of the biblical Leviathan, especially in an age in which allegorical interpretations were eschewed in favour of a literal reading of the bible. How precisely did Hobbes expect his audience to receive his *Leviathan*? And how was it received?

A word of caution might be introduced here about the distinction between a literal and an allegorical reading of the Bible. In his survey of Protestant writing, Tracy Strong in "How to Write Scripture," rightly points out the epistemic significance of the Reformers' claim to "know" the Bible and not merely to "interpret" it.[10] Interpretation as an epistemic rule is post-Kantian, or more accurately, post-Buber. It rests most generally on the claim that we can never know how far our perceptual categories and limitations skew our ideas. Following a line of thought initiated by Hobbes to explain how we can posit the existence of God, as Strong rightly points out, thinkers from Locke to the present claimed that we may *infer* the existence of something if we can name it.[11] However, the faith—for that is what it was—that we can *know* the Bible lay undisturbed by these considerations, which represented precisely a philosophic extension of the Protestant epistemic posture, until the great hermeneutic watershed introduced by Martin Buber, Paul Tillich, and Reinhold Niebuhr, members of the German critical school of the late nineteenth and early twentieth centuries. (It is an open secret that current hermeneutical and phenomenological schools owe their insights once again to a seachange in biblical criticism, once again from the German school.)

A final word of caution: to claim that Reformation commentators believed that one could "know" the Bible is not to suggest that they lacked sophistication about what they were doing—which was essentially a work of "reinterpretation." Reformation exegetes, including Hobbes, knew exactly what they were doing because for the most part they were activists and their methodology was institutionally driven. Up to and including Locke, their epistemology was designed to cut the Church in general, and the clergy in particular, out of the loop between the authorized version and the authorizing civil authority.[12] For this reason, particularly problematic exegesis of obscure and ancient texts, like the Book of Job, was eschewed; texts where, ironically, Hobbes, whose purposes were not so different, found his best proving ground for the new Leviathan.

(2) REFORMATION COMMENTARY
ON LEVIATHAN AND BEHEMOTH

If Hobbes had spun his construction of the mechanical Leviathan out of the Book of Job, among the most cited and most glossed books of the Old Testament in the Reformation, it was surely not done innocently. He must certainly have been aware that the purpose of Reformation retranslation and reinterpretation was to reject allegorical in favour of a literal reading of scripture. The Book of Job was favoured precisely because it addressed the theodicy problem: how a beneficent God may be reconciled with the power of evil. It provided, at the same time, a text enjoining patience on those afflicted or persecuted. But commentators cautioned against making too much of the more difficult parts of the book, allegorical as they clearly are.

Job Expovnded by Theodore Beza, partly in manner of a Commentary, partly in manner of a paraphrase (1589?) is addressed to Queen Elizabeth on behalf of the French Protestants who sought her protection. It is therefore one of the most political readings. It very bluntly states Behemoth to be an elephant and Leviathan to be a crocodile. Beza, conceding the peculiar difficulties of the Book of Job, makes the case for a literal reading by referring to appropriate standards of biblical criticism: "But this booke, then the which there is none in all the Bible, if I be not deceiued, no not Moses himselfe, of greater antiquitie, is in manie places made verie obscure to vs and hard to be vnderstood, partly by reason of the profoundnes of the thinges themselues here debated among most wise men, and not to be conceaued of euery one, partly by diuers straunge words & also phrases differing from the pure *Hebrue.*"[13] He cautions against presuming "to be ouer wise . . . wise aboue that which is meete," expressing the view that: "the wise men of other nations, whome the *Greekes* call Philosophers, haue, touching the true vse, merueilouslie prophaned it." Striking a dark note, he observes: "moreouer . . . the abuse of this Science hath bred that detestable Art *Magick*, which is the welspring of al mischeife, as also that false divining *Astrologie*, which hauing broken the bounds of true Natural knowledge, entreth into the very secrets of God, and at this day hath bewitched the whole world."[14]

Beza, one of the most sophisticated and well read of the Reformation biblical commentators, is as committed to the abandonment of the allegorical interpretation of scripture as the most fundamentalist preacher. And for just the reasons that Hobbes would otherwise endorse: because allegorical constructs were abstractions, they created a host of monsters and phantasms inhabiting the dark regions of superstition and magic, the terrain of the papacy, the Spanish, heretics, and relics of gentilism.

358   POLITICAL THEORY / May 1995

Herbert of Cherbury, in a pioneering English study of "Gentilism," had included the enigmatic statement: "As far as I can find, the great *Leviathan* was known to the Jews only, tho' I question whether the *Rabbins* have left us any Description of it. There are several Reasons may be given, why Fish should exceed all other Animals in Magnitude."[15] Quite plainly in this work, written by an antiquarian and diplomat whom Hobbes knew and admired, Leviathan was a monster and nothing more.

Others agreed with him. Nathaniel Culverwell, in his *Elegant and Learned Discourse of the Light of Nature* of 1646, addressing the question whether the Laws of Nature are binding on beasts, had asked "What are those Lawes that are observed by a rending and tearing Lion, by a devouring *Leviathan?*"[16]—like Herbert, plainly taking Leviathan for a beast, and no extraordinary one in this case. Reformation commentaries on the books of Job and Isaiah are uniformly condemnatory of allegorical interpretations, in particular of these passages of scripture, insisting that Leviathan and Behemoth are simply beasts, although often differing on what beasts they might be. Beza stated flatly "I omit that custome which hath continued euer since *Origenes* time, I say not of inuerting the natural sence of the sacred text to the framing of certaine straunge allegories, but euen of marring and peruerting it."[17]

The beasts of the Book of Job were regularly interpreted as demonstrations of divine omnipotence and nothing more.[18] So George Abbott simply exhorts, "Consider the Elephant [Behemoth]. . . . consider well the Whale [Leviathan]."[19] John Oecolampadius (Halschein), to whom Beza refers, heads up his comments on Job 40:10, "*Voici l'elephant.*"[20] He hopes to lay alternative possibilities to rest with a review of the Hebraists as well as the Reformers on the subject of Job's beasts, finding no exception to their treatment as animals, even by such diverse figures as the Hebraists Rabbi Aben Ezra, Rabbi Levi, Rabbi Moshe, Moshe the Egyptian, Zwingli, Luther, and Thomas Aquinas.[21] Oecolampadius makes certain observations on the use of the Hebrew plural, Behemoth, for the elephant, singular, noting the derivation of Leviathan from the Hebrew verb "Lauah," signifying "addition." He is one of the few to comment on Behemoth's "tail stiff like a Cedar,"[22] attributing the metaphor, rather unconvincingly, to a "hyperbolic mode of speaking."[23]

John Calvin, in his *Sermons of Maister Iohn Calvin, vpon the Booke of Iob,*[24] addressing the question of Behemoth, noted also that "the worde *Behema* signifieth simply a Beast, and vnder that name are Oxen and all other beastes comprehended"; *Behemoth* is simply the plural of *Behema*. "Neuertheles it cannot be coniectured what kinde of beast it is that hee speaketh of, except it bee an Elephant, by reason of the hugenesse of that beastes body." The hugeness serves a purpose: "if we were wise ynough, we needed not to goe out of our selues to behold the maiestie of God: howbeit men must be sent to the beasts bicause of their vnthankfulnesse, in that they know not God as he sheweth hymselfe vnto them"; for this reason the unregenerate "haue need of suche mirrours as are set before vs here in respect of the Elephants & other like beasts."[25] Calvin, like other Reformation commentators reads Leviathan and Behemoth as simple demonstrations of unfathomable divine power: "it is purposely said, that *these Elephants were created with us* . . . so as men must be rauished besides themselues when they thinke thereon."[26] He adds, Leviathan is simply another "like beast," in this case a whale. It is a reading of the Book of Job on which Hobbes's extrapolation to the secular sovereign Leviathan depends, as we have argued here.

Calvin quickly forestalls any other possible interpretation, with a lengthy discursus on the necessity of a literal interpretation.[27]

> There is one peremptorie reason to shewe vs that we must take this text simply as it standeth, & not shiftingly. For we have seen heretofore how it was Gods intent to teach men after a grosse and homely maner, according to their owne small capacitie, and that his doing thereof is to the end that his mightie power should be the better proued vnto them.[28]

About Leviathan he is even more emphatic: "As touching the worde *Leuiathan*, through the whole scripture it signifieth a Whale." But he makes some concession to allegorical interpretation, in allowing men to infer the power of the devil from the strength of these beasts.[29]

Calvin certainly concedes that allegorical interpretations abound,[30] but so strongly was the new Protestant biblical criticism committed to disposing of them, as relics of Catholicism and the power of the Church to interpret scripture, that he enjoins his congregation to reflect on the whale, "is it not an incredible thynge to see so huge a creature, liuing in the water? Who were able to fashion the moulde of so great, huge, and strong a beast."[31]

In fact, in his *Commentary vpon the Prophecie of Isaiah*, dedicated to Henry, Prince of England, son of James I, and Princess Elizabeth, his wife, and perhaps intended for a different audience, Calvin does give an allegorical interpretation, making of Leviathan not only a figure for the Devil but also for the King of Egypt. Commenting on Isaiah 27:1 ("In that day the Lord will visit Leuiathan that pearcing Serpent, and Leuiathan that crooked Serpent, with his sore and great and mightie sword: and will kill the Dragon that is in the sea"), he remarks: "For mine owne part I make no question but by way of Allegorie he speakes here of Satan and his whole kingdome, describing it under the figure of some monstrous beast." The signification of Leviathan as a figure for tyrants, Egypt, and Satan is quite explicit:[32]

> The Prophet speakes heere of Gods iudgement in generall, and so comprehends the whole kingdom of Satan. For hauing spoken before of the vengeance of God against tyrants and vnbeleeuers which had shed innocent blood, he now passeth on further, and publisheth the edict it selfe. The word *Leuiathan* is diuerslie expounded, but generallie it signifies a serpent, or the whales and fishes of the sea, which are as monsters in regard of their excelliue greatnes. Now howsoeuer this description agrees to the king of Egypt, yet vnder this one he meant to comprehend all the enemies of the Church.

Martin Luther understood full well the allegorical force of Leviathan and Behemoth. In his *Magnificat*,[33] he shows how the Bible demonizes "the proud, those "forlorn people" of the Book of Job: "Sometimes it calls them adders who stop their ears lest they hear;[34] sometimes stubborn unicorns;[35] sometimes roaring lions;[36] sometimes great immovable rocks;[37] sometimes dragons;[38] and much else besides." Leviathan and Behemoth are demonizations too: "Equally well are they depicted in Job 40 and 41, where the same kind of people are called Behemoth [Job 40:10ff, 41:10ff]. Behema means a single animal, but behemoth means a number of such animals, in other words, a race which has an animal mind, and does not allow the spirit of God in it."[39] In the sixteenth century, Luther had already given a racial reading of the terms: "The Bible describes them [Behemoth] as having an eye like the red of dawn, for there is no measure to their cunning, and their skin is so tough that they only scoff at a stab or a sting." Referring now to Leviathan, he continued: "the monsters" scales overlap, and leave no intervening space; for these people hold closely together, and the spirit of God cannot enter them."[40] (A famous sexual harrassment case at the University of Pennsylvania in 1993 turned on whether the Hebrew word for "water-buffalo" constituted a racial slur; the word in question was "behema.")

It seems then that Reformation commentators were well aware of the allegorical referents for Leviathan and Behemoth in the powerful states of ancient Egypt and Assyria. But perhaps because these allusions implied an immanent critique of secular nation states—already alarmingly fragile, and the readier to persecute, the more fragile they were—or because the Reformers discouraged apocalyptic speculation—and these were apocryphal texts—they found it politic to play them down. This Hobbes was not willing to do, finding fertile material in the Book of Job for his mortal commonwealth, personified by the sword-wielding sovereign, a work of artifice both fearsome and fragile, mandated by God to reign in historical time, that sliver of temporality created in the interstices of eternity.

(3) BRAMHALL CATCHING LEVIATHAN

It was quite a sheer perversity on Hobbes's part to make such play of the beasts of the Book of Job, and, true to form, he seemed to intend it as a provocation. When, in a series of exchanges with Bishop John Bramhall, Hobbes challenged Bramhall to put in print his objections to his religious doctrine, he offered him the title *"Behemoth against Leviathan."*[41] Bramhall, whose systematic rebuttal of the theological chapters of *Leviathan* has never been surpassed, and who referred to that work as *"Monstrum horrendum, informe, ingens, cui lumen ademptum,"* countered with, *"The catching of LEVIATHAN, or the Great Whale."*[42] The irony was not lost on Bramhall that Hobbes, who argued so systematically against phantasms, should have resorted to a mythical monster to characterize his commonwealth.[43] Bramhall was not the only critic to remark on this peculiarity, the subject of Alexander Ross's, *Leviathan Drawn out with a Hook* (1653), but he was certainly the most thorough. He dared Hobbes to show that he himself was not Leviathan—a possibility on which subsequent commentators, pointing to the resemblance that Leviathan's head in one of the versions of the frontispiece bears to the author, have speculated.[44] Bramhall taunts Hobbes, whose Leviathan, he says, is a man-fish, like the Palestinian idol Dagon,[45] rather than a whale-fish, the biblical original:

> his Leviathan, or mortal God, is a meer phantasme of his own devising, neither flesh nor fish, but a confusion of a man and a whale, engendered in his own brain: not unlike Dagon the Idol of the Philistims, a mixture of a god and a man and a fish. The true literall Liviathan is the Whale-fish.

Bramhall challenges Hobbes the rhetor, who tried to summon into existence a polity by persuasion, invoking classical heroes, Hercules, Pericles, and the proverbial Pythagoras. No one saw more clearly than Bramhall the brazenness of Hobbes's heresy. He who in work after work had damned the opinionated philosophers of the Greek schools for contaminating early Christianity with their teachings, dared himself to offer an opinion on the Christian commonwealth that convicted him as an heresiarch—"a second Pythagoras, at least." Hobbes himself was the monster, among all the children of pride, the great Leviathan incarnate:

> And for a metaphorical Leviathan, I know none so proper to personate that huge body as *T. H.* himself. The Leviathan doth not take his pastime in the deep with so much freedom, nor behave himself with so much height and insolence, as *T. H.* doth in the Schooles, nor domineer over the lesser fishes with so much scorn and contempt, as he

doth over all other authours, censuring, branding, contemning, proscribing whatsoever is contrary to his humour; bustling and bearing down before him whatsoever cometh in his way, creating truth and falsehood by the breath of his mouth, by his sole authority, without other reason; A second Pythagoras at least. There have been self-conceited persons in all Ages, but none that could ever *King it* like him *over all the chldren of pride.* (Job 41.34.) Ruit, agit, rapit, tundit & prosternit.[46]

Bramhall has Hobbes's measure and knows that he can convict him of inconsistency:

> I have provided three good harping irons for my self to dart at this monster, and am resolved to try my skill and fortune, whether I can be as successful against this phantastick Leviathan, as they are against the true Leviathan.[47]

Bramhall's discursus on the whale-fish Leviathan is shaped to the structure of theological rebuttal, each line of argument a harpoon with which to spear Hobbes, more vulnerable than he thinks to the small fry who assail him. The passage may also be read as an elaborate allegory of the threat posed to the unitary state by nonconformists, namely the Protestant sects. Hobbes's heterodoxy opens the door, ironically, to the very proliferation of opinion he is most concerned to forestall. Bramhall paints frightful images of the consequences in the little mouse that "stealeth up thorough the Elephants trunke to eat his brains, making him die desperately mad"; the Indian rat that "creepeth into the belly of the gaping Crocodile, and knaweth his bowels asunder"; and the sword-fish and the thrasher-fish that join forces with the Greenland fishermen to overwhelm Leviathan, "at last to draw this formidable creature to the shore, or to their ship, and slice him in pieces and boile him in a Cauldron, and tun him up in oil."[48] The metonymy of Leviathan was the synecdoche of the state.

Hobbes had offered to his critics the intolerable provocation of an allegorical interpretation of scripture, against which they so heavily enveighed— even as he denied the spiritual and ghostly beings to which they, inconsistent by turn, subscribed in notions of the soul, angels and demons.[49] Leviathan's point was the spectre of countervailing power. The ghostly powers of the pope, as King of Fayrieland, were real enough; just as real had been the demonized power of pharaonic Egypt and Assyria to the fledgling Israelite state. Is the commonwealth then a Leviathan by inversion to render the papacy anti-Leviathan? Perhaps Hobbes saw himself as Leviathan with respect to the Church, fish-man and demon in the service of the state, and revelled in it, just so long as it did not cost him his head. In the *Historia Ecclesiastica*, his enchiridion in elegaic prose, he nicely turns the metaphor of Leviathan. The ancient imperial states, those mighty beasts, Egypt,

Assyria, and Rome, have all been hooked; and snares are being prepared for the rest. The *Historia Ecclesiastica* includes a long discursus on the serpent and the ensnaring arts of the papacy, its hooks and lures of many colours:[50]

> But now the Pope his end compleatly gains,
> And leads the People, and their Prince, in Chains:
> Now vast *Leviathan* the Hook receives,
> And *Behemoth* his wounded Nostrils grieves:
> All gently own the Pope's Imperial Sway
> Where'r the *Roman* eagles wing their Way. . . .
> No crafty Angler will his Art despise,
> Though in his Nets a scanty Profit lies;
> And ever busy'd in his small Affairs,
> He mends his Nets, or strictly views his Wares,
> His Lines new models, or his Hooks surveys,
> And ev'ry Thing in decent Order lays;
> Gay gaudy Flies of ev'ry Sort are seen,
> The bright Carnation and the lovely Green. . . .
> There skimming cross the Streams, with sov'reign Skill,
> The pointed Hooks th'unwary Fishes kill.

The inversion of *Leviathan* was now complete: the Papacy usurps the role of ancient Israel, "draw[ing] out Leviathan with an hooke or his tongue with a corde," piercing the nostrils of Behemoth. Those pitiable (but Satanic) monsters personifying the ancient Egyptian and Assyrian states, respectively, have given way to the great whale, the Christian commonwealth, and now the Pope acts the role of God the Father. Hobbes's play on the beasts of Job goes far beyond allegory and enters the realm of blasphemy. Is it any wonder the man was accused of heresy?

(4) LEVIATHAN AND THE GALLIC HERCULES

But perhaps we are looking in the wrong place to establish the meaning of Leviathan. The kingly figure wearing the four-arched crown, wielding scepter and sword, naked, his body composed of the many persons of his realm, may not be "the coiled one" at all. Presiding almost benignly over a model town spread out before him, the spires of churches and the orderly streets a model of civility, Leviathan, if that is who this figure is, would seem a guardian of civilization and no monster.[51] Arrayed under the insignia of power civil and ecclesiastical, respectively, are symmetrical cameos. A castle is juxtaposed to the ark as seat of power; the crown versus the mitre, potent symbols. Over against the canon stands the divine thunderbolt; and the banners and battle standards of jostling civil powers are pitted against the three pronged, Trinitarian forks, and the two horned dilemmas of ecclesiastical controversy. The dénouement is in each case different: war, the outcome of civil strife; the court of excommunication, the outcome of doctrinal malfeasance. Who is the guardian of cities, villages, shires, and fields, shown in the frontispiece? Is it the Godly Prince, and if so, how could he be Leviathan?[52]

The depiction of Leviathan in the frontispiece is counterintuitive. Neither a ship nor a whale, it is much more an image drawn from medieval organic theories of kingship than a biblical image. There is a more obscure tradition to which Hobbes may be appealing, one to which he makes allusion in the body of the text, and that is the Gallic Hercules, mentioned by Diodorus Siculus,[53] alluded to by Apuleius, and of whom the Syrian Rhetor Lucian tells such a strange story.[54] Named by the Celts "Heracles Ogmios," he was old, bald, naked except for lion's skin, wrinkled, and "burned as black as can be, like an old sea-dog." But he carries the equipment of Heracles, the club and the quiver, and "is Heracles from head to heel as far as that goes."[55] He differs from the classical Heracles in a surprising respect: "That old Heracles of theirs drags after him a great crowd of men who are all tetherd by the ears" to his tongue.[56] Lucian reports a Celtic stranger, fluent in Greek, who offered to "read [him] the riddle of the picture":[57]

> We Celts do not agree with you Greeks in thinking that Hermes is Eloquence: we identify Heracles with it, because he is far more powerful than Hermes. . . . In general, we consider that the real Heracles was a wise man who achieved everything by eloquence and applied persuasion as his principal force. His arrows represent words, I suppose, keen, sure and swift, which make their wounds in souls.

Not by chance, Hobbes invokes the image of the Gallic Hercules to describe his "Artificiall Man, which we call a Common-wealth," tied by "Artificiall Chains, called *Civill Lawes*, which [citizens] themselves, by mutual covenants, have fastned at one end, to the lips of that Man, or Assembly, to whom they have given the Soveraigne Power; and at the other end to their own Ears."[58] With this allusion, Hobbes demonstrates not only his classical knowledge but also his acquaintance with traditions of monarchy learned at first hand in France. Henry II, for his carefully scripted triumphal entry into Paris in 1549, had chosen the Gallic Hercules as an effigy of the king. Clad only in an animal skin, his pediment was a ship, flanked by two naked men raising a cartouche with the legend: "trahimur, seqvimurque volentes."[59] Referring to the four accompanying statues that personified the

Estates, their ears chained to the lips of the king, it translated: "we are pulled and we follow freely."[60]

The message that rhetor Lucian reports: "you know the kinship between ears and tongue,"[61] is one that Henry II had learned well. Eloquence was the lesson that the Renaissance rhetoricians and authors of mirrors taught. Gaullaume Budé had first proposed the model of the Gallic Hercules to Francis I in his 1518 *Institution du Prince*.[62] Jean Bodin, who in the *Methodus* observed that "before the time of Henry II . . . we never used the word 'Majesty' in addressing the king,"[63] in *De la République* declared, "there is nothing more natural, than for the sujects to conforme themselves unto the manners, unto the doings and sayings of their prince . . . having their eyes, their senses, and all their spirits, wholly bent to the imitation of him."[64] He then took the liberty of advising the prince on his proper comportment:

> Wherefore a prince that is wise is, so oft as he should show himself unto the people (which he should most seldom do) should so prepare himselfe, as that he may unto all men seeme even in his face and countenance to carry with him a certaine state and majestie yet still mixt with modestie, but especially in his speech, which should always be maiesticall and sententious.

The Heracles who taught by eloquence forsaking the club, his arrows words, became a Renaissance image for *lex animata*, the king as animate law. While Petrarch spoke of "healing speech," and Francis I aspired to "doulce eloquence et royal bonte," the eloquence of which Bodin was mindful was the language with which Francis I had in fact dealt with the rebels of La Rochelle: "with the maiesite of his speech [he] terrified them" into obedience.[65]

Nor was eloquence the only lesson the Gallic Hercules taught. The classical hero took over the characteristics of his rival Hermes, as the civilizer of peoples, who taught agriculture, protected cities. His Eastern provenance crept back in Geofrey Troy's 1510 edition of the false Berosus [Babylonicus]; and in 1529 Champfleury made him "not only King of Gaul but also a great magician, astronomer, and even founder of Paris."[66] Henry II himself at his 1550 ceremonial entry into Rouen had been greeted by a pageant depicting the Christian king as the antique Hercules, slaying the hydra, accompanied by Orpheus and the nine muses.[67] The bestiary of the Book of Job relates etymologically to the hydra and other monsters of the East Mediterranean myth cycle, Leviathan among them.

Hercules' nakedness, as portrayed in the 1649 royal entry statue, at first a potent classical pagan symbol, was both an evocation of the medieval doctrine of the King's Two Bodies and a satire upon it. It evoked the man, as distinct from the king, who in the classical "double funeral" was represented quite simply as an old man's body in a shroud.[68] In France, the *persona* of the king, decked out in royal regalia, represented the office of kingship under a special aspect: the king-in-parlement as opposed to one man rule. It was to this ideal of the *robed* king that the ceremonial statue of the naked king Henry II, drawing the four estates in tow, bound by their ears to the lips of the king, was a direct affront. It suggested a rupture of traditional patterns of consultancy, of listening and speaking, between king and people, and a turn to government based upon imperial edicts and fear associated with Hispano-Papalism, the courts of Charles V and Philip II.[69]

What could the Gallic Hercules have meant to Hobbes, whose only mentions of the classical hero by name are disparaging? In book 1 chapter 12 of *Leviathan* on Religion, Hobbes refers to Hercules with Bacchus as "mongrill Gods," added by the "Legislators of the Gentiles" for the benefit of the ignorant to the panoply of "ministeriall Gods," anthropomorphized and "endowed . . . with lands, and houses, and officers, and reveunues, set apart from all other humane uses; that is, consecrated, and made holy to those their Idols."[70] Hercules appears again in book 2 chapter 30, devoted to the "Office of the Sovereign Representative," in a discussion of the psychology of rewards and punishments as levers of power that might well have been written by the great commentator on the Roman Empire, Polybius. Preferment and benefices are signs not "of Gratitude, but of Fear: [nor] does it tend to the Benefit, but to the Dammage of the Publique":[71]

> It is a contention with Ambition, like that of *Hercules* with the Monster *Hydra*, which having many heads for every one that was vanquished, there grew up three. For in like manner, when the stubornnesse of one Popular man, is overcome with Reward, there arise many more (by the Example) that do the same Mischief, in hope of like Benefit: and as all sorts of Manifacture, so also Malice encreaseth by being vendible.

Although apparently observations in passing, Hobbes's references are reliable clues to the Gallic Hercules as celebrated in sixteenth century France. His career did not end with Henry II, who aspired both to unfettered one-man rule of Polybian *monarchia*[72] and the territorial ambitions of civilizing Hercules, who turned swords into plough shares and spears into pruning forks.[73] Henry IV, the former Protestant Henry of Navarre, who, judging Paris worth a Mass, converted to Catholicism, fathered the Catholic Henrietta Maria, Queen consort of Charles I, and later, with Sully, authored the Edict of Nantes, could be said to demonstrate the sort of religiosity of which Hobbes approved.[74] Succeeding Henry III (1551-89), whose reign oversaw bitter civil war between Protestants and Catholics, the latter united in a holy league under the Duc de Guise, Henry IV, in the failing days of the Emperor Rudolf II, harboured ambitions to become King of the Romans and take up the cudgels of Christianity against the Turks, whose success in the Balkans at the battle of Kanizsa had shamed the Hapsburgs.[75] Henry's marriage to Maria de' Medici brought with it vistas of a Christendom, from the dominions of Austria to Italy and Spain, united against Islam, seen to herald a *renovatio* of Christian empire in which the Gallic Hercules was radically redeployed. Henry IV, who in 1594 had entered Paris as Perseus, who slew the dragon Spain, the Medusa, as it threatened to devour a chained virgin, was portrayed variously as Caesar, Alexander, Augustus, Constantine, and Charlemagne.[76] But his most symptomatic personifications were as the Gallic Hercules, just because of the symbolic complexity that the legendary progenitor of so many princely lines permitted.[77]

In 1592 at the height of the civil war, Henry as Hercules, armed with a club, was portrayed "dragging the [three-headed] dog Cerberus up from the under-world with a rope, signify[ing] that by his resplendent virtue the Prince subdues and expels vices from his nation with just and hallowed laws," the Venetian Antonio Ricciardo Brixiano, reported.[78] His armaments were striking. On medal after medal, Henry IV is portrayed as Hercules-Hermes, bearer of peace, his weapons a caduceus and a club. The caduceus, Hermes' wand surmounted by entwined serpents, conflates images of the serpent staff of Moses and the ecclesiastical scepter, of which it was perhaps the prototype. Of these the equipment of Hobbes's Leviathan is noticeably similar.

By no accident, Henry IV as Gallic Hercules aspired to unite the two heads of the eagle, ecclesiastical and civil, long a dream of the Gallican Church, in which the king was saluted as founder of the Church of France, protector of cities, and "Empereur dans son Royaume."[79] The imperial *renovatio* was to combine the classical civilizing mission of Heracles-Hermes with a Christian peace in which the French king ruled as priest and prince. Vanquisher of the Medusa and the infidel abroad, he conquered "par la ceducée de sa clemence et vertu" at home,[80] an image exquisitely crafted by engravers of medals, architects, and designers of royal entries, humanist historians, philologists, and poets. Isaac Casaubon, who dedicated his commentaries on Polybius to Henry IV, hailed him as "mighty author of peace, haven for those who are in danger and sole anchor of a Europe long storm-tossed and blown off her course."[81] Honoré d'Urfé's famous allegorical-pastoral novel *L'Astrée*, which tells of the Herculean travails of a young prince, finally admitted into the company of the divine Astraea, heralding a new age of civilization and peace, was dedicated to Henry IV, to whom the monumental work of Olivier de Serres, *Le Théâtre d'Agriculture* of 1601, was also dedicated.[82] These pastoral and pacific allegories were dedicated to eloquence, rule by the word instead of by the club.

Hobbes's answer to Davenant's Preface to *Gondibert*, dedicated to him and his theories, shows the master much more attuned than his acolyte to French literary and rhetorical trends. For all that he campaigned against fairies and fantasms, Hobbes had no desire to extinguish the imagination: "fancy," and its works. It is from "*fancy*," "whence proceed those grateful similes, metaphors and other tropes, by which both *poets* and *orators* have it in their power to make things please or displease, and show well or ill to others, as they like themselves."[83] Leviathan's success lies in the economy of rhetoric. The sword-wielding Leviathan must combine the emblems of church and state on a mission of peace. If the project of the Gallic Hercules was a Counterreformation imperial dream, Hobbes's Leviathan was its antithesis: Protestant Prince, vanquisher of the many-headed papal and Presbyterian hydra, who would finally bring peace.

Now we see why Hobbes the materialist and crusader against fantasms dared to invoke images of Job and the *Apocrypha*, setting allegorical riddles officially ruled out by his theory for his followers to solve. Leviathan walked a tightrope between the Godly prince of protestantism and the God-king of pagan tradition. Multiple in its appeals, this synthetic figure, Gallic Hercules, Old Testament king, evocation of the humanist prince and the Book of Job, was as offensive to one tradition as it was attractive to another. Hobbes had overdone it. If "the tongue of man is a trumpet of warre, and sedition," the spectre of a French absolute monarch ruling like Pericles, who "by his elegant speeches thundered and lightend, and confounded whole Greece t'selfe,"[84] was more than the seventeenth century Englishman was prepared to take.

Hobbes indulged in insolent irony in invoking Lucian the rhetor, author of the notorious *Philsophies for Sale*.[85] He paints "rhetors, a vile race, drawn by greed of money and fanning ears to people proud but poor, who take nothing seriously unless told them by bearded philosophers with austere faces, their whole lives an affront to their own teachings."[86] Lucian, historian of the Gallic Hercules and rhetor who deplores all rhetoricians, is Hobbes, and Hobbes, author of *Leviathan*, is Lucian. If Leviathan is the French King, the Spanish Emperor, the Pope, and the Counterreformation league, that makes the English parliament, that nest of Presbyterians, Behemoth.

Hobbes had effected a set of startling reversals that only contrived to make him more heretical, more politically dangerous, and more theologically controversial. Given his irrepressible disposition, this could have been more or less intentional. For he had serious philosophical reasons for naming his books the way he did, which controversy sometimes obscured. Memory of the Old Testament creator God, the God of fear, could not be expunged from the dispensation of the New Testament, he maintained; not only because of the reality of power politics—old states and old scores to settle—but, more seriously, due to the hermeneutics of power. Leviathan, as an aweful figure of might, personated the Old Testament God who had built the world like a temple poised between worlds. Its storm walls and its starry roof were open for all to see. By such a show of strength, the creator God assailed men, who could not deny him or the Leviathans who personified his power—the latter like Beelzebub were beasts, but somehow part of the divine design. That Hobbes should have designated his own Christian commonwealth a Leviathan is as much an expression of his relentless honesty as it is of his desire to provoke. Like the kingdoms of old—as the creation of men no better and no worse—it was the sort of state one might expect a Henry IV to lead or, at one time, a Charles I.

NOTES

1. The *Oxford English Dictionary* (*OED*, 1989 ed., vol. 8, 869) gives several meanings for the term up to and including the seventeenth century including, firstly, a monster, in the seventeenth century meaning of marvel: "the name of an aquatic animal (real or imaginary) of enormous size, frequently mentioned in Hebrew poetry," as in 1382, Wyclif, Job xl[1.] 20 [21] Whether maist thou drawen out leuyethan with an hoc? 1535 Coverdale Ps ciii[i.] 26, There is that Leuiathan, whom thou hast made, to take his pastyme therin. 1555, Eden, Decades, To Rdr. (Arb.) 51 The greate serpente of the sea Leuiathan, to haue such dominion in the Ocean. 1591, Spenser, Vis. World's Van. 62, The huge Leuiathan, dame Natures wonder; secondly, "a man of wast and formidable power or enormous wealth": 1607, Dekker, Knts Conjur. 60, The lacquy of this great leuiathan promisde he should be maister. c. 1630, Sanderson, Serm. II.310, So can the Lord deal . . . with the great . . . leviathans of the world; thirdly, "After Isaiah xxvii.I.) The great enemy of God, Satan": 1382 Wyclif, Isa. xxvii.I, In that dai viseten shal the Lord in his harde swerd . . . vp on leuyathan . . . a crookid wounde serpent. c. 1400 Destr. Troy 4423, This fende was the first that felle for his pride . . . that lyuyaton is cald. 1412-20, Lydg. Chron. Troy, II. xvii, The vile serpent the Leuiathan. 1447 Bokenham, Seytnys (Roxb.) 150, By the envye deceyvyd of hys enmy Clepyd serpent behemoat or levyathan. 1595, B. Barnes, Spir. Sonn. li, Breake thou the jawes of old Levayathan, Victorious Conqueror; and fourthly, "attrib. passing into adj. when sense: Huge, monstrous: 1624, Middleton, Game at Chess, II. ii, This leviathan-scandal that lies rolling Upon the crystal waters of devotion. The *Oxford English Dictionary* (*OED*) acknowledges that after 1651 the meaning of the term was changed forever, by Hobbes use of it to mean "The organism of political society, the commonwealth" (*OED*, 1989 ed., 869).

2. See Keith Brown, "The Artist of the *Leviathan* Title Page," *British Library Journal* 4, no. 2 (1978): 24-36; Arnold A. Rogow, *Thomas Hobbes: Radical in the Service of Reaction* (New York: W. W. Norton, 1986), 156-60; A. P. Martinich, *The Two Gods of Leviathan* (Cambridge: Cambridge University Press, 1992), 362-5; and Tracy Strong, "How to Write Scripture: Words, Authority, and Politics in Thomas Hobbes," *Critical Inquiry*, 20 (Autumn 1993): 128-59, esp. 128-30. I wish to express my sincere gratitude to the Folger Institute of the Folger Shakespeare

Library and its staff, where I began this work and from whom I was the recipient of a grant-in-aid; to Larry Bryant, Alan Cromartie, Johann and Margaret Sommerville, and Patricia Harris Stäblein, my colleagues there, for useful discussion and assistance; to the Woodrow Wilson Center, Washington, D.C., where as a Fellow for the 1993-4 academic year I have had the pleasure of completing it; and to the Editor and anonymous readers of this journal. I am indebted to Alan Cromartie for specific information on Herbert, Culverwell and the biblical commentaries; to Larry Bryant for his excellent work on the Gallic Hercules; and to Patricia Harris Stäblein for sources on big fish stories, including her own (unpublished) "No Whale Is an Island."

3. Iconographic investigations are less fruitful. Of the books consulted on monsters and marvellous beasts: Christopher Hill, *Antichrist in Seventeenth Century England* (Oxford: Oxford University Press, 1971); C.J.S. Thompson, *The Mystery and Lore of Monsters* (London: Williams and Norgate, 1930); Heinz Mode, *Fabulous Beasts and Monsters* (London: Phaidon, 1975); Claude Kappler, *Monstres et Démons et Merveilles à la fin du Moyen Age* (Paris: Payot, 1980), only Mode makes mention of Leviathan or Behemoth. Mode (1975, 118, 119, 120, 153) reproduces the text of Isaiah 27:1, setting it in the context of a brief discussion of Tiamat and dragon figures of earlier Mesopotamian and Near Eastern literature, accompanied by an excellent line drawing of Leviathan (a dragon) and Behemoth (a hippopotamus) by William Blake, 1825, too late for our purposes. Even the compendious work of P. Gaspar Schott, S. J., *Physica Curiosa, sive Mirabilia naturae et artis* (1667), ranging from angels and demons to biological and astronomical marvels, includes no mention of Leviathan or Behemoth. This despite mention of Egyptian conjurors turning rods into serpents (Schott, 1667, bk. 1, chap. 20, 58); brief mention of Job 1:3 of the Book of the Apocalypse on the precursor to Antichrist (Schott, 1667, bk. 1, chap. 19, 51) and Isaiah 13:5, 20 on the extermination of the Babylonians and their place being taken by dragons (Schott, 1667, bk. 3, chap. 2, 360); and a chapter devoted to Egyptian monsters and deformities (Appendix to bk. 12, chap. 6, 1377-8), matters of related interest to Hobbes.

4. Strong, "How to Write Scripture," 147. Victoria Silver, in her "Critical Response, I: A Matter of Interpretation," *Critical Inquiry* 20 (Autumn, 1993): 160-71, argues against Strong that the Leviathan is a figure for "the world's fundamental intransigence—its resistance to explanation" (p. 164). This is, I think, quite wrong, if only, as I shall show, on the grounds of anachronism.

5. Quoted in Silver, "Critical Response," 164-5, as evidence of God flexing his muscles in the creation of Leviathan, symbol of the intransigence of the world and resistance to explanation.

6. *Leviathan*, 1, 1991 ed., 9.

7. Ibid., chap. 17, 87, 1991 ed., 120.

8. Ibid., 166, 1991 ed., 220

9. Ibid., 166-7, 1991 ed., 220-1.

10. Strong, "How to Write Scripture," 132-3, 149.

11. Ibid. It is important to emphasize that Reformation epistemic revisions to the allegorical tradition of Catholicism represented an institutional challenge in the first instance, and philosophic changes only as a consequence. Allegorical interpretation had opened up a vast terrain of possible meanings, giving the Church the scope it needed to claim institutional authority over the sacred books. The Protestant attempt to claim the scriptures back for the common reader had its analogue in Hobbes's attempt to claim back civil society and its full array of institutions, including philosophy and government, from the domain of an imperial church. It represented at once a democratic appeal to the equality of all believers and an institutional counterclaim against the Church. For this reason, I think that Tracy Strong is right to see the Protestant position on the question of how we can know the scriptures as Hobbes's paradigm for how we can know God and, further, how we can know that civil government is divinely sanctioned. In each of these cases, "know" is the operative word, the "leap of faith" that Silver objects to and that Strong

reasserts. (See Strong's "Critical Response II: When Is a Text not a Pretext? A Rejoinder to Victoria Silver," *Critical Inquiry* 20 (Autumn 1993): 172-8, esp., 172-4). Seventeenth century propositions concerning matters for which we have even fewer guidelines than for understanding scripture do not lend themselves to redescription as, for instance, " 'interpreting' the existence of God," or " 'interpreting' the legitimacy of the sovereign." Semantically incongruous and politically dangerous, they offer no warrant for the redescription " 'interpreting' the Bible," either, language that exegetes are careful not to use.

12. For Hobbes's preoccupation with disempowering the Church, see Patricia Springborg, "Hobbes on Religion," in the *Cambridge Companion to Hobbes*, ed. by Tom Sorrell (Cambridge, forthcoming); and "Hobbes, Heresy and the *Historia Ecclesiastica*," *Journal of the History of Ideas* (October 1994). On anti-clericalism as the obsession in the age of Locke, see J.A.I Champion, *The Pillars of Priestcraft Shaken: The Church of England and its Enemies, 1660-1730* (Cambridge: Cambridge University Press, 1992).

13. Theodore Beza, *Job Expovnded by Theodore Beza, Partly in Manner of a Commentary, Partly in Manner of a Paraphrase* (Cambridge, 1589, STC 2020), Dedicatorie, 4.

14. Ibid., 8-9.

15. Edward Herbert, *The Ancient Religion of the Gentiles and Causes of Errors Considered* (London: 1705 ed.; Folger Library, 153296), 134. English translation of *De religione gentilis, errorumque apud eos causis* (Amsterdam, 1663; Folger Library: 150363.B1805).

16. Nathaniel Culverwell, *An Elegant and Learned Discourse of the Light of Nature* (1646), ed. by Robert A. Green and High MacCallum (Toronto: University of Toronto Press, 1972), 41.

17. Theodore Beza, *Job Expovnded*, Dedicatorie, 4-5.

18. Hugh Broughton, an Hebraist and scholar, noted in his title the time he expended on interpretation compared with translation: Hugh Broughton, *Iob. To the King. A Colon-Agrippina studie of one moneth, for the metricall translation. But of Many Yeres, for Ebrew Difficulties. Part 2 is Iob. Brought on to familiar dialogue and paraphrase for easier entendement* (n.p., 1610, STC 3868). He skips over Job, chapters 38 to 42, with the general comment that God's point here is to teach people: on the one hand, that his demonstrations of power are visible; on the other, that probing them too deeply for meaning is a show of pride of just the sort for which Job took our punishment. Broughton's comment amounts to a confession of failure with this particular set of "'ebrew difficulties," which is to say that he is more open than most of his contemporary commentators (Ibid., 144). This translation, with a political purpose no doubt, had been made for King James I. Earlier, in his translation of *The Lamentation of Ieremy* (1606, 34), dedicated to "Henry, Prince of Great Britany," Broughton had cross-referenced the dragon and ostrich of chapter 4:3 of the Lamentations ("Even the Dragons open their breast, they give suck to their whelps: the daughter of my people is like the cruell: as the ostrich in the wildernes") to the unicorn of Job 39:14, suggesting some unfathomable association between these apocalyptic beasts. The choice of Job and the Lamentations of Jeremiah as texts for royal dedication could, as in the case of Beza, simply be to exhort the Prince to constancy and courage in times of trial, with no particular, or negative, focus on the apocalyptic content, as the Broughton's subtitle for the *Lamentations* (1606), which "Stirreth all to attention of God's Ordered Providence in Kingdomes confusion," would suggest.

19. George Abbott, *The Whole Booke of Iob Paraphrased, or Made easie for any to understand* (London, 1640, STC 41), 256, 259.

20. Jean Oecolampadius, *Exposition de M. Iean Oecolompade svr le Livre de Iob*. Traduit de Latin en François (Edition premiere, Geneve, 1562, Floger Library 218-628q), 487.

21. Ibid., 488-9. Oecolampadius' account is one of the most comprehensive surveys of interpretatons of Behemoth and Leviathan in Bible commentaries.

22. Job 40:17.

23. Behemoth's tail stiff like a Cedar in the Book of Job, would have been read as a figure for Lebanon.

24. John Calvin, *Sermons of Maister Iohn Calvin, vpon the Booke of Iob*, trans. Arthur Golding (London, 1584 STC 4447), 730b, 43ff.

25. Ibid., 731a, 4-11.

26. Ibid., 731a, 16-21.

27. Ibid., 732b, 33ff.

28. Ibid., 732a, 53ff: "Howbeit before I goe any further, wheras here is so long a discourse vpon the said king of beasts of the land whiche I said was an Elephant, (albeit that it bee named here by the general terme of Behemoth) & also vpon the Leuiathan: we haue to marke therupon how men haue bin of opinion, that by an allegory the diuel is spoken of here, rather than either the Elephant or the Whale, and that they haue gone aboute to proue that fanastical deuise of theirs by this, that in the end is said, that the said whale is the king of the children of pride."

29. Ibid., 733a, 6-11: "Neuertheles truely, by conueying the discourse from the one to the other, a man might as wel vse this similitude of the Whales and Elephantes, to make men perceiue how greatly the power of the Deuil ought to fray vs, seeing he is termed the prince of the ayre and of the world."

30. The most common usage of the words "allegory," "allegorical" up to and including the sixteenth century, was to designate a particular tradition of biblical interpretation, Tyndale in his *Obedience of a Christian Man*, of 1528 (Works, vol. I, 303) declaring: "They divide the scripture in four senses, the literal, tropological, allegorical and analogical." Wyclif, on Gal. 4:24, remarked eliptically, "The whiche thingis ben seid by allegorie, or goostly undirstandinge." W. Fulke (*Heskins. Parliament*, 1579, 11) referred to "wicked allegorizing vpon the scriptures"; and, in the same vein, Jortin (Serm, 1571, 1771 ed., I.i.2,) declared: "The Pagan Philosophers fell into the Allegorizing way," *Oxford English Dictionary*, 1989 ed., vol. 1, 333.

31. Calvin, 1584 ed., 733b, 11ff, 28ff; "If we beare away this singlenes, it will stand vs in better steed then all curious expositions that canne be deuised, as when these Allegorimakers serched out his ribs & backbones, & treated also of his skin & of this & that, & to be short, there was not that peece of him, wherein they found not some toy or other. But this is as it were to make the holy scripture a nose of waxe, by transfourming it from the natural sense."

32. John Calvin, *A Commentary vpon the Prophecie of Isaiah* (Translated ovt of French . . . by C. C. London (1609, STC 4396), 260b.

33. *The Reformation Writings of Martin Luther*. Translated from the definitive Weimar edition by Bertram Lee Wolf (London: Lutterworth Press. 1956, 2 vols.), vol. 2, 231.

34. Ps. 58:4.

35. Ps. 22:21.

36. Ps. 7:2.

37. Jer. 5:3.

38. Ps. 74:13

39. Luther, *The Reformation Writings*, 1956 ed., vol. 2, 232.

40. Ibid.

41. Hobbes's challenge is issued in his "Animadversions upon the Bishop's Epistle to the Reader," in *The English Works of Thomas Hobbes*, ed. by Sir William Molesworth (London, 1839-45; 11 vols, referred to as E.W.), vol. 5, 25-6, prefacing *The Questions Concerning Liberty, Necessity and Chance, Clearly Stated and Debated between Dr. Bramhall, Bishop of Derby and Thomas Hobbes of Malmesbury* (1654). It is interesting to speculate at what point Hobbes decided to use the title Behemoth himself, the work that was completed in 1668 and published only in 1679. Hobbes is mute on the significance of its title, at which we can only guess. Did the

Long Parliament in any way resemble Behemoth as a figure for the Assyrians, land of Nebuchadnezzar and the Tower of Babel?

42. John Bramhall, *Castigations of Mr. Hobbes his Last Animadversions, in the Case Concerning Liberty and Universal Necessity. With an Apprendix Concerning the Catching of LEVIATHAN, or the Great Whale* (London, 1658, STC B4215), Preface, ii.

43. Ibid., iii: "*I do believe there never was any Authour Sacred or Profane, Ancient or Moderne, Christian, Jew, Mahumetan, or Pagan, that hath inveighed so frequently and so bitterly against all feigned phantasmes*, with their first devisers, maintainers, and receivers, as T. H. hath done, excluding out of the nature of things the souls of Men, Angels, Devils, and all incorporeal Substances, as fictions, phantasmes, and groundlesse contradictions. Many men fear the meaning of it is not good, that God himself must be gone for company, as being an incorporeal substance, except men will vouchsafe by God to understand nature. So much T. H. himself seemeth to intimate."

44. Brown, "The Artist of the *Leviathan*"; Strong, "How to Write Scripture."

45. *OED*: sea monster, half man half fish. There was a long tradition of big fish stories, in Norse, French Romance, Celtic, and Old English legend, and other folklore far afield. See, Cornelia Catlin Coulter, "The 'Great Fish' in Ancient and Medieval Story," *Transactions of the American Philological Association* 57 (1926): 32-50; Michael N. Nagler, "Beowulf in the Context of Myth," in *Old English Literature in Context*, ed. by J. D. Niles (Totowa, NJ: Rowman and Little field, 1980), 143-56; S. J. Parsons, "Lest Men Like Fishes . . . ," *Traditio* 3 (1946): 381-8.

46. Bramhall, *Castigations of Mr. Hobbes*, iv.

47. Ibid. Bramhall expands on his image: "My first dart is aimed at his heart, or Theological part of his discourse, to shew that his principles are not consistent either with Christianity, or any other Religion. The second dart is aimed at the chine [*OED*: backbone], whereby this vast body is united and fitted for aminal motion, that is, the political part of his discourse; to shew that his principles are pernicious to all formes of Government, and all Societies, and destroy all relations between man and man. The third dart is aimed at his head or rational part of his discourse; to shew that his principles are inconsistent with themselves, and contradict one another. Let him take heed, if these three darts do pierce his Leviathan home, it is not all the Dittany [*OED*: pepperwort, cure for monsters] which groweth in Creet that can make them drop easily out of his body, without the utter overthrow of his cause."

48. Ibid.

49. For more detailed studies of Hobbes on these particular religious doctrines see the following pieces by Patricia Springborg, "Leviathan and the Problem of Ecclesiastical Authority," *Political Theory* 3, no. 3 (1975): 289-303; "Leviathan, the Christian Commonwealth Incorporated," *Political Studies* 24, no. 2 (1976): 171-83.

50. Thomas Hobbes, *Historia ecclesiastica carmine elegiaco concinnata*, ed. with a preface by Thomas Rymer (London: Andrew Crooke, 1688). English paraphrase, *A True Ecclesiastical History From Moses to the time of Martin Luther, in Verse* (London, 1722), lines 1225-35, 1688 ed., 57, 1722 paraphrase, pp. 97-100.

51. This is the spirit of Tracy Strong's description of the frontispiece in "How to Write Scripture," 130.

52. Henry VIII claimed a super-king role in medieval mystical body language "We as head and you as members, we are conjoined and bound together in one body politic," cited by Ernst H. Kantorowicz, *The King's Two Bodies: A Study in Medieval Political Theology* (Princeton, NJ: Princeton University Press, 1957), 228; but even he does not quite qualify for the might and terror of Leviathan.

53. Diodorus Siculus, *Library of History*, trans. C. H. Oldfather (London: Heinemann, Loeb ed., 1935), 4.19, 405.

54. Cited by Corrado Vivanti, "Henry IV, The Gallic Hercules," *Journal of the Warburg and Courtauld Institutes* 30 (1967): 185.

55. Lucian, "Heracles," in *Works*, ed. by A. M. Harmon (London: Heinemann, Loeb ed., 1913), vol. 1, 63.

56. Ibid., 65.

57. Ibid., §3-6, 1913 ed., 65-7.

58. *Leviathan*, 1991 ed., 147; noted by Quentin Skinner, "Thomas Hobbes on the Proper Signification of Liberty," *Transactions of the Royal Historical Society* 40 (1990): 121-51.

59. For this account of Henry IV as the Gallic Hercules, I am indebted to Lawrence M. Bryant, "Politics, Ceremonies, and Embodiments of Majesty in Henry II's France," in *European Monarchy, its Evolution and Practice from Roman Antiquity to Modern Times* (Stuttgart: Franz Steiner Verlag, 1992) 127-54.

60. Ibid., 136-7.

61. Lucian, "Heracles," 5, 1913 ed., 67.

62. Bryant, "Politics, Ceremonies, and Embodiments," 140.

63. Ibid., 136.

64. Jean Bodin, *The Six Bookes of a Commonweale*, trans. R. Knolles (Cambridge: Harvard University Press, 1962), 503, 506, cited Bryant, "Politics, Ceremonies, and Embodiments," 135-6.

65. Bodin, *The Six Bookes*, 3.3, 378, cited Bryant, "Politics, Ceremonies, and Embodiments," 141-2.

66. R. E. Hallowell, "Ronsard and the Gallic Hercules Myth," *Studies in the Renaissance* 9 (1962); cited Bryant, "Politics, Ceremonies, and Embodiments," 141 n. 47.

67. Bryant, "Politics, Ceremonies, and Embodiments," 150.

68. Ernst H. Kantorowicz, *The King's Two Bodies: A Study in Medieval Political Theology* (Princeton, NJ: Princeton University Press, 1957), 498 n. 6.

69. Bryant, "Politics, Ceremonies, and Embodiments," 144-5.

70. *Leviathan*, 1991 ed., 80-1.

71. Ibid., 241.

72. Polybius, 6.7.9-6.9.1.

73. Vivanti, "Henry IV, The Gallic Hercules," 190.

74. As Tracy Strong has pointed out.

75. Vivanti, "Henry IV, The Gallic Hercules," 177-8.

76. Ibid., 179-83.

77. See Jean Seznec, *La Survivance des dieux antiques* (Paris, 1940), 28ff, cited Vivanti, "Henry IV," 183.

78. Antonio Ricciardo Brixiano, *Commentaria Symbolica...in quibus explicantur arcana pene infinita ad mysticam, naturalem et occultam rerum significationem attinentia* (Venice 1591, 33), cited Vivanti, *"Henry IV,"* 184.

79. Antonio la Penna, *Orazio e l'ideologia del principato* (Turin, 1963), 180-1; Ernst Bloch, *Les Rois Thaumaturges* (Paris, 1961), cited Vivanti, "Henry IV," 180-1. Rousseau referred to Hobbes as that "Christian author," who united the two heads of the eagle, *The Social Contract*, 1762, bk. 4, chap. 8, trans. Maurice Cranston (Harmondsworth: Penguin, 1968), 180.

80. Vivanti, "Henry IV," 190.

81. Isaac Casaubon, *Epistolae...eiusdem deicationes, praefationes, prolegomena* (Rotterdam, 1709), vol. 1, 87; cited Vivanti, "Henry IV," 193-4.

82. Vivanti, "Henry IV," 194-5.

83. See Hobbes's Answer to "The Author's Preface to his much honour'd Friend Mr Hobs," by Sir William D'Avenant, and Hobbes's Answer, in *Gondibert: an Heroick Poem* (London, 1651, STC D325), 78-9.

84. Hobbes, *De Cive*, chap. 5, on Imperium, in *The English Works of Thomas Hobbes*, ed. by Sir William Molesworth (11 vols, London, 1839-1845, referred to as E.W.), vol. 1, 88.

85. I thank the anonymous reader of this journal for reminding me of the title of Lucian's other famous work. For the Lucianic tradition more generally, see D. Duncan, *Ben Jonson and the Lucianic Tradition* (Cambridge: Cambridge University Press, 1979).

86. Hobbes added, while "anyone who decries the priests is hunted down as a blasphemer, atheist, heretic." *Historia Ecclesiastica*, lines 385-460, 1688 ed., 19-22; 1722 ed., 28-33.

Patricia Springborg teaches in the Department of Government at the University of Sydney. A Woodrow Wilson International Scholar in 1994-95, she is now a Guest Fellow at the Brookings Institution as the recipient of a MacArthur Foundation Research and Writing Grant.

[21]

Thomas Hobbes and the external relations of states

MURRAY FORSYTH

HOBBES' conception of relations between states has attracted attention from two directions. Students of political theory who have focused on Hobbes have from time to time looked beyond their central pre-occupations and noted briefly the relevance of his doctrine for the international arena.[1] The external relations of Leviathan are for them on the fringe of Hobbes' theory. Students of international relations on the other hand invoke Hobbes' name frequently as a kind of shorthand for a particular approach to the international world, one that is also associated with Machiavelli, and usually called the 'realist' approach. By contrast with the political theorists, they tend to look from the outside *into* Hobbes' theory and to ask whether and how far the 'domestic' situation of individuals in a Hobbesian state of nature bears an analogy with the 'external' situation of states in relationship to one another.[2]

In this study I wish to try and take the discussion of Hobbes and the international world a little further. I do not propose to start from the outside looking in, nor from the inside looking out. I wish to argue that behind the question of whether there are analogies between the 'domestic' and 'external' worlds there lies the deeper question of why Leviathan has external relations at all. Hobbes, after all, never begins his political theory with this or that particular group of men, but always with a consideration of *man*. Why then is the political com-munity that emerges in his theory a body designed for common defence against 'the invasion of foreigners'?[3] Why does not Leviathan logically embrace the whole of mankind? In other words the primary question is not one of analogies or parallels but one of the simultaneous

1. Howard Warrender, *The Political Philosophy of Hobbes* (Oxford, 1957), pp. 118–20 and David P. Gauthier, *The Logic of Leviathan* (Oxford, 1967), pp. 207–212, provide good examples of this tendency. There is also a close similarity in the substance of their arguments.

2. For Hobbes' name used as a shorthand for the 'realist' approach see, for example, Martin Wight, *Systems of States* (Leicester, 1977), pp. 38–39; Geoffrey Stern in *The Bases of International Order* (ed.), Alan James (Oxford, 1973), p. 134; and Hedley Bull, *The Anarchical Society* (London, 1977), pp. 24–27. For the best discussion of the 'domestic analogy' between Hobbes' state of nature and the condition of international relations, see Bull, *op. cit.* pp. 46–51, and also Bull's article, 'Society and Anarchy in International Relations', in *Diplomatic Investigations* (London, 1966), pp. 35–50.

3. *Leviathan*, Michael Oakeshott (ed.), (Oxford, 1960), p. 112.

emergence of 'inner' and 'outer', or 'us' and 'them' in the development of Hobbes' concept of the state.[1]

The search for the answer to this question leads, as might be expected, to a consideration of the process of generation of Hobbes' commonwealth, and more specifically of the way in which the state of nature is transformed into the state proper. This is a field well trampled over by political theorists, and it is difficult not to cover ground which has been explored before. If, however, attention is kept firmly fixed on the crystallization of man as originally conceived by Hobbes, into man divided into discrete groups facing one another, perhaps it is possible to say something fresh about this well-studied subject, and to illuminate not merely this or that side of Hobbes' teaching, but the central core of his theory.

Textual exegesis is unfortunately wearisome, and I shall therefore begin by sketching the general direction of the argument which I wish to develop. First, the subject obliges one to look with particular attention at two junctures in Hobbes' argument: the point at which he moves from a definition of the 'mere' or 'bare' state of nature to a definition of the natural laws, and the point at which he moves from a discussion of the natural laws to the situation that immediately precedes the creation of the commonwealth. Hobbes' argument at these points and elsewhere, I shall argue, make it necessary to differentiate the Hobbesian state of nature into two: a condition in which individual men are governed solely and entirely by self-directed passions, and by their own reason and judgement, and a condition in which the laws of reason, or reason as by definition the taking into account of the *other* person's rights as well as one's own, are immanently at work. Most important of all, this second condition is synonymous with one in which men are woven together into distinct groupings or confederations. It is a condition in which a differentiation between 'allies' and 'enemies' has taken place. Leviathan is the perfection of a discrete group of allies of this sort – it stands for the final expulsion of the right of war from *within* the group and the restriction of the exercise of the right of war to relations *between* groups.

Such is the broad outline of the argument. It is necessary now to show how it derives from Hobbes' own words. In reading Hobbes' three main political texts – *The Elements of Law, De Cive,* and *Leviathan* – it is always difficult to be sure what is most impressive about his writing: the extraordinary tenacity with which he retains in each successive work the arguments of the preceding one, or the subtle changes that he makes in these arguments, accentuating a theme here and paring

---

1. This question must also be distinguished from the problem posed by Kant in his *Idea for a Universal History from a Cosmo-political Point of View*. Kant here assumed that the same unsociability which forced men to create the state obtained between states, and argued that it was therefore essential to create an international federation in the likeness of a state. His later writings, however, show that he progressively modified this argument, and came to see that logically an international federation would have to be *different* from a state.

away another there. Both these characteristics strike the eye when one tries to follow the process of the crystallization of men into groups. The main line of differentiation would seem to run between the argument he develops in his two earlier works, and the one propounded in *Leviathan*. I shall therefore treat the former first, and then the latter. This division should not however be taken to imply that there is a total break in continuity.

The discussion in the early works

In the *Elements* and *De Cive* Hobbes gives the original or 'bare' state of nature a peculiarly sharp definition by attributing to man a natural underived right to all things. In the *Elements* he defines this right as follows:

> Every man by nature hath right to all things, that is to say, to do whatsoever he listeth to whom he listeth, to possess, use, and enjoy all things he will and can. For seeing all things he willeth, must therefore be good unto him in his own judgement, because he willeth them; and may tend to his preservation some time or other; or he may judge so . . . it followeth that all things may rightly also be done by him.[1]

This original underived right of all to all – which I shall call hereafter the raw right to all – is not the only reason why the 'bare' state of nature is a state of war, but it is an important one. The other causes that Hobbes enumerates are the passions – vanity, competition, and appetite for the same thing – and the right to do what in one's own judgement is necessary for one's preservation. The latter right, it should be observed, is not contrary to "right reason", but is something "that all men account to be done justly, and with right".[2] It has an element of reciprocity in it. The raw right to all however is not, and cannot be based on right reason or reciprocity – to recognize the right of another to all things is necessarily to deny oneself this right. By making it an original element of man's nature Hobbes in effect makes each man a totally 'windowless' atom.

The peculiar characteristics of a state of nature founded on the raw right to all are worth dwelling upon. Such a state can only be described as a not-world, a fortuitous or Epicurean concurrence, a 'dissolution' rather than a 'resolution' of civil government. A plurality of men exist each of whom can claim and assert the right to exist *alone*. Each man – each state if we wish to transpose the notion to international affairs – may in other words act not as *a* representative of God, but as

---

1. *The Elements of Law Natural and Politic*, Ferdinand Tonnies (ed.), M. M. Goldsmith (second ed.) (London, 1969), p. 72. The corresponding definition in *De Cive*, for which I have used the translation entitled, *Philosophical Rudiments concerning Government and Society* in volume two of Hobbes' *English Works*, Molesworth (ed.), is on pp. 9–11. The footnote Hobbes added later to this passage in *De Cive* is already a modification of his original position, and prepares the way, like several of the other footnotes, for his ultimate standpoint in *Leviathan*.

2. *De Cive, op. cit.* pp. 8–9.

the representative of God, and may direct his or its actions so as to gain sole lordship over the world. Man is assumed to be free, but as free to pursue his welfare not as distinct from the welfare of others, but as if there were no others from whom 'his own' could be, or need be, differentiated. There is, there can be no notion of ownership either potential or actual in this condition. To talk of a distinct *ius belli* in this condition also seems inappropriate, for to exist is *necessarily* to fight, until at last fighting is unnecessary.

As these multiple 'jets' of blind freedom expand they encounter one another and mutual destruction results. Fear of such destruction, to revert to Hobbes' own words, provokes men to use their "right" or "true" reason to find a way out of this "estate". They consult the laws of nature. Before passing on to a discussion of the impact of the laws of nature on the bare estate of nature, however, it is worth considering the latter's significance and meaning. Why does Hobbes posit as a distinct "estate" something that is merely a not-world, a formless chaos, a buzzing, booming confusion that even the word "estate" distorts?

There would seem to be at least two reasons. The first is that Hobbes was concerned to combat the doctrine that man naturally sought society in the abstract, and followed reason in the abstract, as if the formation of one and the use of the other were disconnected from self-interest and passion. Against this he wished – rightly I think – to argue that society and reason were related to man's self-interest and passion, they did not exist in some pure ethereal world of their own. The positing of a not-world, or the 'position' of a 'negation', which provoked fear of destruction, and hence roused reason to its work, was a potent if crudely linear way of making plain the rootedness of both society and reason in self-interest and passion, or of showing that society and reason were both *will*.

The second reason for Hobbes' posited not-world is that it is an anatomy of the evil which he saw around him when he was writing. The 'bare' state of nature is not, as we have already noted, a resolution of civil government, it is the dissolution of civil government. More precisely, it is the dissolution of the dissolution of civil government. It is an anatomy, in other words, of religious – or as we might put it to-day – of ideological civil war. It portrays a situation in which not merely each sect or party but each man claims to possess absolute truth and absolute right, and feels justified thereby in smiting down his fellow men as mere obstacles to the spread of 'his' truth and right. Such men, as Hobbes put it in *Leviathan* betray "their want of right reason, by the claim they lay to it".[1] By pretending to be Gods, they reduce mankind to brutishness.

The positing of a not-world, an Epicurean concurrence of atoms, thus has its own logic. Let us now turn to the state of nature in its

---

1. *Leviathan, op. cit.* p. 26.

second guise, as it is moulded by the laws of nature. These laws pre-scribe the forms by which free beings establish relationships between themselves. They command men basically to exchange right – that is to engage in the mutual self-limitation of their original freedom. The use of right reason is hence synonymous with the voluntary establish-ment of relationship. Men are no longer 'windowless' atoms, they look out and recognize one another. They do not however establish relation-ships with everyone indiscriminately because reason commands it – that for Hobbes would be a destruction of the nexus between reason and interest on which he was so insistent. Rather men enter into exchange – or form pacts – with *some* men in order the better to meet the enmity of *others*. The awakening of reason means not the extinction of enmity, but the distinction of 'enemies' from 'allies', the ending of ubiquitous enmity.

To demonstrate this simultaneous process Hobbes' own words must be quoted. In the brief passage in *De Cive* that succeeds his definition of the state of nature and precedes his exposition of the laws of nature, Hobbes makes two revealing statements. "No man", he writes, "can esteem a war of all against all to be good for him".

> And so it happens, that through fear of each other we think it fit to rid ourselves of this condition, and to get some fellows; that if there needs must be war, it may not yet be against all men, nor without some helps. Fellows are gotten either by constraint, or by consent . . .[1]

Then, after showing the mechanism of constraint, or the right of irresistible power in the state of nature, he concludes that men cannot expect any lasting preservation by continuing in the state of nature. "Wherefore to seek peace, where there is any hopes of obtaining it, and where there is none, to enquire out for auxiliaries of war, is the dictate of right reason, that is, the law of nature . . ."[2]

It is clear from these two passages, that to search for "auxiliaries of war" is dictated at once by fear of destruction and by the laws of nature. In the section that comes after his exposition of the laws of nature, Hobbes again discusses this interconnection:

> Since therefore the exercise of the natural law is necessary for the preservation of peace, and that for the exercise of the natural law security is no less necessary; it is worth the considering what that is which affords such a security. For this matter nothing else can be imagined, but that each man provide himself of such meet helps, as the invasion of one on the other may be rendered so dangerous, as either of them may think it better to refrain than to meddle.[3]

---

1. *De Cive, op. cit.* p. 12.

2. *Ibid.* p. 13. The ambiguity of these concluding paragraphs of Chapter One of *De Cive* lies in the fact that Hobbes sees the winning of fellows by constraint as part of the 'bare' state of nature and yet also sees the winning of fellows as the way *out* of the 'bare' state of nature. This ambiguity foreshadows that of the commonwealth by acquisition itself: is it but the state of nature congealed, or a genuine step beyond the state of nature? For Locke and Rousseau it was emphatically the former.

3. *Ibid.* pp. 64–65. The identity of the search for peace, or the exercise of the laws of nature, and the concrete creation of security is also indicated by the later passage in which Hobbes

From here Hobbes argues that the "consent of many" only to "direct all their actions to the same end and the common good", or a "society·proceeding from mutual help only", is liable to fall apart once the common end goes. Something else must therefore be done "that those who have once consented for the common good to peace and mutual help, may by fear be restrained lest afterwards they again dissent, when their private interest shall appear discrepant from the common good".[1] It is only at *this* point that Hobbes asserts that what is necessary in civil government is not merely "many wills concurring in one object", but "one will",[2] and proceeds to discuss the establishment of this one will, or the construction of the state proper.

In this survey of the argument in *De Cive* and the *Elements* I have tried to show that lurking within Hobbes' state of nature there are not merely – as is so often imagined – a multiplicity of individuals engaged in a war of all against all, and vainly trying to follow the laws of nature. There are security-communities, confederations and alliances, forming and reforming as the pressure of a common enemy arises and subsides. Hobbes' state is the perfection of a discrete confederation or security-community as much as it is a union of individuals.

The discussion in Leviathan

In *Leviathan* the argument that has been traced in the earlier works undergoes some interesting modifications. Perhaps the first thing to be noted is that in Hobbes' description of the "natural condition of mankind" the raw right of all to all disappears as a cause of the war of all against all. The war is caused by men who are roughly equal in bodily and mental faculties seeking the same thing and struggling for it; seeking to avert such clashes by anticipatory force; and seeking glory. The war is inferred, writes Hobbes, from the passions. Insofar as right is being exercised in it, it would appear to be rational right or a right which men mutually acknowledge. Thus when a man takes measures of war that are "no more than his own conservation requireth," it is "generally allowed", and when augmentation of dominion over others is "necessary to a man's conservation, it ought to be allowed him".[3] The implication here is that some form of agreement between

---

wrote that "dominions (*imperia*) were constituted for peace's sake, and peace was sought after for safety's sake", pp. 166–167. In stressing the identity of the exercise of the natural laws, the formation of pacts, and the creation of security I differ markedly from the position adopted by Howard Warrender in *The Political Philosophy of Hobbes*. Warrender's constant determination to abstract the purely personal essence of natural law both from its other-directed practical dictates, and from the " circumstances" of "sufficient" or "insufficient security" in which it operates, and to make the individual's interpretation of this purely personal essence the constitutive 'ground' of all obligation seems to me to distort Hobbes' doctrine. Hobbes was not concerned to reduce all obligation to its first starting point, he was concerned to show that the first starting point was *only* a starting point, that man had to act with his fellow men in order to make the reason that was part of his nature a real power.

1. *Ibid.* pp. 65–66.   2. *Ibid.* p. 66.
3. *Leviathan, op. cit.* p. 81.

men makes warlike measures that are necessary for survival permissible. Hobbes heightens this suggestion of reason at work in the original state of nature by indicating that men are capable of combining in it. In the very first paragraph he mentions "confederacy with others"[1] as a means of equalizing the strength of the weak with that of the naturally powerful, and later writes of men coming "with forces united"[2] to drive out the single settler. Hobbes also describes men endeavouring to win respect or esteem from others, and daring to go "far enough"[3] as to destroy some men to win this – which is hardly a description of a blind denial of others' right to exist. Finally the passions driving men to peace in *Leviathan* are more positive than in Hobbes' earlier works – the fear of destruction is joined by men's "desire of such things as are necessary to commodious living; and a hope by their industry to obtain them",[4] and Hobbes draws a peculiarly vivid picture of the positive benefits that men lose by engaging in war.

In sum the original state of nature in *Leviathan* has lost something of the bleak nothingness that characterized it in Hobbes' earlier works. Reason seems more immanent in it. Men are capable of relating, if only in a limited way. Passions are pushing men into war but other passions are positively pushing men out. And yet there can be no denying that Hobbes calls it explicitly a "war of every man, against every man",[5] a condition of multiple *solitude*.[6] He can only do this, it may be suggested, by putting all the factors on one side of his equation instead of placing them in dynamic interrelationship with one another. That is to say, instead of defensive unions *checking* aggressive individuals or confederacies *checking* the war relationship between their members – all measures to balance and combine forces are seen as but an extension of a primitive war produced by the passions.

When Hobbes proceeds to define the right of nature and the laws of nature in *Leviathan* it might seem as if the raw right of all to all characteristic of the *Elements* and *De Cive* re-appears. The position however is more complex than this. The right of nature in *Leviathan* is each man's liberty to use his own power, as he will himself, for the preservation of his own nature, and to use his own judgement and reason to decide if, when, and how far measures to preserve himself are required. The laws of nature are once again, "right" reason, that is to say reason reaching out beyond oneself and telling one for one's own good to engage in mutual exchange of right with others. What then is the "right to everything" which Hobbes also says "every man naturally has"? It would seem to be the right of nature as it is exercised *in* the state of nature that has already been defined. Thus, *in* a condition of universal war man is entitled by the right of nature to do anything he wants to his fellow man. His right

1. *Ibid.* p. 80. 2. *Ibid.* p. 81.
3. *Ibid.* p. 81. 4. *Ibid.* p. 84.
5. *Ibid.* p. 82 and p. 83.
6. *Ibid.* p. 82 ('the life of man, solitary'), and p.83.

reason shrivels into nothing. Total measures are permitted. But the shrivelling of right reason into nothingness is the same as man's total destruction. *Ergo* man has to exercise his right of nature in conjunction with right reason, to limit the total right to total war, if he is to continue to exist. The whole thrust of Hobbes' argument would seem to be that the use of right reason is neither merely technical nor merely spontaneous but existential – linked to man's very survival as man. Paradoxically Hobbes can only express this existentiality of right reason by placing man in an "estate" or condition, or supposing him to be able to exist, *without* right reason.[1]

That in *Leviathan* – as in *The Elements of Law* and *De Cive* – the awakening or application of right reason is synonymous with the making of confederacies or alliances by which one gains additional protection against the threat of enemies is plain from Hobbes' own words. One particular passage, in which he fiercely rebuts the Machiavellian argument that "there is no such thing as justice",[2] and that a man can do whatever he likes to gain his own advantage, making or unmaking covenants at whim, is worth quoting at length. In a condition of war, Hobbes writes,

> wherein every man to every man, for want of a common power to keep them all in awe, is an enemy, there is no man who can hope by his own strength, or wit, to defend himself from destruction, without the help of confederates; where every one expects the same defence by the confederation, that any one else does: and therefore he which declares he thinks it reason to deceive those that help him, can in reason expect no other means of safety, than what can be had from his own single power. He therefore that breaketh his covenant, and consequently declareth that he may with reason do so, cannot be received into any society, that unite themselves for peace and defence, but by the error of them that receive him; nor when he is received, be retained in it, without seeing the danger of their error; which errors a man cannot reasonably reckon upon as the means of his security: and therefore if he be left, or cast out of society, he perisheth; and if he live in society, it is by the errors of other men, which he could not foresee, nor reckon upon; and consequently against the reason of his preservation; and so, as all men that contribute not to his destruction, forbear him only out of ignorance of what is good for themselves.[3]

Nowhere does Hobbes argue more cogently than this that even

---

1. This paraphrase is intended to express the essence of the early paragraphs, and above all the fourth, of Chapter XIV, Part I, of Leviathan, i.e. pp. 84–5. There remains however an ambiguity which I feel is incapable of resolution, namely Hobbes' express statement that the right to all is a *result* of the condition of war, and his concomitant statement, a little later that "as long as every man holdeth this right, of doing any thing he liketh; so long are all men in the condition of war".

2. *Ibid.* p. 94.

3. *Ibid.* pp. 95–96. It is worth noting in this context that the very first law of nature (p.85) states that "*every man, ought to endeavour peace, as far as he has hope of obtaining it; and when he cannot obtain it, that he may seek, and use, all helps and advantages of war*". This is a highly 'circumstance-impregnated' injunction.

before the state proper is established the mere individual perishes and confederations alone exist, or, to put it differently, that the natural law of relationship is working and shaping the 'bare' state of nature before Leviathan. There are many other indications of this interpenetration in the chapters expounding the laws of nature – in particular statements making it quite clear that covenants are being made in the state of nature – but there is no need to cite them all.[1] What requires to be stressed is that these confederations or alliances are based solely on covenants or pacts. They do not abolish each individual's right to levy war, they only restrain it, or to put it differently, they make the right to war into a distinct right exercisable in specific circumstances. Thus in the last resort the partners to the covenants or pacts remain the judges of whether the pacts have been infringed, or whether the situation has altered to such a degree as to make them void. They retain the right to treat those with whom they have compacted once again as enemies. It is not difficult to see in such arrangements the essence of treaties and pacts between sovereign states and also – and this was surely Hobbes' main concern – of bodies politic which fall short of sovereign states, that is to say composite bodies politic, in which the right to *re-bellare* is still retained by the partners to them. Here it should be stressed that it was the general opinion that England was a 'mixed' or composite body politic which, in Hobbes' opinion, had

---

1. The kind of non-state allegiances or alliances that Hobbes discusses in Part I, Chapter X of Leviathan deserve to be mentioned, however. Hobbes here writes of the union of powers typified by the state or commonwealth, on the one hand, and "the power of a faction or of divers factions leagued" on the other (p. 56). In the latter, he points out, the power of the association depends on *the will of each particular*. Hobbes proceeds to describe in some detail the features of such factions, indicating that they exist *naturally*, though within commonwealths, sovereigns regulate, and if necessary outlaw them (p. 59, 118, 154). C. B. Macpherson, in his well-known book *The Political Theory of Possessive Individualism* (Oxford, 1962) considers that the associative relationships which Hobbes describes in this chapter demonstrate that Hobbes was "more or less consciously" taking the model of a modern exchange economy as his model for "society as such" (p. 46). Stressing Hobbes' use of words such as "value" and "price" in the chapter in question, Macpherson concludes that in the relationships characteristic of factions: "A man's power is treated as a commodity, regular dealings in which establish market prices" (p. 37). "We have here the essential characteristics of the competitive market" (p. 38) *etc.* Macpherson's interpretation here seems gratuitous, revealing more about his own convictions than those of Hobbes. The relationship characteristic of factions or leagues, as described by Hobbes, is essentially that of unequal or equal alliances, and has at its heart the reciprocal exchange of protection and allegiance. These are not the relationships typical of modern exchange economies, but are similar to those of protective associations like the Mafia (within states) or hegemonial or 'client' relationships, like that between the United States and Britain at this moment (between states). For "protection" or "allegiance" to be marketable "commodities" they would have to be either tangible objects existing outside persons, or intangible qualities offered for a monetary equivalent, and ideally *both* tangible objects *and* objects with a value expressed in monetary terms. While Hobbes uses the terms "price" and "value" in explaining the nature of the exchange characteristic of factions and leagues, he does not equate protection or allegiance with "commodities" and with good reason. Power in the sense of the power to protect is *not* the same as the material objects of power (guns, tanks etc.) bought and sold for a monetary equivalent. It is at heart the judged capacity of a person to protect in a given situation. Allegiance is likewise not at heart something sold for money, but the alignment of a person's will that is made in return for protection.

led to the Civil War.[1] For him such 'mixed' or composite bodies politic had not really left the 'state of war' behind, they were only quasistates.

When did the confederations, alliances or quasi-states of the state of nature qualify as true commonwealths or states? Hobbes put forward not one, but two criteria: size and unity. A small number of men did not provide the requisite security,

> because in small numbers, small additions on the one side or the other, make the advantage of strength so great, as is sufficient to carry the victory; and therefore gives encouragement to an invasion. The multitude sufficient to confide in for our security, is not determined by any certain number, but by comparison with the enemy we fear; and is then sufficient, when the odds of the enemy is not of so visible and conspicuous moment, to determine the event of war, as to move him to attempt.[2]

Size, however, was not enough. There had to be a real unity of direction. In Hobbes' words:

> And be there never so great a multitude; yet if their actions be directed according to their particular judgments, and particular appetites, they can expect thereby no defence, nor protection, neither against a common enemy, nor against the injuries of one another. For being distracted in opinions concerning the best use and application of their strength, they do not help but hinder one another; and reduce their strength by mutual opposition to nothing: whereby they are easily not only subdued by a very few that agree together; but also when there is no common enemy, they make war upon each other, for their particular interests. For if we could suppose a great multitude of men to consent in the observation of justice, and other laws of nature, without a common power to keep them all in awe; we might as well suppose all mankind to do the same; and then there neither would be, nor need to be any civil government, or commonwealth at all; because there would be peace without subjection.
>
> Nor is it enough for the security, which men desire should last all the time of their life, that they be governed, and directed by one judgment, for a limited time; as in one battle, or one war. For though they obtain a victory by their unanimous endeavour against a foreign enemy; yet afterwards, when either they have no common enemy, or he that by one part is held for an enemy, is by another part held for a friend, they must needs by the difference of their interests dissolve, and fall again into a war amongst themselves.[3]

It is quite clear from this that there could be no question for Hobbes of all mankind coming together to form Leviathan, and that the latter was the heir of communities held together by awe of common external enemies. In fact Hobbes proceeds from this particular passage, by way of a polemic against Aristotle's doctrine of the 'naturalness' of

1. See especially *Leviathan, op. cit.* p. 119.
2. *Ibid.* p. 110.
3. *Ibid.* pp. 110–111.

political communities,[1] to his famous account of the covenant – the truly constitutive and transformatory covenant – which takes men finally and unequivocally out of the state of nature and into the state. The creation of the latter is identical with the abandonment by each individual of the *ius belli* itself; with the exercise of the latter solely by the sovereign against external enemies; and with the replacement of it internally by the *right of punishment* of the sovereign. The last inexpungeable residuum of the *ius belli* that is retained by the citizens is the famous right of individual self-defence against direct physical force. The converse of these changes is that right reason ceases to be merely immanent in the associated individuals and becomes an objective public reality governing them. The state, in the words used in *De Cive*, is the "empire of reason".[2]

Hobbes' account of the way the external factor influences the creation of Leviathan raises at least two interesting questions. It has been shown that the pressure that binds together the loose associations that precede Leviathan is fear of a common external enemy, and that Hobbes argues from this to the need for a more permanent source of fear. Is then Leviathan nothing other than the construction of a permanent common external enemy standing *over* the members of the association in place of the more mercurial common enemy that exists alongside them? Is the state really an 'external' relationship of two bodies, that are superimposed in the interest of peace on top of the other?

In the case of the commonwealth by acquisition this interpretation carries some weight. The commonwealth by acquisition is after all based on a mass of individuals fearful of one and the same man or group of men, and agreeing that henceforth he or they should rule them. The formation of the state is here little more than the conservation of an external relationship, the elevation of a powerful enemy into a ruler. But in the case of the sovereign by institution where there is a positive act of constitution and representation, an act in which the mass of the people identify themselves with the sovereign, the argument that Leviathan is nothing other than submission to a common enemy is far less tenable. Here the problem would seem to be rather different, namely that of the motive or interest that could push men to go beyond a loose association versus a common enemy to a genuinely unified community. Is it solely that peace is good and enmity or hostility is bad? In which case has not the connection between reason and interest,

1. A polemic which is repeated in almost identical language in all three of Hobbes' political treatises. It is directed not only against the doctrine of the naturalness of political communities but also against the idea that they can be held together *merely* by covenant. Hobbes thus wants a covenant rather than nature, and a transformatory covenant rather than an ordinary one.

2. *De Cive* (*Opera Latina*, Molesworth (ed.), Vol. 2, p. 265) '*in civitate, imperium rationis, pax, securitas, divitiae, ornatus, societas, elegantia, scientiae, benevolentia.*' As Schmitt observes (*Der Begriff des Politischen* (Berlin, 1963), p. 121), Hobbes, not Hegel, originated the formula of the state as the "empire of reason".

on which Hobbes is so insistent, been snapped? Or is the interest simply that of meeting even more effectively the threat of the common enemy? Is the Hobbesian state merely a mechanism for pursuing a more efficient foreign policy? In which case, if the presence of a common enemy is sufficient in itself to force men to create fully fledged states, why is it necessary to think of this force creating intermediary situations, such as alliances and confederations? Something additional would seem to be required for Hobbes' logic to be secure, and this additional pressure would seem to be man's need to master and transform nature so as to improve the quality of his life – a factor upon which, as has been noted already, Hobbes harps with particular insistence in *Leviathan*. Thus a loose confederation may be sufficient to provide security against a common enemy, but in order to secure men "in such sort, as that by their own industry and by the fruits of the earth, they may nourish themselves and live contentedly"[1] something more highly and rationally organized is needed. The Hobbesian state thus rises from the dual need for security *and* welfare.

The argument that has been sustained here may be expressed in a compressed, schematic form by the following diagram that shows the three-stage evolution of the Hobbesian state.

The formation of the Hobbesian state

Man prior to the state, or the state of nature or state of war in its broadest sense		The state or commonwealth
The original 'bare' state of nature	The state of nature modified by the laws of nature	
Universal war, = to exist is to struggle with enemies, = religious or ideological civil war anatomised, = absurdity or self-destruction. No distinction between internal and external relationships.	Relationships established between men by pacts and confederations, = enemies and allies distinguished, = *ius belli* a discrete right exercised jointly against common enemies and held in reserve against confederates. Internal and external relationships different, but not completely distinct.	The individual *ius belli* finally abandoned by a transformatory pact, = externally, *ius belli* henceforth exercised exclusively by sovereign, = internally, *ius belli* replaced by sovereign's right of punishment. Distinction between internal and external relationships complete.
Right reason silent.	Right reason immanent	Right reason objective.

It is the ambiguous nature of the middle stage of development which perhaps deserves most to be emphasized. *Vis-à-vis* the 'bare' state of

1. *Leviathan, op. cit.* p. 112.

nature it is a genuine world, that is to say, relationships exist in it. *Vis-à-vis* the state however it is still, like the 'bare' state of nature, a condition of war.

Having traced in Hobbes' writings the evolution of man into discrete unities called commonwealths or states it is possible to define more clearly the relations that exist between these unities. In a well-known passage in *Leviathan* Hobbes, after acknowledging that men might never have been in an original condition of war, "one against another", wrote that persons of sovereign authority were, "because of their independency", in "a posture of war" – adding that because sovereigns upheld the "industry of their subjects"[1] the misery that accompanied the liberty of particular men did not accompany their liberty. Here it might seem as if sovereigns between themselves are in a condition identical with that between men in the 'bare' system of nature, with the one significant reservation about "industry". Again, in *De Cive*, Hobbes wrote bluntly that "the state of commonwealths, considered in themselves, is natural, that is to say, hostile",[2] and he pictured them, with their spies, like spiders sitting in their webs.

Despite these passages, however, it cannot surely be maintained that Hobbes believed that states *vis-à-vis* one to another were engaged in the blind, self-destructive struggle that characterized the original state of nature. States, as we have seen, were for him part of the very process by which man escaped his original condition. By banding together in political unities war, the original primordial condition, was reduced both internally, and, by lessening the risks of attack, externally. Part of the very essence of states was that they were balancing mechanisms. Logically it was impossible for them to be in the same position as that which they transformed.

Moreover, in all three of his works on political theory Hobbes expressly identified the laws of nature with the laws of nations, or the law governing the interaction of states. Thus in the *Elements* he wrote: "For that which is the law of nature between man and man, before the constitution of the commonwealth, is the law of nations between sovereign and sovereign after".[3] The point here is that it is only when human associations have grown into states, only when they have developed beyond mere aggregates into *persons* with a will of their own, that they become the *subjects* of natural law. The emergence of states proper is thus identical with the subordination of man's external relations as such to natural law. This law dictates, it will be recalled, that peace should be sought where there is hope of obtaining it, and that where peace cannot be obtained, it is permissible to seek and use all helps and advantages of war.[4] It thus does not abolish the right of war that states possess, but it dictates to them the mutual transfer of rights, or the making of pacts, the mutual recognition of equality, the

1. *Ibid.* p. 83.
2. *De Cive, op. cit.* p. 169.
3. *Elements, op. cit.* p. 190.
4. *Leviathan, op. cit.* 85.

granting of protection to messengers of peace, the submission of controversies to arbitrators, a willingness not to strive to retain those things which are superfluous to oneself but necessary to others, *etc*. It is hence not surprising that Hobbes considered that "leagues between commonwealths, over whom there is no human power established, to keep them all in awe, are not only lawful, but also profitable for the time they last".[4] Spies too, in the blunt passage to which I have already referred, were not for him the signs of a blind, formless, self-annihilatory struggle, but basically insurance mechanisms, because "contracts are invalid in the state of nature, as oft as any just fear doth intervene".[5]

It will be clear from this that Hobbes saw states as existing in what I have called the state of nature *modified by the laws of nature*. Reason was immanently at work in the interstate arena; states were capable of establishing relationships between themselves. Regarded in this light Hobbes does not stand in the 'realist' tradition with Machiavelli – who was not a natural law philosopher like Hobbes – but rather in the classical tradition alongside Pufendorf. The only reason why Hobbes cannot be unequivocally or completely identified with the 'classical' tradition, a reason to which I have drawn attention throughout this study, is that he tended constantly to see in a distinct 'estate' or 'condition' of total war the 'cause' of such pacts, treaties and agreements as were subsequently made between men and states in accordance with natural law. There was always a formless chaos of enmity generating and producing such humanity as existed. The latter never lost a derivative quality. It is, in other words, the proximity of the abyss in Hobbes' theory, the constant intimation of a dark and horrific underworld of violence, that prevents us from removing him completely from the category of harsh realism in which he is so persistently placed. But then, who are we, in these troubled times, to deny that the abyss exists?

1. *Ibid.* p. 154.
2. *De Cive, op. cit.* p. 169.

[22]

Hobbes's Theory of International Relations

Noel Malcolm

I

A strange asymmetry prevails in modern writings on Hobbes's theory of the relations between states. For specialists in international relations theory, Hobbes is a canonical figure, a key representative of one of the major traditions. He stands alongside Machiavelli (and, in many accounts, Thucydides) as an archetypal proponent of 'Realism'. E. H. Carr portrayed Hobbes as the second great Realist, after Machiavelli; Martin Wight, whose system of classification influenced a generation of modern theorists, called Hobbes an 'extreme Realist'; Michael Walzer located Realism 'at its source and in its most compelling form' in the works of Thucydides and Hobbes. One influential modern text, Charles Beitz's *Political Theory and International Relations*, takes what it calls 'the Hobbesian conception of international relations' as the basis of 'skeptical' or 'Realist' theory, and devotes twenty-three pages of detailed argument to refuting it.[1] No student of international relations theory, it seems, can afford to disregard Hobbes's contribution to that field.

And yet, if one turns from the international relations specialists to the Hobbes specialists, one finds that such disregard is perfectly normal. Writers who have devoted years of their lives to the examination of Hobbes's political philosophy seem content to pass over his theory of international relations in a few paragraphs or sentences: it is rare to find any full-length study of Hobbes giving more than a couple of pages to this topic.[2] Consequently, the insights or advances achieved by

[1] E. H. Carr, *The Twenty Years' Crisis 1919–1939: An Introduction to the Study of International Relations* (London, 1939), pp. 81, 83; M. Wight, *International Theory: The Three Traditions*, ed. G. Wight and B. Porter (Leicester, 1991), p. 36; M. Walzer, *Just and Unjust Wars: A Moral Argument with Historical Illustrations* (Harmondsworth, 1980), p. 4; C. Beitz, *Political Theory and International Relations* (Princeton, NJ, 1979), pp. 14, 27–59.

[2] Howard Warrender devotes just over two pages to what he calls a 'speculation' about how Hobbes's theory might be applied to modern international relations (*The Political Philosophy of Hobbes: His Theory of Obligation* (Oxford, 1957), pp. 118–20); David Gauthier has a 6-page appendix to his book, in which he also speculates about the applicability of Hobbesian principles to international relations in the nuclear age (*The Logic of Leviathan: The Moral and Political Theory of Thomas Hobbes* (Oxford, 1969), pp. 207–12). Raymond Polin has a few pages on Hobbes's theory of the justifiability of wars of conquest (*Hobbes, Dieu et les hommes*

HOBBES'S THEORY OF INTERNATIONAL RELATIONS

Hobbes scholars in their work on other areas of his thought have (with a handful of exceptions) hardly begun to impinge on the study of this aspect of his political theory.[3] And the interpretation of Hobbes put forward by modern international relations theorists, meanwhile, has become fixed and ossified, functioning at best as an 'ideal type' and at worst as a caricature.

That fixed view of Hobbes goes roughly as follows. The basic Hobbesian assumption is that there are no objective principles of morality. In the state of nature, before the existence of the civil state, there are (as Hedley Bull puts it) 'no legal or moral rules'; moral terms, at this stage, are merely the expressions of personal preferences, with (in the words of Thomas Johnson) 'every person defining truth relative only to their own needs or desires'.[4] Morality is determined only by the sovereign, once the state is formed; according to Hans Morgenthau, it is 'Hobbes's extreme dictum' that 'the state creates morality as well as law and that there is neither morality nor law outside the state'.[5] Hence 'the realist view that no ethical standards are applicable to relations between states' (E. H. Carr): for Hobbes, 'there can be no effective moral principles in the state of nature' (Charles Beitz), and relationships between sovereign states can only be a matter of 'simple amorality' (Stanley Hoffmann).[6] This leads in turn to a celebration of power-politics; Hobbes shares Machiavelli's conception of politics as 'the practical art of obtaining and preserving state power as an end in itself'.[7] Where Hobbes goes beyond Machiavelli, however, is in his explicit account of the role played by the urge for power in human psychology: according to Morgenthau, Hobbes posits 'an urge toward expansion which knows no rational limits, feeds on its own successes and, if not stopped by a superior force, will go on to the confines of the political world'.[8] E. H. Carr reached a similar conclusion: 'Nationalism . . . develops almost automatically into imperialism. International politics amply confirms the

(Paris, 1981), pp. 197–200). Hobbes specialists have contributed to two volumes of essays dealing with his theory of war and peace (P. Caws, ed., *The Causes of Quarrel: Essays on Peace, War, and Thomas Hobbes* (Boston, 1989); T. Airaksinen and M. A. Bertman, eds., *Hobbes: War among Nations* (Aldershot, 1989)), but their findings are largely inconclusive or negative. The negativity of the latter volume is intensified by the fact that its contributors were invited to answer the question, 'Is it possible to justify world government on Hobbesian principles?' Not surprisingly, the unanimous answer was 'No'.

[3] Two notable exceptions are M. Forsyth, 'Thomas Hobbes and the External Relations of States,' *British Journal of International Studies*, 5 (1979), pp. 196–209, and L. M. Johnson, *Thucydides, Hobbes, and the Interpretation of Realism* (DeKalb, Ill., 1993), esp. pp. 85–98.

[4] H. Bull, *The Anarchical Society: A Study of Order in World Politics* (London, 1977), p. 47; T. J. Johnson, 'The Idea of Power Politics: The Sophistic Foundations of Realism,' in B. Frankel, ed., *Roots of Realism* (London, 1996), pp. 194–247; here p. 224.

[5] H. J. Morgenthau, *American Foreign Policy: A Critical Examination* (London, 1952), p. 34. Cf. Walzer, *Just and Unjust Wars*, p. 10: 'the sovereign . . . fixes the meaning of the moral vocabulary.'

[6] Carr, *Twenty Years' Crisis*, p. 194; Beitz, *Political Theory*, p. 28; S. Hoffmann, *The State of War: Essays on the Theory and Practice of International Politics* (London, 1965), p. 65.

[7] Wight, *International Theory*, p. 103.

[8] H. J. Morgenthau, *Politics among Nations: The Struggle for Power and Peace*, 2nd edn (New York, 1955), p. 52.

ASPECTS OF HOBBES

aphorism . . . of Hobbes that man "cannot assure the power and means to live well which he hath present, without the acquisition of more". Wars, begun for motives of security, quickly become wars of aggression and self-seeking.'[9] Hannah Arendt, similarly, described Hobbes as a forerunner of imperialism.[10]

The Hobbesian state, on this standard view, is little more than Hobbesian man writ large. Indeed, according to Hobbes's modern critics, the great weakness of his theory lies in its assumption of a complete equivalence between individual human beings in the state of nature and sovereign states in international relations. Hobbes's description of the predicament of individuals in the state of nature assumes that they are all equal, and that assumption is based on the fact that 'the weakest has strength enough to kill the strongest'.[11] As Hedley Bull emphasizes, states are not vulnerable in the way that individuals are, and there is no real equality between states great and small.[12] Charles Beitz agrees, and points out a further weakness in the analogy. Hobbes implies that there is a national right of self-preservation analogous to the individual one, but 'it is not clear what such a right involves or how it can be justified'; the 'death' of a state need not involve the death of its citizens, since individual citizens often survive changes in national boundaries.[13]

Beitz also questions Hobbes's assumption that, just as atomic individuals are the only agents in the state of nature, so sovereign states are the only actors in international relations: Hobbes's account of the interpersonal state of nature is plausible only because it denies the existence of any other actors, such as 'secondary associations, functional groups, economic institutions, or extended families', and it is equally arbitrary of Hobbes to exclude 'coalitions, alliances, and secondary associations' at the international level. Doubling back for a moment on his argument, Beitz admits that Hobbes does allow for the possibility of coalitions and alliances in the interpersonal state of nature: but he observes that, according to Hobbes, 'they would, if anything, increase the chances of violence among coalitions'. At the international level, accordingly, Hobbes believes that alliances 'have made no significant contribution to peace and cooperation'. Also at that level of argument, Hobbes 'denies the possibility' that there might be 'transnational associations of persons' whose 'common interests' could 'transcend national boundaries'. Instead, he sees a simplified world in which the units—sovereign states—are able to order their internal affairs in complete independence of one another: this rules out the possibility that 'the pursuit of self-interest by any one unit might require

[9] Carr, *Twenty Years' Crisis*, p. 144.

[10] H. Arendt, *The Origins of Totalitarianism*, 2nd edn (London, 1958), p. 143.

[11] T. Hobbes, *Leviathan*, p. 60.

[12] Bull, *Anarchical Society*, pp. 49–50; cf. also his article 'Hobbes and the International Anarchy,' *Social Research: An International Quarterly of the Social Sciences*, 48 (1981), pp. 717–38, esp. pp. 733–4.

[13] Beitz, *Political Theory*, pp. 40–2, 52. Robinson A. Grover similarly argues that Hobbes's theory breaks down on the implications of the individual/state analogy: 'Hobbes and the Concept of International Law,' in T. Airaksinen and M. A. Bertman, eds., *Hobbes: War among Nations* (Aldershot, 1989), pp. 79–90.

cooperation with other units in the system'. It follows that, in the absence of either any superior authority or any structural incentives or constraints built into the international system, there can be 'no reliable expectations of reciprocal compliance' in inter-state conduct. Nor are these conditions ever likely to change, given that, on Beitz's view of Hobbes, 'no state has an obligation to improve the system'.[14] The state of affairs Hobbes describes is thus little more than an arena for inherently unstable interactions of mutual fears and ambitions. In modern terminology, this is barely an 'international system', and certainly not an 'international society'. And even those writers whose interpretation of Hobbes goes a little further, allowing for the operation of a few procedural rules and principles at the international level (such as mutual recognition, and an acknowledgement of the desirability of honouring agreements), are willing to describe Hobbes's view only as 'a minimalist conception of international society'.[15]

II

How accurate is this portrayal of Hobbes's theory of international relations? It appears to be based, for the most part, on a handful of passages in one or two of his works (ignoring many comments on international affairs elsewhere in his writings); and even those few passages have been misunderstood. The most commonly cited texts are those in which Hobbes sets up his parallelism between the interpersonal state of nature and the international one. In chapter 13 of *Leviathan*, Hobbes first describes the interpersonal state of nature as a state of war, using the latter phrase in a carefully defined and analytical sense: 'So the nature of War, consisteth not in actuall fighting; but in the known disposition thereto, during all the time there is no assurance to the contrary.' Then he suggests that the most realistic (and perhaps the only universal) example of such a state of war is the one that prevails at the international level:

But though there had never been any time, wherein particular men were in a condition of warre one against another; yet in all times, Kings, and Persons of Soveraigne authority, because of their Independency, are in continuall jealousies, and in the state and posture of Gladiators; having their weapons pointing, and their eyes fixed on one another; that is, their Forts, Garrisons, and Guns upon the Frontiers of their Kingdomes; and continuall Spyes upon their neighbours; which is a posture of War.[16]

Within this international state of nature, Hobbes goes on to argue, the only rules of behaviour that can apply are those he describes as the Laws of Nature:

---

[14] Beitz, *Political Theory*, pp. 37–8, 42, 46, 48.

[15] A. Hurrell, 'Society and Anarchy in the 1990s', in B. A. Roberson, ed., *International Society and the Development of International Relations Theory* (London, 1998), pp. 17–42; here p. 25 (contrasting it with the 'pluralist' and the 'Grotian, or solidarist' conceptions).

[16] Hobbes, *Leviathan*, pp. 62, 63.

ASPECTS OF HOBBES

Concerning the Offices of one Soveraign to another, which are comprehended in that Law, which is commonly called the *Law of Nations*, I need not say any thing in this place; because the Law of Nations, and the Law of Nature, is the same thing. And every Soveraign hath the same Right, in procuring the safety of his People, that any particular man can have, in procuring his own safety. And the same Law, that dictateth to men that have no Civil Government, what they ought to do, and what to avoyd in regard of one another, dictateth the same to Common-wealths, that is, to the Consciences of Soveraign Princes, and Soveraign Assemblies; there being no Court of Naturall Justice, but in the Conscience onely; where not Man, but God raigneth; whose Lawes, (such of them as oblige all Mankind,) in respect of God, as he is the Author of Nature, are *Natural*. . .[17]

These passages, the ones most commonly referred to in support of the standard view of Hobbes's theory, indicate both the basis of the comparison he makes between persons and states, and the limitations of the parallelism between those two levels. The basis is jural, and negative: the rulers of sovereign states resemble individuals in the state of nature 'because of their Independency'—in other words, because they are not under any common authority. And the parallelism, such as it is, does not go all the way. Hobbes does not argue that there is one law of nature based on the preservation of individuals on the one hand, and an equivalent law of nature, based in parallel fashion on the preservation of states, on the other. Rather, he claims that there is a single Law of Nature, 'the same Law', applying to actions undertaken at both levels. This is a key point, the significance of which will be explored below.

The few words already cited on the subject of natural law—which obliges 'all Mankind'—are enough to suggest, also, that the standard view of Hobbes seriously misrepresents his theory when it portrays him as a proponent of moral subjectivism (in the state of nature) or arbitrarism (in the civil state, if morality is whatever the sovereign says it is) or sheer amorality (in international relations). Hobbes's account of morality and law is more complex, and more resourceful, than that. He deals differently with three different levels of evaluation: these might be called the psychological, the moral, and the jural. Psychological evaluative terms, such as 'pleasant' and 'unpleasant' (or, in primitive usage, 'good' and 'bad'), are indeed subjective: 'good', in this pre-moral sense, means 'object of desire', and is therefore always relative to the desirer. Moral terms, on the other hand, relate to a system of values that applies to all human beings: pride, humility, equity, iniquity, and other terms for virtuous or vicious actions and dispositions are of universal application, and can be neither subjective nor arbitrary. Jural terms, such as 'right', 'wrong', 'just', and 'unjust', have meanings that are both universal and analytic: 'unjust', for example, means 'in breach of covenant', the covenant being a transfer of rights.[18]

---

[17] Hobbes, *Leviathan*, pp. 185–6.   [18] Ibid., pp. 24, 71, 79.

HOBBES'S THEORY OF INTERNATIONAL RELATIONS

Hobbes carefully manages the transition in his argument from the psychological level to the moral, and again from the moral to the jural. While the contents of people's desires differ, he suggests, the basic conditions for the fulfilment of those desires are the same for all human beings: the most basic condition is being alive, the situation in which that condition can best be fulfilled is peace, and a set of universally valid rules can be drawn up for 'endeavouring' peace and ensuring its continuance. Those rules are the laws of nature, the rules of morality: they remain the same both inside and outside the civil state, being neither subjective nor determined by the sovereign's will. 'The Lawes of Nature are Immutable and Eternall; For Injustice, Ingratitude, Arrogance, Pride, Iniquity, Acception of persons, and the rest, can never be made lawfull. For it can never be that Warre shall preserve life, and Peace destroy it . . . And the Science of them [*sc* the laws of nature], is the true and onely Moral Philosophy.'[19]

The transition from the moral level to the jural comes about because one of the dictates of the laws of nature is that people should transfer rights to a sovereign: the laws of nature also demand that people keep the covenants through which such transfers are made. (Hence the inclusion of 'Injustice' in the list of violations of morality above.) A special kind of open-ended transfer of rights creates a common authority endowed with sovereignty over a group of people who can then be described as a single jural community. A sovereign power has the right to legislate for its subjects; its laws can never be described as 'unjust', because the sovereign has been authorized to make whatever laws it wants, but they can be called 'iniquitous' (in other words, immoral) if they go against the laws of nature. 'It is true that they that have Soveraigne power, may commit Iniquity; but not Injustice, or Injury in the proper signification.'[20] This shows that morality remains an objective standard, by which the laws or actions of the sovereign can still be judged: it is simply not true that the Hobbesian sovereign 'creates morality as well as law'.[21] Such a misinterpretation of Hobbes's argument arises only because he says that the civil law promulgated by the sovereign 'contains' the law of nature: the sovereign is the only authorized interpreter of the law of nature, and it is the framework of civil laws and punishments set up by the sovereign that makes obedience to the law of nature generally obligatory in act as well as in intention.[22] Although there may be some uncertainty here about the latitude of 'interpretation' allowed to the sovereign, Hobbes clearly does not mean that the law of nature is whatever the sovereign wills it to be. When he turns to the category of 'divine positive laws' (i.e. ones conveyed to mankind by revelation, not by reason), he remarks: 'in all things not contrary to the Morall Law, (that is to say, to the Law of Nature,) all Subjects

---

[19] Hobbes, *Leviathan*, p. 79. Hobbes recapitulates the transition from the psychological level to the moral on pp. 79–80.

[20] Ibid., p. 90.   [21] Morgenthau, *American Foreign Policy*, p. 34.

[22] Hobbes, *Leviathan*, p. 138.

ASPECTS OF HOBBES

are bound to obey that for divine Law, which is declared to be so, by the Lawes of the Common-wealth . . . for whatsoever is not against the Law of Nature, may be made Law in the name of them that have the Soveraign power.'[23]

In the state of nature, whether interpersonal or international, the laws of nature therefore exist as an objective standard, available to all human beings who reason correctly. The problematic thing about them is not their existence or their knowability, but their applicability. They always oblige in the internal court of conscience ('in foro interno'), that is, 'to a desire, and endeavour' to follow them; however, since they are rules for maximizing one's chances of self-preservation, a person cannot be obliged to act upon them in circumstances where doing so would endanger the actor's life.[24] According to the popular view of Hobbes, the laws of nature are permanently in abeyance in the state of nature, because under such conditions it can never be rational to act in accordance with them: as Beitz puts it, 'Hobbes holds that there can be no effective moral principles in the state of nature.'[25] But Hobbes does not say that. On the contrary, he presents specific examples of cases in which the laws of nature do oblige, in act as well as intention, in the state of nature. The laws of nature forbid self-regarding acts, such as drinking to excess, that weaken or destroy the ability to reason; they also forbid acts of cruelty to others—cruelty being the commission of gratuitous harm, which will only reduce the actor's chances of self-preservation by unnecessarily increasing the enmity of the victim. In a note added to the second edition of *De cive*, Hobbes insisted that these particular laws of nature must still oblige, in act, in the state of nature. 'However, there are some natural laws whose observance does not cease even in war. For I cannot see what drunkenness or cruelty (which is vengeance without regard to future good) contribute to any man's peace or preservation.'[26]

It is true that Hobbes writes, in *Leviathan*, that 'The Lawes of Nature oblige . . . in Effect then onely when there is Security'; but 'Security' here means not the general condition of the civil state, but the particular circumstances surrounding an individual action.[27] The key example he gives of a case where the actor does have sufficient security, even outside the civil state, concerns a pact or agreement between two individuals: if one of them shows his good will by performing his side of the bargain first, then it is rational (and a dictate of the laws of nature) that the other should also fulfil his promise. 'For the question is not of promises mutuall, where there is no security of performance on either side . . . But either where one of the parties has performed already; or where there is a Power to make him performe; there is the question whether it be against reason, that is, against the benefit of the other to performe, or not. And I say it is not against reason.'[28] Similarly, Hobbes argues that, once an international agreement is in force between two states, it remains binding unless the relevant security situation changes in a way

[23] Ibid., pp. 149–50.   [24] Ibid., p. 79.   [25] Beitz, *Political Theory*, p. 28.
[26] Hobbes, *De cive*, III.27(n).   [27] Hobbes, *Leviathan*, p. 79, marginal note.   [28] Ibid., p. 73.

HOBBES'S THEORY OF INTERNATIONAL RELATIONS

that may justify its breach: 'if a weaker Prince, make a disadvantageous peace with a stronger, for feare; he is bound to keep it; unlesse . . . there ariseth some new, and just cause of feare, to renew the war.'²⁹

If the laws of nature can apply, in act as well as intention, in the state of nature, then it cannot be true that Hobbes's international state of nature is *ipso facto* a state of 'simple amorality'. Their application may be patchy and sporadic, but they cannot be excluded on principle from the international arena. Indeed, there is something very implausible about the claim that Hobbes's laws of nature cannot apply at the international level, given that one of them relates directly to diplomatic practice: his fifteenth law is 'That all men that mediate Peace, be allowed safe Conduct.'³⁰ Naturally this rule would also apply to someone mediating between two individuals in the interpersonal state of nature; but, in the context of seventeenth-century debates on the structure and basis of international law, the point of the inclusion of this rule in Hobbes's list was evidently to settle the long-standing dispute about the status of 'ius feciale', the special area of international law relating to envoys and mediators, by showing how the basic principle of such law could be located within the natural law.³¹

The fundamental division, among seventeenth-century writers in this field, was between those who thought that some or all areas of international law were 'positive law', based on human will and human agreement, and those who thought that international law was directly derived from (or identical with) natural law. What in retrospect seems the mainstream tradition, represented by Vitoria, Suárez, and Grotius, adopted the former position, while Gentili, Hobbes, and Pufendorf adopted the latter. The debate was a real one, and even those contemporary writers who strongly rejected Hobbes's viewpoint treated it as a serious argument about how to classify international law, not as a rejection of international law as such.³² Modern writers do not do Hobbes justice when they describe him either as completely 'silent' on the subject of international law, or as expressing 'the ever recurrent feeling that international law is no more than an inane phrase'.³³ And the fact that, on this fundamental issue, Hobbes was clearly identified as a 'naturalist'

---

²⁹ Hobbes, *Leviathan*, p. 69. For a useful survey of Hobbes's arguments for the validity of laws of nature in the state of nature, see D. Boonin-Vail, *Thomas Hobbes and the Science of Moral Virtue* (Cambridge, 1994), pp. 72–81.

³⁰ Hobbes, *Leviathan*, p. 78.

³¹ See e.g. F. Suárez, *De legibus*, ed. L. Pereña *et al.*, 8 vols. (Madrid, 1971–81), IV, p. 133 (II.xix.7); H. Grotius, *De jure belli et* [sic] *pacis libri tres*, ed. & tr. W. Whewell, 3 vols. (Cambridge, n.d. [1854]), II, pp. 200–7 (II.xviii.1–2); R. Zouch ['Zouche'], *Juris et judicii fecialis, sive, juris inter gentes, et quaestionum de eodem explicatio* (Oxford, 1650), pp. 1–3, 16–22.

³² For a useful short summary of the debate see P. E. Corbett, *Law and Society in the Relations of States* (New York, 1951), pp. 21–6. For a contemporary reply to Hobbes, taking his argument seriously as a 'naturalist' theory of international law, see S. Rachelius, *De jure naturae et gentium dissertationes* (Kiel, 1676), pp. 306–10.

³³ S. Goyard-Fabre, 'Les Silences de Hobbes et de Rousseau devant le droit international,' *Archives de philosophie du droit*, 32 (1987), pp. 59–69; A. Nussbaum, *A Concise History of the Law of Nations*, rev. edn (New York, 1954), p. 146.

ASPECTS OF HOBBES

arguing against the 'positivists', should give pause to those modern commentators who, classifying Hobbes's theory of international relations as 'realist', automatically align him with the positivist tradition.[34]

If the Hobbesian international state of nature is not a realm of sheer amorality but, rather, one in which the actors must examine the circumstances of each decision to see whether or not the dictates of natural law are applicable, then perhaps Hobbes's international agents are not such 'Machiavellian' figures after all. In fact, readers will search Hobbes's works in vain for anything like a depiction of the Machiavellian prince. It is true that Hobbes states that 'Force, and Fraud, are in warre the two Cardinall vertues'; but this observation flows from his argument that the state of war is the worst possible state for mankind.[35] The Machiavellian analysis of political success, which picks out key qualities of alertness, decisiveness, and forcefulness in the ruler and identifies the operation of those qualities in all forms of political action—internal to the state and external, within the bounds of morality and outside them—finds no echo in Hobbes's account of the sovereign.[36] Nor does Hobbes conceive of anything similar to Machiavelli's republican citizenry exhibiting its own 'virtù'; citizen-soldiers have no special political significance in his theory, which happily allows people to hire substitutes to perform their ordinary military duties.[37] In the words of one modern study of Machiavelli's theory of international relations, 'civil life allows citizens to redirect the satisfaction of their passions from each other toward foreigners. Consequently, Machiavellian republics are warlike and rapacious, for they are constrained to make war abroad to maintain peace at home.'[38] The Hobbesian state performs no such role: it merely

---

[34] Martin Wight, for example, having described Hobbes as an 'extreme Realist', continues: 'There is also a general or conventional Realist position, which can be illustrated from the positivists of international law. It is the basic proposition of legal positivists that international law emanates from the free will of sovereign independent states' (*International Theory*, p. 36). On this classification, Grotius would be to a large extent a Realist and Hobbes an anti-Realist.

[35] Hobbes, *Leviathan*, p. 63. Hedley Bull, although generally a purveyor of the standard view of Hobbes, does comment perceptively on this point: 'There is no sense in Hobbes of the glorification of war, nor of relish for the game of power politics as an end in itself' ('Hobbes and the International Anarchy,' pp. 728–9).

[36] For a powerful elaboration of this contrast, see C. Navari, 'Hobbes and the "Hobbesian Tradition" in International Thought', *Millennium: Journal of International Studies*, 11 (1982), pp. 203–22, esp. pp. 207–12. Friedrich Meinecke, similarly, commented on the profound difference in approach between Machiavelli and Hobbes, characterizing the latter's argument as a mechanistic-utilitarian version of natural law theory: *Die Idee der Staatsräson in der neueren Geschichte*, 3rd edn (Munich, 1929), pp. 263–70. Cf., more generally, P. A. Clark, 'Hobbes and the Enlightenment Rejection of Military Virtue', Catholic University of America Ph. D. dissertation, 1996, pp. 6–9, 106–16, for the contrast between Hobbes's position and classical theories of military 'virtus'.

[37] Hobbes, *Leviathan*, p. 112. The best recent discussion of the significance of this point in Hobbes's overall theory is in B. Dix, *Lebensgefährdung und Verpflichtung bei Hobbes* (Würzburg, 1994), pp. 134–45.

[38] M. Fischer, 'Machiavelli's Theory of Foreign Politics', in B. Frankel, ed., *Roots of Realism* (London, 1996), pp. 248–79; here p. 255. Quentin Skinner similarly concludes that 'The pursuit of dominion abroad is thus held to be a precondition of liberty at home': *Machiavelli* (Oxford, 1981), p. 73. Cf. Machiavelli's formulation: 'Ambition uses against foreigners that violence which neither the law nor the king allows her to use internally; as a result, internal trouble almost always ceases' ('l'ambizion contra l'esterna gente / usa il furor ch' usarlo infra se stessa / né la legge né il re gliene consente; / onde il mal proprio quasi sempre cessa'): *Opere letterarie*, ed. A. Borlenghi (Naples, 1969), p. 154.

HOBBES'S THEORY OF INTERNATIONAL RELATIONS

provides a framework within which people can seek the satisfaction of their desires, whatever those desires may be.

For a Machiavellian, evaluating a state's engagement in wars of aggression or conquest is partly a matter of appreciating the qualities (of vigour, fortitude, and so on) which those actions exhibit. For Hobbes, such considerations are irrelevant; the only point to be considered is whether the action is justified on objective criteria—for example as a necessary act of pre-emptive self-defence. Some wars may be justifiable on that basis; but the general presumption in Hobbes's theory is strongly against wars of aggression or aggrandizement. 'For such commonwealths, or such monarchs, as affect war for itself, that is to say, out of ambition, or of vainglory, or that make account to revenge every little injury, or disgrace done by their neighbours, if they ruin not themselves, their fortune must be better than they have reason to expect.'[39] Noting that Athens and Rome sometimes grew rich from foreign conquests, he comments: 'But we should not take enrichment by these means into our calculations. For as a means of gain, military activity is like gambling ['sicut alea': like throwing dice]; in most cases it reduces a person's property; very few succeed.'[40] Both these passages suggest that Hobbes thinks there is an inbuilt balance of probabilities that weighs against success in such cases; the reason for this is not spelt out here, though one possible mechanism (involving the need for 'confederates', and the dangers of acquiring a reputation for aggression) is presented elsewhere in his writings, and will be discussed below. But even if he does not regard this adverse probability as a necessary truth, he certainly believes it to be a valid generalization from historical experience. In his *Dialogue . . . of the Common Laws*, he writes: 'The subjects of those Kings who affect the Glory, and imitate the Actions of *Alexander* the Great, have not always the most comfortable lives, nor do such Kings usually very long enjoy their Conquests.'[41] And in *Leviathan* he includes in his list of the 'diseases' of a commonwealth 'the insatiable appetite, or *Bulimia*, of enlarging Dominion; with the incurable *Wounds* thereby many times received from the enemy; And the *Wens*, of ununited conquests, which are many times a burthen, and with lesse danger lost, than kept'.[42]

The comments just quoted should also suffice to show that Hobbes was not an enthusiastic proto-imperialist. Having direct experience of colonial policy (he was an active participant in the Virginia Company), he had good reason to consider the question of how colonization could be justified. The most convenient justification available was the neo-Aristotelian argument, which portrayed the native people of the Americas as 'natural slaves'; but Hobbes responded to Aristotle's original

---

[39] Hobbes, *Elements of Law*, II.ix.9 (p. 184).

[40] Hobbes, *De cive*, XIII.14 (tr. p. 150).

[41] T. Hobbes, *A Dialogue between a Philosopher and a Student of the Common Laws of England*, ed. J. Cropsey (Chicago, 1971), p. 60.

[42] Hobbes, *Leviathan*, p. 174.

ASPECTS OF HOBBES

version of this argument with withering scorn.[43] In his view, colonization was a permissible way of employing people who could not otherwise be supported by the economy of the mother-country; however, the colonists were under a moral duty to treat the native people humanely, and to encourage them to use greater productivity to compensate for the loss of territory. As he explains in *Leviathan*, the colonists 'are to be transported into Countries not sufficiently inhabited: where neverthelesse, they are not to exterminate those they find there; but constrain them to inhabit closer together, and not range a great deal of ground, to snatch what they find; but to court each little Plot with art and labour.'[44]

For commentators such as Carr and Morgenthau, Hobbes's alleged endorsement of wars of expansion flows directly from his account of individual psychology, in which the urge to acquire more and more power is the driving force of human life. One of the most commonly cited Hobbesian texts is the statement: 'I put for a generall inclination of all mankind, a perpetuall and restlesse desire of Power after power, that ceaseth only in Death.'[45] It is true that restlessness, in the most literal sense, is a basic condition of human life in Hobbes's view: he sees all activity in the universe as describable in terms of matter in motion, and rejects any teleological metaphysic that would posit a 'summum bonum' of static fulfilment. But his argument is not based on any claim about a universal desire for power in the political sense. Nor does he operate with the concept of a 'will to power', if such a phrase implies that power itself is a primary good, something intrinsically motivating for the human will. On the contrary, power in Hobbes's argument has a purely instrumental character: he defines it as the 'present means, to obtain some future apparent Good'.[46] His concept of power, in other words, is analytic, not psychological; even if all human beings were extremely placid and benevolent, they would still require, at any given moment, the present means to obtain what they saw as a future good—for example, the means to give help to other less fortunate people. Of course, Hobbes's empirical judgement of human nature is much more negative than that: he believes that many people (and many rulers) are indeed willing to attack others in order to acquire the riches or fame that they value. 'Kings,

---

[43] Ibid., p. 77. On the argument (put forward by Sepúlveda and contested by Las Casas), see L. Hanke, *Aristotle and the American Indians: A Study in Race Prejudice in the Modern World* (London, 1959); on English knowledge of this debate see H. C. Porter, *The Inconstant Savage: England and the North American Indian 1500–1660* (London, 1979), pp. 171–80. For details of Hobbes's involvement in the Virginia Company see Ch. 3 above. Hannah Arendt's attempt to identify Hobbes as a forerunner of racism (*Origins of Totalitarianism*, p. 157) is particularly ill-conceived: no writer of the early modern period argued more robustly against the idea that any group of human beings was naturally superior to any other group.

[44] Hobbes, *Leviathan*, p. 181.   [45] Ibid., p. 47.

[46] Ibid., p. 41. For a classic modern account of the analytic or formal nature of Hobbes's concept of power, see F. S. McNeilly, *The Anatomy of Leviathan* (London, 1968), pp. 144–7, 152. For a valuable account of the implications for Hobbes's international theory, contrasting him with those 'realists' who assume a universal 'animus dominandi', see R. Malnes, *The Hobbesian Theory of International Conflict* (Oslo, 1993), pp. 122–9.

HOBBES'S THEORY OF INTERNATIONAL RELATIONS

whose power is greatest, turn their endeavours to the assuring it at home by Lawes, or abroad by Wars: and when that is done, there succeedeth a new desire; in some, of Fame from new Conquest; in others, of ease and sensuall pleasure.'[47] But because Hobbes's account is not based on universalizing or essentializing a psychological drive, it does not imply that such wars of aggression are inevitable—still less that they are desirable. Rather, he regards them as the products of mistaken judgement about what will really serve the long-term interests of those rulers, and he aims to supply a true science of politics from which the correct judgements may be derived.

It should also be observed that, in the passage just quoted, Hobbes referred to the desires and actions of 'Kings', not of states. Much modern commentary on his theory of international relations is fixated on the idea that Hobbes set up a complete parallelism between individuals and states, so that anything he said about the psychology and the predicament of the former in the state of nature must equally apply to the latter. Once this parallelism is assumed, critics find it easy to argue that it cannot properly work; such arguments are then taken to prove the inadequacy of Hobbes's theory in general. A closer analysis of his comparison between states and individuals will show, however, that the parallelism is only partial: it operates at the jural level, but not at the moral one.

As the famous engraved title page of *Leviathan* reminds us, Hobbes does indeed have a theory of the collective person-hood of the commonwealth. But his use of the concept of a 'person' here is not a matter of some generalized psychological comparison between individual and collective behaviour. A group of people can act in a coordinated way, with shared fears and desires—for example the members of a mutual defence association in the state of nature—without being, in Hobbes's special sense, a person.[48] What transforms a 'multitude' of cooperating individuals into a 'person' is something that happens at the jural level. A sovereign authority is created when people transfer their rights to it: by the fact of such a transfer, it becomes their 'sovereign representative', which means that it 'bears the person' of the people, and such a 'person' can exist only by virtue of being 'borne' in this way.[49] What matters is not just that one will is substituted for many wills: the key point is that it is an *authorized* will. It is endowed with a special kind of open-ended authority: sovereignty, the power to legislate, potentially on any aspect of life, for the whole community. For those who live within the realm of this authority, a new jural situation has been created. Inside the commonwealth, individuals now have claims on one another's behaviour: they enjoy legally protected rights to property and other forms of 'meum and tuum', which means that their fellow-citizens have

---

[47] Hobbes, *Leviathan*, p. 47.   [48] Hobbes, *De cive*, V.4 (tr. p. 70); *Leviathan*, pp. 85–6.

[49] Hobbes, *De cive*, V.8–9 (tr. p. 73); *Leviathan*, pp. 87–8. Although the concept of a 'person' is much more developed in the latter text, it is not absent from *De cive*, where Hobbes writes: 'A Union so made is called a *commonwealth*, or *civil society* and also a *civil person* [*persona civilis*]' (V.9; tr. p. 73).

ASPECTS OF HOBBES

a duty of non-interference in those matters, and they have a claim not be interfered with. People practise justice, Hobbes says, when they learn 'not to deprive their Neighbours, by violence, or fraud, of any thing which by the Sovereign Authority is theirs': justice consists in 'taking from no man what is his'.[50] They are now linked in a network of mutual rights and duties: these are direct correlatives, the former being, in Hohfeld's famous classification, 'claim'-rights. Citizen A has a claim on citizen B's behaviour, and citizen B has a duty *to* citizen A.[51]

That is the essential difference between conditions inside the commonwealth and conditions outside it. In the absence of a common authority, there is no overall pattern of jural duties or claims—no duties *to* or claims *on* others in general. (At best, there are particular bilateral jural duties generated by covenants or treaties; these are, however, limited in scope, and liable to be annulled by the advent of any new 'just cause' of fear.) There are moral duties, the duties of the laws of nature; but these are fundamentally self-regarding, in the sense that, according to Hobbes's derivation of morality, they are grounded in each individual's own need for self-preservation. A law of nature is defined as 'a Precept, or generall Rule, found out by Reason, by which a man is forbidden to do, that, which is destructive of his life, or taketh away the means of preserving the same; and to omit, that, by which he thinketh it may be best preserved'.[52] Such laws of nature are indeed universal, but only in so far as they are duplicated in every individual. They do not require a person to respect the good of any other human beings, still less of humanity in general, as a primary good; although they dictate that each individual should act in a way that will benefit others too, they do so only because such behaviour is instrumental to that individual's own good. One might call them 'duties *of behaviour towards*', but they could not be described as 'duties *to*'. (In the same way, one might say that the natural-law duty to refrain from eating poisonous berries is a duty to behave in a certain way towards the berries, but not a duty to them.) Thanks to the peculiar nature of Hobbes's derivation of morality, there is thus an important formal difference between moral and jural duties in his theory. Of course, his argument implies that the jural duties of people as citizens are backed up by their moral duties as human beings: the transition from the moral level to the jural in his argument comes about precisely because people are required by the laws of nature to make the necessary transfer of rights, and thereafter to honour that commitment. In normal circumstances, people always have a moral duty to perform a jural duty. But the conceptual distinction between the two types remains—indeed, the whole Hobbesian theory of the state of nature would be unintelligible without it.

50 Hobbes, *Leviathan*, p. 179 (adapting the standard Ciceronian and scholastic definition of justice, 'suum cuique tribuere').

51 See W. N. Hohfeld, *Fundamental Legal Conceptions*, ed. W. W. Cook (New Haven, Conn., 1946), pp. 36–9.

52 Hobbes, *Leviathan*, p. 64.

HOBBES'S THEORY OF INTERNATIONAL RELATIONS

Outside the commonwealth, the general absence of duties (at the jural level) means that there is a universal right in the other basic sense of that term—not a claim, but a jural freedom. (In Hohfeldian analysis, just as a claim-right correlates with a duty on the part of others, so this sort of freedom-right correlates with a 'no-claim' on the part of others; it might therefore be called a 'no-duty'.[53]) In the state of nature, therefore, we have on the one hand a universal right or freedom at the jural level, and on the other hand a specific set of moral duties. The picture is complicated, however, by the fact that Hobbes's system of morality also generates its own variety of rights. While the laws of nature prescribe the optimum long-term means to self-preservation, it may be necessary in the short term to break those laws in order to preserve one's life. And when breaking the laws of nature is necessary on such grounds, a person has the right to do so: this is the 'Right of Nature', a moral right based on the same justificatory principle (self-preservation) as the laws themselves. Hobbes combines both the right and the laws in a single 'Rule of Nature': '*That every man, ought to endeavour Peace, as farre as he has hope of obtaining it; and when he cannot obtain it, that he may seek, and use, all helps, and advantages of Warre.* The first branch of which Rule, containeth the first, and Fundamentall Law of Nature; which is, *to seek Peace, and follow it.* The Second, the summe of the Right of Nature; which is, *By all means we can, to defend our selves.*'[54]

Much of the obscurity in Hobbes's account of the state of nature arises because he apparently thought that this moral right of nature could be used to explain the universal jural freedom-right. Since almost any conceivable action could be justified as an exercise of the right of nature in some conceivable set of circumstances, he summarized the right itself as 'this naturall Right of every man to every thing'.[55] Such a description ignored the fact that in any particular set of circumstances the individual would not be entitled under the right of nature to do anything and everything: he would be entitled to do only the specific thing that was necessary to preserve his life. Another of Hobbes's formulations went even further beyond what his account of the right of nature would allow: describing the situation of a man in the state of nature, he referred to 'this Right, of doing any thing he liketh'.[56] Evidently, Hobbes was running together two conceptually distinct things: the (moral) right of nature, and the (jural) universal freedom-right. The distinction between the two comes out most clearly if one considers the case of an unjustified breach of the laws of nature in the state of nature—for example, a gratuitous act of cruelty. The reason for saying that the individual does not have the right to inflict cruel harm on other people is drawn from the internal system of natural rights and duties arising from that individual's need for self-preservation.

---

[53] Hohfeld, *Fundamental Legal Conceptions,* p. 36. Hohfeld calls it a 'privilege', because he is concerned with the functioning of such rights within a legal system; but the term 'freedom' seems more appropriate for the universal right in the Hobbesian state of nature.

[54] Hobbes, *Leviathan,* p. 64.   [55] Ibid.   [56] Ibid., p. 65.

ASPECTS OF HOBBES

It is not drawn from any external set of duties *to* other people in general; such duties come into being only when people are united in a jural entity under the authority of a sovereign.[57]

Having made these distinctions, we are now in a better position to see what happens when people come together to form a commonwealth. When they authorize a sovereign to 'bear their person' and to legislate for them, their jural situation undergoes a radical change *vis-à-vis* their fellow-citizens; but their basic lack of jural duties to anyone outside the commonwealth remains the same. The only difference, where external relations are concerned, is that their relationship with outsiders is now managed for them by the sovereign: the sovereign decides when to go to war and when to make peace. The various commonwealths that exist in the world are in the same jural vacuum as individuals in the state of nature. At the jural level, therefore, the parallel between states and individuals holds precisely: each commonwealth is indeed like a giant person, acting with a universal freedom-right *vis-à-vis* other such persons in the state of nature.

However, because the jural universal right is not identical with the moral 'right of nature' derived from the principle of self-preservation, it is simply not necessary to continue the parallelism all the way, in an attempt to ground the international jural situation on some putative principle of self-preservation for states *qua* states. That would be to attribute to Hobbes two justificatory systems (one for individuals, the other for states) so perfectly parallel that they would never actually meet. Critics would be entitled to object to such a structure of argument, pointing out that, if the demands of individual-preservation and state-preservation came into conflict, it would offer no way of adjudicating between them. But in fact Hobbes operates with only one concept of the law of nature, and it is based, as the definition quoted above makes clear, on each individual's need to preserve his or her own life.

How and why does the law of nature guide the actions of the sovereign? Where the citizens or subjects are concerned, the argument is very straightforward: each is obliged by the laws of nature, for the sake of self-preservation, to enter into a commonwealth and to do whatever is necessary to maintain its existence. But the case of the sovereign (at least, in a 'commonwealth by institution') is different. Hobbes insists that the sovereign is not a party to a contract with the people: rather, he—or she, or it—is a third-party beneficiary of their mutual covenanting. Strictly speaking, an instituted monarch in Hobbes's theory remains in a state of nature *vis-à-vis* his own subjects: he is jurally entitled to treat them just as he would treat his enemies. And yet, Hobbes's entire political theory depends on the presumption that living under a sovereign is better than remaining in the state of nature.

Accordingly, Hobbes takes special care to point out that it is in the sovereign's own interests to protect and promote the interests of his subjects. The connection

[57] I develop here an analysis first presented in my 'Hobbes and Spinoza', Ch. 2 above, esp. pp. 32–4.

HOBBES'S THEORY OF INTERNATIONAL RELATIONS

is made very directly: 'The riches, power, and honour of a Monarch arise onely from the riches, strength and reputation of his Subjects. For no King can be rich, nor glorious, nor secure; whose Subjects are either poore, or contemptible, or too weak through want, or dissention, to maintain a war against their enemies.'[58] The use of the word 'secure' in that second sentence indicates the way in which this argument is directly linked to the laws of nature, as they apply to the sovereign. But there is also a more indirect connection. In *De cive*, discussing the duties of instituted sovereigns, Hobbes writes: 'Those who have taken it upon themselves to exercise power in this kind of commonwealth, would be acting contrary to the law of nature (because in contravention of the trust of those who put the sovereign power into their hands) if they did not do whatever can be done by laws to ensure that the citizens are abundantly provided with all the good things necessary not just for life but for the enjoyment of life.'[59] This reference to a 'trust' ['fiducia'] is at first sight somewhat puzzling; it cannot imply a contractual relationship, in other words a conditional sovereignty of the Lockean variety, as that is strictly excluded by Hobbes's overall theory. It must refer to something more like a free gift, made in expectation of an equally voluntary return of benefit. This too is covered by the laws of nature; indeed, Hobbes regards the relevant principle as one of the most important laws, placing it third on his list of them in *De cive*: '*If someone has conferred a benefit on you, relying on your good faith* ['fiducia tua'], *do not let him lose on it.*' (He follows up the statement of this law with the comment: 'Without this precept . . . there would be no mutual assistance nor any initiative to win gratitude. As a result, the state of war will inevitably persist.'[60]) This supplies a more long-term reason for thinking that it is in the interests of the sovereign to requite the trust of his subjects by promoting their well-being.

There is thus a two-fold basis in natural law for Hobbes's claim, repeated insistently in every one of his political treatises, that the sovereign has a duty to look after the interests of his people. As he puts it in *Leviathan*,

The Office of the Soveraign, (be it a Monarch, or an Assembly,) consisteth in the end, for which he was trusted with the Soveraign Power, namely the procuration of *the safety of the people*; to which he is obliged by the Law of Nature, and to render an account thereof to God, the Author of that Law, and to none but him. But by Safety here, is not meant a bare Preservation, but also all other Contentments of life, which every man by lawfull Industry, without danger, or hurt to the Common-wealth, shall acquire to himselfe.[61]

It is important to note that the sovereign's concerns thus go beyond the 'bare Preservation' of his people. Hobbes takes care to emphasize that the Latin phrase

---

[58] Hobbes, *Leviathan*, p. 96.   [59] Hobbes, *De cive*, XIII.4 (tr. p. 144).

[60] Ibid., III.8 (tr. p. 47). In *Leviathan* this is the fourth law of nature (p. 75).

[61] Hobbes, *Leviathan*, p. 175. For similar statements about the principle of 'salus populi' see *Elements of Law*, II.ix.1 (p. 179); *De cive*, XIII.2 (tr. p. 143).

ASPECTS OF HOBBES

'salus populi' implies more than just safety or security: in *Behemoth* he translates it as 'the safety and well-being' of the people.[62] The most general term he uses in this context is 'benefit': discussing the liberty of sovereigns in *Leviathan*, he observes that 'in States, and Common-wealths not dependent on one another, every Common-wealth, (not every man) has an absolute Libertie, to doe what it shall judge (that is to say, what that Man, or Assemblie that representeth it, shall judge) most conducing to their benefit.'[63] Natural law, as it relates to individuals, does not make any direct use of the criterion of 'benefit', because concepts of benefit will vary from person to person. Instead, it starts from one absolute requirement which all humans must share (self-preservation), and draws from it one general condition to be aimed at: the condition of peace—peace being the bare minimum framework within which people are preserved. If Hobbes were positing a state-based natural law, parallel to the individual-based one, he would be obliged to construct an exactly equivalent argument: the absolute requirement would be the preservation of the state, and the aim would be international peace. (This would require states to join together in a super-state, the only guarantor of genuine peace between them, just as individuals unite in a state.) However, because Hobbes's argument here consists not of making some new, parallel, state-based natural law, but of making an *application* of the existing natural law to the particular situation of sovereigns *vis-à-vis* their subjects, he is not obliged to argue for a super-state, and he is enabled to invoke the much more wide-ranging criterion of 'benefit'. In Hobbes's theory 'salus populi', the safety and benefit of the people, is the aim of the sovereign's foreign (as well as domestic) policy. Unlike the caricature version of the Hobbesian position, such a theory can give a prominent place to the pursuit of prosperity through international trade, and of other advantages that may flow from international cooperation. And it might even allow, in special circumstances, the extinction of the state itself—for example, by voting to become part of another state, on terms that would benefit both the people and the sovereign.

Naturally, while promoting the 'Contentments of life' of the people is a genuine policy aim, it must take second place to the requirement of their preservation. The primary role of the sovereign is 'the preserving of Peace and Security, by prevention of Discord at home, and Hostility from abroad'.[64] In Hobbes's discussions of the military role of the state, the emphasis is usually on the protection of the people from external attack. His general presumption, as we have already seen, is that wars of conquest do not conduce to the benefit of the people. However, offensive

---

[62] Hobbes, *Behemoth: Or, the Long Parliament*, ed. F. Tönnies (London, 1889), p. 68.

[63] Hobbes, *Leviathan*, p. 110. 'Their' benefit here should clearly be 'its'. The manuscript of *Leviathan* (British Library, MS Egerton 1910) shows that such mis-matching of single and plural forms in general or impersonal constructions was a common fault in Hobbes's writing, corrected in many cases—but not this one—by the printers.

[64] Hobbes, *Leviathan*, pp. 90–1.

HOBBES'S THEORY OF INTERNATIONAL RELATIONS

warfare may be justified, according to his theory, in some circumstances. Hobbes's fullest discussion of this issue is in the *Dialogue of the Common Laws*, where the 'Lawyer' asks the 'Philosopher' whether it is lawful for a sovereign to make war on another and 'dispossess him of his Lands'. The Philosopher (who speaks for Hobbes) replies: 'The intention may be Lawful in divers Cases by the right of nature; one of those Cases is, when he is constrained to it by the necessity of subsisting.' If the sovereign's subjects cannot otherwise preserve their lives, they are entitled, by the moral right of nature, to invade the more fertile lands of their neighbours: the example given here is that of the Children of Israel seizing the territory of the Caananites. One type of justification for offensive warfare, therefore, is 'Necessity'. The other, according to the Philosopher here, is 'Security': in cases where a state has 'just cause' to fear its neighbour, it is entitled to engage in a pre-emptive attack.[65]

According to the standard view of Hobbes, there is always 'just cause' for every state to fear every other one, and the international state of nature is therefore a situation of permanent anarchic violence. That is not, however, the implication of Hobbes's argument. Indeed, his specifying of cases where the state has just cause to fear its neighbour sets up an implicit contrast with other cases where it does not. A just fear is an assessment of danger that must, presumably, be based on some empirical judgement about matters of fact. For example, a large and powerful state would not have just cause to fear that a small, weak, and solitary neighbouring state was about to attack it. Hobbes clearly thought that it was important for states to form well grounded empirical judgements about such matters: in *De cive* he included a long section on the state's need for intelligence operations, to gather information about 'the plans and movements of all those who have the capacity to do it harm'.[66] And, of course, even when a state does have just cause to fear the intentions of a neighbour, it must still weigh the possible advantage of a preemptive strike against the possible dis-benefit to its citizens of involvement in war. Since the ultimate aim is inherently defensive, the optimum strategy is not belligerence but deterrence. And there are two ways in which a state can raise its level of deterrence: by building up its own defensive military strength, and by entering into alliances with other states.

Alliances or 'confederacies' do in fact play a major role in Hobbes's account of the state of nature. As we have seen, he allows that valid pacts or contracts are possible in the state of nature: where one side has performed first, the other does not have just cause to fear it and therefore is obliged to keep its own side of the bargain. Hobbes sets out his reasoning in *Leviathan*, arguing that a man in the state of nature will damage his long-term prospects of self-preservation if he acquires a reputation as a wilful breaker of covenants:

---

[65] Hobbes, *Dialogue of the Common Laws*, p. 159.   [66] Hobbes, *De cive*, XIII.7 (tr. p. 145).

ASPECTS OF HOBBES

Secondly, that in a condition of Warre, wherein every man to every man, for want of a common Power to keep them all in awe, is an Enemy, there is no man can hope by his own strength, or wit, to defend himself from destruction, without the help of Confederates; where every one expects the same defence by the Confederation, that any one else does: and therefore he which declares he thinks it reason to deceive those that help him, can in reason expect no other means of safety, than what can be had from his own single Power. He therefore that breaketh his Covenant, and consequently declareth that he thinks he may with reason do so, cannot be received into any Society, that unite themselves for Peace and Defence, but by error of them that receive him . . .[67]

Most aspects of this argument are also directly applicable to the case of a commonwealth in the international state of nature: it too can join an alliance, 'confederation', or 'society' for mutual defence, and its natural-law obligation to keep its agreement with its confederates can be explained in the same way. (The same type of argument, about the long-term consequences of acquiring a reputation for untrustworthiness, could also be used to explain why states are bound to suffer in the long term if they get into the habit of waging aggressive war, or of making preemptive attacks with insufficient 'just cause'.) Admittedly, what Hobbes claims in the first sentence here about the utter necessity of 'Confederates' is not so compelling in the case of commonwealths: states, unlike human beings, do not go to sleep at night, and an exceptionally powerful state may conceivably be able to defend itself, on its own, against all those that are likely to attack it. Yet most other states will have a clear incentive to form defensive alliances, if only because they might otherwise be vulnerable to offensive ones. (A common criticism of Hobbes's theory of international relations is that it assumes 'that the units that make up the state of nature must be of relatively equal power in the sense that the weakest can defeat the strongest'—an assumption that is manifestly wrong in simple terms.[68] But when Hobbes makes his claim about the parity of individuals in the state of nature, he makes explicit reference to alliances: 'the weakest has strength enough to kill the strongest, either by secret machination, or by confederacy with others.'[69] This makes the theory much less implausible at the international level: it will be generally true that a weak country can defeat a powerful one, if it joins in an alliance with other sufficiently powerful countries.)

One of the strangest modern misunderstandings of Hobbes is the claim made by Charles Beitz when he refers to 'Hobbes's hypothesis that forming alliances increases the chances of war'. (A few sentences later, he attributes to Hobbes the similar and equally strange belief 'that they [*sc.* alliances] have made no significant contribution to peace and cooperation'.[70]) The passage in *Leviathan* to which

---

[67] Hobbes, *Leviathan*, p. 73.   [68] Beitz, *Political Theory*, pp. 40–1.
[69] Hobbes, *Leviathan*, p. 60.   [70] Beitz, *Political Theory*, p. 37.

HOBBES'S THEORY OF INTERNATIONAL RELATIONS

Beitz alludes says no such thing. In it, Hobbes observes first of all that disunited individuals in the state of nature 'make warre upon each other, for their particular interests', and therefore cannot defend themselves against a common enemy; then he says that if they unite for a limited time in an alliance they may indeed 'obtain a Victory by their unanimous endeavour'; and finally, he points out that, after such a temporary alliance has broken up, the individuals may find themselves back in a state of mutual hostility: 'afterwards . . . they must needs by the difference of their interests dissolve, and fall again into a Warre amongst themselves'.[71] The one positive feature of this account is the period of cooperation and successful mutual defence while the alliance lasts; the return to war here is a consequence of the *ceasing* of the alliance, and to present it as a consequence of the alliance's existence is to commit the fallacy of *post hoc, ergo propter hoc.*

Generally speaking, Hobbes does not argue that alliances as such must either increase or decrease the quantity of fighting (though they must, by definition, increase the quantity of cooperation); he notes that alliances may be either offensive or defensive. The 'Conquests of the ancient Germans', for example, were achieved by a 'Confederacy' of 'many absolute Lords joyning together to conquer other Nations'.[72] Such an alliance may indeed increase the chances of war. Equally, however, a defensive alliance may deter aggression. The primary function of 'mutual aid' associations in the state of nature is deterrence: 'the mutual aid of two or three men is of very little security; for the odds on the other side, of a man or two, giveth sufficient encouragement to an assault. And therefore before men have sufficient security in the help of one another, their number must be so great, that the odds of a few which the enemy may have, be no certain and sensible advantage.'[73]

While Hobbes's account of international relations gives special prominence to security alliances or 'Leagues between Common-wealths' (which, he says, are 'not onely lawfull, but also profitable for the time they last'), those are not the only forms of international agreement or cooperation to be considered.[74] One unusual international (or transnational) agreement which caught his eye was that practised by the ancient Amazons, who 'Contracted with the Men of the neighbouring Countries, to whom they had recourse for issue, that the issue Male should be sent back, but the Female remain with themselves'.[75] Other international agreements are more usual, underpinning as they do the ordinary transnational activities of human beings. Thus, 'he that is sent on a message, or hath leave to travell, is still Subject [*sc.* to his own sovereign]; but it is, by Contract between Soveraigns . . . For whosoever entreth into anothers dominion, is Subject to all the Laws thereof; unlesse he have a privilege by the amity of the Soveraigns, or by speciall licence.'[76]

---

[71] Hobbes, *Leviathan*, p. 86. [72] Ibid., p. 184.

[73] Hobbes, *Elements of Law*, I.xix.3 (p. 101); cf. *De cive* V.3 (tr. p. 70).

[74] Hobbes, *Leviathan*, p. 122. [75] Ibid., p. 103; cf. *Elements of Law*, II.iv.5 (p. 133).

[76] Hobbes, *Leviathan*, p. 114.

ASPECTS OF HOBBES

International trade, in Hobbes's view, was essential for the well-being of a commonwealth, because 'there is no Territory under the Dominion of one Commonwealth, (except it be of very vast extent,) that produceth all things needful for the maintenance, and motion of the whole Body'.[77] In the *Elements of Law* he included in his list of the laws of nature the rule '*That men allow commerce and traffic indifferently to one another*'.[78] He recognized that trade required a system of commercial law in which subjects of different states could litigate and seek redress: in his *Dialogue of the Common Laws* he noted that the Court of Admiralty fulfilled such a function, and observed that this court operated on Roman law principles because 'the causes that arise at Sea are very often between us, and People of other Nations, such as are Governed for the most part by the self same Laws Imperial'.[75] And at sovereign-to-sovereign level, Hobbes also recognized the existence of commonly agreed procedures for such matters as the payment of reparations.[80]

The general picture that emerges here is of cooperation and interaction between states, and between the subjects of states, taking place at many levels. Hobbes's comments on trade, for example, are sufficient to refute the claim made by Charles Beitz that he ignores the interdependence of states in non-security matters and has no idea of the economic advantages of cooperation between them.[81] Overall, Hobbes's account contains many of the ingredients of what modern theorists describe as an 'international society': shared practices, institutions, and values. The widely held belief that no society of any kind can exist in a Hobbesian state of nature is drawn from a few places in his writings (such as the famous 'nasty, brutish, and short' passage in chapter 13 of *Leviathan*) where he sets out the ultimate or worst-case implications of a state of war; however, many other passages go to show that social formations of various kinds can exist in his state of nature, and the extreme case he describes should probably be understood by analogy with an asymptotic limit, a theoretical absolute which may be approached but never reached.[32]

[77] Ibid., p. 127. [78] Hobbes, *Elements of Law*, I.xvi.12 (p. 87).

[79] *Dialogue of the Common Laws*, pp. 89–90. On the nature of this court, which dealt with actions for freight and maritime contracts made on foreign soil, see D. E. C. Yale, 'A View of the Admiralty Jurisdiction: Sir Matthew Hale and the Civilians', in D. Jenkins, ed., *Legal History Studies 1972: Papers Presented to the Legal History Conference, Aberystwyth, 18–21 July 1972* (Cardiff, 1972), pp. 87–109.

[80] Hobbes, *Dialogue of the Common Laws*, p. 159: 'Injuries receiv'd justifie a War defensive; but for reparable injuries, if Reparation be tendred, all invasion upon that Title is Iniquity.'

[81] Beitz, *Political Theory*, p. 42. For a proper appreciation of the positive role of international trade in Hobbes's theory, see D. Boucher, *Political Theories of International Relations: From Thucydides to the Present* (Oxford, 1998), pp. 160–1.

[82] See e.g. G. Schochet, *Patriarchalism in Political Thought* (Oxford, 1975), pp. 225–43; C. D. Tarlton, 'The Creation and Maintenance of Government: A Neglected Dimension of Hobbes's Leviathan,' *Political Studies*, 26 (1978), pp. 307–27; R. Ashcraft, 'Political Theory and Practical Action: A Reconsideration of Hobbes's State of Nature', *Hobbes Studies*, 1 (1988), pp. 63–88. For the most penetrating and wide-ranging recent study of social formations and interactions in Hobbes's state of nature, see K. Hoekstra, 'The Savage, the Citizen, and the Foole: The Compulsion for Civil Society in the Philosophy of Thomas Hobbes', Oxford University D.Phil. dissertation (1998), pp. 8–97; this also includes a valuable discussion of the international state of nature (pp. 70–6).

HOBBES'S THEORY OF INTERNATIONAL RELATIONS

It has often been noted that one of Hobbes's basic causes of conflict in the state of nature, the desire for 'glory', presupposes some sort of social context of shared values. Such a context exists also at the international level: commenting in *Behemoth* on the ill-will of the Scots towards the English in the late 1630s, Hobbes puts forward as a possible explanation 'that from the emulation of glory between the nations, they might be willing to see this nation afflicted by civil war'.[83] Later in the same work he presents a carefully nuanced account of the factors behind the outbreak of the Anglo-Dutch war of 1652. While the main Dutch motive was 'the greediness to engross all traffic', the ostensible *casus belli* was a dispute over the English claim to 'dominion of the narrow seas': 'the Dutch knowing the dominion of the narrow seas to be a gallant title, and envied by all the nations that reach the shore, and consequently that they were likely to oppose it, did wisely enough in making this point the state of the quarrel.'[84] Shared values, relating to a code of honour, can thus play a significant role (though not, in this case, a primary one) in international relations.

The basis of shared values is a common culture. Hobbes had a particular reason for paying serious attention to the common cultural heritage of Europe, or 'Christendom'. He was convinced that the amalgam of Graeco-Roman philosophy and biblical doctrine, developed over the centuries by the Roman Church and taught in all European universities, was the biggest single threat to the stability of states: it undermined them at the most vulnerable point of all, in the minds of the subjects. As 'the Actions of men proceed from their Opinions', the essential rights of sovereignty could be maintained only if the people held correct beliefs about them; and such beliefs had been systematically corrupted and subverted by Papal teachings.[85] In Hobbes's view, the Roman Church was an international conspiracy, a ' *Confederacy of Deceivers . . . to obtain dominion over men in this present world*'; he put it in the category of 'Corporations of men, that by Authority from any forraign Person, unite themselves in anothers Dominion, for the easier propagation of Doctrines, and for making a party, against the Power of the Common-wealth'.[86] It was responsible for fomenting rebellions within states, and wars between them: the false doctrine propagated by it was the prime cause of the fact 'that in Christendome there has been, almost from the time of the Apostles, such justling of one another out of their places, both by forraign, and Civill war'.[87] While it was true that the Pope also happened to be a sovereign, ruling the inhabitants of an area

---

[83] Hobbes, *Behemoth*, p. 30. This passage must cast some doubt both on Jean Hampton's claim that 'Hobbes does not consider the way in which a nation's longing for glory can provoke war with other nations' ('Hobbesian Reflections on Glory as a Cause of Conflict,' in P. Caws, ed., *The Causes of Quarrel: Essays on Peace, War, and Thomas Hobbes* (Boston, Mass., 1989), pp. 78–96; here p. 95), and on William Sacksteder's observation that 'nation' is 'a non-Hobbesian term' ('Mutually Acceptable Glory: Rating Among Nations in Hobbes', in Caws, *Causes of Quarrel*, pp. 97–113; here p. 106). Cf. also the passage quoted above at n. 72.

[84] Hobbes, *Behemoth*, pp. 174, 176.   [85] Hobbes, *Leviathan*, pp. 91 (quotation), 175–6.

[86] Ibid., pp. 333, 121.   [87] Ibid., p. 334.

ASPECTS OF HOBBES

of Italy, the way in which the Church functions in Hobbes's account is obviously very different from the normal operations of one state *vis-à-vis* another: even if the Papacy had lost its own territorial sovereignty, it could have continued to operate as a significant factor in international affairs through its far-flung confederacy of priests. Once again, it is necessary to reject Charles Beitz's assertion that, in Hobbes's theory, the only actors in international relations are sovereign states. And it is also necessary to point out that the Catholic Church, as described by Hobbes, is very much a 'transnational association of persons' with its own collective interest —the sort of association of which, according to Beitz, Hobbes simply 'denies the possibility'.[88]

As several recent studies of Hobbes have emphasized, a programme of political re-education (or, on some accounts, 'cultural transformation') was thus central to his entire political and philosophical project.[89] The aim was to clear out of people's minds the false metaphysical assumptions, bogus religious doctrines, and pernicious political principles that had accumulated there as the products of centuries of priestcraft. Once this cultural lumber had been removed, people could easily be taught the true principles of political science—Hobbes's principles—and would then clearly understand their duties as citizens and subjects. His main concern here was with the internal conditions of states; but he did also suggest that this process of political education could have international ramifications. Describing his project in the dedicatory epistle to *De cive*, he wrote: 'For if the patterns of human action were known with the same certainty as the relations of magnitude in figures, ambition and greed, whose power rests on the false opinions of the common people about right and wrong, would be disarmed, and the human race would enjoy such secure peace that (apart from conflicts over space as the population grew) it seems unlikely that it would ever have to fight again.'[90]

This may have been a maximal claim about what was possible; but it should not be dismissed as a mere rhetorical flourish. Elsewhere Hobbes gave some quite specific indications of how an improved understanding of political principles could lead to a change in international conduct. Commenting in *Behemoth* on the failure of 'the Kings and States of Christendom' to deal with the papal threat to their own power, he wrote: 'if they would have freed themselves from his tyranny, they should have agreed together, and made themselves every one, as Henry VIII did, head of the Church within their own respective dominions. But not agreeing,

---

[88] Beitz, *Political Theory*, pp. 36–8.

[89] See especially D. Johnston, *The Rhetoric of Leviathan: Thomas Hobbes and the Politics of Cultural Transformation* (Princeton, NJ, 1986); R. P. Kraynak, *History and Modernity in the Thought of Thomas Hobbes* (Ithaca, NY, 1990); and M. G. Dietz, 'Hobbes's Subject as Citizen', in M. G. Dietz, ed., *Thomas Hobbes and Political Theory* (Lawrence, Kan., 1990), pp. 91–119.

[90] Hobbes, *De cive*, 'Epistle dedicatory', para. 6 (tr. p. 5). For some perceptive comments on the international implications of Hobbes's educative project, see D. W. Hanson, 'Thomas Hobbes's "Highway to Peace" ', *International Organization*, 38 (1984), pp. 329–54.

they let his power continue, every one hoping to make use of it, when there should be cause, against his neighbour.'[91] This is a clear example of how a better-grounded political understanding would lead to a more cooperative policy at the international level. Later in the same work, the other speaker in the dialogue remarks: 'It is methinks no great polity in neighbouring princes to favour, so often as they do, one another's rebels, especially when they rebel against monarchy itself. They should rather, first, make a league against rebellion and afterwards, (if there be no remedy) fight against one another.'[92] While the last part of that remark shows that such an appreciation of common interests would not suffice to eliminate all other causes of war, this suggestion of a 'league against rebellion' is nevertheless a positive example of how international conflict can be reduced by the application of sound political science. And if sovereigns have a joint interest in taking such political action, they must also have a joint interest in reforming the common culture that nurtures and propagates false political principles—a European culture of writings and teachings that crosses national boundaries.

III

To conclude: although Hobbes has a famously low opinion of human nature in general, he does believe that human behaviour can be improved; and he implies that international cooperation may be both a means towards such improvement and a consequence of it. In this respect, Hobbes is much closer to the ameliorism of the rationalist tradition than to the changeless pessimism of the Realists. However, his utter rejection of teleological metaphysics, and his strict derivation of the natural laws from the principle of individual self-preservation, set him far apart from the mainstream of rationalist natural law theories. Unlike the Stoic, scholastic, or Lockean versions of natural law, Hobbes's theory takes no cognizance of the good of mankind as such. There can therefore be no equivalent in it to Locke's concept of the 'executive power of the law of nature', by virtue of which a third party can intervene in other people's affairs to enforce that which is objectively right.

As has been suggested above, it is this peculiar quality of Hobbes's natural laws—their derivation from purely individual long-term self-interest—that makes it possible to open a conceptual gap in his theory between the nature of 'moral' rights and duties on the one hand, and of jural ones on the other. In the Lockean scheme of things no such gap exists, because the laws of nature set out a single, interpersonal scheme of values: if, in the state of nature, A is justly attacking B, then C cannot be justified in assisting B against A. But in Hobbes's theory, where people are acting in the state of nature in accordance with their 'natural' rights and duties, such clashes are perfectly possible. In his *Dialogue of the Common Laws*, the

---

[91] Hobbes, *Behemoth*, p. 21.   [92] Ibid., p. 144.

ASPECTS OF HOBBES

'Philosopher' remarks that a king will be justified in going to war in support of 'Neighbours . . . born down with the Current of a Conquering Enemy' if he judges that his own state may be next in line for conquest. The 'Lawyer' objects: 'If the War upon our Neighbour be Just, it may be question'd whether it be Equity or no to Assist them against the Right.' But the 'Philosopher' (representing Hobbes) dismisses all such objections as irrelevant: 'For my part I make no Question of that at all . . .'[93]

This is a crucial passage, illustrating the peculiar nature of the Hobbesian international state of nature: moral rights and duties do exist in it, but they are not fixed by nature in any pattern of mutual harmony or reciprocity.[94] Outside the commonwealth, rights and duties may be in direct conflict; only inside the commonwealth can they be presumed to be in harmony. While the rationalist tradition of thought about international relations strives to overcome the distinction between those two realms, Hobbes emphasizes it and makes it central to his theory. That, in the end, is why he has so often been described as a 'Realist', despite all the other features of his thinking that such a description so signally fails to capture.

[93] Hobbes, *Dialogue of the Common Laws*, p. 65.

[94] On this point it is necessary to disagree with Murray Forsyth, whose important study 'Thomas Hobbes and External Relations' is flawed by its assumption that Hobbesian natural law is based on 'reason as by definition the taking into account of the *other* person's rights as well as one's own' (p. 197).

[23]

The Hobbesian Tradition in Twentieth Century International Thought*

R. John Vincent

This essay does not seek to contribute to any debate about what Hobbes said, or meant by what he said, or the context in which he wrote. Nor is it a history of ideas. It is not with the establishment and evolution of a Hobbesian tradition that it is concerned, but rather with its current importance. Accordingly, what it does attempt is first to be self-conscious about the way in which we now think about international relations, to discover the extent to which it is shaped by the legacy of Hobbes. "Of all the restraints upon the political philosopher's freedom to speculate," writes Sheldon Wolin, "none has been so powerful as the tradition of political philosophy itself. In the act of philosophising, the theorist enters into a debate the terms of which have largely been set beforehand." [1] What are the signs of this in contemporary thought about international relations?

If there are difficulties involved in marking out the influence of a tradition from a position within it, a still greater number are attached to the second concern of this paper which is to ask whether the Hobbesian tradition is not now moribund. If that tradition can be characterised as having at its centre the problem, grim and insoluble, of the co-existence of states in the absence of international government, it would be undermined by the decline of the state and the rise of international government. In contemporary international politics we are invited to observe the former in, for example, the dimensions of the global ecological crisis which are beyond the reach of the state or the states-system, [2] and the latter in such developments as the transnational "management of interdependence". [3] The investigation of these matters will be the concern of the third part of this article. The first part, despite the earlier disclaimer, will briefly consider what Hobbes said about international relations, and the second section will give some examples of how it continues to be stated or its framework built upon in the Twentieth century. The result of this enterprise is the depiction of a tradition more complex than is often supposed in the glib categories of the first-year courses.

Hobbes' Thought on International Relations

In Hobbes's account of the state of nature contained in *Leviathan,* men are driven to quarrel with one another because of their competition for gain, because of their haste to defend themselves, or because of their quest for glory. So long as they live together in the absence of a common power to overawe them, their relationship with each other is one of war, consisting either in actual fighting or preparation for it. In these circumstances, there is no prospect of men busying themselves with life in society, and there is continual fear and danger of violent death.

If there never was an actual time when individuals were all in a condition of war one against another, this was the situation in which kings and persons of sovereign authority found themselves. The description of the nature of man which led him to quarrel also applied to states whose independence and continual jealousies produced a posture of war. However, the liberty of states in the state of nature was a less miserable condition than that of individuals, because the industry of the Sovereign's subjects was upheld by the state of war.

This is the Hobbes we find in the well-thumbed Chapter XIII of *Leviathan*. In the same chapter, though less often quoted than the passages already made use of, and not apparently written with international relations in mind, is the paragraph in which the dilemma presented by the international anarchy, the state of war which continues "all the time there is no assurance to the contrary", is, to my mind, best, if somewhat cumbersomely, expressed.

> And from this diffidence of one another, there is no way for any man to secure himselfe, so reasonable as Anticipation; that is, by force, or wiles, to master the persons of all men he can, so long, till he sees no other power great enough to endanger him: And this is no more than his own conservation requireth, and is generally allowed. Also because there be some, that taking pleasure in contemplating their own power in the acts of conquest, which they pursue farther than their security requires: if others, that otherwise would be glad to be at ease within modest bounds, should not by invasion increase their power, they would not be able, longtime, by standing only on their defence to subsist. And, by consequence, such augmentation of dominion over men, being necessary to a man's conservation, it ought to be allowed him.[4]

Here is what in the language of the contemporary arms control community would be called the "action-reaction phenomenon", arising from "third-image analysis" of the causes of conflict in international politics, and with this jargon we are pitch-forked into the Twentieth century.[4]

The Impact of Hobbes on Twentieth Century Thought

There are three senses in which the ideas of Hobbes can be said to have had importance in the Twentieth century. First, there is the notion that we happen to live in a Hobbesian age for the interpretation of which his writings are a better guide than those of, say, Grotius or Kant. Second, there is the more profound assertion that Hobbes, in his account of the international anarchy, captured certain essential truths which would apply regardless of time and place. And third, there is the idea that while Hobbes did nothing so grand as to discover scientific laws of politics, he did state, with clarity and force, a view of international relations without an understanding of which no student of the subject is properly equipped.

Concerning the question of a Hobbesian era in international politics, K.C. Brown has written of "a general climate of our age . . . [that is] extremely well-suited to a growth of interest in Hobbes's work": the Third Reich, the hydrogen bomb, the division of men's loyalty between patriotism and some international ideology, and the manner in which "civilised communities [are] prepared to commit atrocities whose obscenity would have surprised The Dark Ages", all of which make it less easy to dismiss Hobbes for having too cynical and pessimistic a view of human nature.[6] Brown goes on to observe that the "present time is one in which the world appears to be dramatising in international terms the story which Hobbes himself told in inter-personal terms: every line of the past twenty years' debate on the difficulties of turning the United Nations into an effective instrument of world government could stand as a gloss upon Hobbes's text".[7]

David P. Gauthier remarks that "Hobbes would have approved [of] our phrase *cold war*" because "it expresses well what he took to be the permanent relationship of nations".[8] In the statement quoted above on the implications of anarchy, Hobbes showed himself to be the father of what Kenneth Waltz has called the "third image": "Because any state may at any time use force, all states must constantly be ready either to counter force with force or to pay the costs of weakness. The requirements of state action are, in this view, imposed by the circumstances in which all states exist".[9] These circumstances of anarchy give international politics the character that distinguishes it from other politics, so that "it is roughly the case that, while in domestic politics the struggle for power is governed and circumscribed by the framework of law and institutions, in international politics law and institutions are governed and circumscribed by the struggle for power".[10] In this struggle, as Sir Herbert Butterfield writes in his brilliant evocation of the "dominion of fear", fear and suspicion play a part not merely as factors in the story, but "they give a certain quality to human life in general, condition the nature of politics, and imprint their character on diplomacy and foreign policy".[11] Men are not absolutely brutish, and do not want to be, but are made so by suspicion and fear of each other.[12] And so long as they remain grouped together in independent communities, there is no way of removing the causes of disagreement among them, and to think otherwise "is to display political imbecility in its most exaggerated form".[13]

There will be occasion in the next section of the essay to cast doubt on the enthronement of this wisdom as the essential truth of international politics. Meanwhile, there is the third sense in which Hobbes has been important in the Twentieth century: his provision of a starting place for thought about international politics. This starting place is often thought to be a realist one, indeed to constitute, with Machiavelli, the definition of Realism, so that to take Hobbes as a guide is to side with Martin Wight's "blood and iron and immorality men".[14] International politics is a struggle for power; war is inevitable in the international anarchy; there is no right and wrong, only competing conceptions of right; there is no society beyond the state; international law is an empty phrase. With buckets half-full of cold water of this kind many a lecturer has dampened the enthusiasm of the undergraduate idealist meting out just the treatment that E.H. Carr administered to the League of Nations utopians in *The Twenty Years'*

Crisis.[15] Members of this society of drenchers have included, in the Twentieth century, in addition to Carr and Wight (in some of their moments), other long-standing residents in reading lists like Morgenthau, Kissinger, Aron, Kaplan, and Bull (in some of their moments).

However, there is a tendency for the drenchers, in other moments, to dry their pupils off, and to rekindle their enthusiasm, not indeed for utopian illusions, but certainly for a version of international politics that is not classically Realist. Carr's realist critique is followed by a chapter on the limitations of Realism. The realist Martin Wight of *Power Politics* is different from the rationalist Martin Wight of "Western Values in International Relations".[16] Morgenthau's account of international politics as a struggle for power includes a treatment of the balance of power as a stabilising factor in the politics of states, and even of the importance of a moral consensus on which the stability of a system in the end depended.[17] Kissinger's deep sense of the adversarial nature of international relations did not diminish his enthusiasm for engaging his own opponents in their joint management. Raymond Aron, in analysing the "enemy-partnership" between today's two superpowers, prefers to see in it continuity with the past rather than discontinuity, treating it as banal rather than paradoxical.[18] Morton Kaplan, while calling the international system a "null political system" because it has no counterpart to government in a municipal system, nevertheless deals with processes of regulation within it which mimic some of the functions of government.[19] And Hedley Bull finds no good reasons why anarchy should exclude society.[20]

There is then among these Hobbesians the influence of "the law and order and keep your word men" whose description of the international world includes order as well as disorder, and whose inclination is to discover an order even in those institutions which ordinary people might be forgiven for counting as disorderly, such as the institution of war. This is especially true of British thought about international politics in the Twentieth century, to the point that the vindication of the concept of international society has been a concern of academic international relations since the subject's arrival on the university curriculum.[21] How far can this concern be said to belong to a Hobbesian tradition?

Against the objection that it is the tradition of Hobbes to deny the possibility of international society, there is one telling observation. Hobbes's remark that the international anarchy is, because it upholds the industry of the subjects of sovereigns, more bearable than anarchy among individual human beings, has been the starting place, and a very productive one, of much thought about the nature of international politics. Reflection about why this is so, and about the larger question of whether or not international society is unique, can be taken as being in a Hobbesian tradition: Hobbes first had the wit to notice the important distinction.

There are three principal answers to the question why the international anarchy is more tolerable than anarchy among individuals. In the first place, there is the strength of states: they are not vulnerable to a single deadly blow as individuals are; the death of kings is not the death of kingdoms.[22] Moreover, the state of war, by upholding the industry of the citizens of a state, might even add to their and its strength, whereas the state of nature among individuals prevents the establishment of any kind of industry. And while states are not necessarily self-sufficient, there is more prospect that they can meet some of the needs of their citizens, than there is of an individual meeting any of his, in the state of nature.

The second reason why the international state of nature is more tolerable than that condition among individuals is the inequality of states. The approximate equality of men makes it possible for the smallest among them to challenge the strongest: even giants sleep. Competition among them is in consequence ceaseless, for the hope of gain at a neighbour's expense is never dead. In international politics, however, where there are great powers outclassing their companions and thus setting limits to their aspirations, there is the possibility of ordering affairs according to the principle that "might is right",[23] and an approximation to international government might result from the establishment of a Concert among the great powers.

A third mark of difference between an international and an inter-individual state of nature concerns the possibility of establishing rules of the game in recognition of common interests. If it is always possible for a vanquished state to live to fight another day, and if there is always the threat that it can bring force to bear to defend its interests, then other states cannot simply despatch it in the manner of an outlaw gunning down the marshal in the old West.[24] Further, "each state has an essentially domestic interest in self-restraint, since, should it implicate its population in all-out wars of extermination, the subject's duty of obedience to it would disappear".[25] And if, in Hobbes, international relations are conducted among states sharing a concern to maintain order domestically, then this is the path to the principles of state sovereignty and non-intervention. Further down the same route is the institution of the balance of power to preserve the independence of states. The argument then, for Hobbes as a Rationalist, draws on him for the defence of the sovereign state as an agency of international order, and complicates the more conventional realist account of the plurality of states leading to international disorder.

Unless one thinks of Hobbes as a Rationalist as well as a Realist it is hard to explain his complacency about international politics. Indeed, it is even reasonable to ask why, if Hobbes's view of international politics was really as the Realists take it to be, he did not seek to bring the international anarchy to an end in the same way as *Leviathan* ordered relations among individuals. Why, in other words, was Hobbes not a Revolutionist, to add to his other accomplishments? Not perhaps a Revolutionist who could join the club of "the subversion and liberation and missionary men", but certainly a Revolutionist in regard to the structure of international politics. It is a common interpretation of Hobbes that if he did not follow this path, then his own logic ought to have impelled him to.[26] If peace and security were invariably the highest political values, and if the Leviathan was always able to provide for their achievement, then there would be no grounds on which princes could object to the establishment of a global sovereign to overawe them and thereby keep them in order. Hobbes's failure to draw this conclusion might be attributed to three things. In the first place, there is his attachment to the doctrine of self-preservation for states (no less than individuals) in the state of nature, which has been said to link Hobbes with the tradition of *raison d'état*.[27] The point here is again that of Hobbes's complacency: presumably most states most of the time were successfully self-preserving. Second, there is the view of Hobbes as an English patriot who could not countenance the extinction of the English state's independence.[28] And third, there is the argument that for the establishment of the Leviathan, external threats are quite as important as the need for internal order, so that it is not a question of the state being established and then appointing a minister of defence, but of defence prompting every step in the direction of the Leviathan.[29] If this is a correct interpretation of Hobbes then a world state must await an extra-terrestrial threat.

There are arguments, then, for cataloguing Hobbes under all three of Martin Wight's categories purporting to distinguish the great contending patterns of thought about international politics. No doubt this raises general questions about the whole enterprise of treating great thinkers like parcels at the post office. And the particular question of the violence this does to Hobbes is an interesting one. We tend to treat Hobbes as either blood and guts in the state of nature, or the repose of the graveyard in the Leviathan. Murray Forsyth has recently argued, very persuasively, that Hobbes is not like this.[30] What Forsyth calls Hobbes's "raw" state of nature, with all the telling phrases about brutishness, is, Forsyth argues, a deliberately fabricated "not-world" invented to satirise the writers who argued that reason alone, unshackled to interest, could establish civil society.

Forsyth also argues that the traditional interpretation of Hobbes overlooks the area in between the raw state of nature and the Leviathan, in which alliances and confederations are formed, where reason and interest go hand in hand, and on which Hobbes spent a good deal of time. This world-in-between, where the state of nature is modified by the law of nature, gives a more plausible account of the emergence of the Leviathan, and more closely resembles the reality of international politics. The Leviathan is the perfection of a confederation, not something from nothing, and international relations are characterised by co-operation as well as conflict.

Where then do we put Hobbes if we still insist on a location within Wight's categories? If we can rule out Revolutionism as something that belongs to a Hobbesian tradition, but not to Hobbes himself, we can do the same with neither Realism, nor Rationalism. Hobbes occupied the marchlands between these two, and constantly kept one as a check on the enthusiasm of the other. Academic international relations in Britain in the Twentieth century has, in this regard, flattered Hobbes by imitating him.

The Continuing Relevance of Hobbes's Thought

However, the question arises: is this imitation mistaken? It may be argued that the Hobbesian tradition is moribund in three senses. First, there is the argument that the "state of war", or "the international anarchy", no longer depict the context of international politics in a way that would make it distinct from every other part of the international system, and no longer convey the essence of international relations. In the second place, there exists not merely international society, which may laboriously be co-opted into the Hobbesian tradition, but also transnational society for which the same labour is, it may be argued, fruitless. Third, there is the criticism which might derive special support from the happenings of the Twentieth century, of the whole tradition of the preoccupation with the state, denying the need for the Leviathan to impose peace and security, and having rhetoric to this effect as statist ideology. The argument in this final point is not that the Hobbesian tradition is now moribund, but that it should never have been born.

The view of international politics as the uneasy relations of sovereign states co-existing in a state of nature which causes them to make security their first obligation sheds very little light on some of the great issues of our time: the relations among the rich North Atlantic states; North-South relations; that growing segment of East-West relations which is not taken up with security. The vocabulary of Realism makes little sense of the global politics of "complex interdependence",[31] and there is the call for a "reformulation of international relations theory"[32] to accommodate actors other than states, motives for action outside the balance of power, and techniques of diplomacy distinct from the use of military force.[33]

A good part of this reformulation is taken up with the attempt to make coherent a new kind of society, or at least a society of which formerly too little account has been taken. This is transnational society which exists by virtue of neither a contract among individuals to establish a Sovereign, nor a compact among Sovereigns, but of the reality of social relations across state frontiers. General Motors, the Roman Catholic Church, holidaymakers going abroad, and international telephone calls, are all, it is said, kinds of transnational society or evidence for its existence. The assertion of the existence of transnational society is subversive of Hobbesian doctrine in a weak and a strong sense. First, it is a society which exists in a state of nature. But this is the weak sense, since it is a possibility which can be said to derive from Hobbes rather than doing him violence, as was argued in the second part of this essay. The strong sense is more fundamental. If a new tribe of "masterless men" is emerging, whose relations are governed by some transnational function which is not the preserve of the state, and yet the relations are socially ordered, then is not the institution of civil government in some respects called into question? Hobbes's show-stopping argument for the Leviathan is then at risk for he can be quoted against himself:

> For if we could suppose a great Multitude of men to consent in the observation of Justice, and other Lawes of Nature, without a common Power to keep them all in awe; we might as well suppose all Mankind to do the same; and then there neither would be, nor need be any Civil Government, or Commonwealth at all; because there would be Peace without Subjection.[34]

The possibility of peace without subjection is the idea which informs the most radical protest against the Leviathan, and this leads to the third objection to the Hobbesian tradition, the one that regretted its ever being established. The point has recently been made that the assumptions made by Hobbes (and Hume) about human behaviour in the absence of the state might "more accurately describe what human behaviour would be like immediately after the state has been removed from a society *whose members had for a long time lived under states*".[35] The assumptions which hold that the state is necessary to coerce men into co-operating are, the argument runs, "*self-fulfilling*, in the sense that, if they were not true before the introduction of the state, . . . they would in time become true as a result of the state's activity".[36] Human nature is not an attribute which can be considered separately from civil society, but is conditioned by the society that surrounds it, and the state has played a considerable part in the atrophy of voluntary co-operative behaviour by itself insisting on the provision of public goods.[37] Thus the argument for the Leviathan as the only means to peace and security is statist special-pleading.

Some attempt will be made in the conclusion to judge the extent to which the Hobbesian tradition survives this onslaught. At the same time there is not only the argument that Hobbes's thought has survived, but also that Twentieth century developments have given him a new lease on life. It is commonplace to remark that the advent of nuclear weapons has reduced states to the position of men in the state of nature, the prospect of their total destruction equalising their misery in just the condition of Hobbes's individual.[38] In this situation, it may be said that Hobbes's arguments can be used more forcibly than they were earlier in support of the establishment of a global Leviathan.

This argument from the advent of nuclear weapons to the need for a world state has more recently been extended to the ecological crisis. In this form, the nuclear threat becomes but one item on a dismal list of potential disasters including pollution of the environment, resource depletion and escalating population growth. Garret Hardin has called attention to the politics of the ecological crisis in his famous account of the "tragedy of the commons".[39] There is no conflict between the interests of individual herdsmen and those of the group of herdsmen using the commons so long as it has the capacity to accommodate additional animals without affecting the grazing of the animals already pastured. But once this point is passed, the tragedy of the commons is set in train, for while it is in the interests of an individual herdsman to add to his stock of animals, his yield increasing albeit at a reduced rate, the interests of the group of herdsmen is damaged by diminishing marginal yields. So long as an individual's gain outweighs his costs he continues to add stock to the commons. But the inevitable result of the overgrazing that follows is damage done to the interests of every herdsman. The failure to articulate a group interest, and to create an institution to enforce it, has reduced the welfare of each individual.

According to Michael Taylor, there is nothing new about this; it is essentially Hobbes's argument.[40] If each individual pursues his own interest, in the absence of government, then the resulting war of all against all is more miserable than the peace and security produced by government. Enter the Leviathan, in response to a global threat, albeit not an extra-global one, to protect our interests by overawing us.

Hobbes's Thought in the Changing Context of International Relations

One of the problems with this point of view is that states are unlikely to adopt it. Even supposing that they accepted the worst-case analysis of the ecological crisis, it is hard to imagine them accepting with it the argument that their sovereignty should be abandoned for its solution. In view of this the better strategy for those who would interdict the tragedy of the commons might be, not the establishment of power at the centre, but the acceptance of anarchy and the encouragement of co-operation within it. In this way the international community is invited merely to solve the one problem of the ecological crisis, and is not burdened with the second requirement of dismantling the international system and rebuilding world politics in an ecologist's design.

As to the particular significance in this regard of the advent of nuclear weapons, Martin Wight notes that it has often been argued that their invention "has transcended the Hobbesian predicament, by transferring fear from the potential enemy to war itself".[41] He goes on to deny this by asserting that every great power fears atomic warfare less than not using it in certain circumstances. In this view, the international anarchy has led states to so highly prize their independence that they would suffer devastating damage rather than surrender it. The tenacity of this view might be explained by the threat of disaster in the international state of nature still having an abstract quality. While in the state of nature among individuals it is possible to imagine the provision of daily evidence of the need for the Leviathan, in the international anarchy this evidence is removed from the mundane preoccupations of individuals. The nuclear disaster, or any other of the ecological threats which are in prospect, are what might happen if the worst comes to the worst. Meanwhile there are other things to be done. Thus the international anarchy is still taken to be less wretched than the same condition among individuals. In this way the Hobbesian tradition continues, though it may now be a delusion.

However, the argument of the writers on "complex interdependence" and "transnational society" was not a delusion but simply irrelevant. While it is true that the "state of war" can give little account of these concepts, and that Hobbesian analysis is pushed by them into the background, the background may be crucial to them in the sense that it deals with the problem of security whose solution, in some degree, has allowed international and transnational co-operation to flourish. The politics of interdependence are not here opposed to the politics of security in a manner that requires a reformulation of international relations theory whenever foul weather turns fair, but the one is made possible by the other. Hobbesian analysis recedes, but it does not disappear.

The final argument is that Hobbes's human nature is in fact the nature of stateman, and that his assumptions were shaped by his conclusions. Since there is little evidence of the behaviour of stateless men, tarring with this brush is difficult to escape. However, an argument was made earlier that Hobbes's human nature on view in the "raw" state of nature was a straw-man fabricated to counter the other straw-man of his more sentimental opponents. In yoking reason to interest in his non-straw-man, and by insisting on an interplay between nature and environment in his account of politics, Hobbes may not be so far removed from a view of human nature that is recognisably modern, and defended in books on anthropology.[42] Whether this is a point in his favour or against him is another question. In either case, we have seen that there are reasons to remark on, if not to celebrate, the vitality of the Hobbesian tradition.

R. John Vincent is a Lecturer in the International Relations Department of the University of Keele

REFERENCES

* An earlier version of this article was read at the Political Studies Association Conference at Sheffield University in April 1979.

1. Sheldon Wolin, *Politics and Vision* (London: Allen & Unwin, 1961), p.22.

2. See for example, Richard A. Falk, *This Endangered Planet* (New York: Random House, 1971), *passim*.

3. See, for example, Miriam Camps, *The Management of Interdependence* (New York: Sage, 1974), *passim*.

4. *Leviathan* (London: Everyman edition), p.64.

5. The "action-reaction phenomenon" refers to that part of the theory of arms races which locates their momentum in the participants' decisions continually to arm against each others new or planned arms. I do not know who first used the expression, but it can be found in C.S. Gray, "The Arms Race Phenomenon", *World Politics* (Vol. XXIV, October 1971). "Third image analysis" has now become so familiar as to almost need no reference due to Kenneth Waltz's *Man, the State and War* (New York: Columbia, 1959).

6. K.C. Brown (ed.), *Hobbes Studies* (Oxford: Basil Blackwell, 1965), p.ix.

7. *Ibid.*

8. David P. Gauthier, *The Logic of Leviathan* (Oxford: Clarendon Press, 1969), p.207.

9. Kenneth Waltz, *op. cit.*, p.160.

10. Martin Wight, *Power Politics*, H. Bull and C. Holbraad (eds.) (Leicester: Leicester University Press, 1978), p.102.

11. Herbert Butterfield, *International Conflict in the Twentieth Century: A Christian View* (London: Routledge and Keegan Paul, 1960), p.85.

12. *Ibid.*, p.84.

13. R.G. Collingwood, *The New Leviathan* (Oxford: Clarendon Press, 1942), p.228.

14. See H. Bull, "Martin Wight and the Theory of International Relations", *British Journal of International Studies* (Vol. 2, No. 2, July 1976), p.102. What follows makes use of Wight's distinction between Realists, Rationalists and Revolutionists.

15. E. H. Carr, *The Twenty Years' Crisis* (London: Macmillan, 1962) 2nd edition, see especially Chap. 5.

16. M. Wight, *Power Politics* (London: RIIA, 1946) and "Western Values in International Relations" in H. Butterfield and M. Wight (eds.) *Diplomatic Investigations* (London: Allen & Unwin, 1966), pp.89 – 131.

17. H. Morgenthau, *Politics Among Nations* (New York: Alfred Knopf, 1963) 3rd edition, see Chap 14.

18. R. Aron, *Peace and War* (London: Weidenfeld, 1966), see Chap. 18.

19. M. Kaplan, *System and Process in International Politics* (London: J.E. Wiley & Sons, 1957), pp.14 and 89.

20. H. Bull, *The Anarchical Society* (London: Macmillan, 1976), *passim*.

21. In addition to E.H. Carr, M. Wight and H. Bull, see C.A.W. Manning, *The Nature of International Society* (London: Bell, 1960), and A.M. James (ed.), *The Bases of International Order* (Oxford: OUP, 1973).

22. The final section of this article examines how true this is in the nuclear age.

23. For this argument and its complications, see H. Bull, "Society and Anarchy in International Relations", in H. Butterfield and M. Wight, *op. cit.*, pp. 46 – 47.

24. Stanley Hoffmann's idea of "reciprocity of interests" emerges from this. See his book *The State of War* (New York: Praeger, 1965), p.61.

25. *Ibid*

26. See for example, H. Morgenthau, *op. cit.*, p.501.

27. See H. Bull, "Hobbes and the International Anarchy", Hobbes Tricentenary Lecture, delivered at Oxford, 1979, p.5.

28. See Christopher Brewin, "Hobbes and War", unpublished paper.

29. See Murray Forsyth, "Thomas Hobbes and the External Relations of States", *British Journal of International Studies* (Vol. 5, No. 3, October 1979), p.205.

30. *Ibid.*, pp. 196 – 209, from which the following argument is taken.

31. R. Keohane and J. Nye, *Power and Interdependence: World Politics in Transition* (Boston: Little, Brown, 1977).

32. Peter J. Katzenstein, "International Relations and Domestic Structures: Foreign Economic Policy of Advanced Industrial States". *International Organization* (Vol, 30, No. 1, Winter 1979), p.9.

33. K.J. Holsti, "A New International Politics? Diplomacy in Complex Interdependence", *International Organization* (Vol. 32, No. 2, Spring 1978).

34. *Leviathan, op. cit.*, p.88.

35. Michael Taylor, *Anarchy and Co-operation* (London: John E. Wiley & Sons, 1976), p.141. Emphasis in the original.

36. *Ibid.*, p. 142.

37. *Ibid.*, pp. 134 – 135.

38. See, for example, D. Gauthier, *op. cit.*

39. Garret Hardin, "The Tragedy of the Commons", *Science* (Vol. 162, No. 3859) December 13, 1968.

40. M. Taylor, *op. cit.*, p. 3.

41. M. Wight, *Power Politics,* H. Bull and C. Holbraad (eds.) *op. cit.*, p. 142.

42. See, for example, Derek Freeman, "Human Nature and Culture", in *Man and the New Biology* (Canberra: ANU Press, 1970).

Name Index